LAm
10/97

STAGES ON LIFE'S WAY

KIERKEGAARD'S WRITINGS, XI

STAGES ON LIFE'S WAY

STUDIES BY VARIOUS PERSONS

by Søren Kierkegaard

Edited and Translated
with Introduction and Notes by

Howard V. Hong and
Edna H. Hong

PRINCETON UNIVERSITY PRESS
PRINCETON, NEW JERSEY

Copyright © 1988 by Howard V. Hong
Published by Princeton University Press, 41 William Street
Princeton, New Jersey 08540
In the United Kingdom: Princeton University Press, Chichester, West Sussex

Library of Congress Cataloging-in-Publication-Data

Kierkegaard, Søren, 1813-1855.
[Stadier paa livets vej. English]
Stages on life's way: studies by various persons / by Søren, Kierkegaard;
edited and translated with introduction and notes by Howard V. Hong and
Edna H. Hong.
p. cm.—(Kierkegaard's writings ; 11)
Translation of: Stadier paa livets vej.
Bibliography: p.
Includes index.
ISBN 0-691-07323-6 (cloth)   ISBN 0-691-02049-3 (pbk.)
I. Hong, Howard Vincent, 1912- . II. Hong, Edna Hatlestad,
1913- . III. Title. IV. Series: Kierkegaard, Søren, 1813-1855.
Works. English. 1978 ; 11.
B4373.S832E5 1988
198'.9—dc19

Second printing, with corrections, 1991

3   5   7   9   10   8   6   4

Preparation of this volume has been made possible in part by a grant from
the Division of Research Programs of the National Endowment for the Humanities,
an independent federal agency

Designed by Frank Mahood

Printed in the United States of America by Princeton Academic Press

CONTENTS

HISTORICAL INTRODUCTION

On the front flyleaf of the newly published work *Either/Or* (February 20, 1843), Kierkegaard wrote:

> Some think that *Either/Or* is a collection of loose papers I had lying in my desk. Bravo! —As a matter of fact, it was the reverse. The only thing this work lacks is a narrative, which I did begin but omitted, just as Aladdin left a window incomplete. It was to be called "Unhappy Love." It was to form a contrast to the Seducer.[1]

He later wrote in his journal:

> Even while I was writing *Either/Or* I had it [the narrative] in mind and frequently dashed off a lyrical suggestion.[2]

How much of the narrative was written is not known. What Kierkegaard had in mind did, however, eventuate as *Stages on Life's Way*. During the first half of 1843, even though Kierkegaard was immersed in the writing of *Two Upbuilding Discourses*, *Fear and Trembling*, *Repetition*, and *Three Upbuilding Discourses* (the first published on May 6 and the remaining three on October 16, 1843), the journal entries of that time contain seeds of most of the special interpolations[3] in the second half of *Stages*, " 'Guilty?'/'Not Guilty?' "

In a letter (May 25, 1843) from Berlin[4] to his friend Emil

[1] *JP* V 5628 (*Pap.* IV A 215). See "The Seducer's Diary," *Either/Or*, I, pp. 301-445, *KW* III (*SV* I 273-412).

[2] *JP* V 5866 (*Pap.* VII¹ B 84).

[3] "A Possibility," "A Leper's Self-Contemplation," "Solomon's Dream," and "Nebuchadnezzar." See Supplement, pp. 502-03, 504-05, 511, 507-08 (*Pap.* IV A 65, 68, 105, 147, 110, 111, 114, 119).

[4] Kierkegaard left for Berlin on May 8, 1843, for a short but intensive period of writing. His return date is not known, but in the May 25 letter to Boesen he states that he will return soon (*Kierkegaard: Letters and Documents*, Letter

Boesen, Kierkegaard mentions having finished a work, presumably *Repetition*, and then goes on to describe his usual day.

> I have never worked as hard as now. I go for a brief walk in the morning. Then I come home and sit in my room without interruption until about three o'clock. My eyes can barely see. Then with my walking stick in hand I sneak off to the restaurant, but am so weak that I believe that if somebody were to call out my name, I would keel over and die. Then I go home and begin again. In my indolence during the past months I had pumped up a veritable shower bath, and now I have pulled the string and the ideas are cascading down upon me: healthy, happy, merry, gay, blessed children born with ease and yet all of them with the birthmark of my personality.[5]

Among the cascading ideas was the beginning of " 'Guilty?'/'Not Guilty?' "[6] Therefore, it appears that, like Part II of *Either/Or*, the second half of *Stages* was begun, and most likely written, first. It was not, however, intended as the second half of *Stages*. At the last minute, two separate works, "The Wrong and the Right"[7] (consisting of " '*In Vino Veritas*' " and the pseudonymous Judge William's piece on marriage) and " 'Guilty?'/'Not Guilty?' " were placed together (ostensibly by Hilarius, a bookbinder, not one of the authors or an editor) in one volume under the title *Stages on Life's Way*, and the title "The Wrong and the Right" was omitted. Indeed, each of the two final manuscripts (transcribed by Israel

---

82, *KW* XXV). The printing manuscript of *Repetition* originally had the superscription "Berlin in May 1843" (*Pap.* IV B 97:3). In Søren's letter (no. 83, June 29, 1843) to his brother Peter Christian Kierkegaard, mention is made of his return from Berlin, but no date is given.

[5] *Letters*, Letter 82, *KW* XXV.

[6] See Supplement, pp. 505-07 (*Pap.* IV A 107).

[7] Danish: *Vrangen og Retten*, literally, "the wrong and the right," said, for example, of a piece of cloth with the reverse side out and the right side in rather than in a specifically juridical or ethical sense.

Levin[8]) has its own pagination.[9] The preface to "The Wrong and the Right"[10] was ready but was omitted. The use of the singular "manuscript" by William Afham[11] may also be a token of the original independent character of the first half of *Stages*, a view confirmed by Hilarius Bookbinder's statement about publishing not one book but several.[12] The initial section of *Stages* was the last to be completed and was difficult to write, as Kierkegaard discloses in a journal entry titled *Report*.[13]

" 'In vino veritas' " is not going well. I am constantly rewriting parts of it,[14] but it does not satisfy me. On the whole I feel that I have given far too much thought to the matter and thereby have gotten into an unproductive mood. I cannot write it here in the city; so I must take a journey.[15] But perhaps it is hardly worth finishing. The idea of the comic as the erotic is hinted at in *The Concept of Anxiety*. The Fashion Designer is a very good figure, but the problem is whether by writing such things I am not deferring more important writing. In any case it must be written in a hurry. If such a moment does not come, I will not do it. At present the productivity has miscarried and makes me constantly write more than I want to write.

August 27, 1844

[8] Israel Salomon Levin (1810-1883), later a well-known philologist and writer, served Kierkegaard as amanuensis and proofreader for a number of years. See Johannes Hohlenberg, *Sören Kierkegaard* (London: Routledge & Kegan Paul, 1954), p. 146. See also *Pap.* VI B 126, 127; VII¹ B 81, 82; X⁵ B 7, 8.

[9] Pages I-CCLIV and 1-452.

[10] See Supplement, p. 568 (*Pap.* V B 191).

[11] See p. 85.

[12] See p. 85.

[13] See Supplement, p. 515 (*Pap.* V A 109).

[14] On the whole, there are more changes in the various drafts of *Stages* (as the Supplement indicates) than is customary in Kierkegaard's manuscripts.

[15] Kierkegaard did not take another writing sabbatical in Berlin. He did, however, make a considerable number of excursions to areas outside Copenhagen. See *JP* V, note 1127.

The relation of *Stages* to the earlier pseudonymous works[16] is one of continuity and contrast, epitomized in the title itself. *Either/Or* presents two qualitatively distinguished stages of life, the immediate or esthetic (that by which one is what one immediately is) and the ethical (that by which one becomes what one becomes[17]), and an intimation of the third stage, the religious, in the concluding "*Ultimatum* [A Final Word]." Both *Fear and Trembling* and *Repetition* center on the question of a justified exception to the ethical. In turn, *Stages* embodies the esthetic and the ethical and the exception to the ethical, and in the reflections of Frater Taciturnus the work delineates more expressly the religious in relation to the esthetic and the ethical.

It may seem curious, therefore, that the term "stages" is almost never used in the text of *Stages*. The terms "sphere" and "existence-sphere"[18] are more frequent, and they are an aid to an understanding of the concept. "Stage" and "stages" may predispose one to the notion of an unbroken line of development from level to level, like childhood, adolescence, and adulthood. "Sphere" and "existence-sphere" more readily denote qualitative possibilities involving the discontinuity of a leap, reflection, and an act in freedom. Furthermore, the spheres are not discrete logical categories, and therefore the lower qualitative sphere is not annihilated but is caught up and transformed. If to a reader this understanding of "stage" and "sphere" is not clear in *Stages* (the diary writer in " 'Guilty?'/ 'Not Guilty?' " is "in the direction of the religious"[19]), it becomes manifest in the next pseudonymous work, *Concluding Unscientific Postscript*, which uses "sphere" and "existence-sphere" more frequently than "stage" and proceeds further in distinguishing between religiousness *A* and religiousness *B*.

[16] The best discussion of the relation of *Stages* to the earlier pseudonymous works is by Johannes Climacus in *Concluding Unscientific Postscript to Philosophical Fragments*, *KW* XII (*SV* VII 242-56). See also Supplement, pp. 651-53, 658, 663 (*Pap.* VI A 41, 78, B 41:10; X¹ A 88; XI¹ A 164).

[17] See *Either/Or*, II, p. 178, *KW* IV (*SV* II 161).

[18] See, for example, pp. 476-77.

[19] P. 398.

The most illuminating relation of *Stages* to the earlier signed works is to the work that appeared (April 29, 1845) just one day before the publication of *Stages*. *Three Discourses on Imagined Occasions* comprises "On the Occasion of a Confession," "On the Occasion of a Wedding," and "At a Graveside"— three parts, just as *Stages* has three parts. That the second part of each work (Judge William on marriage and the discourse at a wedding) is a counterpart of the other is readily seen. At first, Kierkegaard scholar Emanuel Hirsch considered the other parts to be related in serial order, but later he discerned that the substance in each of the others indicates a relation in reverse order of first and third: " 'Guilty?'/'Not Guilty?' " and "Confession," and " '*In Vino Veritas*' " and the discourse "At a Graveside."[20] Viewed in this way, each of the three discourses is seen to clarify and interpret the contents of the counterparts in *Stages*.

If the projected narrative "Unhappy Love," which became " 'Guilty?'/'Not Guilty?' " of *Stages*, is a contrast in substance to "The Seducer's Diary," there is also a difference in form and tone.[21] Quidam's diary is an epistolary novel, or, as Kierkegaard called it, an imaginary psychological construction [*Experiment*].[22] An unincorporated note for *Postscript* states: "This imaginary construction (" 'Guilty?'/'Not Guilty?' ") is the first attempt in all the pseudonymous writings at an existential dialectic in double-reflection. It is not the communication that is in the form of double-reflection (for all the pseudonymous works are that), but the existing person himself

---

[20] See Hirsch, *Kierkegaard Studien*, I-II (1930-33; repr., Vaduz, Liechtenstein: Topos, 1978), I, p. 150 [278]; II, p. 150 [752].

[21] In form and tone, " '*In Vino Veritas*' " also is a contrast to Part I of *Either/ Or*. The participants are older and more discerning in self-knowledge, and their self-disclosure is more manifest in their speeches. Judge William in *Stages* writes as he did before but with deeper insight.

[22] See p. 185. On "imaginary construction [*Experiment*]" and "psychological," see *Fear and Trembling* and *Repetition*, pp. xxi-xxxi, 357-62, *KW* VI. A variant, *Tankeexperiment* (a suppositive case, experiment in thought; see pp. 31-32, 403), was used by Poul M. Møller in *Om populære Ideers Udvikling* (1825), *Efterladte Skrifter*, I-III (Copenhagen: 1839-43; *ASKB* 1574-76), II, p. 17.

exists in this. Thus he does not give up immediacy, but he keeps it and yet gives it up, keeps erotic love's desire and yet gives it up."[23]

In the unpublished "The Book on Adler," Kierkegaard expands his view of the imaginary construction with reference not only to the characters but to the imaginary constructor (Frater Taciturnus) and to the intended result for the reader.

> The art in all communication is to come as close as possible to actuality, to contemporaries in the role of readers, and yet at the same time to have the distance of a point of view, the reassuring, infinite distance of ideality from them. Permit me to illustrate this by an example from a later work. In the imaginary psychological construction [*psychologiske Experiment*] " 'Guilty?'/'Not Guilty?' " (in *Stages on Life's Way*), there is depicted a character in tension in the most extreme mortal danger of the spirit to the point of despair, and the whole thing is done as though it could have occurred yesterday. In this respect the production is placed as close as possible to actuality: the person struggling religiously in despair hovers, so to speak, right over the head of the contemporaries. If the imaginary construction has made any impression, it might be like that which happens when wing strokes of the wild bird, in being heard overhead by the tame birds of the same kind who live securely in the certainty of actuality, prompt these to beat their wings, because those wing strokes simultaneously are unsettling and yet have something that fascinates. But now comes what is reassuring, that the whole thing is an imaginary construction, and that an imaginary constructor [*Experimentator*] stands by. Spiritually understood, the imaginatively constructed character is in a civic sense a highly dangerous character, and such people are usually not allowed to walk along without being accompanied by a pair of policemen—for the sake of public security. Thus, for the reassurance of public security, in that work an imaginary

[23] *JP* V 5865 (*Pap.* VII[1] B 83, *n.d.*, 1846). See Supplement, pp. 654–55.

constructor is along also (he calls himself a street inspector) who very quietly shows how the whole thing hangs together, theoretically educes a life-view that he completes and rounds out, while he points interpretively to the imaginatively constructed character in order to indicate how he makes the movements according to the drawing of the strings. If this were not an imaginary construction, if no imaginary constructor were along, if no life-view were represented—then such a work, regardless of the talent it could display, would merely be debilitating.[24]

Inasmuch as "A First and Last Explanation" was appended in unnumbered pages to *Concluding Unscientific Postscript*[25] and acknowledgment was thereby made of Kierkegaard's poetic relation to the "pseudonymity or polyonymity"[26] of the earlier works, *Stages* was the last of the works published under the veil of pseudonymity. Kierkegaard regarded *Either/Or* as the *beginning* of his authorship[27] and *Postscript* as the *concluding* of his authorship. The surrounding or the accompanying of the pseudonymous works by signed works is readily apparent in the publication schedule culminating in *Postscript* and its appendix.

Pseudonymous Works 1843	Signed Works 1843
Feb. 20 *Either/Or*, I-II edited by Victor Eremita	May 16 *Two Upbuilding Discourses*

---

[24] *Pap.* VII² B 235, pp. 14-15. See Supplement, pp. 656-57.
[25] *SV* VII [545-59].
[26] Ibid. [545].
[27] See, for example, *Two Discourses at the Communion on Fridays, Without Authority*, *KW* XVIII (*SV* XII 267); *On My Work as an Author*, *KW* XXII (*SV* XIII 494, 500); *The Point of View for My Work as an Author*, *KW* XXII (*SV* XIII 517, 521, 569); *JP* VI 6238, 6444, 6770 (*Pap.* IX A 227, p. 124; X¹ A 541, p. 344; X⁶ B 4:3, p. 15).

Oct. 16	*Repetition* by Constantin Constantius *Fear and Trembling* by Johannes de Silentio	Oct. 16	*Three Upbuilding Discourses*
		Dec. 6	*Four Upbuilding Discourses*
	1844		1844
		March 5	*Two Upbuilding Discourses*
		June 8	*Three Upbuilding Discourses*
June 13	*Philosophical Fragments* by Johannes Climacus		
June 17	*The Concept of Anxiety* by Vigilius Haufniensis *Prefaces* by Nicolaus Notabene		
		Aug. 31	*Four Upbuilding Discourses*
	1845		1845
April 30	*Stages on Life's Way* published by Hilarius Bookbinder	April 29	*Three Discourses on Imagined Occasions*

1846

Feb. 27 *Concluding Unscientific Postscript*
by Johannes Climacus, with the appended
"A First and Last Explanation"
by S. Kierkegaard

Even if *Stages* were not a pseudonymous work and a heightened example of Kierkegaard's "indirect method," his conception of the relation of a writer to his work and to his own experience would still apply. "An author certainly must have his private personality as everyone else has, but this must be his ἄδυτον [inner sanctum], and just as the entrance to a house is barred by stationing two soldiers with crossed bayonets, so by means of the dialectical cross of qualitative opposites the equality of ideality forms the barrier that prevents all access."[28]

No writer can totally expunge his experience from his writing, but, as Paul Sponheim observes, it would be an error to regard *Stages* "as an exercise in biography"[29] or autobiography. Just as the creative writer transmutes whatever leaden elements of experience enter into his imaginative work, the assiduous hunter after autobiographical data tends to reverse the process from gold to lead. A better approach is given by Emanuel Hirsch, who points out that *Stages* is the work of one who, out of his suffering and thought, seeks to guide a reader to a personal understanding of penitence and faith.[30] The distinction between recollection and memory, so splendidly and insightfully developed in the beginning of *Stages* (pp. 9-15), applies to the experiential element in the entire work.

In one of the few contemporary reviews of *Stages* (and *Three Discourses on Imagined Occasions*), the veil of pseudo-

---

[28] *Two Ages*, p. 99, *KW* XIV (*SV* VIII 92). For a discussion of autobiography and the works, see *Fear and Trembling* and *Repetition*, pp. ix-xi, *KW* VI.

[29] Sponheim, Introduction, *Stages on Life's Way*, tr. Walter Lowrie (New York: Schocken, 1967), p. xiv. Walter Lowrie in the Introduction by the Translator (p. 3) says, "I must acknowledge with shame that what I said about the *Stages* in a few pages of my book on *Kierkegaard* (pp. 282-5) is not only inadequate but in one respect misleading." Yet a few pages later (p. 13) there is the very misleading line: "Quidam's Diary is in every detail the story of S.K.'s unhappy love." A few details like the ring note in *Stages* (pp. 329-30) scarcely legitimize the claim that "every detail" is autobiographical.

[30] *Einleitung, Stadien auf des Lebens Weg*, Sören Kierkegaard, *Gesammelte Werke*, Abt. 1-36 (Düsseldorf, Cologne: Diederichs Verlag, 1952-69), XV, p. xi.

nymity was publicly drawn aside for the first time. "One would think that Mag[ister] Kierkegaard possessed a kind of magic wand by which he instantaneously conjures up his books, so incredible has his literary activity been in recent years, if we dare believe the rumor that presumably is correct in claiming him to be the author of *Either/Or* and the series of books that apparently comes from the same hand."[31] Kierkegaard responded obliquely by denying a rumor that attributed to him the sermon at the end of *Either/Or*, II, on the basis of his having once delivered a sermon at the theological seminary.[32] Thereupon *The Corsair* [*Corsaren*] printed a fictional report of a fictional court case brought by Kierkegaard against the *Berlingske Tidende* because the latter had "respectfully praised one of the plaintiff's unwritten books."[33]

The main review of *Stages*, by Peder Ludvig Møller, appeared in his annual, *Gæa*.[34] Cleverly written and marked by a polemic stance toward the writer and by a skewed perception consciously calculated to provoke, the review did achieve that purpose, and more, in Kierkegaard's response, "The Activity of a Traveling Esthetician and How He Still Happened to Pay for the Dinner," by Frater Taciturnus.[35] The end of the piece contains the sting: Frater Taciturnus complains that he had *not* been abused in *The Corsair*, as others had, that Hilarius Bookbinder had been flattered and Victor Eremita immortal-

---

[31] *Berlingske Tidende*, 108, May 6, 1845, col. 3-4 (ed. tr.). See *The* Corsair *Affair and Articles Related to the Writings*, pp. 274-75, n. 55, *KW* XIII. The review two days later in *Nyt Aftenblad*, 105, col. 1, repeats the rumor (ed. tr.): "The present work [*Stages*] . . ., to judge according to its themes and style, owes its existence to the pseudonymous or, more correctly, polyonymous author of *Either/Or*, *Fear and Trembling*, *Repetition*, *Philosophical Fragments*, *The Concept of Anxiety* . . .." Thereafter, the review consists of two and one-half columns of quoted text from the end of *Stages* and seemingly is signed *Dixi*, which, however, is the last word in *Stages*.

[32] See Corsair *Affair*, pp. 22-23 (*SV* XIII 416-17), 156-57 (*Pap.* VI B 185), *KW* XIII. See also Supplement, pp. 646-51 (*Pap.* VI B 184).

[33] *Corsaren*, 245, May 23, 1845, col. 13 (ed. tr.). See Corsair *Affair*, pp. 275-76, *KW* XIII.

[34] See Corsair *Affair*, pp. 96-104, *KW* XIII.

[35] *Fædrelandet*, 2078, Dec. 27, 1845, col. 1-6. See Corsair *Affair*, pp. 38-46, *KW* XIII (*SV* XIII 422-31).

ized by *The Corsair*—followed by the declaration: *ubi* P. L. Møller, *ibi The Corsair* [where P. L. Møller is, there is *The Corsair*]. This was the beginning of the most famous literary controversy in Danish history, with very important consequences for P. L. Møller, for Meïr Goldschmidt, the editor and owner of *Corsaren*, and for Kierkegaard.[36]

Despite the unexpected publicity given to *Stages*, public interest in the book, as indicated by sales, was not spectacular. After twenty-six months, about 245 copies had been sold (at five rix-dollars, approximately $25.00 in 1973 money), and 280 copies were then remaindered.[37] In a journal entry, Kierkegaard repeated the prediction of scant response made at the end of *Stages*:

> The *Stages* will not have as many readers as *Either/Or*, will barely make a ripple. That is fine; in a way it rids me of the gawking public who want to be wherever they think there is a disturbance. I prophesied this myself in the epilogue to " 'Guilty?'/'Not Guilty?' "[38]

In *Postscript*, Johannes Climacus corroborates the report and also explains that the lack of attention was perhaps because *Stages* did not have, as *Either/Or* had, "The Seducer's Diary," "for quite certainly that was read most and of course contributed especially to the sensation."[39]

Other, later estimates diverged from the contemporary estimate expressed by indifference. Thirty-two years later Georg Brandes extolled " '*In Vino Veritas,*' " as well as its counterpart in *Either/Or*. "In the literary sense, they are surely the most excellent things Kierkegaard has written. If they had been written in one of the main European languages, they would have made their author world famous, especially since they appeared, not isolated, but as parts in a whole contrasting

---

[36] See Corsair *Affair*, pp. vii–xxxiii, 38–50 (*SV* XIII 422-35), 96-152, 157-240, *KW* XIII.

[37] See Frithiof Brandt and Else Rammel, *Søren Kierkegaard og Pengene* (Copenhagen: Munksgaard, 1935), pp. 18-19.

[38] *JP* V 5824 (*Pap.* VI A 79). See p. 653.

[39] *Postscript*, *KW* XII (*SV* VII 242).

spirit. . . . And if one places " '*In Vino Veritas*' " alongside Plato's *Symposium*, to which it was ostensibly a companion piece, one must acknowledge with amazement that it sustains the comparison as well as any modern composition could. Greater praise can hardly be given."[40] Speaking of the entire volume, Hirsch declares that *Stages*, despite earlier lack of attention, "has become, in Denmark as well as in Germany, Kierkegaard's most famous and influential poetic work," even though it is still "the most difficult to understand and the most misunderstood"[41] of Kierkegaard's works. With reference to " 'Guilty?'/'Not Guilty?' " Kierkegaard would be in some agreement: it is "the richest of all I have written, but it is difficult to understand."[42]

[40] Georg Brandes, *Søren Kierkegaard* (Copenhagen: 1877), pp. 156-57 (ed. tr.).

[41] *Einleitung, Stadien, Werke*, XV, p. vii.

[42] *JP* V 5866 (*Pap.* VII¹ B 84).

STAGES ON LIFE'S WAY

STUDIES BY VARIOUS PERSONS

Compiled, Forwarded to the Press, and Published
by
HILARIUS BOOKBINDER

Exactly What You've Been Looking For.

420 E. Main Street
Galesburg, IL 61401
Lyndon & Sherry Graham
Owners

Bring this card in for a <u>special drawing</u> for Three

Gift Certificates Up To $300

SEE YOU HERE!

Sheilah, Mary, Dan, Sherry & Lyndon

Special <u>12 months same as cash</u>, *with approved credit*
NO PAYMENTS TILL APRIL 2001---PRIOR SALES EXCLUDED

Thomas Moses
1442 N. Cherry
Galesburg, IL 61401

Inasmuch as there ought to be honesty in everything, especially in the realm of truth and in the world of books, also
since no distinguished professor or man of high standing
should resent it if a bookbinder, instead of minding his own
business, mingles unauthorized with the literati, a shameless
boldness that could also prompt severe judgment on the book
and possibly have the result that many, scandalized by the
bookbinder, would not read the book at all—there follows
hereupon the truthful history of the book.

Several years ago a literatus well known to me sent a considerable number of books to be bound, *item* [also] several
books in manuscript to be bound in quarto. Since it was the
busy time of the year and Mr. Literatus was in no hurry about
them, being always a gentle and tractable man, the books, I
am ashamed to say, remained with me more than three
months. And just as things go as the German proverb says:
Heute roth morgen todt [Today red, tomorrow dead], and just
as the preacher says: Death recognizes no status and no age,[2]
and just as my late wife declared: We all must take this road,
but our Lord knows best when it is beneficial,[3] and then it
indeed happens with God's help, and just as it also happens
that even the best of people[4] must depart from here, so in the
meantime the literatus died, and his heirs, who were abroad,
received the books through the probate court, and through
the same court I received payment for my work.

As a hard-working man and a good citizen who conscientiously gives everyone his due, it never occurred to me that I
had not sent everything back to Mr. Literatus, and then one
day I find a small package of handwritten papers. I ponder in
vain who could have sent me these, what should be done with
them, whether they should be bound, in short, all the
thoughts that can occur to a bookbinder in a situation like this,
or whether the whole thing was a mistake. Finally it dawned

VI
8

on my now deceased wife, a singularly faithful aid and support to me in the business, that this packet must have been lying in the big box in which Mr. Literatus's books had come. I arrived at the same opinion, but by now so much time had elapsed, and no one had thought to ask for the return of the papers, so I thought that it all presumably had little value and let the papers lie after I had, however, stitched them together in a colored paper folder so that they would not lie around and clutter up the shop, as my late wife used to say.

In the long winter evenings when I had nothing else to do, I sometimes picked up the book and read it for diversion. But I cannot say that there was much diversion, for I did not understand very much but had my diversion by sitting and speculating over what it might all be. And since a large portion was written in well-executed calligraphy, I now and then had my children copy a page so that they might practice penmanship by imitating the beautiful letters and flourishes. Sometimes they also had to read it aloud in order to practice reading script, something that inconceivably and inexplicably is utterly neglected in school instruction, and probably would long continue to be neglected were it not for the deservedly esteemed literatus Mr. I. Levin,[5] who, according to the newspapers, has sought to remedy this deficiency and has taught me to understand the truth of my late wife's words to the effect that "the reading of handwriting is necessary in the various positions in life and should never be neglected in school." And what indeed is the use of being able to write if one cannot read what one writes, as Henrich says in the comedy: He can write German, all right, but he cannot read it.[6]

My eldest son had turned ten years old when I decided last summer to have him begin more rigorous instruction. A reputable man recommended to me an especially qualified normal-school graduate and candidate in philosophy whom I knew somewhat and had heard with real edification at vespers in Vor Frelsers Church.[7] Although he had not taken the examination and had entirely abandoned studying to be a pastor since he found out that he was an esthete and a poet (I think that is what he calls it), he nevertheless was well educated and gave good sermons, but above all he had a splendid pulpit voice. Our agreement was that in return for his dinner he should instruct the boy two hours daily in the most important subjects.

It was truly fortunate for my humble household that the said normal-school graduate and candidate in philosophy became the boy's teacher, for not only did Hans make great progress, but, as I shall now relate, I became indebted to this good man for something far more important. One day he becomes aware of the book stitched together in a colored paper folder that I had been using for my children's instruction; he reads a little of it and thereupon asks to borrow it. I say to him and really mean it, "You may very well keep it, for now that the boy has a teacher who himself can show him how to write, I do not need it." But he was too honorable, as I now perceive, to want to do that. So he borrowed it. Three days later—I remember it as clearly as if it were yesterday; it was the fifth of January this year—he comes to us and wishes to speak with me. I thought he possibly wanted to borrow a little money, but no! He hands me the well-known book and says, "My dear Mr. Hilarius! You presumably were unaware of what a glorious gift and donation providence has allotted to your household in this book you so casually wanted to give away. If it comes into the right hands, a book such as this is worth its weight in gold. It is by the printing of worthwhile books such as this that one contributes to the advancement of good and beneficial learning among the children of men in these days when not only money but also faith is becoming a rarity among the people. Not only that, but you, Mr. Hilarius, who have always wished to be able to benefit your fellowmen in some other way than as a bookbinder, as well as to honor your late wife's memory by some outstanding good deed, you to whose happy lot it has fallen to be able to do this, you will by this undertaking also be able to earn a not inconsiderable sum when the book is sold." I was deeply moved and became even more so when he raised his voice and continued in a raised voice: As far as I am concerned, I ask nothing or as good as nothing; in consideration of the anticipated large profits, all I

VI
10

ask is ten rix-dollars right now and a half pint of wine for dinner on Sundays and holidays.

So it has come to pass as the good normal-school graduate and candidate in philosophy advised me; I only wish I were as sure of the large profits as he of the ten rix-dollars, which I paid him gladly, all the more so because he made me aware that my service was greater because it was not one book I would publish but several books, probably by several authors. In other words, my learned friend assumes that there must have been a fraternity, a society, or an association of which that literatus had been the head or president and therefore had preserved the papers. Personally, I have no opinion on this matter.

That a bookbinder would aspire to be an author could only arouse understandable resentment in the literary world and be instrumental in making people turn up their noses at the book, but that a bookbinder stitches together, guides through the press, and publishes a book so that he "might be able to benefit his fellowmen in some other way than as a bookbinder," no fair-minded reader will take amiss.[8]

And herewith may the book and the bookbinder and the undertaking be respectfully recommended.

Christianshavn, January 1845.[9]

Yours most respectfully,

Hilarius Bookbinder

"IN VINO VERITAS"[10]

A RECOLLECTION

Related
by
WILLIAM AFHAM[11]

Solche Werke sind Spiegel: wenn ein Affe hinein guckt,
kann kein Apostel heraus sehen
[Such works are mirrors: when an ape looks in,
no apostle can look out].

LICHTENBERG[12]

PREFACE[13]

What a splendid occupation to prepare a secret for oneself, how seductive to enjoy it, and yet at times how precarious to have enjoyed it, how easy for it to miscarry for one. In other words, if someone believes that a secret is transferable as a matter of course, that it can belong to the bearer, he is mistaken, for the [riddle] "Out of the eater comes something to eat"[14] is valid here; but if anyone thinks that the only difficulty entailed in enjoying it is not to betray it, he is also mistaken, for one also takes on the responsibility of not forgetting it.[15] Yet it is even more disgusting to recollect incompletely and to turn one's soul into a transit warehouse for damaged goods. In relation to others, then, let forgetting be the silken curtain that is drawn, recollection [*Erindring*] the vestal virgin who goes behind the curtain; behind the curtain is the forgetting again—if it is not a true recollection, for in that case the forgetting is excluded.

The recollection must be not only accurate; it must also be happy. The bottling of the recollection must have preserved the fragrance of the experience before it is sealed. Just as grapes cannot be pressed at any time whatsoever, just as the weather at the time of pressing has great influence on the wine, so also what is experienced can neither be recollected nor be inwardly recollected at any time whatsoever or under any and all circumstances.

To recollect [*erindre*] is by no means the same as to remember [*huske*].[16] For example, one can remember very well every single detail of an event without thereby recollecting it. Remembering is only a vanishing condition. Through memory, the experience presents itself to receive the consecration of recollection. The distinction is already discernible in the difference between generations. The old person loses memory, which as a rule is the first faculty to be lost. Yet the old person has something poetic about him; in the popular mind he is prophetic, inspired. But recollection is indeed his best power, his consolation, which consoles him with its poetic farsightedness. Childhood, on the other hand, has memory and quickness of apprehension to a high degree but does not have recollection at all. Instead of saying, "Old age does not forget what youth apprehends," one could perhaps say, "What the child remembers the old person recollects." The old person's glasses are ground for seeing close at hand. When youth wears glasses, the lens is for seeing at a distance, for it lacks the power of recollection, which is the power to distance, to place at a distance. But the happy recollection of old age, just like the happy apprehension of the child, is nature's gracious gift, which preferentially embraces the two most helpless and yet in a certain sense happiest periods of life. But for this very reason recollection, as well as memory, is sometimes only the holder of accidental happenings.

Although the difference between memory and recollection is great, they are frequently confused. In human life, this confusion lends itself to studying the depth of the individual. [17]That is, recollection is ideality, but as such it is strenuous and conscientious in a way completely different from indiscriminate memory. Recollection wants to maintain for a person the eternal continuity in life and assure him that his earthly existence remains *uno tenore* [uninterrupted], one breath, and expressible in one breath. Therefore it declines to have the tongue be constrained to chatter on and on in order to ape the chattering nature of life's content. The condition for man's immortality is that life is *uno tenore*. Strangely enough, Jacobi is the only one who, as far as I know, has commented on the terror in thinking oneself immortal.[18] At times it seemed to him as if the thought of immortality, if he held on to it a little longer in the single moment, would confuse his mind. Is the reason for this that Jacobi had bad nerves? A robust man who has acquired callouses on his hand simply by pounding the pulpit or the lectern every time he proved immortality feels no such terror, and yet he surely knows all about immortality, for in Latin[19] to have callouses means to understand something completely. However, as soon as one confuses memory and recollection, the thought is not so terrible—in the first place because one is bold, manly, and robust, and in the second place because one is not thinking the thought at all. No doubt many a man has written memoirs of his life in which there was not a trace of recollection, and yet the recollections were indeed his proceeds for eternity. In recollection, a person draws on the eternal. [20]The eternal is sufficiently humane to honor every claim and to regard everyone as solvent. But it is not the fault of the eternal that a person makes a fool of himself—and remembers instead of recollects and as a result forgets instead of recollects, for what is remembered is also forgotten. But in turn, memory makes life free and easy. One cavalierly goes through the most ludicrous metamorphoses; even at an advanced age one still plays blindman's buff, still plays the lottery of life, and still can become almost anything, although one has been an incredible number of things. Then one dies—and thereupon becomes immortal. And precisely by having lived in such a way, should one not have richly provided oneself with enough to recollect for a whole eternity? Yes, if recollection's ledger were nothing more than a notebook in which one scribbles anything that comes to mind. But recollection's bookkeeping is a curious thing. [21]One could assign oneself a few such problems—but not in fellowship. One person talks day in and day out to general assemblies and always about what the times demand, yet not repetitiously in a Cato-like, tedious way,[22] but always interestingly and intriguingly he follows the moment and never says the same thing; at parties, too, he imposes himself and doles out his fund of eloquence, at times with full even measure, at times heaped up, and always to applause; at least once a week there is something about him in the newspaper; also at night he bestows his favors, on his wife, that is, by talking even in his sleep about the demands of the times as if he were at a general assembly. Another person is silent before he speaks and goes so far that he does not speak at all; they live the same length of time—and here the question of the result is raised: Who has more to recollect? One person pursues one idea, one single idea, is preoccupied only with it; another is an author in seven branches of scholarship and "is interrupted in this significant work" (it is a journalist who is speaking) "just as he was about to transform veterinary science"; they live the same length of time—and here the question of the result is raised: Who has more to recollect?

Actually, only the essential can be recollected, for the old man's recollecting, as stated, is basically of an accidental character; the same holds true of analogies to his recollecting. The essential is conditioned not only by itself but also by its relation to the person concerned. The person who has broken with the idea cannot act essentially, can undertake nothing that is essential; the essential would then be to repent, which is the only new ideality. Despite external indications, anything else he does is unessential. To take a wife is indeed something essential, but anyone who has ever dallied with erotic love [*Elskov*] may very well strike his brow and his heart and his r--- in sheer seriousness and solemnity; it is still frivolity. Even if his marriage involved a whole nation and the bells were rung and the pope married them, it nevertheless is not anything essential to him but essentially is frivolity. The external noise makes no difference, just as the fanfare and presentation of arms do not make the lottery-drawing an essential act for the boy who draws the numbers.[23] Acting essentially does not depend essentially on the blowing of trumpets. But what is recollected cannot be forgotten either. What is recollected is not inconsequential to recollecting in the way that what is remembered is inconsequential to remembering. What is recollected can be thrown away, but just like Thor's hammer,[24] it returns, and not only that, like a dove it has a longing for the recollection, yes, like a dove, however often it is sold, that can never belong to anyone else because it always flies home. But no wonder, for it was recollection itself that hatched out what was recollected, and this hatching is hidden and secret, solitary, and thus immune to any profane knowledge—in just the same way the bird will not sit on its egg if some stranger has touched it.

Memory is immediate and is assisted immediately, recollection only reflectively. This is why it is an art to recollect.

Rather than remember, I, along with Themistocles, wish only to be able to forget;[25] but to recollect and to forget are not opposites. The art of recollecting is not easy, because in the moment of preparation it can become something different, whereas memory merely fluctuates between remembering correctly and remembering incorrectly. For example, what is homesickness? It is something remembered that is recollected. Homesickness is prompted simply by one's being absent. The art would be to be able to feel homesickness even though one is at home. This takes proficiency in illusion. To go on living in an illusion in which there is continual dawning, never daybreak, or to reflect oneself out of all illusion is not as difficult as to reflect oneself into an illusion, plus being able to let it work on oneself with the full force of illusion even though one is fully aware. To conjure up the past for oneself is not as difficult as to conjure away the present for the sake of recollection. This is the essential art of recollection and is reflection to the second power.

To bring about a recollection for oneself takes an acquaintance with contrasting moods, situations, and surroundings. An erotic situation in which the salient feature was the cozy remoteness of rural life can at times be best recollected and inwardly recollected in a theater, where the surroundings and the noise evoke the contrast. Yet the direct contrast is not always the happy one. If it were not unbecoming to use a human being as a means, the happy contrast for recollecting an erotic relationship might be to arrange a new love affair merely in order to recollect.

The contrast can be extremely reflective. The ultimate in the reflective relationship between memory and recollection is to use memory against recollection. For opposite reasons, two people could wish not to see again a place that reminds them of an event. The one has no inkling at all that there is something called recollection but merely fears the memory. Out of sight, out of mind, he thinks; if only he does not see, then he has forgotten. Precisely because the other wants to recollect, he does not want to see. He uses memory only against unpleasant recollections. One who understands recollection but

VI
19

does not understand this indeed has ideality but lacks experience in using *consilia evangelica*[26] *adversus casus conscientiae* [the evangelical counsels against a matter of conscience]. Indeed, he will probably even regard the advice as a paradox and shy away from enduring the first pain, which, nevertheless, just like the first loss, is always to be preferred.[27] When memory is refreshed again and again, it enriches the soul with a mass of details that distract recollection. Thus repentance is a recollection of guilt. From a purely psychological point of view, I really believe that the police aid the criminal in not coming to repent. By continually recounting and repeating his life experiences, the criminal becomes such a memory expert at rattling off his life that the ideality of recollection is driven away. Really to repent, and especially to repent at once, takes enormous ideality; therefore nature also can help a person, and delayed repentance, which in regard to remembering is negligible, is often the hardest and the deepest. The ability to recollect is the condition for all productivity. If a person no longer wishes to be productive, he needs merely to remember the same thing that recollecting he wanted to produce, and production is rendered impossible, or it will become so repulsive to him that the sooner he abandons it the better.

Strictly speaking, a fellowship of recollection does not exist. A kind of *quasi*-fellowship is a contrast-form that the one recollecting uses on his own behalf. Sometimes recollection is prompted best by seeming to confide in someone else only in order to conceal behind this confidence a new reflection in which the recollection comes into existence for oneself.[28] As far as memory is concerned, people can certainly join together for mutual assistance. In this respect, banquets, birthday celebrations, love tokens, and expensive mementos serve the same purpose as turning a dog-ear in a book in order to remember where one left off reading and by the dog-ear to be sure of having read the whole book through. The wine press of recollection, however, everyone must tread alone. In itself, this is far from being a curse. [29]Inasmuch as one is always alone with recollection, every recollection is a secret. Even if several persons are interested in what is the object of recol-

let overtakes, which indeed explains why the deer now became so still but does not explain why it was so restless. No
one travels this road except the wind, about which it is not
known whence it comes or whither it goes.[40] Even he who let
himself be deceived by that beguiling beckoning with which
the shut-in-ness tries to catch the wayfarer, even he who followed the narrow footpath that lures one into the inclosures
of the forest, even he is not as solitary as someone at the eight
paths that no one travels. Eight paths and not a traveler! Indeed, it is as if the world were dead and the one survivor were
in the awkward situation that there was no one to bury him,[41]
or as if the whole tribe had gone off on the eight paths and had
forgotten someone! —If what the poet says is true: *Bene vixit
qui bene latuit* [He who has hidden his life has lived well],[42]
[43]then I have lived well, for my nook was well chosen. It certainly is true that the world and everything therein never look
better than when seen from a nook and one must secretly contrive to see it; it is also true that everything heard and to be
heard in the world sounds most delectable and enchanting
heard from a nook when one must contrive to hear.[44] Thus I
have frequently visited my sequestered nook. I knew it before, long before; by now I have learned not to need nighttime
in order to find stillness, for here it is always still, always
beautiful, but it seems most beautiful to me now when the
autumn sun is having its midafternoon repast and the sky becomes a languorous blue when creation takes a deep breath
after the heat, when the cooling starts and the meadow grass
shivers voluptuously as the forest waves, when the sun is
thinking of eventide and sinking into the ocean at eventide,
when the earth is getting ready for rest and is thinking of giving thanks, when just before taking leave they have an understanding with one another [45]in that tender melting together
that darkens the forest and makes the meadow greener.

VI
23

[46]O friendly spirit, you who inhabit these places, thank you
for always protecting my stillness, thank you for those hours
spent in recollection's pursuits, thank you for that hiding place
I call my own! Then stillness grows as the shadows grow, as
silence grows: a conjuring formula! Indeed, what is as intoxi-

cating as stillness! For no matter how quickly the drunkard raises the glass to his lips, his intoxication does not increase as quickly as the intoxication created by stillness, which increases with every second! And what is the intoxicating content of the glass but a drop compared with the infinite sea of silence from which I drink![47] And what is all the seething of the wine but a fleeting illusion compared with the spontaneous bubbling of silence, which seethes more and more vigorously! But then, too, what vanishes as quickly as this reveling—once there is speaking! And what is as nauseating as the condition of being suddenly cut off from it—even worse than the drunkard's awakening, when one in silence is bereft of speech, shy at the sound of words, stammering like someone who is tongue-tied, weak as a surprised woman, too weak at the moment to be able to beguile with words! Thank you, then, you friendly spirit, for holding surprise and interruption at bay, for the intruder's apology is of little help.

How often I have thought about this! In the human swarm, one does not become guilty if one is innocent, but solitary stillness is holy, and thus everything that disturbs it becomes guilty, and the chaste association of silence, if violated, tolerates no excuse nor is helped by it any more than modesty by explanations. How painful it was when it happened to me— to stand there with the nagging pain in the soul, ashamed of my offense: to have disturbed someone in his solitude! In vain will repentance seek to fathom it: this guilt is inexpressible, just like silence. Only someone who sought solitude unworthily can benefit from surprise, as if a pair of lovers did not even there have the power to shape a situation. If this is the case, then one can serve Eros and the lovers by making an appearance, even if to the lovers one's service remains a mystery, just as the guilt does—they cling closer together out of irritation with the intruder, to whom they are nevertheless indebted for their so doing. But if they are two lovers who worthily seek solitude, how oppressive it is then to take them by surprise, how one could curse oneself as every animal was cursed when it approached Sinai![48] Who does not feel this way, who, when he sees but as yet is unseen, could not wish

VI
24

[50]It was on one of the last days in July, about ten o'clock in the
evening, that the participants gathered for that banquet. The
date and the year I have forgotten; such matters, after all, are
of interest only to memory, not to recollection. The only subject matter for recollection is mood and whatever is classified
under mood. And just as noble wine is improved by crossing
the line[51] because the particles of water vaporize, so recollection also is improved by losing the water particles of memory;
yet recollection no more becomes a figment of the imagination thereby than does the noble wine.

[52]The participants were five in number:[53] Johannes, called
the Seducer, Victor Eremita, Constantin Constantius, and
two more whose names I have not exactly forgotten, which
would not have been important, but whose names I did not
learn. It seemed as if these two had no *proprium* [proper name],
for they were always named only by an epithet. The one was
called: the Young Man. He presumably was in his early twen-
ties, of slender and delicate build, and of rather dark complexion. He had a thoughtful expression, but even more pleasing
was his charming, engaging demeanor, which betokened a
purity of soul that completely harmonized with the almost
femininely luxuriant softness and transparency of his whole
figure. [54]But in turn one forgot this external beauty with the
next impression or kept it only *in mente* [in mind] while contemplating a young man who, cultivated—or, to use an even
more delicate expression, fostered—by intellect alone, nourished by the content of his own soul, had had nothing to do
with the world, had been neither awakened and inflamed nor
disquieted and disturbed. Like a sleepwalker, he carried the
law for his behavior within himself, and his loving sympathetic demeanor involved no one but reflected only the fun-
damental mood of his soul.

The other one they called the Fashion Designer, which was his occupation in civil life. It was impossible to get a genuine impression of this man. He was dressed in the very latest fashion, was curled and perfumed and smelled of *eau de Cologne*. One moment his behavior was not without aplomb, but the next moment his walk assumed a certain dancelike festiveness, a certain floating motion, to which his corpulence nevertheless set limits at some point. Even when he was talking most maliciously, his voice always had an element of boutique-pleasantness and polite sweetness, which certainly must have been extremely nauseating to him personally and only satisfied his defiance. When I think about him now, I certainly understand him better than when I saw him step out of the carriage and could not help but laugh.[55] But a contradiction still remains. He has charmed or bewitched himself, by the wizardry of his will has conjured himself into an almost silly character, but has not quite satisfied himself with it, which is why now and then reflection peeks out.

When I now think of this, it seems almost absurd to me that five such people planned a banquet. Most likely nothing would have come of it had not Constantin Constantius been along. The subject had been broached one day in a coffee shop[56] where they sometimes met in a side room, but it had been completely dropped when the question arose of who should organize it. The Young Man was declared unsuited for it; the Fashion Designer did not have the time. Victor Eremita, of course, did not excuse himself by saying that he had taken a wife or bought a yoke of oxen and had to examine them,[57] but even if he would make an exception and come, he would decline the courtesy of being the organizer and "hereby spoke now."[58] Johannes considered this to be a good word in the proper place,[59] for in his opinion there was only one who was able to arrange a banquet, and that was the tablecloth that spreads itself and sets everything out if one merely says: Spread yourself.[60] It was not always proper to enjoy a young maiden in haste; a banquet he could not wait for and ordinarily was bored with it far in advance. If, however, this was going to be carried out, he insisted on one condition—that it allowed to be reduced to something of insignificance, and in turn the speeches are not allowed to have the importance of being given *inter pocula* [between the glasses]. Up to this point we no doubt agree, and our number, if anything would come of our banquet, is also properly chosen by that beautiful rule: no more than the Muses, no fewer than the Graces.[69] Now, I insist on the richest overabundance of everything imaginable. Even if everything is not right there, the possibility of it must be immediately at hand, hover temptingly over the table even more seductively than the sight of it. To banquet on matches or, like the Dutch, on a sugar lump of which everybody takes a lick, no, thanks. But my demand is difficult to satisfy, because the meal itself must be calculated to awaken and incite that unmentionable craving that every worthy member brings with him. I insist that the earth's fruitfulness be at our service, as if everything sprouted the very instant desire craves it. I insist on a more lavish abundance of wine than Mephistopheles had just by boring a hole in the table.[70] I insist on more voluptuous lighting than the trolls' when they lift the mountain up onto pillars and dance in an ocean of fire. I insist on what arouses the senses most of all, I insist on that delicious refreshment of scents more glorious than those found in the *Arabian Nights' Entertainments*. I insist on a coolness that voluptuously inflames desire and cools the satisfied desire. I insist on the ceaseless exhilaration of a fountain. If Maecenas could not sleep without hearing the splashing of a fountain,[71] then I cannot dine without it. Do not misunderstand me; I can eat dried fish without it, but I cannot eat at a banquet without it; I can drink water without it, but I cannot drink wine at a banquet without it. I insist on a staff of servants, select and handsome, as if I were sitting at the table of the gods. [72]I insist on dinner music, intense and subdued, and I insist that it be my accompaniment at all times. And with regard to you, my friends, I make incredible demands. You see, on the basis of all these demands, which are just as many reasons against it, I think that a banquet is a *pium desiderium* [pious wish], and in this respect I am so far from wanting to talk about a repetition that I assume that it cannot be done even once.

The only one who had not actually taken part in that conversation, or in the defeat of the banquet, was Constantin Constantius. But for him it would never have been anything except talk. He had arrived at another conclusion and believed that if one took the others by surprise the idea could very well be carried out. Some time went by, and both the banquet and the discussion about it were forgotten, until suddenly one day the participants received an invitation from Constantin to a banquet the same evening. The motto for the banquet was specified by Constantin: *in vino veritas*, because certainly there must be speeches, not just conversation, but there must be no speeches except *in vino*, and no truth must be heard except that which is *in vino*, when wine is a defense for truth and truth is a defense for wine.

VI
30

[73]The place chosen was in a wooded area a few miles from Copenhagen.[74] The salon in which they were to dine had been redecorated and altered recently beyond all recognition; a small room separated from the salon by a corridor was prepared for an orchestra. Shutters and curtains were placed before all the windows, and behind these the windows stood open. Constantin's wish was that, as a preliminary, they arrive by carriage in the evening. Even though one knows that one is driving to a banquet and consequently indulges momentarily in imagining the sumptuousness of it, yet the impact of the natural environment is so powerful that it must prevail. The only fear Constantin had was that this would not happen, for just as there is no force so proficient as the imagination in embellishing everything, so, too, there is no other force able to play havoc with everything when things go wrong for one in the moment of encounter with actuality. Driving on a summer evening does not, however, turn the imagination toward the sumptuous but does the very opposite. Even if one does not see and hear it, the imagination nevertheless involuntarily creates an image of the evening's cozy, comfortable longing; thus one sees girls and farmhands on their way home from their field work, hears the hurried clattering of the harvest wagon, interprets even the bellowing far off in the meadow as a longing. In this way the summer

between man and woman;[86] love affairs, however, should not be related, but indeed they might very well be the basis of the point of view.

The conditions were accepted. —All of a host's just and reasonable demands upon guests were fulfilled: they ate, drank and drank, and became drunk,[87] as it says in Hebrew—that is, they drank mightily.

The dessert was served. If Victor had not yet had his request fulfilled to hear the splashing of a fountain, something that fortunately for him he had forgotten about since that conversation, now the champagne effervesced to overflowing. The clock struck twelve; then Constantin asked for silence and toasted the Young Man with a glass and these words: *Quod felix sit faustumque* [May it be to good fortune and success][88] and asked him to speak first.

The Young Man arose and declared that he did feel the influence of the wine, which was rather visible, for the blood pulsed violently in his temples, and his appearance was not as handsome as before the meal. He spoke as follows.

If there is any truth in the poets' words, dear drinking companions, then unhappy erotic love is indeed the saddest of pains. If this needs any proof, then listen to what lovers say. They say that it is death, certain death, and the first time they believe it for two weeks. The second time they say it is death; the third time they say it is death, and finally one day they die—of unhappy love—for there is no doubt that they die of love, and that it takes love three times to succeed in taking their lives is like the dentist's having to try three times before extracting the impacted molar. But if unhappy love is certain death in this way, then how lucky am I, I who have never loved and hope that I shall manage to die only once and mercifully not from unhappy love! But perhaps precisely this is the very worst misfortune; how unhappy, then, must I not be! The significance of love presumably must be (for I am speaking as the blind person speaks about colors) its bliss, and this again expresses that the cessation of love is the lover's death. This I understand as an imaginary construction in

VI
35

thought that relates life and death. But if love is just an imaginary construction in thought, the lovers who actually go and fall in love are indeed ludicrous. But if it is supposed to be something actual, then the actuality must in fact confirm what the lovers say about it. But even if we hear this said, do we hear or perceive that it actually happens? Already in this I see one of the contradictions in which love entangles a person; whether it is otherwise for the initiates, I do not know, but to me love seems to entangle a person in the strangest contradictions. No other relationship between human beings lays claim to the ideality that love does, and yet it is never judged to have it. Just on this basis I am afraid of love, because I fear it might have the power also to make me gush about a bliss I did not perceive and a pain I did not feel. I am saying this here since I am bound to speak about love, although unversed in it; I am saying this here in surroundings that are as gratifying to me as a Greek symposium, for otherwise I have no desire to talk about it, have no desire to disturb anyone's happiness, but am satisfied with my own thoughts. Perhaps in the eyes of the initiates these thoughts are merely stupidities and cobwebs; perhaps my ignorance is explained by my never having learned or cared to learn from anyone how one comes to love, by my never, because it was bold, having challenged a woman with a glance but having always looked down, unwilling to surrender to an impression before I have fully comprehended the significance of the power to whose control I am surrendering.

At this point the Young Man was interrupted by Constantin, who pointed out that by confessing that he had never had a love affair he had disqualified himself from being able to speak. The Young Man declared that at any other time he would gladly comply with an order that called for silence, because he had often enough felt bored in speaking, but here he wanted to defend his rights. Precisely this, that he had had no love affair, was also a love affair, and the person who could say this was especially qualified to talk about Eros,[89] because in his thought he could be said to have a relationship to the whole sex and not to individuals.[90] He was given permission to speak, and he continued.

Inasmuch as doubt has been cast on my right to talk, this doubt presumably has served to spare me your laughter, for I am well aware that just as anyone who does not have a pipe is not considered by farmhands to be a real man, so also anyone without any experience in erotic love is not considered by males to be a real man. If someone wants to laugh, then let him laugh—to me the thought is and remains the primary point. Or does erotic love perhaps have the privilege of being the only thing one must not think about beforehand but only afterward? If this were the case, what would happen if I, the lover, came to think afterward that it was afterward? This, you see, is why I choose to think about erotic love beforehand! To be sure, lovers also declare that they have thought about it beforehand, but this is not so. [91]They presuppose that to love belongs essentially to a human being,[92] but that, after all, is not thinking about erotic love but is presupposing it in order to be intent on acquiring a beloved for oneself.

Everywhere, therefore, where my reflection wants to comprehend erotic love, I see only contradiction. To be sure, at times it seems to me as if something has escaped me, but what it is I cannot say; on the other hand, my reflection is again able to show me immediately the contradiction here. Therefore, you see, in my view Eros is the greatest contradiction imaginable—and comic as well. The two go hand in hand. The basis of the comic is always in the category of contradiction,[93] a subject I cannot elaborate upon here, but what I do wish to point out here is that erotic love is comic.[94] By love, I understand here the relation between man and woman and am not thinking of Eros in the Greek sense, for example, as so beautifully eulogized by Plato,[95] but with him it was so far from being a matter of loving women that this is mentioned only in passing and is even considered to be imperfect in comparison with loving young men. I am saying that erotic love is comic to a third party—more I do not say. Whether this is why lovers always hate a third party, I do not know, but this I do know, that reflection is always a third party, and therefore I cannot love without also being a third party to myself in my reflection. [96]This cannot seem strange to anyone, inasmuch as everyone, after all, has doubted everything,[97] and I am making an attempt to doubt everything only with respect to erotic love; but on the other hand it seems strange to me that one has doubted everything and has found certainty again and yet never drops a word about the difficulties that have fettered my thought so that I have at times longingly wished deliverance with the help of the one, please note, who first thought of the difficulties and did not in his sleep receive the suggestion to doubt and then doubted everything, and again I say, did not in his sleep receive the suggestion to explain and then explained everything. So give me your attention, dear drinking companions, and if you yourselves are lovers, nevertheless please do not interrupt me, do not shush me up because you do not want to hear the explanation; rather turn away and listen with averted faces to what I have to say, what I have a mind to say now that I have begun.

In the first place,[98] I find it comic that all human beings love, and want to love, and yet one can never learn what the lovable, what the actual object of erotic love, is. I am not taking the words "to love" into consideration, for they say nothing, but as soon as the subject comes up, the first question is: What is it that one loves? To that there is no other answer than that one loves what is lovable. In other words, if the answer along with Plato is that one should love the good,[99] then one has overstepped in a single step the whole sphere of the erotic. But then the answer may be that one should love the beautiful. If I then were to ask whether to love is to love a beautiful region of the country, a beautiful painting, we would promptly see that the erotic is not related as a species to the sphere of erotic love but is something utterly distinctive. Thus if a lover, desiring to express how much love there really was in him, were to talk as follows: I love a beautiful countryside, and my Lalage,[100] and the beautiful dancer, and a beautiful horse—in short, I love everything that is beautiful—then Lalage, even though otherwise satisfied with him, would not be satisfied with his eulogy, even though she was beautiful. And fancying that I am thinking about life when I, with regard to something important, say: Let it pass.

A human being consists of soul and body; on that all the wisest and best men agree. If we now place the power of erotic love in the relation between female and male, the comic will once again manifest itself in the reversal that occurs when the psychical at its loftiest expresses itself in the most sensual. I am thinking here of all of erotic love's very strange gesticulations and mysterious signs—in short, all the freemasonry that is a continuation of that first inexplicable something. The contradiction in which erotic love here involves a person is this— that the symbolic does not mean anything at all, or, what amounts to the same thing, no one is able to say what it is supposed to mean. Two loving souls assure each other that they will love each other for all eternity; thereupon they embrace each other and seal this eternal pact with a kiss. I ask any thinking person whether he ever thought of that. And so it continually alternates in erotic love. The psychical at its loftiest finds its expression in the extreme opposite, and the sensual wants to signify the psychical at its loftiest. *Posito* [Suppose] that I had fallen in love. It would then be of the utmost importance to me that the beloved would belong to me for all eternity. This I understand, for here I am actually speaking only of the kind of Greek eroticism in which one loves beautiful souls. Then when the beloved had assured me of this, I would believe it, or if any doubt remained, I would contest it. But what happens, for if I were in love, I presumably would behave like all the others; I would seek some other assurance than believing her, which nevertheless is the only assurance there is. Here again I confront the inexplicable. When Kakkadue all of a sudden begins to plume himself like a gorged duck and thereupon stutters the word "Mariane,"[107] everyone, including me, laughs. The spectators perhaps find the comic in the fact that Kakkadue, who does not love Mariane at all, is in such rapport with her; but now suppose that Kakkadue loved Mariane—would it then not be comic? To me it seems just as comic, and the comic lies in this, that erotic love has become commensurable and is supposed to be regarded as

VI
42

commensurable with an expression such as that. Whether this has been the custom since the beginning of the world does not alter the case; the comic has eternity's prescriptive right to consist in contradiction, and here is a contradiction. There is really nothing comic about a puppet, for there is no contradiction in its making the strangest motions when the string is pulled. But to be a puppet in the service of something inexplicable is comic. The contradiction is that there is no apparent rational reason for having a twitch now in this leg, now in the other. If I cannot explain to myself what it is I am doing, then I will not do it; if I cannot understand the force to whose power I am surrendering, then I will not surrender to its power. And if love is a kind of mysterious law that combines the most extreme contradictions, who will guarantee to me that confusion may not suddenly arise in it? But this is of minor concern to me. For instance, I have certainly heard that some lovers find the behavior of other lovers ludicrous. [108]What that kind of laughter really means, I do not comprehend, for if that law is a law of nature, then it is certainly the same for all lovers; and if it is a law of freedom, then those laughing lovers must, after all, be able to explain everything— which they nevertheless are not able to do.

As far as that goes, I can better understand that generally it is the case that the one lover laughs at the other because he finds the other ludicrous but not himself. If it is ludicrous to kiss an ugly girl, it is also ludicrous to kiss a pretty one. And the notion that doing it in a certain manner justifies laughing at someone else who does it in another way is nothing but superciliousness and a conspiracy that still does not save such a discriminating person from the general ludicrousness because of the inability of everyone to say what it is supposed to mean, whereas it nevertheless is supposed to mean everything, and to mean that the two lovers will belong to each other for all eternity—indeed, what is still more amusing, is supposed to assure them that they do.

If a man, all of a sudden tipping his head to one side or shaking his head or kicking out his foot, answered me if I asked him why he did it: I really do not know, I just happened to do it that way; next time I'll do it differently, for it is in-voluntary—ah, then I would understand him very well. But if he said—as the lovers indeed say of those gesticulations—that all the bliss consists in this, how ludicrous I would find it, as I also found that first instance ludicrous, admittedly in a somewhat different sense, until the man forestalled the laugh-ter by explaining that they were not supposed to mean any-thing. Hereby precisely the contradiction underlying the comic is nullified, for it is not ludicrous to declare that some-thing that is meaningless does not mean anything at all, whereas it certainly is ludicrous to declare that it means every-thing. As for the involuntary, the contradiction is initially present: that we do not expect the involuntary from a free ra-tional being. Suppose, for instance, that the pope started coughing the very moment he was about to place the crown on Napoleon's head or that in the solemn moment of ex-changing vows the bride and bridegroom began to sneeze—the comic would be apparent. The more the given occasion emphasizes the free rational being, the more comic the invol-untary becomes. The same applies to erotic gesticulations, where the comic appears for the second time when people try to explain that contradiction by giving them absolute mean-ing. Children, as is known, have a great sense of the comic—in substantiation of this one can always rely on children. Or-dinarily, children can never help laughing at lovers, and if we induce them to tell what they have seen, no one can refrain from laughing. Perhaps this is because children leave out the point. How strange that when the Jew left out the point no one laughed, but here it is just the opposite: when someone leaves out the point everyone laughs. But since no one can say what the point is, then it certainly is left out. The lovers ex-plain nothing; those who eulogize love explain nothing but are only prepared, as ordered by the Danish constitution, to say everything that may be kind and pleasant.[109] But the per-son who thinks gives an account of his categories, and the per-son who thinks about love also promptly thinks about the cat-egories. But people do not do this with love, and we still lack a science of rural life [*Pastoral-Videnskab*], for even if a poet

VI
44

tries to have love come to life in a *pastorale* [pastoral poem], everything is smuggled in again with the aid of another person from whom the lovers learn [110]to love.[111] —Consequently, I found the comic in the erotic reversal whereby the highest in one sphere does not find its expression in this sphere but in something totally opposite in another sphere. It is comic that erotic love's lofty soaring (wanting to belong to each other for all eternity) always ends up, like Saft, in the pantry,[112] but it is still more comic that this conclusion of the matter is supposed to be the highest expression.

[113]Wherever there is contradiction, there is the comic. I am continually following this track. If it upsets you, dear drinking companions, to follow me, then follow with averted faces; after all, I myself am speaking as if I had a veil over my eyes, for since I can see only the enigmatic, I cannot really see, or I am really seeing nothing. What is a consequence? If in one way or another it cannot be identified with that of which it is the consequence, then it becomes ludicrous if it nevertheless should claim to be a consequence. For instance, when a man who wants to take a bath jumps into the tub and as he somewhat confusedly surfaces again grabs for the bath rope to steady himself but mistakenly grabs the chain of a shower, which then with excellent motivation and with every possible justification streams down on him, the consequence is entirely proper. The ludicrousness consists in his grabbing the wrong chain, but there is nothing ludicrous in a shower gushing forth if one pulls the chain; indeed, it would rather be ludicrous if it did not, as if—to demonstrate the correctness of my proposition about contradiction—as if a man deliberately steeled himself to be prepared and rightly able to tolerate that cold shower, pulled the chain with the zest of resolution—and no water came.

[114]Let us now see how it is with erotic love. The lovers want to belong to each other for all eternity. This they expressed in that strange manner of embracing each other in the fervency of the moment, and all the desire of the bliss of love is supposed to be in that embrace. But all desire is selfish. The lover's desire presumably is not selfish in relation to the be-

loved's, but the desire of both together is absolutely selfish
insofar as they in union and in love form one self. And yet
they are deceived; for at the very same moment the species
triumphs over the individuals, the species is victorious while
individuals are subordinated to being in its service. I find this
more ludicrous than what Aristophanes found so ludicrous.[115]
For the ludicrousness in that bisection lies in the contradiction,
which Aristophanes did not adequately emphasize. When one
looks at a human being, one should still believe him to be a
complete entity in himself, and one believes that—until one
sees that in the obsession of love he is only a half running
around after his other half. There is nothing comic in half an
apple; the comic would become apparent only if a whole apple
were half an apple. In the former case there is no contradiction, but certainly in the latter case. If the colloquialism that a
woman is only half a person is taken seriously, she would not
be at all comic in erotic love. But the man who has enjoyed
social esteem as a whole man becomes comic when he suddenly begins to run around and thereby betrays that he is but
half a person. The more one thinks about it, the more ludicrous it becomes, for if the man actually is a whole, then he
certainly does not become a whole in erotic love, but he and
the woman become one and a half. No wonder the gods
laugh, and especially at the man. But I turn back to my consequence. Now, if the lovers have found each other, one
would expect them to be a whole, and that would account for
the truth of their living for each other for all eternity. But
look, instead of living for each other they begin living for the
human race, and this they do not suspect.

[116]What is a consequence? If, when it appears, one cannot
see it in that from which it emerged, then such a consequence
is ludicrous and those involved in it are ludicrous. Now if
those separated halves have found each other, this certainly
means perfect satisfaction and rest, and yet a new life
[Tilværelse] results from it. It is understandable that the lovers'
finding each other becomes a new life for them, but it is not
understandable that a new life for another person dates from
it. And yet this resulting consequence is even greater than that

from which it is a consequence, and yet a completion like that of the lovers who found each other surely must be a sign that no further consequences are thinkable. Is any other desire analogous to this? Quite the reverse. [117]Indeed, gratified desire always means[118] a more or less stagnant state, and even if *tristitia* [sloth, dejection, moroseness] sets in, suggesting that all desire is comic, such *tristitia* will be a simple consequence, even if no *tristitia* is such strong evidence of a prior element of the comic as is the *tristitia* of erotic love. On the other hand, such an enormous consequence as the one of which we speak is another matter, a consequence of which no one knows whence it comes or if it comes, whereas it nevertheless, if it comes, comes as a consequence.

[119]Who can comprehend this? And yet for the initiates what is erotic love's highest desire is also its deepest significance; it is so significant that the lovers even take new names that are derived from the consequence, which then curiously enough acquire retroactive force. The lover is now called "father," and the beloved is called "mother," and to them these names are the most beautiful of all. And yet there is one for whom these names are even more beautiful, for what is as beautiful as piety? To me it seems the most beautiful of all, and fortunately I am able to understand its idea. We are taught that the son ought to love his father. This I understand. I do not have even an intimation of a contradiction. I feel blessedly bound in piety's beautiful bonds of love. [120]I believe that it is the most sublime to owe life to another person; I believe that this debt cannot be settled or discharged by any reckoning, and this is why I feel that Cicero is right in saying that in relation to the father the son is always in the wrong,[121] and it is precisely piety that teaches me to believe this, teaches me not even to want to penetrate what is hidden but rather to go on being hidden in the father. Yes, I am happy to be another human being's greatest debtor, but conversely, before I decide to make another person my greatest debtor, I certainly want to be clear in my own mind, because in my opinion there is no comparison between being another person's debtor and making another person one's debtor so that he cannot become free

everything, and if he has been so fortunate as to find the right one, then, presto, he has an authoress who wants to lay eggs, and he himself adoringly shades his eyes with his hand while he marvels at what the little black hen produces in other respects.[143] It is incomprehensible that Socrates did not choose to play this part instead of squabbling with Xanthippe, but then, of course, he wanted to practice, just like the riding master who, even if he has the best broken-in horse, still knows how to tease it in such a way that there may be sufficient reason to break it in.[144]

I shall proceed a bit more concretely in order to shed light on a particular and really interesting incident. The faithfulness of woman is much discussed, but it is seldom discussed correctly. From the purely esthetic point of view, it belongs with the phantom the author has walk across the stage looking for the beloved, the phantom sitting at the spinning wheel waiting for the beloved—for when she has found him and he has come, well, then esthetics is at a dead end. Her unfaithfulness, which can be directly connected with that previous faithfulness, if viewed mainly ethically, then encounters jealousy as a tragic passion. There will be three examples, and the relation is to the woman's advantage, because two of them show faithfulness, the third unfaithfulness. [145]Incomprehensibly great is her faithfulness as long as she is not sure of her beloved, and just as incomprehensibly great when he declines her faithfulness. The third instance is unfaithfulness. Once one has the mind and the disinterestedness to think, sufficient justification will readily be found for the category of jest in what has already been said.

[146]Our young friend, who in a way misled me at the outset, started out as if he wanted to deal with this, but backed away from it, terrified by the difficulty. [147]But the explanation is not difficult if one is really serious about relating unhappy love to death, if one is sufficiently earnest to hold fast to this idea— and that much earnestness we ought to have at all times—for the sake of the jest. All the talk naturally comes from a woman or an effeminate male. It is recognized at once, for it is one of those absolute outbursts that, spoken with much self-assur-

ance at the moment, are sure of much applause at the moment. Even though it is a discussion of life and death, it nevertheless is calculated to be enjoyed as one enjoys a whipped-cream meringue—at the moment; even though it concerns a whole life, it nevertheless does not at all obligate the one who is dying but obligates only the listener to hurry at once to the aid of the dying one. If a man were to hold forth in this manner, it would not be one bit amusing, for he is so despicable that one is unable to laugh at him. But woman is a genius, is lovable in her genius, and is amusing from first to last. So, then, she in love dies of erotic love; that is certain, for did she not say so herself. Here lies her pathos, for woman is man; at least she is man enough to say what hardly any man is man enough to do. Man she is. In saying this, I have viewed her ethically. Do likewise, dear drinking companions, and then understand Aristotle. He makes the correct observation that woman is really not usable in tragedy.[148] This is, of course, obvious; she belongs in the pathos-filled and serious divertissement, in the dramatic half-hour jest, not the five-act play. And then she dies. But should she therefore not be able to love again? Why not—that is, if she can be revived. If she revives, then she is indeed a new human being; and a new human being, a different human being, begins, loves for the first time, and there is nothing remarkable about that. O death, how powerful you are; the most powerful emetic, the strongest laxative could not purge so clean.

The confusion is superb—if only we pay attention to it and do not forget. A dead person is one of the most amusing figures to be met in life. Strange that this is not used on the stage more frequently[149]—now and then in real life we can meet such a one. Even one feigning death has an essentially comic oddity about him, but a person who is actually dead furnishes all the amusement one can reasonably require of a contribution to amusement. Just keep on the alert; I myself actually became aware of this one day while walking along the street with an acquaintance. We met a passing couple. My companion's demeanor led me to assume that he knew the couple, and I asked him about them. "Oh," he answered, "I know them very well and very intimately, especially the lady, for she was my late departed." "What late departed?" I asked. "Oh, my late departed first love; yes, it was a strange story. 'I am dying,' she said, and at the same moment departed, as is natural with death—otherwise one could have invested in the widows' pension fund. It was too late; dead she was and dead she remained, and now I am wandering about, as the poet says, 'looking in vain for my beloved's grave so that I can offer her a tear.'"[150]

VI
56

So it was with that dejected man who was left alone in the world, notwithstanding that it comforted him to find the late beloved already so far along, if not because of someone else nevertheless with someone else. How fine it is for the girls, I thought, that they do not have to be buried every time they die; if parents hitherto have regarded boys as the most expensive, girls could then easily become even more expensive. A simple case of unfaithfulness is not nearly so amusing, I think, as when a girl falls in love with someone else and says to her husband: I can't help it; save me from myself. But to die of sorrow because she cannot bear to have her beloved be far away on a journey to the West Indies, to have to reconcile herself to his going, and then upon his homecoming not only be dead but united forever to someone else—that is really a strange fate for a lover. No wonder that the dejected man sometimes comforted himself with the chorus of an old ballad: Cheers for you and me, say I; this day will never be forgotten.[151]

Forgive me, dear drinking companions, if I have spoken too long; and now let us empty a glass to erotic love and to woman. Beautiful is she and lovely when she is viewed esthetically—no one can deny it. But as is said so often, so I, too, will say: One should not stop with that but should go further.[152] Look at her ethically; just start doing that, and you have the jest. Even Plato and Aristotle assume that woman is an incomplete form,[153] consequently an irrational quantity that perhaps in a better existence can be led back to the male form; here in life one must take her for what she is. What that is will soon be manifest, for she, too, is not satisfied with the esthetic. She goes further; she wants to be emancipated—she is man enough to say that. If that happens, the jest will exceed all bounds.

When Constantin had spoken, he promptly invited Victor Eremita to begin; the latter spoke as follows.

[154]Plato, as we know, thanks the gods for four things, and for the fourth he gives thanks because he had been contemporary with Socrates.[155] An earlier Greek philosopher[156] had already thanked the gods for the three first good things that he mentions, and I conclude that they are thankworthy.[157] Ah, but no matter if I wanted to give thanks as those Greeks did, I still cannot give thanks for what has been denied to me. Hence I will summon my soul to give thanks for the one thing that was in fact given me—that I became a man, not a woman.

To be a woman is something so special, so mixed, so compounded that there are no predicates to describe it, and the many predicates, if they were used, contradict one another in a manner only a woman can tolerate, indeed, even worse, can relish. That in actuality she signifies less than man is not her misfortune, even less if she were to find out about it, for that, of course, can be endured; no, the misfortune is that her life in the romantic consciousness has become meaningless. Thus, one moment she means everything, nothing at all in the next, yet without ever finding out what significance she actually does have, and still this is not the misfortune—it is mainly that she cannot come to know it, because she is woman. [158]For my part, if I were a woman, I would rather be one in the Orient, where I would be a slave, for to be a slave—either more nor less—is still always something compared with being "hurrah" and nothing.

Even if a woman's life did not have such contradictions, the distinction she enjoys and that is correctly assumed to be due to her *qua* woman, a distinction she does not share with the man, already points to meaninglessness. This distinction is that of gallantry. To be gallant toward woman befits the man. Now gallantry, quite simply, consists in conceiving in fantastic categories the person toward whom one is gallant. Thus to be gallant to a man is an insult, for he declines the use of fantastic categories. On the other hand, gallantry is a tribute to the fair sex, a distinction to which she is essentially entitled. Alas! Alas! Alas! It would not be so bad if it were a matter of one gentleman who is gallant. But such is not the case. Basically every man is gallant; he is instinctively gallant. This means, then, that it is life [*Tilværelse*] itself that has regaled the fair sex with this *provenue* [perquisite]. On the other hand, woman instinctively accepts it. This, again, is unfortunate, for there would have to be another explanation if one woman were to do so. Here again we have life's own irony. If gallantry is to be genuine, it must be reciprocal and be the quoted rate for the specified difference between beauty and power, cunning and strength. But this is not the case, woman is essentially entitled to gallantry, and the fact that she instinctively accepts it can be explained by nature's solicitude for the weaker, the stepmotherly treated, for whom an illusion provides more than compensation. But this illusion is precisely the calamity.[159] Not rarely is it the case that nature comes to the aid of a deformed person by consoling him with a delusion that he is the handsomest of men. Thus nature has compensated for everything; he possesses even more than a reasonable claim could request. But to possess this in a delusion, not to be enslaved in wretchedness but to be tricked into a delusion—this is indeed an even greater mockery. Woman is a long way from being *verwahrloszt* [neglected] in the sense in which a deformed person is,[160] but certainly in another sense insofar as she cannot ever shed the illusion with which life has consoled her.

If a feminine existence is summed up to show the decisive elements in its totality, then every feminine existence makes a thoroughly fantastic impression. The critical turning points in her life are quite different from man's, for her critical turning points turn everything upside down. In Tieck's romantic plays we sometimes find a character who, formerly king of Mesopotamia, is now a grocer in Copenhagen.[161] Every feminine existence is precisely as fantastic as this. If the girl's name is Juliane, then her life is as follows: "Formerly empress in the vast outskirts [*Overdrev*] of erotic love and titular queen of all exaggerations [*Overdrivelser*] of giddiness, now Mrs. Petersen on the corner of Badstustræde [Bathhouse Street]."

As a child, a girl is regarded as inferior to a boy. When she is a little older, one does not quite know what to do with her; finally comes that decisive period that makes her the sovereign. Adoring, man approaches her; he is the suitor. Adoring, for every suitor is that; it is not an invention of a cunning deceiver. Even the public executioner, when he lays down his *fasces*[162] to go a–wooing, even he bends the knee, even though he intends as soon as possible to devote himself to domestic executions, which he takes so much for granted that he is far from trying to make the excuse that public executions are becoming so rare. The cultured gentleman conducts himself in the same way. He kneels, he adores, he conceives of the beloved in the most fantastic categories and thereupon very quickly forgets his kneeling position and would know full well while he was kneeling that it was fantasy. If I were a woman, I would prefer being sold by my father to the highest bidder, as in the Orient, for a business transaction nevertheless does have meaning. What a misfortune to be a woman, and yet the misfortune is really that if one is a woman then one does not comprehend it. If she complains, she does not complain about the former but about the latter. If I were a woman, I would first and foremost decline all wooing and reconcile myself to being the weaker sex, if that is what I am, but I would take care—and this is the main point if one wishes to be proud—not to step outside the truth. This concerns her less. Juliane is in seventh heaven, and Mrs. Petersen is reconciled to her fate.

So I thank the gods I became a man and not a woman. And yet how much I have to renounce! From the drinking song to the tragedy, poetry is the idolization of woman. Worst of all for her and for him who admires, for if he does not take care he will suddenly pull a long face as he is standing there. Beauty, excellence, man's achievements are attributable to woman, for she inspires him. Woman is the inspiring influence—how many amorous flutists have played this theme, and how many shepherdesses have listened to it! Truly my soul is without envy and is only grateful to the god, for I would rather be a man and a little inferior, and actually be that, than be a woman and be an undefinable quantity and made blissful in fantasy; I would, however, rather be a concretion that means something than an abstraction that means everything. [163]So it is altogether true: ideality came into life because of woman—what would man be without her? Many a man became a genius because of a girl, many a man became a hero because of a girl, many a man became a poet because of a girl, many a man became a saint because of a girl—but he did not become a genius because of the girl he got, for with her he became only a cabinet official; he did not become a hero because of the girl he got, for because of her he became only a general; he did not become a poet because of the girl he got, for because of her he became only a father; he did not become a saint because of the girl he got, for he got none at all and wanted only to have the one and only whom he did not get, just as each of the others became a genius, a hero, a poet with the aid of the girl he did not get. [164]If woman's ideality were in itself inspiring, then the one who inspires would have to be the one to whom he is bound for life. Life expresses it another way. It says: In a negative relationship woman makes man productive in ideality. Understood in this way, she is inspiring, but to say it directly is to become guilty of a paralogism, which one must be a woman to ignore. Indeed, who ever heard that anyone became a poet because of his wife? As long as man does not have her, she inspires him. This is the truth that is the source of poetry's and woman's fantasy. That he does not have her means that he is still fighting for her (for example, a girl has inspired many a man and made a knight of him, but has anyone ever heard that someone became valiant because of his wife!), or that he does not have her means that he cannot get her at all. In this way a girl has inspired many a man and awakened his ideality, that is, if he has any to display. But a wife who has ever so much to give scarcely arouses ideality. Or that he does not have her means he is pursuing ideality. He may love many, but loving many is also a kind of unhappy love, and yet his soul's ideality actually consists in this striving and aspiring, not in the fractions of charm that constitute the *summa summarum* [sum total] of the contributions of all the individuals.

The highest ideality woman can awaken in man is really to awaken the consciousness of immortality. The nerve of this proof consists in what could be called the necessity for final lines. Just as we say of a play—it cannot end until this one and that one have been given final lines—so ideality says that life cannot end with death; I demand final lines. Positive proof of this is often to be found in *Adresseavisen*.[165] I find this quite as it should be, for if it is to be carried in *Adresseavisen*, it must be carried out positively. Mrs. Petersen had lived so and so many years until the night between the twenty-fourth and the twenty-fifth it pleased providence etc. On this occasion, Mr. Petersen has an attack of nostalgic memories of the courtship period, and to put it quite specifically—reunion is his only consolation. In the meantime, he prepares himself for this blessed reunion by taking a second wife, for it may be true that a second marriage is not quite as poetic as the first, but it is still a good reprint. This is the positive proof. Mr. Petersen is not satisfied with demanding final lines—no, reunion in the hereafter. It is well known that imitation metal sometimes has the sheen of the genuine—this is the brief silver-flash. For the imitation metal this is tragic, for now the imitation metal must put up with being an imitation. Not so with Mr. Petersen. Every person is rightly entitled to ideality. If, then, I laugh at Mr. Petersen, it is not because he, if he was actually imitation metal, had but a single silver-flash, but because this silver-flash betrays that he has become imitation metal. Thus the bourgeois-philistine mentality looks most ludicrous when, decked out in ideality, it provides an appropriate occasion to say with Holberg: Isn't the cow, too, wearing a Parisian gown?[166]

[167]The point is this—if woman awakens ideality and thereby proof of immortality in man, she always does it negatively. The person who because of a woman actually became a genius, became a hero, became a poet, became a saint, that person in the very same instant seized the immortal. If the ideal-

izing element were positively present in woman, then the wife and only the wife might awaken the consciousness of immortality in the husband. Life expresses the very opposite. If she is really going to awaken ideality in her husband, she must die. Yet she does not awaken it in Mr. Petersen. If by her death she does awaken ideality in the husband, she then does all the great things poetry says of her; but, please note, whatever she did positively for him did not awaken ideality. Her meaning, however, becomes more and more questionable the longer she lives, because she actually has begun to want to have a positive meaning. The more positively the proof is produced, the less it proves, for then the longing will be for something experienced, the content of which must be assumed to be essentially exhaustive, inasmuch as it is experienced. The proof becomes most positive when the object of longing is those trifles of marital life: the time we were in Deer Park together. In the same way one can suddenly have a longing for a pair of old shoes one once wore so comfortably, but this longing is no proof of the immortality of the soul. The more negative the proof, the better it is, for the negative is higher than the positive, is the infinite, and thus the one and only positive.

Woman's entire meaning is negative; her positive meaning is nothing in comparison—indeed, it probably is even corruptive. It is this truth that life has concealed from her, and life has consoled her with a fancy that surpasses anything that can arise in any man's mind[168] and has paternally arranged existence in such a way that language and everything else strengthens her in the fancy. Even when she is viewed as the opposite of being inspiring, as the source of corruption, whatever it may be—that sin entered the world through her, or it is her unfaithfulness that destroys everything—the conception is at all times gallant. [169]When one hears such talk, one would indeed think that woman is really capable of becoming infinitely much more guilty than man—which certainly is a prodigious acknowledgment. _{VI 62}

Alas, alas, alas! It isn't that way at all. There is a secret way of reading that woman does not understand; for the very next moment all life acknowledges the same point of view as the state, which makes the husband responsible for his wife. She is condemned in a way no man has ever been condemned, for he receives only an actual sentence. It all ends not with her receiving a lighter sentence, for then, of course, her whole life would not be an illusion, but with dismissal of the charge and letting the public, that is, life, pay the costs. One moment she is supposed to know all the tricks, and the next moment we laugh at the one she is deceiving, which certainly is a contradiction, and even over Potiphar's wife there hovers a possibility of being able to give the appearance that she has been seduced.[170] Thus woman has a possibility that no man has, an enormous possibility; but her actuality is in proportion to it, and the most terrible of all is the witchcraft of the illusion in which she feels so happy.

[171]Let Plato, then, thank the gods that he was contemporary with Socrates—I envy him; let him give thanks that he became a Greek—I envy him; but when he gives thanks that he became a man and not a woman, then I wholeheartedly join in. If I had become a woman and could understand what I now understand—how terrible! If I had become a woman and consequently could not even understand that—how much more terrible!

But if this is the way it is, then it follows that one must stay out of any positive relationship with her. Wherever woman is involved, there promptly is this unavoidable hiatus that makes her happy because she does not notice it and is the death of man if he discovers it.

A negative relationship with a woman can infinitize—this must always be said and be said to the honor of woman, and can be said absolutely unconditionally, because it does not depend essentially on the particular woman's unique character, her loveliness, or on the continuance of her loveliness. It depends upon her making her appearance at the right moment, when ideality is acquiring its vision. It is a brief moment, and then she does well to vanish again. For a positive relationship with woman makes man finite on the largest possible scale. Therefore the highest a woman can do for a man is to make her appearance before him at the right moment. This, however, she cannot do; it is the courtesy of fate. But now comes the greatest thing she can do for a man—that is to be unfaithful to him, the sooner the better. The first ideality will help him to an intensified ideality, and he is helped absolutely. To be sure, this second ideality is purchased with the deepest pain, but it is also the greatest blessing. To be sure, he can by no means wish it before it has happened, but this is why he thanks her that it has happened; and since he, humanly speaking, does not have much reason to be so very thankful, all is well. [172]But woe to him if she remains faithful to him!

So I thank the gods that I became a man and not a woman; in the next place, I thank the gods that no woman continually makes me have afterthoughts because of a lifelong commitment.

What a strange invention is marriage! And what makes it even more strange is that it is supposed to be a spontaneous step. And yet there is no step as decisive, for with regard to human life there is nothing as self-willed and as tyrannical as marriage.[173] And then something so decisive one is supposed to do spontaneously. Yet marriage is not something simple, but is extremely complex and has many meanings. Just as turtle meat has a taste of all kinds of meat, so marriage has a taste of everything, and just as the turtle is a slow creature, so also is marriage. Falling in love is indeed something simple, but a marriage! Is it something pagan or something Christian, or something sacred or something secular, or something civil or a little of everything? Is it the expression of that inexplicable eroticism, that *Wahlverwandtschaft* [elective affinity][174] between kindred souls, or is it a duty, or is it a partnership or an expediency in life or the custom in certain countries, or is it a little of everything? Is the town musician or the organist to furnish the music—or should one have a little of both; should the pastor or the police sergeant give the talk and inscribe their names in life's register—or in the municipal register; is it in comb-and-paper music that marriage can be heard or does it listen to that whisper that sounds like "the fairies' from the grottos on a summer night"?[175] Every benedict believes that when he entered upon marriage he performed a very composite number, a very complex passage, [176]more complicated than anything else, and expects to go on performing it as a married man.

My dear drinking companions! For want of another wedding gift and congratulations, should we not give each of the married folks *one* NB [*nota bene*, note well] and marriage *two* NBs for repeated inattention! To express a single idea in one's life can be strenuous enough, but to think something so complex and then to give it unity, to express something so complex in such a way that justice is done to each separate part and everything is present at the same time—yes, he who does that is truly impressive. And yet, after all, every benedict does that, and he does it, that is for sure; does he not say that he does it spontaneously? If it is to be done spontaneously, it must be done by virtue of a higher immediacy that has permeated the entire reflection. But there is not even a hint of this. It is not worth the trouble to ask a married man about this. Anyone who has ever done something stupid is continually afflicted by the consequence. The stupidity is to have become involved in all this; the revenge is that he will see with hindsight what it is he has done. [177]Now he strikes an emotional note and believes he has done something extraordinary by marrying; now he sticks his tail between his legs; now he eulogizes marriage in self-defense—but I wait in vain for the unifying idea that holds these most heterogeneous *disjecta membra* [separated members][178] of life-views together.

[179]So, then, to be a plain and simple benedict is rubbish, to be a seducer is also rubbish, to want to experiment with women for the sake of amusement is also rubbish. After all, the two last-named methods are as great concessions from the man's side to woman as is marriage. The seducer wants to assert himself by deceiving, but that he deceives, that he wants to deceive, and that he takes the trouble to deceive are also manifestations of his dependence on woman, and the same holds true for the experimenting male.

If a positive relationship with woman is thinkable, then it has to be so reflective that for that very reason it would not become a relationship with her. To be an exceptional husband

and yet secretly seduce every girl, to seem to be a seducer and yet hide all the ardor of romanticism within one would really be something—yet the concession to the first power is invariably destroyed in the second. Nevertheless man has his true ideality only in a reduplication.[180] [181]Every immediate existence must be annihilated and the annihilation constantly safeguarded by a false expression. Woman cannot grasp a reduplication such as that; it makes it impossible for her to state man's nature. If it were possible for a woman to have her nature in a reduplication such as that, then an erotic relationship with her would be unthinkable, and since her nature so obviously is as it is, there is a disturbance of the erotic condition of man's nature, which continually has its life in the annihilation of that in which she has her life.

So, then, am I perhaps preaching the monastery, and am I justifiably called Eremita?[182] By no means. Away with the monastery. It, too, is still only an immediate expression of spirit, and spirit cannot be expressed immediately. It makes no difference whether someone uses gold or silver or paper currency, but the person who does not pay out even a farthing unless it is false, he knows what I mean. The person for whom every immediate expression is only forgery, he and he alone is better safeguarded than if he entered the monastery; he becomes an Eremita even if he rides the omnibus night and day.

[183]Scarcely had Victor finished before the Fashion Designer leaped to his feet, upset a bottle of wine standing in front of him, and then began as follows.

[184]Well spoken, dear drinking companions, well spoken! The more I hear you talk, the more I am convinced that you are fellow conspirators. I greet you as such, I understand you as such, for one understands conspirators even at a distance. And yet what do you know, what is your bit of theory that you pass off as experience, what is your bit of experience that you remake into a theory, and finally you even on occasion believe it for a moment and are inveigled for a moment. No, I know woman from her weak side; that means, I know her. In my study, I shun no terror and shun no means to make sure of what I have understood, for I am a madman, and a madman

one must be in order to understand her, and if one was not that before, one becomes that once one has understood her. Just as the robber has his hideout beside the noisy highway and the anteater its funnel in the loose sand and the pirate ship its hiding place by the roaring sea, so I have my fashion boutique right in the middle of the human swarm, as seductive and irresistible to a woman as Venusberg[185] to the man. Here in a fashion boutique one learns to know her practically and from the ground up without all that theoretical fuss. [186]Indeed, if fashion meant nothing more than that a woman in the concupiscence of desire put everything aside, that would still be something. But that is not the way it is; fashion is not open sensuality, is not tolerated dissipation, but is a sneaky trafficking in impropriety that is authorized as propriety. And just as in pagan Prussia the marriageable girl carried a bell whose ringing was a signal to the men, so a woman's existence in fashion is a perpetual carillon—not to the profligate but to sweet-toothed sensualists. Fortune is thought to be a woman—oh, to be sure, it is indeed fickle, but nevertheless it is fickle in something, for it can give much, provided it is not a woman. No, fashion is a woman, for fashion is fickle in nonsense, which knows but one consequence: that it inevitably becomes more and more extravagantly mad. If one wishes to learn to know women, one hour in my boutique is worth more than years and days on the outside; in my fashion boutique there is no thought of competition, for it is the only one in the royal city. Who would dare to compete with someone who has completely dedicated himself and dedicates himself as high priest in this idol worship? No, there is no distinguished social gathering where my name is not first and last, and there is no middle-class social gathering where the mention of my name does not inspire holy awe as does the king's, and there is no costume so crazy that, if it is from my boutique, it is not accompanied by whispering as it walks through the salon. And there is no aristocratic lady who dares to walk past my boutique, and no middle-class maiden walks past without sighing and thinking: If only I could afford it. But then she was not deceived, either. I deceive no one; I supply the finest and the most expensive things at the cheapest prices—indeed, I sell below cost. Hence I am not out to gain—no, every year I lose huge sums. And yet I want to gain; I do want it; I spend my last farthing in order to suborn, in order to bribe, the organs of fashion so that my game may be won. [187]To me it is a sensual pleasure without rival to take out the costliest fabrics, to cut them, to clip genuine Brussels lace in order to create a fool's costume; I sell genuine and fashionable material at the lowest prices.

You may think that it is only in odd moments that she wishes to be in fashion. Far from it, she wants to be that at all times, and it is her one and only thought. Woman does have spirit, but it is invested just about as well as the prodigal son's resources;[188] and woman is reflective to an incomprehensibly high degree, for there is nothing so sacred that she does not immediately find it suitable for adornment, and the most exclusive manifestation of adornment is fashion. No wonder she finds it suitable, for fashion, after all, is the sacred. And there is nothing so insignificant that she does not in turn know how to relate it to adornment, and the manifestation of adornment most devoid of ideas is fashion. And there is nothing, not one thing in her whole attire, not the smallest ribbon, without her having a notion of its relevance to fashion, and without her detecting at once whether the lady passing by has noticed it—because for whom does she adorn herself if it is not for other ladies![189] Even in my boutique, where she comes, of course, to be fitted out in fashion, even there she is in fashion. Just as there are a special bathing costume and a riding costume, so there is also a special attire that is in vogue to wear for going to the boutique. This costume is not as casual as the negligee in which a lady likes to be surprised earlier in the forenoon. The whole point then is her femininity and coquetry in letting herself be surprised. Her boutique attire, on the other hand, is calculated to be casual, a bit frivolous without thereby causing embarrassment, because a fashion designer has a relation to her quite different from a cavalier's. The coquetry consists in appearing this way before a man, who, because of his position, does not dare claim the lady's feminine recognition but must be satisfied with the uncertain profits that richly pay off but without her thinking about it or without her dreaming of wanting to be the lady in relation to a fashion designer. Thus the whole point is that femininity is in a way left out and coquetry is invalidated in the exclusive superiority of the distinguished lady, who would smile if anyone were to allude to such a relationship. In her negligee on the occasion of a [surprise] call, she covers herself and thereby gives herself away; in the boutique she uncovers herself with utmost nonchalance, for it is only a fashion designer—and she is a woman. Now the shawl slips down a bit and shows a little white skin—if I do not know what that means and what she wants, then my reputation is lost. [190]Now she puckers her lips apriorally, then gesticulates aposteriorally; now she wriggles her hips, then looks in the mirror and sees my admiring face; now she lisps, walks with a mincing gait, then hardly seems to touch the floor; now she trails her foot daringly, sinks weakly into an armchair, while I obsequiously hand her a scent-flacon and cool her with my adoration; now she roguishly hits at me with her hand, then drops her handkerchief and lets her hand remain in a loose, drooping position, while I bow low and pick it up, offer it to her, and receive a little patronizing nod. This is how a woman of fashion deports herself in a boutique. [191]Whether Diogenes disturbed the woman praying in a somewhat immodest position by asking her whether she did not believe that the gods could see her from behind,[192] I do not know, but this I do know—if I were to say to her kneeling ladyship: The folds of your gown do not fall in a fashionable way, she would dread this more than offending the gods. Woe to the outcast, the Cinderella who does not understand this. *Pro dii immortales* [By the immortal gods], what is a woman really when she is not in fashion; *per deos obsecro* [I swear by the gods], what is she when she is in fashion!

Is this true? Well, test it: just when the beloved sinks ecstatic upon the lover's breast and whispers incomprehensibly "yours forever," hiding her head in his bosom, have him say to her: Sweet Katy, your hairdo is not at all in style. Perhaps men do not give this any thought, but the one who knows this and has a reputation for knowing it is the most dangerous man in the kingdom. What blissful hours the lover spends with the beloved before the wedding, I do not know, but the blissful hours she spends in my boutique pass him by. Without my special license and my sanction, a wedding is still an invalid act or else a very plebian affair. Suppose the time has already come when they are to meet at the altar, suppose she comes forward with the clearest conscience in the world since everything has been bought in my boutique and in every way put to the test before me—if I were to rush up and say: But good heavens, my lady, the myrtle wreath is fastened entirely wrong—the ceremony would very likely be postponed. But men are ignorant of all such things; to know that, one must be a fashion designer. It takes such prodigious reflection to supervise a woman's reflection that only a man who devotes himself to it is able to do it, and then only if he is originally so endowed. Lucky, then, is the man who does not become involved with any woman; even if she belongs to no other man, she does not belong to him, for she belongs to that phantom produced by feminine reflection's unnatural intercourse with feminine reflection: fashion. This, you see, is why a woman should always swear by fashion; then there would be substance to her oath, for fashion, after all, is the only thing she is always thinking about, the only thing she is able to think together with and in the midst of everything else. [193]From my boutique has gone out to the elite world the glad gospel for all ladies of distinction that fashion decrees that a certain kind of headgear be worn when one goes to church, and that in turn this headgear must be different for the morning service and for vespers. So when the bells ring, the carriage stops at my door. Her ladyship steps out (for it has also been proclaimed that no one but me, the fashion designer, can adjust the headgear properly); I rush to greet her with a deep bow, lead her into my dressing room; while she softly vegetates, I put everything in order. She is ready, has looked at herself in the mirror. Swiftly as an emissary of the gods, I hurry ahead, open the door of the dressing room and bow, hurry to the boutique door, place my arm across my chest like an oriental slave, but then, encouraged by a gracious nod, even dare to throw her an adoring and admiring kiss. She sits down in the carriage—but look! she has forgotten her hymnbook; I hurry out and hand it to her through the window, allowing myself once again to remind her to hold her head just a trifle to the right and to adjust her headgear herself if in stepping out she should disarrange it a bit. She drives off and is edified.

[194]You may believe that it is only high-society ladies who pay homage to fashion—far from it. Behold my seamstresses, on whose grooming I spare no pains in order that the dogmas of fashion may be proclaimed emphatically from my boutique. They form a chorus of the half-mad, and I myself as high priest set a shining example and squander away everything just in order to make every woman ludicrous by means of fashion. [195]For when a seducer boasts that every woman's virtue is salable to the right purchaser, I do not believe him, but I do believe that in a short time every woman is going to be made a fanatic by the demented and defiling mirrored image of fashion, which corrupts her in quite another way than if she were seduced.[196] I have tested this out more than once. [197]If I am unable to do it myself, then I set a couple of fashion's slave-women of her own class on her, for just as one trains rats to bite rats, so the bite of the fanatic woman is just like the tarantula's. And it is most dangerous of all when a man enters into it in a supportive role. Whether I am serving the devil or the god, I do not know, but I am right and I am determined to be right. I will be right as long as I have a single farthing; I am determined to be right until the blood spurts from my fingers. The physiologist draws a woman's shape in order to show the terrible results of corsets; alongside he draws the normal shape. This is correct, but only the one has the validity of actuality; they all wear corsets. Describe, then, the wretched, stunted affectation of the fashion-addicted woman, describe this insidious reflection that devours her, and depict the feminine modesty that least of all knows something about itself, do a good job of it and you will also have condemned woman and in reality condemned her terribly. If I ever find a girl who is humble and content and uncorrupted

by indecent association with women, she will fall nevertheless. I bring her into my snare; now she stands at the place of
sacrifice, that is, in my boutique. With the most contemptuous glance that snobbish nonchalance can exercise, I measure her. She is perishing with dread; a laugh from the next
room where my trained minions are sitting demolishes her.
Then when I have her dolled up in fashion, when she looks
crazier than a mad hatter, as crazy as someone who would not
even be admitted to a loony bin, she blissfully sallies forth
from me. No one, not even a god, could dismay her, for she
is indeed in fashion.

Do you understand me now, do you understand why I call
you fellow conspirators, even though at a distance? Do you
understand my view of woman? Everything in life is a matter
of fashion; the fear of God is a matter of fashion, and love and
hoopskirts and a ring in the nose. So, then, I will do my utmost to aid and abet that sublime genius[198] who likes to laugh
at the most ludicrous of all animals. If woman has reduced
everything to fashion, then I will use fashion to prostitute her
as she deserves. I never rest [*raste*], I, the Fashion Designer;
my soul rages [*rase*] when I think about my task; eventually
she is going to wear a ring in her nose. So do not go looking
for a love affair, stay clear of erotic love as you would the most
dangerous neighborhood, for your beloved, too, might eventually wear a ring in her nose.[199]

[200]Thereupon Johannes the Seducer spoke as follows:

[201]Esteemed drinking companions, are you possessed by the
devil? You certainly are talking like undertakers; your eyes are
red from tears and not from wine. You are almost moving
even me to tears, for an unhappy lover endures a most miserable role in life. *Hinc illae lacrymae* [Hence these tears].[202] But
I am a happy lover and merely wish to keep on being that. Is
it perhaps a concession to woman that Victor fears so much?
Why not? It is a concession. That I loosen the tie of this champagne bottle is also a concession, that I let its effervescence
plunge into the goblet is also a concession, that I raise the goblet to my lips is also a concession—now I empty it—*concedo* [I

concede]. But now the goblet is empty—consequently I am making no concession.

So also with the girls. If an unhappy lover has paid too much for a kiss, that merely proves to me that he knows neither how to take nor how to leave off. I never pay too much; I leave that to the girls. What does that mean? To me it means the most beautiful, the most delicious, the most persuasive, and almost the most convincing *argumentum ad hominem* [argument based on the opponent's personal circumstances], but since every woman at least once in her life possesses this argumentative originality, why should I not let myself be convinced! Our young friend wishes to think it. As far as that goes, he can buy a candy kiss and gaze at it. I want to enjoy. No chattering. That is why an old ballad says of a kiss: *Es ist kaum zu sehn, es ist nur für Lippen, die genau sich verstehen* [It is scarcely to be seen, it is only for lips that agree precisely][203]— so intimately that reflection is a piece of impertinence and foolishness. Anyone who, when he is twenty years old, does not understand that there is a categorical imperative—Enjoy—is a fool, and anyone who does not start doing it is a Christiansfelder.[204] [205]But you are unhappy lovers, and that is why you want to remodel woman. Heaven forbid. She pleases me as she is, just as she is. Even Constantin's joke contains a secret wish. I, however, am gallant. Why not? Gallantry costs nothing and brings everything and conditions all erotic enjoyment. Gallantry is sensuality's and pleasure's freemasonry between man and woman. Like the language of erotic love on the whole, it is a natural language. It consists not of sounds but of disguised cravings that are continually changing roles. That an unhappy lover is so ungallant as to want to convert his deficit into a bill of exchange on eternity, I can perhaps understand. Yet I do not understand it, for to me woman has a high exchange rate. I assure every woman of that, and it is the truth, and it is also certain that I am the only one who is not deceived by this truth. Whether a ruined woman is worth less than a man is not found in my current price list. I do not pick broken flowers; that I leave for married men to use in decorating their Shrovetide birch branch.[206]

Whether Edward, for example, wanted to reconsider and fall in love with Cordelia[207] again or repeat his love affair inwardly, I leave up to him—why should I become involved in things that do not concern me. What I thought of her I explained to her at the time, and indeed she has also convinced me, absolutely and completely convinced me, that my gallantry was in the right place. *Concedo. Concessi* [I concede. I did concede]. If a new Cordelia comes along, I will perform *Ring No. 2*.[208] But you are unhappy lovers and conspirators, and, despite your being very talented, you are more deceived than the girls. But resolution, desire's resolution, is the whole point in life. Our young friend will always remain on the outside. Victor is a fanatic; Constantin has paid far too much for his intellect; the Fashion Designer is a madman. What good is that! All four of you after the same girl will turn out to be a fizzle. Have enough fanaticism to idealize, enough appetite to join in the jolly conviviality of desire, enough understanding to break off in exactly the same way death breaks off, enough rage to want to enjoy all over again—then one is the favorite of the gods and of the girls. But what's the use of talking about it here? I am not out to make proselytes. Nor is this the place for it. Certainly I am enjoying the wine; certainly I am enjoying the overabundance of the banquet, it is good; but give me the company of a girl, and then I shall talk. [209]So thank you, Constantin, for the banquet and the wine and the excellent arrangements; the speeches, however, have been scarcely anything to write home about. But lest it end this way, I shall speak in praise of woman. Just as the person who is supposed to talk about the divine must be inspired by the divine in order to be able to talk worthily and therefore is taught what he is to say by the divine itself, so it is also with speaking about woman. Woman, even less than the god, is a whim from a man's brain, a daydream, something one hits upon all by oneself and argues about *pro et contra*. No, only from her herself does one learn to talk about her. And the more one has learned from, the better. The first time one is a pupil; the second time is already an improvement, just as in the public defense of a doctoral dissertation one uses the polite compliments of the previous opponent against the next one. But despite all that, nothing is lost. For as little as a kiss is a smack or an embrace is a strain, as little is this exhausted, like a demonstration of a mathematical theorem, which remains the same no matter if other letters are inserted. Such things are suitable to mathematics and phantoms, but not to erotic love and to woman, where every new thing is a new proof and demonstrates in another way the correctness of the same theorem. I rejoice that the female sex, far from being more imperfect than the male, is more perfect. But I shall clothe my speech in a myth, and on behalf of woman, whom you have so unjustly offended, it will please me if the speech may pass judgment on your souls, insofar as enjoyment makes an appearance but shuns you as the fruit shunned Tantalus,[210] because you have shunned them and because you have offended woman. Only in this way is she offended, even though she is elevated far above offense, and anyone who dares to offend in this way is punished. I offend no one. To say I do is merely the invention and backbiting of married men, inasmuch as I, on the contrary, appreciate her much more than the husband does.

Originally there was only one sex, so the Greeks tell us;[211] it was the male sex. Gloriously endowed was he, thus doing honor to the gods, so gloriously endowed that the same thing happened to the gods as sometimes happens to a poet who has burned up all his powers in his poetic creation: they became envious of man. Indeed, worse yet, they feared him, feared that he would not voluntarily bow beneath their yoke; they feared, even though groundlessly, that he might even shake the foundations of heaven. Thus they had conjured up a dynamic force they felt scarcely able to control. So there were misgivings and concern in the council of the gods. They had been very extravagant in creating man, which was magnanimous, but now they had to risk everything; it was in self-defense, for everything was at stake—so thought the gods. Man could not be retracted as a poet retracts his thought. He could not be compelled by force, for in that case the gods themselves could have compelled him, but that was the very thing they despaired of doing. He had to be taken captive and compelled by a force that was weaker than his own and yet stronger—and strong enough to compel. What wonderful power that had to be! But necessity teaches even the gods to surpass themselves in inventiveness. They searched and pondered and found. This power was woman, the wonder of creation, even in the eyes of the gods a greater wonder than man, a discovery on which the gods in their naïveté could not help congratulating themselves. What more can be said to her honor than that she would be able to do something of which even the gods did not think themselves capable; what more can be said than that she was capable of doing it; how wonderful she must be to be capable of it! This was a stratagem on the part of the gods. The enchantress was created full of deceit; the instant she had cast her spell on man, she transformed herself and made him a prisoner of all the prolixities of finitude. That was what the gods wanted. But is there anything more delicious, more delightful, more enchanting than what the gods, contending for their dominion, thought up as the only thing that could entice man? And it is really so, woman is the one and only, and the most seductive thing in heaven and on earth. By comparison, man is very much inferior.

And the stratagem of the gods succeeded. But it did not always succeed. In all ages there were some men, individual men, who became aware of the deception. To be sure, they saw her loveliness, more than anyone else, but they suspected the truth of the matter. These I call devotees of erotic love, and I count myself among their number. Men call them seducers; woman has no name for them—to her such a person is unmentionable. These devotees of erotic love are the happy ones. They live more luxuriously than the gods, for invariably they eat only what is more costly than ambrosia and drink what is more delicious than nectar: they eat the most seductive whims of the gods' most cunning thought; they always eat only the bait. Ah, what incomparable sensual pleasure, what a blissful way to live!—they always eat only the bait—they are never trapped. The other men fall to and eat the bait the way peasants eat cucumber salad and are trapped. Only the devotee of erotic love knows how to appraise the value of the bait, to place an infinite value on it. Woman has an intimation of this, and this is why there is a secret understanding between him and her. But he also knows that this is bait—this secret he keeps to himself.

That nothing more wonderful, nothing more delicious, nothing more seductive can be devised than a woman—this the gods guarantee, and their need, which sharpened their inventiveness, is in turn their guarantee that they have staked everything and in forming her nature have prevailed upon the powers of heaven and of earth.

I abandon the myth. The concept of man corresponds to the idea of man. Therefore one needs only one man in existence and no more. [212]The idea of woman, however, is a generality that is not exhausted by any woman. She is not *ebenbürtig* [of equal standing] with man but subsequent, a part of man and yet more perfect than he. Whether the gods took a part of him while he was sleeping[213] out of fear of waking him by taking too much, or whether the gods divided him in half and the woman was the other half,[214] it was the man, after all, who was divided. Consequently it is in subdivision that she first became equal with man. She is a deception, but this she is only in the next moment and for the one who is deceived. She is finiteness, but at her beginning she is finiteness raised to the highest power in the delusive infinity of all divine and human illusions. As yet there is no deception. But a moment later, and one is deceived. She is finiteness; thus she is a collective noun; the one woman is the many. Only the devotee of erotic love understands this, and that is why he knows how to love many, is never deceived, but imbibes all the sensual pleasures the cunning gods managed to prepare. This is why woman cannot be exhausted in any formula but is an infinitude of finitudes. Trying to conceive the idea of woman is like gazing into a sea of misty shapes continually forming and reforming, or like becoming unhinged by looking at the waves and the foam maidens who continually play tricks, because the idea of woman is only a workshop of possibilities, and once again for the devotee of erotic love this possibility is the eternal source of infatuation.

[215]So the gods formed woman as delicate and ethereal as if of the mists of a summer night, and yet rounded as ripe fruit; light as a bird although she bears a world of desire within her, light because the play of forces is unified in the invisible center of a negative relationship in which she relates herself to herself; slim and firm, with clearly defined contours and yet to the eye surging with the undulations of beauty; complete and yet continually as if she were just now finished; cool, delicious, refreshing as the new-fallen snow, and yet blushing in tranquil transparency; happy as a pleasantry that lets one forget everything, soothing as the objective of the desiring, gratifying by being herself the incitement of the desiring. And the gods planned the situation in such a way that man, upon seeing her, would be as amazed as one who sees himself and yet in turn as if he were familiar with this sight, as amazed as one who sees himself in the reflection of perfection, as amazed as one who sees what he never suspected and yet sees, so it seems, what must necessarily have occurred to him, sees what is necessary in life, and yet sees it as the riddle of life. [216]It is this very contradiction in man's amazement that coaxes out [*elske frem*] the desire, while his amazement pushes him closer and closer until he cannot stop looking, cannot stop feeling familiar with this, yet without really daring to come closer, even if he cannot stop desiring.

[217]Having imagined woman's shape and character, the gods themselves feared lest they not be able to express it. But what they feared more was woman herself. For fear of one who is in on the secret and could spoil the stratagem, they did not dare let her know how beautiful she was. Then the crown was placed on the work. The gods finished her, but they hid everything from her in the ignorance of innocence, and hid it once again from her in the impenetrable secrecy of modesty. She was finished, and victory was certain. Inviting she was, and that she was by being elusive, constraining by her fleeing, irresistible by her own continual resisting. The gods rejoiced. Nothing as alluring as woman had been devised in the world,

and nothing is as absolutely alluring as innocence; no temptation is as entrapping as that of modesty, and no deception as
matchless as woman. She knows nothing, and yet her modesty possesses an instinctive presentiment; she is separated
from man, and the partition of modesty is more decisive than
Aladdin's sword that separates him from Gulnare;[218] and yet
the devotee of erotic love who, like Pyramis,[219] places his ear
against the partition of modesty senses dim intimations of all
the passion of desire behind it.

This is how woman tempts. Human beings set out the most
excellent fare they have as food for the gods, they know nothing better to offer; in the same way woman is a display fruit;
the gods knew of nothing to compare with her. She is, she is
right here, present, close to us, and yet she is infinitely far
away, concealed in modesty until she herself betrays her hiding place—how, she does not know; it is not she, it is life itself
that is the cunning informer. She is roguish, like a child at play
who peeks out of its hiding place, and yet her roguishness is
inexplicable, for she herself is unaware of it, and she is always
enigmatic—enigmatic when she hides her eyes, enigmatic
when she sends out the emissary of a glance that no thought,
even less any word, is able to pursue. And yet if the glance is
the soul's "interpreter," where then is the explanation when
the interpreter himself speaks incomprehensibly. She is calm,
like the stillness of evening when not a leaf is stirring, calm,
like a consciousness that as yet is not aware of anything; her
heart beats as regularly as if it did not exist, and yet the devotee of erotic love who listens with stethoscopic probity discovers the dithyrambic beat of desire as an unconscious accompaniment. Carefree as a breeze, contented as the deep sea,
and yet as full of longing as the unexplained always is. My
friends, my mind is appeased, indescribably appeased! I perceive that my life, too, expresses an idea, even if you do not
understand me. I, too, have spied out the secret of life; I, too,
serve something divine,[220] and certainly I do not serve for
nothing. Just as woman is a deception by the gods, so is this a
true expression of her wanting to be seduced; and just as

woman is not an idea, so also is the truth of this, that the devotee of erotic love wants to love as many as possible.

What a sensual pleasure it is to enjoy the deception without
being deceived, only the devotee of erotic love understands.
How blissful it is to be seduced, only woman really knows. I
have learned this from woman, even though I have not allowed any time to explain it to myself but have held my
ground and served the idea by a breach as abrupt as death's,
because a bride [*en Brud*] and a breach [*et Brud*] correspond to
one another as female and male.[221] Only woman knows this,
and knows it along with her seducer. No married man comprehends such a thing. Nor does she ever speak to him about
it. She is reconciled to her fate; she suspects that it has to be
this way, that she can be seduced only once. This is why she
is really never angry with her seducer. That is, if he actually
has seduced her and expressed the idea. A broken marriage
vow and the like are, of course, pure nonsense and no seduction. Thus far it is not such a great misfortune for a woman to
be seduced, and it is her good fortune if she is seduced. A girl
who has been seduced in a first-rate way can become a first-
rate wife. If I myself were not good at being a seducer, even
though I, when I consider myself along those lines, [would]
deeply feel my inferiority, if I wanted to be a married man, I
would always choose a woman who has been seduced, lest I
should begin by seducing my wife. Marriage, too, expresses
an idea, but in relation to this idea what is absolute in relation
to my idea is a matter of indifference. Therefore, marriage
should never be established with a beginning, as if it were the
beginning of a seduction story. This much is certain, that for
every woman there is a corresponding seducer. Her good fortune is precisely to meet him.

With marriage, on the other hand, the gods prevail. Then
the once-upon-a-time seduced woman walks through life at
her husband's side, occasionally looks back wistfully, recon-
ciles herself to her fate, until she has reached the borderland of
life. She dies, but she does not die in the same sense as the man
dies, she evaporates and dissolves into that indefinable something from which the gods formed her; she vanishes like a

dream, like a temporary character whose time is up. For what else is woman but a dream, and yet the highest reality. This is how the devotee of erotic love sees her and in the moment of seduction leads her and is led by her outside of time, where as an illusion she belongs. With a husband she becomes temporal, and he through her.

Wonderful nature, if I did not admire you, a woman would teach me to do so, for she is the *Venerabile* [something worthy of veneration][222] of life. Glorious you made her, but even more glorious in that you never made one woman like another. With man the essential is the essential and thus always the same; with woman the accidental is the essential and in this way an inexhaustible heterogeneity. Brief is her glory, but the pain is also quickly forgotten, and when the same glory is offered to me again, it is as if I had not even felt the pain. True, I also am aware of the unloveliness that can appear later, but in that case she is not with her seducer.[223]

The signal was given to rise from the table. It took but a sign from Constantin; with military timing the participants understood one another when it was a matter of right-about-face. With the invisible baton, which in Constantin's hand was as pliable as a divining rod [*Ønskeqvist*, wishing twig], he touched them once again in a fleeting reminiscence to remind them of the banquet and the mood of enjoyment that had been partially vanquished by the speakers' trains of thought, so that, as in an echo, the sounds of festivity that had vanished might reverberate over the guests in the brief instant of resonance. In farewell, he saluted them with a full glass; he emptied it; he hurled it against the door in the back wall. The others followed his example and consummated this symbolic act with the solemnity of an initiate. Thus the pleasure of breaking off had its due, this imperial pleasure that, even though briefer than any other, is still more liberating than any other. Enjoyment ought to begin with a libation, but this libation whereby one hurls away the glass into annihilation and oblivion and, as if in mortal danger, passionately tears oneself away from every memory, this libation is to the gods of the underworld. [224]One *breaks* off, and it takes strength to do it, even more strength than to cut a knot in two, for the obstacle of the knot provides the passion, but the passion it takes to break off, one must oneself provide. In a certain external sense the result may be the same, but artistically they are poles apart—whether something stops, comes to an end, or it is broken off by means of a free act, whether it is a happening or a passionate decision, whether it is over like the schoolmaster's ditty when there is no more or something caused by pleasure's Caesarean incision, whether it is a triviality everyone has experienced or that secret that escapes most people.

It was a symbolic act on Constantin's part when he flung away the goblet, and yet in a way this fling became a decisive blow, for at the last blow the door opened, and, like someone who has presumptuously knocked on death's portal and when it is opened sees the forces of annihilation, we saw that demolition crew ready to destroy everything—a memento that instantly changed the participants into refugees from that place and in the same instant had already transformed, as it were, the whole surroundings into a ruin.

A carriage stood ready at the door. At Constantin's invitation they took their seats and drove away in high spirits, for that tableau of annihilation in the background had given their souls new resilience. A few miles away the carriage stopped; here Constantin as host said goodbye and informed them that there were five carriages at their service; each of them could follow his own inclination, drive wherever he wanted, alone or if he so desired in the company of whomever he wished. So it is that a skyrocket is propelled in one single shot upward by the force of the gunpowder, comes to a standstill for a moment, totally concentrated in that one split second, and then explodes to the four winds.

While the carriages were being made ready, the nocturnal guests went for a little walk down the road. The brisk morning air tempered their fevered blood with its coolness and they surrendered completely to its invigoration, while their silhouettes and the group they formed made a fantastic impression on me. That the morning sun shines upon field and meadow

and upon every creature that found rest in the night and
strength to enable it to rise up jubilantly with the sun—in this
is but a salutary mutual understanding—but nocturnal rev-
elers seen in the morning light in a smiling rustic environment
have an almost *unheimlich* [disquieting] effect. One comes to
think of ghosts surprised by dawn, of the subterranean creatures that cannot find the fissure through which they disappear because it is visible only in the dark, of the poor unfor-
tunates for whom the difference between night and day has
vanished in the monotony of suffering.

A footpath took them across a little field to a hedged-in garden, behind which a modest country house was visible in the
background. At the end of the garden over toward the field
was an arbor formed by trees. Aware that there was someone
in the arbor, they all became curious, and with the searching
gaze of spies the besiegers surrounded that friendly hideout,
themselves as concealed and tense as police agents out to surprise someone. [225]As police agents, well, as far as that goes,
their external appearance made a confusion possible—the police agents could be out looking for them. Each one had taken
his place in order to peek in when Victor stepped back and
said to his neighbor: Oh, my God, it's Judge William[226] and
his wife.

They were surprised—not those two hidden by the leaves,
that happy couple much too absorbed in domestic pleasure to
be watchers, much too secure to think of themselves as objects
of observation by anyone but the morning sun, which with
delight was peeking in at them, while a soft breeze stirred the
branches and while the peacefulness of rustic simplicity, like
everything around them, protected this little arbor. The
happy married couple were not surprised and did not notice a
thing. That they were a married couple was quite obvious,
that was immediately apparent—alas, at least to someone with
the observer in his blood. Even if nothing, nothing in the
wide, wide world, nothing undisguised and nothing disguised
has any disguised or undisguised intention or desire to disturb
the happiness of lovers when they are sitting close to each
other, they are not secure in the same way. Blissful they are,

and yet they cling so closely to each other as if there were
some power that wanted to separate them; it is as if there were
some enemy against whom they are protecting themselves
and as if they could never feel sufficiently secure. [227]It is not so
with married people, and not so with that married couple in
the arbor.

How long they had been married could not, however, be
stated definitely. To be sure, the way the wife busied herself
at the tea table had a practiced sureness, but nevertheless there
was so much almost childlike zeal about it as if she were just
married, in that intermediate state where she still did not
know for sure whether marriage is jest or earnestness,
whether being a housewife is a task or a game, a pastime. Yet
she may have been married for some time but did not usually
function at the tea table; perhaps she did it only out here in the
country, or perhaps she was doing it only this morning,
which possibly had a special significance for them. Who can
say for sure? Up to a point, all conjecturing runs aground on
every individuality with an originality in his soul, because this
prevents time from making its marks. When the sun shines in
all its summer brilliance, one immediately thinks that there
must be some festive occasion or other, it cannot be this way
every day, or that this is the first time or at least one of the
first times this is being done, for this cannot be repeated for a
long time. So thinks anyone who sees it only once or sees it
for the first time, and I was seeing the Judge's wife for the first
time. The person who sees it every day presumably thinks
otherwise, provided that he sees the same thing. But this is
the Judge's affair. So, then, our charming housewife was
busy; she poured boiling water into two cups, supposedly to
heat them properly, poured it out, set the cups on a tray,
poured the tea, served what goes with it, and now she was
ready—was this jest or earnestness? If anyone is not ordinarily
a friend of tea, he should have been in the Judge's place. To
me at that moment this drink appeared most inviting, and to
me only the wife's friendly inviting look appeared more inviting. Up until now she presumably had had no time to talk;
now she broke the silence and as she handed him the tea she

said, "Hurry now, dear, and drink your tea while it is hot; the morning air is still somewhat cool, and the least thing I can do for you is to be a little solicitous." "The least?" replied the Judge laconically. "Well, or the most, or the only thing." The Judge looked questioningly at her, and while he was fixing his tea to taste she continued, "You interrupted me yesterday when I started to say this, but I have been thinking about it again; I have thought about it many times, and right now especially, and you know very well on account of whom. It is certain and true that if you had not married you would have become much greater in the world." With the cup still on the saucer, the Judge drank the first mouthful with visible delight and seemed really refreshed, or was this perhaps joy over this lovable woman. I believe the latter; she, however, seemed only to delight in his relishing the tea. Now he set the cup on the table beside him, took out a cigar, and said: "May I light it at your chafing dish?" "Please do," she answered, taking a coal with a teaspoon and handing it to him. He lit the cigar, put his arm around her waist while she leaned against his shoulder, turned his head aside to blow away the smoke, then rested his eyes on her with all the devotion a look can communicate, yet smiling, although this smile of joy was tinged with sad irony. Finally he said: "Do you really believe that, my dear?" "What do you mean?" she asked. He was silent again; the smile spread, although his voice was still very earnest. "Since you yourself have forgotten it so quickly, I forgive your silliness a moment ago, for your talk was like that of a silly woman—what sort of great person was I supposed to be in the world?" The Judge's wife seemed to be momentarily embarrassed by this turn, but she quickly regained her poise and went into detail with feminine eloquence. The Judge looked straight ahead; he did not interrupt her, but as she continued speaking he began drumming on the table with the fingers of his right hand and hummed a melody. The words of the ballad were momentarily audible; just as the pattern in the fabric in a loom becomes visible and disappears again, so the words faded away again into the humming of the melody of the ballad: "The husband went out to the forest and cut the switches white."[228] After this melodramatic discourse, that is, the wife's explication, which was accompanied by the Judge's humming, the dialogue began again. "Very likely," he said, "very likely you are not aware that Danish law permits a husband to beat his wife; the only trouble is that the law does not state in what situation it is allowed." The wife smiled at his threat and went on, "But why can't I ever get you to be serious when I talk about this. You do not understand me; believe me, I honestly mean it, I myself think it is a very beautiful idea. Of course, if you were not my husband I would not venture to think it, but right now I have thought it for your sake and for my sake, and now please be properly serious for my sake and answer me honestly." "No, you are not going to make me be serious, and you are not going to receive a serious answer; I must either laugh at you or make you forget it, as before, or beat you, or you must stop talking about it, or in some other way I must make you be silent. You see it is a jest, and that is why there are so many ways out." [229]He stood up, kissed her on the forehead, put his arm in hers, and they disappeared down a thickly wooded path leading away from the arbor.

[230]So the arbor was deserted, and there was nothing more to do here; the enemy occupation troops retreated without any plunder [Bytte]. None of them seemed gratified by this outcome [Udbytte], but the others were content with making a malicious remark. They turned back but missed Victor. He had gone around the corner, and along the garden he had reached the country house. Here the veranda doors stood open to a lawn; a window facing the road also stood open. Presumably he had seen something that drew his attention. He jumped in through the window, and just as he was jumping out, the others, who had been looking for him, were standing nearby. Triumphantly holding some papers in his hands, he shouted, "A manuscript by His Honor the Judge. If I have published his others,[231] it is no more than my duty to publish this also." He stuck it in his pocket, or rather he intended to stick it in his pocket, but as he bent his arm and

VI
83

already had his hand with the manuscript half in his pocket, I slipped it away from him.

But who, then, am I? Let no one ask about that. If it did not occur to anyone to ask before, then I am saved, for now I am over the worst of it. Moreover, I am not worth asking about, for I am the least of all, and people make me very bashful by asking this question. I am pure being and thus almost less than nothing.[232] I am the pure being that is everywhere present but yet not noticeable, for I am continually being annulled.

I am like the line with the arithmetic problem above and the answer below—who cares about the line? By myself, I am capable of nothing at all, for even the idea of tricking Victor out of the manuscript was not my own notion, but the very notion according to which I borrowed the manuscript, as thieves put it, was in fact borrowed from Victor. Now, in publishing the manuscript, I again am nothing at all, for the manuscript[233] belongs to the Judge, and in my nothingness I as publisher am only like a nemesis upon Victor, who presumably thought he had the right to publish it.

SOME REFLECTIONS ON MARRIAGE
IN ANSWER TO OBJECTIONS

by

A MARRIED MAN[1]

Motto: "The deceived is wiser than one not deceived."[2]

My dear reader, if you do not have the time and opportunity
to take a dozen years of your life to travel around the world
to see everything a world traveler is acquainted with, if you
do not have the capability and qualifications from years of
practice in a foreign language to penetrate to the differences in
national characteristics as these become apparent to the research scholar, if you are not bent upon discovering a new
astronomical system that will displace both the Copernican
and the Ptolemaic—then marry; and if you have time for the
first, the capability for the second, the idea for the last, then
marry *also*. Even if you did not manage to see the whole globe
or to speak in many tongues or to know all about the heavens,
you will not regret it, for marriage is and remains the most
important voyage of discovery a human being undertakes;
compared with a married man's knowledge of life
[*Tilværelse*], any other knowledge of it is superficial, for he
and he alone has properly immersed himself in life. It is true,
of course, that no poet will be able to say of you what the poet
says of the wily Ulysses—that he saw many cities of men and
learned to know their mentality,[3] but the question is whether
he would not have learned just as much and things just as gratifying if he had stayed at home with Penelope. If no one else
is of this opinion, my wife is, and if I am not very much in
error, every wife agrees. Now that is a bit more than a simple
majority, all the more so since he who has the wives on his
side no doubt has the men, too. Of course, the traveling companions on this expedition are few; it is not, as on five- and
ten-year-long expeditions, a large group, which also, please
note, continually remains the same; but then it is reserved for
marriage to establish a unique kind of acquaintance, the most
wonderful of all, and in which every addition is always the
most welcome.

Therefore, praised be marriage, praised be everyone who

speaks in its honor. If a beginner may allow himself an observation, then I will say that the reason it seems to me to be so wonderful is that everything revolves around little things that the divine element in marriage nevertheless transforms by a miracle into something significant for the believer. Then, too, all these little things have the remarkable characteristic that nothing can be evaluated in advance, nothing worked out in a rough plan; but while the understanding stands still and the imagination is on a wild-goose chase and calculation calculates wrongly and sagacity despairs, the married life goes along and is transformed from glory unto glory,[4] the insignificant becomes more and more significant by a miracle—for the believer. But a believer one must be, and a married man who is not a believer is a tiresome character, a real household pest. There is nothing more fatal when one goes out in the company of others to enjoy demonstrations and ventures in natural magic than to have a killjoy along who continually disbelieves even though he cannot explain the feats. Yet one puts up with a calamity such as that; after all, it is seldom one goes out that way, and moreover there is the advantage that a fusty spectator like that gets in on the act. Ordinarily the professor of natural magic has it in for him and makes a fool of him by using him to entertain the rest of us with his cleverness, just as Arv[5] entertains with his stupidity. But a slug of a married man like that ought to be put in a sack like a patricide and thrown into the water.[6] What agony to see a woman exhaust all her lovableness in persuading him, to see him, after having received the initiation that entitles him to be a believer, only spoil everything—spoil everything—because, jesting aside, marriage in many ways is really a venture in natural magic and a venture in it is truly wonderful. It is nauseating to listen to a pastor who himself does not believe what he says, but it is still more nauseating to see a married man who does not believe in his estate, and all the more shocking because the audience can desert the pastor, but a wife cannot desert her husband, cannot do it, will not do it, does not wish to do it—and even this cannot persuade him.

Ordinarily we speak only of a married man's unfaithfulness, but what is just as bad is a married man's lack of faith. Faith is all that is required, and faith compensates for everything. Just let understanding and sagacity and sophistication reckon, figure out, and describe how a married man ought to be: there is only one attribute that makes him lovable, and that is faith, absolute faith in marriage. Just let experience in life try to define exactly what is required of a married man's faithfulness; there is only one faithfulness, one honesty that is truly lovable and hides everything in itself, and that is the honesty toward God and his wife and his married estate in refusing to deny the miracle.

This is also my consolation when I choose to write about marriage, for while I disclaim any other competence, I do claim just one—conviction. That I have it I know in myself, and I share it with my wife, which to me is of major importance, for even if it behooves the woman to be silent in the congregation[7] and not to be occupied with scholarship and art, what is said about marriage ought essentially to be such that it meets with her approval. It does not follow that she is supposed to know how to evaluate everything critically—that kind of reflection is not suitable for her—but she should have an absolute *veto*, and her approval must be respected as adequately reassuring. My conviction, then, is my one and only justification, and in turn the guarantee for my firm conviction is the weight of the responsibility under which my life, like every married man's life, is placed.

To be sure, I do not feel the weight as a burden but as a blessing; to be sure, I do not feel the bond as binding but as liberating, and yet it is there. The bond? No, the innumerable bonds by which I am bound fast in life as the tree is bound by the multiple branching roots. Suppose everything were to change for me—my God, if that were possible!—suppose I were to feel tied down by being married—what would Laocoön's misery[8] be compared to mine, for no snake, no ten snakes, would be able to wind themselves as alarmingly and tightly around a person's body and squeeze as does the marriage that ties me down in hundreds of ways and consequently would fetter me with a hundred chains. So you see, then—if this is a guarantee—while I feel happy and content and give thanks without ceasing for my happiness here on earth, I also have a presentiment of the terror that can overwhelm a man along this way, of the hell that he builds up who as a husband *adscriptus glebae* [bound to the earth] tries to tear himself loose and thereby continually finds only how impossible it is for him, tries to cut one chain and thereby only discovers one even more elastic that binds him indissolubly—if this is an adequate negative guarantee that what I may have to say is not idle thoughts conceived in a spare moment, is not crafty brain webs designed to trap others, then please do not disdain what I may have to say.

I am far from being learned and make no claims to that; it would be embarrassing if I were foolish enough to assume anything like that. I am not a dialectician, not a philosopher, but to the best of my ability respect learning and everything that brilliant people offer to explain life. I am, however, a married man, and when it comes to marriage I am afraid of no one. If I were asked, I would confidently and cheerfully stand at the professor's lectern, even if what I have to say is not entirely appropriate for delivery from a lectern. I boldly argue my thesis with all the world's dialecticians, with Satan himself—he shall not be able to wrench my conviction away from me. Let the nitpicking chicaners pile up all their objections to marriage—their case will collapse. Their objections can quickly be classified in two parts: those which one best answers, as Hamann says, by saying "Bah"[9]—the others can quickly be disposed of. Generally I am somewhat thin-skinned and cannot very well bear being laughed at. It is a weakness I still have been unable to master, but if someone wants to laugh at me for being a married man, then I am afraid of nothing. In this respect I am invulnerable to laughter; in this respect I feel a courage that is almost the antithesis of the life pattern of the poor judge who goes from his home to court and from court to his home and is surrounded by documents. Put me in a group of clever fellows who have conspired to make marriage ludicrous and to mock what is holy—arm them with every witticism there is, tip their mocking arrows

with the barb that an ambiguous relation to the opposite sex
sharpens, dip the arrows in the malice that is not slow-witted
but gained by devilish sagacity—I have no fear. Wherever I
am, even if it were in the fiery furnace,[10] when I am to talk
about marriage, I notice nothing. An angel is with me,[11] or,
more correctly, I am not there, I am with her, her whom I still
continue to love with the blessed resolution of youth, I who,
although a married man for several years, still have the honor
of fighting under the victorious banner of the happy first love
alongside her through whom I feel the meaning of my life,
that it has meaning and in many ways. For what to the rebel
are chains, what to the slave-minded are onerous duties, to me
are titles and positions of honor I would not exchange for
those of the King, King of the Wends and the Goths, Duke of
Slesvig, etc.[12] That is, I do not know whether these titles and
positions of honor would have significance in another life,
whether they, like so much else, are forgotten in a hundred
years, whether it is possible to imagine and clearly ascertain
how the idea of such relationships can fill out an eternal consciousness in recollection. I honor the King, as does every
good married man, but I would not exchange my titles with
his. This is the way I see myself; and I like to think that every
other married man does the same, and really, whether the single individual is far away or nearby, I wish that he also would
be as I am.

See, I secretly wear on my breast the ribbon of my order,
love's necklace of roses. Believe me, its roses are not withered;
believe me, its roses do not wither. Even if they change with
the years, they still do not fade; even if the rose is not as red,
it is because it has become a white rose—it did not fade. And
now my titles and positions of honor—what is so glorious
about them is that they are so equally apportioned, for only
the divine justice of marriage is able continually to give like
for like. What I am through her she is through me, and neither
of us is anything by oneself, but we are what we are in union.
Through her I am Man, for only a married man [*Ægtemand*] is
an authentic man [*ægte Mand*];[13] compared with this any other
title is nothing and actually presupposes this. Through her I

am Father—any other position of honor is but a human invention, a fad that is forgotten in a hundred years. Through her I
am Head of the Family; through her I am Defender of the
Home, Breadwinner, Guardian of the Children.

With so many positions of honor, one does not become an
author in order to acquire a new rank. Nor do I ask for what
I do not dare lay claim to, but I do write so that the person
who is as happy as I may be reminded of his own happiness if
he reads this, so that he who doubts, if he reads this, may be
persuaded. If there were only one, I am still happy; I ask for
only a little—not because I am so easily satisfied, but because
I am indescribably contented. With so many occupations and
all of them so appealing, one writes when there is time and
opportunity and hopes that anyone who could possibly benefit from it might not be disturbed by deficiencies in form and
will refrain from all criticism, for a married man who writes
about marriage writes least of all to be criticized. He writes as
he thinks best, often distracted by those more appealing pursuits. In other words, if I could mean something to more people by being an author, I far prefer to mean as much as possible
to my wife. I am her husband, by marriage—that is, by marriage I become eligible for the prize, the race track that is my
Rhodes and my dancing place.[14] I am her friend—oh, that I
might be that in all sincerity of heart, oh, that she might never
feel the need of anyone more sincere. I am her counselor—oh,
that my wisdom might be equal to my will. I am her comfort
and her encouragement—admittedly not yet summoned—oh,
but if I am ever summoned to serve in this capacity, may my
strength be equal to the disposition of my heart. I am her
debtor, my accounting is honest, and the accounting itself is a
blissful task. And finally, this I know, I will be a recollection
of her when death one day separates us—oh, that my memory
will be faithful, that it will preserve everything when it is lost,
an annuity of recollection for my remaining days, that it will
give me even the most minor details again and that I may say
with the poet when I am anxious about today: *et haec meminisse
juvat* [and it is pleasant to recollect these things], and when I
am troubled about tomorrow: *et haec meminisse juvabit* [and it

will be pleasant to recollect these things].[15] Alas, like the judge in court, one must at times put up with the dismay of reading again and again a summary of a criminal's *vita ante acta* [earlier life], but with a beloved wife's *vita ante acta* one never becomes bored—neither does one need the accurate printed details in order to recollect. It is certainly true that willing hands make light work, and so it is also with the task of remembrance. It is probably true (when said, it sounds infatuated) that in death the picture of the beloved will be found in the faithful lover's heart, but from the marital point of view a resolution of the will is vigilant in the falling in love so that it does not become lost in the infinite. To be sure, love declares that a moment with the beloved is heavenly bliss, but marriage wishes love well and fortunately is better informed. Suppose it is the case that the first effervescent passion of falling in love, however beautiful it is, cannot be sustained; then marriage knows precisely how the best in the love can be sustained. If a child who has received from his parents a copy of his school book has, so to speak, devoured it even before the year is over, is this a sign that he is to be praised as a pupil for his zeal and delight? So it is with marriage—the married man who from God in heaven received his copy (as beautiful as a gift from God can be!) and read it daily, every day throughout a long life, and when it was laid aside, when night came and the reading had to stop, it was just as beautiful as the day he received it: was not this honest discretion, directly proportionate to the delight of the infatuation, with which he reads again and again, was this not just as praiseworthy, just as strong an expression of falling in love as the strongest expression that falling in love has at its disposal?

Only of marriage do I wish to write; to persuade one individual is my hope; to spirit away those who speak against it is my intention. Hence for me marriage is my only chord, but it is so compounded that I, without exactly relying on the virtuosity that is generally required of anyone who has but one chord, dare permit myself to be heard, not exactly as an artist for a large audience, but rather as a wandering musician who stands outside the door of a particular house and does not call

VI
93

anyone away from his work, even though there is a winsomeness to his music when it sounds during work. In other words, I by no means think that what I may have to say would be unlovely. A good deal of it I owe to my wife, even though I do not talk with her in just the way I am writing here, but what comes from her invariably has a certain charm that is a woman's dowry. I am often amazed by it. Just as someone who writes a poor hand must be amazed when he sees his own manuscript executed by an expert calligrapher, and just as one who has sent a closely and crabbedly handwritten sheet to the printer hardly dares to acknowledge as his own the attractive, clean proof he receives, so it often is also with me in my domestic life. I express as well as I can what obscurely moves within her, and then she is amazed that it is just exactly what she wanted to say; hence I say it as well as I can, and then she appropriates it. But now comes my turn, when I see with amazement that my thoughts and my words have acquired an inspiration, an inwardness, and a charm so that I can justifiably say that they are not my thoughts. The trouble is that the attractive elegance of the words and thoughts more or less almost entirely disappears when I want to repeat them and can no more be expressed than I can describe her voice on paper. She is, however, to a certain extent a coauthor, and a literary firm such as that does not seem unlovely to me if one intends to write only about marriage. She sanctions, that I know, my using what I owe to her; she forgives, that I know, my using the opportunity to say one thing and another about her that I otherwise cannot manage to say except in solitude, because I cannot say directly to her how much she means to me, lest my eulogizing become oppressive and perhaps almost disturb our good understanding. As anonymous and as one who wants to preserve anonymity most scrupulously, I have safeguarded myself against what I on the whole hope that a sense of delicacy would forbid everyone: to make my domestic life an object of anyone's curiosity.

Praised be marriage, praised be everyone who speaks in its honor! What I have to say is not some new discovery—indeed, it would be dubious to make a new discovery with re-

VI
94

spect to the oldest institution in the world. Every married man knows the same as I know. The main ideas are and remain the same, just like the root consonants (radicals), but while these remain fixed and unchanged, one can have the joy of adding new vowels[16] and then rereading it. It follows, of course, that this must be taken *cum grano salis* [with a grain of salt] and, however I may go about it, that I do not, as a malicious mocker has said, make erotic love and marriage have the same consonants and the vowels constitute the difference. This, in turn, is like a well-known passage in the book of Genesis, where it says that Esau kissed Jacob,[17] and the learned Jews who did not credit Esau with this mentality but did not dare to change the consonants, either, merely inserted other dots, so that it read: he bit him. The best answer to such a charge is "Bah"; any other objection, precisely the more forthright it is, is welcome, for a consistent objection is a "wanted" notice for the apprehension of the truth and is extremely opportune for one who has the explanation.

VI
95

Erotic love [*Elskov*] does indeed have its own god. Who does not know him by name, how many do not think to benefit greatly by calling this relationship by this name: an erotic relationship. Eros, the erotic, and everything pertaining to it have a claim to the poetic. Marriage, on the other hand, is not so favored, does not have such a lofty lineage, for even if it is said that God has instituted marriage, it is usually the pastor or, if you like, the theologian, who says it, and he or the latter speaks in a totally different sense about God than does the poet. As a result, all that is comfortable and fragrant about Eros disappears, for Eros can become concrete only in the totally specific; the idea of God, however, is on the one hand so earnest that the pleasure of love seems to vanish when the God who is the Father of spirits is himself supposed to be the copula, and is on the other hand so universal that one loses oneself as a nothing that still wants to have a teleological qualification by which one is qualified in relation to the highest being. The clearness, the transparency, and, on the other hand, the roguishness and the semidarkness, which is Eros's relation to the lovers, the God of spirit cannot easily acquire in relation to marriage. The fact that he is involved is in a certain sense too much, and for that very reason his presence means less than that of Eros, who exists wholly and entirely only for the lovers. The relationship is similar to a purely human one. If his royal majesty has his lord chamberlain attend a christening party, it can perhaps heighten the mood of those present; but if the king himself were to attend, it perhaps would disturb, but remember that with respect to marriage there is no status distinction that makes one class stand closer to God than another. Nor is it easy to think of God precisely as spirit and then to think of him involved in the marriage in such a way that the idea does not become an introduction so general in nature that it leads into nothing at all, and in such a way that the idea does not become so spiritual that it promptly leads out again.

If one is willing to be satisfied with the poetic explanation of erotic love, which essentially is pagan—for the attribution of falling in love to a deity is nothing but the beautiful jesting earnestness of immediacy—if one is willing to let marriage shift for itself or at most be something that tags along afterward, then perhaps there is no difficulty, but to find no difficulty in this way is a difficult matter for anyone who is accustomed to thinking. Naturally Eros lays no claim to any faith and cannot become the object of faith—this makes Eros so useful to the poet—but a God of spirit who is the object of a spiritual faith is indeed in a certain sense infinitely removed from the concretion of falling in love.

In paganism there was a god for erotic love and none for marriage; in Christianity there is, if I may say so, a god for marriage and none for erotic love. Marriage is, namely, a higher expression for erotic love. If the matter is not regarded in this way, everything is confused and either one remains unmarried and a mocker, a seducer, a hermit, or one's marriage becomes thoughtlessness. The difficulty is that as soon as one thinks of God as spirit,[18] the individual's relationship with him becomes so spiritual that the physical-psychical synthesis that is Eros's potency easily disappears, as if one were to say that marriage is a duty, that to marry is a duty, that this then is a higher expression than falling in love, because duty is a spiritual relation with a God who is spirit. Paganism and immediacy do not think of God as spirit, but when this is taken for granted, the difficulty is to be able to preserve the qualifications inherent in the erotic so that the spiritual does not burn them up and consume them but burns in them without consuming them. Thus, marriage is threatened with dangers from two sides; if the individual has not in faith placed himself in the relationship with God as spirit, paganism haunts his brain as a fantastic reminiscence and he cannot enter into any marriage; and on the other hand neither can he do it if he has become totally spiritual; even if one of the latter type and one of the former type were married, such falling in love or such a match is no marriage.

Now, even though paganism did not have a god for marriage as it had for erotic love, even if marriage is a Christian idea, there is nevertheless always something to hold to—namely, that Zeus and Hera had a special title as Protectors of Marriage: τέλειος [he who has attained fulfillment] and τέλεια [she . . .].[19] To explain the term more precisely is a matter for philologists. I do not hide my ignorance, and since I am quite aware that I lack the necessary learning, I do not arrogate to myself a spiritual eagle eye[20] that would authorize me to make light of classical learning and classical culture, which still always remains the substantial food of the soul, beneficial in a way entirely different from green fodder and the solutions of the schemers to the question: What do the times require? For me it is of importance only to dare to use these words, τέλειος and τέλεια, about married people; I leave Jupiter and Juno out of this, not wishing to make a fool of myself by wanting to solve the historical–philological problem.

Marriage I regard, then, as the highest τέλος [goal] of individual life; it is the highest τέλος in such a way that anyone who evades it crosses out the whole of earthly life in one single stroke and retains only eternity and spiritual interests, which admittedly at first glance are not slight, but in the *longitude of time* are very strenuous and also in one way or another an expression for an unhappy life. That the highest τέλος, if marriage is so regarded, cannot therefore be exhausted by a succession of finite "whys"[21] is obvious to everyone and need not be elaborated. The highest τέλος always includes the particular qualifications, in which it is exhausted as in its predicates, thus under itself, so that they have their meaning precisely as immanent and, on the other hand, are meaningless as soon as they attempt to go on their own, for a detached thought that wants to be all its own is comical and thoughtless. Thus, in order to eliminate misunderstandings, the main point is that marriage is a τέλος, yet not for nature's striving so that we touch on the meaning of the τέλος in the mysteries, but for the individuality. But if it is a τέλος, it is not some-

thing immediate but an act of freedom, and belonging under
freedom as it does, the task is actualized only through a resolution. Now the signal is given; all the objections that prowl
around society like solitary shapes will, if they have any sense
at all, concentrate on this point. I know it well, the battle is
going to be here; this will not be forgotten, even if I seem for
a time to have forgotten it in order hypothetically to take a
little look around.

The difficulty is this: erotic love or falling in love is altogether immediate; marriage is a resolution; yet falling in love
must be taken up into marriage or into the resolution: to will
to marry—that is, the most immediate of all immediacies
must also be the freest resolution, that which is so inexplicable
in its immediacy that it must be attributed to a deity must also
come about by virtue of deliberation, and such exhaustive deliberation that from it a resolution results. Furthermore, the
one must not follow the other; the resolution must not come
slinking along behind but must occur simultaneously; both
parts must be present in the moment of decision. If deliberation has not exhausted thought, then I make no resolution; I
act either on inspiration or on the basis of a whim.

If the lover ventures out—that is, if his falling in love does
not just remain a state of mind but he is actually united with
the beloved, yet without having any other expression for falling in love than falling in love, if he ventures out, motivated
and blissfully quickened only by the *impetus* that to him seems
a trade wind that unchanged is bound to take him along the
bright, cheerful way in the company of his beloved—this by
no means signifies that a marriage is going to result in the next
moment. In the next moment—for since he is just immediately qualified a next moment is bound to come sooner or
later. Marriage is based on a resolution, but a resolution is not
the direct result of the immediacy of erotic love. Either nothing more is needed at all than the prompting of erotic love,
which then like the magnet steadily points without deviation
toward the same point, or the resolution must be present from
the beginning. If the resolution is supposed to come later, then
something else may also happen. What safeguard is there

against this? Falling in love, they say. Fine, but this is precisely the critical moment of falling in love, its moment of helplessness, for the fact that the light breeze of immediacy does not fill the sail of falling in love, that it fluctuates in the crisis, indicates precisely that there is bound to be a shift of wind, while immediacy is about to be, as it were, brought to a standstill in a dead calm. The second and equally likely consequence of immediate falling in love is—seduction. Who says that a seducer was a seducer at the very first moment? No, he became that at the second moment. When it is a matter of immediate falling in love, it is utterly impossible to determine whether it is a knight or a seducer who is speaking, for the next moment decides that. This is not the case with marriage, for resolution is present from the very beginning.

Consider Aladdin. What young man with wishes and aspiration in his soul, what maiden with longing in her heart, has not read Aladdin's command to the jinni in the fourth act[22] (where he gives orders concerning the wedding) without being kindled, indeed, almost set ablaze, by the passion of the poet and the fire of the words! Aladdin is a knight; to depict being in love like that is moral, it is said. My answer is: No, it is poetic, and by his happy thoughts and extreme richness of presentation the poet has proved for evermore that he is absolutely a poet. Aladdin is altogether immediate; therefore his wish is such that in the next moment he is able to be a poet. All that occupies him is that "cherished, long desired wedding night" that will assure him the possession of Gulnare, and thus the palace, the wedding hall, the wedding.

For me a lovely wedding make, night darkness turn to day,
With incense torches 'round the spacious hall.
Have sybil chor'sters lead a graceful dance,
While others sweetly sing and cithers play.

Aladdin himself is almost overwhelmed; he is about to faint in anticipated delight. Not without a certain tremor in his voice he asks the jinni whether he can do this; he beseeches him to answer honestly, and in this word "honestly" we hear, as it were, the anxiety of immediacy over its own happiness.

What makes Aladdin great is his wish, that his soul has the inner strength to desire. If in this respect I were to make any criticism of a masterpiece—which then would be only infatuated envy—it would be this, that it is never sufficiently clear and emphatic that Aladdin is a justified individuality, that to wish, to be able to wish, to dare to wish, to be rash in wishing, resolute in seizing the initiative, insatiable in aspiring, that this is a genius comparable to any other. We perhaps do not believe this, and yet in every generation there perhaps are not ten young men who have this blind courage, this vigor in the unlimited. Leave out the ten and give everyone else full authority to wish, and in his hand it will nevertheless become more or less a begging letter; he will grow pale around his nose; he will want to think about it. He wants to wish, all right, but now it is a matter of wishing for the right thing—in other words, he is a bungler and not a genius like Aladdin, who is the jinni's favorite because he is exorbitant. Therefore, the fulfillment must not appear as an accidental favor, lest it furnish the poor wretches with the pretext that if they only were sure of the fulfillment they surely would wish. Wrong, all wrong! Already here there is reflection. No, even if no wish were fulfilled for Aladdin, he assumes rank with his wish, with this mightiness of demand which ultimately is worth more than any fulfillment.

Great is Aladdin; he celebrates the wedding, quite true, but he does not marry. Truly, no one can wish him more happiness or be more sincerely happy for him than I, but if I were able, just as the poet gives him the jinni of the lamp, to give him something comparable, if by daily intercession I were able to provide him with the only thing I believe he lacks, a jinni of resolution that in vigor and concretion would correspond to what his wish is in immoderation and abstraction (for his aspiring is certainly unlimited and is burning like the desert sand)—oh, what a married man Aladdin could have become! Now there is nothing that can be said. My enemies, however, robbers who lie in wait for their prey, calmly and coolly make capital of Aladdin. The seducer reinforces himself with Aladdin's immediacy, goes ahead and seduces, and then he says: Aladdin, too, was a seducer, that I know from a very reliable source; he became one the morning after the wedding. Whether it was not exactly the very next morning but not until a few years later is essentially irrelevant and only shows, if it was a few years later, that Aladdin has diminished. Here the seducer is right; if the immediate is to be done with, then the thing to do is break it off quickly (and therefore it is precisely a moral task to depict a seducer); if not, then resolution must already be there from the beginning, and then we have a married man. Only the resolution could vouch for Aladdin—the poet could not, poetry could not, for poetry cannot use a married man. The poet's enthusiasm is for the immediate; the poet is great by virtue of his faith in immediacy and in its power to force its way through. The married man has permitted himself a doubt, an innocent, a well-meaning, a noble, a lovely doubt, for he really is far from wanting to offend erotic love or wanting to do without it. Just as surely as the immediate falling in love does not constitute a husband, so a match in which erotic love has been omitted, whatever the reason, is no marriage. ^{VI 102}

By venturing out, carried along only by the irresistible, blissful incitement of falling in love, the lover is certainly led into the embrace of his beloved, is perhaps led further with her, but he does not arrive at marriage, for if the lovers' union is not a marriage from the beginning, it never becomes that. If the resolution has to tag along behind, the idea is not expressed. Presumably the lovers can live happily, and quite possibly they do not care about objections; yet in a way the enemies are still right. Everything hinges on the ideality. Marriage must not be a fragmentary something that comes along with time and opportunity, something that happens to the lovers after they have lived together for a while—then the enemies are still right. They uphold ideality, the ideality of evil, demonic ideality. Indeed, it is easy to see from the objections whether the one speaking is just a *chicaneur* [chicaner, trickster] or has demonic ideality. One can act altogether properly in not wanting to become involved with the objections, in not wanting to be disturbed by them, but one ought to have a good conscience and an unbroken pact with the idea. To be content with being comfortable, to be happy etc., is perdition if this happiness is based on thoughtlessness or cowardliness or a secular mentality's miserable idolization of life. Compared with such wretchedness, to have kept one's pact with the idea, even if one became unhappy thereby, is a paradise—this I do believe. This is why I dare to speak up; as a married man I do not stick my tail between my legs, I dare to talk with enemies, not only with friends. I know that as a married man I am τέλειος, but I also know what is required of such a person with regard to the idea. No haggling, no compromising, no commiseration between husbands and husband, as if husbands, like women in a seraglio, were prisoners for life who had something private that they dared not have the world know, as if erotic love were the gilded finery we let the poet take and turn the better side out and marriage the threadbare side that is turned in. No, an open fight—marriage's idea is bound to win. Humble before God, submissive to the divine majesty of love,[23] I proudly hold my head high above all witticisms and do not bow my head to any objection.

VI
103

We agree with the enemies in their posing of all the difficulty; we agree that the synthesis that constitutes marriage is difficult, but we do not agree with them in their posing this as an objection, and even less with the expedient they themselves grasp at. When an adversary triumphantly presents his objection in order to terrify with all the difficulty, the thing to do is to have the courage to say with Hamann: That is just the way it is.[24] It is a good answer and in the proper place. The answer will be given here, too, but I ask that it be postponed just a few moments in order that I may give a little orientation with a few brief general comments about marriage as life's highest τέλος.

In paganism, a penalty was imposed on bachelors, and those who produced many children were rewarded;[25] in the Middle Ages it was a perfection not to be married. These are the extremes. As for the former, there is no need to impose a penalty, for life always asserts itself and knows how to punish anyone who wants to emancipate himself. Here the one who wants to emancipate himself is the one who does not will to marry. It must be emphasized that he does not *will* it. Just as marriage is a resolution, so also is its opposite, which can be a subject for discussion, a resolution that does not will. To fritter life away looking for the ideal (as if all such seeking were anything but stupidity and presumption) without understanding the meaning of either erotic love or marriage, without ever understanding the innocent enthusiasm that jestingly reminds youth that time is passing, that time is passing—this is an existence devoid of ideas. The same is true of prudishly rejecting and rejecting (as if all such rejecting expressed anything other than that the rejecter is not pure) and finding no one, which is the objective expression life gives to subjective rejecting.

That marriage, compared with such tomfoolery, has the absolute advantage is so definite that it is almost an insult to marriage to say it. No, to have any significance the objection must vindicate this by a negative resolution. The resolution of marriage is a positive resolution and essentially the most positive of all; its opposite is also a resolution that resolves not to will to actualize this task. Everyone who not only remains outside marriage but also remains outside it without resolution—his passage through life is a waste of time and trouble. Every human existence that does not want to be blather—and no one should want that—does not dare to give up something universal except by virtue of a resolution, whatever causes him to make the resolution, which with regard to not willing to marry can be very different, but it is unnecessary to go into detail here, lest it prove distracting.

The resolution not to marry does, of course, involve an ideality, but not the kind of ideality involved in making the positive resolution. Only in relation to time and circumstances can it become clearer to the single individual that he has made a resolution when he has made a negative one, inasmuch as according to a common opinion a positive resolution can be made easily enough. For example, it is certainly possible to marry, as the saying goes, without having made a resolution, although one has indeed made a resolution, but one resolution and another resolution are very different. A resolution speedily arrived at in line with others and resolved on the basis that the next-door neighbor and the neighbor across the street have also resolved is really no resolution, for whether there is poetry at second hand I do not know, but a resolution at third hand is no resolution. Compared with such marriages, which do not play the best suit either of falling in love or of resolution but pass and pass by, a negative resolution naturally has the advantage. But then marriages of that sort are not marriages, either, but are an aping.

A person's total ideality lies first and last in resolution. Any other ideality is a trifle. To admire him for it is childish, and if the person involved understands himself properly, it is an insult. Consequently, it is a matter only of positive and negative resolutions. The positive resolution has the great advantage that it consolidates life and sets the individual at rest within himself; the negative resolution keeps him constantly *in suspenso*. A negative resolution is always far more exhausting than a positive one; it cannot become habitual, and yet it must be constantly maintained.

A positive resolution is sure in its happy outcome, for the universal, which is its positive element, assures happiness, assures that it will come and provides the happiness with security when it has come. A negative resolution is continually ambiguous, even with respect to a happy outcome. Just like happiness in paganism, it is an illusion, for happiness *is* only when it *has been*.[26] That is to say, not until I am dead can I know whether I *have been* happy. So also with the negative resolution. The individual has initiated conflict with life; therefore at no moment can he be finished; he cannot, like someone who has made and is held by a positive resolution, immerse himself day after day in the original basis of his resolution. A negative resolution does not hold him; he must hold it, however long it takes. Even if fortune favors him, and even if something most significant results for him, he still does not dare to deny the possibility that everything can suddenly have another interpretation. Through his negative resolution he now actually exists hypothetically or subjunctively, and with respect to a hypothesis the rub is that it is never completed until it has explained every phenomenon, for even with an incorrect hypothesis one can for the time being make a lot of headway until the phenomenon comes along that invalidates it, and with respect to the subjunctive *if*, it holds true—yes, if. A positive resolution has only one risk— not to be true to itself; a negative resolution always has a double danger: not to be true to itself, which resembles the danger in the positive resolution with the one difference that all this faithfulness is without reward, is a faded glory and as barren as a bachelor's life; and then the second risk—whether all this faithfulness whereby one is true to oneself in one's negative resolution is not a deviation that for all its faithfulness is eventually rewarded with repentance. Whereas the positive resolution cheerfully refreshes itself with rest, cheerfully rises up with the sun, cheerfully begins where it left off, cheerfully surveys everything thriving around it, and, as does the married man, cheerfully sees with each new day a new demonstration of what needed no demonstration (for the positive is not a hypothesis that must be demonstrated), the person who has chosen the negative resolution sleeps uneasily at night, expects the nightmare that he chose wrongly will suddenly come upon him, wakes up exhausted to see the barren heath around him, and is never restored because he is continually in suspense.

The state really does not need to penalize bachelors; life itself punishes the person who deserves to be punished, for the person who does not make a resolution is a poor wretch of whom it must be said in the sad sense: He does not come under judgment.[27] I do not speak this way because I am envious of those who do not will to marry; I am too happy to envy anyone, but I am zealous for life.

VI
106

I return to what I said before, that resolution is a person's ideality. I shall now attempt to develop how the resolution most formative of the individuality must be constituted, and I rejoice in thinking that marriage is precisely so constituted, which, as stated, I assume for the time being to be a synthesis of falling in love and resolution.

There is a phantom that frequently prowls around when the making of a resolution is at stake—it is *probability*—a spineless fellow, a dabbler, a Jewish peddler, with whom no freeborn soul becomes involved, a good-for-nothing fellow who ought to be jailed instead of quacks, male and female, since he tricks people out of what is more than money and more valuable than money. Anyone who with regard to resolution comes no further, never comes any further than to decide on the basis of probability, is lost for ideality, whatever he may become. If a person does not encounter God in the resolution, if he has never made a resolution in which he had a transaction with God, he might just as well have never lived. But God always does business *en gros* [wholesale], and probability is a security that is not registered in heaven. Thus it is so very important that there be an element in the resolution that impresses officious probability and renders it speechless.

There is a phantasm that the person making a resolution chases after the way the dog chases its shadow in the water;[28] it is the *outcome*, a symbol of finiteness, a mirage of perdition—woe to the person who looks for it, he is lost. Just as the person who, if bitten by serpents, looked at the cross in the desert and became healthy,[29] so the person who fastens his gaze on the outcome is bitten by a serpent, wounded by the secular mentality, lost both for time and for eternity. If a person in the moment of resolution is not so glowingly surrounded by the brightness of the divine that all phantasms created by the fogs of drowsiness vanish, his resolution is but a greater or minor forgery—let him find consolation in the outcome. This is why it is so very important that the object of the resolution be of such a nature that no outcome dares to bid at the auction, because what is being purchased is being purchased *à tout prix* [at all costs].

VI
107   All that is said here applies to every resolution in which the eternal is present and completes the purchase, not only to that resolution of marriage when for the first time it presses to its breast the infatuation of erotic love and clasps [*slutte*] it in the firm embrace of the resolution [*Beslutning*]. It is true of every resolution that has the eternal in it, to that extent also of the

negative resolution, provided that it is negative only toward temporality but is oriented positively toward the eternal. But precisely therein is the basis for its state of suspense. In the resolution of marriage, on the other hand, falling in love is deposited as a trust fund, and love has precisely the power to draw down the resolution maker not exactly to earth, far from it, but down beside the beloved in time. The resolving is the ethical, is freedom; the negative resolution also has this, but the freedom, blank and bare, is as if tongue-tied, hard to express, and generally has something hard in its nature. Falling in love, however, promptly sets it to music, even if this composition contains a very difficult passage. For the bridal couple who in that sacred moment, or when they think about it later, do not find that in a certain sense it is nonsense for the pastor to say to the lovers that they *shall* love one another, and on the other hand do not find, if I dare say so, that it is very splendidly stated—such a bridal couple lack a marital ear. Just as it is delicious to discern the whispering of falling in love, this precious witness at the wedding, so that rash phrase is welcome that says: You shall love her. How dithyrambic a wedding ceremony is; how almost presumptuous that one is not satisfied with falling in love but calls it a duty. No wonder that a resolution that matches such a charge seems to some to be a hard saying: that erotic love, then, is not satisfied with being self-confident but in its daredevilry attempts that *"You shall!"* that marriage, then, has a resolution that is the one and only wish, an eternal duty that is the eye's delight and the heart's desire!

Cheer up, then, venture boldly. Have the courage to will the difficult; then in turn the difficulty will be of assistance, for the difficulty is not an old grump, is not a chicaner, but an omnipotence that wills to do it so very well. Whereas the person who in his eternal resolution relates negatively to the temporal becomes solitary in the moment of resolution and (even if he actually is great, even if he were a Prometheus) is chained, not to a mountain, but is imprisoned in temporality as if by chains, the married man, upon opening his eyes again (insofar as they seemed to be shut in the eternity of resolution), again stands where he was before, in the very same place, at his beloved's side, where he indeed prefers to be, and suffers no lack of the eternal, for it is with him in temporality.

The negative resolution is for the eternal only; the positive, for both the temporal and the eternal, and thus the person is simultaneously temporal and eternal. Therefore, the ideality of the genuine resolution lies first of all in a resolution that is just as temporal as eternal, which is, if I may put it this way, both signed and countersigned, a precaution used for bonds and which the bank even uses for its larger bank notes. The genuinely idealizing resolution then has this characteristic: it is signed in heaven, and then it is countersigned in temporality. But not only this, time after time as life goes on the married man keeps on getting new countersignatures, the one just as precious as the other. Every married man understands what I mean; why should I think anything else: that he was a disgrace, an ingrate, who grudgingly regarded the further assurances as troublesome. A married man with integrity understands that a wife is the principal countersignature, that anyone in the circle growing up under marriage's eye is a new countersignature and a new endorsement. Oh, what a blessed assurance! Oh, what a rich man! Oh, what an assured blessedness—to possess all one's abundance in a single bond that cannot vanish before one's eyes as does the eternal resolution for the person who relates negatively to the temporal. [30]The latter is a poor wretch or a mutineer, and such a person is also a poor wretch; he is a poor wretch who goes through time with his eternal resolution but never gets it countersigned—on the contrary, wherever he goes it is protested. He is an outcast of the race and even though consoled by the eternal is nevertheless a stranger to joy, weeps, and perhaps gnashes his teeth, for the person who in eternity does not wear the wedding garment is thrown out,[31] but here on earth the wedding garment is indeed the wedding garment.

The genuinely idealizing resolution must be just as sympathetic as it is autopathetic. But the person who is negative toward the temporal has no channel for his sympathy; consequently, instead of becoming a refreshment for him when it pours out its blessed overabundance and then accumulates anew, his sympathy becomes a torment that eats away his soul because it cannot express itself. To be suffocated is terrible, but to have sympathy and not be able to give vent to it is equally terrible. I am assuming, namely, that he has sympathy, for otherwise he is not worth talking about. To have sympathy is an essential quality of being human; any resolution that disregards this is in the larger sense not idealizing, and neither is it idealizing if sympathy does not acquire its adequate expression. Let the bachelor become a fool who wastes his sympathy on dogs and cats and pranks; let the recluse who made a negative choice be a noble soul, let his sympathy seek and find tasks far greater than having a wife and children—he still has no joy from it. If heaven's dew was not allowed to fall on the grass and not allowed to have the joy of seeing the flower refreshed by its deliciousness, if it was supposed to diffuse itself over the wide ocean or evaporate before it reached the flower, would that not be terrible? If the milk in the mother's breast flowed in abundance but there was no infant, if the wasted milk was as priceless as Juno's milk, after which the Milky Way is named[32]—ah, how sad! So also with a man whose sympathy is not allowed to see a wife burst into leaf like the tree[33] planted within the blessed hedgerow of sympathy, is not permitted to see the tree blossom and bear its fruit, which ripens under the solicitude of sympathy! How unfortunate the man who does not have this expression for his sympathy and the still more glorious expression for everything his sympathy expresses: that all this is his duty. This contradiction is sympathy's most blissful delight, a bliss that can make him seem to lose his mind for joy. Let a poor wretch who does not have an understanding with the temporal in the resolution of marriage nurse the sick, feed the poor, clothe the naked; let him visit the prisoner, let him comfort the dying[34]—I commend him, he will not miss his reward,[35] but neither is he in divine madness an unprofitable servant. His sympathy is continually seeking its deepest expression but does not find it, seeks it far and wide as his solicitude goes from house to house, whereas the married man finds opportunity in his house, in his home, where to him it is bliss to will to do everything, and an even greater bliss, a divine *poscimur* [we are called upon],[36] that he is and remains without meritoriousness.

The genuinely idealizing resolution must be just as concrete as it is abstract. To the degree that a resolution is drawn up negatively, to the same degree it is solely abstract. But no matter what a resolution pertains to, there is nothing between heaven and earth so concrete as a marriage and the marital relationship, nothing so inexhaustible; even the most insignificant thing has its significance, and while the marriage commitment flexibly spans a lifetime (just like that hide that measured out the circumference of Carthage[37]), it encircles the moment, and every moment, just as flexibly. There is nothing as piecemeal as a marriage, and yet there is no one who can stand a divided heart less than marriage—God himself is not as jealous.[38] Every obligatory relation can be approximately exhausted in stipulations; every task, every achievement, in short, what generally occupies one's time, has its time, but marital life evades such stipulation. Indeed, woe to the person for whom it is a burden; even to be sentenced for life does not give an adequate conception of the torment of his sentence, for that is an abstract term, but such a marital criminal daily feels the horror of being sentenced for life. The more concrete a person becomes in the ideality, the more perfect is the ideality. Consequently, the person who will not marry has rejected the most idealizing resolution. Moreover, it is really an inconsistency to refuse to get married and then to want to decide on some positive objective in temporality. What interest can anyone who refuses to let marriage have its reality [*Realitet*][39] have in the idea of the state, what love can he have for his fatherland, what civic patriotism can he have for everything that pertains to the woes and welfare of society! The more abstract the ideality, the more imperfect it is!

Abstraction is ideality's first expression, but concretion is its essential expression. Marriage expresses this. When they fall in love, the lovers will to belong to each other *forever*; in the resolution they resolve to will to be *everything* to each other, and this prodigious abstraction has its concrete expression in what is so insignificant that no third party dreams of it. The highest expression of falling in love is that the lover feels like nothing before the beloved, and vice versa, because to feel oneself to be something conflicts with falling in love. The resolution has no words, because words themselves are almost too concrete. The vow is silent or that immortal "yes"—and this abstraction is expressed in such a way that if all the writers of shorthand joined together they would be unable to describe what takes place in a week of marriage. This is the marital happiness. I do not mean it in the sense in which one speaks of a particular happy couple—no, this is the happiness of being a married man. What life is happier than his for whom everything has meaning; how could life become long for the person to whom the moment has meaning? And if this happiness is not safe and secure, for indeed an old proverb says that *Ehestand* [marriage] is *Wehestand* [misery],[40] and marriage declares itself in this way; how secure it must indeed feel so that it dares to invite people to attempt it! Is there any other arrangement in life, any other relationship, that begins in this way—alas, all other beginnings are flattering enough and are silent about the difficulties. To excuse the note he has sent to the Count, Figaro tells the Countess that she is the only woman in the kingdom to whom he dared permit himself to do such a thing with certainty;[41] similarly, marriage, I believe, is unique in that it dares to say of itself with certainty that it is a torment; it would be incautious of anything else in life to betray anything.

The genuinely idealizing resolution must be just as dialectical with regard to freedom as to the divine dispensation. No resolution is made without venturing. Now that the resolution has been made, the more abstract it is, the less dialectical it is with respect to the divine dispensation. The ideality of the resolution thereby gradually acquires a certain falseness; it becomes a bit proud, haughty, inhuman; the whole argument of providence in particular is regarded as extrajudicial. The more concrete the resolution is, the more it has to do with a relation to the divine dispensation. This gives it the ideality of humility, meekness, and gratitude. But a married man who is that with his whole life and soul is certainly the one who has ventured and ventured most of all. He ventures out of infatuation's hiding place with the beloved one, with the beloved ones—what cannot happen there? He does not know; if he would devote himself to this thought, his hair would certainly turn gray in a single night. He does not know what would happen, but this he does know—he can lose everything; and this he does know—he cannot evade a single thing, for the resolution holds him firmly there where his love imprisons him but also holds him undaunted there where falling in love laments.

There is an old saying that perhaps has fallen somewhat into discredit, but never mind; the saying goes like this: What does one not do for the sake of wife and children? *Antwort* [Answer]: One does everything, everything. —And what does one then do against the divine dispensation, who fathoms its secret? One flexes one's muscles, one works, one fights, one suffers—ah, there is nothing one will not put up with. The more positive a person's resolution is, the more declinable he himself becomes, and only a married man is declined by the divine dispensation in all *genera* [genders], *numeri* [numbers], and *casibus* [cases]. —From a purely external point of view, there certainly are hundreds and hundreds more who have risked more than a married man, risked kingdoms and countries, millions and millions of millions have lost thrones and principalities, fortunes and prosperity, and yet the married man risks more. For the person who loves risks more than all these things, and the person who loves in as many ways as it is possible for a man to love risks most of all. Suppose that the married man is a king, a millionaire—there is no need for that, there is no need for that; all those other things merely confuse the clarity of the arithmetical problem—suppose that he is a beggar, he risks the most. Suppose that the brave one dares to do the hero-dance on the battlefield, or dance upon the heaving sea, or leap across the abyss—there is no need for that, there is no need for that, for everyday use there is no need for that. In a theater it might be needed, but mankind would be in a bad way if life and our Lord did not have a few reserve battalions of heroes who are not applauded even though they risk more. A married man risks every day, and every day the sword of duty hangs over his head, and the journal is kept up as long as the marriage keeps on, and the ledger of responsibility is never closed, and the responsibility is even more inspiring than the most glorious epic poet who must testify for the hero. Well, it is true that he does not take the risk for nothing—no, like for like; he risks everything for everything, and if because of its responsibility marriage is an epic, then because of its happiness it certainly is also an idyll.

Thus marriage is the beautiful focal point of life and existence, a center that reflects just as deeply as that which it manifests is high: a disclosure that in its concealment manifests the heavenly. And every marriage does this, just as not only the ocean but the quiet lake does, provided the water is not turbid. To be a married man is the most beautiful and meaningful task; the person who did not become married is an unfortunate whose life either did not permit him that or who never fell in love, or he is a suspicious character whom we eventually ought to take into custody. Marriage is the fullness of time.[42] He who did not become a married man is always regarded as unhappy by others or he is that also to himself; in his eccentricity he wants to feel time as a burden. This is what marriage is like. It is divine, for falling in love is the wonder; it is earthly, for falling in love is nature's most profound myth. Love is the unfathomable ground that is hidden in darkness, but the resolution is the triumphant victor who, like Orpheus,[43] fetches the infatuation of falling in love to the light of day, for the resolution is the true form of love, the true explanation and transfiguration;[44] therefore marriage is sacred and blessed by God. It is civic, for by marriage the lovers belong to the state and the fatherland and the common concerns of their fellow citizens. It is poetic, inexpressibly so, just as is falling in love, but the resolution is the conscientious translator that translates the enthusiasm into actuality, and this translator is so scrupulous, oh, so scrupulous! The voice of falling in love "sounds like the fairies' from the grottoes on a summer

VI
113

night,"[45] but the resolution has the earnestness of perseverance that sounds through the fleeting and the transitory. The movement of falling in love is light, like dancing in the meadow, but the resolution catches hold of the weary one until the dance begins again. This is what marriage is like. It is happy like a child, and yet solemn, for it continually has the wonder before its eyes. It is modest and concealed, yet festivity lives within, but just as the storekeeper's door to the street is locked during a divine service, so is marriage's door always shut, because a divine service is going on continually. It is concerned, but this concern is not unbeautiful, since it rests in understanding of and feeling for the deep pain of all life. Whoever does not know this pain is unbeautiful: it is solemn and yet mitigated in jest, for not to will to do everything is a poor jest, but to do one's utmost and then to understand that it is little, so little, nothing at all compared with love's desire and with resolution's demand—that is a blessed jest. It is humble and yet courageous; indeed, courage such as this is found only in marriage, because it is formed from the strength of the man and the frailty of the woman and is rejuvenated by the child's freedom from care. It is faithful; truly, if marriage were not faithful, where then would there be faithfulness! It is secure, at peace, enfranchised in life; no danger is a real danger, but only a spiritual conflict. It is content with little, it also knows how to use much; but it knows how to be beautiful in scarcity and knows how to be no less beautiful in abundance! It is satisfied and yet full of expectancy; the lovers are sufficient unto themselves and yet exist only for the sake of others. It is plain and everyday—indeed, what is as plain and everyday as marriage; it is totally temporal, and yet the recollection of eternity listens and forgets nothing.

This will have to be enough on the subject of marriage. At this moment I have no more that I want to say; another time, perhaps tomorrow, I shall say more, but "always the same and about the same thing,"[46] for it is only gypsies and robbers and swindlers who have the motto: Never go back where you have once been.[47] Yet it seems to me to be sufficient, and the only thing I would like to add is that if marriage were only half as good, it would already be attractive in my eyes, all the more so since I certainly do feel that I have not been eulogizing myself but rather have been passing judgment. But then a man can indeed also be a happy husband without having achieved perfection if only he has his eyes on perfection and humbly feels his own imperfection. All I wanted to do here was to jack up the price a bit,[48] for when one is dealing with chicaners who cavil at everything, with freebooters who devastate and burn, with spies who lurk at the door, with vagabonds who want to burst right in from the street, then one commands respect for what is holy, and incidentally plays a little blind man's buff with them, since one is well aware that they are standing and fumbling at the street door, the blind door of marriage, but along that path one learns nothing about marriage.

Now for the objections. Even if a married man cannot sharpen them as a chicaner can, he knows very well where the trouble lies, knows how to include such things in stating the case for marriage, or at least has acquired ordinary competence in taking a hint. To elaborate the objections as such is only a waste of time, even if one had the talent for it. But this much is certain: anyone who raises an objection is always to be pitied. Either he has gone astray in desire and thereupon become callous or he is infatuated with the understanding. With regard to any objection based on the latter, the only reply, *à la* Hamann, is "Bah!" Let him go on talking as long as he wants to; then ask if he has finished, and then say that magic word. Having closed the door in this manner, one then has a second reply. The Sophist Gorgias is supposed to have said about tragedy that it is a deception in which the one deceiving seems more justified than the one not deceiving and the deceived wiser than the one not deceived.[49] This last remark is an eternal truth and a proper response whenever the understanding goes astray in its own thoughts and precisely out of fear of being deceived is thereby deceived. It is indeed true that it takes a quite different kind of wisdom to remain in the blessed deception of ardor and of mystery and of erotic love and of illusion and of the wonder than to run away from house and home split naked, half-sappy from sheer sapience. The contrast arises in such a strange way. At times absent-mindedness is due to a deficiency of memory, and yet there are cases of a man's becoming absentminded because he has too much memory.

If the objection is going to start at the bottom, it should, insofar as it is leveling its charge against marriage, first of all level its charge at falling in love, for first things must still always come first. This seldom happens. Ordinarily the objections just take love under their wing, and their amorous kiss is a real Judas kiss[50] with which they betray marriage. The enemies who level charges against love are less harmful and only very seldom have a hearing. As soon as the understanding wants to try to explain or think through love, the ludicrousness of it becomes apparent, something that is best expressed by saying that understanding becomes ludicrous. But the matter takes on a different aspect with regard to the person who is doing the talking. If it is a degenerate who ends a perhaps dissolute life by wanting to ridicule everything that always knew how to elude his profane touch, even if he has dabbled quite enough in so-called falling in love, then any response is superfluous. But a more acceptable form of objection is conceivable; it is so acceptable that one can decide to feel sorry for the poor mixed-up fellow and explain his mistake. Then it must be a young man who actually was pure in regard to the erotic, but a young man who, like a prematurely wise child, has skipped a stage in the development of the soul and has begun his life with reflection. Such a thing is certainly conceivable in our reflective age; in a certain sense he can even be regarded as a justified individuality, insofar as all the profuse talk about reflection, the idolization of it, the necessity of it, sharpened by doubting everything, for him expresses itself in his being more earnest than many an irresponsible systematician who wants to make a hit in a book by doubting everything, gets the preposterous idea of wanting to think the erotic, think himself into it—that is, think himself away from it. Such an individuality is an unhappy individuality, and to the extent that he actually is pure, I cannot consider his unhappiness without sympathy. He is indeed like that solitary fairy who has lost her swan's wings and now sits there abandoned, vainly, despite all her efforts, trying to fly.[51] He has lost the immediacy that carries a person through life, the immediacy without which falling in love is impossible, the immediacy, continually presupposed, that has continually taken him a little further; he is excluded from the benevolence of immediacy, for which one cannot really manage to give thanks since the benevolence always hides itself.

Just as it is sad to see the misery of that solitary fairy, so, too, it is sad to see all the mental exertions of such a person, whether he suffers in silence or with a demonic virtuosity in reflecting he knows how to conceal his nakedness with clever words.

All falling in love is a wonder—marvel not, then, that the understanding stands still while the lovers kneel in adoration before the wonder's sacred symbol. In this connection, one should here, as everywhere, continually watch one's expressions. There is a category called "to choose oneself," a somewhat modernized Greek category[52] (it is my favorite category and encompasses an individual's existence), but it should never be applied to the erotic, as in speaking of choosing a beloved, for the beloved is the god's [*Gudens*] gift and just as the person choosing, who chooses himself, is presupposed to exist, so also must the beloved be presupposed to exist as the beloved if the category "to choose" is to be used univocally in both connections. If that phrase "to choose" is used to mean wanting to set someone up as the beloved, instead of wanting to accept the beloved, then a deluded reflection promptly has something to hold to. The young man then dissolves love into loving the lovable—after all, he must *choose*. Poor fellow, that is an impossibility; and not only that, who would still dare to choose if it is supposed to be understood in this way; who would dare to be so doting on his own manliness that he would not grasp that he who proposes must first be proposed to by the god himself, and any other proposing is a foolish having it all one's own way. I decline to choose in this way; instead I thank the god for the gift—he chooses better—and to thank is more blessed. I do not wish to become a laughingstock by starting a silly, critical lecture on the beloved, that I love her for this reason and for that reason and finally for this reason—because I love her. If done right, a lecture of this sort

VI
117

to the lovers themselves can be very amusing by quite humorously placing the whole substance of erotic love in relation to a triviality, as if the husband were to tell his wife that he really loved her because she had blond hair. That kind of talk is a humorous jest that long ago lost sight of the importance of all reflection. I give the god what is the god's,[53] and every human being ought to do that. But he does not do it when he denies him the sacred tribute of admiration and wonder. Precisely when the understanding stands still, it behooves one to have the courage and the heart to believe the wondrous and, continually strengthened by this vision, to return to actuality and not just sit still and want to fathom it. Nevertheless, I still prefer a futile attempt of a sharply sustained critique that drives the reflecting one to despair and perhaps precisely thereby saves him to a silly garrulous reflection, a lady's maid who wants to dress up erotic love and know more than the wonder. Surely erotic love is a wonder, not some town gossip; its priest is a worshiper, not a streetwalker.

In paganism, therefore, love was attributed to Eros. Since the resolution of marriage adds the ethical, that somewhat arch assignation to a deity thereby becomes in marriage a purely religious expression for one's receiving the beloved from the hand of God. As soon as God is present in the consciousness, the wonder is there, for God cannot be there in any other way. The Jews expressed this by saying that the person who saw God must die.[54] This was only a figurative expression; it is literal and true that one loses one's mind in the same way as the lover does when he sees the beloved and, which he also does, sees God. To be sure, I have been a married man for several years. Perhaps one will laugh at my enthusiasm—but laugh then—a married man is always in love, and otherwise he never comes to understand what it means to fall in love.

The rueful knight of reflection goes further; he wants to fathom the synthesis at the basis of erotic love. He does not perceive that a veil is hung before his eyes and that once again he faces the wonder. God creates out of nothing, but here, if I dare say so, he does more—he dresses an instinct in all the beauty of erotic love so that the lovers see only the beauty and are unaware of the instinct. Who lifted the veil? Who would dare to do that? The ideal beauty is veiled beauty, and presumably the moon shines half as beautifully through the cloud veil, and the sky dreams half as yearningly through the curtain of blossoms, and the sea in its half transparency tempts half as strongly as the beloved, as the wife, through the veil of modesty. I dream—I, a poor married man? But what shall I say about the mystery that was, is, and will remain a mystery to me through the years, for I do not know that any explanation is coming; I do not even comprehend this loathsome presumptuousness that believes nature's veil to be more precious than morality's.

So, then, that poor fellow whom reflection reduces to beggary, as always, goes further: his dreaming makes him unhappier; his wealth makes him poorer. He pauses at what he presumably would call the consequences of erotic love. And who does not also pause here; indeed, it is as if the natural course of life paused while the god creatively intervenes. O blessed wonder! Who is not grateful to see the god here, grateful that he does not sink into depression as does reflection's weary warrior. Who is not grateful out of joy over life, not as if the child were a wonder child (vanity, vanity), but it is a wonder that a child is born. Anyone who refuses to see the wonder here must indeed—if he is not utterly lacking in spirit—say with Thales that out of love of children he will not have any children:[55] the saddest of sayings (for it implies that it is a greater crime or misfortune to give a human being life than to take a human being's life) and the most disastrous self-contradiction!

Falling in love, then, is claimed as the wonder, and everything that belongs to love belongs to the wonder. Love, then, is assumed as given. Any attempt on the part of reflection, however flattering or shocking, however rash or insipid, is straightway condemned as false. —The question remains: How can this immediacy (falling in love) find its equivalent in an immediacy reached through reflection? Here the crucial battle will take place.

VI
119

But first of all I would like to point out another aspect of the matter.[56] Love is ordinarily praised enough. Even a seducer does not lack the audacity to join in. But the moment or the brief period of falling in love is supposed to be woman's culmination, and therefore the point is to leave off again. In that case the objections take another direction, and the amorous, seductive worship of the sex ends with insults.

Incidentally, I was brought up in the Christian religion, and although I can scarcely sanction all the improper attempts to gain the emancipation of woman, all paganlike reminiscences also seem foolish to me. My brief and simple opinion is that woman is certainly just as good as man—period. Any more discursive elaboration of the difference between the sexes or deliberation on which sex is superior is an idle intellectual occupation for loafers and bachelors. A well-brought-up child is recognized by his being satisfied with what he receives, and likewise a well-brought-up married man is recognized by his being happy and grateful for what has been allotted to him—in other words, that he is in love. We sometimes hear a married man lament that marriage gives him too much to attend to—how much more he has if he also is shameless enough either to want to be only his wife's censor and critic, who torments her every other moment of the day with his insipid claims that she must smile this way, hold her head up this way, curtsy this way, dress this way, and pronounce this way—or he wants to be a married man and also a critic and censor.

As a critic of marriage, I am a *tiro* [novice]; I have no shallow introductory studies from a man-about-town period, which at times is more poisonous than one thinks. My love story is in a certain sense short. I have minded my own business and tended to my studies; I have not inspected the girls at parties and on the promenades, at theaters and concerts. I have not entered into it recklessly, nor have I done it with the idiotic seriousness in which a marriageable male is pleased to think that a girl must be extraordinary to be good enough for him. Thus without any experience I became acquainted with her who now is mine. I have never been in love before, and my prayer is that I may not fall in love later on, but if for a moment I were to think what for me is indeed unthinkable— that death took her from me, that my life underwent a change such that I would be dedicated to being a husband a second time, I am convinced that my marriage has not spoiled me or made me more competent to criticize, select, and inspect. No wonder one hears so much silly talk about love, since to hear so much talk is already an indication that reflection is universally forcing its way in to disturb the quiet, more modest life where love prefers to reside because in its modesty it is so close to piety.

Thus I am well aware that Messrs. Esthetes will promptly declare me incompetent for discussion, and all the more so when I do not conceal that despite being married for eight years I still do not definitely know in a critical sense what my wife looks like. To love is not to criticize, and marital faithfulness does not consist of detailed criticism. Yet this ignorance of mine is not entirely due to my being uncultured; I, too, am able to observe the beautiful, but I observe a portrait, a statue, in that way, not a wife. I thank her in part for that, for if she had found any vain delight whatsoever in being the object of a philanderer's critical adoration, who knows whether I, too, might not have become a philanderer and as usual ended up becoming a grumpy critic and husband. Neither do I see myself able to move easily and routinely in some of the *termini* [technical terms] the connoisseurs sling about; I do not ask for that and do not go to banquets with connoisseurs. To put it as mildly as possible, to me such connoisseurs seem like those who sit and change money in the forecourt of the sanctuary;[57] and just as it must be nauseating for someone entering the temple in an exalted frame of mind to hear the jingling of coins, so is it nauseating to me to hear the noise of words such as "slim," "shapely," "svelte," etc. When I read these words in a primitive[58] poet, flowing out of originality of mood and of the mother tongue, I am delighted, but I do not profane them, and, as far as my wife is concerned, I am not sure to this day whether she is slim. My joy and my being in love are not that of a horse dealer or the irascible unwholesomeness of a cunning seducer. If I were to express myself about her in that way, I am sure I would talk nonsense. Having refrained from it up to now, I am very likely saved from it for the rest of my life, for just the mere presence of an infant

makes being in love even more bashful than it is intrinsically.
I have often pondered this, and for that reason I have always
found it unbecoming for an older man with children to marry
a very young girl.

Precisely because my love [*Kjærlighed*] is everything to me,
all critical output is in my opinion sheer nonsense. If I were to
praise the female sex in the esthetic way people speak about
praising, I would do it only humorously, for all this slimness
and svelteness and the eyebrows and flashing eyes do not constitute falling in love, still less a marriage, and only in marriage does being in love have its true expression; outside marriage it is seduction or flirtation. There is a little book by Hen.
Cornel. Agrippa of Nettesheim: *De nobilitate et praecelientia
foeminei sexus, eiusdemque supra virilem eminentia libellus* [On the
Nobility and Excellence of the Female Sex, and the Superiority of the Same over the Male Sex].[59] This little book in a very
naive way says the most remarkable things in honor of
women. Whether the author has demonstrated what he
wanted to demonstrate, I am not exactly sure, although he
speaks *bona fide* [in good faith] and well and is good-natured
enough to believe that he has demonstrated it; I do, however,
fully approve of the poem (at the end of the book) that refuses
to have anything to do with any turgid [*vaniloquax*] praise of
man. When in the absolute assurance of the happiness of being
in love and of marriage one reads this naive argumentation,
when one adds a very pathos-filled *ergo* [therefore] or *quod erat
demonstrandum* [that which was to be demonstrated] to each
argument, whereas the genuine pathos is the rich substance of
that assurance, which needs no proof, then a purely humorous
effect is produced.

I shall explain this a bit more precisely. A speech was delivered to the Twenty-eighth of May Society[60] by a young
scholar who in his enthusiasm for the natural sciences was of
the opinion that every new discovery, for example, the recent
discovery that soap could be made from flintstone, led us
closer to God and convinced us of his goodness, wisdom, etc.
If the speech is supposed to be considered a serious attempt to
come closer to God, it is, it seems to me, very miserable. It is
different, however, if an individuality who is a millionaire and

"better" than the Bank of England when it comes to his faith in the goodness and wisdom of God, if he, when reflection began to show signs of wanting to demonstrate something with regard to this, were to interrupt its demonstration with the argument that now we are even able to wash our hands in soap made of flintstone. He could then end his speech something like this: Look! Now I am washing my hands; if this is not a convincing demonstration, then I despair of producing any. In that little book it is adduced as proof that in Hebrew woman is called Eve (life), man is called Adam (earth)[61]—*ergo*. Something like this is excellent as a jest in an *altercatio* [exchange of words] in which everything is absolutely decided and signed and sealed with both the notary public's seal and God's. So it is also when the author cites as another demonstration that when a woman falls into the water she floats on top whereas a man, if he falls into the water, sinks—*ergo*. This demonstration lends itself to other uses, which helps explain the fact that so many witches were burned in the Middle Ages.

It is a few years since I read that little book, but it was highly amusing to me. The most comical things in the natural sciences and philology appear in the most naive way. Various things imprinted themselves on my memory, and while I never speak to my wife about her being slender etc., which would certainly displease her and be a failure for me, yet sometimes, if I do say so myself, I am very good at the kind of arguments and observations that please her, probably because they demonstrate nothing at all and therefore simply demonstrate that our marriage needs no prolix critique but that we are happy.

In that connection, it has often amazed me that no poet really portrays a married couple conversing. If they are ever portrayed—and they are meant to be a happy couple—they usually talk like a couple in love. Ordinarily they are only minor characters and so much older that they are the father and mother of the lover the poet is portraying. If a marriage is to be portrayed, it at least must be unhappy in order to be able to come under consideration. They are viewed so differently: falling in love is supposed to be happy and have dangers outside; marriage must have its dangers within in order to be poetic. I regard this as a sad indirect demonstration that marriage is far from enjoying the recognition that it deserves, for it indeed seems as if a married couple were not just as poetic as a couple of lovers. Let the lovers talk with all the effervescence of infatuation, which appeals to the young man and the young maiden; married folk are not so bad, either.

I assume that it is a poor husband who does not become a humorist through his marriage, in the same sense as it is a poor lover who does not become a poet; and I assume that every husband becomes somewhat humorous, gets a touch of it, just as every lover becomes somewhat poetic. I cite myself, not so much with regard to the poetic as with regard to a sense of humor, a certain touch of it, which I owe solely to my marriage. In falling in love much of the erotic has an absolute meaning; in marriage this absolute meaning alternates with the humorous view, which is the poetic articulation of the quiet and contented security of married life.

I shall cite an example and beg the reader to have enough sense of humor not to regard it as demonstrating anything. Together with my wife, I made a little summer excursion through southern Sjælland. We traveled entirely at our own convenience, and since my wife wished to gain an idea of what certain people call rambling around on country roads, we stopped at all the country inns we could, sometimes stayed overnight in such a place, but first and foremost took our own good time. At the inn, we had an opportunity to look around. Now, it so happened, strangely enough, that in five successive inns we found a posted advertisement that, pursuing us in this way, was impossible to ignore. The advertisement had the following contents: A worried paterfamilias most cordially thanked an experienced and expert practitioner for having easily and painlessly, with an expert hand, relieved the paterfamilias, and also his family, of some bad corns and thus restored him and his family to social life. The members of the family were specified, and among them there was also a daughter, who, since like an Antigone she belonged to this unfortunate family, was not exempted from this family evil either. After we had read this advertisement at three stops, it is no wonder

that it became a subject for conversation. I thought it tactless
of the paterfamilias to inform on the girl, for even if it was
now generally known that she was completely healed, it
nevertheless was bound to make a suitor have second
thoughts, which was totally unnecessary, for corns should be
reckoned among the infirmities one could find out about after
the wedding.

I now ask a poet to tell me whether the subject of this conversation, although I probably was not the man able to develop it altogether humorously, is not humorous; but on the
other hand whether it is not also true that this is a proper subject only in the mouth of a married man. A lover would feel
offended, because this nasty corn, even after it was removed,
has a most disturbing effect on an esthetic romantic view of
the beautiful. A jest such as that in the mouth of a lover would
be utterly unforgivable. Now, even if the conversation, because of my humble self, turned out to be simple, everyday
chitchat, I do know that it amused my wife; it amused her that
an accidentality of that sort was placed in the category of an
esthetic absolute—as, for example, by asking whether it
would not be sufficient grounds for divorce etc. And at times
when some connoisseur and some superclever miss discourse
grandiloquently in my living room about falling in love and
slenderness and say that the lovers must really get to know
each other in order to be sure of their choice, in order to make
no error of judgment, I put in a few words, actually playing
to my wife, and say: Yes, it is difficult, it is difficult—take
corns, for example: no one can know for sure about them,
whether someone has them or has had them or is going to
have them.

But enough of this. It is precisely marriage's sense of security that sustains the humorous; based upon experience, it
does not have the restlessness of erotic love's first bliss, even
if marriage's bliss is far from being minor. And when I as a
married man, a married man of eight years, rest my head on
her shoulder, I am not a critic, who admires or sees the lack of
some earthly beauty; nor am I an infatuated youth who celebrates her bosom, but nevertheless I am as deeply moved as
the first time. For I know what I knew and what I am repeat-

VI
124

edly convinced of—that there within my wife's breast beats a
heart, quietly and humbly, but steadily and smoothly; I know
that it beats for me and my welfare and for what is mutually
ours; I know that its calm, tender movement is uninterrupted—ah, while I am busy about my affairs, while I am distracted by so many different things, I know that at whatever
time, in whatever situation I turn to her, it has not stopped
beating for me. And I am a believer: just as the lover believes
that the beloved is his life, so I spiritually believe that this tenderness—like mother's milk, which, as also stated in that little
book, natural scientists maintain is lifesaving for someone
who is sick unto death—I believe that this tenderness that un-
failingly struggles for an ever more intimate expression, I believe that this tenderness that was her rich bridal dowry, I believe that it returns rich dividends; I believe that it will double
itself if I do not squander her resources. I believe that if I were
ill, sick unto death, and this tender gaze rested upon me—ah,
as if she herself and not I were the dying gladiator—I believe
that it would summon me back to life if God in heaven did
not himself use his power, and if God does use his power, then
I believe that this tenderness once again binds me to life as a
vision that visits her, as one deceased whom death cannot
really persuade, until we are again united. But until then, until
God uses his power in this way, I believe that through her I
absorb peace and contentment into my life and many times
am rescued from the death of despondency and evil torment
of vexation of spirit.[62]

This is the way every husband talks—better, provided he is
a better husband, better, provided he is talented. He is not an
amorous youth, his expressions do not have the passion of the
moment, and what an insult to want to give thanks for a love
like that in the emotional blaze of the moment. He is like that
honest bookkeeper who once almost became the object of suspicion, because, when the stern auditors, in a case of fraud,
came to his door and demanded to see his account books, he
replied: I have none; I keep all my accounts in my head. How
suspicious! But all honor to the old man's head, his accounts
were absolutely correct! A husband may even be talking a bit
humorously when he speaks of this to his wife, but this hu-

mor, this carefree giving of thanks, this receipt—not on paper but in the ledger of recollection—demonstrates precisely that his accounting is trustworthy and that his marriage has an abundant supply of the daily bread of demonstration.

With this I have already suggested in what direction I seek woman's beauty. Alas, even upright people have contributed to the deplorable mistaken notion at which, all the worse, a rash young woman snatches all too eagerly, without considering that it is despair—the mistaken notion that a girl's only beauty is the first* beauty of youth, that she blossoms for only

⁶³* Precisely because it would be dubious, yes, even misleading, with respect to the thesis that woman's beauty increases with the years, to call to mind the theater arts, since here everything focuses on the demand of the moment and differences are required primarily, I perceive with all the more joy a beautiful, and to me so cherished, truth happily confirmed in the midst of the swiftly changing scenes of theatrical life. The actress on our stage who really portrays femininity—without being narrowly confined to one aspect of it, without being supported and without suffering under an accidentality in it, without being assigned to one period of it—is Mme. Nielsen.⁶⁴ The character she presents, but not immediately, the voice she uses so skillfully in the play, the inwardness that animates the interaction, the introverted absorption that makes the spectator feel so secure, the calmness with which she grips us, the authentic soulfulness that disdains all sham mannerisms, the even, full sonority of mood that does not come in gusts, does not strain by coyly absenting itself, does not drift into wild ranting, does not pretentiously procrastinate, does not violently erupt, does not pant for the inexpressible, but is true to herself, is responsible to herself, always promptly at every moment and continually reliable—in short, her whole performance brings to a focus what could be called the essentially feminine. Many an actress has achieved fame and adulation by her virtuosity in one accidental aspect of femininity; but this admiration, which also usually finds its appropriate expression in all kinds of momentary jubilation, is from the beginning the victim of time once the accidentals disappear on which the triumphal performance was based.

Since Mme. Nielsen's power is the essentially feminine, her range encompasses the essential even in the more insignificant, when in the play she is still seen in an essential relation (as the sweetheart in a vaudeville piece, as the mother in a pastoral play, etc.), the essential in the noble character, the essential in the ignoble character, who although femininely corrupted essentially belongs to her gender, so that one does not become uncomfortable at the sight of unloveliness, does not become suspicious because of the exaggeration, does not tend to explain the corruption by upbringing, the influence of environment, etc., since precisely in the ideality of the performance one sees the depth of the corruption and its origin. But just as her range is essential, so also is her triumph not the transitory triumph of a moment but the triumph that time a moment, that this is the time of falling in love, and that one loves only once.

Quite true, one does love only once, but with the years
woman increases particularly in beauty and is so far from diminishing that the first beauty is somewhat questionable when compared with the later. Indeed, who, unless he is desperately in love,[66] has not looked at a young girl without sensing a certain sadness because the fragility of mortal life shows itself here in its most extreme contrasts: vanity as swift as a

---

has no power over her. In every period of her life she will have new tasks and will express the essential as she did at the beginning of her beautiful career. And if she attains her sixtieth year, she will continue to be perfect. I know of no more noble triumph for an actress than this—that the one person who in perhaps the whole kingdom is most concerned not to give offense here dares to mention with confidence, as I do, the sixtieth year, which ordinarily is the last thing one should hasten to mention in connection with an actress's name. She will portray the grandmother perfectly, once again produce her effect through the essential, just as the young girl did not produce her effect by some extraordinary beauty that infatuated the critics, or by a matchless singing voice that charmed the connoisseurs, or by being able to dance, something that aroused the public's special interest, or by a bit of flirtation that every spectator pleasantly turned to his own account, but produced her effect by the dedication that is the pact of pure femininity with the imperishable.

Although at the theater one ordinarily tends to think about the vanity of life and youth, beauty and charm, one is safe in admiring her, because one knows that this does not perish. Perhaps others are affected in a different way, so that admiration, because there is no reason to hurry (and in this case there certainly is plenty of time), sometimes fails to appear, and this actress is considered to be second-rate, which she is indeed if the requirement is to strive to excel in the moment and to produce an effect not by what endures but by what is transitory. For this reason she may not have her admirers among the critics who register the pulse of the moment, or among the devotees of the theater who are obliged to have seen this one and that one, or among the messengers who want something to gossip about, or among the triumph-bearers who like other carriers seek day labor bearing someone away, or among young men who, failing otherwise to situate an adolescent love, cast it upon an actress, or among the dissipated who sustain themselves by a momentary excitation, but instead has her admirers among those who, themselves happy and contented in life, do not miss the theater, do not hanker after it, whose right hand does not promptly run to the left in applause on the spot,[65] whose pen is not busy on paper that same evening in connection with some detail, but who are slow to speak and perhaps rejoice all the more discriminatingly [*skiønsomt*] in seeing the *beautiful* [*skjønne*] when *in truth* it *is*.

dream, beauty as fair as a dream. But however fair that first beauty is, it is still not the truth; it is an envelope, a garment, from which only with the years does the true beauty extricate itself before the husband's grateful eyes. VI
128

On the other hand, look at the woman of years. You do not instinctively snatch at her beauty, for it is not the fleeting kind that hurries away like a dream. No, sit down beside her and observe her more closely. With her motherly solicitude, whose busy time, however, is now over, she belongs entirely to the world, and only the solicitude itself remains, and inside it she hovers like an angel over the ark of the covenant.[67] Truly, if you do not here feel what reality [*Realitet*] a woman has, then you are and remain a critic, a reviewer, a connoisseur perhaps—that is, a person in despair who rushes along in the fury of despair, shouting: Let us love today,[68] for tomorrow it is all over—not with us, that would be sad, but with erotic love—and that is abominable. Take some time now; sit down beside her. This is not the delightful fruit of desire; beware of any presumptuous thoughts or of wanting to use the connoisseurs' *termini*; if you foam within, then sit here so that you may calm down. This is not the froth of the moment; do you dare to surrender something like that in her presence, or would you dare to offer her your hand in a waltz! Then perhaps you prefer to avoid her company. Oh, even if the young generation milling around her are discourteous (so presumably thinks the fashionable gentleman who feels that she needs his conversation), no, are delinquent enough to let her sit all alone, she does not miss the pleasure of their company, she feels no sting of insult. She is reconciled with life, and if you once again feel the urge for a reconciling word, if you should feel the urge to forget the dissonances of life, then go to her, sit worthily with this worthy one—and which one, then, is more beautiful, the young mother who nourishes with the power of nature or the mother full of years who nourishes you again with her solicitude! Or if you are not so badly taken up with the troubles of the world, just sit worthily with this worthy one. Her life, too, is not devoid of melody; this age also is *non sine cithara* [not without its lyre],[69] and nothing of what has been experienced is forgotten—when this voice touches the strings of memory, all the sounds from life's various ages sweetly harmonize. You see, she has arrived at life's solution; indeed she herself is the solution to life, audible and visible. A man never finishes his life in this way, ordinarily his accounts are more complicated; but a housewife has only elementary events, the everyday distresses and the everyday joys, but therefore also this happiness, for if a young girl is happy, then the woman of years is even happier. Tell me, then, what is more beautiful—the young girl with her happiness or the woman full of years who accomplishes a work of God, who provides the solution to the worried person and for the cheerful person is the best eulogy on existence by being life's beautiful solution!

VI
129

Now I leave the woman of years, whose company I am not, however, really avoiding; I go back in time, happy that with the help of God I still have a beautiful part of my life left, but also without knowing any of that cowardliness that fears growing old, or fears it on his wife's behalf, for I do indeed assume that woman becomes more beautiful with the years. To my eyes, as a mother she is already far more beautiful than a young girl. A young girl, after all, is a phantasm; one scarcely knows whether she belongs to actuality or is a vision. And is that supposed to be the highest? Well, let the fantasts believe it. As a mother, however, she belongs totally to actuality, and mother love itself is not like the longings and presentiments of youth but is an inexhaustible source of inwardness. Neither is it so that all this was present as a possibility in the young girl. Even if it were so, a possibility is still less than an actuality, but it is not so. Inwardness is no more present in a young girl's breast than mother's milk. This is a metamorphosis that has no analogy in the man. If one can jokingly say that the man is not completely finished until he has his wisdom teeth, then one in all seriousness can say that a woman's development is not complete until she is a mother; only then does she exist in all her beauty—and in her beautiful actuality. So let that nimble, light, flirtatious, happy girl skip over the meadow, duping anyone who wants to catch her—ah, yes, I also delight in looking at it, but now, now she has been caught, imprisoned. I certainly did not catch her (to that end how futile and vainly foolish). I certainly do not imprison her (how weak a prison!). No, no, she has trapped herself and sits imprisoned beside the cradle; imprisoned, and yet she has complete freedom, a boundless freedom in which she binds herself to the child; I am sure that she is willing to die in her nest.[70]

Here only a word parenthetically. To speak as inoffensively as possible, I will assume that it was the mother's partiality for the child that made the husband a bit jealous—well, good Lord, that jealousy will certainly be surmounted. So now I have mentioned the word "jealousy." It is a dark passion, "a monster that befouls the food by which it is nourished."[71] Anger is also a dark passion, but from this it does not follow that there cannot also be a noble anger. It is the same with jealousy. In a noble love there is also a righteous indignation that really is both troubled and resentful and is an altogether normal psychical condition if the terrible thing has happened. I have no fault to find with it. Indeed, I demand of a husband that his soul show in this way the last honor to her who dishonored him, and to her to whom he also concedes, if you like, the abundant significance in being able to dishonor him. I consider this psychical condition as love's ethical sorrow over someone who has died. However, I also know that there are demonic powers in life; I know that there is a not very commendable fearlessness that, plagued by an evil spirit, wants to be pure spirit, and also wants to have the power to become what is just as reprehensible as raging in jealousy—the power to become cold, thoroughly chilled in the icy passion of wittiness. For there is a hell whose heat blights all life; but there is also a hell whose cold kills all life.

But I am not even jealous of the mother. A woman's life as a mother is an actuality so infinitely rich in variety that my love has enough to do day after day to discover something new. As mother, woman has no situation of which one might say that in this she is her most beautiful; as mother she is constantly in that situation, and mother love is soft as pure gold and pliant in every decision, and yet whole. And the husband's joy is new every day; it is not consumed even though he feeds on it, for it is like the food in Valhalla;[72] and even though he does not live on it, [73]it is nonetheless certain that he does not live on bread alone[74] but also on the approving admiration that accompanies the mother's achievements; he has in his home *panis et circenses* [bread and circuses].[75]

To what a multiplicity of collisions mother love is exposed, and how beautiful the mother is every time her self-renouncing, self-sacrificing love comes out victorious! I am not speaking here of what certainly is well known and is a given, that the mother sacrifices her life for the child. That sounds so exalted, so sentimental, and does not have the proper marital stamp. It is just as discernible, just as great, and just as endearing in small things. Wherever I see it, I admire it, and not infrequently one sees it even where one does not expect it— on the street, for example. The other day, I was walking steadily at my businesslike pace from the other end of the city to the courthouse to render a verdict; it was about half past one. Inadvertently I looked across the street; there was a young mother who was walking along hand in hand with her little son. The little fellow was probably about two and a half years old. The mother's attire, her demeanor, seemed to suggest that she even belonged to the upper class, and thus I was surprised to see that no servant or maid accompanied her. I immediately made numerous guesses—that her carriage very likely was standing in another street or several houses away, or she perhaps was just going a few houses from the place where she lived or was etc. I stop guessing and hope that the reader is grateful to me for carrying out my energetic and radical economies. But basically it was indeed wonderful enough. The boy was a charming child; he asked curiously about everything, stood still, looked, and asked: What's that? I quickly put on my glasses so that I could see properly and properly enjoy the lovable countenance, the tender motherliness with which she entered into everything, the fond joy with which she regarded her little darling. The boy's questioning made an awkward situation for her—perhaps no one has told her what a profound wise man has said, that talking with a child is a *tentamen rigorosum* [rigorous examination];[76] perhaps the circle to which she seemed to belong did not even consider it an art—how terribly awkward, then, to be placed in a dilemma by a tiny tot's questioning, together with his loudness, which invited passersby to listen—and the scene was on Østergade.[77] Embarrassment—I found none; it was easy to read the beautiful motherly joy on her friendly face, and the situation did not mark it as false.

Suddenly the little one stands still and demands to be carried. This clearly was contrary to the arrangement they had made when they left home, a breach of agreement—otherwise a nursemaid would have been along. Here was a vexing dilemma—but not for her. With the most loving look in the world, she picked him up and walked straight ahead without looking for a side street. To me this was as beautiful and solemn as a procession, and I devoutly joined it. Several people turned around. She noticed nothing; altogether unchanged, absorbed in her motherly happiness, she did not walk faster. I have sat as an examining judge on a commission of inquiry, and because of that I have a certain competence in reading faces; but at the risk of dismissal from my office, I affirm that there was not a trace of embarrassment or of any repressed anger or of any growing impatience; that there was no attempt to let her face show any reflection upon what was almost ludicrous in the situation. She walked along Østergade as if she were walking the floor at home, with her little one in her arms.

VI
132

Mother love will offer its life for the child; in this clash it seemed to me equally beautiful. If the little one was in the wrong, if he perhaps was well able to walk, if he was being naughty, no attention would be paid to it at home; and what, then, would have made the difference, what else but that the mother had reflected upon herself. There perhaps are few collisions in which even affectionate parents more easily make a mistake than when the whole matter is a trifle, but this little trifle makes an awkward situation for them. Perhaps a child has bungled his manners a bit; in everyday life we laugh at it and the child does not suspect in the least that it is supposed to be a fault. Then there is someone present, and the vain mother wants to be flattered a bit—and see, the child's greeting is a bit clumsy, and the mother becomes angry—not over a trifle, no, but her reflection upon herself suddenly changes the trifle into something important. Indeed, if that little lad had fallen down, if he had bumped himself, or if he perhaps had come too close to a carriage, if the task had been to save the child at the risk of one's life, I certainly would have seen mother love, but to me this undemonstrative expression of it was just as beautiful.

Mother love is just as beautiful in the routine of everyday life as it is on the most crucial occasion, and it is actually essentially beautiful in the routine of everyday life, for there it is in its element, because there, without receiving any impulse or any increment of force through external catastrophes, it is motivated solely within itself, is nourished by itself, quickens itself through its own original drive, is unpretentious and yet always up and doing its beloved work. Poor man, who must go out in the world to seek a daisy [*Tusindfryd*[78]] such as that and yet does not find it; poor man, who at most has a notion that his neighbor grows it; happy the married man who really knows how to rejoice in his thousandfold joy [*Tusind-Fryd*]. If he finds this flower somewhere else than in his own yard, this flower that—just as that century plant is remarkable for blossoming only once every hundred years—has the even more seldom rarity that it blossoms every day, and does not even close at night—then he has the joy of telling at home what he has seen out in the world.

VI
133

Yesterday I told my wife of a little incident that attracted my attention to such a degree that it made me what ordinarily I am not—an inattentive and distracted listener to a sermon. Perhaps the young mother who provided the occasion for my becoming distracted was wrong in taking a little child along to church; perhaps, but I forgive her, for presumably she did so in order not to entrust it to a nursemaid during the mother's absence. I draw that conclusion from the fact that she really was a mother who goes to church, not a fine lady who pays a

French visit. Do not misunderstand me, as if it were the length of time one spends in church that matters, far from it— indeed, in my opinion a poor hired girl who has all she can do to slip away from home and yet despite all her haste does not manage to arrive there in time for more than hearing the pastor say Amen, in my opinion she is able to bring blessing home from her church attendance, but anyone who otherwise has plenty of time for all sorts of things in life could also find time to go to church properly. Thus our churchgoer came in good time and along with her came little Fidgets; yet I am convinced that the sermon and the whole divine service did not have a more devout listener or a more worthy participant than she. She was ushered into a box pew; the unauthorized member of the congregation was placed on the seat, presumably in the hope that he would sit there like a legitimate member. But this assumption does not seem to have occurred to the little one. The mother bowed her head in prayer, covered her eyes with a handkerchief. Long before she raised her head again, the little one had jumped down and began to crawl around in the box pew. She was praying and went on praying, quite undisturbed. Having ended her prayer, she set him up on the seat again and presumably spoke a few chiding words to him. The service began, but the game had indeed already begun before the service, and the little one seemed to find his own kind of fun in this up again, down again, and up again. Until this time he had sat at his mother's right and had another woman at his right, while the mother sat at the end of the box pew. Now they changed places. After first seeing that the door was shut, the mother then moved over, shared fairly with him so that he had the corner of the box pew at his disposal. He made no noise, but like a child accustomed to look after himself he started to play with his mother's parasol, and only insofar as he wanted to crawl farther along on the seat was the way blocked for him. The mother was and continued to be absorbed in her devotion; only when the pastor paused did she lovingly look down at the little underworldling. Her face aglow with joy in the child, she again turned her gaze to the pastor and listened to the discourse with the devotion of

VI
134

her whole soul. To be able to divide equally this way, to have joy in the child even when he is disturbing, or at least seems to be about to disturb, or is being somewhat of a nuisance, to be free of any foolish demands upon the child—for many parents demand almost more devotion from a little fellow like this than from themselves and thus disturb both themselves and the child by sitting and scolding, rebuking and rearranging—consequently, to be able to divide equally in such a way that she also was concentrated on her devotions with undivided soul—that is indeed a beautiful expression of mother love. Insignificant? Oh, yes, but mother love is essentially beautiful precisely in what is insignificant.

Only a married man, however, has a live feeling for the beautiful performances of mother love; he also has the genuine sympathy that is formed by the earnestness in grasping the infinite significance of the task and the joy in life in wanting to make the discovery, although he does not therefore simply burst into words and jubilation. Or are jealousy and evil passions alone supposed to make a married man clear-sighted and alert, should not faithful love [*Kjærlighed*] be able to do the same—indeed, be able to keep him alert longer? Or did not the wise virgins stay awake longer than the foolish ones?[79] In this respect a married man is—in the good sense of the word— like a deceiver portrayed by Shakespeare:* *ein Gelegenheitshascher, dessen Blick Vortheile prägt und falschmünzt, wenn selbst kein wirklicher Vortheil sich ihm darbietet* [a finder-out of occasions, whose eye can stamp and counterfeit advantages, even when no true advantage presents itself to him].[80] In other words, a married man does it with the quiet joy that shows that he does not pretend to be an expert; neither does he counterfeit, and he is rarely in the situation where he does not find such advantages.

As a bride, woman is more beautiful than as a maiden; as a mother she is more beautiful than as a bride; as a wife and mother she is a good word in season,[81] and with the years she becomes more beautiful. The young girl's beauty is obvious

---

* *Othello*, II, 1, Iago.

to many; it is more abstract, more extensive. This is why they flock about her, the fantasts, [82]the pure and the impure. Then the god [*Guden*] brings the one who is her lover. He really sees her beauty, for one loves the beautiful, and this must be understood as being synonymous with: to love is to see the beautiful. Thus reflection inevitably misses the beautiful. From now on her beauty becomes more intensive and concrete. The housewife does not have a flock of adorers; she is not even beautiful, she is beautiful only in the eyes of her husband. To the same degree this beauty becomes more and more concrete, she becomes less and less subject to evaluation by ordinary appraising and selecting. Is she therefore less beautiful? Is an author less rich in ideas because ordinary observation finds nothing, while the reader who has made him his sole study nevertheless discovers an ever-greater wealth? Is it a perfection in human works of art that they look best at a distance? Is it an imperfection in the meadow flower, as in all the works of God, that under microscopic scrutiny it becomes lovelier and lovelier, more and more exquisite, more and more delicate?

But if the wife and mother is so beautiful in her happiness or, more correctly, if she is a blessing to those to whom she belongs, then in her unhappiness and in her day of distress she is in turn more poetic than the young girl. Let her child die, and then see the grieving mother. There is indeed no one who welcomes the arrival of a baby as joyfully as a mother, but neither is there anyone who is able to grieve in this way when death comes and takes it again. But a grief that is precisely just as ideal as it is actual is the most poetic grief.

Or a husband dies; he leaves nothing, as they say, but a grieving wife—to me it seems that he leaves behind him an infinite wealth. Let the young girl lose her beloved, let her grief be ever so deep, let her dwell in the memory of him— her grief is still abstract, likewise her memory. For this daily requiem for the dead, which is the occupation of the grieving wife, the young girl lacks the dedication and the epic presuppositions.

Truly, I am not eager to leave behind me a great and famous

name. If it must be this way, if in death, which is the last of all, I must take the last step, must seek separation from her whom I love, my wife, my earthly joy, if I nevertheless leave her grieving, then I have left behind me what I shall miss, indeed, the very last thing I would do without, but I have also left behind me what I most reluctantly would do without: a memorial that many times and in many ways will preserve the recollection of me better than the poet's song and the stubborn immortality of a monument, a memorial that will subtract from itself in order to give to me.

Finally, let the wife be tried and tested in the worst of fates: let her be unhappily married. What is the brief suffering of a deceived girl compared with this daily torment, what is the core of her pain compared with the thousand-tongued misery, this wretchedness that no one can bear to look at, this slow torturing that no one can track down—and this may be why we forget how beautiful, in turn how far more poetic, the wife is than the young girl. Great is Desdemona because of her "sublime lie";[83] we admire her, we should admire her. And yet she is greater for her angelic patience, which if it were to be described would fill more books than the largest library contains, even if it fails to fill up the boundless abyss of jealousy and disappears as if it were nothing—indeed, almost stimulates the hunger of passion.

But woman is the weaker sex. In the present context, this remark seems to be rather *mal à propos* [misapplied], for she certainly has not manifested herself as such. Indeed, a silk cord can be just as strong as an iron chain, and the chain that bound the Fenris wolf[84] was indeed invisible, was something that did not exist at all—what if it were the same with woman's weakness, that it is an invisible power that expresses its strength in weakness. If the objections still want permission to use the expression "the weaker sex" about woman, well, let them have it—language usage, too, is certainly on their side. One must, however, always beware of promptly making a rule on the basis of particular observations. Hence I shall not deny that it certainly could happen that a young girl may look odd, and ultimately comic if one is so depraved as to laugh when things get out of control, when she is thrown into the extreme dismay of a decision, into a state of confusion in which a man could hardly stand and keep from being blown away. But who says that she must be hurled into this? The same girl, quietly and solicitously and lovingly treated, would perhaps become a lovable creature as wife and mother. Hence, we should not laugh at such things, for there is something very tragic in seeing the storm demolish the peaceful hedge where it could have been pleasant to live in security. Nor indeed should the woman be strong in such a way that the distress of dismay perhaps issues from the husband himself. If he stands firm, then the woman stands just as firm beside him, and together they stand more firm than either of them alone.

VI
137

Moreover, the trouble with the objection [that woman is the weaker sex] is that those who talk this way about woman view her only esthetically. This is again the perpetually gallant and rude, titillating and insulting talk about her having but one moment in her life or a brief time—namely, the first awakening of adolescence. But anyone who really wants to talk about her strength or weakness must, of course, see her when she stands fully armed, and that is as a wife and mother. Moreover, then she need never struggle or undergo tests of strength, and if one finally wants to talk about strength, then the first condition or the essential form of all strength is endurance [*Udholdenhed*]. When it comes to this, the man perhaps cannot equal [*holde ud med*] her. Then, too, what energy does every simulated movement require? But what else is devotedness than a secret manifestation of strength, a manifestation of strength that expresses itself by its opposite, just as, for example, good taste and concern for one's appearance can express itself by effecting a kind of carelessness, although not the carelessness that every Tom, Dick, and Harry understands, just as, for example, the mature intellectual work completed with great effort has a simplicity that is not, however, the simplicity that, in his simplemindedness, every normal-school graduate admires.

If I picture two actors, one playing the role of Don Giovanni, the other the role of the Commendatore, in the scene where the Commendatore is holding Don Giovanni by the hand while the latter desperately tries to wrench himself free,[85] I ask myself which one is using the greater force. Don Giovanni is the one who suffers; the Commendatore stands calmly with his right hand extended. Yet I am betting on Don Giovanni. If the actor playing Don Giovanni were to use only half his strength, he would make the Commendatore totter; on the other hand, if he does not writhe, does not shake, he spoils the effect. So what does he do? He uses half his strength to express the pain, the other half to support the Commendatore, and while he appears to be trying with all his might to wrench himself away from the Commendatore, he is holding on to him so that he will not totter.

So it is, so it is in actuality with a wife, for this was just idle conjecturing. She loves her husband so much that she always wants him to be dominant, and this is why he appears to be so strong and she so weak, for she uses her strength to support him, uses it as devotedness and submission. What wonderful weakness! Even though the gallery believes that the Commendatore has greater powers, even though the profane praise masculine strength and misuse it to humble the woman, the married man has another interpretation, and the deceived is wiser than the one not deceived, the one deceiving is more justified than the one not deceiving.

Moreover, there are different ways of measuring strength. When Holger Danske squeezes sweat out of an iron glove,[86] that is strength, but if he were handed a butterfly, I am afraid that he would not have sufficient strength to take it properly. To mention the sublime example, God's omnipotence appears great in having created everything, but does it not appear equally great in the omnipotent moderation that can permit a blade of grass to grow its season. Woman is assigned the less significant tasks, which for that very reason require strength. She chooses her task, chooses it gladly, and also has the joy of continually equipping man with the conspicuous strength. I for my part believe that my wife can do wonders; and I more readily understand the greatest feat I read about than the dainty embroidery with which she clothes my earthly life.

If, however, one has it fixed in one's head that woman is the weaker sex, which chicaners ordinarily interpret more explicitly to mean that she has her first moment in adolescence, when she exhausts, indeed, surpasses all eulogy, and with that it is over, that her strength was an illusion, and that the only real strength she has left is the strength of the scream—well, of course, one can then make all sorts of oddities out of it. Jean Paul says somewhere: *solchen Secanten, Cosecanten, Tangenten, Cotangenten kommt Alles excentrisch vor, besonders das Centrum* [to such secants, cosecants, tangents, cotangents, everything seems eccentric, particularly the center].[87] Precisely because marriage is the center, woman must be seen in relation to it, and the same goes for man, and all this talk about and viewing of each sex separately is confused and profane, for what God has joined together,[88] what life has destined for each other, thought must also think together. If a male hits upon the idea of separating the two, he presumably thinks he has the advantage of making the woman the victim, whereas he himself becomes just as ludicrous, a male who in a superior manner wishes to be disengaged from a relation to which he certainly is, after all, just as bound by life as is woman.

VI
139

If this happens, then the bachelor (for however experienced in what one likes to call the erotic, even if one were a scoundrel or what probably is more common, a braggart—the unmarried man in ordinary language is called a bachelor) reserves the ethical categories for himself. At best this can be regarded as a caprice, for to use ethical categories to insult or at least to want to insult woman is not exactly the mark of an ethical individuality. Such a hodgepodge of paganism, which Platonically makes woman an imperfect version,[89] and of Christianity, which imposes the ethical upon her, I have never seen carried through. It must indeed be a very confused brain in which an idea such as that could become so self-important that it wished itself to be given a more detailed expression.

On the other hand, the objection to woman can have a touch of deep irony that when propounded with a certain good-naturedness, indeed, with sympathy for her presumably unhappy fate of being sheer illusion, is not without a tragic and comic effect. It maintains, then, that she is the weaker sex; the tragedy is due to its being hidden from her in illusion, and hidden from her externally in man's gallantry. It is as if all existence were playing blindman's buff with her. Here irony has really acquired a task. Too bad the whole thing is a fiction. Nowadays woman is continually characterized in the highest terms, in the most flattering phrases, up to, indeed, far beyond the boundaries of the fantastic. Everything that is great in life is ascribed to her; on this point poetry and gallantry agree. And irony is naturally most gallant of all, for gallantry is indeed irony's mother tongue, and it is never so gallant as when it regards the whole thing as a false alarm. Woman's existence in the world becomes a parade of fools and irony is gallantry's master of ceremonies; the procession itself is reminiscent of [90]Hoffmann's insane school teacher, who, holding

a ruler like a scepter as he graciously bows to all sides, declares that his general has just returned from a victory over the Lombards; whereupon he takes some cloves out of his vest pocket, hands them to someone present with these words: Do not disdain this small token of my grace.[91] Irony prostrates itself and worships most obsequiously.

The good aspect of this objection is that it carries the stamp of fiction to such an extent that it cannot insult even the weakest. On the contrary, it is entertaining, amusing, and one can without hesitation indulge in it, unless one became somewhat dubious by seeing it advanced in dead earnest. If the objection attempts to explain some aspect of life, then one can one-two-three reduce it to its most lofty expression—that marriage or any positive relation to woman is a hindrance. In unhappy love she has her supreme reality [*Realitet*], and here her meaning is so doubtful that she signifies nothing positive but is negatively the occasion for the arousal of the unhappy lover's ideality. Thus the objection is reduced to its briefest expression and thereby also *in absurdum* [to absurdity], just as the objection itself is making a show of wanting to have all life take the same path. Indeed, to condense the whole content of existence in this manner is a devil's haste, the speed of a Caesar—not in capturing but in losing. Lichtenberg declares somewhere that there are critics who with a single stroke of the pen have crossed every boundary of sound reasoning;[92] similarly, an impatient thinker of this sort seems not to find time even to begin the conclusion of his conditional clause. This kind of thinker seems to want to carry out Augustine's teaching that by means of celibacy *multo citius civitas dei compleretur, et acceleraretur terminus seculi* [God's Kingdom will be filled much faster, and the end of the world will be hastened],[93] although as a jest, for we cannot expect an objection of this kind to have a religious background such as Augustine has. But as a secular observation on life it truly is, as is usually said of women's letters, "in haste," and lacks what we generally say women's are usually said to consist of essentially—postscripts. Along with Hamann one can appropriately shout at this speedy fellow, who naturally considers a married man a procrastinator—"Bah"—if there is even time for that and the fellow is not already so far away that "scarcely his coattails remain behind in existence."[94]

VI
141

I return to the subject of falling in love. It remains intact, no thought reaches it, it is a wonder. The resolution of marriage is so far from wanting to invalidate it that, on the contrary, it presupposes it. But falling in love is no marriage, and a resolution alone is no marriage, either. Now someone may think that it is because of the miserableness of life and of existence that falling in love is unable to carry through by itself and therefore it has to accept the convoy of marriage. Far from it. No, falling in love penetrates all existence and does this in marriage. The situation is just the reverse. It is an insult to love to be unwilling to have marriage intervene, as if love were something so spontaneous and immediate that it cannot be harnessed with a resolution. On the contrary, it is no insult to a genius to say of him that his power of resolution is just as highborn as his inborn immediacy, that as guarantor he takes charge of his genius. It is insulting to him to say that he lacks resolution or that his resolution is not in proportion to his genius. This does not mean that the resolution would gradually take over as the genius subsides, so that finally he is attired in the resolution and has become another person than when at-

tired in his genius. The beautiful meaning, however, is that
the resolution is contemporary with the genius, and in its own
way is just as great; thus the person who received the gracious
gift of immediacy lets himself be married to it in the resolution—and this is indeed the beautiful meaning of marriage.

It is even easier to show this in marriage than in genius,
because by this time love is already a subsequent immediacy,
a heat lightning that commences at a time when the will may
be sufficiently developed to comprehend a resolution just as
crucial as falling in love, taken in its immediacy, is crucial.
Understood in this way, marriage is the deepest, highest, and
most beautiful expression of love. Love is the gift of the god,
but in the resolution of marriage the lovers make themselves
worthy of receiving it. Be life ever so paradisiacal, to leave out
the resolution is unbeautiful, and just as unbeautiful in the direction of spirit as it is unbeautiful in the opposite direction,
that adolescents marry.

Later, I shall go into this subject further, but here it might
be best to look around a little, to pause a moment at falling in
love in its critical aspect. Of course, what is established here
on the basis of experience will not and cannot serve to diminish marriage but serves merely to illustrate. Falling in love has
always been much sought after, and some people grow no
more weary of seeking (*sit venia verbo* [pardon the expression])
and desiring the wonder of falling in love than "the nanny
goat wearies of cropping green buds." But precisely here is
the difficulty; here it is that the enemy sows evil seed[95] while
the lovers are not thinking about it. Even the seducer lets falling in love stand as something he cannot give himself (so it is
only very young apprentices or Münchhausens[96] who carry
on about making conquests), but the demonic in him makes
him decide with demonic resolution to make the enjoyment
as brief and thus, so he thinks, as intense as possible. By means
of this demonic resolution, the seducer, in relation to evil, is
actually great; without this resolution, he is really no seducer.
Nevertheless, he can do plenty of damage and his life can become quite warped, even though it is more innocent than an
actual seducer's life, and it acquires a more innocent appear-

VI
142

ance because the forgetfulness of time intervenes. Such a person is aware of falling in love; he is not evil enough to make a demonic resolution, but neither is he good enough to make the good resolution; he is, to express myself concretely, not good enough to become a husband in the noble sense in which I take this word for what it is, in the noble sense in which a man is a husband only when he is worthy of the gift of the god.

If I were to give an example of deviation in falling in love, I would mention Goethe—that is, Goethe as he portrayed himself in *Aus meinem Leben*.[97] His personal life is extraneous; I refrain from any judgment. I do not credit myself with sufficient esthetic refinement to evaluate his poetic works, but there are certain things I can understand as well as a child; and there is one thing marriage does not understand, even if, to repeat, it is tempered in jest. It does not understand jest, and in addition to the seducer's, there is still another counterpart to the good resolution—namely, subterfuges.

In *Aus meinem Leben*, an existence is portrayed that is not a seducer's; it is too chivalrous for that, even though in the direction of spirit (ethically understood) this chivalry is inferior to a seducer's, for it lacks decisive resolution; but a demonic resolution is, of course, also ethical—that is, ethically bad. But an existence such as this more readily finds forgiveness in the world, indeed, all too readily, for the existing person is actually in love. But then, yes, then the ardor cooled; he had made a mistake; he goes away "in a courteous manner."[98] A half year later he even knows how to give reasons, good reasons, why the break and the distancing were sensible and almost praiseworthy: After all, it didn't amount to much, just a little village belle; there was too much passion, passion doesn't last in the long run, etc. etc., for this chatter can be as prolonged as one wishes. By means of a half year and with the aid of a theory of perspective, the fact of falling in love has become a happening (this is both an impiety against erotic love and a fraud against the ethical, and a satire upon oneself) from which it is now a bit of luck to have escaped. Everything becomes confused to me the moment I consider that such an

VI
143

existence is supposed to be a poetic life. I feel as if I were sitting on a conciliation board, far from the boldness of immediacy and far from the high-mindedness of resolution, far from the heaven of falling in love and far from the judgment day of resolution; I feel as if I were sitting on a conciliation commission[99] surrounded by fatuous folk listening to a talented attorney defend blunders with a certain poetic ingenuity. If the attorney himself were the hero of those burlesque love affairs, one might very well, from the ethical point of view, lose patience. The cast of actresses is absolutely without blame for their being burlesque love affairs (all honor to Goethe's portrayal, be it *Dichtung* [poetry] or *Wahrheit* [truth]), for as far as I recall there is no reason to assume that any one of them left tragedy for vaudeville. In other words, if a little village belle has been so unfortunate as to misunderstand His Excellency, if she remains true to herself, I know from what I learned as a child—and still know nothing better—that she advances: from the idyll to tragedy. But if His Excellency has been so unfortunate as to misunderstand himself and furthermore is additionally unfortunate in the way in which he wants to make amends for it, I know from what I learned as a child—and still know nothing better—that he has left tragedy and drama and is established in vaudeville.

Time has a strange power. If that poetic character in *Aus meinem Leben* had acknowledged that it was nevertheless bound to end rather soon or if, having had no inkling of it beforehand and having no other way of making amends, he nevertheless had been ethical enough to regard himself as a scoundrel, then he would have been declared a seducer, and the warning bell would have been sounded every time he approached a village. But now, now he is a knight—well, not exactly a knight, but then we are not living in the age of chivalry, either—but still something of a knight, a person of status who perfectly fits the saying *aut Caesar, aut nihil* [either Caesar, or nothing].[100]

Some time goes by; he himself sorrows over the broken relationship, which, however, as circumspectly as possible is kept from taking on any of the more serious aspects of a break. He sorrows a little over the poor girl, it is not pretense, he really sorrows—no, really! This, however, is carrying politeness rather far; it is, after all, a sympathy and condolence that will only increase the pain. The break itself or, to put it more precisely and accurately, this polite and amicable agreement about a departure is precisely what is most insulting; this final forgery, that any girl, when it is established that a man has a contractual obligation, should not be a peremptory creditor, this forgery, that a bankrupt will not report his total deficit, is really the most shocking thing of all, and yet it is with this politeness that he bought the world's forgiveness. Oh, the sorrowing lover! He is sorrowing not over his instability, over this flare-up of ardor, over this shift in the world of the spirit, not over his sins. That poetic character would probably call such a sorrow depression, for he expressly laments that the age and he as a part of it have become depressed by reading English authors—Young,[101] for example. Well, why not? If one is so constituted, one can become depressed by listening to a sermon, if it really has substance, as Young has, but Young is far from depressing.

This kind of existence, which essentially is scarcely a paradigm, can nevertheless figuratively assume a paradigmatic character or be paradigmatic by the accident of being an irregular declension, according to which several lives are indeed formed. One dare not say that they form their lives according to it, for they are too innocent [*uskyldig*] for that, and this is precisely their excuse [*Undskyldning*]: it happens to them; they themselves do not know how it happens. Indeed, at times such people are even visionaries who are pursuing the ideal. They do not learn any more from their love affairs than what a lottery player learns from losing. This last observation does not apply, of course, to that poet in *Aus meinem Leben*. He is too great not to learn, too superior not to harvest advantage, and if he had been just as ethically inspired as he is gloriously endowed, he, more than anyone else, would have discovered and solved the problem: whether there is an intellectual existence so eminent that in the profoundest sense it cannot become commensurable with the erotic, for the response that one loves many times, that one parcels out one's superiority, is merely a disorientation that neither esthetically nor ethically satisfies what could be termed a decent man's more serious demand upon life. That poet seems to have learned a great deal; indeed, just as the latest philosophy has made it a term of abuse to speak of Kant's honest way, in the same way Goethe smiles in a superior manner at Klopstock because he was so concerned whether Meta, his first love who had married again, would belong to him in another life.[102]

So what has happened in such an existence? One does not stop with falling in love, but neither does resolution enter in. The reflection out of which the resolution comes into existence in order to grasp the falling in love blunders; it becomes a reflection over falling in love. The reason I have dwelt on this is to point out what will be shown again later[103]—that the reflection behind resolution just lets falling in love stand and pays attention to totally different matters. Hence that existing poet in *Aus meinem Leben*[104] arrives at no resolution; he is not a seducer, he does not become a married man, he becomes—a connoisseur.

To what extent every poet-existence should itself be a poem, also under what angle of refraction his life in this respect should stand to his poetry, I do not venture to decide. However, this much is certain: an existence such as the one in *Aus meinem Leben* is bound to have an influence on the poetic production. If this is Goethe's own life, then this seems to explain that what one misses most of all in Goethe is pathos. The pathos of immediacy he does not have; for that he is too intellectual, but neither has he made his way through to win the highest pathos. Every time that existing poet faces the crisis, he backs out. This he does in every possible direction. He relates that he has had a strict religious upbringing.[105] This is an impression of childhood and certainly not part of the nonsense one sheds over the years, since with respect to religion it is really true that one learns the best things as a child and acquires a presupposition that can never, never be replaced. A period comes later in his life when the impression of this piety almost overwhelms him. This is the crisis and is entirely in order; the more intelligent an individuality, the more difficult his assigned task to preserve and regain childhood's pious faith. Now what does that poet do, he who otherwise, as he himself relates, has done all sorts of exercises to train himself not to be afraid in the dark, not to be upset by seeing a corpse or by being alone at night in a graveyard[106]—he backs out, separates it and himself, avoids contact.[107] Good Lord, if a person was indeed a bit afraid of walking alone in the dark it would not be so dreadful, but to retreat when it is a matter of being true to oneself in one's impression of childhood, where it is a matter, with the renunciation of every claim upon life or for a meaningful existence even to the point of despair, of fighting for the precious recollection of one's parents (for even if that poet repeatedly recalls his mother, can he believe that in her or in his father's eyes it was accidental that they allowed the religious to have such a great influence on the child?), of fighting for the fellowship of faith with the dead, for what they had regarded as the one thing needful, what he himself once upon a time in childlike innocence wholeheartedly accepted—at this point to leap away—should this not be avenged by the absence of pathos in the poetry? If that poet is Goethe himself, might this not then explain that the idolized hero, whose most accidental utterances and statements are collected, published, read, worshiped as holy relics, this idolized hero who is called king in the realm of thought, that he, to put it mildly, is titular king of the eternal kingdom of religion? In Goethe's sound wisdom there is supposed to be a cure for mental aberration and above all for depression, which he himself knew how to avoid.[108] How strange. Everyone knows from what he learned at his mother's knee that diversion is most dangerous for the person who has a disposition toward depression—indeed, it is even dangerous for the person who is not so disposed. How strange—that he who has grown a little older and a little more mature (provided he then believes that the wiser person is supposed to be different from the simple soul in that he understands what the latter understands and understands it better, and understands somewhat more and does not think that the wise man is supposed to be

distinguished because the only thing he does not grasp is what
the simple soul understands) knows that to back away from a
task is to indenture himself and his soul to depression sooner
or later; but Goethe knew how to avoid this another way.
This, however, is only in order to illuminate the erotic.

The experts will perhaps also agree with me that Goethe's
women are his best-drawn characters. But on closer scrutiny
the best of them are not perceived in true feminine ideality but
in the light in which an equivocator sees them, one who is
especially adept at discovering what is lovely, at kindling a
blaze, but also knows how to look at this conflagration with
an exclusive superiority. They are lovely, very much so, superbly portrayed, and yet it is not so much they who are dishonored as it is womanhood that is dishonored in their persons, because in relation to them the condescending
sensibleness that knows how to enjoy, to relish, but also how
to distance them and itself when the pleasure is over, almost
seems to be justified or at least excusable.

In *Aus meinem Leben*, that poet is a master in this distance
theory. He himself has been so good as to explain the procedure.[109] Yet it must be remembered that the poet does not
wish to be instructive—far from it; he is well aware that this
is not something given to everyone. It is a natural characteristic; he is a privileged individuality. Admittedly, that poet is
a hero, and I who am so rash as to talk about him am a bourgeois-philistine, but fortunately there are certain things that
every child can understand and about which it makes no difference whether one is a hero, a judge, or a pauper. Hence,
every time a human relationship is about to overwhelm him,
he must distance it from himself by poetizing it. How different temperaments are, or are they perhaps not so different!
What does it mean to poetize a human relationship? Whether
or not one obtains a poetic masterpiece out of it is beside the
point—alas, in this respect there is a glaring difference between a hero and a poor judge, and also an inmate of the
workhouse. To poetize an actual human relationship by
means of distancing (which, please note, one must defend as
guarantor) is neither more nor less than to falsify the ethical in

it and to give it a false stamp as an event and an intellectual pursuit. Indeed, if one has a lightning conductor such as that in one's pocket, no wonder that one is safe in the storm! How many bunglers and dabblers have servilely and obsequiously admired this natural characteristic? And yet every person has this natural characteristic more or less; to put it very simply, it is the natural and covetous person's warding off of the ethical. This talent to poetize, that is, to distance the actual life relationship in poetic contours, is often found among criminals; it is frequently found among the depressed also, but with the difference that the esthetically depressed thereby gain a mitigation, but the ethically depressed an aggravation. Possibly the cheerful Goethe was a little depressed, just as the wise Goethe had a fair share of superstition. Thus the natural tendency to poeticize an actual human relationship is both rather common and dubious. Of course, not everyone who "poetizes" therefore writes masterpieces—who would be so foolish as to say anything like that? But with regard to the ethical, that distinction whereby one person is a hero, yes, perhaps even as unique as a hero, another a bungler, is totally irrelevant. The ethical is so incorruptible that if our Lord himself had been obliged to allow himself a little irregularity in creating the world, ethics would not let itself be disturbed, although heaven and earth and everything found therein is nevertheless a quite fine masterpiece.

Now, if that poet-existence in *Aus meinem Leben* is poetic, then goodbye to marriage, which then at most becomes a refuge for the declining years. If that existence is poetic, then what does one do for woman? Then she, too, must take care to become poetic. It is bad enough for a man who is tried and experienced in the erotic—indeed, is a burned-out case—brazenly to take a young girl for a wife in order to be rejuvenated a little and to have the best nursing care now that he is beginning to become old; but it is revolting for an elderly woman, an experienced spinster, to marry a young man in order to assure herself of a safe shelter and a sophisticated stimulation now that the poetic is beginning to vanish.

Marriage likes deserters just as little as it allows one to serve

two masters.[110] Solomon puts it beautifully when he says that
he who finds a wife finds a good thing and obtains a good gift
from God[111]—or, to modernize the saying a bit, to him who
falls in love, the god has been gracious. If he marries the beloved, he does a good deed and does well to finish what he has
begun.[112]

What has just been said will not, of course, in any miserable
way recommend the resolution of marriage. The resolution of
marriage is its own best recommendation, since, as stated, it
is the only adequate form of being in love.

Consequently, the point now is to see how the resolution
can intervene, how the reflection that is presupposed in the
resolution can reach a point where it coincides with the immediacy of falling in love. As soon as falling in love is eliminated, it becomes ludicrous to want to reflect upon whether
one ought to marry or not. This is quite true, but this does
not justify the elimination of being in love, which is done
every time one tries to keep the resolution separate from falling in love and then makes reflecting upon it ludicrous.

That such reflection upon whether to marry is silly when
there is no love has already been correctly perceived and profoundly propounded by a few wise men of antiquity, but not,
as we will see, in order to put weapons into the hands of the
mockers. It is told that Socrates is supposed to have answered
someone who asked him about marriage: Marry or do not
marry—you will regret both.[113] Socrates was an ironist who
presumably concealed his wisdom and truth ironically lest it
become local gossip, but he was not a mocker. The irony is
superb. The questioner's stupidity lies precisely in asking a
third person for something one can never learn from a third
person. But not all are as wise as Socrates, and they often become quite earnestly involved with the one who poses a stupid question. If the falling in love is lacking, then reflection
cannot be exhausted at all, and if one is in love, one does not
ask such a question. If a mocker wants to use the Socratic saying, then he acts as if it were a discourse and makes it into
something other than what it is: namely, a deeply ironic, infinitely wise answer to a foolish question. By changing the
answer to a question into a discourse, one can produce a cer-

tain crazy comic effect, but one loses the Socratic wisdom and does violence to the trustworthy testimony that expressly introduces the story thus: Someone asked him (Socrates) whether one should marry or not. To which he answered: Whether **you** do the one or the other, you will regret it. If Socrates had not been so ironic, he presumably would have expressed it this way: As far as **you** are concerned, you can do as you wish—you are and remain a dunce. For not everyone who regrets demonstrates thereby that now, in the moment of regret, he is a stronger and better individuality than in the moment of the thoughtless action; sometimes regret can demonstrate most of all that the regretter is a fusspot. —There is a story about Thales that when his mother was urging him to marry he first answered that he was too young, that the time had not yet come, and when she later repeated the request, he replied that the time was now past.[114] There is an irony also in this answer that chastises the worldly common sense that would make marriage an undertaking like buying a house. In other words, there is only one age at which it is timely to marry, and that is when one is in love; at any other age one is either too young or too old.

Such things are always pleasant to consider, for if frivolousness in the realm of the erotic is disastrous, then a certain kind of commonsensicality is even more disastrous. But this one saying of Socrates, properly understood, is able to cut down, like death with his scythe, the whole luxuriant growth of commonsensical chatter that wants to talk itself into a marriage.

Here, then, I pause at the crucial point: a resolution must be added to falling in love. But a resolution presupposes reflection, but reflection is immediacy's angel of death.[115] So the matter stands, and if it was right that reflection should attack falling in love, then there will never be a marriage. But that is precisely what it should not do—indeed, what is more, even prior to and simultaneously with this process, which through reflection comes to the resolution, there is the negative resolution that fends off any reflection of this nature as a spiritual temptation. While reflection's destroying angel of death ordinarily goes about calling for death to the immediate, there is still one immediacy it allows to stand—the immediacy of falling in love, which is a wonder. If reflection attacks falling in love, this means that one is supposed to inspect whether the beloved meets the ideal abstract conception of an ideal. Any reflection of this sort, even the scantiest, is an offense just as it is also a stupidity. Even if the lover had, on the face of it, the purest enthusiasm in wanting to discover the loveliness, suppose that he had a voice "so sweet, oh, so sweet," suppose that he had a lightness of desire, suppose that he had a poet's eloquence in reflecting so keenly that even the most delicate feminine soul would hear only the sweet melody and sense only the sweet fragrance of the offering and would not discover the offense—it is still an attempt to deplete erotic love. But just as the god of love is blind and love is itself a wonder, something that both the lover and the most preposterous reflection acknowledge or must acknowledge, just so the lover should preserve himself in this clairvoyance.

VI
151

There is a modesty to which even the most adoring admiration is an affront; it is a kind of unfaithfulness to the beloved. Even if this admiration, as the lover believes, binds him even more inseparably to her, it nevertheless has already, so to speak, separated him; it is a kind of unfaithfulness, because there is a criticism dormant in this admiration. Moreover, beauty is transitory and loveliness can vanish. Thus it is an affront to the beloved to want to have all her lovableness consist in the synthesis that is the basis of the modesty in falling in love. On the other hand there is feminine lovableness, which again is essentially that of the wife and mother, that does not require this bashfulness, whereas, even if she had the face of an angel, wanting to admire this beauty is an offense that already suggests that the equality in falling in love is no longer in balance.

But, I hear the lover say: precisely in this admiration I feel the sublimity of the beloved, and thus there is basically no reciprocity, none at all, in my being loved in return. Oh, even the person who calculates in infinite quantities nevertheless calculates! Hence, whether the beloved is the fairest among women[116] or she is not so favored, the only appropriate, brief, pithy, adequate phrase for the whole content of falling in love is: I love her. Truly, someone who at the beginning had nothing else to say and later just as taciturnly kept his soul terse in true expressions of love is more faithful to her than someone who could invite the races of men and of gods to a banquet of descriptions of the beloved's loveliness and do it so consummately that they all, all, would go away overwhelmed and envious.

But what dares to be scrutinized, dares to be admired, is the lovable substance of her nature. Here to admire is not an affront, although admiration will learn from love not to become an insipid babbler of words or a birthday poet but an incorruptible little humming of quiet joy. This substance of the soul gains its only real opportunity to disclose itself in marriage, which has at its disposal the cornucopia of tasks, the best gift one receives on the wedding day. Even if the beloved, just to delight the one for whom she would sacrifice her life, since there is no opportunity for a greater proof, demonstrates it equally well in lesser ways, even if she adorned herself only to please him and now, she, the beautiful one, in her lovely apparel was so lovely that the old men followed her sadly with their eyes as they followed Helen walking through the hall[117]—if with one single nerve in his eyes the lover looked at her in the wrong way and admired instead of comprehending the proper expression of being in love, that it was to please him—then he has taken a wrong turn, he is on the way to becoming a connoisseur.

VI
152

Thus if one imagines a time of love, especially a time such as the engagement, consequently outside of marriage, one may often make a mistake, precisely because erotic love lacks the essential tasks and therefore at times can make both parties faultfinding. What Bedreddin says about Gulnare's gaze,

> Gently as when the grave opens and sends
> The redeemed soul to paradise,
> She opens her lovely eyelids
> And heavenward turns her gaze,[118]

could be understood of the whole disclosing of the lovable content of the soul with respect to the immediacy of falling in love. This immediacy is the obscure element, but just as gently as when the grave opens, the transfigured one extricates herself from the concealment of love into a beauty of soul, and in this transfiguration she belongs to the husband.

Since reflection does not dare to set foot in the holy place of love and on the consecrated ground of immediacy, what direction shall it then take until it arrives at the resolution? Reflection turns toward the relation between falling in love and actuality. For the lover, the most certain of all things is that he is in love, and no meddlesome thoughts, no stockbrokers run back and forth between falling in love and a so-called ideal—this is a forbidden road. Nor does reflection inquire whether he should marry; he does not forget Socrates. But to marry is to enter an actuality in relation to a given actuality; to marry involves an extraordinary concretion. This concretion is the task of reflection. But is it perhaps so concrete (defined in terms of time, place, surroundings, the stroke of the clock, seventeen relationships, etc.) that no reflection can penetrate it? If this is assumed, one has thereby also assumed that, on the whole, no resolution is possible. A resolution is still always an ideality; I have the resolution before I begin to act in virtue of this resolution. But how, then, have I come to the resolution? A resolution is always reflective; if this is disregarded, then language is confused and resolution is identified with an immediate impulse, and any statement about resolution is no more an advancement than a journey in which one drives all night but takes the wrong road and in the morning arrives back at the same place from which one departed. In a perfectly ideal reflection the resolution has ideally emptied actuality, and the conclusion of this ideal reflection, which is something more than the *summa summarum* [sum total] and *enfin* [finally], is precisely the resolution: the resolution[119] is the ideality brought about through a perfectly ideal reflection, which is the action's acquired working capital.

"But," someone says, "that is all very fine, but it will take a long time, and meanwhile the grass is growing—a husband of that sort certainly does not become an apprentice [*Pebersvend*] but the oldest journeyman in the shop [*Oldgesel*]." By no means. Moreover, the same charge can be made against any

VI
153

resolution, and yet resolution is the true beginning of freedom, but it is required of a beginning that it be timely, that it
have a proper relation to that which is to be carried out, that
it not come to be like an introduction that anticipates the
whole book or a petition that cuts short the entire parliamen-
tary debate. But delight actuates any work, and the delight of
one in love, which during all this is the same, quickens him
early and late, keeps him awake and unremitting in his chivalrous wanderings, for truly this expedition of the lover to
find the resolution is more chivalrous than a crusade against
the Turks, than a pilgrimage, more winsome to the eyes of
erotic love than any feat whatsoever, for it is concentric with
erotic love itself.

So, led by the hand of his guardian spirit, the happy young
man [*Ungersvend*] (that a young man in love is happy goes
without saying) goes his way and surveys that ideal image of
actuality that appears to him, while the beloved sits waiting,
safe and happy; for every time he has returned to her (in order
once again, after having rested in his wanderings, once again
to continue until he finds the jewel, the wedding gift, the resolution, the most beautiful and the only worthy gift), she has
never seen a change in him, as little as his amorousness has
changed, not even to becoming an admiring amorousness.

And the young man does not have many moments to give
away. He knows that any moment he gives away is a bliss he
is giving away—this is bound to be a perfect means to teach
speed. But the good gift of resolution is also the highest gain,
the wedding garment without which he is an unworthy—this
is bound to be a good means to prevent his becoming so rash
that in his haste he would rush away from the resolution.

Precisely because this is how it is with the resolution or the
one making the resolution, the reflection becomes ideal, and
one quickly takes a wonderful shortcut. And why should one
not go by a shortcut when it is certain that it takes one faster
to the goal, faster than any other, but also unerringly, more
unerringly than any other? It has been correctly observed that
reflection cannot be exhausted, that it is infinite. Quite right—
it can be exhausted in reflection no more than someone, be he

ever so hungry, can eat his own stomach, and thus one dares to look upon anyone who says he has done this, be he a systematic hero or a newsboy, as a Münchhausen. On the other hand, reflection is discharged into faith, which is precisely the anticipation of the ideal infinity as resolution. Thus through the purely ideally exhausted reflection the resolution has gained a new immediacy that corresponds exactly to the immediacy of falling in love. The resolution is a religious view of life constructed upon ethical presuppositions, a view of life that is supposed to pave the way, so to speak, for falling in love and to secure it against any external and internal danger. See, in infatuation the lovers are, as it were, carried away paradisiacally out of actuality to some place like remote Asia, on the shores of a quiet lake, or in a primeval forest where silence reigns and where there is no trace of human beings, but the resolution knows how to find the road to the society of human beings and to pave the safe way, whereas falling in love does not look for such things but is happy as a child who lets his parents take care of all inconveniences. The resolution is not the man's power, the man's courage, and the man's ingenuity (these are only immediate categories that do not correspond uniformly to the immediacy of falling in love, since they belong to the same sphere and are not a new immediacy), but it is a religious point of departure. If it is not this, the person making the resolution has only been finitized in his reflection; he has not taken the shortcut with the speed of falling in love but has remained en route, and such a resolution is too shabby for love not to disregard it and rely upon itself rather than to entrust itself to the guidance of such a smatterer.

The immediacy of falling in love recognizes but one immediacy that is *ebenbürtig* [of equal standing], and that is a religious immediacy; falling in love is too virginal to recognize any confidant other than God. But the religious is a *new* immediacy,[120] has reflection in between—otherwise paganism would actually be religious and Christianity not. That the religious is a new immediacy every person easily understands who is satisfied with following the honest path of ordinary common sense. And although I imagine I have but few readers, I confess nevertheless that I do imagine my readers to be among these, since I am far from wanting to instruct the admired ones who make systematic discoveries *à la* Niels Klim,[121] who have left their good skin [*Skind*] in order to put on the "real appearance [*virkelige Skin*]."[122]

To penetrate reflection successfully in this way until one gains the resolution is not so difficult, especially if one has the impetus of the passion of falling in love, and without passion one never arrives at any resolution but, most likely, in chats along the way with every Tom, Dick, and Harry, with thinkers and trinket salesmen, learns a lot about the world and gets much to talk about, just like the man who inadvertently, by remaining on board ship too long, traveled around the world; or, to express myself less facetiously: the person who does not have passion never sees the promised land but perishes in the desert.

What the resolution wants now is first of all to hold fast to love. In this new immediacy, which reaches far beyond any reflection, the lover is rescued from becoming a connoisseur; he himself is bowed down under the imperative of duty and raised again in the optative of the resolution. With respect to falling in love, he is directed toward essential matters and repudiates the reflection game of criticizing.

The resolution wants next to triumph over all danger and spiritual trials. Precisely because the reflection that precedes the resolution is altogether ideal, a single imagined danger will be enough to bring the one making the resolution to resolve religiously. Let him think what he will, even if the danger is only that he cannot take the future in advance by thinking. In using his powers of thought and his concerned love to think this, he *eo ipso* [precisely thereby] thinks it [the danger] to be so terrible that he cannot surmount it by himself. He has run aground; he must either let go of love—or believe in God. In this way the wonder of falling in love is taken up into the wonder of faith; the wonder of falling in love is taken up into a purely religious wonder; the absurdity of falling in love is taken up into a divine understanding with the absurdity of religiousness. Cheer up! A simple, decent person who respects

VI
156

ordinary common sense can well understand that the absurd exists and that it cannot be understood; fortunately this is hidden from systematic thinkers.

Finally, in the resolution he will, through the universal, place himself in relationship with God. He does not dare cling to himself as a singular individual if he is going to venture out with his love. His comfort is precisely that he is just like other human beings and in this common humanity is in relationship with God by faith and by the resolution. This is the resolution's bath of purification, which is just as beautiful as the Greek's bath before a banquet[123] or as the bath Aladdin wished to have before the wedding.[124] Everything that comes under the name of earthly vanity, selfishness, disagreeable manly intrepidity, the itch to be critical, etc., is consumed, and in the resolution the husband is worthy of the divine gift of falling in love.

If in his quest for the resolution the lover encounters anomalies, finds that he has become singular, not in the sense that this singularity promptly comes off in the washing of resolution, but singular in such a way that he does not dare to trust that he is a universal human being, in other words, if he encounters repentance, then it may last a long time, and if he is really in love, as is indeed assumed, then he can regard himself as someone selected to be examined by life, for when he is questioned by love up one side and by repentance down the other side about the same thing, his examination can become much too rigorous.

But I shall not pursue this here; difficulties of that sort have no place in a general consideration. The person making the resolution does not encounter such anomalies; he returns home from his expedition as the knight from the crusade, and so:

> If he comes home with a feather in his hat
> Hip, hip, hurrah! We'll dance and drink to that![125]

Thus that happy young man (that a young man in love is happy goes without saying) has found what he was looking for. Like the man in the Gospel story, he has purchased the field in which the pearl lay,[126] but he is different from that man inasmuch as he in a way owned the field before he sold everything in order to buy it, for in the field of love he also found the pearl of resolution. He returns home from his holy pilgrimage; he belongs to her; he is prepared—prepared to meet her at the foot of the altar where the Church will proclaim him to be a lawful husband.

So now we have come to the wedding ceremony. Our young man has not become an old man—far from it—it does not take years to become mature in this way. Indeed, if he is not truly in love, and if he has no ethical needs and no religious presuppositions in his soul, he will never become mature anyhow. But the eternal does not need to intervene many times in order to find the really opportune moment, and in this he is matured. To be sure, this maturing makes him older in a certain sense, but it is precisely the youthfulness of the eternal that it gives to him, and in this way falling in love also makes a person older.

That a young lover is a pleasing sight need not be said, but it may be necessary to say that a husband is an even more refreshing sight, unless the altar is unto offense, because it is wrong, of course, to be only a young lover when one steps up there. But the husband is the young lover, totally so. His love is unchanged, except that it has something the youth does not have, the holy beauty of the resolution. Is he not just as rich and happy as the young man? Is my wealth less because I possess it in the only adequately secure way; is my claim upon life less because I have it on stamped paper; is my happiness less because God in heaven guarantees it, and not in jest, as Eros would do it, but in earnestness and truth, as truly as the resolution holds him fast! Or is the language the young lover knows how to use supposed to be more divine than the married man can understand? Is not the wedding ceremony itself such obscure discourse[127] that it takes more than a poet to understand it; is it not such a boldly ventured promise that anyone who understands but half is bound to lose his senses? To talk about duty to a pair of lovers—and to understand it and still be in love, bound to the beloved with the strongest bond of immediacy! To talk about the curse that rests upon the human race, about the difficulties of marriage, about woman's pain and man's sour sweat—and still be in love and in the immediacy of being in love be convinced that nothing but happiness awaits them! To hear this, to envision the resolution, to keep one's mind fixed upon it, and also to envision the myrtle wreath upon the beloved's head—truly, a married man, a genuine husband, is himself a wonder! To be able to hear his beloved's voice while the organ plays! To be able to hold on to the delight of erotic love while life concentrates the full force of earnestness upon him and his beloved!

But now to her, for without resolution there is no marriage. A feminine soul does not have and should not have reflection the way a man does. Therefore, this is not the way she is to come to the resolution. But swiftly as a bird she comes from esthetic immediacy to the religious, and one can say of a woman in quite another sense than of a man that it is a depraved woman whom falling in love does not make devout. They meet in the religious immediacy as a married couple. But the man reaches it through an ethical development. A Greek sage has said that daughters should be married when they are maidens in years but women in understanding.[128] Very beautifully said, but one must remember that a woman in understanding is not a man in understanding. The highest understanding a woman has—and has it with honor and with beauty—is a religious immediacy.

It has often given me joy to consider how a girl and a young man must be counterparts in order to be a proper married couple. To be honest, anyone who does not have joy in considering this may have a sense for the most beautiful sight in the sphere of nature—a couple in love—but not the spirit's sense and not faith in spirit. If someone declares that such a phenomenon, a marriage that expresses the idea, is indeed rarely seen, well, perhaps it is just as rare to see that a person who, as of course we all do, believes in immortality, in the existence [*Tilværelse*] of God, actually expresses the idea in his life.

In her immediacy, woman is essentially esthetic, but precisely because she is that essentially the transition to the religious is also close by. Feminine romanticism is in the next moment the religious. If it is not this, it is only sensual ardor and the demonic inspiration of sensuality; the holy purity of modesty is transformed into a darkness that tempts and incites.

VI
159

Immediate love, then, is in the woman. Here is the common ground. But the transition to the religious occurs without reflection. That is, when an intimation of the thought, the content of which the man's reflection ideally exhausts, passes through her consciousness, she faints, while her husband hurries off and, equally moved but also through reflection, is not overwhelmed; he stands firm, the beloved leaning on him until she opens her eyes again. In this swooning, she is transferred from the immediacy of erotic love into that of the religious, and here they meet again. Now she is prepared for the wedding, for without resolution there is no marriage.

Has something now been lost? Has the happiness of falling in love diminished because the bliss of erotic love reflects the blessing of heaven? Has the lovers' wanting to belong to each other forever become a temporal stipulation because it has come to be in earnest? Is the highest earnestness as a resonance in the most lovable jest less beautiful than everything that love wants in immediacy, for the person who talks entirely in immediacy still talks only in jest. When the lover wants to risk his life for his love and she the beloved says Amen to it, even when he does risk his life, it is noble, it can move a stone to pity—woe to the one who laughs, but in a certain sense it is still only a jest, for the one who loses and ventures in immediacy has still not understood himself.

There is a picture that portrays Romeo and Juliet[129]—an eternal picture. Whether it is an exceptional work of art, I leave undecided, or whether the forms are beautiful, I do not judge—I lack both the aptitude and the competence for that. The eternal element in the picture is that it portrays a pair of lovers and portrays them in an essential expression. No commentary is necessary; one understands it at once, and on the other hand no commentary provides this repose in the beautiful situation of love. Juliet has sunk in admiration at her lover's feet, but from this adoring position her devotion raises her up in a gaze filled with heavenly bliss, but Romeo stops this look and with a kiss all the longing of erotic love is set at rest forever, for the reflection of eternity surrounds the moment with a halo, and no more than Romeo and Juliet does anyone who looks at the picture think that there will be a next moment, even if it were only to repeat the sacred seal of the kiss. Do not ask the lovers, for they do not hear your voice, but out in the world ask in what century this happened, in what country, at what time of the day, at what hour it was—no one replies, for it is an eternal picture.

They are a loving couple, an eternal subject for art, but a married couple they are not. Am I not supposed to dare to mention a married couple; is the other supposed to be more glorious because there is lacking some of the invisible glory that marriage has? If that were the case, why, then, would I be a married man? In other words, no married couple is perfect any more than every pair of lovers is a Romeo and Juliet, but it is every loving couple's beautiful joy to have this prototype; but here it is indeed a matter only of the prototype according to the supremacy, if I may say so, that determines the rank of the ministrants.

She is, then, not kneeling adoringly, for the difference that is fixed in the immediacy of erotic love, the man's strength that gives him the advantage, is sensed to be raised into a higher unity, into the divine equality of the religious. She is only sinking down; she wants to kneel in the admiration of love, but his strong arm holds her upright. She is drooping, yet not before the visible but before the invisible, before the excessiveness of the impression; then she grasps him, who is already holding her supportively. He himself is moved as he grasps her, and if the kiss were not their mutual support, they both might falter. This is no picture, there is no repose in the artistic situation, for as one looks at her almost sinking in adoration, one sees beyond this interrupted posture the necessity of a new one, that she stands upright at his side. One has intimations of a new prototype, the authentic prototype of marriage, because married people are contiguous angles on the same base. What is it that produces that incompleteness in the first picture, what is being sought in this faltering—it is the equality of the resolution; it is the higher immediacy of the religious.

So forget all objections, which merely exclude themselves. Even when the objection declares with scorn: *Habeat vivat cum illa* [Let him have her, live with her],[130] it just plays up to the married man, for this is what he wants, and the objection surely cannot want one to refrain from marrying, for then, of course, it would have nothing to mock and we would all become just as exclusive as the one making the objection. Hence marriage seems to me to be the most secure of all. Love says: Yours for eternity. The wedding ceremony says: You *shall* leave everything to belong to her;[131] the objection says: Keep her. But then there is indeed no objection; for even if the objection thinks that the married man becomes ludicrous, the married man is not thereby prevented from leaving everything (the mockery as well) in order to remain with her. Indeed, even if the mocker himself wanted to have her, if he stepped forward in connection with the objection that is called for—but that cannot happen, for it is only the licit that is sought after, and even if the licit "forever holds his peace,"[132] there is never anyone who has sent for the illicit.

Since, however, as the occasion requires and as it behooves a married man, I have hastily shadowboxed with the objections, which usually are snatched out of thin air, I shall also look at the matter from another side.

I do not say, then, that marriage is the highest life; I know a life that is higher, but woe to the person who gratuitously wants to leap over it. It is in this narrow pass that I choose my checkpoint in order, if I may say so, to inspect in thought those who want to slip past. It is easy to see what direction that feigned outcome of life must take. It must take the direction of the religious, in the direction of spirit, in such a way that because of being spirit one wants to forget that one is also a human being and not pure spirit, as is God alone.

The Middle Ages' disdainful view of marriage may conceivably return in a totally different form, as an intellectuality that renounces marriage not on dogmatic and hypermoral grounds, but rejects it out of recklessness of spirit. The extreme counterpart to this is already expressing itself, for precisely because inflated intellectuality has missed the ethical point, it can prate about the idolization of the flesh, but the idolization of the flesh is one manifestation that the flesh has become indifferent in relation to intellectuality. The opposite expression is that it is totally annulled, that spirituality does not want to recognize the corruptible body in which it lives, this temporality in which it has its home, its transient residence,[133] this piecemealness[134] out of which it must collect itself. There are various kinds of eccentricity; the theocentric kind has a reasonable claim to be assigned to the place to which it belongs. But speculation, after all, is theocentric, both the theocentric speculator and the theocentric theory. As long as it remains at that and the theocentric limits itself to being theocentric behind the lectern three times a week from 4:00 P.M. until 5:00 P.M. but otherwise is a citizen and a married man and a captain of the popinjay shooting club just like the rest of us, one cannot say that temporality has not been given a fair deal; a theoretical digression of that sort three times a week, a sidetracking, can be regarded as being without further consequences.

VI
162

If, however, one takes the idolization of intellectuality seriously, if the individual has sufficient demonic ideality to shape his whole life according to his hypothesizing resolution, just as the married man does with respect to his good resolution—that is, in the sense that every objection, every counterargument of life is regarded as a spiritual trial—then he has done what he could to take his stand as an exception. It cannot be denied that for a period, at least, an individual can risk everything for his hypothesizing resolution; neither can it be denied that he can even risk his life for it, but he acquires no justification that way, no more than one acquires a prescriptive right to stolen goods. In a certain sense, such a person is certainly an exception; he is also an exception in the sense that he, as a demoniac, has more will power than average people, who, to speak demonically, do not go so far as to be evil.

Such a person, however, is utterly devoid of anything that could impress a judge and keep him from declaring him unjustified; he has nothing at all that could touch and move the *viscera* [bowels] of compassion when one sees him plunge into the abyss he has prepared for himself. In other words, pure intellectuality is a prodigious abstraction, and on the other side of abstraction there is nothing, nothing, not even the remotest hint of a religious idea. The exception is an emigrant, but of a peculiar kind, for he does not emigrate to America or to another continent on the other side of the ocean, or on the other side of the grave—no, he vanishes. We have let his negative comments be aimed at marriage in particular; to that extent it seems that he could still have many temporal interests. But this is not the case. In other words, marriage is central in temporality, and the individual personality is unable to relate directly and immediately to the idea of the state. It might be that he wanted to sacrifice himself totally to the state and for that reason does not marry. But this is a futile contradiction, in which he does not respect the consistency of his idea, to which, however, obedience is dearer than the fat of rams.[135] If in relation to his idea he is to be justified in leaping over marriage, then his idea must be indifferent toward the idea of the state. But here as everywhere one must remember that it is not a matter of the accidental point that an individual does not marry; here it is a matter only of not willing to marry. Every individuality of rank, if I may put it that way, in the world of spirit has resolution, and the rank is in relation to the resolution.

The infinite abstraction acquires a foothold behind itself; the fervor of annihilation becomes but a small risk compared with what is to be gained as soon as the person who renounces the world and makes the *votum castitatis* [vow of chastity] has a religious base. Such a person does not take this step, with which he passes beyond life, for nothing. To be sure he does not stare fixedly at the reward, but still he trustfully works his way toward it; just as the rower rows toward the goal but continually turns his back to it, so he works himself out of life.

That such conduct is a religious abstraction is entirely true, but that something like this might be so obsolete that it could not recur in a repetition is less true. It is obvious that the religious has been lying fallow long enough; when it begins to move with ideal energy, it is not to be wondered at if it makes a mistake again. To find the true concretion for the religious is not easy, for the religious continually has the infinite abstraction as its presupposition and is no simple immediacy. At times, in a way that is well meant, to be sure, people may talk very beautifully and very truthfully about the religious, and at times, perhaps with a single word, retract everything without being aware of it themselves, since it appears that they are speaking of the purely immediate. I am continually aiming at marriage. To find a proper religious expression for marriage, to find precisely and categorically defined what the Middle Ages despaired of, something to which the last few centuries (which are proud enough of being far more advanced than the Middle Ages—which must be understood to mean advanced not in piety but in worldliness) have contributed very little, I still regard as a *pium desiderium* [pious wish]. I think it is good for a married man to ponder this and, if he wants to be something of an author, to write about such things; besides, everything else has been treated, even astronomy.[136]

VI
164

Yet, from the essentially religious point of view, it cannot be denied that it makes no difference whether or not a person has been married. Here the religious opens the infinite abyss of the abstraction. And speaking with a forked tongue does not help, either. If in concern one seeks guidance in the religious discourse, one will perhaps find an ambiguity more frequently than one thinks and than the speaker himself realizes. Marriage is extolled when it is the subject of the discourse. But if someone dies unmarried, then—well, then the discourse is indeed not about marriage, and then, with an almost humorous turn, it is said that it makes no difference whether a person has been married or not. But what of the person who listens to both discourses? For when the discourse is like that, it is far and away more difficult to be a good listener who is looking for guidance and instruction than to be an orator who in every way is at your service. The importance of temporality is emphasized, its ethical importance; it is called the time of grace, the arena of conversion, the period of the decision that decides for eternity. But then a child dies and a funeral oration is delivered, or in a sermon one alludes to the troubled parents who have lost a child, and one is humoristically above all the vanity of temporality. Mention is made of the seventy years as toil and as spiritual wear and tear,[137] of all the rivers running into the sea without its ever becoming full.[138] Thus the Romans were more consistent in letting these infants weep in Elysium because they were not permitted to live.[139] Meanwhile work is being done on the system—good Lord, compared with this prodigious effort, to demand a view of life would be already too much. This much, then, is certain; it will never do to have many beautiful discourses with meaning in all of them but not one meaning in all.[140]

However, even if it were so that the religious abstraction was something vanished, something antiquated, something *surmounted* (this last expression stems from the systematic assistance that is so good as to confuse, if I may say so, the development of an eternal generation with each generation's repetitions of what has been experienced), suppose it were so; it could then very well find its place here as the subject of discussion. Even if it is not exactly an everyday sight to see genuine love, then it is, of course, even more rare to see a real marriage. Higgling and haggling is futile; it only plays the victory into the hands of chicaners, who also know how to distill a caustic substance from the religious. Even if it is an objection of the utmost chicanery, it is a mediocre defense to make light of it if one does not have a good conscience and know one is right.

The religious abstraction desires to belong to God alone. For this love [*Kærlighed*] it is willing to refuse, renounce, sacrifice everything (these are the nuances); from this love it will not allow itself to be disturbed, diverted, captured by anything else. In relation to this love it refuses to have any duplic-

VI
165

ity in the accounting; every transaction must always take place in a pure relationship with God, who is not related to him through anything else. Pride in an abstraction of that kind can be very religiously tempered with humility in relation to God, but for the time being the abstraction must be regarded as unjustified because it relates itself altogether abstractly to that which it renounces. It does not concern itself with trying to grasp more concretely (to stick to my theme) the beautiful reality [*Realitet*] of falling in love and the true reality of marriage—an occupation with that would be spiritual trial. This is actually the inhumanity of this abstraction, about which one nevertheless should make a cautious judgment, and above all one should not commend railway speculation and committee foolery, and other such busyness—as if such hurly-burly or such hurry-scurry were the actual content of temporality!

Inhumanity toward human beings is also importunity toward God. To repeat, the inhumanity does not consist in willing the highest; that is not at all inhumane. And proclamations or anathemas from a worldly affluent but at the same time spiritual poorhouse where one has status by being like the majority, and where even now the envy of ostracism and the argument of potsherds[141] are continually directed against anyone who is better, mean nothing at all here. Neither does the inhumanity consist in wanting to base one's life-view upon something accidental, whereby many are excluded, for the exception does not deny that everyone can do just as he does, and all this chatter—it is admittedly something great, but not everyone can do it, and what would become of the world in that case—comes from the poorhouse, where they cannot understand and refuse to understand that if this is correct, then they must leave the rest up to God, who certainly is competent and is not so down at the heels that he needs the assistance of the poorhouse. No, the inhumanity consists in his not wanting to have any concrete idea of what for most people is the reality of their lives. But this concrete idea is and remains a condition just for his being able to have the appearance of being in the right. Importunity toward God is a kind of impertinent camaraderie, even if he himself does not understand it that way. He can even be truly humble, but in the very same way, humanly speaking, a subordinate can have the most loyal enthusiasm for his king and be far superior to those who are neither hot nor cold[142] but are *numerus* [numbers] and *pecus* [cattle],[143] but yet when he seeks an audience with the king he can wish to be permitted to enter through a door different from the one assigned to all subjects. To me it seems that there must be something terrible about his being turned away and hearing these words: The other way, then we shall see what can be done. For the person who has actually had sufficient inwardness to comprehend that the religious is the highest love, how heartbreaking, how annihilating it must be to discover that he has allowed himself too much, that he has been too free, has grieved the spirit,[144] has offended his love [*Forelskelse*]—alas, all the more grievously if he actually was intending to give his relationship the highest expression.

Consequently, such a religious exception will ignore the universal; he will outbid actuality's terms. It is promptly seen thereby that he is unjustified. It becomes even more difficult when he wants to underbid. He recognizes entirely *in abstracto* the reality [*Realitet*] of temporality or, to stick to my theme, the reality of marrying. But he is unhappy, unfit for this joy, for this security in existence; he is depressed, a burden to himself, and feels he must be that to others. Do not be quick to judge—the weaker person also has his rights; and depression is something real that one does not delete with a stroke of the pen. So, then, having accounted for life in this way, he finds consolation in a religious abstraction. When the person who seeks an audience with the king in an unconventional way almost arouses sympathy, it seems to be a different story and quite appropriate that he gains a hearing.

Yet here again the dubiousness is that he speaks altogether abstractly about what he wants to give up. Precisely because he is depressed he has an abstract notion that life for others is so pleasant and happy. But what the unfamiliar is like one cannot know *in abstracto*. Here, too, is the fraudulence that is inseparable from all depression. Whatever distress the depressed person struggles with, be it ever so concrete, for him it always has an admixture of fantasy and thereby of abstraction. But if on occasion the depressed person is down in existence, it is just a minor manner, a little falsification, which still does not prevent him from participating in common affairs and being like other people, although even in the slightest thing he undertakes or suffers he receives a little admixture from imagination's inexhaustible funds *ad usus privatos* [for private use]. If, however, he is allowed to gather up all existence *in abstracto*, then he never really finds out what it is he is giving up. The joy of life, such as he thinks others relish, becomes a burden to him, a double burden, since he already has enough to bear. Here is the comic side of depression, for the experience of the depressed person in relation to life is often like that of the journeyman tailor Hebel[145] tells about. He wanted to take passage on a ship being towed up the Rhine and was bargaining about the price when the skipper said that he could come along for half price if he would walk alongside and help with the pulling. Alas, so it goes with the depressed person; by relating abstractly to life he thinks he is slipping through for half price and does not notice that he is pulling as hard as the ship's crew and paying money to boot.

What these two forms of exception lack is obvious: having experienced. From this it is easy to perceive that no one can become a justified exception on his own. First of all something has to happen. Incidentally, I am speaking, as stated before, theoretically, for I do not know whether there is or ever has been a justified exception, but I shall come as close as possible to it. It must happen in a different way; it must be someone who has been living on in a secure understanding with life and then suddenly is halted. Therefore, he must experience falling in love, real falling in love. True, there is an old saying that one cannot resist the god of erotic love,[146] but the person who from the beginning resolutely takes his stand against actuality will always have the power to drive off the inspiration of erotic love or to slay it at birth. Face to face with an immediate existence, erotic love is the stronger force, but face to face with a resolution armed in advance against it, it is not.

First of all, then, I require him to be really in love. [147]A broken love affair is enough for a person, but if the lover must himself break it, then this breaking is a double-edged sword in his hand, a sword without a hilt, although he still must hold it. Then this operation pains just as deeply autopathetically as sympathetically. Someone may say, "If falling in love is assumed first of all, then it is impossible to find the exception along this road, because in falling in love everything is at stake, it is playing for high stakes. And in love everything is at stake for the beloved, it is a doubling of the highest stake. How impossible, then, to back out of it, to be willing to lose everything, honor as well; it is impossible if he really loves."

Well, if he does not really love, then it is impossible for him to become the exception, provided there is such a one, but the other is not impossible. It is terrible, a horror, but so it has to be. The person who wants to break with actuality must at least know what it is he is breaking with. I am far from being cruel; I am no more cruel here than I am cruel when I am calmly sitting in an inquiring capacity and conjure up all sorts of horrors in order to frighten back within the peaceful enclosure of law and justice. The person who in falling in love has bent the branch of happiness down to the ground may cut it off and himself be hurled by its force into deadly torment, just as the poor fellow condemned to death suffers even more because he also rends asunder his beloved. When he is sailing along secure in his happiness, it is possible to descend and bore a hole in the ship and bring himself and another into distress at sea. It is possible for him to do it if he is really in love; if he is not, it is impossible for him to be the exception, provided there is such a one. It is terrible to put a sword in the hand of one who is in a frenzy, but it is just as terrible that happiness is placed in his hands when he is the way he is, for he does not have to be demented as yet. What motivates him, I shall not go into here; I shall only depict the psychological presuppositions, the psychical conditions that must be present if there is to be any question at all of a justified exception.

Next, I require him to be a married man. There is something more terrible to lose than to lose honor, and the crying of fatherless children calls out more loudly than all the disgrace of dishonor; even more terrible than the loneliness of the betrayed girl is the thousand-tongued misery of the deserted wife and mother. "It is impossible," someone says. "If he is actually bound to life this way, then it is impossible to break off." Well, if he is not so bound, it is impossible for him to become an exception, provided there is such a one. The other, however, is not impossible, even if it is so terrible that it freezes the soul and suffocates the emotions. Yet the person who is sitting in an inquiring capacity must not be moved from the truth, not by any terror, must not defraud justice of a farthing; and the exemption must not purchase justification for a round sum but must pay to the last penny.[148] If it is doubtful whether falling in love is from God, if falling in love does not even need to presuppose a religious view, marriage is unconditionally of religious origin. Thus the person who breaks it not only makes himself and those whom he loves totally miserable, but he places life in contradiction with itself, he places God in contradiction with himself. It is not impossible for one who is in a frenzy, and yet he does not have to be demented. I shall not propose or try to propose here what possibly may motivate him—I only expound the psychological presuppositions. If these are not present in all their horror, then he does not become the justified exception.

Now, then, the break has occurred; I continue. I require that after this he is to love life; if he becomes inimical to life, he is unjustified, because being an exception does not make less beautiful that from which he is excepted. That with which he broke he must love with an enthusiasm exceeding anyone else's, and in this enthusiasm he must find each beautiful thing even more lovely and delightful than does the person who rejoices in happiness, because the one who wills to reject something universal has to be better informed about it than the person who is peacefully living in it. You see, if such a person, provided there is such a one, would speak about marriage, he would have a glow that scarcely any married man has—at least I yield to him. He would speak with an intimate knowledge of all its quiet joy such as no married man has, for the torment of the broken responsibility is bound to keep his soul vigilant and diligent in the contemplation of what he destroyed, and the new responsibility requires first and foremost that he know what he did. If such a person, provided there is such a person, would speak about the justification of the exceptions, then my role is only that of a subordinate compared with that of him who is a general inspector, for he must indeed know every hiding place, every nook and corner, every wrong turn where no one imagines there is even a road; he must be able to see the irregularities in the dark where someone else assumes there is nothing at all to separate him from justification.

VI
170

The break itself he must feel as a fatality and a horror, for the suffering in it is that he is halted and is not like an adventurer romantically renouncing the concrete content of life. He has actually comprehended and comprehends its full substance, even though he guilelessly became a bankrupt whom life itself ruined. On the other hand, he must look upon the afterpains of the break as punitive suffering, for although his understanding despairs of discovering the guilt, since he is indeed actually in love, actually belongs wholeheartedly to his married life, even if the pain of tearing himself away is just as great, indeed, greater, than is the pain of shattering for the beloved, nevertheless the intense feeling of despair must still find its joy in making honorable amends to God, in signing the same charter as the happy one does—that the way of providence is sheer wisdom and justice.

He must comprehend the break in such a way that he who had found security in life (for the most loving upbringing is to be formed by a wife's humble submission, and the most rejuvenating instruction is to bring up his children, and the best refuge is behind the sacred walls of marriage) is now hurled out into new, into the most horrible peril. In other words, even if it is definite that he cannot do otherwise, in making this step he has ventured out into the trackless infinite space where the sword of Damocles[149] hangs over his head if he looks up toward heaven, where the snare of unknown temptations clutches at his feet if he looks toward the ground, where no human help reaches out, where not even the most daring pilot willing to sacrifice his life ventures out because here there is more to lose than life, where no sympathy reaches out for him, indeed, not even the tenderest sympathy can spy him, for he has ventured out into the void from which mankind shrinks. He is a rebel against the earthly, and he has made an enemy of the sensate, which in well-disposed harmony with the spiritual is a supporting staff, just as time is; therefore the sensate has become for him a serpent, and time has become the moment of the bad conscience. It is believed to be so easy to be victorious over the sensate; well, so it is, if one does not incite it by wanting to annihilate it. One does not speak of such things to lovers, for their love keeps them ignorant of the dangers that only the rebel discovers; love does not know why marriage was instituted, but an earnest discourse, nevertheless, knows that it was instituted: *ob adjutorium, ob propagationem, ob evitandam fornicationem* [for assistance, for propagation, for the avoidance of illicit sex],[150] and experiences in monasteries could add terrible footnotes to this text. Here is the proper psychological source of the catastrophe of Faust, who precisely by willing to become sheer spirit finally succumbs to the wild revolt of sensuality. Woe to the one who is solitary in this way! He is abandoned by all existence; yet he is not without company, because at every moment an anxious recollection, in which all the passion of sympathy burns and consumes, conjures up for him pictures of the misery of the shattered ones and at any minute the sudden[151] can come over him with its terror.

He must comprehend that no one can understand him and must have the composure to reconcile himself to the fact that human language has only curses for him, and for his sufferings the human heart has only the feeling that he suffers as guilty. And yet he must not harden his own heart against it, for at the same time he does he is unjustified. He must feel the torturing of misunderstanding just as the ascetic constantly felt the prick of the hair shirt he wore next to his bare body— and thus he has attired himself in misunderstanding, which is just as dreadful a costume to be in as the one Hercules received from Omphale and the one in which he was burned.[152]

To repeat the most essential points, he must not feel himself above the universal, but lower; he must *à tout prix* [at all costs] want to remain within it, for he is actually in love and, what is more, is a married man; he must want to remain within it for his own sake and must want it for the sake of them for whom he is willing to sacrifice his life, whereas instead he now sees their misery as if he were someone whose hands and feet have been cut off and whose tongue has been torn from his mouth—that is, without a single means of communication. He must feel himself to be the most wretched of men, the scum of humanity,[153] must feel it doubly precisely because he knows, not *in abstracto* but *in concreto*, what the beautiful is. Then he sinks down, desperate in all his wretchedness, when that single word, that final, that ultimate word, so ultimate that it is not within human language, is not forthcoming, when the testimony is not with him, when he cannot tear open the sealed dispatch that is only to be opened out there and that contains the orders from God. This is the start of becoming an exception, if there is such a one at all; if all this is not a given, he is without justification.

Whether out of this wretchedness—which surely is the deepest, the most agonizing, in which the pain does not cease except in order that repentance can swing its whip over him, where all human suffering is personally present to torment, in which the suffering does not let up any more than a city stops being besieged because the guard is changed or because the new guard is from another enemy detachment, and they relieve each other thus: if one's own pain takes a nap, the pain of sympathy stays awake; if the pain of sympathy takes a nap, one's own pain stays awake, and at any moment repentance making its rounds can come to see whether the guard is awake—whether out of this wretchedness, I repeat, a sense of being blessed can develop, whether in this dreadful nothingness there can be any divine meaning, what faith it must take to believe that God could intervene [*gribe ind*] in life this way, that is, in such a way that it manifests itself as such to the one suffering and acting, for if God actually is the one who intervenes, then he has well provided for the rescue of the annihi-

lated ones, except that at the critical moment the one apprehended [*den Grebne*], the one selected, cannot know about it—
all this is beyond my comprehension. I do not know whether
there is a justified exception, and if there is such a person, he
does not know it either, not even at the moment he droops,
for if he has the slightest intimation of it, he is unjustified.

[154]It has not been my wish to become involved with what
brings a person to despair in such a way as to want to trick
spirit out of the divine and not to receive it in the way it has
pleased the divine to apportion it, or how a person could become the object of a divine partiality that, jealous of itself,
uses as its first expression the terrible spiritual trial of envy—I
have merely wished to delineate the psychological presuppositions. See here a candidate for the monastery who does not
dare indulge in the concession of the Middle Ages but, alien
to the contemporary consciousness, buys the highest priced
suffering at the highest price. My description is similar to
ready-made clothing; it is the hair shirt of sufferings that the
exception must wear—I do not believe that anyone out of
mistaken pleasure would take a fancy to this costume.

I am not cruel. Oh, if one is as happy as a husband can be,
if one loves life so highly, loves it so highly during the repeated taking of oaths that the one oath is more precious to
one than the other because in this love of life one clings firmly
to her whom I still embrace with the victorious resolution of
the happy first love, to one's wife, for whose sake one must
leave father and mother,[155] clings firmly to what compensates
for the loss, what beautifies and rejuvenates my married life,
my darlings, whose joy, whose cheerfulness, whose innocent
minds, whose progress in the good make plain and simple
daily bread an inestimable overabundance, make giving
thanks for my livelihood and my intercession just as important in my eyes as a king's for his country—then one is too
happy to be cruel. But when one sits on the commission of
inquiry one is undaunted by everything that will make the
road of justice crooked, by everything that will lead truth
astray. I do not go around trying to find someone to wear this
hair shirt; on the contrary, I cry out to the rash person, if he

will listen, that he should not venture on these paths—anyone who ventures on his own initiative is lost. But to me it is a new demonstration of the gloriousness of life that it is enclosed in such a way that no one is tempted to want to venture outside, is so constituted that the mere thought of the terror must be enough to crush all foolish and frivolous and inflated and fallacious and neurotic talk about wanting to be an exception; for even if all my requirements are met, I still do not know whether there is a justified exception. Indeed, I shall add this as the worst of terrors, that the very person who wants to be an exception never finds out in this life whether he is. So, then—with the loss of everything, with torment beyond all bounds, not to be able to buy oneself a certainty!

What I do know definitely, however—something that shrewdness no more than mockery, no more than the terror of these deliberations, can wrench away from me—is the happiness of my marriage, or, more correctly, my conviction of the happiness of marriage. The terror is now far removed, I am no longer sitting on the commission of inquiry but in my study, and just as a thunderstorm makes the landscape smile again, so my soul is again in high spirits for writing about marriage, with which I will in a certain sense never be finished. In other words, marriage is no more something that can be explained at once than a married man is a hothead. I have been performing a painful task, now I have come home, and I am with her whom all the powers of life have united to authorize me to have lawfully as my own, her who shortens the dark days for me and adds an eternity to our happy understanding, her who subtracts from my sufferings and shares my cares and increases my joys. Look, she just went by my door; I understand why—she is waiting for me but does not come in lest she disturb. Just one minute, my beloved, just one moment—my soul is so rich, I am so eloquent at this moment that I want to write it down on paper, a eulogy on you, my lovely better half, and thus convince the whole world of the validity of marriage. [156]And yet in due time, tomorrow, the day after tomorrow, in a week, I shall throw you away, you wretched pen[157]—my choice is made, and I follow the

VI
174

beckoning and the invitation. Let a wretched author sit trembling when a thought presents itself in a lucky moment, shivering lest someone disturb him—I am afraid of nothing, but I also know what is better than the most felicitous idea in a man's mind and better than the most felicitous expression on paper of the most felicitous idea and what is infinitely more precious than any secret a poor author can have with his pen.[158]

[1]"GUILTY?"/"NOT GUILTY?"

A STORY OF SUFFERING

AN IMAGINARY PSYCHOLOGICAL
CONSTRUCTION
by
FRATER TACITURNUS

NOTICE: OWNER SOUGHT[2]

Every child knows that Søborg Castle[3] is a ruin that lies in north Sjælland about two miles from the coast near a little town of the same name. Although the castle has long since been destroyed, it still survives in folk memory and will survive inasmuch as it has a rich historical and historically poetic past to draw upon. In a certain sense, this is true also of Søborg Lake belonging to the castle. Originally it was about nine miles in circumference and had a depth of several fathoms to draw upon and therefore has not yet disappeared and will probably claim its existence as a lake for some time even though the mainland tricks it out of one transitional boundary after another and thus squeezes it together more and more.

It was in Helsingør last summer that I met an elderly friend, a naturalist, who had traveled the coast north from Copenhagen in order to make observations of marine plants. His plan was then to visit the region around Søborg, which he supposed might provide a rich yield. He invited me to come along, and I accepted the invitation.

The lake is not easy to approach, for it is surrounded by a rather wide stretch of quagmire. Here the boundary dispute between the lake and the land goes on night and day. There is something melancholy about this battle, of which, however, no trace of destruction gives any indication, for what the earth gradually wins from the lake is transformed into a smiling and exceedingly fertile meadow. Ah, but the poor lake that is disappearing in this way! No one has any pity on it, no one feels for it, because neither the pastor, whose land borders one side of it, nor the peasants farming on the other side have anything against gaining one piece of meadow after the other. The poor lake is abandoned both on the one side and on the other.

What gives the lake an even more inclosed [*indesluttet*] look is that the quagmire is thickly overgrown with reeds; indeed, there is nothing like it in Denmark, at least so says my friend the naturalist. Only in one place has a little waterway been opened up; here there is a flat-bottomed boat, in which we two, he on behalf of science and I on behalf of friendship and curiosity, poled ourselves out. With effort we brought the boat out, for the channel has hardly a foot of water. The reed growth, however, is as dense and thick as a forest, probably eight feet high. Concealed by it, one seems as if eternally lost to the world, forgotten in the stillness broken only by our struggling with the boat or when a bittern, that secret voice in the solitude, repeats its cry three times, and then repeats it again. Strange bird, why do you wail and lament this way— after all, you indeed wish only to remain in solitude!

Finally we made our way beyond the reeds, and the lake lay before us, clear as a mirror, sparkling in the afternoon light. Everything was so still; silence rested over the lake. If, while we were poling through the growth of reeds, I felt as if I were in the lush fecundity in India, now it seemed as if I lay out on the calm sea. I became almost anxious; to be so infinitely far from people, to be in a nutshell out on an ocean! Now there was a flustered clamoring, a blended screaming of all sorts of birds, and then, when the sound suddenly ceased, stillness again, almost to the point of anxiety, and the ear grasped in vain for a support in the infinite.

My naturalist friend took out the implement with which he uprooted marine plants, cast it out, and began his work. Meanwhile, in the other end of the boat I sat in reverie, absorbed in the scenery. He had already brought up some plants and was busying himself with the find when I asked if I might borrow his instrument. I resumed my former place and cast out. With a muffled sound it sank into the deep. Perhaps it was because I was inexperienced, but it seemed to me that when I wanted to pull it up something held back so much that I was almost afraid of being the weaker one. I pulled, and a bubble rose from the depths. It lingered a moment, and broke, and then success. Deep down I had a strange feeling; yet I had no idea at all of the nature of my discovery. Now that I think about it, now that I know everything, now I understand it. I understand that it was a sigh from below, a sigh

de profundis [out of the depths],[4] a sigh because I wrested from
the lake its deposit, a sigh from the inclosed lake, a sigh from
an inclosed soul from which I wrested its secret. If I had had
any intimation of this two minutes earlier, I would not have
dared to pull.

The naturalist sat totally absorbed in his work, asking just
once if I had found anything, a question that did not seem to
expect a reply since he quite appropriately did not regard my
fishing as being on behalf of science. Well, I had not found
what he was searching for, either, but something totally different. And so each of us sat in his end of the boat, each one
occupied with his find, he for the sake of science, and I for the
sake of friendship and curiosity.

Wrapped in oilcloth provided with many seals lay a box
made of palisander wood. The box was locked, and when I
forced it open the key was inside: inclosing reserve [*Indesluttedhed*][5] is always turned inward in that way. Inside the box
was a very carefully and neatly handwritten manuscript on
very fine letter paper. There was an orderliness, a meticulous-
ness about the whole thing and yet a solemnity as if it had been
done in the sight of God. To think that by my meddling I had
brought disorder into the archives of heavenly justice! But
now it is too late, and I beg the forgiveness of heaven and the
unknown person. Undeniably the hiding place was well chosen, and Søborg Lake is more reliable than the most solemn
vow—absolute silence is promised—for it never once makes
this vow. Strangely enough, however different happiness and
unhappiness are, at times they agree in wishing for one thing:
silence. We commend a lottery operator who distributes the
lucky prizes if he withholds the name of the lucky person, lest
the good fortune become an affliction to him; but as a matter
of fact the unlucky fellow who gambled away all his assets
also wants his name withheld.

There were also a few pieces of jewelry in the box, some
even of considerable value, ornaments and precious stones—
alas, precious stones, the owner probably would say, precious, dearly purchased, although he did indeed receive permission to keep them. It is this valuable find I feel duty-bound

to advertise. There was a plain gold ring with an engraved date, a necklace consisting of a diamond cross fastened to a light blue silk ribbon. The rest was partly of no value whatsoever—a fragment of a poster advertising a comedy, [6]a page torn from the New Testament, each one in a neat vellum envelope, a withered rose[7] in a little box with silver overlay, and other similar articles that only to the owner can have a value equal to that of diamonds of two carats.

VI
180

Notice is hereby given to the owner of the box found in Søborg Lake in the summer of 1844 to communicate with me through Reitzel's bookstore[8] by means of a sealed note marked with the initials F. T. May I, however, in order to reduce any possibility of unnecessary delay, remark that the handwriting will immediately betray the owner, and furthermore, that anyone who might honor me with any communication and receives no reply may safely conclude that the handwriting did not match, and only that one can lay claim to a reply. On the other hand, for the comfort of the owner may it be said that even if I have taken the liberty of publishing his manuscript, which by its nature, unlike the handwriting, will not betray anyone, may it be said that I have not taken the liberty of showing anyone, not one single person, either the handwriting or the diamond cross and the other things.

[9]Mr. Bonfils, M.A., has published a table by which the year can be determined with given dates. I, too, benefit from his services; I have calculated and calculated and finally worked out that the year that fits the given dates is the year 1751, or that remarkable year when Gregor Rothfischer joined the Lutheran Church, a year which for anyone who with one deeply profound eye cyclopeanly contemplates the marvels in the course of history is also noteworthy in that precisely five years later the Seven Years' War[10] broke out. Thus one is compelled to go rather far back in time if one does not assume that an error crept into the information or into my calculations. If one is under no such constraint, then one could perhaps assume *mir nichts* and *Dir nichts* [without further ado][11] that a poor wretch of a psychologist who dares to count on but little sym-

pathy for imaginary psychological constructions [*Experimen-*
ter][12] and unreal fabrications has made an attempt to invite
sympathy by giving it the aspect of a novel. A psychologically
accurate sketch that does not ask whether such a person ever
lived is perhaps not very interesting in our day, when even
poetry has snatched at the expedient of wanting to have the
effect of actuality. [13]People certainly want to have a little psychology, a little observation of so-called actual people, but
when this science or art goes its own way, when it ignores the
many inadequate manifestations of the psychical states that actuality offers, when it slips away by itself to create an individuality out of its own knowledge and to make this individuality
the object of its observations, then many people get weary.
That is, in actual life the case is that passions, psychical states,
etc. are found only to a certain degree. This, too, delights the
psychology, but it also has another kind of delight in seeing
passion carried to its extreme limit.

VI
181

As far as reviewers are concerned, I would ask that my request be understood simply and altogether literally as my
honest intention and that the result might be according to the
petition of the request: that the book would not be subjected
to any critical mention, be it in the form of acknowledgment
or approval or disapproval. If one is able to acquire a claim to
a person's gratitude in such an easy manner, one could very
well indulge him.

F. T.

In Norway the rich farmer places a new copper kettle over his door for every thousand dollars he acquires, and the innkeeper makes a mark on the beam for every time the debtor becomes more indebted—in the same way I add a new word for every time I consider my wealth and my poverty.[14]

Periissem nisi periissem
[I would have perished had I not perished].[15]

January 3. *Morning.*[16]

So it is a year ago today since I saw her for the first time, that is, for the first time with a resolute soul. I was no fantasizer, was not in the habit of becoming intoxicated on fine words and brief dreams; therefore my resolution certainly did not mean that I would die if she did not become mine. Neither did I think that my soul would be scattered and my life become completely empty for me if she did not become mine—I had too many religious presuppositions for that. For me my resolution meant: Marry her or do not marry at all. That is what was at stake. In my soul there was no doubt that I loved her, but I also knew that in connection with such a step there were so many anomalies that for me it became a most difficult task. An individuality like me is not nimble; I cannot say: If I do not have this one, I'll take another. I do not dare to allow myself the presupposition, which comes easily to many, that a person is himself always all right, if only the other one is also worthy of him. As far as I am concerned, the emphasis must be placed elsewhere—whether I was actually capable of giving my life the kind of expression that a marriage requires. I was as much in love as anyone, even though not many would understand that I, if my deliberation had not allowed me this step, would have kept my falling in love to myself. I marry her or I do not marry at all.

Should a soldier stationed at the frontier be married? Does a soldier stationed at the frontier, spiritually understood, dare to marry—an outpost who battles night and day, not exactly with Tartars and Scythians but with the robber bands of a primordial depression, an outpost who, even though he does not fight day and night, even though he has peace for some time, still can never know at what moment the battle will begin again, since he never even dares to call this tranquillity a truce?

Depression is my nature, that is true, but thanks be to the

power who, even if it bound me in this way, nevertheless also gave me a consolation. There are animals that are only poorly armed against their enemies, but nature has provided them with a cunning by which they nevertheless are saved. I, too, was given a cunning such as this, a capacity for cunning that makes me just as strong as everyone against whom I have tested my strength. My cunning is that I am able to hide my depression; my deception is just as cunning as my depression is deep.

This is no groundless opinion. I have trained myself in deception and train myself every day. I often think of a child I once saw on the Esplanade.[17] He used crutches, but with his crutches he could hop, jump, and run a race with all but the healthiest of boys. I have trained myself from earliest childhood; ever since I saw her and fell in love, I have carried on the most rigorous exercises before there could be any question of making a resolution. I am able at any time of the day to divest myself of my depression or, more correctly, put on my disguise, because depression simply waits for me until I am alone. If there is anyone present, no matter who it is, I am never entirely who I am. If I am taken by surprise in an unguarded moment, by talking for less than a half hour I am able to wrest this impression from anyone I have encountered in my practice. My deception is not hilarity. When it comes to depression, this is nature's own deception and therefore at once should make one suspect in the eyes of even a second-rate observer. The safest deception is good common sense, dispassionate reflection, and above all a candid face and an openhearted nature. Behind this deceptive self-confidence and security in life there is a sleepless and thousand-tongued reflection that, if the first pose becomes unsure, throws everything into confusion until the opponent does not know whether he is coming or going, and once again one attains one's security. And so deep within—depression. This is true; it stays on and continues to be my misery. But I do not want to throw this misery upon any other person. That is certainly not my real reason for wanting to marry.

Am I perhaps being somewhat sophistical toward myself? I

am in love—is it the delight of falling in love that fooled me
into thinking that I was capable of this? But I have indeed been
exercising myself so many years and until now it has never
failed. In fact, my father was married, and he was the most
depressed person I have known. But he was calm and happy
all day long; and, like Loki's wife, used an evening hour to
drain the bowl of bitterness,[18] and thus he was healed again. I
do not need even that much time. I need only a moment according to the time and the occasion; then everything goes
properly. From the bitterness of depression there is distilled a
joy of life, a sympathy, an inwardness, that certainly cannot
embitter life for anyone. [19]My joy, such as sometimes over-
flows in my heart, belongs entirely to her; for everyday use I
work honestly to earn a livelihood of joy for her; only the
occasional dark moments do I have for myself—she must not
come to suffer under them.

VI
187

That is how things stand. With all the heroes who hover in
my imagination, it is indeed more or less the case that they
carry a deep and secret sorrow that they are unable or unwilling to confide to anyone. I do not marry to have another person slave under my depression. It is my pride, my honor, my
inspiration to keep in inclosing reserve what must be locked
up, to reduce it to the scantiest rations possible; my joy, my
bliss, my first and my only wish is to belong to her whom I
would purchase at any price with my life and blood, but
whom I still refuse to weaken and destroy by initiating her
into my sufferings.

Her, or I shall never marry. A person does not more than
once go through all the strain to which only falling in love can
give all the glory of magic. For I am well aware that for me a
marriage can become the most difficult task, a matter of concern, even though it is my supreme wish.

January 3. *Midnight.*

When a despairing person dashes through a side street of life
in order to find peace in a monastery, he does well to consider
first of all whether there is something in the circumstances of
his life that for the time being binds him and makes it his first

duty to work at getting another person afloat if that other one can be rescued. If he has given his all to this, then, even if he was not knighted in his lifetime, he places his hope on the honor that the Middle Ages granted the scholastic when he died—to be buried as a knight. So be calm. The point is to remain as apathetic and undecided as possible. After all, I am a murderer; I do indeed have a person's life on my conscience! But then can one justifiably take refuge in a monastery? No! Ordinarily the only thing a murderer has to wait for is his verdict; I am waiting for a verdict that will decide whether I was a murderer, for she is indeed still living. Oh, how dreadful if it was an exaggeration, a momentary mood, if it was the defiance of powerlessness that drew this word from her lips and the lips of those around her! Oh, what profound sneering at life if there was no one in the whole world except me alone who took that word seriously! My mind comes up with one suspicion after another;[20] the demon of laughter is continually knocking; I know what it wants—it wants to whirl her off like an abracadabra.[21] Depart from me, you unclean spirit! My honor, my pride order me to believe her; my depression is on the lookout for the most secret idea therein lest I be allowed to sneak away from something. She and the others who spoke have the responsibility for having said something terrible; it is my responsibility if I do not scrupulously stick to the word. After all, I am not an observer, not a counselor for the conscience, but one acting—that is, the guilty one. Consequently, my imagination is permitted to picture her in all her misery; my depression is permitted to lecture on the application: You are the murderer. If the first thing I said to myself at the time of the separation ever comes true: She chooses the scream; I choose the pain—if it ever comes true, I do not want to know it now and cannot know if it ever comes true.

Oh, that she might not die; oh, that she might not be blighted! If it is possible, God in heaven, you indeed know; it was indeed and it is my one and only desire—if it ever should be possible and it is not too late!

I saw her on the street yesterday afternoon. [22]How pale, how suffering, [23]how utterly like the figure of someone who summons one to appear in eternity. This almost glazed look, this trembling in my soul because death is walking over my grave. And yet I do not wish to forget any of it, not any; only to the faithfulness of an alarmed imagination that returns to me what has been confided more terrible than it was, only to the memory of a troubled conscience that sets a high interest rate on guilt, only to an honesty such as that will I and dare I entrust myself!—She is dying. How loathsome that I could believe for a moment the craftiness of the understanding or almost heed the demon of laughter—abominable!

And yet perhaps she was so pale only because she saw me. Perhaps! What a mean tormentor resides in this word! Is it not as when a child has tortured a butterfly long enough and when in the next moment it is about to die the child pokes at it, and the butterfly for one second again snatches at life, snatches at freedom with its wings.

VI
189

But if she does die, I cannot survive her; that I cannot do. But not a moment before, lest my death give her an explanation that I would certainly sacrifice my life to keep from her.

So be cold, calm, composed, unchanged. Strangely enough, when I was courting her I was anxious lest I be too intriguing; now I am compelled to be that.

January 5. *Midnight*.

Quiet Despair[24]

When Swift became an old man, he was committed to the insane asylum he himself had established when he was young. Here, it is related, he often stood in front of a mirror with the perseverance of a vain and lascivious woman, if not exactly with her thoughts. He looked at himself and said: Poor old man![25]

Once upon a time there were a father and a son. A son is like a mirror in which the father sees himself, and for the son in turn the father is like a mirror in which he sees himself in the time to come. Yet they seldom looked at each other in that way, for the cheerfulness of high-spirited, lively conversation was their daily round. Only a few times did it happen that the father stopped, faced the son with a sorrowful countenance, looked at him and said: Poor child, you are in a quiet despair. Nothing more was ever said about it, how it was to be understood, how true it was. And the father believed that he was responsible for his son's depression, and the son believed that it was he who caused the father sorrow—but never a word was exchanged about this.

Then the father died. And the son saw much, heard much, experienced much, and was tried in various temptations, but he longed for only one thing, only one thing moved him—it was that word and it was the voice of the father when he said it.

Then the son also became an old man; but just as love devises everything, so longing and loss taught him—not, of course, to wrest any communication from the silence of eternity—but it taught him to imitate his father's voice until the likeness satisfied him. Then he did not look at himself in the mirror, as did the aged Swift, for the mirror was no more, but in loneliness he comforted himself by listening to his father's voice: Poor child, you are in a quiet despair. For the father was the only one who had understood him, and yet he did not know whether he had understood him; and the father was the only intimate he had had, but the intimacy was of such a nature that it remained the same whether the father was alive or dead.

January 8. *Morning.*

A year ago today I saw her at her uncle's, where I was together with her. How secretively I brood over my love, how clandestinely I absorb the nourishment of love. And why so secretively? It certainly is not as if love needed the incitement of any mystification; but it is partly due to my being accustomed to it from an earlier time and even more from the time of preparation for this *tentamen rigorosum* [rigorous examination], and it is partly due to my thinking that I owe it to her. It is indeed indefensible for a man to misuse the more free association with the opposite sex that our milieu permits, as they say, to make passes. It is entirely unpredictable to what extent

and in what way this making passes can have a disturbing effect on a girl or have a disturbing effect on the one to whom
she will some day belong. I know very well that falling in love
can eliminate insignificant cares, and yet if I were in love with
a girl it would always pain me, it would always upset me, to
know that she had been the object of a philanderer's attention.
She might far better have been actually engaged or married,
for every more earnest expression of the erotic does not disturb as does this indeterminate kind that for precisely this reason is a flirtation. This is the attitude I would want someone
else to have toward me; this is the attitude I want to have toward him, for I am far from being so brazen as to take it for
granted that she is going to belong to me. But whether she
becomes mine or she does not become mine (what a short
process language can make of it, and yet at other times language is in loving connivance with the prolixity of sorrow),
my judgment remains unchanged. If she is to belong to another, then it is my wish that my thought, swiftly slain, may
flee back into my interior being and leave nothing, not a trace,
in the outer world.[26]

Nor am I so reserved because I wish to take her by surprise
by means of some mystification. Of what help would that be
to me? Then, of course, I would have to presuppose that I was
a first-rate fellow who could easily make her happy if only she
were good enough. I do not know whether any such thought
can arise in the brain of someone who is in love; in mine it has
no lodging. I feel all too keenly the responsibility, and what it
would mean to take by surprise with cunning and then—cun-
ningly shift the weight of responsibility onto myself? If she
ever did become mine and I were obliged to admit to myself
that I had used scheming against her, [27]I would be as if demolished in all my happiness, for the past could not be undone—
indeed, not even fabricated for the imagination, since even her
own interpretation would contain nothing about how everything would have been different if this had not happened. I do
not know if cunning can ever be united with the erotic, but
this I do know, that when one is struggling with God and with
oneself whether *to dare* to follow the beckoning of love,

VI
191

whether to dare to reach for the desire that is the eye's delight and the heart's craving, then one is protected against this kind of going astray. But this is the reason I am so cautious, cautious to the very last moment—ah, what if there came to my interior being a counterorder that I should not have presumptuously intervened disturbingly there, and I should not only have the pain of an unhappy love affair [28]but would also have to make the retreat of repentance. If there were a magic word, if there were a rune that could make her mine, I do not know whether I would have sufficient earnestness with respect to the erotic, sufficient sensitivity, to see how ugly any such expedient is, sufficient strength to reject it, but this I do know, when one is bound as I am, one is not tempted.

However, the fullness of time is approaching. For about a whole year now, ever since I realized I was in love with her (for prior to that time I had, of course, seen her), I have secretly and clandestinely been absorbed in this love. I have seen her at parties, seen her in her home; I have followed her path without being observed. In a way the last was my favorite, partly because it satisfied the secrecy of love, partly because it did not make me uneasy with the fear that someone would discover it, which could affront her and prematurely snatch me, irresolute, out of the school of experience. This year, my year of preparation, has its own fascination for me. Through everything else I undertook, the silken cord of erotic love [*Elskov*] was entwined as in the Americans' anchor ropes,[29] and everything in which I engaged was in exact proportion to it. Whereas an anchor rope can have no presentiment of the storms in which it will be tested, I imagined many a terror and drilled myself in it while the pleasure of love hummed along with the task. An enthusiastic student studies diligently for his examination; how much more, then, was I bound to be inspired to engage in such exercises that in a totally different sense were to me the *conditio sine qua non* [indispensable condition].

How expert I became is comprehensible only to someone who knows what it means to attempt nothing, not the slightest thing, except by virtue of reflection, which is like someone's having to use an artificial leg for walking and not being able to take a step without it, and at the same time wanting to conceal from people (something that can be successfully done in regard to reflection) that it is an artificial leg. A person needs to know only how much he does spontaneously in order to know what it means not to do the slightest thing without calculation. He needs to know the difference between coming to a lively gathering and being promptly happy and, on the other hand, coming out of the deepest darkness of depression and yet arriving precisely at the time stipulated in the invitation and with the kind of blithe spirit that the company and surroundings demand. If one is not in love, one becomes weary on the way.

Once a week she went to singing lessons—this I knew. I knew where her singing teacher lived. Far from making any attempt to force my way into this circle, I wished only to watch her secretly. Fortunately, it so happened that on the same street there lived a pastry baker whose shop she passed when she went to her lessons and when she returned. Here I had my resting place. Here I sat and waited; here I watched her, myself unseen; here the secret growth of love increased and was enjoyably encouraged before my eyes. It was a second-rate café and I could be fairly sure of not being taken by surprise. Some of my associates, however, became aware of it. I made them believe that the coffee was incomparably the best in the entire city—in fact, with great feeling I even urged them to try it. A few of them went there one day and tasted it—and of course found it to be poor, as it indeed was. I argued with them vehemently. As a result, when they and some others were discussing why I always went to that café, one of them said, "Ah, it's just his usual contrariness! Just as a whim he claimed that the coffee was superb, and now merely to be in the right he forces himself to drink the bilge. That's the way he is—a good head but as stubborn as they come, and the way to pay him back, as with Diogenes, is not by contradicting him but by ignoring him[30] and *in casu* [in this case] his visits to the café." Another one thought that I was quite disposed to fixed ideas, and he found it amusing that I could actually be-

VI
193

lieve that the coffee was good. Basically, however, all of them
were wrong, because to my taste, too, the coffee was bad. On
the other hand, they were not wrong in paying me back by
granting my wish to be left in peace with my pastry baker and
his coffee. If I had pleaded with them about it, I could hardly
have been so secure. I drank the coffee, did not think much
about it, but here was the place I waited, here it was I nourished my love with the longing and refreshed it with the sight,
and from here I took much home with me when the sight had
vanished. I never dared sit by the window, but when I sat in
the middle of the room, my eye could take in the street and
the sidewalk on the other side where she walked; but the passerby could not see me. Oh, what a beautiful time, what fond
recollection, what sweet unrest, what a happy sight—when I
adorned my hidden life with the magic of love!

When I attended grammar school as a boy I had a Latin
teacher whom I frequently recall. He was very capable, and
by no means was it the case that we learned nothing from him,
but at times he was somewhat strange or, if you choose to
look at it that way, somewhat absentminded. Yet his absent-
mindedness was a matter not of losing himself in thought,
falling silent, etc., but of occasionally speaking suddenly in a
completely different voice and from a completely different
world. One of the books we read with him was Terence's
Phormio. It tells of Phaedria, who fell in love with a cither
player and was reduced to following her to and from school.
The poet then says:

> *ex advorsum ei loco*
> *Tonstrina erat quaedam; hic solebamus fere*
> *plerumque eam opperiri, dum inde rediret domum*
> [right opposite
> was a barber's shop; that's where we used
> generally for the most part to wait for her to
> come out and go home].[31]

With pedagogic gravity the teacher asked the pupil why *dum*
in this instance takes the subjunctive. The pupil answered: Because it means the same as *dummodo* [if only]. Correct, replied

the teacher, but thereupon began to explain that we were not to regard the subjunctive mood in an external way as if it were the particle as such that took the subjunctive. It was the internal and the psychical that determined the mood, and in the case at hand it was the optative passion, the impatient longing, the soul's emotion of expectancy. Thereupon his voice changed completely, and he went on to say: The person sitting and waiting there in that barber shop as if it were a café or a public place such as that is not an indifferent man but a man in love waiting for his beloved. In fact, if he had been a porter, a chair carrier, a messenger, or a cabdriver who was waiting there, then the waiting could be thought of as occupying the time while the girl was at her music and singing lesson, which is not to be considered subjunctive but indicative, unless it was the case that these gentlemen were waiting to be paid, which is a very mediocre passion. Language really ought not to be allowed to express that kind of expectation in the subjunctive mood. But it is Phaedria who is waiting, and he is waiting in a mood of: If only she, if she would only, would that she might only soon, soon come back; and all this is appropriately the subjunctive mood. There was a solemnity and a passion in his voice that made his pupils sit as if they were listening to a spectral voice. He fell silent, then cleared his throat, and said with the usual pedagogical gravity: Next.

This was a recollection from my school days. Now it is clear to me that my unforgettable Latin teacher, although he concerned himself only with Latin, could have taken on other subjects as well as Latin.

A year ago I escorted her home in the evening. There was no one else who could be asked to do it. In the company of several others, I walked happily along at her side. And yet it seemed to me that I was almost happier in my hiding place; to come so close to actuality, yet without actually being closer, results in distancing, whereas the distance of concealment draws the object to oneself. [32]What if the whole thing were an illusion? Impossible. Why, then, do I feel happier in the distance of possibility? For the reason I myself have given; anything else is dark imagining. She is indeed the only one I love and have loved, and I will never love anyone else. But neither will I stoop to learn, as they say, to know her by testing and investigating her nature. She is my beloved, and the secret task of my love is to imagine everything lovable about her until I almost perish from impatience. The time and the hour may not yet be at hand; my soul is resolved.

January 9. *Morning.*
A year ago today. I count the moments; if only a chance to talk with her is granted to me, the die is cast. I have thought the whole thing over anew—her or nothing at all. God in heaven, would that this might turn out happily! To pray about her, I would not dare, except with the boundless reservation that makes me pray not about her but about what is beneficial for me. I have never dared to pray to God about anything in any other way, have never wished to pray in any other way. No doubt a person is closest to God on the shortcut of resignation, but this shortcut is a complete journey around life. In a certain sense I fear her Yes almost more than her No. Intimate as I am with silence and with dark thoughts, a No suits me better. But a Yes—yes, that is my only wish. After all, it does not have to suit the rest of me; to me it will mean that just as I have a dark corner in my soul where I am a lodger in depression, so now joy will also live with me; when I belong to her, I shall be able to concentrate my whole soul on making her as happy as it is possible for me. I ask no more in the world than that my soul might still have one abode where joy is at home, one object upon which I can concentrate in order to make happy and to be made happy.

I have not cared to test her or, as they say, to learn to know her. Constantly running through my mind is the verse: Martha, Martha, you have so many cares; one thing is needful.[33] This one thing needful is: she is the beloved. I think that we do suit each other in this way: if I am good enough, she is always so. Of dangers I have no fear, nor of self-sacrifices, either, so far from it that I almost find a joy in the absurd wish that she was unhappy. Truly, the only thing I fear is that she might be far happier without me.

I have, however, almost spied on her surroundings, her life situation. Fortunately these are propitious for me. Her family lives in almost idyllic peace. Her father is a serious man, and the mother's death has mollified his nature and diffused a friendliness that certainly has something sad about it but also something open and inviting. Cheerfulness is not turned away from this place, but neither is happiness sought outside or in the prolix company of every Tom, Dick, and Harry. The mother's death has helped the children to draw closer together more earnestly and to center their thoughts on their home, where the father, not without sadness but all the more solicitously, protects his children and not ungraciously lets himself be rejuvenated by the legitimate demands of the young people upon life. That is just as I wish it to be. Her surroundings are the kind that favor my undertaking and the happiness of my future more than a duenna favors the knight's understanding with his beloved. I would not dare to tear a girl out of her accustomed surroundings and transplant her in an alien way of life.[34]

So come, then, hour of opportunity. I want to speak to her; I do not want to write or to appeal to any third party. It is my belief that a love in all honesty, an inwardness of conviction, a resoluteness of choice give the short word, give the voice itself, an expressiveness, a trustworthiness that to the person involved is more convincing and more satisfying than the result of the deliberations of fathers and friends, who still do not know one. What I want to say can be short, the shorter the better, just so it is said face to face. If I had eloquence, if I had the power to fascinate, how uneasy I would be lest I use it, and if I did use it, I would eventually pay most dearly for it. I fear no one as I fear myself. Woe is me if I discovered that there had been a single deceitful word in my mouth, a single word by which I had tried to prevail upon her.

January 11. *Morning.*

A year ago today. It is really exhausting, almost too much for me to keep my soul at the peak of resolution. In the same way a woodcutter swings his ax over his head and this posture multiplies the force many times; with all his might, he sets himself, as it were, in opposition, every muscle quivers in the effort. But just for one moment. Oh, that these moments might be shortened! Oh, that I do not make a false step! If in this almost preternatural state I do not grasp an actuality, if this potentiation in the service of a new reflection turns against me, then I am exhausted, perhaps demolished forever. O time, time, how terrible you are to struggle with! O man, how strangely you are constituted: to be able to be so strong and to be able to fall before nothing! Although I now feel strong, strong as a Greek god, I also realize that if nothing happens, I am crushed.

So then I met her. We met as we both were visiting the family who lived on Kronprindsesse Street.[35] The mistress of the house was upstairs with her grandparents; since my errand was to her, her daughter was so kind as to fetch her. —Thus we were all alone. Very likely a more propitious occasion would not offer itself so soon or such a safeguarded moment. The grandmother was somewhat deaf but, as old people frequently are, very inquisitive; hence everything had to be said loudly and clearly, which does, however, take some time. As she ran out, Juliane had slammed the hall door behind her and thus had locked out herself and her mother. The situation, however, did not facilitate any more prolonged expectoration or the natural deceptions of an ardent feeling, but it would compel her to use all her powers so that no one would notice anything, and if on their entering they should find her to be a little different than usual, they would naturally attribute it to Juliane's tactlessness in leaving us alone and even more so since my having to go out in the hall and open the door would give occasion for a little hilarity. The dramatic, however, is much quicker; a half minute was enough for me to survey what becomes rather prolix when I want to call it forth for recollection.

Am I, then, not perfidious; is there not something calculated in everything I undertake? Good God, if I use my sagacity precisely out of concern for her, what more can I do? The words spoken could now remain a secret between her and me;

no one, not a soul, could suspect that a moment such as this was used in this way; if it so pleased her, the words spoken could be as null and void as if they were never spoken. The situation was precisely such that it prevented her from saying anything—if in her agitation she might otherwise have uttered a word to someone, a word that she perhaps would bitterly regret.

What I did say, I do not know, but I shivered inwardly, and although my voice was calm, it was nevertheless deep with emotion; I cannot describe how, but it was an indescribable relief to pour it out. I am convinced that what I said had all the interior truth of my passion. She stood as if paralyzed; she trembled visibly; she answered not a word. —I heard footsteps on the stairs, the doorbell rang, I opened it. The laughter was a great help, and the conversation began—it had worked out as planned. Now my wish was that she would be the first to go and thereby avoid our leaving together, which could be suspicious. By leaving first, she would also be safeguarded against any questions. Very likely she realized the same, for she departed. I stayed for an hour to divert attention.

VI
198

Thereupon I went home and wrote to her father asking for her hand. Now every mundane deliberation, every sympathetic and concerned consideration on the occasion of such an important step was welcome to me and in my opinion entirely appropriate. Far from desiring to avoid this, I want every difficulty, every doubt, definitely to have its say; every danger must become clear to her. But my first words, my declaration of love, must be affirmed; it must not be thrown in with all these deliberations as just one more document. If I have kept silent so long, I also have the right to make my declaration without art, without guile, but just as my mood commands when it concentrates the full power of silent passion into a crucial declaration and at a crucial moment. This is the impression I want her to have of me, the impression I myself want to have—the rest I commit to God, as also this, but in another way.

Have I overwhelmed her? Have I made too strong an impression? Are the unexpected and a passionate outburst combined in one statement too much for a young girl to bear? Why was she silent? Why did she tremble? Why did she become almost alarmed at me? When the castle gate has not been opened for many years, it is not opened noiselessly like an inside door that turns with springs. When the door of silence has been shut for a long time, then the word does not come out like the hello and goodbye of a quick tongue; when one has staked everything on one word, when someone has willed one thing for years and years and now is to say it—not to a friend but to the one in whose hands lies its fulfillment—then the voice is not as disinterested as that of a watchman who calls out what time it is, and is interested in a way quite different from that of someone who is counting slabs of peat. Why, then, am I afraid; why am I restless; why does my reflection already want to wound me, as if there were something subtle in being silent so long, something demonic in being able to do so, something cunning in utilizing the moment, something unjustified in using the simplest means and the most honest course of action because this is perhaps the most effective?

January 12. *Morning.*
A year ago today. It is settled. So they did not make the testing period long for me. Well, I needed that, for I am very exhausted. O possibility, you sinewy, agile athlete, in vain one tries to lift you off the ground in order to take away your strength,[36] for you can be stretched as long as an eternity and yet keep your footing; in vain one tries to put you at a distance, for you are one's self. Yes, I know that you will still be the one who some day takes my life, but not this time. Let go of me, you withered hag, whose embrace is as revolting to me as was the forest hag's to Roland's squires.[37] Shrivel up to the nothing that you are; lie there like a wind-dried grass-snake until once again you come to life and once again become tough and elastic and able to eat away at my soul! At this moment your power is broken. The testing period is over—if only it has not been too short, if only no one hurried her into making a resolution, if only they made the whole matter difficult enough for her.

So rejoice, my soul! She is mine! God in heaven, I thank you! Now for a little day of rest so that I can really rejoice in her, for I know very well that I can indeed do nothing, nothing at all, without seeing her and thinking of her.

The first kiss—what bliss! A girl with a joyful temperament, happy in her youth! And she is mine. What are all dark thoughts and fancies but a cobweb, and what is depression but a fog that flies before this actuality, a sickness that is healed and is being healed by the sight of this health, this health that, after all, is mine since it is hers, is my life and my future. Riches she does not have; this I know, I know it very well; nor is it necessary either, but she can say, as an apostle said to the paralytic, "Silver and gold I do not have, but what I have I give you; stand up, be well!"[38]

VI
200

If yesterday I became ten years older, today I became ten years younger—no, younger than I have ever been. Is this a crisis? Is this the wavering of decision? *Estne adhuc sub judice lis* [Is the case perhaps still before the court]?[39] Have I really become ten years older, I who was almost an old man—the poor girl, who has to nurse one who is dead; or have I become young as I never was young—what an enviable fate to be able to be so much to a person.

January 12. *Midnight.*

Everything is asleep; at this hour only the dead emerge from the grave and live their lives over again. And I am not doing even that, for since I am not dead I cannot live my life over again, and if I were dead, I could not relive it either, for, after all, I have never lived.

In order to keep my nocturnal pursuits as hidden as possible, I take the precaution of going to bed at nine o'clock. At twelve o'clock I get up again. No one imagines that, not even the sympathetic who have enough sympathy to take exception to my going to bed so early.

Was it chance that brought us so close, or what power is pursuing me with her, from whom I am fleeing and yet do not wish to escape. To see her is as horrible as it must be for the sinner to hear the death sentence read aloud, and yet I do not dare to avoid this sight any more than I dare to seek it, which could very well be disturbing to her. If I were convinced that in order to avoid her I had gone a step out of my usual way, in order to avoid her had stayed away from some place where I am in the habit of going, I believe I would go out of my mind. Only by enduring and suffering, by deferring to every argument against my shattered soul, do I maintain any meaning in my existence. If I were to walk the street, take one step, to look for her, I think I would go out of my mind out of worrying that I had prevented her from helping herself. I dare not do a thing, dare not refrain from doing anything; my situation is like the everlasting torment of the condemned.

And today it was our engagement day! She was crossing the street diagonally to the sidewalk; I was on the sidewalk and had the right of way. She could not set her foot on the curb before I had passed; a carriage driving by made it impossible for her to have recourse to the street. If I had wanted to talk to her, the situation was as favorable as possible. But no, not a word, not a sound, not a movement of the lips, not a problematic hint in the eyes, nothing, nothing on my part. Good God, if she were sick with a fever, if this word from me were the glass of cold water she wanted, would I deny it? So I am a brute, then! No, my little lady, no, we have talked together enough! Oh, that I can talk this way about her in my thoughts, her for whose sake I will risk everything if only I understood that it is beneficial to her. But why does she pursue me? I am wrong, it is true, very true—scandalously wrong. But am I not being punished, do I not have a murder on my conscience? Have I no rights at all? Will she not be able to understand at all what I am suffering? Is it a loving girl who behaves this way? And why does she look at me that way? Because she believes that it makes an impression on me deep within. So she does believe there is something good about me. And then to want to wound someone who is tortured to death!

I made the moment last as long as possible. In this kind of encounter there is always a halt, because the one has to wait until the other has passed. I used my advantage to judge how

she looked and if possible her state of mind. I had taken out
my handkerchief and, just as one quite leisurely holds it out to
see what part one wants to use, I stood there impassive as if I
did not know her, although I was looking at her and with the
exactitude of despair. But not a word, my whole expression
as meaningless as nothing. Yes, just boil inside, for I, too,
have warm blood, perhaps only too warm; burst, my heart,
and then I shall topple over dead. That is more like it; one can
put up with that. Palpitate in the fingertips if you must, beat
upon the brain with the blow of terror, but not visibly in the
temples, not on the lips, not in the eyes—that I do not want,
I do not want that. Why did I get so worked up; why was I
compelled to discover my capacity to dissimulate when it
serves a good cause!

She was less pale, but perhaps that was due to the fresh air;
perhaps she had been walking more. Her glance ventured to
judge me, but then she dropped her eyes, and she looked almost imploring. A woman's pleas! Who inexcusably put this
weapon into her hands, who gives the madman a sword, and
how powerless he is compared with the pleading of the powerless!

When I turned the corner, I had to lean against the building.
Now if there were an intimate acquaintance to whom I would
say, "So it is," I would be able to look quite calm and collected, but when I turn the corner I am almost fainting, and if
this acquaintance were an inquisitive fellow who wanted to
spy on me, what then? Then I would become aware of it, for
just as Kaspar Hauser[40] could feel metal through countless lay-
ers of clothing, so I feel deception and cunning through any
covering. What then? Then I would not become faint as I
turned the corner, but when I had gone down the street and
the inquisitive acquaintance had perceived nothing, then I
would find the nearest cross street in order to fall in a heap.

Sleep, my beloved, sleep well! Would to God that she might
sleep all her pain away and sleep herself happy and rosy for
tomorrow! Do tightrope dancers who are parents have no father love and mother love, have they none when they place
their child on that thin rope and walk beneath it in deathly

anxiety? If the verdict that I am a murderer has not yet been pronounced, what worse can happen than that she dies, and yet there is no likelihood of that now. Either she is the rarity among girls, and then my procedure contributes something so that she is not disturbed in becoming the outstanding one, a girl whose deification did not begin with death but with grief—or she is, indeed, I would rather not say it, or she has fancied etc., and thereupon she becomes commonsensical etc.—that is, she fancies herself to have become commonsensical etc. —Stop! I have no factual information that justifies me in any conclusion. Therefore, I remain in my misery and hold her in honor. But my understanding, my understanding, it tells me this, indeed, it tells me this in order to insult me, for it certainly was not my wish that she should appear to be less than what she seemed, and neither for her sake nor my own could I wish to be saved in this manner, that is, to become the butt of ridicule.[41]

But there is nothing, nothing at all, that can help me with a little information. I impatiently and to no avail throw myself from one side to the other; when one is stretched on the torture rack, it pains all over. She can despise me—good God, that is what I want, that is what I am working for, and yet I shudder at the thought of such a lifelong martyrdom. Whether I shall be able to stick it out, whether I shall not utterly despair, I do not know; but I do know, and the power knows who by his very nature shares the most hidden thoughts, he knows that I pulled the cord of the shower bath. Whether it will crush me I do not know. —She can prepare her soul for patience, can take the veil of sorrow with an unscathed conscience—what can I do? Where shall I hide from myself, where is the resting place where the weary one can gather new strength, where is the bed on which I can slumber quietly and recuperate? In the grave? No, Scripture is not true when it says that there is no recollection in the grave,[42] for I shall recollect her. In eternity! Is there time to sleep? In eternity! In what way shall I see her again? Will she come toward me accusingly and condemningly? How terrible! Or will she perhaps have passed the whole thing off as if it were a childish prank? [43]How revolting! And yet not revolting but something worse, for was not her becoming such a one perhaps due to my silence. And I, who feared precisely that a word from me might make her a chatterbox and set her mind at rest in gossip!

January 15. *Morning.*
A year ago today. Is this how it is to be engaged? I knew what it is to be in love, that I knew—but this new thing, to be convinced that the object of love is secured, that she is mine, mine forever.

Is this the way it is to be a mother? wailed Rachel when the twins' struggle began in her womb,[44] and many a person presumably has said this to himself when he obtained what he craved: Is this the way it is?

And is it not as if there were two natures struggling within me: have I become ten years older or have I become ten years younger?

Yet how strange it must be to be a young girl, to enter into life so briskly. I believed that I would be released, that I would be changed, that I would have seen myself in love and by looking in love at her I would see myself saved—then I would have become like her, a bird on a branch, a song of joy in youth. I believed that we would have grown up together, that our life would be happy for us in our union and in its happiness understandable to others, like a happy person's greeting as he hurries by and throws us a kiss.

I understand a great deal; every reflection I hear or read is as familiar to me as if it belonged to me. But this life I do not understand. To think about nothing and yet be so lovable, to live a mixture of wisdom and folly and not rightly know which is which. If a jeweler who had become such an expert in genuine precious stones that distinguishing them was his life—if he saw a child who was playing with various stones, genuine and imitation, which the child mixed together, and had equal joy from both kinds—I think the jeweler would shudder to see the absolute distinction canceled; but if he saw the child's happiness, his happy mood in his play, he perhaps would humble himself under it and be fascinated by this ap-

VI
204

palling sight. Similarly, for the immediate person there is no absolute distinction between the idea that bursts into thought and language, as does the precious stone in its radiance, and the idea in which this is lacking. There is no absolute distinction that makes the one into the most precious of all and the other into nothing, the one into that which defines everything and the other into what cannot even be defined in relation to this.

Lovers ought to have no differences [*Mellemværende*] between them. Alas, alas, we have been united too briefly to have any differences. We have nothing between us, and yet we have a world between us, exactly a world.

At particular moments I am happy, perfectly happy, happier than I have ever dreamed of being; to me this is rich compensation for my pain; if only she has no intimation of it, then all is well.

She is silent, at least quieter than she usually is, but only when we are alone. Might she be thinking? If only she does not begin to reflect!

January 17. *Morning*.

A year ago today. What is this? What does it mean? I am as agitated as the forest's anxious quivering before the storm. What kind of presentiment oppresses me? I do not recognize myself. Is this love? Oh, no! This much I certainly do realize—that it is not with her, it is not with Eros that I must struggle.[45] It is religious crises that are gathering over me. My life-view has become ambiguous—how, I cannot as yet say. And my life belongs to her, but she suspects nothing.

January 17. *Midnight*.

What I write in the morning is from the past and belongs to the past year; what I am writing now, these "night thoughts"[46] of mine, are my diary for the current year. The current year! What a terrible mockery of me there is in that phrase! If a human being had invented language, I would believe that he had invented this phrase to ridicule me. In former days, the army used a very cruel punishment—riding the wooden horse. The poor wretch was forced by weights down on the horse, which had a very sharp back. Once when this punishment was being executed and the culprit was groaning with pain, a peasant came walking along the embankment and stopped to look down at the parade ground where the culprit was suffering his punishment. Desperate with pain and incensed at the sight of such a callous clod, the poor wretch shouted to him: What are you gawking at? But the peasant answered: If you can't stand to have anyone look at you, then you can ride around to another street. And just as that riding wretch was riding, so the current year is running for me.

Something must be done for her. My brain spins nothing but schemes from morning till night. If my conduct prior to her becoming mine in all sincerity anxiously avoided anything that could be regarded as cunning, then I have now become all the more scheming. Who would not think me a fool if I told him that now in this current year she preoccupies me more than ever. But the difficulty is that I do not dare do anything, for the slightest intimation of how she preoccupies me would be the absolutely most dangerous thing; it might lead her in false hope out into the indeterminable and let her be saved—that is, perish, be lost in half measures.

To be willing to pay for every bit of information, every word, with gold and not to dare to do it because it is perilous, since it could arouse her suspicion and hinder her in helping herself! To be forced into a thousand circuitous ways to beg for a remark *en passant* when one could have communication in overabundance, but not to dare, for her sake not to dare to have it! If I were to observe absolute silence toward my so-called nearest ones, that, too, could easily arouse a suspicion. Therefore, I have devised a formula that I say to them. Only I do not say it as a formula but say it in such a way that one does not notice that it is a formula. One can learn this from a clergyman. He is well aware that it is an old cast-off sermon he is delivering, but if he declaims it and wipes away the sweat the listener thinks that it is a real speech. In the same way, the persons concerned believe that I am conversing, although I am only reciting a formula that is decidedly stereotyped and every

VI
206

word chosen after lengthy premeditation. The opposite method is also usable—to speak about it *ad modum* [according to custom]: Your highly esteemed of the 25th inst. *styli novi* [according to the new calendar][47] duly received. There is nothing that makes passion less transparent than the style of the office, of the bookkeeper, and of the business. [48]The latter method is better. I have studied it in my own dealings with an inclosingly reserved person, and thus I know it. One should never attempt to press in upon a reserved person; then one loses. But just as a rheumatic is worried about drafts, so one can reach him by a casual reference one does not pursue at all.[49] Or one waylays him once he has let a little something slip. One can immediately form an estimate of his inclosing reserve by the difficulty he has in stopping. He regrets having said something, wants to dispel the impression. One is silent—now he is dubious about himself, that he has not succeeded, wants to make a conversational transition, and this fails. One is silent—he is annoyed at the lull, betrays more and more, if not by anything else, then by his eagerness to conceal. But when one knows this, then one performs one's exercises in time. And the art is to speak about it a little (for complete silence is unwise) and thus deftly to keep a consuming passion in firm control of the conversation so that, just like an equestrian, one can guide it with a sewing thread and, just like a driver, swing around in a figure eight.

To scheme is a distraction, nevertheless; to examine witnesses and receive information, to confer and verify, to run around the world, to be on the watch for the moment is indeed doing something even if nothing is gained; but it is unbearable to sit and bring forth wind,[50] to conceive one plan more ingenious than the other and not dare to use it because it is still more sagacious to desist lest one be betrayed; to see these tantalizing, inviting fruits that tempt sympathy by promising everything! To have passion as a gambler has, and not dare to move from the spot and to be tied only by oneself! To have the soul full of reckless courage and the mind of plans and the words available—and then to have a pen that cannot write or with great toil write one letter of the alphabet every other hour! To have passion as a fisherman has, to know where the fish will bite and not dare to cast out, or to see the float jerk and not dare to pull on the line lest the movement betray something! To have in your power the one who could tell everything, [51]to have the knife at his throat if he betrayed something, and yet not dare to use him because for me, after all, there is no relation between revenge on him and the harm he could do her. Instead of this kind of information, to have to be satisfied with a chance word from a maidservant, a manservant, a cabdriver, a passerby, and to have to make something out of that because it is a matter of one's salvation. To have to make soup from a sausage peg[52] and have to do so because one regards it as the most important thing of all! To have to sit here at night and imitate different ones to see if the voice has not betrayed something, to see that the conversational tone was maintained! Not to dare to trust anyone! Indeed, what does it mean if a person wanted to trust someone but had not dared to trust a girl he loved and whom he could encompass with a hundred spying observations! If a person were going to confide in someone and then dared to choose only the one whom he could not trust—that is, to confide in him in the form of a deception.

The only person I actually manage to learn anything from is a long way from being in my service. Yet we have a secret understanding. He knows everything; he is perhaps the most dependable of all. Fortunately he hates me. If possible, he will torture me—indeed, that I understand. He never says anything directly, never mentions any names, but he tells me such strange stories. At first I did not understand him at all, but now I know that he is talking about her but using fictitious names. He believes I have sufficient imagination to understand every allusion, and that I do, but I also have enough sense to pass it off as nothing. Yet I must count on his being malevolent.

[53]Would that she were dead; would that she had died immediately, that she had fallen dead before my eyes in that crucial moment; would that the family had come running; would that I had been arrested; would that there had been a criminal

trial! If only that had happened! I would have immediately petitioned to be executed and be freed from all these empty complications. Human justice, after all, is just nonsense, and three
authorities only make the joke boring. The prosecuting attorney and the defense attorney are like Harlequin and Pierrot,[54]
and justice is like Jeronymus or Cassandra,[55] who are led by
the nose. Everything here is ludicrous, including the guards
who parade at the execution. The executioner is the only acceptable character. Then if my petition was not rejected, provided that I myself would pay all the costs, then along with
my confidant I would have looked for a setting appropriate to
my state of mind. There I would have demanded of him what
the knight ordinarily demands of his faithful squire—to run a
sword through my breast; indeed, it makes no difference
whether it is a squire or an executioner—on the contrary, the
latter has the advantage of not needing to have it on his conscience. —Then there would have been meaning in the whole
affair.

But in this there is no meaning. I am a rogue. Correct—if I
were what I am considered to be, but I am just the opposite.
What am I then? A fool, a fantast, a quixotic knight who will
take a young girl's words so to heart. Why? Is this a theological proceeding against me, as Aristotle requires? Is there no
third position?[56] Was it a careless word? Damn and blast it, if I
examine evidence, I do it to some purpose. I took two
months; I have made attempts in all moods; she has said it in
as decisive a manner as possible. Is it a careless word? [57]Then
it must be that a girl according to her very nature is also mentally rejuvenated and begins all over again.

See, now I am certainly ready to go to bed; I feel like sleeping, I the perfidious one. Then I shall not think about anything, and above all will abominate anyone whose view of
life, by wanting to go to the defense of a girl, insults her more
deeply than I have done. In closing, I think of you, immortal
Shakespeare; you are able to speak passionately. I shall think
of the lovable Imogen in act three, scene four, of *Cymbeline*,
where she says:

Falsch seinem Bett? Was heiszt das falsch ihm seyn?
Wachend d'rinn liegen und an ihn nur denken?
Weinend von Stund zu Stund? Erliegt Natur
Dem Schlaf, auffahren mit furchtbarem Traum
Von ihm; erwachen gleich in Schreckensthränen
[False to his bed? What is it to be false?
To lie in watch there and to think on him?
To weep 'twixt clock and clock? if sleep charge nature,
To break it with a fearful dream of him
And cry myself awake][58]

At this point an eminent poet would stop, but Shakespeare knows how to speak the language of passion fluently, a language that *sensu eminenti* [in the eminent sense] then has the characteristic that if a person cannot speak it fluently he cannot speak it at all—that is, it simply does not exist for him. Therefore Imogen says:

> *Heiszt das nun falsch seyn seinem Bette? heiszt es*
> [That's false to his bed? is it]?

Allow that Imogen is right in this, that *der Männer Schwüre sind der Frauen Verräther* [men's vows are women's traitors],[59] but cursed be the paltry consolation that a woman's vows cannot deceive anyone because she cannot take an oath or swear.

January 20. Morning.

A year ago today. I cannot keep my soul in the immediacy of falling in love. I am well aware that she is lovely, in my eyes indescribably so, but I do not feel like throwing the passion of my soul in that direction. Alas, loveliness is ephemeral; it is a shame to grasp it at once. She shall not complain that in this respect I am leading her erotically astray. Indeed, I am so reserved for still another reason, because I am most unhappy when she is most beautiful. Then it seems to me that she has such an indescribable claim upon life; I cannot comprehend that every human being has a claim upon life—I alone do not. I wish that she were ugly—then everything would go better. I wonder if Socrates would understand this interpretation of

loving ugly people?[60] And yet this is the way it is: like loves
only like. If she were unhappy, it would help. But this childlike happiness, this buoyancy in the world, which I cannot
understand and with which I cannot deeply and essentially
sympathize (because my sympathy for it is through sadness,
which indicates precisely the contradiction)—and my battle,
my courage (to say something positive about myself), my
buoyancy in dancing over abysses of which she has no idea
whatsoever and with which she can sympathize only unessen-
tially, as with a dreadful story one reads and whose actuality
one cannot conceive, that is, through the imagination—what
will come of this?

So I have chosen the religious. This is closest to me; my
faith is in it. So leave loveliness in abeyance; let heaven keep it
for her. If I attain a common point of departure along this
road, then come, you smiling freedom from care; I shall rejoice with you as sincerely as I can, braid rosebuds in your
hair; I shall handle you as lightly as is possible for me, as is
possible for someone who is accustomed to reach for what is
crucial with the passion of thought and at the risk of his life.

[61]Yesterday I read a sermon aloud to her. What emotion!
Never has my soul been shaken in this way. Tears pour out of
my eyes; a dreadful intimation comes over me; the dark cloud
of care sinks lower and lower over me. I can scarcely see her,
although she is sitting with me. Poor girl, I wonder what she
is thinking! Nevertheless, let come what may along this road!
I wonder what she is thinking. She is silent, quiet, but entirely
calm. That I am so overwhelmed by her—I wonder if she
would attribute this effect to love. Impossible, to me that
would be the most unlovely thing I can imagine. When I
humble myself under God, then to believe that it was under
her! No, she does not have that effect upon me. I have been
able, can still bear, to live without her if only I retain the religious. But I suspect that the religious crisis is to bring it into
what I have begun here.

Might it be possible, might my whole attitude to life be
askew, might I have run into something here in which secre-
tiveness is forbidden? I do not understand it. I who have be-

come a master in my art, I who—alas, I do confess it—
proudly ranked myself with the heroes I found in the poets'
writings because I knew I could do what was said of them,[62] I
who for her sake and the sake of this relationship had just
brought this to perfection! Suppose a pilgrim had been wandering for ten years, taking two steps forward and one back,
suppose that he finally saw the holy city in the distance and
was told: That is not the holy city—well, presumably he
would keep on walking. But suppose he was told: That is the
holy city, but your method is completely wrong; you must
break yourself of the habit of walking in this way if you want
your journey to be pleasing to heaven! He who for ten years
had been walking in this manner with most extreme effort!

VI
211

January 20. *Midnight.*
Is there nevertheless no third party? No. Everything is dark;
the lights are out all over. Of course, if anyone was suspicious
of me and curious, the best thing would be to stay in a dark
room oneself. How rewarding it is to be inclosed within oneself; I truly cannot say that I do not have my reward.[63]

If a third party did think about my love-relationship, or
someone else—for when all is said and done I am perhaps the
only one who thinks about it and am not even a second party
on the subject. But that, after all, is what I want and what I
am fighting for. Yet it is alarming to think this way in the
stillness of the night. All existence thereby becomes somewhat askew, somewhat turned around, and thereby somewhat weird. When will the time come when I shall be allowed
to examine more closely how things are going with me, what
I have suffered? —Consequently, if there were a third party
who thought about my relationship—I shall begin in that
way, and I can then begin anywhere; the only thing I cannot
do is to finish. There is a contradiction in all my desperate
exertion. To myself I seem like a person who wanted to take
his *examen artium* [final comprehensive examination] and had
studied beyond measure for seven others but had not studied
what was prescribed and therefore failed. A third party, be it
a stage hairdresser, a silk, wool, and linen merchant, a young

girl at a finishing school, to say nothing of the gentlemen who write short stories and novels—a third party would be informed at once. So this is the situation. I am a depraved man who in the intoxication of new sins has promptly forgotten the girl and the relationship. That is certain, and if everything is just as certain, we shall probably make some sense of it. And certain it is—that is precisely my consolation. Surely not many know me, but if the girl were to go to any one of those who do know me, there is not a single one who would not say that. If it is the grocer's clerk across the street—when he is engaged and all dressed up on a Sunday, he thinks of such a man with disgust; if it is one of Østergade's more common dilettantes, he feels like a knight when he considers such villainy; if it is a husband who worries his wife to death with his marital fidelity, he is appalled at the thought of such treachery. But the girl, reports the third party, she sits and grieves, she broods over every little recollection, she listens for a footstep.[64] —But the first is not the case; does it follow that the second is not, either? Would that this conclusion were right, but what does Aristotle say?[65]

Every word she has said, every look on her face, I can remember as clearly as if it were yesterday, and every flimsiest hint about her is promptly set in circulation among my deliberative thoughts. The most nonsensical thing becomes the object of the most enormous efforts. In antiquity there were those who assumed that the principle of existence was a vortex.[66] So is my life. At times it is an atom, which cannot be seen by the naked eye, a mere nothing, that sets the vortex seething. [67]My pride prohibits me from disdaining the least thing; my honor does this, and if one is so alone in this as I am, one is obliged to be very careful. Things that I ordinarily would let go in one ear and out the other must now have significance, absolute significance. If a religious fanatic had but a single dubious Bible passage to cite, to what effort he would go to demonstrate its authenticity so that he could erect his system upon this sure foundation! And a Bible passage is nevertheless always something, but one word from her, a comment she did not know she made about the tea, that is little. Yet it is indeed possible that a secret lay therein—it is just possible. Who but me understands this? But I do, after all, have a support in myself, for who would ever dream that I could be such as I am. *Ergo*—yes, it is correct, absolutely correct: it is possible. It is possible that she was just as skilled in reflection as I am. Indeed, if my honor and my pride, my depression, did not put the thumbscrews on me, I would hardly feel the force of this syllogism. But I do not want it any different. If it could be undone, if it were possible—oh, if this were so, I would be convinced that I had acted to the best of my ability, had done everything that understanding and madness can dredge up; I would be convinced that undoing it would not come as a new whim but as a potentiation of the logical consequences; I would be convinced that I had done everything to thrust her from me, if this could save her, and everything to keep my soul at the peak of desire so that I might be the same. Heaven be praised, that is what I am right now; my hope is that I shall keep on as long as it is required. There is indeed nothing as strengthening as consistency, and nothing as consistent as consistency itself. I have still not counseled with flesh and blood;[68] my soul's passion steadily keeps the sail set for the wind of resolution. Just as the sailor says that the ship is sailing steadily at the same speed, so I dare say that I am steadily standing still at the same speed. She has pleaded with me; it is her plea that plunges me into despair.

My suffering is a punishment. I accept it from God's hands; I have deserved it. In my youth I have often quietly smiled at erotic love. I have not scoffed at it, have not done a thing to hold it up to ridicule—it occupied me too little for that. [69]I have lived only intellectually. When I read in the poets the speeches of lovers, I smiled because I could not understand that such a relationship could occupy them so much. The eternal, a relationship with God, a relationship to the idea—this stirred my soul, but I could not grasp something so intermediate. Now—well, now I am suffering, I am doing penance, even if I am not suffering in a purely erotic way.

VI
213

January 25. *Morning.*

A year ago today. Religious presuppositions she does not
seem to have at all. So a metamorphosis can occur. And yet
what will my little influence be when compared with the originality of childhood. If only I would not gain too much power
over her, either. If only the awkward situation that may come
about along this road does not intervene—that I become her
religion teacher instead of her lover, that I become the autocrat
instead of her beloved, that I become superior to her and manage to destroy the erotic element, that I barbarically cross out
her feminine loveliness and assert myself. Would that I might
lift her or rather that she might swing herself over into the
religious freedom where she will feel the power of the spirit
and feel religiously assured and secure, then everything will
be all right. Would that she not become unjustifiably indebted
to me for anything, that she not ever foolishly fancy that she
is. Even if my depression cannot fulfill her youthful, beautiful
claim on life (and God knows whether or not it is my depression that tortures my feelings with exaggerations), well, then
I shall regard her love as a sacrifice she makes. Can love
[*Kjærlighed*] be appraised or paid for more highly! Spiritually
I shall always be able to be something for her. We shall then,
both of us, grow older; there indeed comes a time when youth
does not crave in the same way, and then in a distinctive sense
our love will have the years ahead of it. Or is, then, the most
enviable love that whose most beautiful time was when the
lovers could sweep out onto the floor in a waltz?

She is reserved, quiet, entirely calm; when someone is present, she is as cheerful as ever.

January 26. *Midnight.*

Alas, if it were possible, if it were possible! My God, every
one of my nerves is probing, as it were, out in existence; they
are feeling their way to see whether there would be some indication that we still might turn out to be suitable for each
other, that until then I would have maintained the strength to
keep my soul and my love at the peak of desire *per tot discrimina*
[through so many perilous chances],[70] and that she would

VI
214

have promptly found her bearings without looking to the
right or to the left. What a tremendous reward for all my misery! If the whole thing were to be but a day, if my wedding
day and the day of my death were to be the same, what over-
payment for all my toil and trouble, for what I, regarding the
matter from a comic angle, have given up outwardly and
what I, tragically suffering, call the overtime work of a prisoner! Ineffable bliss! What are Romeo and Juliet compared
with an understanding through such spiritual trials, compared
with a victory through such perils, compared with the happiest outcome of the deepest despair! Great, yes, it would be
truly great! If it were to happen in the wintertime, methinks
the flowers would spring up for joy; were it to happen in sum-
mertime, methinks the sun would dance for joy, and at any
time the kinsfolk would be proud of the happiness that made
us too blissful to be proud of our happiness. —But what if,
what if I grew weary and lost my energy and enthusiasm for
desire; what if, what if she perished—but, no, that is out of
the question; but what if she languished and faded away, what
if she is languishing, is fading away! Or what if she could not
persevere with me in the desert of expectancy, what if she
longs for the more secure life in Egypt;[71] or what if she married someone else! If she does, may God bless her marriage—
after all, in a certain sense that is what I want, what I am
working for. And yet at this point I have other thoughts on
the matter. Do I then have more than one understanding; is
this a sign of sagacity or insanity? Or what if she were totally
unchanged, had suffered nothing either in soul or body, but
she did not understand me, did not understand me entirely;
what if the heart in the young girl's breast did not beat violently as it does in the breast of the faithless one; what if the
blood of youth did not rush to her head as it does to mine;
what if it coursed calmly in the inexperienced girl and not as
it does in the cool soul of the sensible person; what if she did
not understand my suffering and its degree, did not understand my chilling composure, the necessity for it; what if the
word "forgiveness" between us were to be earnest, the earnestness of judgment, and not a ball we both hit in the game

VI
215

of erotic love while fidelity jubilated over its victory; what if she did not entirely understand that there is only one way to be zealots in our day and to preserve romance of soul in the nineteenth century's risible commonsensibleness, and that is to be just as cool outwardly as one is warm inwardly; what if she did not understand, did not entirely understand, that it is infamous to help by half measures and that it is being faithful to reject illusory relief; what if, when the hint came from heaven, the sign for our happiness, what if she were out of step and could not follow it—what then, what then, what then? —Ah, I am at the end of my tether, I am relapsing. If only she may be saved, I shall manage. She may do what she wishes, if only she is outside, really outside me, belongs to another, has become tired of the whole affair, or has never understood me. If I am convinced of it, if she wished it or if it just could be done (something I do not fear, for if I dare give full rein to my passion, it makes a place for me everywhere), what a sophist I would become to prove to her that she had chosen the highest.[72]

So I wish her every good. Right now I can think of ten possibilities at once—yes, twenty, despite my deplorable bias, which has a sense only for the possibilities of unhappiness; I can think of an explanation for each one in particular, and then, in turn, an explanation that will demonstrate to her that she has done the proudest thing. Suppose that she were so proud that she would not dare to admit her love for me, she who nevertheless was going to die of it; suppose she defends herself by scorning me—if only I dare, I will not be ashamed of her, I will calmly say: I have lost much, very much, or, more correctly, I have had to deny myself my dearest wish. Should I be afraid of confessing an unhappy love [*Kjærlighed*], should I change myself and my opinion of her because she changed toward me? What is a human life, after all—it is like grass, withered tomorrow[73]—perhaps I, too, shall die tomorrow. If a fool laughs at me, what does that demonstrate but that I have acted wisely? If a lost soul shrugs his shoulders at me sympathetically, what does that demonstrate but that I may still dare to hope for my salvation beyond and before God?

But for myself and for both of us, I still wish again my most blessed wish, which is beyond all measure and passes all understanding.[74] Sleep well, my beloved, sleep well; stay with me in my dreams, stay with the lonely solitary, you heavenly perhaps with your ineffable bliss. And then to rest:

> *Zu Bett, zu Bett wer einen Liebsten hätt*
> *Wer keinen hätt musz auch zu Bett*
> [To bed, to bed who a beloved has
> Who has none must also to bed].[75]

February 1. *Morning*.

A year ago today. Erotically speaking, I surely am not harming her; I am as shy in my association with her as if she were not my fiancée but merely entrusted to my care. But surely this would not have a disturbing effect on her; surely this would not act as an indirect incitement? Faithless reflection, [76]you faithless one, when a person keeps his eyes fixed on you, you look trustworthy enough and like a seasoned fighter who guarantees victory, but the instant he turns his head he sees what you are: a deserter, a deserter by profession, a deserter for whom it is impossible to be true to anyone. That she is encircled by reflection such as this, she scarcely notices at all.

She is quiet and reserved with respect to every religious impression; if I approach her somewhat poetically and lightly in conversation, she seems to find pleasure in it.

If only she is not proud; in that case she is bound to misunderstand me completely. I do not deny that once in a while there is something that seems to suggest it; in the company of others even I myself have been the subject of comments that could very well be so explained.

VI
217

February 2. *Midnight*.

[77]God created man in his image,[78] and in return man creates God in his, declares Lichtenberg,[79] and it is true that the kind of person one is personally has an essential influence on one's

conception of God. For example, I think of God as one who sanctions solicitude's calculation if a person does not have his own welfare in mind but someone else's; I believe that he sanctions intrigues, and what I have read in the sacred books of the Old Testament does not seem to discourage me. I cannot think of God without this poetic vigil over the honest invention of a troubled passion. If it were otherwise, I would be bound to become anxious and afraid for myself. The Bible lies on my table at all times and is the book in which I read the most; my second book of guidance is a rigorous devotional book[80] from an earlier Lutheranism—[81]and nevertheless I have found nothing at all to prevent acting as sagaciously as possible toward her and devising as sagacious a plan as possible for me—provided I have not my welfare in mind but hers.

This collision between sagacity and purely ethical-religious obligations, abstractly understood, is difficult enough. From great theorists and admired poets, whose remarks dropped at a luncheon are picked up and published, objects of veneration just as the evacuations of the Dalai Lama, we learn that the devil never totally reveals himself and that consequently an inclosing reserve is demonic. No attention, then, is paid to the contrast—that the whole Old Testament gives plenty of examples of a sagacity that is regarded as acceptable to God; that in a later age Christ says to his disciples: I did not say these things to you from the beginning; that he has more to say to them, but as yet they cannot bear it[82] (consequently a teleological suspension of the ethical[83] principle of speaking the whole truth). If it so happens that an individuality who was great by virtue of his inclosing reserve offers himself as a subject for poetic treatment,[84] or such a person is encountered in the course of world history, which, of course, speculation is supposed to reconstruct, then we sneak up to admire, assured by the outcome that we shall be able to understand him very well. What consolation for the person who in his need seeks guidance! Inclosing reserve, silence (the teleological suspension of the duty to speak the truth), is a strictly formal qualification and therefore can just as well be the form for good as for evil. To resolve the collision by nullifying sagacity actually means not even to think of the collision, for there is indeed also a duty that orders the use of one's sagacity. But as soon as one acknowledges this, one has *eo ipso* won God for intrigue (in the good sense). Thereby subjectivity is in turn maintained in its rights, just as every individuality who has acted and not limited himself to talking about others, to poetizing or speculating with the help of the outcome, must understand it. Most people never come as far as these spheres at all, for there always are only a few who act in the eminent sense of the word. Now, if we want to separate by designation those who experience what is permitted every human being to experience—to act—if we separate them, then we can use the demonic as the main rubric and divide as follows: every individuality who solely by himself has a relation to the idea without any middle term (here is the silence toward all others) is demonic; if the idea is God, then the individual is religious; if the idea is that of evil, then he is in the stricter sense demonic. This is how I have understood it and have found it helpful. Basically, it is easy enough except for someone who has ever been lent the helping hand of the privateer-wealth of the system and thereby in turn the beggar's staff. Only if one is so circumspect as to want to construct a system without including ethics does it work; then one obtains a system in which one has everything, everything else, and has omitted the one thing needful.

Perhaps I have not loved her at all; perhaps on the whole I am too reflective to be able to love? Now I shall proceed as follows. Should I not have loved her at all? But, my God, why all these sufferings, then? Is it not love that I think of her night and day, that I am spending my life solely to save her, that I in no way ever consider whether life will become terrible for me because I am thinking only of her? And yet I have language, I have her, I have the human race, I have every external evidence against me, I have nothing to plead in self-defense, nothing to support me. I do not love her? Is this what it is to love, she and the language and the race reply—to forsake her? See, I could not have carried on that conversation; I cannot bear it. This is why I turn to you, you all-knowing one—if I am guilty in this way, then crush me. Alas, no! Who dares to pray thus? Then illuminate my understanding so that I may see my error and my depravity! Do not believe that I want to evade sufferings; that is not my prayer. Destroy me, erase me from the number of the living; recall me as a miscarried idea, a wicked venture, but let me never be healed in such a way that I prematurely cease to grieve. Do not dampen my fervor, do not put out its fire; it is still something good even if it must be purified. Let me never learn to bargain; I still must win, even if the method is vastly different from anything I can imagine.

What a comfort to have language on one's side, to be able to say as she can: I have loved him! But if my first premise is wrong, then there is nothing to be concluded from it. But here it is not a matter of a few paltry premises one wishes to draw to a conclusion but [85]of the most dreadful thing of all, an eternal torment: a personal existence that cannot coalesce in a conclusion.

Now I want to go to sleep. For a lover it is quite possible that he cannot sleep because of the restlessness of love; perhaps I am sleepless because I cannot know for sure whether I love or do not love.

February 5. *Midnight.*

A Leper's Self-Contemplation[86]

(The scene is among the graves at dawn. Simon *leprosus* [the leper][87] is sitting on a stone, has dozed off, wakes up, and shouts:)

Simon! —Yes! —Simon! —Yes, who is calling? —Where are you, Simon? —Here; with whom are you speaking? —With myself. Is it with yourself; how loathsome you are with your leprous skin, a plague upon all the living. Get away from me, you abomination, flee out among the graves. —Why am I the only one who may not speak this way, may not do accordingly? Everyone else, if I do not run away from him, runs away from me and leaves me alone. Does not an artist hide in

order to be a secret witness to how his work of art is admired;
why cannot I part company with this loathsome shape and
only secretly witness people's abhorrence? Why must I be
condemned to carry it around and display it, as if I were a vain
artist who insisted on hearing the admiration in person? Why
must I fill the desert with my shrieking and keep company
with wild animals and while away the time for them with my
howling? This is no exclamation, this is a question; I ask the
one who himself said that it is not good for a person to be
without companionship.[88] Are these, then, my companions,
are these the equals I am supposed to seek: the hungry mon-
sters, or the dead, who are not afraid of being infected?

(Sits down again, looks around, and says to himself:)

[89]Where has Manasse gone? (With raised voice) Manasse!—
(Is silent for a moment.) So he has gone off to the city, after
all. Yes, I know. [90]I concocted a salve by which all the muti-
lation turns inward so that no one can see it, and the priest
must pronounce us healthy. I taught him to use it; I told him
that the disease did not thereby terminate, that it turned it inward, and that one's breath could infect another so that he
would become visibly leprous. That made him jubilant. He
hates life; he curses men; he wants to have revenge. He runs
off to the city; he is breathing poison on all of them. Manasse,
Manasse, why did you give the devil a place in your soul—
was it not enough that your body was leprous?

I will throw away the rest of the salve so that I may never
be tempted. God of Father Abraham, let me forget how it is
prepared! Father Abraham, when I die, I shall awaken in your
bosom;[91] then I shall eat with the purest of the pure—you,
after all, are not afraid of lepers. Isaac and Jacob, you are not
afraid to sit at table[92] with someone who was leprous and
loathed by men. You dead who are sleeping here around me,
wake up, just for a moment; listen to a word, just one word:
Greet Abraham from me so that he has a place prepared
among the blessed for the one who was not permitted to have
a place among men.

What is human compassion anyhow! Who is entitled to it if
not the unfortunate one, and how is it paid to him? The pov-

erty-stricken man falls into the hands of the moneylender, who ultimately helps him into captivity as a slave—the fortunate practice usury in the same way and regard the unfortunate as a sacrifice and expect to purchase the Lord's friendship at a bargain price, indeed, in an unlawful manner. A contribution, a mite, when they themselves have overabundance, a visit if there is no danger, a little sympathy that by its contrast can season their wastefulness—see, that is the sacrifice that compassion makes. But if there is danger, they drive the unfortunate one out into the desert in order not to hear his screaming, which could disturb the music and dancing and opulence and pass judgment on compassion—the human compassion that wants to deceive God and the unfortunate one.

So look in vain for compassion in the city and among the fortunate, look for it out here in the desert. I thank you, God of Abraham, that you allowed me to concoct this salve; I thank you that you helped me to renounce the use of it. I still understand your mercifulness, that I voluntarily bear my fate, freely suffer necessity. If no one has compassion on me, no wonder, then, that compassion has fled as I have out among the graves, where I sit comforted as one who offers his life to save others, as one who freely chooses exile to save others, comforted as one who has compassion on the fortunate. God of Father Abraham, give them new wine and grain in overabundance, and happy times; build their barns bigger and give them surplus bigger than their barns; give wisdom to the fathers, fertility to the mothers, and blessing to the children; give victory in the struggle that they may be a people of your own.[93] Hear the prayer of him whose body is infected and unclean, an abomination to the priests, a horror to the people, a trap for the happy; hear him if his heart is still not infected.[94]

Simon *leprosus* was a Jew; if he had lived in Christianity, he would have found an utterly different kind of sympathy. Whenever in the course of the year there is a sermon about the ten lepers,[95] the pastor affirms that he, too, has felt like a leper—but when it comes to typhoid . . . . .

February 7. *Morning.*

A year ago today. She has seen me overwhelmed by the power of the religious, but she does not have an eye for the religious. She knew me long before our engagement, has often enough been witness to my usual conduct as a cool, hardheaded man, almost a scoffer; [96]she believes that I scoff at everything, only not at her. Now if she were proud—I shudder to think of it; it certainly would be seductive food for pride to be adored (and thus she could perhaps misunderstand the religious emotion) by someone who scoffs at everything else.

In the presence of others, her pride emerges more clearly; perhaps it was present from the beginning, but I did not have time to discover it. Even I am a victim of it; the other day it happened in such an unbecoming way that the people present were startled by it. Of itself it is a trifle. A young girl is allowed much leeway—such a thing may only be playfulness. If only I were reassured myself, but I am afraid of worse conflicts. And if it were something other than playfulness, then I sense a colossal misunderstanding. If only she does not believe that what in her eyes is probably odd symptoms is merely erotic impressions, that this is an adoring lover who worships a goddess. Then in an erotic way she would be taking my religiousness in vain. One does indeed humble oneself under God and the ethical relationship, but not under a human being. It is true, my outer being is entirely different from my inner being, but I have never religiously scoffed at anyone. The religious is my principle of equality, and [97]my soul is not exactly suited to erotic bickering about which of us was somewhat extraordinary.

Far from asking any extravagant tenderness of amorous affection on her part, I merely want her to express herself a little more so that I can see what is taking place within her. Despite all my endeavors, I really do believe that she regards me as a very sharp critic, and this stifles her freedom of expression.

February 7. *Midnight.*

When the whale is wounded, it plunges to the bottom of the ocean and spouts jets of blood; in its dying it is most terrible.

VI
222

The herring dies at once, and once it is dead is as dead as a doornail. But sometimes, even though the whale is not dead, it lies perfectly still. If at times I spout blood in the moment of passion, and it seems to me as if I have broken a blood vessel when the words pour out, then I, too, can be absolutely still, but that does not mean that I am dead. What a mysterious power is pathos! In one sense the whole thing can be wrapped up in a package and carried in a vest pocket, but when passion lights the fire, then this little insignificant thing is seen to be a flaming sea.

VI
223

Now I want to begin in another way; I want to reflect on the relationship as if I were only an observer who has to file his report. I am fully aware that this objectivity does not help me, nor is it supposed to; I simply feel a need to drain off the almost comic aspect of the affair. Having done that, having shaken the foolishness from me, I shall again feel disposed to drag and lift tragically the same affair as a burden.

Here is the report. It is a young girl who, in other respects fortunately endowed with feminine charms, lacks one thing: religious presuppositions. Religiously she is just about at the following level (a level that presumably is seldom recorded by the pastor in the official record, for she certainly can recite her catechism)—for her God is very much like what one pictures as a kind elderly uncle who for a sweet word does everything the child wants, just as the child wants it. That is why one is so very fond of this uncle. One also has a certain unexplainable awe of God that does not become anything more. When one is sitting devoutly in church, it makes a lovely sight, viewed purely esthetically. But resignation, infinite resignation, the relationship of spirit, the absolute relationship of spirit with spirit—there is no thought of that. This girl takes up the religious and talks away about it nonchalantly. And just as the youthful temperament as a rule presumptuously says the first thing that comes to mind, which is precisely a feminine charm, she does this with religion as well. She loves a person more than she loves God. [98]She swears by God, she beseeches in God's name, and yet with regard to the religious she is only romantic in the little multiplication table,[99] and with regard to the religious she is, *valore intrinseco* [according to intrinsic value], only an ordinary dollar.[100]

Now if the opponent with whom she is matched were a thoroughly commonsensical person, he would probably respond to this rhetoric by recalling the schoolchildren who say to each other, "Do you dare to say 'by God'?" But he is just the opposite, he is religiously constructed; his romanticism has the magnitude of infinity, in which God is a powerful God, and seventy years a stroke of the pen, and a whole life on earth a period of probation, and the loss of his one and only desire is something for which one must be prepared if one wishes to be involved with him, because as the eternal he has a round concept of time and says to the one who seeks him, "No, the moment hasn't come yet—wait just a bit." "How long?" "Well—seventy years." "My God, meanwhile a person could die ten times!" "That must certainly be left up to me, without whose will not one sparrow falls to the ground,[101] so then—tomorrow, tomorrow very early." In other words, in seventy years, for since a thousand years for him is as one day,[102] so seventy years is precisely one hour, forty-six minutes, and three seconds. This is how the opponent is constituted. He thinks the task in relation to this is not to be angry with God because he is great but is to bear in mind that he himself is of low degree, is not to wrangle with God because he is eternal, for this, after all, was never a fault, but is to bear in mind that he, admittedly a miserable entity in the temporal, is nothing, that the task is to endure, not to disturb for himself the only love that is happy,[103] not to forfeit the only admiration that is blessed, not to lose out on the only expectation that endures, since the task, after all, is to endure. Now, when he is so constructed, it follows that if a person is capable of bringing her relationship with him under a relationship with God, then the schoolchild's "by God" becomes absolute—he is bound both in time and in eternity. He has, of course, enough circumspection not to respect this word in the mouth of every passerby, but he is bound to that girl, and she has no compunctions about using the oath. It is no help to him at all to know that in her mouth the word is an interjection to which she does not want to feel religiously bound at all, because, on the whole, her dialectic is the dialectic of the desire, of the pleasant and the unpleasant: by virtue of his relationship with God he must honor the claim down to the last farthing.

There is something profoundly comic in this misrelation. Every human being is indeed permitted to swear by God. Ethical categories are usually employed in forming an opinion of the conduct of the one swearing, that he either is of the truth or is a hypocrite. But this approach is utterly inadequate and can do great wrong, for such an individual might indeed just be comic. Otherwise I can make nothing of it. It is adequate even when I take a more eminent example. When the Pharisee in the Gospel is portrayed as a hypocrite,[104] this is true only insofar as he feels himself superior to other people, but the rest of what he says is comic as soon as one gives it any thought. Imagine an individual who is speaking with God in prayer and now it occurs to him to speak as follows: I fast three times a week, pay the tithe of mint and cumin.[105] It is altogether comic, like the man who lay in the ditch and thought he was riding horseback. In other words, the Pharisee thinks he is speaking with God, whereas from what he says it is clear and distinct enough that he is speaking with himself or with another Pharisee. If, for example, a saloonkeeper were to stand in a church and talk this way with God in prayer, saying: I am not like the other saloonkeepers, who give only the prescribed measure; I give generous measure, and in addition that extra at the New Year—he is not thereby a hypocrite, but he is comic instead, since it is clear that he is not speaking with God but with himself *qua* saloonkeeper or with one of the other saloonkeepers. Therefore, one should never appeal to God for help with a wish, because one thereby binds oneself absolutely. That is, if the wish is not granted, God and I are not therefore quits, by any means, for that, after all, must be left to God, but I am obliged to hold to my word. I must at all times firmly maintain that it was and is my only wish, so earnestly, so eternally my only wish that I dared to give it a religious expression. In other words, if after the passage of some time I come with a new wish and promptly send for God again just as fussy parents send for the physician for nothing, what then? Then I have made a fool of God and also made manifest that I am a comic character who, far from being a hypocrite, assumed that *to pray to God* was the same as petting papa on the cheek and saying: *Bitte, bitte* [Please, please].

Here ends the report; my understanding has received its tribute—now I owe it nothing. Come now and stay with me, you, my beloved pain! Externally she cannot now be mine (or were it possible, oh, if it were possible!), but the thought that spiritually she might not be where I am confuses everything for me. Can one human being, then, not understand the other; is there, then, no equality in the religious? —Why did I sweep her along out into the current with me, why did I make myself guilty of applying a standard to a girl's existence that only disturbs both of us! Well, now, now it is too late. Even if everything turns out all right and she really does help herself out of her misery or never was so deeply immersed in it, for me the religious nevertheless is so much the true meaning in life that it terrifies me if she is healed only in temporal categories. If one does not have this kind of concern, it is easy enough to retire into empty, glittering glory, like a chosen one; but if my, if you like, high standard has disturbed her life, then she in turn holds me with her, if you please, lesser standard; she with her lesser standard is a mighty sovereign to me, because without her I am unable to complete any view of life, since through her I sympathize with every human being. For me, without much knowledge of people, it has been my comfort and likewise my victory over life, my relief from the differences in life, that one may require the religious of every individuality. And yet here I have run up against an individuality from whom I am not sure I dare to require this, to whom I might be doing a wrong thereby. But on the other hand, if just one single individuality like this exists, consequently if religiousness is supposed to join hands with genius and talent,[106] then I am powerless, for this thought is really my life's idea, which gives me the bold confidence not to envy the outstanding and the talented, the calmness of mind not to be alarmed to the point of irresoluteness by the misery of someone who externally is more miserable than I am.

To go on. Suppose, when all is said and done, she perhaps admired me more than she loved me; suppose she cherishes the dismal thought that I was an important personage. Then how difficult it will be for her, perhaps at one time intoxicated with a fantasy dream that I worshiped her, to recover from such an impression. And here again it is my fault that she is humiliated in this way! When one does not have such an anxious concern, then I can well understand that it is tempting to be counted among the elite, the object of much attention. This does not tempt me: I wished to be a rank-and-file soldier, indistinguishable from all the rest.

Fearing that she would misunderstand and would venture out into the infinite, I do not even dare to give my external existence a proper religious expression. She is unable to do that, not yet. What will save her, as I thought at first and still do, is a certain healthiness of temporality. I am convinced that even in the most crucial moment, when I made the separation between us, she did not comprehend resignation. Either she believed: now I shall die and then it will be over, but that is not resignation; or she hoped altogether spontaneously, but that is not resignation; or she picked herself up internally by virtue of her natural healthiness and was stimulated precisely now to take hold of temporality—but that is not resignation.

VI
227 Be still, then. It is a matter of being as insignificant as possible. Any suggestion from me would merely confuse and, most dangerous of all, would perhaps help momentarily. She must, however, be stimulated lest her suffering state become habitual. Her suffering state—I really do not know for sure whether she is suffering.

Reflection, however, is utterly inexhaustible. It acts just the way Tordenskjold[107] did: it uses the same troops—when they have marched by, they turn down a side street, don another uniform, and thus the parade goes on—the countless garrison.

February 12. Morning.

A year ago today. She is not inattentive when I read to her from some religious book; I myself am growing more and more in the direction of the religious. As yet I cannot attain enough freedom from care to express love more erotically, nor do I find it in my heart to do so. First comes the hard part—the pleasure of being in love will no doubt come later.

If only I have not made the whole scheme too big, if only the whole thing is not too serious for her, even though all religious moroseness and severity are foreign to my nature, and especially with regard to her, whose presence makes me as gentle as possible.

[108]So I also speak a bit more lightly to her; I converse. For me this conversation truly has a charm I had never suspected. What pleasure it is when I think of the future, for in my eyes this conversation will continue to have something so appealing, something so refreshing for my soul, that I crave no other balm than this. She is as good as entirely without reflection, but she does not chatter, either: she says one thing and then another as it occurs to her. My reflection instantly seizes upon what she said, a little modification, and I have transferred it over into my sphere, and in this way the conversation goes by turns. Then she says something in her spontaneous way, a little modification, sometimes just a change of tone, and I am satisfied by the remark and have enjoyment over it. She cannot understand how such a comment by her can amuse me so much; however, she seems really gratified out of joy over the intimated high spirit that prevails in the conversation. She finds satisfaction in expressing herself, and then is surprised to see her remarks as the object of so much attention; I understand some level of reflection, add to it, rejoice over her—and thus we are both gratified. I do actually seem to be discovering that I have some qualities that could make me into an excellent husband: I have a sense for insignificant matters; I have a memory for trifles; I have some talent in introducing a bit of meaning—all of which is very good over the passage of time. If I only knew how I could become a model husband, I would spare neither time nor energy. But my trouble is that in my inclosing reserve I have an elemental flaw. And for me to be something by halves is a bitter pill.

VI
228

February 13.[109] *Midnight.*

If only something might happen. To maintain one's soul in ecstasy week after week, to maintain all my countless reflections ready to leap, to have everything ready, ready at any moment because one cannot know whether it is going to be used or when it is going to be used or what is going to be used!

[110]Today I saw her. She was pale. Oh, if one's soul is filled with anxiety, if through this one has a sense for portents, then such paleness can have significance. Macbeth becomes furious simply because a messenger coming with an unfavorable report is pale,[111] but in this case the paleness itself is the report. And yet the medical report is that in general she feels well—at least so I heard at the Hansens, where the physician was present and where she was being discussed, for when I by reason of the relationship between her family and the Hansens and the presence of the physician had a suspicion and repeated the words as a question: Who is it who is feeling so well (the physician had said these words just as I entered), they became embarrassed. And when I, not without some sarcasm, said that it did not amaze me if a physician was himself surprised at having said what he so seldom says—she feels well—but who is it, then, the physician recovered his composure and answered: Ah, it was Mrs. Fredriksen. Good Lord, I replied, Mrs. Fredriksen! Has she been ill? It was she whose husband was the judge in Skanderborg, and who later was transferred here to Sjælland. How strange etc. Then I conversed for a full hour with the esteemed family and the physician about the lady in question. It was obvious that for them the situation was as painful as it could be. Then the physician left, and I turned the conversation to the physician and the many families for whom he was the family physician, but said that I had never known that he was Mrs. Fredriksen's physician. As long as the physician was present, I did not dare say this, for it was very possible that he had spoken the truth, but the family may not have known it and knew, on the other hand, that he had resorted to a subterfuge. This way one never lacks a topic for conversation. But it was of her they were speaking: I am certain of that, for I knew that a half hour before the physician had been at her house and undoubtedly had come straight from there. So this is the medical report. On the other hand, I saw that she was pale. What torment to have to ob-

serve a phenomenon when the phenomenon itself changes in relation to the observer.

[112]At one time she had wanted to be something extraordinary—an artist, writer, a virtuoso, in short, to shine in the world. It was indeed possible—at least it is psychologically correct that an unhappy event can be a decisive impetus in this direction. True enough, but I never comprehended how she got this idea and how she could misunderstand herself in this way—as lovable as she was, she was not particularly talented. If she had been talented, I certainly would have discovered it, for my depression would promptly have seen in it an additional suffering, because I would have understood that she was bound to have enormous claims on life. But a catastrophe can certainly transform a person, and this wish, this hankering could perhaps be a valid presentiment in her soul. No wonder I did not understand it, I who from earliest youth have lived in the continual contradiction between [113]seeming to be talented in comparison with the particular individual and secretly being convinced that I was good for nothing.

I am free and independent, unemployed, the servant of no man, of no other woman, of no conditions of life. I lie along the shore in my boat and wonder whether some phenomenon will show up out there. If she could emerge that way as an object of admiration, that would suit me fine, it would be the happiest existence I could imagine—secretly to see her admired, secretly to stake my last thought and my last penny so that the admiration could be jubilant. How impatience already boils within me! I can coax people, I can lie, demonstrate everything, flatter, squeeze the hands of the journalists, write articles day and night myself—and admiration, after all, is for sale for money and for sagacity. I give up everything; it would be my happy fate to work secretly for her. And when it is achieved, when pain has energized her soul, when fortune and favor and flattery compete with each other to adorn the honored one, when her soul swells to the point of overweening pride—and she then passes by me triumphantly, then I shall dare to look calmly at her, my gaze will not be able to disturb her, for life will certainly have vindicated her against me.

[114]But still one must have a little something to hold on to. It will be a long while before I run after anonymous novels again—the last one made me really feel the ridiculousness of my fancy. If I have not learned anything else from it, I have gained some idea of how reviews come about. I have never been able to take seriously the idea of the work of a reviewer, but merely on the vaguest suspicion that she could be the writer (for rumor had it that it was by a woman), I set everything in motion to convince people that it was something superlative.

February 20. *Morning.*
[115]A year ago today. No, I cannot understand it in any other way than that I am making her unhappy. There is and continues to be a vast misrelation between us. She does not understand me, and I do not understand her; she cannot rejoice in what gives me joy and cannot sorrow over what gives 'me sorrow. But I began this, so I will persevere, but I insist on being honest. I confess to her that I regard her relationship with me as a sacrifice on her part; I have asked her forgiveness for sweeping her along out into the current. More I cannot do. I really never dreamed that I would ever humble myself this way before a human being. But of course it is certainly not before her that I humble myself; it is before the relationship and the ethical task; yet I do have to prevail upon myself in order to say it to a human being, and if I do say it, my frame of mind is not exactly that of saying it as a joke. But basically it does not make much difference, for since she does not come to know a word she cannot understand it, but here again is the misrelation.

February 20. *Midnight.*
[116]I saw her today on Hauser Square.[117] Everything as usual. It is very fortunate that she sees me so often. I myself am sure that I never go out of my way, not one foot, in order to see her. I dare not: my existence must express complete indifference. [118]If I dared to do it, and if I did not have my hypochondriacal keenness for keeping secret watch over myself and for

having intimations of possibilities, I would have taken up residence in her neighborhood long ago merely to compel her to see me. There is nothing more dangerous for a girl in her condition than to avoid seeing someone, and thereby to give the imagination the opportunity to dream.

[119]She must be stimulated so that she does not get listless and become neither one thing nor the other, neither grieve nor win. Now I suppose it will succeed. My correspondence by letter with a friend in the country, that is, a person whom I do not trust, is shared in copy with my confidant, who plagues me. Naturally it was done under the pledge of absolute silence on the part of my friend, and the confidant in turn entrusts it in writing to his sweetheart in Holbæk,[120] with the demand of absolute silence, and so it travels, all right, and at top speed. We sometimes complain of the slowness of the postal service—when one is so lucky as to have a friend's girlfriend carry the letters, they travel at top speed. I suppose that she will run on foot to the metropolis just to trot out her secret for the information of the woman for whom it is destined. Indeed, there is nothing in the world more trustworthy than a friend one is sure will betray everything confided to him, nothing more trustworthy if only one is careful about what is confided to him. It is unsafe to ask a friend to tell this or that, but if one confides to him under the pledge of secrecy something one wishes to come out, then one can be absolutely sure, for then it must come out. Furthermore, it is a rare good fortune if in turn such a friend has a friend, and in turn this friend has a girlfriend—then it travels with the speed of lightning. [121]Thus my correspondence is transmitted by way of friendship.

The more one suffers, the more sense, I believe, one gains for the comic. Only by the most profound suffering does one gain real competence in the comic, which with a word magically transforms the rational creature called man into a *Fratze* [caricature]. This competence is like a policeman's self-assurance when he abruptly grips his club and does not tolerate any talk or blocking of traffic. The victim protests, he objects, he insists on being respected as a citizen, he demands a hearing—immediately there is a second rap from the club, and that

means: Please move on! Don't stand there! In other words, to want to stand there to protest, to demand a hearing, is just a poor, pathetic wretch's attempt to really amount to something, but the comic turns the fellow around, just as the policeman who gets him turned around in a hurry and, by seeing him from behind, with the help of his club makes him comic.

Yet this sense of the comic has to be acquired so painfully that one cannot quite wish to have it. But the sense of the comic presses in on me particularly every time my suffering brings me in contact with other people.

The correspondence contains a confidential communication concerning my love affair. Everything is correct, especially the names and years and days—the rest for the most part is fiction. I am fully convinced that she herself cannot possibly have a reliable conception of me and of our relationship; I have confused the affair for her far too much for that and changed it into a witch's letter[122] that can mean just anything. Everything must be left up to her, and on no account must she have an authentic interpretation from me, for then she would never be healed. That she might be able to find herself completely again is my greatest wish for her, and I shall risk everything for that. Just a single reliable word of instruction from me would be enough for her to preserve in secret an impression of me that she must not have.

My peroration in these two months, my definitely not brilliant but nonetheless true-to-character departure, was calculated to make me seem a depraved person. This is the primary interpretation. Such an interpretation has the effect of instantly making her suffering totally autopathetic, free of all sympathy, with the result that her suffering does not become at all dialectical to her, as if she had any fault, something for which to reproach herself. The same approach must now be followed. What would be the most provocative thing to do next? I suppose even a scoundrel like that is not without a certain concern for the poor girl. A villain does indeed stand completely outside the good, but if he is brazen enough to want to communicate with it through an almost cavalier kind of sympathy—I know of nothing more outrageous. That confidential forgery bears precisely the stamp of this sympathy. It is devoid of passion but in courteous form. To keep the mood proper, I have, while writing, continually imagined someone who has had or has a toothache, someone about whose state of health one is not without concern.

In other respects, it has been abhorrent to me to write all that, not because of her, for my hope is that it will be of benefit to her, but because of those through whose hands it goes, and in turn for a very special reason. I am convinced; I bet a hundred to one that all three of them after reading it will say, "Well, he is nevertheless not as bad as I thought, he is indeed not entirely without concern." It is unbelievable how stricken with stupidity people are with regard to the ethical. By being sufficiently brazen to want to be utterly despicable, one becomes a pretty decent fellow, almost as good as most folk— because, good heavens, many a man has had a love affair and has let a girl sit and wait, but if he just shows a little sympathy, then he is really a nice fellow. And yet being a rogue is not so hopeless; salvation is possible. But to be able to show sympathy in that way is indisputable evidence that one has damaged one's own soul.

And now for a rest. I recall all my thoughts from the labor of scheming; I concentrate them on her, on my concern and on my wish. I refuse to be disturbed by anything, but I also wish to do what I regard as my duty. If it can be right to be a fool in the world for the sake of a good cause,[123] then it presumably can also be defensible to be scheming, or rather I am afraid of a belated misgiving and regret if I have left anything unattempted. I do not think much of schemes, not because I do not calculate everything to the best of my ability but because the matter is so important to me.

Oh, pain compounded! We grow further and further apart; a lifetime lies between us, and to me it seems as if now an eternity must lie between us if she really tears herself loose from me. It is as if I served two masters:[124] I do everything to work her loose, to wipe out everything between us, and then I also discipline my soul so that it may keep itself at the peak of my wish, so that if its fulfillment were ever possible it

VI
233

might be just as much aflame at the moment she is lost to me forever as it was when everything favored our union, as it was most intense of all when she knelt at my feet and pleaded. To wish is not so difficult while one is young, but to keep the soul concentrated upon the wish when secret resentment and when mortal anxiety waste away one's powers is not easy. To caper about when the horse is young and fiery and long-winded is not difficult; it is instead difficult not to do that. But when the horse is tired, when it totteringly stumbles ahead, when it almost falls down at every step—then the horse cannot caper about. But the Spirit gives life,[125] and just as an old king said: A king may die, but he must not become ill, so it is my consolation that I can die but I must not become tired. For what is it to have spirit but to have will, and what is it to have will but to have it beyond all measure, since the person who does not have it beyond all measure but only to a certain degree does not have it at all.

VI
234

[126]February 28. *Morning.*

A year ago today. Courage and perseverance! I shall reach the religious with her. This is a security that gives life assurance, or, alas! is it only a precaution, akin to putting money in the widows' pension fund. In other respects I am able to do everything with proficiency and am developing it more and more. Her youthfulness demands all my effort, and I am as youthful as it is possible for me to be. I believe it is working. A few days ago there was a man who said of us that we were a proper young engaged couple. Obviously, we are that indeed: she by virtue of her seventeen years and I by virtue of the artificial leg I use. The deception is working, as it always does for me. To express myself directly seldom succeeds for me, but to express myself indirectly and deceptively succeeds beyond measure. It is a natural aptitude I have, a reflectiveness I was born with. But I am also learning something else; I am learning the comic from the bottom up: a young fiancé with an artificial leg! To me I am just another Captain Gribskopf.[127] Yet this comedy, my secret, is nothing to joke about. The effort I do not fear, for I rejoice in her, but I do fear misunderstanding.

February 28.[128] *Midnight.*

Only this was lacking—she seeks me out; that is obvious. So, then, I have been shadowboxing; she must have a backlog of sympathy, a nerve in which I still pain her sympathetically. She cannot have received that confidential communication yet; so it was lucky that I thought of sending it. In my countenance she will find nothing. My face is no advertising publication or, if it must be, it is for miscellaneous announcements that are so miscellaneous that no one can make head or tail of them.

VI
235

As early as last Wednesday it struck me that this was the second time and on a Wednesday that I had seen her on Hauser Square. She knows from before that every Wednesday at precisely four o'clock I go down this street; she knows that I have business with a man who lives there. If she is seeking me out, then I dare to bear witness within myself that I have not gone a step out of my way to seek her out. I am so uneasy, almost to the point of madness, lest I do something that could prompt suspicion on her part, and my uneasiness then makes me assume that she is just as sensitive to the least little thing as I am.

This had to be investigated. At five minutes to four I was on Hauser Square and went into the goldsmith's shop. Correct! Two minutes later she came along. She was walking slowly, looking around; she turned in the direction of Tornebuske Street, from which I usually came. In itself, it is an excellent idea to meet on the street, where chance is always ready with an explanation. But since I separated from her, I have declared perpetual warfare on the power we call chance, in order, if possible, to do away with it—which does not need force of arms but particularly memory, a memory that is just as niggling as chance itself. I quickly bolted out of the shop, ran around by Suhms Street, and came down Tornebuske Street precisely at four o'clock, exactly as usual.

We met, passed each other; she was a little self-conscious, perhaps because she was a little disquieted by what amounted almost to taking a forbidden path or because she was a little fatigued by having reconnoitered the terrain. She quickly dropped her eyes and avoided my glance.

So this much is clear—my machinations are more or less futile; but this much is also clear—that she still does have strength.

For me there is nothing to do. Precisely at four o'clock every Wednesday I come to Hauser Square. To stay away would be most imprudent. I believe I have never been so scrupulous about time as I am with this exact hour and minute lest my coming too early or not coming might prompt her suspicion that I was waiting for her or was avoiding her, which in different ways would demonstrate the same thing—that I was concerned about her.

VI
236

[129]March 5. *Morning.*

A year ago today. No new symptom.[130] When a brighter prospect appears before me, when it seems to me that everything must work out, when a happy thought visits my soul, then I hurry to her. I am really young, as young as one must be in the days of one's youth. At times like this, I do not look for some roundabout way; I rush with the speed of longing in order to be able to rejoice with her. If it would always be like this, if I were capable of always being this way, no matter what it would cost me, then it would be easy to marry.

What her state is in a deeper sense, I do not know, nor do I wish to know it. I prefer not to push her or take her by surprise, but her circumspect reticence makes me wonder. And it is somewhat unfree; it is as if she is afraid of my criticism, that what she says would not be brilliant enough. That is how difficult my external nature has made our mutual understanding for me.

March 5. *Midnight.*

Solomon's Dream[131]

Solomon's verdict[132] is quite familiar; it was able to separate truth from deception and to make the judge famous as the wise prince. His dream is less familiar.

If there is any agony of sympathy, it is to have to be ashamed of one's father, of the person one loves the most and

to whom one owes the most, to have to approach him backward, with face averted, in order not to see his disgrace.[133] But
what greater blessedness of sympathy is there than to dare to
love as the son wishes to love, and then to have the added
good fortune of daring to be proud of him because he is the
chosen one, the distinguished one, a nation's strength, a country's pride, God's friend, the future's promise, celebrated in
his lifetime, highly praised in his memory! Fortunate Solomon—that was your fate! Among the chosen people (how
glorious was this alone, to belong to them!) he was the king's
son (enviable fate!), [134]the son of the king who was the chosen
one among kings.

So Solomon lived happily with the prophet Nathan.[135] The
father's vigor and the father's achievements did not inspire
him to great exploits, for, after all, there was no opportunity
left for that, but they inspired him to admiration, and admiration made him a poet. But if the poet was almost envious of
his hero, the son was blissful in his devotion to the father.

Then one night the youth paid a visit to his royal father.
During the night he is awakened by hearing movements
where his father is sleeping. He is seized with horror; he fears
it is a knave who wants to murder David. He approaches
stealthily—he sees David crushed in spirit, he hears the cry of
despair from the penitent's soul.

Faint, Solomon goes back to his bed; he falls asleep, but he
does not rest. He dreams—he dreams that David is an ungodly man, rejected by God, that the royal majesty is God's
anger with him, that he must wear the purple as a punishment, that he is condemned to rule, condemned to listen to
the people's approval, while the righteousness of the Lord secretly and hiddenly passes judgment upon the guilty one. And
the dream intimates that God is not the God of the godly but
of the ungodly, and that to be singled out by God one has to
be an ungodly person, and the horror of the dream is this contradiction.

As David lay on the ground crushed in spirit, Solomon rose
from his bed, but his mind was crushed. Horror seized him
when he thought of what it means to be God's chosen one.

VI
237

He suspected that the saint's intimacy with God, the uprightness of the pure and faultless man before God, was not the explanation, but that secret guilt was the secret that explained everything.[136]

And Solomon became wise, but he did not become a hero; he became a thinker, but he did not become a man of prayer; and he became a preacher, but he did not become a believer; and he could help many people, but he could not help himself; and he became sensual, but not repentant; and he became crushed but not raised up again, for the power of the will had been overstrained in lifting what was beyond the lad's strength.[137] And he staggered through life, tossed about by life, strong, supranaturally strong—that is, womanly weak in the bold infatuations of the imagination and in amazing fabrications, ingenious in the explanation of ideas. But there was a split in his being, and Solomon was like the invalid who cannot carry his own body. He sat in his harem like a decrepit old man, until desire awakened and he shouted: Strike up the tambourines; dance before me, you women. But when the Queen of the East came to visit him, lured by his wisdom, his soul was rich, and the wise answers flowed from his lips like the precious myrrh that flows down the trees in Arabia.[138]

VI
238

March 7. *Midnight.*

[139]On Wednesday I did not see her. Presumably she has now received the confidential communication; confidential it certainly was—it was entrusted to frailty and dishonesty. Or perhaps she came a bit earlier or a bit later—I do not know, for I always come on the dot, not a minute before, not a minute after, not a tempo faster one time than the other—I do not dare. Only someone who has an idea of the sagacity and cunning involved in utilizing what is most insignificant will grasp what such an ascetic renunciation of the most insignificant means.

My head is tired. Oh, if only I dared to surrender to rest and sing myself to sleep in sad recollection! If only I dared, like a deceased person, to take away the pain and recall what was beautiful. But I dare not do that, for I promptly would be deceiving her. I dare not do that, for I am alive; after all, I am still in the middle of the action, the play is far from over. Is the play not over? For me it certainly is not over, for the recent past is so far from being an epilogue that the engagement was rather a prologue and the play began when it was broken. And yet there is no action; nothing happens. Nothing happens visibly and externally, and all my efforts go to keep me from acting and yet keep me personally acting κατὰ δύναμιν [according to potentiality]. What is all this for? Why do I do it? Because I cannot do otherwise. I do it for the sake of the idea, for the sake of meaning, for I cannot live without an idea; I cannot bear that my life should have no meaning at all. The nothing I am doing still does provide a little meaning. Any other attempt to forget, to begin all over again, to clink glasses with a friend and drink *dus*[140] with a congenial person is impossible for me, although I well realize that my life would then be regarded as having deep meaning. Perhaps there is something wrong with my eyes, but I have never seen a friendship in which the one fired up the other to risk the utmost for an idea that has a bearing on personal existence. But I certainly ὁ have seen that—because the other (ὁ ἕτερος) does not have the modesty about oneself that everyone has in his innermost being for a period—I have seen that their association taught them both to haggle and not to take the world too seriously. Only a relationship with God is the true idealizing friendship, for the thought of God penetrates to the point of separating mind and thoughts[141] and does not arrive at an understanding through chatter.

I am doing this nothing and this everything because it is the highest passion of my freedom and the deepest necessity of my being. If Simon Stylites[142] in any way was able to relate the idea of God to standing on a tall pillar and bending himself into the most difficult positions and frightening away sleep and searching for terror in the crises of balance, then in my opinion he did well to do that. His mistake was that he did it in the eyes of men, that he was nevertheless a ballerina, that he, just as she, bending in the most difficult positions on the floor, seeks public applause. This I have never done, but I certainly am doing as he did—I am frightening away sleep and wrenching my soul.

This is not morbid reflection on my part, for during this whole affair my principal idea has been as clear as day to me: to do everything to work her loose and to keep myself at the pinnacle of my wish. I do not think up a new purpose every day, but my reflection certainly can think up something new in connection with my purpose. I wonder if the man who wants to be rich in this world is morbidly reflective when he sticks firmly to his resolve but in the form of calculation reckons everything without changing his first plan; I wonder if he is morbidly reflective when he sticks firmly to his resolve but when he sees that it will not work with one method then chooses another? If I had been morbidly reflective, I would have acted externally long ago and broken my intention to remain absolutely still and yet absolutely alert. Indeed, it would be much easier if I only had to stay awake like one of the bridesmaids,[143] only keep my lamp lit, and otherwise be able to let my soul be without passion, but I do not dare to do that, for then I would be imperceptibly changed and would not hold myself entirely unchanged on the pinnacle of my wish with the flexibility of passion. This is what I really want; if I am changed, then it is against my will; praise God, to date this has not happened.

March 9. *Morning*.

A year ago today. No new symptom. Where we are, I do not know, and I shall not be in a great hurry with any exploration.

March 15. *Midnight*.

[144]I did not see her yesterday, either. Perhaps that meeting on Hauser Square was just accidental, or perhaps it was an attempt she wanted to make out of concern for me. Perhaps she has received my confidential communication; perhaps it did not have a stimulating but merely a depressing effect; perhaps she chooses finally to pine away, to be drugged in the analgesic relief of quiet sorrow. Suppose she were to move to the country, suppose she did not wish to live in the old surround-

ings, could not stand it but preferred to have a strong, decisive way to express that she was offended; suppose she became a lady's companion in a noble family or a governess.[145] Good God, to have a creditor like that who has the power of life and death over me! And not to dare to discharge the debt, and that not daring to do it must be precisely one's humiliation! She probably does not dream what a powerful force she is for me, that she determines the course of my life, that by a step such as the one feared she can plunge me into the deepest despair. So this is the situation: if I manage to work her loose or she works herself loose—in short, if she becomes herself again—I shall have arrived at the very point where, concerned about my own pain, I can work for my own cause. My life before I was joined to her was like my being subject to the painful third degree; then I was interrupted and called out into the most appalling decisions, and when I am through, if I ever am through, then I can begin with myself again where I left off. Of course, I have learned what is even more painful. And if this does not happen, if she remains as she is, then I am a beggar, a pauper, yes, a slave in the outermost darkness.

And yet she did remark that she might wish to be located in the country. And such a remark, a word from her, a whim, a comment of which she perhaps was no more aware than one is aware of what one says while sleeping, such a word is sufficient for me. I myself seem to be like a child just beginning school and trying his hand at his first exercises in the practice of his mother tongue: forming a sentence from a given word.

Today I accidentally heard from a cabdriver that her father had hired a carriage to drive about forty miles out to a country manor. What could he want there, he who almost never goes beyond the city ramparts except when riding horseback, and then four miles at most, he who has no connections out in the country. —Just suppose—the phrase rings in my memory, and the drill exercises commence. The drill exercises! Suppose she really has made a decision, suppose she insists on being offended, wants it to be in the open, wants to despair and to have a distinctive form of desperation.

Good God! Only not this, everything else, only not this!

Cursed be wealth and earthly tinsel and being or seeming to be somebody important in the eyes of the world! Would that I were a workhouse inmate, a poor wretch of a man, then the misrelation would be something else again. True enough, in the eyes of the world I am a scoundrel. In the eyes of the world—what are the eyes of the world but blindness, and what is the world's verdict? I have not found ten men who are capable of judging rigorously. Or am I not honored and esteemed as before, do I not enjoy more recognition than before, and in the eyes of the world is this not the necessary qualification, the justification for being a scoundrel, or at least for having an extraordinary *ingenium* [natural talent] for becoming one? Let it choose between an abandoned girl who bows her innocent head in sorrow and seeks a hiding place in the country so that she can grieve—and an actor in the theater of life, a brazen fellow who keeps his head up and defies everybody with his proud eyes—the world's choice is soon made. A man is given a lifelong fine for an accidental injury, but I, I have no verdict pronounced on me. Condemned! I incite people against me, and they shout, "Bravo!"; I wait for them to kill me, and they carry me in triumph. I tremble, I doubt whether I have the strength and the courage to bear the world's verdict, whether I do not owe it to myself to place myself in a better light, but I do not falter, and I pull the cord to the shower—and the world's judgment is utterly favorable.

But, merciful God, do not let this happen, do not let it happen. I despair, I wrestle with you, I rush out there, I win her once again, I give up everything in order to challenge with gold all the splendor of the manor house, I have a wedding, and I shoot myself on the wedding day.

But I must go out there; I must see what he wants out there. Alas, I do not dare to ask anyone about anything, not for anything. It is easy enough to take the vow of silence when one would rather not have anything more to do with the world, but to have to be silent when one is as concerned as this!

March 17. *Midnight.*

False alarm. Right now I have driven a hundred miles in sixteen hours, I have been nearly dead with anxiety and impa-

tience—and for nothing. My life has been endangered in a ludicrous way—and for nothing. A clumsy lout of a mail-coach
driver falls asleep and the horses along with him. In a fury, I
jump from the carriage and hit the fellow without taking into
consideration that he was a giant compared with me. But
what one will not do in such a mood! And then they praise the
mail-coach service, and the special coach service! It is miserable. If Richard III would give his kingdom for a horse,[146] I
believe I would have given half my fortune for a team of run-
ners. The coach driver threw me to the ground. It was no use
to walk, I had to apologize, give him a big tip—and we drove
on.

The whole thing is a private matter. There is a farm to rent,
and a man in Jylland has a son who wants to rent it. The father
is an old friend of her father, and he is out there now to obtain
some information about the terms.

How can a brain stand all this! This is a higher and rougher
sea than is known in the Atlantic Ocean, for the swell swings
between nothing and the most dreadful of all.

March 20. *Morning.*

A year ago today. No new symptom. Whether this security
and stillness are a good sign I do not know; whether in the
spiritual sense this is growing weather and the beautiful flower
is sprouting in secret or whether stormy weather is brewing,
I do not know; I do not even dare to investigate lest I do it
prematurely and thereby disturb.

March 20. *Midnight.*

[147]There is no time at all to think about myself, and yet my
inner life is such that it can provide enough to think about. I
am really no religious individuality; I am just a regular and perfectly constructed possibility of such a person. With a sword
hanging over my head, in peril of my life, I discover the religious crises with a primitivity[148] such as if I had not known of
them before, with such a primitivity that if they had not been
discovered I would have to discover them. But this is unnecessary; in that regard I can jumble and discipline myself as I
once consoled a somewhat slow-witted man of whom an-

other jokingly said: He won't invent gunpowder. I answered: That is not necessary, after all, since it has been invented. But it is one thing to learn from the catechism and memorized lessons, and it is one thing to be able to recite to the pastor, indeed, even to the bishop when he makes a visitation, and it is one thing to be able to hold forth like a preacher—primitivity in appropriation is quite another thing.[149] It is good that I do not have to teach others. I gladly pay the church dues and also put money in the offering plate; fortunate is the person who is so sure of himself that he dares to accept money for teaching.

As possibility, I am all right, but when at the turning point I want to appropriate the religious prototypes [*Forbilleder*], I encounter a philosophical doubt [150]that I would not express as such to one single person. What it depends upon is the element of appropriation. Predisposed as I am, at the turning point of the religious crisis I reach for the paradigm, but look, I cannot understand the paradigm at all, even though I venerate it with a childlike piety that does not want to abandon it. The one paradigm appeals to visions, another to revelations, the third to dreams. To talk about it, to inflame the presentation with imagination and yet retain the presupposition, the presupposition that specifically involves the appropriation element for the one who comes later, is easy enough—but to understand it!

If someone realizes his religious need so deeply that he presumably could even do without the pastor and then has a philosophical skepticism that exactly matches it, the prospects are not quite the best. But if I only manage to get through that year of mourning when I shall mourn for her (and my year of mourning is not defined astronomically, it can come to be five and ten years and my whole lifetime, but it is defined by her), then I can plunge into these conflicts, and things will go all right. I am determined to persevere to the end; I will not run away from it. [151]I will not be clever with phrases by which one deceives, like schoolboys who in the front of the book write "See the middle," and in the middle write "See the end of the book," and at the end of the book jeer at the one who was tricked. It is my conviction that the will is of primary importance even in connection with thinking, that talents ten times as good without an energetic will do not constitute as good a thinker as talents ten times as poor combined with an energetic will: the superb talents help to understand much, the energetic will helps to understand the one thing. But just because a person wants to persevere and will persevere does not mean that one becomes a yodeling saint who, when he contemplates the course of life and of existence and world history, looks at it, and see, it is so wonderful.[152] Just let him look at life and world history and see that it is so wonderful—when I look at him, I see that he is a blockhead for sure, just like the preacher who does an entrechat in the pulpit[153] in honor of Christianity, or becomes so earnest that he is as amusing as the pastor in the snuffbox.[154] Stupidity or sweating and getting red in the face is no more earnestness (because the sweater is so stupid he is not even able to laugh) than silly gaping is religiousness. If I know nothing else, I do know that the comic ought to be used to keep order in the sphere of the religious. Aberration should not be called hypocrisy but stupidity. Calling a person a hypocrite helps him, inasmuch as it acknowledges that he has a relationship with God. [155]A pathos-filled indignant rage at speculation's embezzlement and systematic cheating, which like the Roman proconsuls drains the provinces and enriches itself, makes the system rich and life empty. Obviously what is sorely needed is a good comic drawing of a religious enthusiast. A skipper can go on swearing all day without giving it a thought, and in the same way an enthusiast can be solemn all day long without a complete or sound idea in his soul. That Gothic king refused to be baptized when he learned that he would not be together with his forefathers.[156] The natives in America feared heaven more than hell and wished to remain pagans lest they be together with the orthodox Spaniards in heaven. Similarly, many an enthusiast, if he does nothing else, makes a person nauseated by the religious.

About this conflict within me, I do not dare as yet to say "today,"[157] but I feel that I owe her much with respect to venturing. The one who has made another person unhappy can be very useful for persevering in battles such as this: the one who is sentenced to life is given rasp work[158] to do, which is mortally dangerous, but then, after all, he is condemned.

This, too, I also realize—that the unmarried person can venture more in the world of spirit than the married, and risk everything and be concerned only about the idea, and is qualified in a totally different way to be in the *discrimen* [crucial moment] of decision, where it is almost impossible to stand, to say nothing of taking up residence. But definitely this was not my reason for not wishing to marry. [159]Indeed, I, too, wished for a somewhat quieter happiness in life, and her beseeching made my own wish my one and only wish. And even if I had not wished it, I would have done it, because I always believe that obedience is more precious to God than cosmopolitan, philanthropic, patriotic sacrifices upon the altar of humanity,[160] that quietness in the fulfilling of a modest duty is infinitely more valuable and more befitting to every human being than luxuriance in the world of the spirit and prodigality of concern for the whole human race, as if one were God in heaven. Let them talk vehemently about God's wrath and the consuming fire[161] —there is also something I fear and fear just as much, and that is that I might force God to pull rank on me, make me vanish as a lie before his stately and superior majesty. An enthusiast would probably find this expression is not earnest enough; he no doubt would want me to curse piously just as the skipper curses impiously. For me it has earnestness enough, and more terror in it than the sensate notions of an excited imagination. As soon as I disdain duty, God becomes exclusive, for only in duty am I in humble harmony with his sublimity, and therefore his majesty is not exclusiveness. Therefore it is not God who makes himself exclusive, which he never does (this is paganism), but it is I who make him exclusive, and this is a punishment. This is the profound consistency: that the person who wants to come closer to God by disdaining what is simple, distances God in his exclusiveness, in an exclusiveness that not even the most wretched of human beings has to experience. Here, too, I am quick of

VI
245

hearing, and even though many a philosopher who shouts to the world Δός μοι που στῶ; [*Dos moi pou sto*; Give me a place to stand][162] does not hear it, I hear a voice that says: I will give you your *Dosmoi*, you dunces [*Dosmere*]!

No! If I had not believed that I had a divine counterorder, I never would have retreated, and as soon as this order is revoked I shall choose my wish again. [163]God forbid that the effort and the tension weaken my wish before this is allowed! My counterorder I can understand, for it goes through repentance. A repentant individuality who is able to take a whole lifetime to recant cannot advance. This is a very simple protest against a marriage. I have neither visions nor dreams to guide me; my collision is quite simply the collision of repentance with existence, a collision of suspension with a present actuality. Until it is resolved, I am *in suspenso*; as soon as it is resolved, I am free again. This is why I am doing all I can to keep myself at the pinnacle of love. As soon as she is free, the religious crises are my task.

VI
246

Just suppose, to think quite theoretically, suppose that she found herself again; just suppose that the remark about death had been only an exaggeration, not intended as a pathos-filled reply but something like the utterance when one says in the course of a conversation: I am almost dying from the heat in this cramped apartment. Just suppose she had meant it but did not understand herself, or suppose she had suffered unto death but had been victorious; just suppose I had contributed a little to this victory or nothing at all; [164]just suppose she seized the defense that she had never cared about me at all—what then? Then I would have cared about her more than ever. Good God, as if this were possible! How my soul snatches at every explanation from this quarter! Even if in some of these instances it would make me sorry for her, I ask no more. Then I would have suffered more than she; I ask no more. I would have taken the girl's *partes* [role], would have been better at the task of sorrowing, or at least just as good; I ask no more. I did not leave her in order to become the lead dancer in a public dance hall or the lead lover in a perpetual Friendship Society.[165] What for her has had no meaning, or perhaps only as a decision in the temporal realm, for me has had eternal meaning. I regret nothing, not a tear, not a single one, that I have shed for her sake; I am not ashamed of it, for it is not unmanly to be able to cry, but it is effeminate to be unable to conceal it from everyone. Indeed, if there were a scoffer who had counted every tear (oh, what a contemptible thing to do, how deceived the poor fellow is who counts the tears that soothe my soul!), suppose the number were great, suppose he were to mention the number in order to ridicule me: a man who weeps!—I will not regret them. If I were to die tomorrow, my existence would still be an epigram that makes any epitaph superfluous. I do not regret it; she has indeed benefited me, benefited me infinitely, simply by a rash word and an exaggerated expression.

You see, if this was the situation, then my position becomes difficult in an odd way. I would have to have a human life on my conscience in order to be awakened and torn out of the lethargy of depression. I humble myself under the earnestness of this thought. But then along comes my understanding and says: No, this is not true; you perceived, of course, that it was not a question of a human life, it was your imagination that created this hallucination and showed it to your depression, and both agreed that it was indeed possible. But then it was not a human life; it was a word that you perhaps would even have laughed at in many another's mouth. Yes, in one sense that is true. And yet I regret nothing; I do not regret having suffered all this pain, which nevertheless has not yet paralyzed me, although it would do that if I were to talk about it. I have felt it in loneliness, in sleeplessness, when in one second one can think more thoughts together than one can write in months, when the imagination conjures up anxieties with which no pen dares to become involved, when the conscience gives a start of alarm and terrifies with optical illusions.

But, alas, all this is indeed only a theory.

VI
247

March 25. *Morning.*

A year ago today.

[166]What is the happiest life? It is that of a young girl sixteen years old, when she, pure and innocent, possesses nothing,

neither a chest of drawers nor a tall cupboard, but makes use of the lowest drawer of her mother's bureau to hide all her treasures: a confirmation dress and a hymnbook. Fortunate is he who possesses no more than he could manage with the next drawer.

What is the happiest life? It is that of a young girl sixteen years old, when she, pure and innocent, indeed can dance but goes to a ball only twice a year.

What is the happiest life? It is that of a young girl sixteen summers old, when she, pure and innocent, sits busy at her work and still has time to steal a glance at him, at him, who owns nothing, neither a chest of drawers nor a tall cupboard, but is only a copartner in the shared wardrobe, and nevertheless has a completely different explanation, since in her he possesses the whole world, although she possesses nothing at all.

And who, then, is the unhappy one? It is that rich young man, twenty-five winters old, who lives across the street.

If someone is sixteen summers old and another sixteen winters, are they not the same age? Alas, no! Why not? Is the time not the same when it is the same? Alas, no! The time is not the same.

Alas, why were nine months in the womb enough to make me an old man! Alas, why was I not swaddled in joy? Why was I born not only in pain but to pain?[167] Why were my eyes opened not to what is happy but only to peer into that kingdom of sighs and to be unable to tear myself away from it?

VI
248

March 27. *Midnight.*

To grasp a theory is just like embracing a cloud instead of Juno,[168] and it is also unfaithfulness to her. But to use the theory as a means of exercising, to unbuckle the soul in it so as to give one's energy new elasticity, that is permissible—indeed, it is what one ought to do. After that kind of strengthening I am once again entirely hers, entirely. If I no longer hold her in my embrace, I nevertheless still embrace her, for the task of recollection in the morning hours and the rescue attempt at midnight do, after all, constitute a kind of embrace in which she is inclosed. The rescue attempt—can it really be called that? [169]Indeed, even if I had everything in readiness, of what use is it if I dare not use it? Even if I were ever so willing, of what use is it if I am bound, and keeping myself bound is the only thing that can possibly help her a little? If only I dared to get myself afloat, I would promptly be there in my boat, if it could somehow be of any help to her, for it is possible, of course, that what would have rescued her at one time has no significance at all for her now. It is unbelievable how many avenues of escape possibility knows, especially for the person who does not dare to set foot on a single one of them, for then there would be one fewer, indeed, perhaps several fewer. And yet it is a rescue attempt.

What a strange power a single word has when, as in this case, it does not accommodate itself in the context of a speech or a sentence, so that one pays attention to it only in passing, but without linguistic connection it stares at one with the incitement of an enigma and the assiduousness of anxiety! I am as depressed as if there were another kind of real truth in this word, as if I were floating on the rush-fringed lake one quiet evening, as if I heard her scream, and I took to the oars—and I saved her life, but she never became a human being again. Anxiety and pain and perplexity would have slowly picked at the lock of consciousness until despair managed to dissipate the lovely nature of this lovable womanliness.[170] Terrible! Do I not dare to order this thought to take flight? Do I not dare to ask that this thought might be taken away from me? No! After all, it is a possibility. And yet if I were just sitting with her, just that I dared to be in her presence, that I dared to do everything even if it is nothing—that would still be a relief, a relief that, like a smoldering, is an uninterrupted dull pain but not so much a suffering. Then she would confuse everything; she would believe that as before we were sitting in the boat on that lake we sailed together, and then we would exchange, if not winged words, then expressions of madness, and would understand each other in madness, and speak of our love as Lear wanted to speak with Cordelia about the royal household and ask for news from it.[171] —But to be separated from her! And if she died—then the one who was nearest and dearest, perhaps the only one who had a whole lifetime, be it short or long, to mourn for her, he would be the only one not seen among the mourners or, rather, he would be prevented from riding in the carriage when the funeral procession followed her to the grave, even though he would know as well as anyone that one who is dead is the most powerful of all!

Oh, any expression of grief, even the most painful, is nevertheless a relief compared with having none at all. To live as if I were a mute and yet have torment in my soul and the language within, not such as is learned from a phrase book but as the heart invents it; to be as if mute, indeed, as if disabled,[172] and yet have sufferings that crave the eloquence of a mime! To have to be suspicious of the voice lest it tremble if one were to speak of her, something that could be to her ruin; to have to be suspicious of the feet lest they go off the usual path and leave a betraying clue; to have to be suspicious of the hand lest it suddenly move to the heart and suggest what is hidden there, of the arms lest they reach out to her! To sit at home in sackcloth and ashes or, rather, naked in all one's misery, and when one wants to dress to have no clothes in which to disguise oneself except the clothes of joy and good cheer!

"Where exactly do you suffer?" the physician asks the patient. "Alas, dear doctor, everywhere," he answers. "But how are you suffering?" continues the physician, "so that I can diagnose the illness." No one asks me this, nor do I need it. I know very well how I suffer—[173]I suffer sympathetically. This is exactly the suffering that is really able to shake me deeply. Even though I am depressingly and sincerely convinced that I am good for nothing, as soon as there is danger I really have the strength of a lion. When I suffer autopathetically, I am able to stake all my will, and depressed as I am and depressingly brought up, the appalling finds me all the more prepared for what is even more appalling. But when I suffer sympathetically, I have to use all my power, all my ingenuity, in the service of the appalling to reproduce the other's pain, and that exhausts me. When I myself suffer, my understanding thinks of grounds for comfort, but when I suffer sympathetically, I dare not believe a single one of them, for I cannot, of course, know the other one so accurately that I can know whether the presuppositions are present that are the condition for its effectiveness. When I suffer autopathetically, I know where I am; I place signs along the road of suffering so that I can have something to hold to, but when I suffer sympathetically I go astray, for I cannot really know where the other one actually is, and at every moment I must start all over again, prepared at the next moment to be able to think an even more appalling possibility, the dreadfulness of which I must endure in order not to shirk anything.

As soon as she is free, I certainly shall not be without sorrow, but then I shall have reached the point she most likely thought I was at when she begged me to remember her once in a while. Yes, then I shall remember her, but then I shall also have found relief; I shall be sad and say with Ossian: Sweet is the sorrow of melancholy.[174] Then I shall have peace, for the person who depressingly recollects is also blessed and soothed and is as happy as the weeping willow when it is swayed by the evening breeze. But not at present. I do not fear the whole world; at least I do not think that I do—but I do fear this girl. A glimpse of her in passing, and she determines my fate until the next time. Thus she is essentially everything, everything, absolutely everything; if she is free, she is essentially nothing at all. She is the lovable, it is true, but this does not essentially mean anything. If she were lovelier than an angel, that would not concern me; a girl's beauty does not essentially concern me. I have been in love, but my soul is structured too eternally for it to despair over an unhappy love affair, [175]but on the other hand I can certainly despair over an unhappy responsibility, an unhappy understanding with the eternal meaning in life. Only the person who himself is being tried can grasp how dialectically difficult my position is. When an inexperienced person reads through a legal document, he presumably understands it, but only the practiced lawyer can reconstruct its coming into existence, only he can read the invisible writing of the surmounted difficulties, only he is informed about the contribution past generations have made to the drawing up of this document. He knows this boundary dispute between ingenuity and ingenuity, the ingenuity in the service of righteousness and the ingenuity in the service of deceit, and thus for him the single phrases do not have relative meaning but absolute meaning; therefore to him the particular expression does not have significance to a certain degree but has absolute significance, and to him a document such as this is also a contribution to the history of the human race. The inexperienced person certainly can understand it, but he cannot draw it up—indeed, he can scarcely copy it with certainty.

April 2. *Morning.*

[176]A year ago today. It was either the first or the second of this month that I decided to check on where we were. I arranged an occasion and posed a situational question to give her the chance to express her feelings. What happens? In the most candid way of the world, indeed, with an unbecoming intensity bordering on bad temper, she declares that she does not care for me at all, that she had accepted me out of sympathy and could not at all understand what I wanted with her. [177]In short, a little improvisation *ad modum* [in the manner of] Beatrice in *Viel Lärmen um Nichts* [*Much Ado about Nothing*].[178]

O depression, how you do make fun of the one who is depressed! What the poet says is true: *Quem deus perdere vult primum dementat* [Whom a god would destroy he first makes mad].[179] These days I have been wandering through the valley of the shadows of concerns in order to try to do everything as well as possible. I would not dare to admit to anyone how much I have humiliated myself. I have sat in the darkness of death deeply wounded by the thought that I could not make her happy—and what was right under my nose never occurred to me, what I can perfectly understand, now that she says it, that she does not care for me at all.

But it may have been only a rash remark, an intense outburst; perhaps she was irritated, by what, however, I am not sure. I am not going to let myself be irritated. [180]If only I were absolutely confident in my view of life so that I would dare to use force, then the whole thing would be tomfoolery. But, on the other hand, she does open up for me a bright prospect. This much is sure, that marriage is and remains for me the most difficult of tasks. I have now come to understand this much, that if I had understood myself this way earlier, I would not have entered into this. And now she seems to be far the stronger in relation to me than I in relation to her.

The exploration became an explosion, and I received the full force of it right in my face. Just as someone who has been sitting in the dark for a long time cannot immediately see when a bright light shines, so it was with me: although she was sitting at my side, I could scarcely see her. This ideal figure whom I embraced with the concerned responsibility of an eternal commitment became, I must say, somewhat smaller, so insignificant that I could scarcely discern her. My depression is as if blown away; I see what I have before me—by Jove, such a little miss!

Yet I ought to repeat the attempt in order to see if this is in earnest or not. That is, I miss a consistency of action: that she revokes the whole thing and I am rejected. But it seems that she does not have this in mind at all; what does something like this mean? We shall see.

April 2. *Midnight.*

[181]What if she actually became insane! Probably there has never been any question of danger to her life; at least now it seems to have been avoided (even if for me there always remains a troubling consistency that confused a *cum hoc* [simultaneous with this] with a *propter hoc* [because of this], but insanity! Let us see what happened.

[182]First and foremost, my exit as a scoundrel will make a substantial change, since it will set her into a quite different kind of pathological motion; it will stir up her wrath, bitterness, and defiance toward me, and her pride in particular will quicken her to go to extremes to keep herself afloat. If I had been true to her, then it would satisfy love, as well as the other aspects of the soul, to have its all in the beloved and therefore to lose its all in the beloved, but since I did not turn out to be a worthy object of her love, it would take a rare heroism to reject the consolation that offers itself most easily: to make the unworthy one as insignificant as possible. In this regard I have

supported her to the best of my ability, and I believe that if I had not taken this precaution, in which I also respected the judgment of the universal on me, I would have been directly to blame if she became insane, because my wanting to be a worthy object of her love and then wanting to behave in this manner poses for her a dialectical task that counts on a single individuality's relationship with God in such a way that only with God can he grasp the issue. Therefore it is his duty to be reconciled (indeed, to assist in the process) to being regarded as a depraved person in the eyes of everyone involved in this affair, above all in her eyes. Toward those not involved, he certainly can keep silent. This I have done.

Psychologically speaking, it is possible for a feminine psyche to become insane in two ways. The first is by the transition of the sudden, when the understanding comes to the end of its rope. One can become blind because of the sudden change of light and darkness; the heart can stop beating because of a sudden change of temperature, because the breathing is hindered by the incoming air. So also with the understanding in relation to the shift of the sudden—reflection cannot breathe, and the understanding stands still. Thus the insanity is petrifying. There is no relation or, rather, there is an absolute misrelation between what the understanding is capable of doing and the task here enjoined. The insanity manifests this misrelation. One moment decides it all; just one moment more, then this would not have happened.

It occurs in the other way when a secret passion wears out the will through reflection, and the sufferer sinks slowly into insanity. The sufferer does not become petrified but becomes deranged in a composite of conceptions that displace one another with natural necessity but have no relation to the freedom that once freely gave rise to the conceptions, until they now unfreely give rise to themselves.

The former could not possibly be the case with her; the transition was as shaded as possible; moreover, it also would have to be manifest that it had happened. The second way, which is almost the more dangerous, seems to be the one, if anything, that could commence. That is, in a certain sense the situation was made as dialectical for her as it was possible for my reflection to make it. I do not think that I have neglected to set forth any possibility; I have always tossed it off so hypothetically that it was left to her herself to find an explanation. This I have deliberately done; humanly speaking, I believe it is the only thing to do. Ah, but it was hard work, and it was almost rather to be feared that I myself would have lost my mind. She was not very reflective by nature or, rather, almost not reflective at all, but still one can never know what influence an event can have. Just a tenth of the reflection-possibilities I have set in motion—if she herself had found them out—would be sufficient to disturb a feminine head. But in her eyes the reflection-possibilities must have ceased to be tempting. That was my aim, and, humanly speaking, it is correct. Secret sorrow must itself invent and produce the reflection-possibility; then it is seductive for sorrow to hold on to it; and this is the earnest money of insanity. This is not the case with her. She can produce whatever reflection-possibility she wants to—it does not have the refreshing coolness of novelty, the alluring attraction of surprise; it has no secret prepossessing power, for she is acquainted with it. In the next place, I have introduced every reflection-possibility as completely as possible—to me, at least. I have wanted to give her the impression of a superior reflection. One does that as well as one can. Then the moment she wants to begin reflecting, it will occur to her: Ah, what's the use of my reflecting; if I could reflect as he does, but of what help was it to him? For a feminine psyche, reflection is like candy for the child. A little of it is tempting but *en masse* the candy loses its seduction.

Furthermore, if she thinks of me at times, if she hopes for a possibility of the reestablishment of the relationship, then a new kind of reflection could sneak in, one of which she herself would be the inventor. In this respect, I have worked and I work with all my powers to keep my existence completely unchanged. But meanwhile she may come to a conclusion from something she hears about me or from something in my external appearance she thinks she sees. Quite so, but at the very same moment she will consider that my reflection has

VI
254

shown her so much possibility that she cannot possibly keep up. This cannot humiliate or insult her, for it is in the order of nature that a reflective individuality has more, much more reflection than a girl. If she had not, as I hope, even to the point of nausea, acquired a concrete idea of what reflection is capable of doing, then it perhaps might still have tempted her. Now I believe it does not. I have done everything to make reflection disgusting to her (because the omnipotence of reflection when it broods on one idea naturally becomes omnipotence in dialectical rubbish when the one idea is taken away) and to make every attempt at reflection to appear futile to her even before she starts on it. I myself have suffered enough under this and still suffer; one can suck poison out of another person and oneself die—in order to divest another person of reflection one can become all too reflective. But if reflection is disgusting to her, then she will be close to a resolution and will not walk at all on the slippery path that can lead to insanity. If she becomes free, she will become free through her own resolution and not free by way of some observation and view I have slipped to her.

In all human probability, she could not become insane from love. Precisely because she was not very reflective, the transition of the sudden would have been the most dangerous for her. This has been prevented, and I have done my best to preclude the mistake of reflection. If insanity does come, then it would have to be an offended feminine pride over being rejected, which, despairing of taking revenge, inclosed itself within itself until it lost its way. Alas, I am well aware of the judgment of the world. I perhaps have felt the pain more agonizingly than she; I shudder to think that someone by daring to give her a proud look—or, what is just as terrible, a sympathetic look—would lead her to understand that she was insulted and consequently to prolong the insult. In olden days, it was sometimes the custom, so they say, that a prince was educated along with a boy of humbler birth, who had to take punishment every time the prince deserved it. People have spoken of the cruelty to the poor lad who had to take the thrashings; to me it seems to be far more cruel to the poor prince, who, if he had any sense of honor, must have felt the blows far more forcefully, far more painfully, far more crushingly than they were felt physically. I also know how it pained me to expose her to this pain. I know that I was willing to do everything to prevent it by giving the separation a false expression, so that in the eyes of the world I became the one who suffered, for if it is only I myself, I know how much it pains and what I have to do about it—but it could not be done. Several times in our conversations I dropped a few hints in a joking and chatty tone in order to make her aware—but in vain. Just a word from her and it would have happened, even if I had had enough foresight to undertake in a joking and chatty tone what for me was an indescribable relief. More than that I dared not do. Ah, if I had talked about it with all my passion, she would *eo ipso* have detected from my eagerness how much she preoccupied me, and then everything would again have been postponed and drawn out, and she again would have allowed herself every resource to move me, that is, to torture me, for I must not be moved.

It is a comic contradiction to talk with pathos or with systematic decisiveness about something of which a person is not himself convinced or does not himself understand, but it is a tragic, a deeply tragic contradiction to have to talk in vague terms, in joking hints, in chatty platitudes about what preoccupies and worries one to death. It is a comic contradiction to be willing to stake four shillings[183] when there is enormously much to win, but it is a tragic, a deeply tragic contradiction to have to make the form of the stake as if counters were being played for when one is all too aware of how much is at stake. I suppose it would be one of the most terrible collisions, perhaps the most horrible, if one were to imagine that concern for a person made it necessary for an apostle to talk in ambiguous terms and in a light chatty tone about the truth of Christianity.

But to the subject. I am loath to think that insanity would advance along this path, not because it is terrible, for the terrible requires of my honor that I must think it, but because a less favorable light would fall on her conduct toward me.

Every outburst of passion by which she placed a murder on
my conscience, every such passionate outburst that my honor,
until some other information is at hand, bids me regard as
truth, despite all objections by the understanding, every such
outburst that, if clearly an exaggeration, nevertheless can be
associated with feminine purity and feminine lovableness,
every such outburst, on the presupposition that pride was the
mainspring, would be an ugly falsehood on the part of self-
love against me. Admittedly I have taken the liberty of many
a falsehood against her, but it truly was in order to save her,
and it was motivated by sympathy. Therefore I am so loath to
imagine this terrible thing. Furthermore, here again I have
done everything I could and I do it undauntedly. If my existence expressed something positive, it would indeed be conceivable that this could incite her pride. If I could maintain a
masculine existence that is precisely that through its relation
to the other sex, consequently by handsomeness, poise,
charming personality, affability, etc., then the prior judgment
on me could actually be prejudicial against her, it would be
able to incite her that the person to whom the sex granted
competency to judge passed this judgment on her. But fortunately I am removed from this as far as any person can be. If I
were an artist, who consequently has a sense for beauty and
femininity, if I were a poet, who is indeed the darling of the
sex, then the fact that the person whom the sex acknowledged
did judge this way about her could possibly inflame her pride.
If I were a thinker, a scholar, then it would already be more
difficult to imagine how such an existence could further tempt
the offended feminine pride. But an existence such as that
would nevertheless be something. But the something that I
am is precisely nothing. With her *in mente*, it satisfies me and
my guardian spirit to hold my whole existence at the critical
null point between cold and warm, at the critical null point
between being something and being nothing, between being
perhaps, perhaps wise and then perhaps, perhaps silly and stupid. An existence such as that is utterly incongruous with a
feminine existence, it cannot engross a woman, far less incite
her. I am not so feebleminded that she could have sympathy

VI
257

for me, but I am just half-crazy enough that she can disinter-
estedly say, "Oh, he is mad, you know"; and if an offended
pride is interested in opposition to me, it will easily be able to
feel superior to a *Sonderling* [eccentric] like that. It already
takes considerable dialectic to conceive of a null-point existence and to maintain it, but then in turn to conceive of such
an existence as a polemic against oneself—that would take an
extraordinary dialectician. A woman rarely has much dialectic. She did not have it; if she later has become such an extraordinary dialectician, then she is lucky, and if she has not, then
my method of approach is proper and well calculated.

This is my medical diagnosis. It has not, I am sorry to say,
given me much consolation, even if it is always necessary for
me to make everything clear. If I had been consulted and if I
had dared to say that this was the sufferer's condition, my
mind would be set at rest with regard to the onset of delirium.
Since I am not the physician but the guilty party, this does not
help me. The poison works on me myself: the poison of reflection that I have developed within myself in order if possible to absorb all reflection out of her. I remember that she once
said to me that it must be dreadful to be able to explain everything this way. At this point she could have gained an idea of
how little she understood my reflection, because she hardly
grasped how welcome this remark was to me, or in what way
it was welcome.

But I have come to understand and to experience that it
could be possible; my depression has also stamped this possibility on my mind. If the unfortunate person, ensnared by insanity in its infatuation, suffers nothing, to have to experience
sympathetically the insanity of another, ceaselessly gazing at
the dubious interpretation of an eternal responsibility—alas,
the mere thought of it is enough to get the better of a person.
And yet if it were to happen, I certainly would dare to seek
her out, and it would be a relief to me, but then suppose she
recovered, and my problem came back; then it probably
would be my turn. I can watch and keep vigil beside her night
and day, but I cannot sleep, and my agony is not overcome by

"every night resting at my wife's side"[184] when it is not decided whether she can be my wife.

Now I shall put out the lights—I feel best when everything
is dark around me and I myself am silent. What is the use of
talking—after all, everybody would say it is a lie. Be that as it
may. It is not my intention to defend my case against oppo-
nents, *neque thesin meam publico colloquio defendere conabor* [and
I shall not attempt to defend my thesis in a public debate].[185]
And what, then, is the case in which I dispute with God?
Just suppose it were about nothing, suppose she had changed
her mind, suppose she were delighted to take back every word
[186]that is working together with my depression to create this
terrible thing—what then? The inevitable result would be that
she would bring a nemesis upon her own head—it would be
apparent that she had confused her person with an eternal relationship of duty and responsibility to God and that she
thereby revealed herself in all her insignificance. The case has
gone to a higher court. I have granted her every possible ideality; neither for her sake nor for my own could I wish ever
again to have the comic so close to me.

April 5. *Morning.*

A year ago today. Sure enough, today I received the declaration and the last will and testament witnessed to and confirmed by—my little confirmand, for this is precisely the
impression she makes on me, such a little miss. And yet she
does not want to act; she seems rather to want to incite me so
that I must become a worshiper. In anyone else, I would say
that this is the beginning of a bit of coquetry; of her I dare not
and shall not say that, not even think it. But this is one of the
most ridiculous situations I have experienced. I am, as I have
all too deeply felt, much too old for her, but by acting in this
way she certainly makes me so disproportionately older that I
involuntarily think of an old schoolmaster[187] who *ex cathedra*
[from the chair, with authority] said to a pupil, "If you do this
again, you are really going to have your ears boxed . . . . .
and I do believe you are going to get it right now."

This, then, is the result of my ideal conception of duty. If it could become clear to me that, literally speaking, I had a duty to all people, I would be the most troubled person in the whole country. I have an ideal conception of every relationship of duty, and since my independent position has resulted in my not assuming any, this conception still has a primitivity of childhood, an enthusiasm of youth, a concern of depression that makes the conception itself perhaps the best I have but also commits me to the most uncompromising effort.

Why, then, should she introduce into this relationship what to me is ridiculous? If she really did not care for me, well, I am ready to travel. I have been religiously crushed and very likely will be so again as soon as I take on the responsibility, but I cannot be erotically crushed. If she is in earnest about this, then the thing to do is to say something like this straightforwardly, say it decorously, respect oneself in everything one does in this regard, but not become peevish and lash out, for that only makes everything ludicrous. [188]Even in her behavior there may be an acknowledgment of me against her will, for it is a kind of obstinacy. She must know, of course, that she has just as much power as I, and a person who has the power does not act that way.

April 5. *Midnight.*

A Possibility[189]

Langebro [Long Bridge][190] has its name from its length; that is, as a bridge it is long but is not much as a roadway, as one easily finds out by passing over it. Then when one is standing on the other side in Christianshavn, it in turn seems that the bridge must nevertheless be long, because one is far, very far away from Copenhagen. It is immediately evident that one is not in the capital and royal-residence city; in a certain sense one misses the noise and traffic in the streets; one seems to be out of one's element by being outside the meeting and parting, the haste and hurry in which the most diverse matters equally assert themselves, outside the noisy community in which everyone contributes his share to the general racket. [191]But in Christianshavn a quiet peacefulness reigns. People

there do not seem to be acquainted with the aims and goals
that prompt the inhabitants of the capital to such noisy and
busy activity, do not seem to be aware of the heterogeneity VI
260
that is at the root of the capital's boisterous movement. Here
it is not as if the earth moves—indeed, shakes—under one's
feet; one stands as securely as any stargazer or a submarine
telescope gazer could wish for the sake of his observations.
One looks about in vain for that social *poscimur* [we are sum-
moned][192] of the capital, where it is so easy to go along, where
at any moment one can get rid of oneself, at any hour find a
seat in an omnibus, everywhere encompassed by diversions;
here one feels abandoned and imprisoned in the stillness that
isolates, where one cannot get rid of oneself, where one is encompassed on all sides by lack of diversion. In some sections
the streets are so empty that one hears one's own footsteps.
The enormous warehouses contain nothing and bring in nothing, for echo is certainly a very quiet tenant, but when it
comes to business and payment, it is no good to the owner.
In the really populated sections, life is far from being extinct;
nevertheless, far from being strident; it is like a quiet human
noise that at least for me resembles the droning of summer,
that by its droning suggests the stillness out in the country.

How sad one becomes upon entering Christianshavn, for
out there among the empty warehouses recollection is sad,
and what one sees in the overpopulated streets is sad, there
where the eye finds only a scene of poverty and misery.
[193]One has crossed the salt water to reach it, and now one is
far, far away, off in another world where lives a butcher who
deals in horsemeat, where in the only city square stands but
one ruin from that great fire[194] that did not, as superstition
usually has it, burn everything and leave the church intact, but
burned the church and left the reformatory standing. One is
in a poor market town where only the haunts of suspicious
characters and the special surveillance of the police are reminders of the nearness of the capital city. Otherwise it is just
as in a market town: the quiet noise of people, that everyone
knows everyone, that there is a poor wretch who at least

every other day serves as a drunkard, and that there is a mentally disordered fellow, known to all, who shifts for himself.

Some years ago at a specific hour of the day, a tall, slender man could be seen walking with measured steps back and forth on the flagstones in the southern section of Overgaden over Vandet.[195] Hardly anyone failed to notice the peculiarity in his walks, for the distance he covered was so short that even the uninitiated were bound to become aware of him, that he did not enter shops and that he was not, like others, out for a stroll, either. Anyone who observed him frequently could see in his gait an image of the force of habit. A skipper who is accustomed on shipboard to stroll the length of the deck chooses on land a stretch of similar length and then mechanically walks back and forth: so also this wanderer or bookkeeper, as people called him. When he came to the end of the street, the tug of habit was apparent, the reverse of an electric shock: he came to a halt, almost in a military tempo, stood, lifted his head, swung around, dropped his eyes to the ground again, and thereupon walked back, and so on.

He was, of course, well known in the whole neighborhood, but even though he was mentally disordered, he was never exposed to any insult; on the contrary, the neighbors treated him with a certain respect. Conducive to this were his wealth and also his charitableness and his attractive appearance. It is true that his countenance had the impassive expression characteristic of a certain kind of mental disorder, but his features were handsome, his figure erect and well formed, his attire very meticulous, even elegant. Moreover, his mental disorder manifested itself most clearly only in the forenoon between eleven and twelve o'clock, when he paced the flagstones between Børnehus [Orphanage] Bridge and the south end of the street. The rest of the day he presumably spent trailing after his unhappy concern, but it did not express itself in this way. He spoke with people, went on longer strolls, involved himself in many things, but between eleven and twelve o'clock no one for all the world could stop him from walking, make him walk farther, answer any question, or even respond to a greeting—he who otherwise was courtesy itself. Whether this hour had any special significance for him or there was a physical condition that occurred periodically—there are such cases—I never found out when he was alive, and after his death there was no one who could furnish me with more detailed information.

Now, although the conduct of the nearby residents toward him was almost reminiscent of the conduct of the Indians toward a mentally disordered person, whom they venerated as a wise man, in private they possibly had many conjectures as to the cause of his misfortune. It happens not infrequently that by this kind of conjecturing the so-called sagacious people betray just as much disposition to lunacy or perhaps more foolishness than anyone mentally disordered. The so-called sagacious people are often so stupid as to believe everything a lunatic says, and not infrequently stupid enough to believe that everything he says is lunacy, although many a time no one is more cunning at hiding what he wants to hide than a mentally disordered person, and although many a word from him contains a wisdom of which the wisest need not be ashamed. This no doubt explains how the same view that thinks that in the governance of existence a grain of sand or an accident determines the outcome can hold also in psychology, for it is the same view if one sees no deeper cause for insanity but regards insanity as easily explained by nothing, just as mediocre actors believe that acting the role of an intoxicated person is the easiest of tasks, which is true only if one is sure of having a mediocre audience to see the acting.

The bookkeeper, however, was spared because he was loved, and the conjectures were so well kept in private that I actually never heard more than one. Maybe they did not have more in private, either. That, too, I may assume and am not averse to it, lest my stubborn suspicion that they had many conjectures in private might betray in me a disposition to foolishness. The conjecture was that he had been in love with a queen of Spain, and this conjecture was an attempt doomed to failure because it did not even pay attention to a very noteworthy piece of evidence concerning him—a decided partiality for children. Along this line, he did a great deal of good,

VI
262

actually used his wealth for this, which explains why the poor people sincerely loved him; and many a poor woman impressed upon her child that, among other things, he should greet the bookkeeper respectfully. But between eleven and twelve o'clock in the morning he never responded to any greeting. I myself often witnessed how many a poor woman walked past him with her children and greeted him in such a friendly and respectful way, and the children likewise, but he did not look up. And after passing him, the poor woman shook her head. [196]The situation was touching, for in a singular way and in a peculiar sense his charitableness was gratis. The pawnbroker takes six percent for a loan, and many a rich man and many a successful man and many a man in power and many a middleman between these people and the poor sometimes take usurious interest on a gift, but with regard to the bookkeeper the poor woman is not so ready to envy him or to be dejected by his misery or to be dismayed by the public-welfare tax [*Fattigskat*], which the poor [*Fattige*] do not pay in money but expiate with bent backs and humiliated souls, for she probably felt that her honorable and noble benefactor (this, of course, is the poor people's expression) was more unfortunate than she—she who received from the bookkeeper the money she needed.

[197]But it was not merely to have an opportunity to do good that children occupied him—no, it was the children themselves, and in a most singular way. Except for the hour between eleven and twelve o'clock, as soon as he saw a child, the flat look in his countenance became animated and all sorts of moods were reflected in it. He paused with the child, spoke with him, and during all this regarded the child as attentively as if he were an artist who painted nothing but children's faces.

This is what one saw on the street, but anyone who saw his apartment was bound to be even more astonished. Often we gain a completely different impression of a person when we see him in his home or apartment than when we see him elsewhere in life, and this is far from being the case only with alchemists and others who devote themselves to the secret arts and sciences or with astrologers like Dapsul von Zabelthau,[198] who while sitting in his living room looks like any other man but when he is sitting in his observatory wears a high peaked cap on his head, a gray calamanco cape, has a long white beard, and talks in a dissembled voice so that his own daughter cannot recognize him but thinks he is a Christmas goat.[199] Ah, we often discover an entirely different kind of transformation when we see a person in his home or apartment and then compare what appears there with how the same person appears in life. This was not the case with the bookkeeper, and one only saw with amazement how earnest he was in his concern for children. He had collected a not inconsiderable library, but all the books were of physiological content. He had the costliest copper engravings and, in addition to that, whole series of his own sketches. These included faces executed with portraitlike detail, and then a series of faces related to each portrait, with the resemblance gradually disappearing, although a trace of it always remained. There were faces executed according to mathematical proportionality and the transformation in the whole face, conditioned by a change in the proportions, made graphic in clear outline. There were faces modeled according to physiological observations, and these in turn were tested by other faces that were sketched on the basis of hypotheses. It was family likeness in particular and consistencies in the relation of generations that concerned him physiologically, physiognomically, and pathologically. It is perhaps lamentable that his works did not see the light of day, for it is true that he was mentally disordered, as I subsequently learned in more detail, but such a person is not the poorest observer if his fixed idea becomes an instinct for discovery. An inquisitively interested observer sees a great deal, a scientifically interested observer is worthy of respect, a concerned interested observer sees what others do not see, but a mentally disordered observer perhaps sees the most of all; his observations are sharper and more persevering, just as certain animals have sharper senses than do human beings. But, of course, his observations must be verified.

As soon as he was busy with his passionate research, generally at all times other than between eleven and twelve o'clock, to many people he did not seem mentally disordered, although it was precisely then that his disorder was most pervasive. And just as at the base of every scientific investigation there is an *X* that is sought, or, looked at from another side, just as the inspiration for the scientific investigation is an eternal presupposition, the certainty of which seeks its corroboration in the observation, so also did his troubled passion have an *X* that was sought, a law that indicated precisely the relation of resemblance in the family line, in order with its help to come to a more accurate conclusion. Hence it had a presupposition to which his imagination lent, for him, a sorrowful certainty that this discovery would confirm for him something sorrowful concerning himself.

He was a son of a minor public official who lived in modest circumstances. At an early age he was employed in business by one of the richest merchants. Quiet, reserved, somewhat shy, he applied himself to his trade with an acumen and punctiliousness that soon led the head of the firm to realize that he was a very useful person. His free time was devoted to reading, practice in foreign languages, the development of a decided talent for drawing, and a daily visit to his parental home, where he was the only child. He went on living this way, unacquainted with the world. As an office employee he had favorable arrangements, and soon he was receiving a considerable annual salary. If it is true, as the English say, that money makes virtue, then it is also true that money makes vice. The youth, however, was not tempted, but as the years passed he became more and more a stranger to the world. He himself was quite unaware of it, for his time was always filled. Only once did an intimation of it dawn in his soul; he became a stranger to himself, or to himself he seemed to be like someone who suddenly stops and concentrates on something he must have forgotten without even being able to grasp what it is—but it must be something. And indeed there was something he had forgotten, for he had forgotten to be young and to let his heart be cheered in the manner of youth while days are still there.[200]

[201]Then he learned to know a couple of other employees who were men of the world. They soon discovered his helplessness but yet had so much respect for his competence and knowledge that they really never let him know his deficiency. At times they invited him to go along with them for a little merriment, on little outings, to a play; he did so and it pleased him. On the other hand, the others certainly were not harmed by his company, for his shyness placed a beneficial curb on the merriment of others, so that it did not become too wild, and his purity gave the amusement itself a more elevated touch than that to which they perhaps were otherwise accustomed. But shyness is not a force that can assert itself and make its claim, and whether it was that sadness which sometimes seizes the person unacquainted with the world that stirred him to rebellion, or whatever the reason was, an excursion to the woods ended with an unusually splendid dinner party. Wanton as the two already were, his shyness was merely an incitement to them, and his own painful awareness of it incited him in turn, and all the more so as the three of them became heated with wine. Carried along by the others and overexcited, he became a completely different person— and he was in bad company. Then they also visited one of those places where, strangely enough, one pays money for a woman's contemptibleness. What happened there, even he himself did not know.

The following day he was dejected and dissatisfied with himself; sleep had blotted out the impressions, but he did recollect enough so that he never again sought the decent, even less the indecent, company of these friends. If he had been diligent before, he now became all the more diligent, and the pain over his friends' having led him astray, or his having had such friends, made him even more withdrawn, to which the death of his parents also contributed.

[202]His reputation with the head of the firm increased as his diligence increased. He was a very trusted employee and was already being considered for partnership in the business when he became sick, sick unto death. At the moment he was closest to death and already prepared to set foot on "the solemn

bridge of eternity," there suddenly awakened a recollection, a recollection of that event which up until now actually had not existed for him. In his recollection, the event took on a definite shape that for him terminated his life with the loss of his purity. He was restored to health, but when he rose from his bed cured he took along with him a *possibility,* and this possibility pursued him, and he pursued this possibility in his passionate investigation, and this possibility incubated in his silence, and this possibility animated the features of his face in many ways when he saw a child—and this possibility was that another being owed its life to him. And what he was seeking in his concern, what made him an old man although scarcely an adult in years,[203] was this unhappy child or whether there was one; and what made him mentally disordered was that every more specific way to finding out was barred to him since the two whose company had been his ruin had long ago gone to America and vanished; and what made the disorder so dialectical was that he could never know for sure whether it was a result of the illness, a feverish hallucination, or whether death had actually come to the aid of his memory with a recollection of an actuality. This, you see, is why with bowed head he wandered that short street between eleven and twelve o'clock and the rest of the time he wandered the enormous detour along the desperate twistings of all possibilities, to find if possible a certainty, and then that for which he was seeking.

Nevertheless, at the beginning he was well able to take care of duties at the office. He was as painstaking and punctual as ever. He looked up things in ledgers and letter copybooks, but in occasional glimpses it seemed to him that the whole thing was pointless toil[204] and that there was something altogether different he should be looking for; he concluded the accounting for the year, but in occasional glimpses it struck him as a joke when he thought of his own enormous account.

Then the head of the firm died, leaving a considerable fortune, and since he was childless and had loved the bookkeeper like a son, he also made him an heir as if he had been a son. Thereupon the bookkeeper closed the accounts and thus became a scientist.

Now he had *otium* [leisure]. His troubled recollection still might not have become a fixed idea for him if life had not brought about one of those coincidences that sometimes tip the scale. The only relative he had left was an old man, his late mother's cousin, "the cousin," as he was called κατ᾽ ἐξοχην [in an eminent sense], a bachelor, to whose house he had moved after his parents' death. He took his meals there every day, which he continued to do even after the firm was dissolved. The cousin delighted in a certain kind of double-entendre witticism that, as is easy to explain psychologically, is heard more frequently from the elderly than from young people. If it is true that the plain, simple word that remains when everything has been heard and most of it forgotten can acquire in the mouth of an old man a weight that it ordinarily never has, then it is also true that a double meaning, a frivolous word, in the mouth of someone advanced in years can have a disturbing effect, especially upon someone so disposed as the book-keeper. [205] Among the cousin's witticisms that he continually repeated was the stock one that no man, not even the married man, could know for sure how many children he had. For better or for worse, this was the cousin; otherwise he was a good fellow, what is called a good mixer, fond of lively parties, but double entendres and snuff were a necessity for him. There is no doubt that the bookkeeper had many times suffered the cousin's whole repertoire, including that particular double entendre, but he had not grasped it and had not really heard it. Now, however, it continually aimed at his tender spot, as if calculated to wound him there where his weakness and suffering were. He fell to brooding, and when the cousin's words should have spiced the conversation, this chance contact developed the resiliency of his fixed idea so that it took hold more and more. His silence, self-inclosed as he was, and the joking of the blabber worked together upon the poor fellow so long that eventually his understanding became earnest about making a change because it could not go on serving in such a household, and the bookkeeper exchanged understanding for mental derangement.

In the capital there is traffic and bustling; in Christianshavn,

VI
267

however, a quiet peacefulness reigns. People seem unaware of the aims and goals that set the residents of the metropolis in such frantic and noisy motion, unaware of the diverse things that motivate this boisterous movement of the capital. The unfortunate bookkeeper lived in Christianshavn; literally speaking, there he had his home, and there, figuratively speaking, he was at home. But whether he tried to penetrate to the source of that recollection by way of specific historical research or by way of the enormous detour of ordinary human observations and, supported only by treacherous theories, wearily tried to change that unknown X into a denominated quantity, he did not find what he sought. At times it seemed to him that what he was seeking must be far away; at times it seemed so near that when the poor thanked him on behalf of the children for his rich gifts he was aware only of his own crushed condition. It seemed to him as if he were buying his freedom from the most sacred duty; it seemed to him to be the horror of horrors if a father gave alms to his own child. Therefore he wanted no gratitude lest this gratitude be a curse, but he could not stop giving, either. And rarely did the poor find so honorable and noble a benefactor, assistance on such favorable terms.

Through some more general observations, an intelligent physician would, of course, have been able to do a great deal to remove the first possibility, which conditioned everything, and even if he, in order to make an approach in another way, had expediently admitted this as a sad certainty, with his professional knowledge he in turn would have been able, through so many possibilities, to eliminate the consequence of this certainty to such an extent that no one would be able to discern it—except the mentally disordered person, whom such treatment would perhaps only disturb. Thus possibility works in various ways. It is used as a file: if the material is hard, the sharp edge is filed off, but if the material is softer like that of a saw, then the teeth of the saw only become sharper. Every new possibility the unfortunate bookkeeper discovered sharpened the saw of concern that he was drawing all by himself and the bite of which he himself suffered. It would not have helped him if someone had wanted to help him.

I often saw him out there when he walked on Overgaden over Vandet; and I saw him on other occasions as well, but once I met him at a local café. I soon learned that he came there on every fourteenth day in the evening. He read the newspapers, drank a glass of punch, and talked with an old ship captain[206] who came regularly every evening. The captain was in his late seventies, white-haired, healthy in appearance, his vitality unimpaired; his whole person showed not a trace of—which most likely was not the case, either—of having been knocked around in life in any other way than as a sailor. How these two had become acquainted I did not know, but it was a café-relationship, and they met only there and spoke sometimes English, sometimes Danish, sometimes a mixture of both languages. The bookkeeper was a completely different person. He came through the door, greeted the old sailor in English, which perked him up; he looked so roguish that he was hardly recognizable. The captain's eyes were not the best, and with the years he had lost the ability to judge people's appearance. This explains how the bookkeeper, who was only forty years old and in this particular place appeared much younger than usual, could fool the captain into thinking he was sixty years old, a fiction he maintained. In his youth, the captain had in all decency been a jolly fellow, as a sailor may well have been, but certainly in all decency, for his countenance had such dignity and his whole character was so attractive that one would indeed dare to vouch for his life and for his dash as a sailor. Now he was indefatigable in telling lively stories about dance halls in London and escapades with the wenches, and then about India. Thereupon they clinked glasses in the course of the conversation, and the captain said, "Yes, that was in our youth; now we are old—well, maybe I shouldn't say 'we,' for how old are you?" "Sixty," answered the bookkeeper, and they clinked glasses again. —Poor bookkeeper, that was his only compensation for a lost youth, and even this compensation was like a contrasting corollary of the all too heavily brooding earnestness of his mental disorder.

VI
269

The whole situation had such a good humorous pattern, the deception of being sixty years old so profoundly reinforced by the English language precisely as a presupposition for the humorous, that it impressed upon me how much one can learn from a mentally disordered person.

[207]Eventually the bookkeeper died. He was ill several days; and when death came in earnest and when he really had to step onto the dreadful bridge of eternity, the possibility vanished; it had been an aberration, after all. But his deeds followed him[208] and the blessings of the poor along with them, and in the souls of the children remained the memories of how much he had done for them. I went to his funeral. I happened to ride back from the cemetery with the cousin. I was well aware that he had made a will and also that the cousin was far from being avaricious. Therefore I took the liberty of saying that there was something sad in his having no family to inherit whatever fortune he might have left behind, in his not having married and left children. Although really moved by the death more than I had expected, and on the whole impressing me more favorably than I had anticipated, he still could not refrain from saying: Well, my good friend, no man, not even the married man, can know for sure how many children he leaves behind him. The redeeming part for me was that it was an old saying that he perhaps was not aware of at all; the sad part was to have a saying like that. I have known criminals in prison who were really reformed, really had gained a vision of something higher, and whose lives testified to it, but with whom it nevertheless happened that in their earnest discussions of religion the most loathsome reminiscences were interspersed— and in such a way that they themselves were completely unaware of it.

Langebro has its name from its length; that is, as a bridge it is long but is not much as a roadway, as one easily finds out by passing over it. Then when one is standing on the other side in Christianshavn, it in turn seems that the bridge must nevertheless be long as a roadway, because one is far, very far away from Copenhagen.

April 6.[209] *Midnight.*

How dismaying it is when one is concerned about a single solitary thing and then nothing at all happens that pertains to it. There is life enough in the street, events and bustling and noise in the houses—but not a single word is heard about my affair. In the same way a haberdasher sits in his little shop on a side street and waits for customers and hears scarcely a footstep—on Østergade the boutiques are full of people. But then the haberdasher does not pay such a high rent as the rich shopkeeper does on Østergade. That is true, but I, on the other hand—I certainly pay just as stiff taxes and fees as any married man, and yet nothing happens with regard to me.

Suppose the actor knew his role, had memorized it perfectly, felt inspired in delivery and in demeanor and was only waiting for the cue, but the prompter had fallen asleep and he could not manage to summon him!

Suppose a lantern semaphor were set up on the other side of the strait;[210] it was lighted, and the first word was legible, but then the fog rolled in and one could learn nothing without the help of the semaphor, and what one wished to know was as important as the soul's salvation!

Suppose the noble steed understood why it was saddled, knew that she was about to come, the equestrienne, the royal maiden, the steed's pride, and therefore it puffed and snorted and stamped its feet, flaunting its strength so that it might please her with the sensual rapture of constraining this fiery mettle, but the groom went away and did not return, and when he finally did come the equestrienne was not with him, and yet the riding gear was not removed, but the fiery steed became afraid of losing its wind and mettle and joy of jumping and the satisfaction of obeying the touch of the royal equestrienne!

Suppose Scheherazade[211] had made up a new story more entertaining than any of the previous ones; suppose that she placed all her confidence in this story, that it might save her life and not merely postpone the death verdict if she could manage to tell it as grippingly as she could at this very moment, but she was not summoned at twelve o'clock, and one o'clock drew near and she was afraid she had forgotten it or forgotten how to tell it!

[212]Last evening I had the good fortune to converse with a couple clever women. It went very brilliantly, and without exaggeration I dare almost believe that my presence inspired the clever ladies. They were women of fashion, and I—I, after all, am a man of the world, that is, an intelligent but corrupt man. No wonder that such clever people are in sympathy! What a voluptuous delight to take a fling in that exultation that is a combination of laxity and witty understanding. It is so auspicious to have along in the operation someone in relation to whom one in an emergency may withdraw and say, "Good heavens, we are indeed far from approving his shabby behavior, but he certainly is clever." Thus I learned a great deal about what it takes to have a happy erotic understanding, that when a man does not have intelligence enough to follow the emancipated creature in her lofty flight or, more correctly, in her stampeding, then it is a cross and is extremely painful to be bound—indeed, the association is really invalid. No more was said, but I do not doubt but that my heroines, who were so confident of spirit, were also willing to reverse the statement and show their sympathy to the person bound to a girl like that or rather demand that he make short work of it and find himself a more clever girl. Even a hint was dropped, obviously meant for me and obligingly intended. O silence, silence, how you can bring a person into contradiction with himself!

So it was an indulgence that was offered to me, an attempt to evaluate my conduct. That one woman dares to insult another woman in this way, and in this case a girl whose shoelaces they are not worthy to untie![213] If I had been emperor, they would have been banished straightway to a desert island. It is also really a nemesis on my head that my external existence, even if unfamiliar to many, contributes its part to encouraging someone in this loathsome snobbish cleverness. If only I were free and did not have this consideration that an authentic conception of my situation can become a dangerous precedent for her; truly, if the girl who is grieving, or causes me my grief, if she desires to place a man in the field as her contingent for the good cause of falling in love, if she makes me free, I will *pro virili* [as a token of manliness] hold the banner up.

Come on, then, you clever women with your devastating witticisms; a good cause stretches the bow tightest and hits the target most surely. That a love should not be held in honor in some other way! Indeed, I do feel that I could make use of an unhappy love affair; it is appropriate to my existence. If only I were free in my expression of my love, rejected but also the freeholder of my love, if only I did not fear that by admitting its meaning for me I would suddenly disturb her, who must be supported by the very opposite. Then I would say: Yes, I am the unmanly male (for I dare not be called a man), the poor manikin who could not manage to love more than once, the straitlaced bungler who was so narrow-minded as to take seriously that beautiful phrase about the first love and could not regard it as a coy cliché that experienced and at least half-experienced young women banteringly toss around among themselves at the supper table. But take a little pity on me. I myself feel what a sorry figure I cut these days when even the girls die as passionately of love as Falstaff passionately falls in the battle with Percy[214]—and then rise up again, vigorous and nubile enough to drink to a fresh love. Bravo [*Peteheia*]![215] —And by this kind of talk, or rather, by a life that justifies talking this way, I would think—provided that one person can benefit another at all—I would think that I have benefited my esteemed contemporaries more than by writing a paragraph in the system. What it depends upon is the positing of life's pathological elements absolutely, clearly, legibly, and powerfully, so that life does not come to be like the system, a secondhand store where there is a little of everything, so that one does everything to a certain degree, even the most foolish thing of all, believing to a certain degree, so that one does not tell a lie but is ashamed of oneself, does not tell a lie and then, erotically speaking, romantically dies of love and is a hero, but does not stop at that or just lie there but gets up again and goes further and becomes a hero in novels of everyday life,[216] and goes further yet and becomes frivolous, witty, a hero in Scribe.[217] Imagine eternity in a confusion like that; imagine a man like that on Judgment Day; imagine hearing the voice of God, "Have you believed?" Imagine hearing the answer, "Faith is the immediate;[218] one should not stop with the immediate as they did in the Middle Ages, but since Hegel one goes further;[219] nevertheless one admits that it is the immediate and that the immediate exists but anticipates a new treatise." My old schoolmaster was a hero, a man of iron. Woe, woe to the boy who could not answer yes or no to a direct question. And if on Judgment Day a person is no longer a boy, God in heaven can still pass for a schoolmaster. Just imagine that this paragraph-madness, this curriculum-craze, and this systematic sliding about have so taken over that eventually, to make a long story short, we want to brief our Lord on the most recent philosophy. —If God is unwilling, then I imagine the trumpet angel will take the trumpet and hit such an assistant professor on the head so that he is nevermore a man.

But the person who bungles in one thing bungles in all, and the person who sins in one thing sins in all.[220] If you only knew, you clever people, how comic the cleverness is that you admire. If you only knew, not how bad a seducer is, but how comic a character he is. If you only knew how loathsome but also how ludicrous it is that falling in love, the ultimate in earthly life, is supposed to be nothing more than an invention of sensuality, being in heat as the animals are, or a game of wittiness and a partnership of clever people! But you do not know that all this is nothing but themes for vaudeville and that your company is that of Pryssing and Klatterup.[221] Assume that a woman as beautiful as the concubine of a god and as clever as the Queen of Sheba were willing to squander the *summa summarum* [sum of sums] of her hidden and manifest charms on my unworthy cleverness; assume that on the same evening one of my peers invited me to drink wine with him and clink the glasses and smoke tobacco in student fashion [*studenticos*][222] and enjoy the old classics together—I would not ponder very long. What prudery, they shout. Prudery? I do not think that is so. In my opinion, all this beauty and cleverness, together with love and the eternal, have infinite worth, but without that a relation between man and woman, which nevertheless essentially wants to express this, is not worth a pipe of tobacco. In my opinion, when falling in love is separated from this—please note, the eternal from falling in love—one can properly speak only of what is left over, which would be the same as talking like a midwife, who does not beat about the bush, or like a dead and departed one who, "seared to spirit,"[223] does not feel stimulus. It is comic that the action in the vaudeville[224] revolves around four marks and eight shillings, and it is the same here also. When falling in love—that is, the eternal in falling in love—is absent, then the erotic, despite all possible cleverness, revolves around less than four marks and eight shillings, revolves around what becomes nauseating because spirit *qua* spirit wants to have an ambiguous involvement with it. It is comic that a mentally disordered man picks up any piece of granite and carries it around because he believes it is money, and in the same way it is comic that Don Juan has 1,003 mistresses, for the number simply indicates that they have no value. Therefore one should stay within one's means in the use of the word "love." [225]Language has but the one word and none more holy.[226] When there is need, one should not shy away from using the descriptive terms that both the Bible and Holberg use, but neither should one be so superclever that one believes that cleverness is the constituting factor, for it constitutes anything but an erotic relationship.

But to keep up an unhappy love affair, to become happy in the highest sense by means of it, to make meaningful what seemed so meaningless to me when in Prussia an order was established for those who participated in the War of Independence and an order also for those who stayed home,[227] to make this rich in beautiful meaning so that the one who stayed home was happy in his order, happy in his love, even if one saw the cross more clearly in the star-insignia on his breast than in that of the fortunate one, even if he wore the order, as the Prussians say of the second order, more for the will than for the deed—I realize that it would indeed be an inspiring task for the person who knows how to be content with ideas, with himself, and the knowledge of heaven. Let them fall on his right-hand side, the individuals who collapsed during the battle for an unhappy love. They rest in honor, they deserve an epitaph and a tombstone, but he must not want to bury the dead[228] lest he himself be disturbed. Let them rise up again, the apparently dead who are resuscitated by use of the customary means; let them amuse themselves by playing the ring game again and then again. Let them recover from everything now that they are plump mistresses of the house; let them *ganz völlig hergestellte* [most completely reestablished] feel happiness by being taken with the best of care into a third marriage. Let them munch in unison on the scraps of falling in love, and drool life away in a marital association, but he must not be willing to take time to watch it, lest he be delayed.

My pledge to silence makes me strong on monologues, but even an excursion like this continually leads me all the more definitely back to her. It must be glorious, so it seems to me, if the fatherland is in the distress of war and a woman has the means to arm a ship. That will never be my lot, but she—she can launch a warship that will battle for a good cause.

April 7. *Morning.*

A year ago today. She is unmanageable; she breaks off and breaks off and yet she does not break off. Damn blast it, if this is the way the match is going to be, if we come to blows— well, so we will start tomorrow.

April 7. *Midnight.*

How do things stand with the wish? Surely I am not about to wish for another, wish for compensation in a new love affair? Indeed, if someone holding a cane in his hand were as sure of actually holding it in his hand as I am sure that there is not a thought of that in my soul, he would be very sure. But is the passion of the wish completely unchanged? It is difficult to test oneself in possibility; it is like someone's testing whether he has a strong voice without daring to use his voice. Hitherto I have frequently speculated in vain about finding a means for being able to check myself in possibility.

Nevertheless, I do believe that the passion is the same, and if it should have changed, then I am sure that a hint, the slightest hint, of a more imminent possibility would be sufficient to make the wish more fervent than ever, for actually it is only with the breaking of the engagement that I can say of myself in every sense and every respect what is said of Phaedria: *amare coepit perdite* [he fell desperately in love].[229]

[230]In a way, everything is ready; all that is lacking is the approval of the idea and the consent of the thought-context, although I privately have examined and am examining every version. Scarcely any stage manager can know more reliably than I do that the change of scene is all in order when he gives the signal. At my expense I have a complete set of furniture in readiness at a secondhand dealer's, my apartment is arranged, everything is planned for a wedding—if only the moment arrives. I shall give the signal, and the change of scene is done in no time at all.

Suspicious of myself, I have arranged my personal existence exactly like that of a married man. Punctuality and order prevail everywhere. Darius or Xerxes, no matter which one, had a slave who reminded him about waging war against the Greeks.[231] Since I dare not confide in anyone, I must be satisfied with having my reminder within myself. In my whole existence, I produce a halfness that is a memento. Everything I buy, I buy double. My table is set for two; coffee is served for two; when I take a drive I always ride as if I had a lady beside me. Insofar as I live somewhat differently during these nighttime hours, it is not just because this life pleases me so very much.

And if nothing comes of this whole affair, I regret [232]nothing, I would not omit the least thing; for me it is [233]a matter of integrity, which I take with the greatest earnestness, so that if it ever can be done my balance sheet must balance down to the last penny.

April 8. *Morning.*

A year ago today. War is declared. If there is going to be a wrangle, it is important to restrain oneself, and above all no impetuousness. Admission to a menagerie costs three marks at first; later it costs one mark. A deluxe edition of a book costs six rix-dollars;[234] if one is not impetuous, later there comes the cheap edition, and it is still the same book. If there is going to be a quarrel, one must take care to use the opportunity and know where the opportunity is. From a second-hand dealer and in private sale one buys at half price. When a dancer steps out of a carriage, she carefully conceals her feet under her cloak lest someone admire these elegant feet. Not for ten rix-dollars would she do differently, and yet anyone knows, of course, that for only three marks—or for people of quality, eight marks—she dances before one in satin shoes etc.

My mood disgusts me; she has forced all my icy commonsensicality into this relationship from which I had banished it forever. It will not last long.

Today, meticulously dressed, I came in with a hop and a skip, stood hat in hand in an easy conversational stance, in passing kissed her hand obligingly and with polite stateliness, and hurried into the drawing room, where I knew there were guests, since it was a family festivity. It was very fortunate. Sarcasm, satire, and coolness do not show up to advantage at all under four eyes—if it is going to have any effect, some others must be present.

A lady at the party was so good as to invite us for the following evening. As a rule I leave all such things up to her, but in this case I hastened to thank her most cordially for the invitation on behalf of both of us. It was quickly decided, and what I said had been so flattering that if my little confirmand had said a word against it she would have made a fool of herself. Nor did she do it.

As I parted from her, having said good-bye and already gone halfway through the door, I suddenly turned around and said to her: Oh, by the way, you know what—shouldn't we break up? Thereupon I swung around and waved good-bye.

April 10. *Morning*.

A year ago today. I was immeasurably bored last night; but what will one not do for one's fiancée so that she can go out in society—and have her behave with a bit of manners.

She understands me very well, I can certainly see. Now, if everything was all right with the announcement, then I would have it *in optima forma* [in the best form].

Today we are to go to the exhibition, promenade the streets, and pay visits. Everything is going splendidly; although we are seen together more than usual, I keep her at a distance by being extremely polite. The advantage of being regarded as malicious is being utilized: I can be fairly sure of not being disregarded when we are out together; she easily comes to be one too many. Why has she baited me? Of course no third party notices her awkward position, for I continually slip in quotations from her, "It is just as my fiancée says— indeed, she said it just yesterday." [235]Just a look, and then, "Good Lord, my dear, can't you remember? It was yesterday—no, wait a moment, I don't want to be too insistent—it was four days ago, exactly four days ago—can't you remember" etc. She knows very well why four days was mentioned.

But my mood is gone; there is something ominous about the whole thing. An old man has said that it is never good that something which is supposed to be sacred appears in ludicrous form. A young girl, to be sure, is not the sacred, but yet she was something like that to me. I truly did not plague her with demands that she should behave as an ideal; I merely wished her to sit still while I concerned myself only much too earnestly with the relationship.

Yet I hope that this childhood disease is soon over and there is still such a good understanding between us that I ventured to read aloud to her from a devotional book. This makes the whole affair even more strange. A third party would perhaps find it dubious that I can be as I am and also want to be a religious person. If one has nothing else, it is quite easy to disregard sagacity and anything else but simon-pure solemn earnestness. But such opinions are of little use to me. Spiritually it is with an individuality as it is grammatically with a sentence: a sentence that consists only of a subject and predicate is easier to construct than a periodic sentence with dependent and intermediate clauses. That there was someone who was *unable* to behave in this manner to his beloved does not thereby explain anything, but it certainly would if there were someone who could do so and in a situation similar to mine would not do so and for valid reasons. I stick to the idea; she is comic—that is really what I am expressing. And I do believe that she is receiving more justice than if in an erotic relationship I presumptuously wanted to be the one doing the admonishing. I must always have the redeeming equality; here it is the esthetic idea that judges between us.

VI
279

[236]But if this prompted a defiance in her, it could be costly enough for me. But I do not know how to act otherwise.

April 10. *Midnight.*

There once was a person who said to me, "I have suffered something so terrible that I have never dared speak of it to anyone." [237]Most people perhaps would be a little too quick to dispose of such a statement: It is an exaggeration. And while they would be right in saying that it is an exaggeration, yet in another way the man would be right. In other words, when the explanation was at hand, it would show that the object of terror was a sheer triviality; but that it had gripped him in this way, so that he dared not confide in anyone, can indeed have had the effect that he suffered terribly.

[238]Yesterday I read in the newspaper about "a girl of distinguished parentage" who had ended her life by suicide. If the girl had just considered the mortal agony she can cause another person, I believe she would have refrained. [239]But who could ever think of using precautionary care toward me! And then not to dare to question anyone but have to fish for information in the casual language of conversation, by means of innumerable beginnings, leaps, and turns! [240]If my path is generally strewn with thorns, these random contacts are like a hawthorn hedge in which I am stuck. I am continually seeing ghosts: in random comments, in poetry, in mystifications. It is a nemesis upon me that I myself am so practiced.

It is now fourteen days since she received my confidential communication. I have not seen her on Hauser Square since. —Even if the ocean is ever so stormy and wherever one looks there is ocean, the compass still points due north. But on the sea of possibility the compass itself is dialectical, and the deviation of the magnetic needle cannot be distinguished from the reliable pointing.

April 12. *Morning.*
A year ago today. She is rather reticent, not without perplexity; this is quite obvious to me. She would not be altogether unwilling to yield a bit, but she cannot prevail upon herself. Well, so be it. She has trumped too soon and altogether in the wrong place. After my behavior these last few days, what would have been a reasonably defensible accusation came as a completely unmotivated downpour. —It is true I am waging war for the sake of peace, and yet it pains me to think of the purpose of the war, the crisis when she gives up. It will pain me, for I do not want a victory over her. As long as we are in conflict it is, of course, undecided who is the stronger, but if she surrenders as the weaker one, I do not wish to be present. I myself am proud, and in my relationship with her I am prouder on her behalf than on mine.

April 13. *Morning.*
A year ago today. It went splendidly; I can thank her guardian spirit for that, which I have privately done. Yesterday afternoon in my fencing lesson, my mask fell off while I was making a pass; the one who was countering could not stop his lunge and I took it on the head. The whole thing was a minor incident—some bleeding, the application of a bit of bandage, and I went home. But what happens? Fairly late last night she heard an exaggerated story about it, and when I did not come as I had promised she became anxious. The bloodshed, the tension between us or our thrust and counterthrust, and then perhaps a little love combined to keep her sleepless. As I have always said, in one sleepless night one can be unbelievably changed. Today she hurried over to me with [241]her father. She

was agonizing in a way that had to move the most callous person. —So everything went well. We escaped without my being victorious, and mortal danger helped us understand each other.

So much lovableness, such a girl, and then such a little miss! But I will gladly give a hundred rix-dollars to the poor because we so happily bypassed the precariousness of a capitulation. She looked at me now and then in such a way that I understood she had something to tell me, but then I talked about the dangerous wound and about the oddity that it was a mask that had fallen off. Then she laughed, even though there was a tear in her eye. Then I said, "Yes, you may well laugh at me for being unmasked that way." Then she said, "Oh, that's silly—you know very well what I mean." "Yes, that I should challenge him again and say: The whole thing doesn't count if the mask falls off." And then we talked of other things.

After that she goes home, and I watch her as I did when she returned from her singing lesson, and yet she walks in a different way; there is a brash happiness in her walk.

O death, I believe we do you an injustice; what meaning you are able to give life when even such a little reminder has such an effect.

April 14. *Midnight.*
[242]The method must be changed. When an interrogator wants to examine searchingly, he creates a setting as inquisitorial for the accused as possible. He seats the murderer beside the one who was murdered; he awakens at cockcrow the one who is apprehensive at night. For me there is a setting in which my interrogator is able to bring me to the brink of a confession, as near as I think it possible to bring me: it is in a church.[243] Today, contrary to my custom, I went to Trinitatis Church.[244] She is farsighted like a bird and unfortunately has a very good idea of my powers of observation. She caught me with her eyes and could see very well that I saw her. I was standing in the narrow aisle to the right; she came down from the church door, crossed in front of the chancel, and was

about to be shut in a pew on the opposite side. She looked at me, then nodded. I quickly dropped my eyes and leafed through the hymnbook as though I had lost the hymn and by this movement managed to shake my head. [245]Alas, I was afraid that in this greeting a hope was hidden. When I looked up, another glance was exchanged; she seemed to have understood the meaning of the movement of my head, and then she nodded again. Alas! Her expression was altogether different; it seemed to me as if she, giving up hope, were asking only for an admission. I had found the hymn and lustily joined the singing, and, as the parish cantor sometimes does, I lifted my head together with my voice and let it sink down again, a movement resembling that of one who is bidding at an auction and says "Yes." Then the pastor entered and separated us. I did not see where she went, and I went the way I had come, not a foot off the path. A Pythagorean could not step on the earth more anxiously than I in fear of, as they say, taking any step.[246]

VI
282

So, then, I have spoken! No, spoken I have not; I have not even done anything that I could not deny doing. It should not have been in a church; she should not have diverted me from what I still must regard as my duty. But in a church I am so easily tempted to regard the matter eternally, and in an eternal sense I can certainly speak the truth, but not in time, or not yet. She perhaps can be saved for life; she must not say farewell to it because I do. I do not believe she is religiously mature enough really to grasp what it means to break with life in this way, which for a woman is even more decisive than for a man. To want to proceed jointly along this path will produce again that dreadful misrelation that I already feared in that dreadful two-month period: that we would jointly sorrow over an unhappy love affair. It cannot be. What similarity is there between her sorrow and mine, what solidarity is there between guilt and innocence, what kinship is there between repentance and an esthetic sorrow over life, when that which awakens repentance is that which awakens her sorrow? I can sorrow in my way; if she must sorrow, she must also do it on her own account. A girl may submit to a man in many things, but not in the ethical; and it is unethical for her and for me to sorrow jointly in this way. Taking this path, how will she ever come to sorrow religiously when she must leave undecided an ethical issue such as my behavior toward her, when it is indeed over its result that she wishes to sorrow. Would that I might be a woman for half a year so that I could learn how she is dissimilar to man. I fully realize that there are examples of women who have conducted themselves in this way. Psychologically I have them right at hand, but in my opinion they are all wasted individualities. My view of life is meaningless if I must personally experience that one individual is being squandered upon another, and squandered she is if it goes this way.

As soon as she begins to venture along the narrow way to a religious movement, she is lost to me. A woman can have passion as strong as or perhaps stronger than a man, but contradiction in passion is not a task for her, such as the task of simultaneously giving up and preserving the wish. If she works purely religiously to give up the wish, she is transformed; if the moment for its fulfillment ever did come, she would no longer understand it.[247]

And yet I perhaps am talking quite foolishly; my conception of her may be laid out on too large a scale. The religious movement of infinity[248] may not be natural to her individuality. Her pride may not be sufficiently energetic to save her in an intensification of temporality. If she had been thoroughly proud, this would have happened, humanly speaking. This, too, may be why the religious does not take effect with the turning of the infinite. The religious eternity very likely does not become the eternal decision but a spacing out of the temporal. So eternity has paused at her side, consoled her, just as in Homer the god or the goddess hurries to the aid of the hero. She believed it was the decision of eternity, she believed it was her death, she believed all was lost, but see, because she was not so much awakened to this eternal decision as weary from futile wishing and weary of the futile act of renunciation, she gently slumbered on into eternity; then time passed, and she woke up and belonged to life once again. Thus there was even a possibility of a new alliance, a new falling in love.

This was indeed what I wanted; then she is really free. I have imagined three possibilities: that through pride she would gain an intensification in temporal existence, that through an illusory resignation she would gain a new love, that she would become mine. I have not wanted to think of any unlovely possibility in which she certainly would become free but in such a way that she would go down in my estimation. The first possibility must be relinquished. If she still, if after having received my confidential communication she has progressed no further, then she is not proud in the way needed to construct something exceptional upon this foundation. The last possibility is only a wish, which has also the difficulty that she would only have remained at this point if she had not entered into the religious at all but had continued in her feminine naïveté. Only when she has begun to sorrow religiously does the wish vanish like the setting sun when the moon's brilliance begins to shine or like the light of the moon before the break of day. A woman cannot involve herself in double-illumination and double-reflection;[249] her reflection is only single. If she wants to give up the wish, then reflection is the conflict between the life of the wish and the death of the resignation, but to will both at the same time is for her impossible—indeed, perhaps even impossible for her to understand.

So the middle possibility remains: an illusory resignation's slumbering on into an eternity, a relaxation, while time passes by, until she once again opens her eyes and is awakened to new life. If this happens, then no human life has been squandered on me. The girl, who in the illusion of sorrow may once have felt, alas, like a superfluous flower in life and have felt, alas, like the poor little bird that could not be considered when it was a question of a larger one, seems in this manner actually to receive consideration. So let the natural scientists teach us that life squanders on an enormous scale, let whoever wishes talk of love that demands sacrifices; if the state of affairs is as I think it is, then the girl becomes a capitalist to my eyes, and providence makes a very economical conversion. Denmark is said to be the only country that possesses a private fortune, because it has the toll from the Øresund;[250] to me it seems that she, in the smaller proportions in the world of individuality, likewise becomes an exception among wives. Marriage becomes, as it were, the national revenue, but then she has in addition the interest that my life brings to her. But it is good that she nevertheless did not do this for my sake or because I requested it of her. —This looks really inviting to me. Her existence comes to have more meaning than mine. I cannot have meant very much to her, for then one of the incidents laid out *en gros* [on a large scale] would have occurred, and it would have been costly for me.

But even when I think about it purely theoretically in this way, there is still something dubious. What is it precisely that she should do; what should happen? Yes, I am fully aware that she should do what is preached about in perhaps more than one church. The religiousness of infinity is perhaps not proclaimed if one is exacting about the categories. Christianity is not always proclaimed, either, just because without a trace of hypocrisy the holy names and the biblical terms are used, for at times the train of thought might be altogether pagan. That in which she will find consolation is not genuine religiousness. Seen from that point of view, I would in her eyes vanish like an atom, as an occasion, like the sale of Joseph,[251] for her gaining of the eternal; but then neither would there be any question of a new love affair. No, what she will be healed by is a life-wisdom permeated with a certain religiousness, a not exactly unbeautiful compound of something of the esthetic, of the religious, and of a life-philosophy. My view of life is a different one, and I force myself to the best of my ability to hold my life to the category. I know that one can die; I know that one can be slowly tortured—but one can hold to the category and hold it firmly. This is what I will; this is what I ask of anyone I am to admire, of anyone I am really to approve— that during the day he think only of the category of his life and dream about it at night. I judge no one; anyone busily engaged in judging others *in concreto* rarely remains true to the category. It is the same as with the person who seeks in someone else's testimony a proof that he is earnest; he is *eo ipso* not in earnest, for earnestness is first and foremost positive confidence in oneself. But every existence that wills something thereby indirectly judges, [252]and the person who wills the category indirectly judges him who does not will. I also know that even if a person has only one step left to take he may stumble and relinquish his category; but I do not believe that I would therefore escape from it and be rescued by nonsense; I believe that it would hold on to me and judge me, and in this judgment there would in turn be the category.

What power she still has over me. To humor her every wish, to spend the day on delight for her, if I were allowed to do that. Yes, that is a pleasure, but my thought is my life, and its loss would be my intellectual death if it were taken away from me. Long ago I crossed out differences, but that which sustains life for me is that in willing there is an equality of all human beings,[253] that on this point one dares to require the same of everybody. And yet how she has prevailed, just by a slight suggestion, upon me to be—as a third person presumably would say—decent about that dubious resignation. And why? Because I, in turn, am unable to exist intellectually unless she must be able to exist in the same thing. From this it is clear how dangerous it is for a thinker to be in love, to say nothing of being married and having daily arguing from a woman. Should he perhaps be neither the one nor the other, or should he perhaps be both? —Yes, it would be a male who would come up with such a life-view, who relinquishes to a certain degree, and then in turn comforts himself to a certain degree. But no! Be quiet, you passion that wants to provoke my mind to rebellion, even if it may have its reasons, for what I demand of myself to the point of despair, not as something extraordinary but as the right thing—this I cannot bear to see confused with something else, I cannot haggle.

But have not I myself provided the occasion so that something like this could happen? Indeed, the goal of my efforts is that she can become free. Correct, but I have submitted the matter for her decision so dialectically that she can do what she wishes. I believed that I owed it to myself to take all the responsibility upon myself. Perhaps it was still possible in the reign of terror to arrange a more amicable settlement, but if I had done something along that line I would have thought of my own welfare and not hers. She perhaps would not have grasped how she thereby would become dependent on me and far from being respected would be squandered. So the matter was put in such a way that she had the power and the sovereignty to act in the power of the religious infinity. I would thereby be bound forever and would never have gained myself again. If she chooses the other, I have not prevailed.[254]

What consoles me is that infinite reflection is not essential for woman. Therefore that more dubious kind of resignation can keep a woman just as beautiful. If she can fall in love, I am helped as much as I can be, but whatever she does I still cannot refrain from making something beautiful of it. Ah, what a bitter consolation for me if I were helped and she, too, but I secretly had to say of her: This existence has renounced the idea.

And what is the point of all my concerns and plans and efforts? What am I achieving? Nothing. But I am not going to stop for that reason. Precisely for that reason I am not going to stop, for when a person does everything and it is of no help, then he can be sure that he is acting with enthusiasm. Therefore I do not disdain this nothing, just as the widow did not disdain putting three pennies into the temple treasury,[255] this nothing in connection with achieving, which in connection with suffering is very much—something a solitary will understand. For when agony convulses the innermost being and the body trembles, if the sufferer is a man there is still a friendly hand that supports his head until that fury has abated; or when the sigh alarms and pain crushes the heart to the breaking point, if the sufferer is a woman, there is still a compassionate woman to loosen the stays until she can breathe again; but the solitary does not even dare to abandon himself to the sensate relief that passion finds in nausea.

But as yet there is no time to sorrow on my own behalf, for this, too, manifests the dialectical difficulty of my position, that it means two entirely different things if I sorrow on my own and on the family's behalf. But I must see about finding

what to my eyes is the most beautiful form for a new alliance.
The most beautiful would be that she had been in love with
someone else before she pledged herself to me and that this
love could reawaken now, perhaps supported by the self-re-
proach she must feel at having preferred me. Then her relationship with me would become an episode, she would not be
falling in love anew but only returning to her first love, and
the relationship with me perhaps would have taught her to
find it more beautiful than ever. Bravo, bravo! That will do!
If my pen were a living thing—but it is, of course, only a steel
pen—but if it were a bird that came bearing this leaf in its
beak,[256] if it could have any joy from my gratitude, how I
would thank it! —But the trouble is that I do not know anything about all this. And yet a more intimate confidant to
whom I could turn is unthinkable. But why be silent about it,
and why so eager to hold on to me? The answer to this would
show her a responsibility to that unknown person and to me.
Have I taken her by surprise, then? Far from it—I once made
that matter unmistakably clear to myself. [257]If I have taken her
by surprise, then it must have happened through the very circumspection with which I tried to prevent it. If I assume it,
then it can continue. So she has nevertheless feared me more
than she loved me. When the debates over the separation began, what she had forgotten resurfaced, and this painfulness
has been the spur to her despair. —So that is how it is. If this
happens, she will be helped—that is, she will have helped herself; and I shall be helped since she is free, and helped since she
has not become less beautiful. She does not owe me anything,
for she has not followed any advice of mine, since I have given
none and along this line could give none. If she does owe me
something, a little compensation for all the suffering, then it
is that I have had nothing to do with trying to counsel her. I
do not owe her anything directly, for I have not asked her to
do anything for my sake, nor can she be assumed to be doing
anything for my sake. Indirectly I owe her a great deal; yet
this debt is essentially founded on my personality, which precisely on the basis of the assumed presupposition wishes to
acknowledge it.

VI
287

[258]All this is splendid—if only it were not a hypothesis; it is a splendid hypothesis, if only, regarded as a hypothesis, it were not so weak.

It is five minutes to two; my working time is over. I shall think about her passionately from midnight on, but not a minute after this stroke of the clock. It is a matter of perseverance, and after two o'clock every thought about her is a spiritual trial, a deceit against her, for there must be some sleep to sustain passion all the way, which I want to do. —The difference between weak beer and the strongest beer brewed in England is not that the latter foams, for the weakest beer can foam, and foam just as much, but its foam vanishes instantly; the foam of the strong beer, however, lasts.

April 15. *Morning.*

A year ago today. So the weather turned out fine, even clear. If one starts out early in the morning, seeking freedom and beauty, but the weather is unsettled, one sits in the carriage like a schemer, wondering whether this fickleness can possibly show a more beautiful side so it will meet with one's satisfaction—and then the sun itself tires of the wayward whims of the scudding clouds, of the fitfulness of the passing showers, and bursts forth in all its splendor, and now it is settled, the weather is clear—[259]how I do appreciate that it is now settled by her, my sun, and that the season of passing showers is over!

The feminine immaturity with its somewhat feverish expressions seems to be forgotten. I dare to believe that I am loved. It certainly did not occur to me that she would love someone else, but she seemed to me to lack the integration that beautifies, and by its beauty penetrates the soul. The sight of it is a moment of joy comparable to the terrible moment when one sees a person who has taken poison, sees that the poison is working.

And the pain that she could behave so wrongly gives her a gentleness I had not suspected; and that she feels this pain—what does it not prove! How fortunate that death came between us! If we had continued in conflict and settled it between and by ourselves, however amicable the decision, it would nevertheless always be dubious. But I am only afraid that she is taking the whole affair too hard. To ignore it altogether in forgetfulness could result in her being secretly pained, and if I refer to it she is immediately agitated, although I do it as kindly and as jestingly as possible; is that perhaps the reason for it?

April 17. *Morning.*

A year ago today. The trouble is that she has no religious presuppositions at all. In that respect, I have been shadowboxing. She did, however, want to be in conflict with me; she has not exactly been overcome by me, but the anxiety of that night has taught her to understand herself. She considers it a set-back, even though she finds herself happier than before. Here it is a matter of her freedom of infinity in relation to me. Right now she has made me ideal and is using that little deviation against herself. If only this does not develop into a weakness, a devotion to me that I cannot and do not wish to understand. I do not want to be adored; I do not believe that her unfaithfulness could wound me as deeply as the sight of this annihilation in my eyes. I myself am proud, and every person ought to be that in his relation to other human beings; toward God he ought to be humble, and humble in every respect, but not humbled under another's personality. Really and truly, however dreadful this is, there is a kind of devotedness that precisely when it clings tightly to me will compel me to thrust it away. If it is unseemly for lovers to wrangle, then there is a devotedness that in a religious sense is a terrible responsibility.

VI
289

April 18. *Midnight.*

So there is nothing whatsoever for me to do but to keep calm, for it is impossible to do something about a former love affair about which I know nothing at all. Consequently what I have done is futile, as are also [260]part of my sympathetic expectation for her and my trembling for myself.

What, then, is the good of sagacity? But I am not sagacious anyway. If in one sense I am the most sagacious of my peers, then in another sense I perhaps am the most stupid of all. In everything that I have heard and read, nothing has so hit me and struck home as what is said of Periander.[261] He is said to have talked like a wise man and acted like a lunatic. That this saying fits me precisely is proved by my receiving it with the most passionate sympathy and by its nevertheless having not the slightest influence in changing me. This manner of appropriation is entirely *à la* Periander. Within my presupposition, I am sagacious, but the presupposition of my action is so ideal that this presupposition makes all my sagacity foolishness. If I could learn to reduce my presupposition, my sagacity would make a better showing. If I could act sagaciously in this way, I would have been married long ago. To have one's wish fulfilled, in addition to receive gratitude as for a good deed, and in the next place to order things as if one essentially had freedom, this would have been sagacious, and I would have been a respectable person who does not break his given word, a husband worth seeing, who is faithful to his wife and does honor to a girl. My ideal presupposition most likely does not honor her, and that I would rather stake everything and move heaven and earth than smuggle myself into the God-pleasing state and sneak through life most likely demonstrates that I have no honor.

My wish, which is higher than to see her free, my wish, which is the culmination of the divine frenzy in my soul, presumably must be abandoned now. But I will not do it. Once I am set free and dare to act, it would indeed still be possible that my nature could make the wish flare up in her. Let this possibility within a remote possibility, let it be infinitely remote—I still will not relinquish it and will not give it up. Only when it is officially certain that she is free and is another's, only then is the wish dead, but until then it shall not wretchedly visit me as a whim now and then but shall be held high in honor as the highest passion of my synthesis.

[262]It is indeed true that sadness is sorrow's grace, just as despair is its fury, but one first screams in pain before daring to be sad. To become sad immediately is sometimes a mark of a base soul.

VI
290

So sleep well, my girl. He who promised you faithfulness cannot do more than he is doing. Sleep well, then—I could almost say "my dear child," for my concern is indeed almost that of a father who craves to see his daughter in love. See, this is sadness, but I will not. I will persevere with you, will persevere even though I become an old man if nothing happens earlier. I will not call back the night watchman who stands on the look-out for the expectation.

April 20. Morning.

A year ago today. When an interrogator has perhaps been sitting for a long time reading documents, hearing witnesses, gathering evidence, inspecting the setting, he suddenly, sitting there in his room, sees something. It is not a human being, a new witness, it is not a *corpus delicti* [body of evidence]; it is a something, and he calls it: the pattern of the case. As soon as he has seen the pattern of the case, *he*, that is, an interrogator, is effective.

VI
291

I have been aware that there was a restlessness in my whole being, that something terrible was brewing; I have not slept the whole night, and now I see the pattern—alas, I see the pattern not of the case but of the annihilation. She is devoted on a scale that alarms my whole being, and yet in my eyes she is lovable and stirs me profoundly, but this devotion and my agitation are painful to me. Even if I were different from what I am, I could not understand this devotion and I could not be devoted in this way. And I who am so inclosingly reserved— she knows very little about me—what a misrelation! I gain complete power over her; she has none whatsoever over me. Is a relationship such as that a marriage? Indeed, it is like a tale of seduction. Do I, then, want to seduce her? What a loathsome notion! And is there not a still higher kind of seduction, worse than that of lust? She says she has never felt happier than she does now; she cares about nothing but her ecstasy. Is it love on my part to behold such a misrelation? And I am convinced that I am inclosingly reserved. Indeed, I must say I have come to see that my practice can lead to my being allowed to conceal my inclosed reserve. But her devotion becomes the demand that tosses my being up and down. To be sure, she actually does not comprehend this at all; but I know it, and what shall I do?

[263]That misunderstanding has done irreparable harm. In her inward being she may have wanted to contend in earnest. And there is no limit to the expression of devotion as soon as it begins to express itself directly. It is like a person's beginning to complain about his sufferings: very soon the truth no longer moves the listener, and so, unconsciously, he slips in an untruth. That misunderstanding does irreparable harm. If I look serious, she will think it is over that. And when that is not the case at all, but it is my inclosed reserve that is now making me gloomy! Ah, it is enough to make one lose one's mind!

Today she asked me to sit down on a chair. I did so without suspecting anything. Then she backed away a few steps, came up to me, and fell on her knees. No doubt there was a bit of flirtatiousness in it, but essentially there was sadness, and then a kind of bliss—yes, I may call it a demented bliss at having found a right expression for her passion. Instantly I grabbed her and lifted her up. Someone who has committed a crime looks around the room, suspecting every corner; he looks out the window to check the people opposite, and his anxious conscience makes him keen of eye: I do not know how much I would have paid for the certainty that no one had seen it, or how much I would have paid not to have seen it myself! Did I ask for this! Truly, she has never understood me. I myself have never bowed my knee before anyone; perhaps I could do it before her if the relationship called for it, but before her personage and before mine, it should never happen. For me such an act is no prank, no overplayed gesture; if I had done it, my opinion of it is that I would tolerate no such insult, that it was regarded in this way. Here I have my pride again.

I certainly do realize that a girl is different from a man, but I nevertheless still do not ever forget it; it has put a frenzy into my blood, a confusion into my mind, an anxiety into my inclosing reserve, a despair into my resolve, and above all a buzzing into the ear of presentiment, which for me is a harbinger and express messenger of the last extremity.

April 22. *Midnight.*

Just as a sick person habituated to a certain medicine must take the painkilling drops along with him wherever he goes, so I, alas, must have along with me everywhere a short summary of the history of my sufferings so that I can immediately orient myself in the whole—orient myself in what I have threshed over with myself in quite another way than a pupil does his assigned lesson with the teacher. If it happens that I suddenly come to think of it—"suddenly" in this case means that there is an interval of half a day between the last time I repeated the lesson—the most terrible crisis occurs. It is something like a trace of apoplexy in relation to the physical constitution. In an instant I become dizzy; my thought cannot quickly enough grasp anything firm in the hodgepodge, and it seems to me as if I were a murderer. There is nothing to do then except to reject the idea with supreme effort as a religious spiritual trial; then the moment is over, and I once again understand what I have repeated hundreds and hundreds of times. —Or, I suddenly come to think of how much I have suffered, and the thought comes so suddenly that the supervisors of reflection are not quick enough to be able to rush over there, and I am completely overwhelmed. That happened to me yesterday. I was sitting in a café reading a newspaper; suddenly that idea awakened in my soul, so suddenly that I burst into tears. Fortunately there was no one present, but I learned new caution.

April 24. *Morning.*

A year ago today. I have gone astray; I am like someone who has come into a strange country where people speak another language and have other customs. Now, if my suffering were that the strangers treated me with national pride, that would be all right. But that is not my situation. She is very far from making any demands upon me; absorbed in her illusion, she sees in it only her illusion. She is happy, she says; I do believe her to be happy in a certain sense. She is lovable and busies herself with her love like a child who shifts for itself but is merry and happy at its pastime. One could sit and watch her and grow old and go on watching her—there is only one dubious aspect—and that is that I am the object of her love. Everything prior to that little *altercatio* [dispute] which to me had so much meaning: the impact of the idea to which I, yielding myself to the idea, tried to draw her attention—this has not touched her at all. In this respect, she is, so to speak, insensitive. But the conflict, my changed behavior, the intervention of death, transforms her nature; she is displaying a lovableness I sadly admire and that makes me an enthusiast to her. And what, then, does this mean? It means that she has no sensitivity whatsoever to the motives I consider to be supreme. There is a language difference between us, a world between us, a distance that now manifests itself in all its pain.

April 25. *Midnight.*

Patience!

April 26. *Morning.*

A year ago today. So it is upon this rock I am to be wrecked! I have never humbled myself before any human being; neither have I exactly wanted to behave with arrogance. My view of my relation to people was to let everyone be given his due and then period. On the whole, I have not had much to do with people in a more intimate sense. My spiritual existence has occupied me too much. Here I have been humbled. And who is it who humbles me? It is a young girl, and it is not by her pride, for then we could have managed all right, but by her devotedness.

Happy with me she will never be—no, never! It is possible that she can make herself believe it, but I do not understand it, and that, too, certainly belongs to her happiness. And if we are united, it will eventually come to the point where she will someday sense with terror what I ought to have prevented.

To preserve my inclosing reserve in relation to her is easy enough—perhaps that is why I feel the humiliation right now.

What to me is the vital force of my spiritual existence—
equality in the essentially human—she destroys. She does not
care at all about the infinite passion of this freedom; she has
erected an illusion, and she is satisfied with that. I, too, believe
that one can love, can sacrifice everything for one's love, but
whether I am going to see good days or am going to risk my
life, the deepest breathing [*Aandedræt*] of my spirit-existence
[*Aands-Existents*] I cannot do without, I cannot sacrifice, because that is a contradiction, since without it I indeed am not.
And she feels no need for this breathing.

Yet I feel precisely now that I love her, love her more than
ever, and yet I dare not, I who am engaged to marry her, who
indeed, please note, *am obliged* to love her.

April 27. *Midnight.*
I have no desire to record anything, nor is there anything. Yet
I am just as much on the alert. Here in the city the night
watchmen show that they are on duty by shouting. Why this
shouting? In England they walk in utter silence and put a pellet into a box, and in the morning the supervisor sees whether
they have been on duty and have not slept.[264]

April 28. *Morning.*
A year ago today. If only she could put up some resistance to
me. When I fight I am lighthearted, and even when I live in
peace, I want the one with whom I am keeping the peace to
be just as strong as or stronger than I am. The more she surrenders herself, the more responsibility I have. And I am
afraid of the responsibility. Why? Because then I have myself
to deal with, and this conflict I always fear. If God himself
were what is called a man, someone outside oneself with
whom one could speak and to whom one could say: Now let's
hear what you have to say, and then you will soon see what I
can think of—well, then we could manage all right. But he is
the strongest of all, the only strong one, because he simply
does not speak that way with a person. The person with
whom he wants to be briefly involved he takes hold of in such
a way that he speaks to him through the person himself. Their

conversation is not a *pro* and *contra* exterior to each other, but when God speaks he uses the person to whom he is speaking, he speaks to the person through the person himself. This is why he has the power and at any moment he wishes can crush a person. But if it were so that God had once and for all spoken, for example in Scripture, then, far from being the most powerful, God would be in the tightest squeeze, for a person can easily argue with something like this if he is allowed to use himself against it. But such an assumption is an airy notion without any basis, for this is not the way God speaks. He speaks to each individuality, and the instant he speaks to him, he uses the individual himself in order to say through him what he wants to say to him. Therefore in Job it is a weakness in the plot that God appears in the clouds[265] and also speaks like the most skillful of dialecticians, for what makes God that frightful dialectician is that one has him in a quite different way at close quarters, and here the softest whisper is more blessed and the softest whisper is more terrible than to see him on the throne in the clouds or to hear him in the thunder over the earth. This is why one cannot utilize the dialectical with him, for God uses the very dialectical power of the person involved precisely against this person himself.

When an individual fears God, he fears what is greater than himself, and next to this fear is the fear of himself, and the *angustiae* [narrow pass] of this fear is responsibility.

The more she surrenders herself, the unhappier I become. Is this a happy alliance? And what, indeed, is her happiness? Seen from my standpoint, it is the happiness of blind enchantment, of illusion. But Socrates says that being in an illusion is the greatest unhappiness.[266]

April 29. *Midnight.*

[267]The question remains whether or not I could give her a more lenient conception of myself. If she sometimes thinks of me at all, of which there surely is a sad probability, then I do indeed realize what she in all human probability might need. The explanation presumably would go something like this: "To a certain extent I was a corrupt man, yet not totally bad;

I had my good sides as well. I certainly have loved her but lacked earnestness. And then there was my instability, which cannot hold firmly to a resolution. I certainly did regard her as a charming girl but still did not find in her the spirit with which I could become happy. It is therefore beautiful of her to resign herself to her fate. It is magnanimous of her to be reconciled to the girl who some day will captivate me with a greater power: for this much is sure, that if he ever finds a more brilliant girl, he will find no one who would love him in this way. This he himself certainly must admit, and, as far as that goes, he certainly has also repented of his conduct, even though he is too proud to undo anything." —A repenting individuality who repents but is too proud to undo anything he has done wrong when it still can be undone—God knows what repentance is then!

To have to assist with an explanation such as that, in which every sentence is meaningless and also untrue with respect to me! I am either very corrupt, indeed a hypocrite, or even to the point of nausea ensnared in self-deception—or I am really as chivalrous as anyone. Nor do I lack stability in holding firmly to a resolution, unless it should be when the criterion was a young girl who did not really know what a resolution is. I have always regarded her as charming, and I have not changed my opinion one bit. I have not *found* anyone more brilliant since I am looking for none and politely decline feminine brilliance. Her magnanimity is no trump card at all. I do not intend to act out a story of everyday life[268] and barter. That I repent is true, but it is equally true that it is my wish to undo everything.

With the help of this explanation, I advance. I step out of all the qualifications of infinity—and become comic. To be sure, not in the eyes of everyone; in the eyes of a few poets I even become a hero. Truly, one would not think that an eternal and righteous God had originally produced the ethical, but that a bungling theatrical tailor had slapped something together. [269]And this criterion is used for heroes even by poets—in order to show that they are heroes—but Scribe is the cleverest of all. We read and hear lines by him that confound all existence, as if this comedy were played not to human beings, not to the demented, but to "dazed June bugs," and yet these lines are dropped so conversationally and so lightly that one sees that it is as easy as falling off a log. A married woman is portrayed by the author as both sensible and good—indeed, as championing the good cause: a true love affair between a young girl on whom she has an influence and a young man who on this occasion appeals to her for help. I cannot remember the lady's name, so let us call her Madame Scribe. She says to the courting young man: "But have you ever considered that the girl has no fortune?" "I have considered that." "She has only twenty thousand francs in capital." "I know that." "And yet you stand by your word?" "Yes." "Really, this heroism wins me completely to your side."[270] What a satirist Scribe is without knowing it; I thought I was at a Punch and Judy show. The young man is put in a bright light, he wins the girl, twenty thousand francs—and becomes a hero. But that kind of hero is just as comic as a tailor's child with the name of Caesar Alexander Bonaparte Appleorchard; and an author who creates such heroes seems just as foolish to me as the tailor parents who had their child baptized with such a name.

It is my duty, however, to do everything that may seem beneficial, everything, whether or not it eventually benefits her in a specific way. The previous attempts were futile. If she had become a religious individuality in the proper sense, it would have been frightful for me. Yet I have not sought advice from flesh and blood.[271]

My reason has fumed as it shrinks from the harlequin's costume—that is, from becoming a hero in Scribe. Enough of that. I think of her, I see her recuperating, I see the possibility of a happy ending. Well, I submit to the discipline. Truly, this girl is destined for my humiliation. Even if no one is aware of this, even if only few would understand if I spoke out, I do understand it, understand it perfectly.

[272]When the legitimate children of Pericles were living, he issued a law that no one could be considered a citizen of Athens who was not born of Athenian parents. Many suffered because of this law. Then the plague came and all the children

of Pericles died; his distress was so great that when he came up to lay a wreath upon the head of his last child he burst into tears in the sight of all, something never before seen. He had only illegitimate children left; then Pericles petitioned that that law be abolished. It is shocking: Pericles weeps—and Pericles does one thing one day and the opposite the next. But it is moving to read Plutarch—he says that the Athenians yielded to him; they believed that the gods had taken revenge on him and that the people therefore had to deal gently with him.[273]

Pericles was a great man; he could hold firmly to a resolution; after resolving to dedicate himself to the service of the state, he never went out in society again. It is easy for me at this point to feel my inferiority, but would that I might sense the leniency that deals gently with me by letting me realize that I ought to misrepresent my existence! But as a matter of fact have I not continually misrepresented it? True, but this misrepresentation was of such a nature that I hoped it—if she looked at it—would produce something great in her; this misrepresentation, if it does contribute something, will not contribute to greatness. And the first method honored her in an entirely different way than this one.

April 30. *Morning.*

A year ago today. She is no longer effervescent in her expressions of devotion. Perhaps it was all a transition. But I have seen that alarming tableau, and I shall never forget it.

My depression has really won out.

May 1. *Morning.*

A year ago today. Is it possible! She became exasperated over an inattention on my part. Well, I do not deny that it was an inattention. She almost stands up to me. Now or never. It is fine that the word "separation" was brought up between us in that little *altercatio* [dispute]. It always makes it easier to bring up the word again.

Run away from the issue, I will not; it is not in order to have an easy life that I want to be separated from her—it is because I cannot do otherwise. If I cause her pain, I will not, I dare not, excuse myself from the sight. I wish to make this state of affairs as brief as possible; that I believe is beneficial to her. But I am also willing in another way and will respect any argument.

At this moment, she is stronger. So now the issue has been broached.

My verdict on her is brief: I love her, I have never loved anyone else, nor shall I. I want to stop with this and not go further; so I certainly dare to say this but still have the strength to find a new love. My mistake is that I have ventured in where I do not belong. What I have shaped myself to be with all my passion appears to me to be an error, but I cannot be remade now. She does not understand me, nor I her. From the very first time I saw her, during all the time she was my preoccupation in the form of hope, I have been able to imagine her dead without losing my composure. I would have felt pain, perhaps all my life, but the eternal would promptly have been present, and for me the eternal is supreme. Only in this way can I understand that one loves another. In the consciousness of the eternal, in infinity, each of the partners is free, and both of them have this freedom while they love each other. This higher existence is of no concern to her at all. Is this relationship of ours any structure for a marriage? Is, then, a married man a pasha with three horse tails?[274] With such a union, I become unhappy; I am alarmed about my deepest existence. Suppose I could do it, suppose I could go through with this— well, what then, what is her happiness for which I am to risk all this? Am I to risk everything for a delusion? Suppose that someone could guarantee to me that she would be happy; but to be in a delusion, is that being happy? But once she has devoted herself in this way, then I have the responsibility.

That these are premises for a lifelong sentence is apparent. Whether it applies to two or one, I dare not say; the verdict upon me is the more certain. But is it not unreasonable to make two people unhappy when one is enough? Indeed it is, if only I could perceive what it means that I can make her happy.

May 2. *Midnight.*

But do I not still harbor a secret anger against her? I do not deny it; I do not like these direct expressions of feelings; one should be silent and act interiorly. I do not like to talk about dying of erotic love, and if the person speaking without any feminine resignation also does not hesitate to place her life as a murder on the conscience of a depressed man—as if this were faithfulness, true faithfulness, and if a Charlotte Stieglitz[275] committed suicide not because she was overwrought, for that is true, but because she felt herself a burden and understood the situation in a womanly way—I do not deny that if it were someone else I would demand from life that it allow us to have a view of the matter, that it was a false alarm. It would appease my wrath, if it were someone else, to have it be common knowledge that these strong words and these sworn avowals were neither more nor less (with reverence be it said) than some nasty belches, some little hiccups, brought on perhaps by too much reading of novels, that these thoughts of death were dreams, not like those of Shakespeare's Juliet after having taken poison[276] but like Wessel's Grete after having eaten peas.[277] I would demand this from life because what I myself eternally respect must not be made ludicrous, and the person who truly and earnestly respects it must not become a laughingstock because a girl jeers with the same words.

No oath binds me; quite the contrary, I am liberated and on extraordinary terms, by becoming a scoundrel, for usually such people are imprisoned. I did not say a word about death when the anxiety of death went through my soul, and I still feel the same way. If I actually die, I certainly do not need to talk about it; I have not invited anyone to see in me a dashing hero. But this makes little or no difference in the matter if I in my interior self might just be found faithful; for no matter whether a person has appearances on his side or against him, time is and remains a dangerous enemy. External stimuli can help for only a short time, but it is still an illusion. If a person is going to persevere it must be on his own, and not even this is possible if day after day his religiousness does not absorb eternity into temporality's resolution. Hence, every person who truly remains faithful can thank God for it. This is the sharpest, perhaps the most difficult, but also the most inspiring segregation: what that actually is of which a person must say that he thanks God for it and no one else. To have appearances against one always helps to illuminate this distinction, but everyone does it, as does language also—the question is only *how*. It is this *how*, by no means new figures of speech, phrases, and terms, that makes the matter clear. —Yesterday I saw a drunken woman in the street; she fell down, and the boys laughed at her. Then she got up without anyone's help and said: I am woman enough to get up by myself, but for that I thank God alone and no one else—no, no one else! When a person is totally engrossed in this distinction, it is rather humiliating for him to be so far from having made new discoveries that a drunken woman says the same thing. And yet it is something indescribably joyful and moving and inspiring that even a drunken woman says the same thing. How it is said, each one justifies, but I wish only to have my life there where everyone can have it—if he so desires.

A life that will work for the idea, I can understand; outside of that, it is virtually impossible for me to sympathize with anyone, whether he is happy or unhappy.

This does not apply to her. As yet any renunciation of the idea has not entered in, and therefore I shun as an insult to her any idea of it in connection with her. If it does enter in, I ask only the leniency that I be able to abstain from thinking about it. What is death? Only a little pause on the once trodden path if one remained faithful to the idea. But a break with the idea means that one has taken a wrong direction.

May 4. *Morning.*

A year ago today. It has happened. In two days I have already managed to introduce that terrible word into the course of conversation. There is an enormous difference when a warship and a nutshell put out to sea, and the difference is externally visible. It is different with words. The same word can indicate an even greater difference, and yet the word is the same. The word has not come up between us in a pathos-filled way, but it comes up again and again, mixed in among various things in order to clarify the mood. —From what I have observed until now, I could almost be tempted to believe that it will go more calmly than I dared hope.

As for myself, I have indeed taken the responsibility for this step. In my view, this means that I am making a human being unhappy. When I do business with myself, I cannot have it cheaper. What actuality will be able to show me is that I may have overrated the responsibility. This is the way I have resolved to act; I have imagined the worst, and actuality cannot terrify me. What I am suffering inwardly where everything is confused and shaken, what I am suffering at the thought of her pain, at the thought that I probably will never recover from this impression because my whole edifice has been made to reel, my view of life, of myself, of my relation to the idea has failed, and I shall never be able to erect a new edifice without remembering her and my responsibility—that is my share. It is a lion's share, or more accurately, the sorrow is so great that there is abundantly enough for both of us.

VI
302

May 5. *Midnight.*

The Reading Lesson[278]

Periander[279]

Periander was a son of Cypselus, a descendant of Hercules, and succeeded his father as tyrant in Corinth. Of him it is said that he always spoke as a wise man and always acted as a lunatic. It is very curious and in a sense a continuation of Periander's insanity that the person who stamped him with this ingenious phrase was himself unaware of how expressive it was. In his simplicity, its somewhat limited originator introduces the wise remark in the following way: It is very striking that the Greeks could include such a fool as Periander among the wise. But a fool, *un fat* [a fop], to use the moralist's term, Periander was not. It would have been different if he had said that there was another Periander, Periander of Ambracia,[280] with whom he possibly was confused, or that there were only five wise men, or that historians differ in their views, etc. Then the gods would have better understood the epigram about Periander, for in their wrath they led him through life in such a way that they brought these wise words as a mockery down upon the head of the tyrant who by his deeds disgraced his own wise words.

When he became tyrant he distinguished himself by leniency, by justice toward the lowly, by wisdom among the prudent. He stood by his word and gave the gods the carved pillar he had promised,[281] but it was paid for by the women's jewelry. Bold were his undertakings; and this was his aphorism: Diligence accomplishes everything.[282] His explanation was like the saying about digging through the isthmus, for diligence accomplishes everything.

But under his leniency smoldered the fire of passion, and until the moment arrived the word of wisdom concealed the madness of action; and the bold projects evidenced the power that remained the same also in the changed man. For Periander changed. He did not become another person, but he became two who could not be contained in one person: the wise man and the tyrant, which means that he became an inhuman monster. The reason is related in various ways. But this much is certain—there was only an occasion—that is, if it was at all explicable that he could be so changed. It is, however, related that he had had penally culpable relations with his mother, Cratia,[283] presumably before he had heard his own beautiful proverb: Do not do what ought to be kept secret.[284]

And this is Periander's saying: It is better to be feared than to be pitied.[285] He acted accordingly. He was the first to keep mercenaries,[286] and he remodeled the government to meet the demands of tyranny and ruled as an autocrat over the serfs, himself bound by the power he could not get rid of, for as he himself said: It is just as dangerous for a tyrant to relinquish his supremacy as to have it taken away. He also ingeniously avoided the difficulty that subsequently will be described, and not even death took revenge on him—the epitaph is inscribed over the empty tomb. That this was bound to happen Periander himself knew better than anyone, for he said: "Ill gain breeds bad gain." "Tyrants," he said, "who want to be secure must have goodwill as a bodyguard and not armed soldiers."[287] Therefore, the tyrant Periander was never secure, and the only place of refuge he found safe enough in death was an empty grave in which he did not lie. This could also have been expressed in an obvious way by placing the following epitaph over the empty vault: Here **rests** a tyrant. But the Greeks did not do it in this manner; more conciliatory, they allowed him in death to find peace in the bosom of his native earth and wrote over the empty grave words that sound more beautiful in verse but mean something like this: Here Corinth, his native country, hides in its bosom Periander the Rich, the Wise. But inasmuch as he does not lie there, this is untrue. A Greek author composed another epitaph for him, intended primarily for the spectator, so that the epitaph might remind him "not to be grieved because one's wish is not fulfilled but to be happy with the decrees of the gods" as he considers "that the spirit of the wise Periander was quenched in despondency because he was unable to carry out what he wanted to do."[288]

This is enough here with regard to his final end, which teaches posterity about the wrath of the gods, something Periander did not learn from it. The story goes back to report the cause that made Periander's madness erupt, which from that moment so increased over the years that he could truthfully have said of himself a motto that many centuries later a despairing man, so it is said, had inscribed on his shield: "More annihilated than repentant."[289]

As for the reason, we shall leave it open whether it was that there were rumors about his penally culpable relations with his mother, so that he was offended because people knew "he had done what dare not be mentioned"; or whether the reason was a cryptic response by his friend Thrasybulus, tyrant in Miletus,[290] which, significant although tacit, was not understood by the messenger but certainly by Periander in the same way as the same answer was understood by Tarquinius, son of Superbus,[291] as an instructive clue to a tyrant; or finally whether the reason was his despair over having in a fit of jealousy kicked to death his beloved wife Lysida, to whom he himself had given the name Melissa[292]—this we cannot determine. Each event in itself would certainly be adequate: the infamy of disgrace for the proud prince, the temptation of the significant cryptic words for the ambitious man, the anguish of guilt for the unhappy lover. Together they would gradually cause wickedness to replace the wise man's good sense, and indignation would deceive the ruler's soul.

But as Periander altered, his fate also changed. The proud saying that it was better to be feared than to be pitied recoiled upon him, upon his desperate life, and upon him in death. For he came to be pitied, pitied even for having said these words, pitied because the gods, who are the stronger, worked against him, while he, more and more shattered, less and less in repentance understood their wrath.

Melissa[293] was a daughter of Procles, monarch of Epidaurus. When the mother was killed, her two sons, Cypselus and Lycophron, the one seventeen years old and the other eighteen, fled to their maternal grandfather in Epidaurus. Here they stayed for some time, and when they returned, Procles, bidding them farewell, said: Children, do you know who it was who killed your mother? The words made no impression on Cypselus, but Lycophron became silent. After his homecoming to his father's house, he never condescended to answer his father. Periander became indignant, drove him away, and finally, by assisting Cypselus's memory by many questions, learned what Lycophron was hiding in his silence. His wrath now pursued the exile: no one was to harbor him; it pursued the fugitive, who went from house to house until finally some friends took him in. Then Periander issued a proclamation that whoever gave shelter to Lycophron or merely spoke a word with him would die. Now no one dared to become involved with him; thus he was bound to perish of hunger and misery. Periander himself was shaken and went to him after Lycophron had had neither food nor drink for four days and nights. He invited him to become ruler of Corinth and lord of all his possessions since by now he certainly had learned what it is to defy his father. But Lycophron answered not a word; finally he said: "You yourself have deserved death, for you have indeed overstepped your own edict and spoken with me." Indignant at this, Periander banished him to Corcyra, and his wrath turned on Procles, whom he conquered, imprisoned, and dispossessed of Epidaurus.

Periander had now become an old man; weary of dominion, he wanted to relinquish it. "But it is just as dangerous to relinquish tyranny as to have it taken away." This the wise man said, and one learns from the tyrant that it is even difficult to get rid of it. Cypselus was not qualified to rule; not even the words of Procles had made any impression on him. Consequently Lycophron should succeed him on the throne. Periander sent a messenger to him, but "No"; and finally he sent his daughter so that the compliant one might persuade the defiant one and by her temperament lead the prodigal back to respect for his father, but he remained in Corcyra. Eventually they decided to divide their estate not as father and son make division in love but as deadly enemies make division: they decided to exchange their places of residence. Periander would reside in Corcyra, and Lycophron would be ruler in Corinth. Periander was all ready for the departure, but the people of Corcyra had such a dread of him and had understood the bellicose incompatibility of the father and son so well that they decided to murder Lycophron, for then presumably Periander would stay away. And so they did. But they were not thereby saved from Periander; he had three hundred of their children carried off to be ravaged. But the gods prevented it, and Periander was so upset that he could not avenge his son that he decided to take his life.

For the last time the wise man and the tyrant were united. His desperate resolve and fear of being overtaken in death by disgrace led his wisdom to find an ingenious escape from life. He summoned two young men and showed them a secret passage. He ordered them to come there the next night and to kill the first man they met and to bury him immediately. When the two were gone, he summoned four others and gave them the same order—to wait in the passage and when they met two young men to murder them and to bury them at once. Then he summoned double the number and gave them the same command—to murder the four they would encounter and bury them immediately on the spot where they felled them. Then Periander himself came at the appointed hour and was murdered.

May 6. *Morning*.

A year ago today. It goes better and better. The word is acquiring a more and more pathos-filled meaning for us. She seems tranquil. Would to God it were so! If only I had a little earlier understood myself as I do now. When that little *altercatio* erupted would have been the time. By being goaded, she herself perhaps would have broken off, and she would have suffered nothing at all.

My soul is oppressed, my mind troubled, and my hope is like an overcrowded lifeboat on a stormy sea.

But the person who is concerned about someone else does not have time really to feel his own pain, and the dreadful terrors of the imagination far outweigh the terrors of actuality. The misrelation between us shows itself here again and seems to create a new wrong against her. Her actual pain, be it ever so keen, her plaintive cry, be it ever so vehement, is still only weak compared with the inventiveness of my imagination without my having seen anything.

May 7. *Morning*.

A year ago today. The decision does not come to her suddenly. And the sudden would perhaps be most dangerous of all for her. The practicing has come so far that it was almost like a dress rehearsal. If it goes off this well in actuality, I ask no more, even though in another sense it will be rather unexplainable to me.

As for me, I feel homesick for myself, for daring to be with myself. It is shattering to have an imagination and an actuality so contrary to each other. My troubled imagination is terrible. Must I now in turn, in a way just as tragic as it is comic, find actuality easier? Oh, that I might be permitted to keep my fancies, for I am accustomed to grappling with them.

Yet it consoles me to be an eyewitness to all this; even if she were to die, I would want to be an eyewitness to it. Actuality is still not the tormentor that possibility is.

May 8. *Morning*.
A year ago today. The situation repeated, the decision as near as possible in a rehearsal, yet not without passion on her part. She seems to understand, however, that what was too coarse as a jest must be in earnest. She is not without vehemence, and that is good. It must happen even today.

When the merchant stands at the furthest tip of the harbor and watches his ship and its rich cargo in distress and, concentrating his mind on the loss, goes away saying to himself: It is your own fault that you did not insure it—I wonder if he really would be happy if a sailor came running after him and said, "We can see the ship again; it has not gone down!"—and the merchant turned around, and the sailor took the telescope to look out there and said, "Why, now it is gone again!"

Truly, she does mean more to me than a merchant ship and a rich cargo. It is my wish, my most fervent wish, that the whole affair may mean as little as possible to her; but even if she received with laughter the letter that will come today, even if she regarded it as joyful news that now she was free of a burden—would that it were so—but even if it were so, it would not help me. What I have experienced at the core of my being—standing at the furthest tip of possibility and seeing the most extreme terror—the result of having stood there and of seeing that sight is what will pursue me. Wound her—if I mean anything to her so that I am able to do that—I will not. I humble myself under the relationship and under my guilt, and in this way I shall take leave of her. From the rehearsals, I believe I have seen enough to know that actuality's terror will not be such that I will evade something by not seeing it.

I wrote a letter to her as follows: In order not to keep on rehearsing what must nevertheless happen, what, when it has happened, will certainly provide the strength that is needed—let it then have happened. Above all, forget the one who writes this; forgive a man who, even if he was capable of something, was nevertheless incapable of making a girl happy.[294]

In the Orient, to send a silken cord is a death penalty to the recipient; in this case to send a ring is very likely a death penalty to the person who sends it.

Now it has happened. I stagger around like a drunkard; I can scarcely walk, cannot concentrate on anything. Indeed, there is nothing on which to focus, either. These moments are really like the hyphen or dash between two words.

What happens? My God, she has been at my apartment while I was out. I find a note, composed in passionate despair—she cannot live without me, it will be the death of her if I leave her, [295]she beseeches me for God's sake, for my salvation's sake, in memory of all that binds me, in the blessed name I rarely mention because my doubt has kept me from appropriating it, even though for that very reason my veneration for it is unmatched.

So, then, I am wedded to her! What else does a wedding ceremony mean than that one gives love a religious expression, a religious obligation. It has happened. [296]There are two powers that bind me and bind me indissolubly: the power of God and the power of one who is dead—there is no arguing with them; there is a name that will obligate me forever, even if all my thinking only remotely perceives it—that name, too, she commandeers. If these powers are obliterated, I do not exist; and if I exist, I am bound, and in these thoughts I shall constantly come to think of the one who commandeered them.

Erotically she is in the wrong; that is certain. A girl has no right to use such means. The fact that she uses them demonstrates basically how little understanding she has of them. Truly I would not dare to use such means. The person who uses them against another binds himself just as firmly as the person he wants to bind: lest it ever be demonstrated that he has taken these sacred means in vain. But my capital crime gives her the most open account.

But how rash to go up to my apartment! Someone may find out that she was in my apartment that day and perhaps not know that I was not at home. So now her honor may also be called in question. And I, who have carefully watched so that no such indignity would venture to come near her! It is bad enough that it will appear as if I rejected her. My only wish had been that it actually was she who rejected me. The terror of responsibility considerably lowers the price of direct erotic sufferings.

And where did she go when she left here? Perhaps she ran away in a delirium, desperate over not being good enough. Good enough—that is the only thing I believe to be out of the question. O death, who gave you permission to practice usury? Or do you not practice usury worse than the most bloodthirsty Jew, worse than the most bloodthirsty miser, every time you merely threaten or merely torture a person with anxiety about death!

So the terminus of our separation has been postponed, if for no other reasons, then for the sake of her honor, and because the whole affair has taken on a terrible shape: I have a human life on my conscience and an eternal responsibility. But what relationship am I now to have with her? [297]A religious point of unity is nonsense; that we two will sorrow together is madness if I am the guilty one and she the one who suffers. How meaningless to be father confessor and murderer simultaneously, to be the one who guiltily crushes and the one who sympathetically raises up!

No! She will see me—I have no intention of running away from anything. If she has rashly bound me for life to this relationship, fastened me with a band that she indeed can tie but cannot untie, then she may be in for something, for I am certainly going to see this through. But it does not follow that she becomes mine or I hers, but if she thinks she can make some impression on me, if she has an argument that I may not have taken into consideration—well, I will not sneak out of anything.

Separated we are, but I will do what is humanly possible to help her. Take complete control of me, then, you formidable passion, you forger who are truth's changeling but in the deception are not distinguishable from it. [298]Brace me up for two

VI
310

months; that is the time, not one day more, but punctually and conscientiously that long. Change all the agony in my breast into foolishness on my lips, all the pathos therein into nonsense when it is uttered. Take away, take it away, hide every trace, every look, every feeling, every hint of a feeling that could please her, hide it all so well that no truth glimmers through the deception. Transform me; when I sit beside her, let me sit like a nodding mandarin, with a thoughtless smile on my lips, reeking of nonsense.

I went to see her. She was relatively more calm than I had expected. —A pair of secret lovers need to be circumspect in order to conceal their understanding with each other. We, of course, are lovers openly and yet it is necessary for us to conceal *our* understanding.

Tomorrow, then, begins the last battle, the reign of terror. I have no impression of her at all. The religious, which always has occupied me, occupied my mind to the point of despair and surely will occupy me as long as I can think, she has enlisted on her side. Perhaps it is such a ferocious skirmish that she did not know what she should think up to use against me and so she has used this. Be that as it may, I must respect it. What I shall venture to do now is to pull myself away from her, if possible, scramble her image of me into sheer inanity and utterly confound her. Every counterargument will be respected. I know very well what these will be. All sympathy for me must be wiped out, and she must also be run weary in reflection. In all human probability she will then be over the worst suffering with me and, humanly speaking, will not be inclined to begin all over again the moment I leave her. —One becomes almost calm when it is a matter of acting, even if what one will do is the most desperate and in the most difficult form—namely, in the form of time and of duration. But if I cannot be calm, then I might just as well not begin this work.

May 8. *Midnight.*[299]

So now all is quiet—not in the sense of the stillness acquired by a passion that is stronger than the noisiest outburst. No, it is quiet in the sense in which the merchant says that the grain market is quiet at present, there is no demand; quiet in the sense in which one says of a village that it is quiet because there is no real event and none is expected, although the usual events are taking place: the cock crows on the manure pile and the duck splashes in the water, and the midday smoke rises out of the chimney, and Morten Frandsen drives home, and everything is in motion until the farmer shuts his door and looks out into the quiet evening, for until then it was not quiet. Quiet, not in the eerie sense in which one says it of an ominous, secretive, closed-up house, but in the common-ordinary sense one says it of a house where peaceful families live, with each one taking care of the appropriate task, and everything goes on as is customary; quiet as one says it of the "quiet people in the land"[300] who go about their business all week long, keep up their account books, shut up shop, and go to church on Sunday.

The more I ponder this stillness, the more changed my nature. Hope for any impassioned decision has been relinquished; the whole thing presumably will go off quietly. But to me this stillness, this security, seems to be the most subtle fraud of existence. Yes, when stillness is an infinite nothing and for that very reason possibility's capacious form for an infinite content—well, then I love it, for then it is the spirit's element and more copious than successions to thrones and world events. This is why I love you, you stillness among the graves, for the dead are sleeping, and yet this stillness is the form for eternity's consciousness of their deeds! This is why I love you, you stillness of the night, when nature's innermost being more clearly discloses itself in intimations than when it loudly proclaims itself in the life and movement of all things! This is why I love you, you stillness of the witching hour here in my room, where no sound and no human voice restrict the infinity of thinking and of the thoughts, where Petrarch's words are appropriate: The sea has not as many creatures in its waves, night has never seen as many stars in the vault of heaven, there are not as many birds in the forest or as many blades of grass in the field and meadow as my heart has thoughts every evening![301] This is why I love you, you solemn

stillness before the battle; let it be the quiet of unspoken pray-
ers, let it be the quiet of the whispered password, your stillness signifies more than does the uproar of battle! This is why
I love you with a shiver, you stillness in the desert; you are
more terrifying than anything that happens or has happened!
This is why I love you, you stillness of solitude, more than
anything that is multifarious, for you are infinite!

But this vegetating stillness in which human life is bewitched, in which time comes and goes and is filled with
something so that there is no felt need, for all rivers flow into
the sea and yet cannot fill the infinite sea, but this and that can
fill up time for people—this is foreign to my soul. And yet it
is this with which I must now seek to become familiar. Down
there in the village lives pretty Marie. She, too, had a love
affair; now the pain is over, now the musician scrapes away
on the violin, and Marie is dancing with a new lover. No! No!
That upsets my whole being! Let infinity separate us—my
hope was that eternity would also unite us. Come, death, and
keep her for eternity; come, madness, and suspend everything
until eternity removes the probate court's seal; come, hate,
with your infinite passion; come, proud distinction, with
your withering wreath of honor; come, godly piety, with
your incorruptible blessedness; come, one of you, and take
her whom I myself cannot take—but not this, not the dab-
blings of the finite. —If that happens, oh, then I am deceiving
her, then I must deceive her. I steal her image as I love to see
it in my imagination; I shall gaze at it, but it will not remind
me of her as it formerly did when I renounced the anesthetiz-
ing relief of recollection, for then it is only a recollection.

Alas, when we separated, my understanding taught me that
I must be prepared, indeed, that I ought to expect this. Now,
now it seems so difficult if it were to happen.

But presumably it will happen—I do not know. But this I
do know—that I owe it to her to accommodate myself to
everything that is possible for me! And it is possible for me to
give her or try to send her a more lenient explanation (and for
me the decisive factor is not whether I in all human probability achieve something) of my conduct, an explanation that is
abhorrent to me, more abhorrent than the most brazen lie I

used when I was hoping that in an infinite sense it would be beneficial to her.

May 12. *Midnight.*

[302]Today I saw her. It was during the noon hour just outside Kongenshave.[303] She came out from the gardens; I was walking on the other side of the street toward the gardens. It was actually my intention when I left home to go there; had it not been my intention, I would not have gone a step out of my way. Yet this scrupulousness is indeed only a leftover from a bygone method, by which, through ascetic abstinence from every, even the remotest, intervention with self-tormenting cruelty, I acknowledged the infinite in her. As far as that goes, I had never once needed the favor. So we met. She had seen me a little beforehand and thus was prepared but perhaps was also somewhat agitated. What a task for observation! To have half a minute to see, to see what will become the object of many hours of consideration! And then to have to watch myself and to be careful to include in the appraisal the impression the sight of me might make. Her face showed some movement; was it the suggestion of a suppressed pain or was it the beginning of a smile. I have never known a girl or any person in whom the expressions of the preliminaries to tears and laughter were so much alike as in her. And in this case the contrasts were not even so pronounced, for a stifled laugh is detectable in the movements of the muscles of the neck, and a stifled sob by the expansion of the chest, but here the doubtfulness of the relations lay in lesser contrasts, and then there was no time to look. The movement could also have been due to her drawing a deep breath in such a way, namely, that I did not see it the moment she opened her mouth but when she closed it.

VI
314

One could go mad trying to extort something definite out of an impression like that, and yet that is what I want to do. [304]If one hears the strokes of the church clock and counts them, it does not necessarily mean that one knows what time it is, for the transmission of sound in relation to the distance in space can result in one's hearing only the last strokes and then making a mistake if one begins to count.

She even looked vigorous, somewhat pale, but I never dare attach much importance to this paleness, for it may be caused by the sight of me. But I do dare to rejoice over vigor, or could it be an illusion that it was the fresh air that had given her the appearance of health. What is a hasty physician able to say! I really am not a hasty physician, for I am not the one who hurries through the patient's room; it is the patient who is rushing so fast past me; and I am not a physician, either, but rather a patient myself.

May 15. *Morning.*

A year ago today. I have frequently laughed at the story of an engaged man who kept another suit coat at his fiancée's to put on in order not to wear out the new one. Now I do not laugh at it; I, too, have a second coat, not at her house, of course, but outside in the passageway. There I put it on and renounce every expression of my love, every hint of my sympathy, every tempting little wish which, if our relationship were secure, would crave to gladden her with trifles. As soon as the coat is on, then begins the everlasting weaving of nonsense, jumbling together the physical and the moral, driveling it all together, continually prating about our being in love, and our being in love, and all that.

It is an agonizing self-punishment, as agonizing as the scene in Tartarus:[305] to have to sit that way and make faces at myself. But so it must be. Through this approach I hope that our whole relationship, when the moment to sever it comes again, will have no appeal whatsoever for her, not even the temptation of terror, but that she will loathe it, be fed up with it, and be nauseated just as someone is sick of oranges who has eaten them along with taking a medicine. If all on her own she is able later to idealize the relationship, then she is quite another individuality than I believed her to be and is far from needing me.

May 16. *Midnight.*

As I said before, the whole thing will probably go off quietly. Yesterday and the day before I spoke with my friend, who is well informed, and who also with true friendship has tortured me, even though at the same time he rendered me a service, with all sorts of pieces of information under fictitious names. He went on with the stories and his fictitious names. And his friendship is unaltered. At first he wanted to alarm me with the peril to life. Now his pipe has another tune; he is out to arouse me, if possible, by stirring up a little jealousy in me— but in that case she must be in rather good health. The benefit I have from this man is incalculable. He is the one I am going to use now; the comedy began today. When he was in the middle of his story, I stood up, embraced him warmly, and said with emotion, "Now I understand you! Oh, what a fool I was not to have seen in you a friend! Do not deny it—you are talking about her, alas, about her whom I have made un-happy and whom I still have loved and to whom I have wished many a time to return but cannot. No, I cannot do it; to be honest, my pride has too much power over me." My friend was rather dumbfounded; indeed, it must be rather awkward to be sitting amicably and with simple Christian malice trying to torment someone and then to be enfolded in the embrace of friendship. It is as if a robber meeting a traveler on a solitary road and on the point of assaulting his victim felt himself tenderly embraced and heard these touching words: O sweet fate, to send me a guide, to me who am lost, and you, my kind benefactor, mankind's precious representative in these desolate places, etc. It would certainly be possible for the robber to be reduced to embarrassment. At least my friend was. I am well aware that occasionally she must make inquir-ies about me. I do not know this from him, but I know it because there is someone else who has been very quick to gather something from me to run with, and my friend is much closer to her.

VI
316

In a way, he now became my friend. Of course, I do not trust him an inch. But it is grist for his mill that he thinks he has me in his power and that I am still so concerned about her that he can have his fun in torturing me. At first, I wanted with his help to initiate a correspondence with her. I very ur-gently assured him that I dared not see her and therefore had to write. That I have seen her, no one knows, and she would scarcely ever dream of telling it. This plan, however, was rejected. Then he promised to get into her hands some letters I am writing to a third man. For safety's sake I have used three kinds of ink so that there can be a little difference in the color, inasmuch as the dates differ.

So, with united efforts, it is now going well. He has nothing against her falling in love again, because he believes it will prod me, and he perceives that I may even be of some help along this line.

An author, I do not remember who, has said that honesty is the best policy, only not when it comes to pleasing women. I, too, really do believe that truth does not make a woman happy, nor do lies, either, far from it, but just a little dose of untruth.

The schemed jealousy is hardly my concern. *Non enim est in carendo difficultas, nisi quum est in habendo cupiditas* [For there is no difficulty in abstaining unless there is lust in enjoying], declares Augustine.[306] It is certainly true that I have desired her, indeed, that I do desire her, but that I had no external obstacle shows that there was something higher that binds my desire. That higher something is the idea. Together with it, I desire her, infinitely; without it, I hold to what is higher than both of us. Thus my concern is of a different sort: essentially (for in actuality and on the basis of my chances I may achieve nothing) with these letters I am writing a bill of divorcement that sets infinity between us, and with these letters, I have essentially done my part (truly not my sympathetic desire) to procure some ease in my life, which grieves me.

VI
317

May 19. *Midnight.*

Presumably she has received my letters now. My conception of the relationship is not devoid of repentance and contrition. This concession grieves me most. With every other deception I was at least blazing with enthusiasm,[307] because my reason for it and my motivation in it was the hope that she would concentrate herself in an infinite sense. This time I am dejected, and yet this time I may have an entirely different influence on her than with all my efforts when I was bound to her and my efforts when, by breaking away, I became bound to her even more. My repentance and contrition, of course, run into many words, and the upshot of those many words naturally is that it cannot be undone now. I repent of the past; I wish to undo it, but I cannot—no, I cannot do it, but I want to do so. If only it were not for my pride, I would do it etc. As a rule repentance is identified by one thing, that it acts. In our day, it perhaps is less subject to being misunderstood in this way. I believe that neither Young nor Talleyrand nor a more recent author was right in what they said about language,[308] why it exists, for I believe that it exists to strengthen and assist people in abstaining from action. What to me is nonsense will perhaps have a great effect and perhaps most of my acquaintances, if they were to read these letters, would say: "Well, now we have understood him."

It is indeed hard; one would certainly prefer to enjoy the general reputation of not being regarded as a loony-bin inmate. That, too, I am achieving. I really do believe that no matter what I say, provided it is not the truth or my most sincere opinion, I would even be regarded as sagacious; by doing the latter I would unconditionally provide grounds for my deportation. If I were to say, "I took that crucial step because I felt bound, because I had to have my freedom, inasmuch as the lustfulness of my desire embraces a world and cannot be satisfied with one girl," then the chorus would reply, "That makes sense! Good luck, you enlightened man!" But if I were to say, "She was the only one I have loved; if I had not been sure of that when I left her, I would never have dared to leave her," then the answer would be, "Away to the loony bin with him!" If I were to say, "I was tired of her," then the chorus would answer, "Now you're talking! That is understandable!" But if I were to say, "Then I cannot understand it, for one certainly does not dare to break a relationship of duty because one is tired of it," then they would say, "He is crazy." If I were to say (in the words of my most recent interpretation), "I repent of it, I would like to undo it, but I cannot do it—no, I cannot do it, my pride does not permit it—no, I cannot do it"—then the verdict would be, "He is just like everyone else and like the heroes in French poetry." But if I were to declare that nothing, nothing would so satisfy my pride as to dare to undo it, that nothing, nothing would so allay the cold fire of revenge that demands amends, then the response would be: "He is delirious; do not listen to him; away to the loony bin with him."

Mundus vult decipi [The world wants to be deceived];[309] my relationship to the environment that I must call my world can hardly be more definitely expressed. In fact, I believe that in a wider sense it is the best that has been said about the world. Thus speculators should not cudgel their brains trying to fathom what the times demand, for it has been essentially the same since time immemorial: to be tricked and bamboozled. If one just says something silly and drinks *dus* with humanity *en masse*, then one comes to be, like Per Degn, loved and esteemed by the whole congregation.[310] It is not any different now, and anyone who with visible signs of deep concern strikes an attitude of brooding in public over how to find out what it is the times demand has already, when all is said and done, discovered it. In this respect, anyone can serve the age, whether it is to be understood as a whole nation, the human race as a whole, all the future generations, or a little circle of contemporaries. I serve the participants by being a scoundrel. There is no doubt that I satisfy their demand. In fact, I myself also benefit from it and in a certain sense find this outside appraisal really desirable.[311] To be a model of virtue, a bright normative human being, is, for one thing, very embarrassing—and also very dubious. But, on the other hand, I am not being persecuted, either. This, too, is desirable, lest I should draw wrong conclusions and think well of myself because I am persecuted in the world.

With regard to people, I have never hesitated to follow my guardian spirit in yielding to a certain elemental modesty about the good and a somewhat gloomy distrust of myself—in other words, to deceive in such a way that I perhaps am always a little better than I seem. I have never been able to understand it in any other way than that every human being is essentially assigned himself and that outside of this either there is an authorization such as an apostle's, the dialectical nature of which I cannot grasp, although out of respect for what is handed down to me as sacred I refrain from drawing any conclusions from my nonunderstanding—or there is maundering. It is quite true that a person who cannot shave himself can set up shop as a barber and serve others according to their needs, but in the world of spirit this is meaningless.

It is, however, regarded as part and parcel of earnestness to want to be readily available to exert an influence upon others, yet without necessarily wanting to be an apostle (how humble!)—and yet without being able to determine one's similarity to and one's dissimilarity from such a person (how meaningless!). Everyone wants to work for others. This is a rule in the civic address, although it is more understandable there, but it is also a rule in the rhetorical form of the religious address. I do not doubt that it is found in printed sermon outlines, and one hears it ever so often, unless one is listening to an individual who has been personally tested and knows how to speak and knows whereof he speaks.

If the sermon is about preparing the way of the Lord,[312] then the first point is that everyone does his part in spreading Christianity, not just we pastors but also everyone else as well etc. This is indeed fascinating! Not just we pastors. Here at the outset the dialectical middle terms, whether a pastor is an apostle, are lacking, and if not, then how is he different from one and how is he like one? The ecclesiastical points of difference with regard to ordination increase the difficulties, and the principal middle term is pushed back by decisions in the realm of the undecided. So, then, not just we pastors. This passage looks very hopeful at the beginning. But that to which "not just" refers is not given at all, and now follows the apodosis with the earnestness of exhortation: Heed my words, dear listeners, it is not just I and we pastors who should work in this manner, but you also should work in this way! How? Well, that is the only thing that does not become clear in this earnest discourse, the earnestness of which does not lie exactly in the subject matter. Now the first point has been made; the pastor wipes away the sweat, and the listeners do likewise just at the thought that in this way they have become missionaries.

The speaker begins again. One hopes to receive a little more detailed enlightenment, but look! The next point is that each person prepares the way of the Lord within himself. This, of course, is what ought to be spoken about, and on this point a life-view can be built. One understands that the single individual has essentially with himself to do, that performance is the incidental, which one is not to anticipate and essentially does not dare to attribute to oneself, and which only in the retrospection of eternity will be seen for what it is—essentially God's extra bonus and incidentally the individual's work. In other words, life and the Governance in it are something more than a flat sum of all individual human beings' deeds. Therefore a person must have his absolute idea *in mente* wherever he goes. If this is lacking, one deceives in two ways: one captivates people in daydreams, and one does an injustice to the one who suffers. Actually, that first point requires prosperity of everyone. It is very easy to talk about things like this, which immature and lazy natures prefer to hear; it is meaningless to *require* it, for prosperity is not freedom's extra bonus, but Governance's, and suppose, then, that one had suffered adversity. But if it is understood that the single individual essentially has with himself to do, then it will also be understood that he exists in such a way that his life, what he says, etc., can *possibly* have meaning for others; possibly, because first it is the affair of Governance and second it is not the direct influence of example and teaching. Thus a speaker could begin here and turn the first point around somewhat like this, "Although it may seem so, not even I can essentially do more than to attend to myself. Do not let yourself be trapped by an illusion."[313] But the design of the discourse is just the reverse. One appeals to the example of John the Baptizer, but John the Baptizer is not a straightforward paradigm; he is ἀφορισμένος [set apart][314] in the exceptional, and consequently middle terms are required. Moreover, one must always be circumspect in using world-historical characters. [315]That is, they have a completion that makes the observation sure—and also

VI
320

the misunderstanding. Every character that is to be used must come into existence for thought, clear in its dialectical structure; otherwise it is only a jest to offer him as a paradigm.

Since I myself am an existing person and consequently must use ethically what is said, I have pondered this very much. When one chooses differently, chooses to instruct or to listen, but leaves out the crises of realization, then it is easy to have much to say, much advice to give, and easy to find peace of mind. Through what I have thought about this, I have reached the conclusion that I benefit a person most by deceiving him. The highest truth with respect to my relation to him is this: essentially I can be of no benefit to him (this is the expression for the most profoundly optative sympathetic pain, which one can keep from experiencing only through giddiness, but also for the highest enthusiasm in the equality of all), and the most adequate form for this truth is that I deceive him, for otherwise it would be possible for him to make a mistake and learn the truth from me and thereby be deceived, namely, that he would believe that he had learned it from me. I am well aware that the majority of those I would initiate into my skeptical line of thought would smile at me and censure my frivolousness, for the captivating—that was the earnestness. This cannot disturb me without making me guilty of an inconsistency, and this cannot be, since I do not wish to confide in anyone lest I myself make a mistake and think I should go out and proclaim this closehandedness instead of staying close to myself. Let every human being be closehanded; then God will be the only openhanded one.

VI
321

This I have learned best and also most grievously in my relationship with her, in which the optative sympathy continually has wanted to make an exception, in which I have wished to the point of despair to be able to be everything to her, until in pain I learned that it is infinitely higher to be nothing at all to her. It consoles me that in my relationship with her I have never fancied myself to be a teacher or felt called upon to say a few admonitory words. Even if the wisest of persons spent six hours a day on someone, even if he spent six other hours considering how best to do it, if he continued in this for six years, he would be a deceiver if he dared to say that he had benefited him *essentially*. And for me, at least, this thought is the deepest fount of inspiration. A person can teach language, the arts, manual skills, etc., to another, but ethically-religiously one cannot essentially benefit another. And this is why it is beautiful and inspiring to express this in the utmost exertion of the deception, because a deception under ethical responsibility is no easy matter and can always cope with the admonitory words. Now after what happened later, it consoles me that she does not have a learner's relation to me, which could be disturbing. What I have spoken I have spoken as if it were to myself, and I have made neither gesticulations nor applications. If she appropriates it, she does it on her own, not depending on "his word and gown."[316] It is quite easy to jump on an omnibus and ride around and say a few admonitory words; there may also be something beautiful in wanting to do it, but it is stupid to be able to teach that a person is capable of nothing whatsoever and then to be able to ascribe such enormous influence to a few admonitory words. Wonder's and admiration's thanksgiving for the effect belongs to God. For every human being should see to himself in life; in eternity there is time to see what God has brought out of this. And this does not mean the conspicuous influence of particular individuals, but the minutest fraction of influence in connection with the deed of the least important person.

This is how I have tried to understand life. The person who has understood it the same way presumably will conduct himself in the same way and, above all, continually express himself so circumspectly and in the form of deception that he avoids the danger of which everyone, right down to the most insignificant newspaper reporter, must be aware of in our age—that there nevertheless were a couple of people who had the preposterous idea that what was said directly was the truth and that their task was to sally forth into the world etc. But sallying forth into the world must be left to knights-errant; true earnestness is aware of every danger, of this one also— that someone might *bona fide* become a thoughtless follower, something best prevented by using antithesis as the form of presentation. In my opinion, no one, with the exception of such authorized individualities as the apostles, whose dialectical position I do not grasp,[317] has been more earnest than the person who clothed his thoughts in the form of jest, and no one has so sympathetically loved his fellow beings, and no one has so deeply admired the divine.[318] So let the history books tell of kings who introduced Christianity—I am of the opinion that a king can introduce an improved breed of sheep and railroads etc., but Christianity and spirit, ethically understood, not even an emperor should go to the trouble of introducing—that is, essentially understood.

A change is now occurring in my relationship with her. Until now, I have kept very quiet and respected the infinity in her. Now I offer an explanation. This I regard as a deception. Earlier the form was deception and the contents interest for the infinity in her. Thus my stillness, my silence, my annihilation was deception's form of an infinite interest for her. Now it is otherwise. What I say I do not mean, but neither do I mean that in the form of deception it is the adequate guise or disguise for my true meaning. Whether it actually influences her makes no difference. My only concern is the essential, and the essential is that this is my motive and intention. My explanation that I repent but cannot undo what I am guilty of doing is nonsense. In other words, if I cannot give the reason why I cannot undo it, I should never speak of repenting, but least of all give pride as the reason (i.e., that I do not want to), for that is actually to make a fool of her. Therefore I have never represented myself as repenting before now, although I do indeed repent and have repented that I entered into that relationship and find my humiliation in not being able to undo it, precisely what my pride desires, since it is crushed because I, who have had an almost foolhardy conception of willing, must wince because there is something I will, will with all my passion, but cannot do. Why I cannot (which is due to my relation to the idea, until either this is changed or I am), I cannot tell her in such a way that she can understand it, but for this very reason I have never said that I repented. Thus there was meaning in my conduct. But to repent and to give pride as the hindrance

VI
323

to the expression of repentance, since, on the contrary, it ought to be the object of repentance, is high treason against God. How anyone can understand it and find it plausible, I do not comprehend, but in return most people presumably say the same thing about my view.

For the first time in my life, perhaps, I am doing something that I myself regard as meaningless. I have done much that the majority perhaps would regard as that; this has not disturbed me since it also could be because the majority do not have enough understanding to think it through and the courage to venture out into the extremities where I have my life. I have also done much that I myself later perceived to be foolish, and even though repentance does not respect excuses when it makes inspection, I still find a kind of consolation in the fact that when I did it I did not regard it as meaningless. Incapable as I am of understanding such tasks as the future of all mankind or what it is that the times demand, I have concentrated entirely on myself. When the right thing becomes doubtful to me, I have usually said my name aloud to myself, with the addition: One may die, one may become unhappy, but one can still preserve meaning in one's life and faithfulness to the idea. Now that is at an end. [319]And who is to blame for that? Someone else would perhaps say: It is she, to whose apron strings you still are tied. But I would not say that, for I usually refrain from such nonsense, that someone else is to blame when I do something wrong. I prefer to say that I myself am at fault. The fault is mine, is my weakness, and the difficulty is that my understanding guarantees me that it can be beneficial to her in the finite sense, whereas my sympathy would rather love her in the infinite sense. This relationship has humbled me, and now, whether she reads my letters or not, whether they have any influence on her or not, she now triumphs over me in a way that makes me dejected.

VI
324

May 21. *Midnight.*
There is nothing new under the sun, says Solomon.[320] Well, so be it, but it is worse when nothing at all happens. With this observation alone I assure myself how absurd it would be if I

sought out any confidant. Yes, if my pain were rich in incidents, in changes of scene and setting, then it would have interest. But my suffering is boring. It is true, I am still continually involved in the exposition of this nothing, and the scene
unchanged is the same.

[321]Suppose that I traveled in order to make time pass, *per
mare tristitiam fugiens per saxa per ignes* [fleeing sorrow through
sea, through rocks, through flame],[322] but it cannot be done. I
still ought to keep entirely quiet. A journey, of which she
would easily be informed, could possibly upset her and delude
her into thinking that after a longer passage of time I had
changed. But time must be dispensed to her as scantily as possible. I only wish that Governance will lead our paths together
frequently, because she benefits from seeing me; she thereby
has the opportunity to reassure herself that I am here and living as usual and that I am not in a foreign country—and possibly thinking of her and possibly being homesick. If I were
to travel, I ought to have gone a long time ago, ought to have
given out a false indication of time for the journey, and then
suddenly have come back. It might have occurred to her that
this suddenness pertained to her; until she perceived that it did
not pertain to her, it perhaps would have been beneficial. But
the time for such things is over.

VI
325

Just now the clock struck one. This inconsolable indication
of time! For twelve is indeed a large number of strokes, and a
person is conscious that it is time that is being indicated, and
two, of course, is counting,[323] but one is like a declaration of
eternity. If there is a kind of eternity of punishment, and the
poor wretch wanted to lament to someone, why would not
people shun him, for he is not only wretched but his suffering
is boring—if it were not boring, one very likely could show
him sympathy.

As for me, I want no one's sympathy. God in heaven is not
disgusted with what is boring. It is supposed to be a duty to
pray, it is supposed to be beneficial to pray, there are supposed
to be three reasons, perhaps even four, for praying. I have no
intention of depriving anyone of his reasons; he is welcome to
keep them if only I may keep *daring* to pray as something so

inspiring that in a far deeper sense than Plato and Aristotle one can say that wonder [*Forundring*] is the starting point of knowledge.[324] In this respect, I have no confidence in many arguments and sixteen reasons; it would perhaps be better, especially with regard to the educated (for it comes easier to the poor, wretched, and simple to pray), if permission to pray were made to cost something—then there perhaps would be a great demand for it. If it holds true of earthly love that it seeks secrecy, it is even more true of prayer that it prefers solitude and being as secret as possible in order neither to be disturbed nor to embarrass others by its emotion; one does not need to have witnesses, either, and it helps very little to have them. A prince who travels incognito can lay aside his incognito at any time; it seems to me that the external appearance of the one who is praying is also an incognito that he certainly cannot lay aside in order to become an object of worldly admiration [*Beundring*], but he can lay it aside when in prayer he is lifted to a new and infinite wonder [*Under*] that God in heaven is the only one who does not become weary of listening to a human being. And this holy wonder in turn will keep the one who is praying from thinking whether he receives what he is praying about. [325]Falling in love is not beautiful if one looks to see if it pays, and even if one sees that it pays exceptionally well, it is not a happy falling in love. Prayer was certainly not devised in order to rebuke God but is a favor that is graciously granted to every human being and that makes him more than a nobleman. But if one understands to the point of wonder—indeed, to the point where wonder shipwrecks one's understanding—that it is a favor, then arguments are perceived to be not necessary, either, for it is only the problematic that is commended by arguments. Every external reflection *eo ipso* nullifies prayer, be it reflection squinting at the temporal advantage or be it reflection on the individual himself and his relation to others, as if a man were so earnest that he could not pray within himself and alone but had to step forward and benefit the whole congregation with his intercession and his example as one who prays; [326]likewise there are also people who are

VI
326

unable to speak except to a general assembly, and Madame Voltisubito cannot ride without hearing the whip crack.[327]

But her, her! What if she still refuses to understand this within herself but instead seeks finite consolation! How hard it is for a person who has not scattered his soul in diffusive concern for every Tom, Dick, and Harry, or for the whole human race, to dare in solitude to express his concern for himself alone, like shadowboxing, and not dare to do all that which certainly in a higher sense is a nothing but which does, nevertheless, provide sympathetic relief.

May 22. *Morning.*

[328]A year ago today. Laughter is and continues to be the best method of exploration. She joins in the laughter, but then she is unable to laugh any more and her laughter is exhausted. So, then, she does not have infinite passion but only to a certain degree. Then I shudder, for I know what is coming. Then come pleas and tears, until she becomes tired again, but my prattling away has not become tired, it continues steadily.

It is terrible to be jabbed where the most delicate nerves are, but it is still more terrible not once to dare to alter one's features while it goes on but to have to sit there perfectly calm and to chatter away.

For only ten minutes I was earnest today. I intend to act that way once a week. I calmly said to her: "End it, break up; in the long run you will not resist me." [329]But then her passion flares up most violently; she declares that she would rather have all this than not to see me. This is only a passionate outburst, and its violence shows me definitely that my approach will contribute to working her afloat.

May 25. *Midnight.*

Recollect her I dare not. If death had separated us as it separates lovers, if she had broken with me, then I would dare to recollect what was beautiful and lovely, every moment that was once happy for us. Then when spring youthfully breaks into bud, I would remember her; when the foliage throws its shadow, I would rest in the recollection of her; in the evening

VI
327

when the summer mists gather, I would see her image; beside the quiet lake, when the reeds whisper, I would be reminded of her; [330]along the seashore, when the ship is coming in, I would imagine that I would meet her until the monotonous waves rocked me away into recollection; at my favorite old café I would seek a vestige of it and often, often deceive myself, as if I were going to her. But I dare not. For me there is no change of the seasons, just as for me there is no change; [331]recollection does not bloom and blossom in my hands; it is like a judgment hanging over me, or like a mysterious sign, the meaning of which I am not quite sure. [332]Indeed, did Adam dare to recollect Eden; did he dare, when he saw thistles and thorns[333] at his feet, did he dare to say to Eve: No! It was not like this in Eden. In Eden, oh, do you recollect? Did Adam dare to do this? Even less do I.

May 27. *Midnight.*
Forget her? —It is impossible. My edifice has collapsed. [334]I was depressed, but in this depression I was an enthusiast, and that bleak idea of my youth that I was good for nothing was perhaps only a form of enthusiasm because I required an ideality, under which I sank. This secret I wanted to hide within myself and within this secret an ardor that certainly made me unhappy but also indescribably happy. Early, all too soon, I thought I detected that the enthusiasm one finds on the highways and byways is not the kind I wanted to have any part of. Then I would put on a cold and callous front in order to have no association with what is cosmeticized or self-deluding. That was a proud thought, something that could occur to a depressed person. But even if there were shrill cries against me, that I was an egotist, I did not want anyone to be right in opposition to me. All this is thrown into chaos; I am disarmed. I have become a prisoner in the appearance I wanted to conjure up. I have indeed acted shabbily toward a human being. Even if I see it differently and even if I am as sure as the sun rises in the east that I shall always have enthusiasm on my side, whatever I do—I cannot make myself comprehensible to any human being.

Governance has made me captive. The idea of my existence was proud; now I am crushed. I do know that. I can conceal it from others, but I have lost the very substance of my existence, the secure place of resort behind my deceptive appearance, lost what I shall never regain, precisely what I myself must prevent myself from regaining, for my pride still remains but has had to *referre pedem* [give ground] and now has the task, among other things, of never forgiving myself. Only religiously can I now become intelligible to myself before God; in relation to people, misunderstanding is the foreign language I speak. I wanted to have the power to be able to express myself in the universal any time I wished; now I cannot do it.

Ah, to have an understanding with God is blissful, but that through Governance or myself I am so encompassed with misunderstanding that I am continually being forced back into this solitary understanding still has its pain also. Who would think twice about choosing a relationship of confidence, but my choice is not free. Here I am sensible of freedom only when in necessity I surrender myself and in the surrender forget it. I cannot say "to whom should I go but to you,"[335] for I cannot go to anyone, since one cannot, of course, entrust oneself to the intimacy of misunderstanding; I cannot go to anyone, for I am a prisoner, and misunderstanding and again misunderstanding and again misunderstanding are the heavy iron bars before my window, and I choose not to go to God, for I am constrained. But then comes the moment of understanding, and then it is once again blessed that there are iron bars before the windows, for the result of this is that the understanding cannot be an illusion, something acquired, a yield at second hand, and that it cannot become some chattering blabbing, for to whom should I speak?

VI
329

My idea was to structure my life ethically in my innermost being and to conceal this inwardness in the form of deception. Now I am forced even further back into myself; my life is religiously structured and is so far back in inwardness that I have difficulty in making my way to actuality.

To whom, indeed, would it occur to want to be self-impor-

tant in relation to God, but my relationship is of such a nature
that it is as if God had chosen me, not I God. Not even the
appearance of the negative expression of being something—
that it is I who come to him—is left to me.[336] If I am unwilling
to resign myself to bearing the pain of necessity, I am annihilated and have nowhere to be but among men in misunderstanding. If I endure the pain of necessity, then the transformation occurs.

My loss I shall never get over, and it will probably be a long
time before I learn to bear it. As I walk about among men, it
seems to me as if my lost pride walked by, as if I read in another's face that he was judging me in this way. Then I could
rush like a desperate man in among the people to try to grasp
my lost shadow, to claim it,[337] to avenge myself, to console
myself with revenge until I would sink down from exhaus-
tion. Yes, woe to the woman whose look moved me in this
way. But one can have revenge upon a woman. [338]I know that
the person who is offended by natural conditions can be possessed by dreadful thoughts. How did it happen that Richard
III could overpower the woman who was his sworn enemy
and change her into his lover?[339] And why, I wonder, did he
do it? Was it politics? Was the derision with which he ponders
the ease of his conquest politics also? When he dwells on his
own deformity with the passion of despair, was it self-exam-
ination, whereby he would perceive himself fit to be king?
No, it was a hatred of life; it was by the power of the spirit
that he wanted to scoff at nature, which had scoffed at him; he
wanted to hold nature up to ridicule together with its invention of erotic love and love of the beautiful, for he, the injured
one, he, the cripple, he, the desperate one, he, the devil,
wanted to demonstrate, despite language and all the laws of
life, that he could be loved. Then he learned, then he discovered that there is a power that works upon woman with certainty, the power of falsehood and lies, when they are declared
with the flame of wild enthusiasm, with the unhealthy excitement of lust, and yet with the chilling coldness of the understanding, just as the strongest wines are served cooled with
ice. He himself hated, and yet he aroused erotic love, even

though women do not love someone like that but are disgusted with him and succumb to him only when dizzy and
stunned. There is an evil spirit such as that, and it offers huge
sums of earnest money: the anticipation of suprahuman powers; and it tempts with mirages, as if an insane revenge were
the true way to save one's pride and avenge one's honor. And
the way is bound to be hard even though it is possible—the
way back over the chasmic abyss that separates good and evil
in time as well, the transition from being of supranatural size
by the power of evil to being nothing, nothing at all, less than
nothing in repentance.

"What is honor?" says Falstaff. "Can it put on a leg? No.
Can it put on an arm? No. Ergo, it is a fancy, a word, a
painted escutcheon."[340] No, this "ergo" was foolish, for if
honor can do none of these things if one wins it, it can do the
opposite if it is lost, it can take off a leg and an arm—indeed,
it can maltreat a person worse than is done in Russia and can
send one to Siberia. When it can do that, it is not something
we imagine. Go to the battlefield and look at the fallen, go to
the disabled-soldiers' hospital and look at the wounded—you
will never find a dead or wounded man as maltreated as one
with whom honor has finished.

Thus, understanding comes inside the iron bars. Where,
then, is the field of honor? It is wherever a man falls with
honor. But the person who, rather than sneaking through life
with honor, preferred to lose his honor and give it to God, he,
too, falls on the field of honor. If there is a new heaven and a
new earth[341] to expect, then there is also a new honor. Even if
I fall where no one dreams that a field of honor can be, even if
I am buried in the graveyard of the dishonorable, if there
nevertheless is one single individual who, passing by my
grave perhaps thinking other thoughts, suddenly stops and
delivers this funeral oration to me, "How did this person
come to lie here? Can one then lie without disgrace among the
dishonored—and he certainly lies here with honor"—then I
ask no more. I shall picture it more clearly and more deci-
sively than the crisis of my life. Suppose that Mary Magdalene
had had no witness to her shame[342] and she could have sneaked

VI
331

through life with honor and in death sneaked out of the world with a myrtle wreath upon her brow—it seems to me that through her courage she won another honor; it seems to me that in death she lies more honored without the myrtle wreath than with it.

So it also seems to me that the person who admitted that he had begun what he could not finish still did not lose his honor but preserved it better than if he had obtained cheap what he would give everything to possess, better than if he had sneaked through life as a girl's benefactor when he did not even dare admit to himself to being the more unassuming person that he merely wished to be, instead of holding her in high esteem while she youthfully had too high an opinion of herself, instead of holding her in high esteem when she despondently very much undervalued herself, and holding her in highest esteem as her deceiver when for the lowest price he could be her husband. It seems to me that the benedictions of the grateful pronounced over him would be like mockery, and the venerable designation of his relationship with her an abomination, but the severest judgment of language and of rage upon his conduct would be a restitution of honor.

May 30. *Morning.*

[343]A year ago today. Is it not possible that she could be victorious and carry through her wish? We shall see. What I am shipwrecked on is that my whole view of life, which was not snatched out of thin air but was indeed essential to my individuality, is rejected. I cannot become happy; she cannot become happy; our relationship cannot become a marriage. Can she not become happy? What does that mean when she herself so passionately desires it. But what is the use of passion when it is a question as to whether she understands herself? Her passion shows precisely that she does not even have freedom of thought in relation to another view. If we separate and I use force to break up, she becomes unhappy. But then there is nothing, either, that will make manifest that she is happy, and there is meaning in her unhappiness and in my guilt. But if she becomes unhappy by remaining with me, then this is non-

sense, and if the passionateness is gone because there is no provocative opposition, what then? Our relationship cannot become a marriage. Why not? Because I am inclosed by my
depression. I knew that from the beginning and believed that
my task was to conceal it; so I have understood it, but a marriage is not like that. But if she would nevertheless put up with
what would amount to a morganatic marriage? But I myself
will not put up with that, for as I see it now it would be an
insult to her. Indeed, should one merely ask if one can put up
with something and not ask what this something is, whether
it is true, whether it is beautiful, whether it is by virtue of the
idea? She does not ask about this at all, she who once was
proud. This shows that she is so passionate that she cannot
have any judgment at all.

VI
332

For a marriage, a wedding is required. What is a wedding?
It is the making of a vow that is mutually binding. But a mutual commitment certainly requires mutual understanding.
But she does not understand me at all. What does my vow
become, then? It becomes nonsense. Is it a marriage? No, it is
a profanation! If we were to be wedded ten times, I would not
be married to her, but she would be to me. But if she is altogether unconcerned about this? Is one merely to ask about carrying through one's passionate wish and ask nothing about
the idea; is one merely to believe in one's passionateness and
have no faith or confidence that the person one loves can mean
well, as they say, even though he does not have the same
meaning? Does this not demonstrate her passionateness and
its contradiction? Precisely in that which should bind us together most intimately, I see a divine protestation against the
whole thing. At the time of the wedding, we are not united
but I find out what I knew beforehand—that we are separated.
Is this a marriage? Or am I married to her because she lives in
my house, because I do not wish any other woman? Then I
am essentially married to her, for she still remains with me,
and I certainly will know how to honor myself and her by not
looking for any new love, as if I had rejected her, something
she no doubt imagines, and this again shows that she does not

understand me and again shows that in her passionateness there smolders a secret pride.

What a strange and wonderful creature is woman, and what a strange power is love! I cannot stop loving her, and yet her fidelity is of a dubious kind. Is it love to love the way she loves at this time, is it an art? No, it is weakness. Is it beautiful? No, for it is unfree. Is it a power? No, it is a weakness. Is it fellow feeling? No, it is self-love. Is it faithfulness? No, it is a subtlety of nature. And yet when it is a woman who does it . . . . . . No, I do not believe I would like this in anyone else, but when she does it, she does it in such a way, or I look upon it in such a way, that she loses nothing at all in my eyes. She uses every means against me, and it never occurs to her to suggest by a single word that she could believe me and therefore would give in, that she would resign herself [344]and thereby give me my freedom, that she will scorn me and on that condition give me up. In a way we have traded roles, for in a certain sense she is the strong one and I the weak, inasmuch as I am always fearful on her behalf. And truly, if it were one to one, I would be no match for her, but the trouble is that I am more than one since I have the category and the idea on my side. Therefore I am not qualified to be a hero, for it is not my victory I am seeking; it is the victory of the idea, and I am willing to be annihilated. Thus when I have won and it is settled, I will not say as did Pyrrhus: One more victory like this, and it is over—for this victory is enough. [345]

June 3. Midnight.

So once again I am sitting on watch. If I were to say that to a third party, it no doubt would need an explanation, for it is readily understood that the pilot along the coast, the sentinel at the top of the tower, the lookout at the bow of the ship, and the robber in his lair sit on watch because there is something to watch for. But someone sitting alone in his room—for what can he be watching? And someone who anticipates that everything—that is, the minor little affair that everyone else would perhaps disregard—will pass quietly, he, of course, is on watch for nothing. No wonder it is a strain for his soul and his head, because to look for something is good for the eyes, but to look for nothing strains them. And when the eyes look for nothing for a long time they finally see themselves or their own seeing: in the same way the emptiness surrounding me presses my thinking back into myself.

So I am beginning all over again to scrutinize the dialectical difficulties of my expectation. The culmination of my existence, that almost mad wish, my enthusiasm's utmost exertion and ultimate delight, is that the whole thing could be undone. I have focused my whole being on this extreme peak; admittedly, I feel that the weight of the finite has now dragged me down from it at times. So, then, more practice. From this wish, the paths branch off; the wish becomes one thing for her, something else for me. Autopathetically, I must wish that she would become another's; for my personality in its egoity, this is the easiest solution of all. Sympathetically, I do not wish it, insofar as it does not happen in a way that is incomprehensible, such as returning to a first love, for otherwise it is a finite healing and not the highest. Otherwise, a religiously oriented infinitizing would be the highest and is the highest, thus something I must wish for her, even though, autopathetically understood, such an existence would become a heavy burden for me. For her it would not be difficult to find a religious solution. She has nothing for which to reproach herself; she can live in blessed friendship with the eternal, she can die gently and quietly in God "*wie das Wiegenkind mit seiner Mutter Brust im Munde sterbend* [like the cradle babe dying with its mother's breast between its lips]."[346] For me such an existence would become a sentence to penitence *in perpetuum* [in perpetuity]. Hard on the heels of a religious infinitizing, my next sympathetic wish for her would be that she might be intensified in her temporal existence, become something great and exceptional. If this were to happen, my life would once again be impounded. —I scarcely need to list the terrible crises; they may be considered a thing of the past.

Despite this long series of steps, there is still meaning in my existence. What I have done already, up to the last letters, is consistent. I have kept perfectly quiet, silent, as if nothing

VI
334

were happening. What a strain this has been on me is understood only by the person who understands my passions, not by others. How true it is, what Heiberg says in an excellent novella, *Den farlige Taushed* [The Perilous Silence], "No matter how strong our reasons for regarding a person as unhappy and inwardly shattered, if he appears collected, cheerful, and in good spirits, all our reasons are put to flight and we believe what we see instead of what we know."[347] —We have laughed often enough at the bear that severely mauled its master as it tried to drive away a fly. Indeed, it is comic, but the situation can easily be made deeply tragic. Suppose the bear were aware of the consequences of using its strength as only the bear can use it. And suppose it saw its master being pestered and then had to sit there restraining itself lest it make everything more dangerous. This was bound to be very irksome and hard, for of course it knew that it could easily kill the fly.

It is the art of the actor to have to seem agitated while he is calm (if he is actually upset, it is a fault); it is the art of the inclosingly reserved person to seem calm although he is agitated. If he is not agitated and shaken, then his art = 0, and he is not inclosingly reserved.

June 5. *Morning.*

A year ago today. So I could, of course, do without the wedding and make an erotic arrangement, of which there are examples.[348] She is willing to put up with everything. Put up with everything—but then must one not inquire about what one is willing to put up with? The situation is so preposterously inverted [349]that I could easily elicit the seduction from her. But now if she also in her pain, alas, believes that I will easily be able to find a more exceptional girl, or if she believes in her mistaken belief, alas, that I can so easily forget her and find ever-new joy some other way in the world, ought she then also to believe that I value my honor so little that for the sake of a whim I will forfeit what can never be regained, for honor I certainly will not regain, or last of all; she will much sooner fall in love again. But from the point of view of the idea, to circumvent the wedding, whether she is willing to put up with that or not, whether she could depend on my fidelity or not, is an outrage. And she may die and she may place a murder on my conscience, and she may curse me, and she may loathe me, and she may write an epigram on my depression when she has calmed down in a new love affair and I am unchanged there where she fancied herself to be: but dishonored she shall not be, and least of all in such a way that I become a knight thereby.

If there were one person to whom I could turn, I would go to him and say: *Bitte, bitte* [Please, please], put a little meaning for me into my confusion. To me the most appalling meaning is not as appalling as meaninglessness, and this is all the more dreadful, the more thoughtlessly it smiles.

Laughter explores in all directions, and by its help and under its false flag I bring everything into the discussion[350] in order that my reflection can scrutinize the thought paths in her soul and her strengths. This much I certainly do see—that she does not have the strictly ideal conception of what it is to sorrow. In the finite sense she is healthy and sound, and yet it is by finitude that she must be saved. She must be brought to the point of loathing the whole affair; then we separate. Then she lies down to sleep; then she sleeps it away—and thus she is saved again for time. It is not with the powers of ideality that she fights; it is a finite hope to which she clings, and my presence helps her. My being present and being forced to be a spectator give her a self-importance she will not have when I am gone.

If I were not convinced that I am suffering more than she does and more will come, for the worst awaits me when I have only myself to deal with, then I would not endure it. But so it goes, and one can inure oneself to all suffering. I am becoming inured to what I shrank from as from entering into a fiery furnace.[351] I am succeeding so uncommonly well at jabbering and drooling that at home I have to make the opposite motions lest for me, too, it end with the whole thing disintegrating into nonsense. If she had infinity in her soul, [352]it would be easy for her to be magnanimous toward me (oh, enviable condition), to give me my freedom, to accept the pain and have a religious transfer for it, and thus to make me her debtor, a debtor in proportion to nobleness of soul. This condition has been offered; I have not dared to deny her that; but it truly would have been a frightful punishment for me. What is all her anger and contempt in comparison with nobleness of soul?

June 5. *Midnight.*

Nebuchadnezzar[353]

(Daniel)[354]

[355]1. Recollections from my life when I was a beast of the field and ate grass,[356] I, Nebuchadnezzar, to all peoples and languages.

2. Was not Babylon the great city, the greatest of the cities of all the nations—I, I Nebuchadnezzar, have built it.

3. In renown, no city was like Babylon, and no king like me, because of Babylon, the glory of my lordship.

4. My royal house was visible to the ends of the earth, and my wisdom was like an obscure saying that none of the wise men could explain.

5. Thus they could not interpret to me what I had dreamed.[357]

6. And word came to me that I would be changed to become like a beast that eats grass in the field, while seven times passed over me.

7. Then I gathered all my chieftains with their armies and sent out urgent messages so that I might be prepared when the enemy came, as the word intimated.

8. But no one dared approach proud Babylon, and I said: Is this not the proud Babylon that I, I Nebuchadnezzar, have built.

9. Now a voice was suddenly heard, and I was transformed as swiftly as a woman changes color.

10. Grass was my food; dew fell upon me; and no one knew me, knew who I was.

11. But I knew Babylon and cried out: Is not this Babylon?

And no one discerned my words, for they sounded like the bellowing of an animal.

12. My thoughts terrified me, my thoughts in my mind, for my mouth was bound and no one could discern anything but a voice similar to an animal's.

13. And I thought: Who is this Mighty One, the Lord, the Lord whose wisdom is like the darkness of the night and as unfathomable as the depths of the sea,

14. indeed, like a dream that he alone controls and whose interpretation he has not given into the power of any human being when it comes suddenly upon one and holds one with its strong arms.

15. No one knows where this Mighty One resides, so that one could point, saying, "See, here is his throne," so that one could journey through countries until one hears, "See, here is the boundary of his dominion."

16. For he does not reside on the borders of my kingdom as my neighbor, nor from the farthest ocean to the boundaries of my kingdom as an entrenchment surrounding it.

17. Neither does he reside in his temple, for I, Nebuchadnezzar, have taken his gold and silver vessels and destroyed his temple.

VI
338

18. And no one knows anything about him, who his father was, and how he gained power, or who taught him the secret of his might.

19. He has no advisers from whom his secret could be bought with gold, no one to whom he says: What shall I do?— and no one who says to him: What are you doing?

20. He does not have scouts to scout out the occasion, so that one could capture them, for he does not say "tomorrow" but says "today."

21. For he does not make preparations as a human being does, and his preparations give the enemy no time, for he says, "Be done," and it is done.

22. He sits quietly and speaks to himself; one does not know whether he exists before it has happened.

23. This he has done against me. He does not take aim as

the archer does, so that one can dodge his arrow; he speaks to himself, and it is accomplished.

24. In his hands kings' brains are like wax in the melting furnace, and their might like a feather when he weighs it.

25. And yet he does not reside on earth as the Mighty One, so that he could take Babylon from me and leave me a little or so that he could take everything from me and be the Mighty One in Babylon.

26. This is how I thought in the privacy of my mind when no one knew me, and the thoughts in my brain terrified me, to think that the Lord, the Lord, was such a one.

27. But when the seven years had passed, I became Nebuchadnezzar again.

28. And I summoned all the wise men so that they should explain the secret of this power to me and why I became like a beast of the field.

29. But they all prostrated themselves and said: Great Nebuchadnezzar! This is a fantasy, an evil dream; who would be capable of doing this to you?

30. But my anger was at the wise men in the whole land, and I had them cut down in their folly.

31. For the Lord, the Lord has all power as no human being has, and I will not envy him his might but will praise it and will be second to him because I have taken his gold and silver vessels.

VI
339 32. Babylon is no longer the renowned Babylon; I, I Nebuchadnezzar, am no longer Nebuchadnezzar, and my armies no longer protect me, for no one can see the Lord, the Lord, and no one can observe him

33. if he should come, and the watchmen would shout in vain, for I would already have become like a bird in the tree or like a fish in water, recognized only by the other fish.

34. Therefore I do not wish to be renowned because of Babylon, but every seventh year there shall be a festival in the land,

35. a great festival among the people, and it shall be called The Festival of the Passing.

36. And an astronomer shall be led through the streets and

be dressed as an animal, and he shall carry with him his reckonings, shredded like a bundle of hay.

37. And all the people shall shout: The Lord, the Lord, the
Lord is the Mighty One, and his deed is as swift as the great
fish's leap in the sea.

38. For soon my days are numbered, and my dominion is
over like a night watch, and I do not know where I shall go,

39. whether I shall come to the distant, invisible land where
the Mighty One lives so that I might find favor in his eyes—

40. whether it is he who takes from me the breath of life so
that I become like a discarded garment, like my predecessors
so that he might find pleasure in me.

41. This, I, I Nebuchadnezzar, have had announced for all
peoples and languages, and great Babylon shall accomplish
my will.[358]

June 7. Midnight.

[359]When I was a child, a little pond in a peat excavation was
everything to me.[360] The dark tree roots that poked out here
and there in the murky darkness were vanished kingdoms and
countries, each one a discovery as important to me as antedi-
luvian discoveries to the natural scientist. Activities were in
good supply, for if I threw a stone, what tremendous movements were produced, one circle greater than the other, until
the water once again became still, and if I threw a stone in
another way, the movement was different from the other and
in itself rich in new variety. Then I would lie on the edge and
look over its expanse and see how first out in the middle the
wind began to ripple the water until the channeled undulation
disappeared among the rushes on the opposite side. Then I
climbed up into the willow tree that leaned out over the excavation, sat as far out as possible, and weighed the branch
down a little in order to gaze down into the darkness; then the
ducks came swimming to foreign lands, climbed the small
tongue of land that ran out and along with the rushes formed
a bay, where my raft lay in harbor. But if a wild duck flew
from the woods over the excavation, its cry awakened dim
memories in the heads of the sedate ducks and they began to

beat their wings, to fly wildly along the surface.[361] Then a longing awoke in my breast also, until I once again gazed myself into contentment with my little peat excavation.

It always happens that way—so charitable, so rich is life: the less one has, the more one sees. Take a book, the poorest one written, but read it with the passion that it is the only book you will read—ultimately you will read everything out of it, that is, as much as there was in yourself, and you could never get more out of reading, even if you read the best of books.

The time of childhood is long since over; therefore, with regard to imagination, I do not have very much to draw upon—in this way I have changed. But the object of my consideration has not become much greater compared with what an older person ordinarily has. There is one person, one single person, about whom everything revolves. I gaze and gaze so long at this girl—until I draw out of myself what I perhaps would otherwise never have come to see, even if I had seen ever so much, for this would not imply that my inwardness had become transparent to me. If she had been unusually gifted with spirit, she would never have affected me in this way. She is quite enough for me when it comes to responsibility, and again the responsibility is mine, and yet it is she who in this responsibility brings my inwardness to consciousness. I was far too much and far too definitely developed for her to be able to influence me by means of communication, nor was she equipped so as to enrich me spiritually with new content. But in order ultimately to understand oneself, it is a question of coming into the proper situation. To this end she has helped me in terms of responsibility. [362]In this respect, all my suffering is even a favor. The testing quietness of responsibility teaches a person to have to help himself by virtue of spirit; achievement, action, activities, so often lauded and deservedly so, can still have an admixture of diversion so that one does not find out what one is capable of by virtue of spirit and what the manifold external stimuli help one to attain; one also escapes many a terror that does not have time to reach one, but to escape them does not mean to have conquered them or to have understood oneself.

She will go on helping me with responsibility, for I will not
be finished where she is finished. Suppose she became another's and I became free. Then I am not finished, for then I
would still have the possibility that it would suddenly strike
me—perhaps prompted by some thinker or by a chance word,
which at times has the greatest power—that it would suddenly
strike me that a marriage could have been built out of our relationship. Precisely because in that case I would not have the
sympathetic consternation on her behalf, the pain would grip
me again, but autopathetically. What will responsibility be to
me then? It will become my very consolation, and in that very
responsibility I shall come to understand myself.

From this standpoint of self-understanding, I am well
aware that as a human being I am very far from being a paradigm; if anything, I am a sample human being. With a fair
degree of accuracy, I give the temperature of every mood and
passion, and when I am generating my own inwardness, I understand these words: *homo sum, nil humani a me alienum puto*
[I am a human being, I hold that nothing human is alien to
me].[363] But humanly no one can model himself on me, and
historically I am even less a prototype for any human being.
[364]If anything, I am someone who could be needed in a crisis,
a guinea pig that life uses to feel its way. A person half as
reflective as I would be able to be of significance for many
people, but precisely because I am altogether reflective I have
none at all.

As soon as I am outside my religious understanding, I feel
as an insect with which children are playing must feel, because
life seems to have dealt with me so unmercifully; as soon as I
am inside my religious understanding, I understand that precisely this has absolute meaning for me. Hence, that which in
one case is a dreadful jest is in another sense the most profound
earnestness.

Earnestness is basically not something simple, a simplex,
but is a *compositum* [compound], for true earnestness is the
unity of jest and earnestness.[365] I am best convinced of that by
considering Socrates. If, in accord with one of Plato's
views,[366] one quite ingeniously takes Socrates to be the unity

of the comic and the tragic, this is entirely right; but the question remains: in what does the unity consist? A new kind of literature and anything such as that is completely out of the question; no, the unity is in the earnestness. Thus Socrates was the most earnest man in Greece. His intellectuality was absolutely commensurate with the ethical in him (otherwise one can become earnest about trifles); his sense of the comic was just as great as his ethical pathos—therefore he was secured against becoming ridiculous in his pathos; his earnestness was concealed in jest—therefore he was free in it and needed no external support whatsoever in order to be earnest, which is always an indication of a lack of the specific worth of earnestness.

In all immediate existence, the point is not to come to see contradiction, for then immediacy is lost; in spiritual existence, the point is to endure contradiction, but also to keep it at arm's length in freedom. For this reason, bigoted earnestness always fears the comic, and rightly so; true earnestness itself invents the comic. If this were not the case, then stupidity would be the privileged caste with respect to earnestness. But earnestness is not mediation[367]—that is jest and a new theme for the comic. Mediation has no place at all in the existence-sphere of freedom and can only in a ludicrous way want to force itself from metaphysics into the sphere where freedom is continually becoming. Earnestness sees through the comic, and the deeper down from which it fetches itself up, the better, but it does not mediate. What earnestness wills in earnest it does not regard as comic insofar as it itself wills it, but for that reason it can readily see the comic therein. In this way the comic purifies the pathos-filled emotions, and conversely the pathos-filled emotions give substance to the comic. For example, the most devastating comic perception would be the one in which indignation is latent—yet no one detects it because of the laughter. *Vis comica* [Comic power] is the most responsible weapon and thus is essentially present only in the hands of someone who has a fully equivalent pathos. Hence, anyone who could in truth make a hypocrite a butt of laughter will also be able to crush him with indigna-

VI
342

tion. But anyone who wants to use indignation and does not have the corresponding *vis comica* will readily degenerate into rhetoric and will himself become comic.

But here I sit and forget her! No, definitely not, for the unity of the comic and the tragic concerns me very much. Often enough my fractious understanding has wanted to whirl the whole affair into laughter for me, but out of this very whirl my tragic passion has developed more intensely. So I understand myself better and understand that I have indeed maintained earnestness in my relationship with her. If it had not been this way from the beginning, if I had not step by step perceived the comic and under its surveillance kept the tragic to myself, then in all probability, if it so happened that she became another's, either a certain passionateness (which for all its vehemence is not earnestness) or laughter (in an unwarranted way in its separation from the pathos-filled) would have gained the upper hand over me. Now that the situation is reversed, it is indeed comic that I am the villain and she the one who wants to die. But this blow I certainly can bear, for my pathos is saved from the very beginning. My pathos does not stem from her or from her vehement outburst—it is my soul's inwardness. This is why change cannot play games with me; I hold firmly to the idea, and the comic from the outside has no power over me. That I have believed everything, every word of hers, as earnestly as is humanly possible, that I feel myself bound by it as tightly as a person can feel it, is not at all comic. If she did not mean it at all, it makes no difference whatsoever in this matter; if like Jacob v. Thyboe she says: *Wir haben uns bedacht* [We have reconsidered],[368] it makes no difference whatsoever. Indeed, if I had believed it only because of her, because she said it, if I had believed it out of confidence in her reliability, then I would be comic and in a certain sense would already have been comic. But I have believed her because she stood in an ethical relationship to me; therefore it was my duty to believe. On my own initiative I have given her words the weight of eternity for me because I respected the relationship; I have not established my life on her word and gown.[369] That is why I have perceived the comic

VI
343

from the very beginning, and precisely for that reason I can never in all eternity become comic. I can produce the comic at any moment I wish, but I do not want to do it, and this is the control for my pathos, that it is not vehement and blind—and thereby comic.

This is how the matter stands; even in case this "if" enters in, I am and remain unaltered.

June 11. *Midnight.*

Today I saw her. Yet this seeing does not help me much, for I dare not believe what ordinarily is considered to be the surest of all—my own eyes. But today the situation favored me. I was walking with another person when we met her; I knew that he was not acquainted with her. As we approached I commented on how much the girl appeared to be suffering. That certainly was an untruth, but what will one not do to get an opinion on the matter. Quite impassively he answered, "It does not seem that way at all to me." It is really strange to talk with a person this way; I doubt that he will ever in his life say anything as significant as that to me, although for him it meant nothing at all. But that was not the end of it. We had something to discuss and therefore walked up and down the street; a half hour later she came out of a shop and returned the same way. As she passed us, which she could not avoid doing inasmuch as there was no cross street and she had seen us too late, I called his attention to her again, and when she had passed us I said, "You were quite right. She certainly looks almost radiant." He replied quite phlegmatically, "Yes, that's what I said, but I can't see why you bother your head about it." It is strange to talk with a person this way; I doubt that he will ever make a remark that touches me to this degree, and yet he scarcely gave it a thought. I explained that it was one of my diversions to pay attention to people's exteriors in order to draw conclusions about their interiors. Thus I would readily admit that this last time she did look well, indeed, quite contented, but I was convinced that on her walk something must have happened that produced this effect, because the first time she looked as if she were suffering. He became somewhat angry and insisted that he was as much a judge of faces as I was, and she had looked the same both times. I felt as if I were standing on live coals, fearing that I had made a blunder, but to save myself from the snares of imagination lest in solitude it might worry me that he could have become aware of her and later would find out who she was, I took a desperate risk: "Well, we will soon settle the matter; do you think you can recognize her again so that together we can find out more about her, for I am not sure of recognizing her myself, although I looked at her a bit more closely than you did." "Quibbling," he replied, "you are quibbling just to be right. How could I recognize her when I looked at her so very fleetingly, even though I saw enough to vouch for what I said." It is strange to talk with a person in this way; I doubt that he will ever say anything that so dispels my concern as what he said merely to carry his point against me.

This was indeed like an expert appraisal; the person with whom I was walking was truly an impartial man. Consequently, I certainly dare to believe this. When one has to do something on the sly this way, one really does appreciate it. —To have pleasure on the sly, there is some reason in that, but not even to dare to be concerned, to walk the road of concern as one who is walking the forbidden path—and what if the outcome had been that she did appear to be suffering—that, too, I would have had to take on the sly.

VI
345

June 12. *Morning*.
[370]A year ago today. [371]Now, if a marriage could be built despite my inclosing reserve, then this union is indeed my wish. Most certainly, even if at this moment I cannot determine whether it is purely erotic or is a mixture of agitation over her pain and of my pride, which in a certain sense she has on her side. Then I could really make myself believe that my break with the idea was commendable since it was for her sake; without worrying about her I could take her at her impassioned word and thus have as much as possible of the joy that I wished for myself and that always is in possession of her, and thus be unrepentant and free of all complications and ter-

rors. When I look away from the idea, I am very tempted by this. And now if she will not only put up with all this but thank me for it as for a benefaction, then . . . . . I cannot bear this confusion. How will my exhausted mind find something on which to rest? The situation is changed, and everything is spinning around for me. It was my wish that she become mine; it becomes my pain to give it up. It was my duty to continue in the relationship; to break a binding relationship becomes something on which one can dwell—but God in heaven, save my sanity, save me from one thing: let me not become her benefactor. Totally without meaning I cannot live. I must have a little; it can be very little. Suppose I become her murderer—if it has to be this way, I understand that I have forced my way ahead where I ought not to have ventured, then with some effort I can understand that it is a severe sentence that is imposed upon me, and conscious thought can still breathe in me—but to be her benefactor! No, it is impossible. Away with you, deranged meaninglessness with your grinning mug, make me miserable if there is meaning in it, but do not make me blissful in nonsense. [372]If I cannot do it even though it is my wish, if I cannot do it even though it is my duty, then no more is needed, then anything else proceeds not from evil but from madness.

VI
346

Come what may, though I drop dead today, it is still not as terrible to depart this life with perhaps an attempted murder on one's conscience as to live as her benefactor. There must be a mistake on her side; a condition such as this should never be offered to me. There is in it an implicit insult to both of us, for it seems to say: You do not really love me; you pay no attention to your duty, but still you are miserable enough to let yourself be moved and I am weak enough to want this.

If she is perhaps suffering because her breast is so oppressed by stifled sighs, because she cannot cry, then my consciousness likewise suffers from not being able to exhale but groans under stifled thoughts and perishes in meaninglessness. Just as the fish when it lies on the shore gasps in vain for the sea in which it can breathe, so I gasp in vain for meaning.

She is suffering—that is obvious, and the person who sees it is I! No one else suspects what is taking place between us. As soon as someone else is around, my manner is as usual. She is quiet, and I keep vigil with a hundred eyes on every word that is spoken lest there suddenly be an explosion. She would find relief in talking to someone, but it would merely be a cooling off, and the worst symptoms would perhaps come over her in solitude; she is much better off to persevere with me.

[373]A casual remark can be most disturbing. Just when one has calculatingly covered everything, a remark may suddenly be dropped that hits close to home without one's anticipating it. Yesterday we were at a party. At the dinner table there was talk about engagements. One of the ladies made the comment that "engaged people always become thin." How δεικτικῶς [close to home]! For her and for me it was a shattering truth. As I was about to draw attention away from this subject lest further use be made of this empirical maxim, a gentleman went on to say, "But in recompense one usually takes on weight when one is married." The poor girl. I managed, however, to keep my composure enough to add as lightly as a heavily armed person can, "But yet there are examples to the contrary," and when I mentioned a man's name that was enough to provoke laughter, I said, "He has been married three times, and yet he is thinner than I am." People deigned to laugh; she had time to collect herself. But a torture such as that is ruinous to both soul and body.

VI
347

She is, however, and continues to be unresigned. She bids lower and lower, but to perceive the task sympathetically does not occur to her at all. When she is willing to throw herself away as a slave girl, as a nothing, as a burden, she thinks that she is carrying resignation to the limit. God knows that in this way it is indeed being carried infinitely much further than I could bear to see it. On the other hand, she either cannot or will not understand what she should do and that she is torturing me unjustly, since for one thing there has never been contention about her lovableness, and for another, that kind of behavior strengthens me in my resolve precisely out of my concern for her.

What I fear most of all is that she nevertheless has built me up in her imagination as something important. If that is the case, this humiliation is the worst of all disasters. Here I have found a limit to my deception. If I were to speak in the form of nonsense about my unimportance, then I am only strengthening such a fancy, if it exists. Thus, just as once a week I earnestly urge her to break the engagement, so I have also opened a little communication with my inner being in regard to the latest mistake. Next to becoming her benefactor ranks the absurdity that I am supposed to be something important and disdain her. It is only momentary, for as soon as I have said that she is always good enough, the nonsense begins again. In this regard, I console myself that when I have left her everyone will confirm her opinion that it was no great loss. With regard to my callousness in treating her this way, she will, I hope, also find corroboration in everyone's judgment of me.

It would be superb if she herself could be brought or if it would occur to her to break the connection, for then she would be spared the humiliation. I drop hints about it, for I do not dare to speak of it with full voice and total passion; then she would discover how much she preoccupies me and then she would try all means once again; for this reason I must speak with muted voice and false passion.

June 14. *Midnight.*

[374]In the Middle Ages a person saved his soul by telling his beads a certain number of times; if in a similar manner I could save my soul by repeating to myself the story of my sufferings, I would have been saved a long time ago. If my repetition is perhaps not always imploring, ah, it nevertheless preferably ends in this final solace. She helps me with that in a singular way. If I did not have to keep myself in the passion of action, if it were all over and I were quiet—that is, at rest dared to reflect on the whole affair—then I would say that she has benefited me in that I, humbled by seeing her prostrate

herself before me, find all the more joy in prostrating myself before a higher one. Her misfortune was that she had nothing higher than a human being. Just as Scripture says that an idol has no real existence in the world,[375] so it may well be that I end up as a nonentity simply because I was an idol to her.

But how strange it all was. It is so dialectically deceptive that it seems as if I could lose track of it at any minute, as if I had not left her because I loved her but because I loved myself! I find everything to be just as I wished it, all her surroundings just as I had imagined them after the ordeal. They suit me as no others do; I could travel around the world and perhaps not find any so favorable to me. If a step prior to a marriage is required, a rational deliberation, then I dare to say that I have proceeded by trial and error. I did not, however, wish by any means to offend her by reconnoitering. I find her somewhat different than I imagined; a little scene lends us a helping hand, and to my eyes she becomes more lovable than ever—and look, then all the difficulty stems from me. But then am I perhaps rash? [376]All my earlier (prior to the step) deliberation upon her circumstances and upon the family's individuality proves the exact opposite; and I dare to testify on my own behalf that I entered into the relationship with the most honest will, convinced that I knew the nature of the task, perhaps a little proud of being able to accomplish it: to control my inclosing reserve—and behold, I am shipwrecked precisely on that, not in such a way that I cannot do it, but in such a way that this proves not to be the task. After that little incident [*Begivenhed*], her devotion [*Hengivenhed*] becomes more and more reckless in its expression and demonstrates to me precisely that my inclosing reserve is an absolute misrelation, that her relationship with me [377]will become a misalliance for her, even if she does not understand it. That this is the way things stand is my pain, and yet I cannot renounce my inclosing reserve for that reason. If I have taken fifteen years to form a view of life for myself and to mature in it, a view of life that both inspired me and was altogether compatible with my nature, I cannot suddenly be altered in this way. Indeed, I cannot even tell her that I wished it, because such a wish is a thoroughly indefinite stipulation, and it would be very irresponsible to use it to have her life at one's disposal. Insofar as she has struggled with all her might to show her devotion, she has worked against herself with all her vitality.

And now I realize clearly that my depression makes it impossible for me to have a confidant, and I of course know that what the wedding ceremony would require of me is that she should be the one. [378]But she would never have become that even if I had opened myself ever so much, for we do not understand each other. This is because my consciousness has one more extension. According to the intermediate court, which actually is the court of everyday life or of actuality, according to the intermediate court where she essentially has her life, as indeed the majority have, I am out of my mind. Only by a long roundabout way do I become once again, in a higher sense, calm and secure like other men. Mentally disordered I am not, for I can take care of myself very well. I need no confidant, and I burden no one with my unhappiness; neither does it disturb me in my work. My depression hunts for the terrifying in all directions. Now it seizes me with all its dreadfulness. [379]Flee from it, I cannot and will not—I must bear the thought; then I find a religious reassurance, and only then am I free and happy as spirit. Although I have the most inspired conception of God's love, I also have the conception that he is not an old fussbudget who sits in heaven and humors us, but that in time and temporality one must be prepared to suffer everything. It is my conviction that it is only a Judaizing relic, a truncated particularism in Christianity, or ordinary cowardliness and laziness that has the idea of being in relationship with God and of being exempted from such things. Officious spiritual or secular advice about keeping the terrible away is simply nauseating to me, because this advice does not understand what the terrible is. Indeed, anyone who is busy willing or became great by willing something in this finite world does well to keep and has been compelled to keep the terrible away, lest it change him and his goal into nothing or hinder him from attaining the fancied greatness. But the person who wills religiously must have receptivity precisely for the terrible; he must open himself to it and needs only to take care that he does not stop halfway, but that it leads him into the security of the infinite. This takes place gradually with each instance of the terrible. He becomes intimate with it, intimate with the thought that what he most fears will happen to him, but he also becomes expert in practicing this thought in his assurance of God's love. Hence the thought perhaps visits him off and on, but it stays only a minute; in that very instant he is religiously oriented in it, and the whole thing does not disturb him. But then comes another terror, and he does not maunder about it to others but tends to his work, and he succeeds also with this etc.

If she had become mine, I am sure that on the wedding day I would stand beside her with the thought that one of us would die before evening, or with some such gloomy notion. I guarantee that neither she nor anyone else would notice it in my countenance. I would also be inwardly at peace, but religiously at peace, and yet I would still have the thought. This, you see, is a deception! If I did have a confidant, I would ask him something like this: "Isn't it a shame for a person who is depressed to torture his wife with his depressing ideas?" And he would answer, and along with him perhaps everyone else, "Yes, indeed! A man ought to constrain himself and thereby show that he is a man." "Fine," I would answer, "I can do just that, I can look like a smiling hope. And yet it is precisely on this that I am stranded, for it is a deception that marriage does not tolerate, [380]whether the respective wife understands it or not." And the trouble is that I myself believed this was the task until I began to realize that the wedding ceremony is a divine protest against it.

Speak with a confidant, that I cannot do. A confidant will not think my depressing idea with the same passion as I do, and consequently he will not understand, either, that for me it becomes a religious point of departure. To live confidentially with another person requires either that one not have such thoughts, that one's world of consciousness end at the scarcely Greek, even less Christian, systematic board fence— the outer is the inner and the inner is the outer[381]—or that one not have them on such a large scale that they do not retreat before what is called reasonable grounds. In other words, most people have a fractional idea of life's fraudulence, but then along come experience and probability etc. and patch the pieces together, and then they are safe and secure and have reasonable grounds for it. Of this I am personally well informed. An elderly woman once picked up the idea that she would be buried alive. She confided in me. Sure enough, she had thought up three precautionary measures, but since she was depressively worried, her worry had in turn quite naturally deprived her of all three—that is, she could conceive of the possibility that they were not adequate. Now, if she had not been depressed, she would have become happy in the assurance that there are such prudential measures and priceless truths that are able to guarantee a person something in the finite world. Now I was obliged to make her happy in this nonsense, for since I realized that the infinite would perhaps upset her completely, I chose the finite. I myself had once been plagued with the same idea and was richly supplied with precautions. This overabundance had not helped me, for my depression had taken it away from me—until I found comfort in the infinite. I then thought up the fourth and fifth precautionary measures of which she had not dreamed, and she was helped and has continually thanked me; but I have never known whether I should laugh or cry over it.

What if I were married and my wife were my confidant—what then? I shall assume that it is in the time of suffering before I became mature and that it was that old woman's depressing notion that plagued me. Then I would speak and initiate her into it. She would really laugh now, for sure, because it would be inconceivable to her where anybody could pick up such notions. Now, if for me my depression were not continually the point of departure for a religious fulfillment, if it were an empty caprice that ended in nothing, then perhaps this innocent laughter would be the very best cure, for a charming youthfulness does have considerable power. But for me the religious fulfillment is worth more than all youthfulness, and therefore it would not help me except to help me

find sad pleasure in her happiness, which I nevertheless do not
crave. But I must speak, for being silent was for me the easiest. Then she probably would become worried and would try
her hand at the reasonable grounds. Suppose she thinks up
five precautionary measures, and now it is her dialectic that is
to take the wind out of my sails. The whole thing becomes so
clear to me that I want to hear her voice in order positively to
assure myself that I have done the right thing in keeping myself from hearing it. Then she would name the four precautionary measures and would say: And finally you do have me,
I who would indeed do everything for you, believe me, if it
would dispel those dark thoughts; believe me, I promise you
that it will not happen; everything will be done as if my soul's
salvation depended on this matter—and therefore be happy
again. It seems to me that this situation would be enough to
make stones cry. The poor wife! She has thought of everything she could imagine. If I contradict her, she thinks I do not
have confidence in her that she is what she wishes to appear to
be, and this grieves her; and then on the other hand, this is the
dialectic that is supposed to bind me. Even the simplest objection, one that will occur to anybody—that she could die before I do—she would not understand, for precisely because it
is essentially her nature to expect everything happy and in this
hope and faith and confidence of immediacy she has her assurance in life, she would be speaking most sincerely if she said:
How can you believe that! That I should die before you—now
I know how important it is to you etc. Once again she would
make stones cry by her genuine fervent emotion, but then on
the other hand, this is the dialectic that is supposed to bind the
one who for fifteen years day and night has improved himself
in handling thoughts dialectically, just as the Arab handles the
snorting steed, as the juggler plays with sharp knives.

What would the result be? That I could not bear to see her
distressed, could not have the heart to let her go away feeling
the indignity of my not having trusted her. And what then?
Then I would let a day go by, would put on my disguise, look
as friendly as possible, and say to her, "Yes, my dear, it is as
you said, I do have you, and you have convinced me, if not

by your reasons, then by what you said about yourself." And then she will look so happy and contented, she, my eyes' beloved delight—and I would have deceived her. And this I cannot bear, because if I were in her place I could not bear it, and because I will and must honor her by loving her as much as I love myself, which I can do only by leaving her. With regard to others, the deception is permissible, for they are not bound to me, are not divinely installed as my confidants, and if they are weary of me, they can, of course, go, which she cannot do if she ever dimly realizes the misrelation.

If I actually were calmed when I spoke this way to her, it would make no difference to the matter at hand, for if I had been calm, I would have been that within myself. In that case the misrelation is again evident. For her a depressing idea cannot acquire the significance of becoming the point of departure for a religious fulfillment. If she were to have one opinion about a drama and I another, if the difference in opinion perhaps showed that I was an estheticist and she anything but that, it would have nothing at all to do with the basis of a misrelation, and if it were based on that, I would gladly surrender my opinion for her sake. But the singular ideas of depression I do not surrender, for these ideas that a third person perhaps would call whims and she perhaps would sympathetically call sad fancies I call reminders: if I just follow them and endure them they lead me to the eternal certitude of the infinite.

Thus in my solitude these ideas are precious to me even though they terrify me; they have great significance for me and teach me—instead of wanting to congratulate myself on matchless discoveries[382] in the sphere of the religious and to make mankind blissful with them—to discover, as it were, to my own abasement, the most simple things and to be infinitely satisfied with them. —Furthermore, implicit in the concept of the fear of God is the idea that one is to fear him; and if it is dangerous for a person's soul to make God into a despot, then it is also dangerous for his piety to speculate God into a subordinate servant, and if it is troubling to a person's soul if God were inclosed in eternal silence, then it is also dan-

gerous to revise God's accounts speculatively or to parade
prophetically into world history.[383] Indeed, why is it that
there is more fear of God in the out-of-the-way places where
there are two or three miles between each little cottage than in
the noisy cities, that the sailor has more fear of God than the
inhabitant of a market town,[384] why, indeed, unless it is that
these people experience something and experience it in such a
way that there are no escapes. When the storm rages in the
night and in it the hungry howling of the wolves sounds fore-
bodingly, when someone in distress at sea has saved himself
on a plank—that is, has to be rescued by a straw from certain
ruin, and consequently one cannot send a message to the next
cottage because no one dares to venture out into the night, and
thus one can save one's shouts: then one learns to be content
with something other than confidence in night watchmen and
policemen and the efficacy of distress signals. In big cities both
people and buildings are packed in together much too tightly.

If someone is really to have a primitive[385] impression in such
a place, either there must be an event or one must have another way, as I have in my depression. If not, then there is
danger that the proceeds of a person's life add up to this: he
was young and still remembers many enjoyable impressions
from that time, many happy days; then he was married, and
everything went well, except that he once became very ill, and
a physician, the first one available, was hastily summoned,
and so Professor D. came and proved to be a very careful physician, and thus became the family physician; also in Pastor P.
he found an earnest spiritual counselor, of whose deep religiousness and sincerity he was more convinced than of his
own religiousness and therefore he became fonder of him year
after year. Then he became acquainted with many congenial
families, associated with them, and then he died. And why
should it not be beautiful to have had a happy youth and to
remember it; why should it not be gratifying to have learned
to know Professor D. and Pastor P., but if this is supposed to
be the ultimate when all is said and done—then I would rather
not have inconvenienced either the professor or the pastor but

VI
354

would rather have heard the howling of the wolves and learned to know God.

In love stories, the messenger the lover uses is often a dwarf, a deformed person, an old hag—who would ever believe it was a love message; my depressing ideas are likewise a messenger from what was my first love [*Kjærlighed*], from what must always remain my one and only love. They terrify me, but they have never had the sender's permission to annihilate me, to weaken my spirit, to make me a burden to others. Whether that will happen, I do not know; whether it will happen at once or soon, I do not know, for then I would not be depressed. But this I do know, they have led me to the most blessed certainty—and thus it can be the same with the mode of conveyance, "whether one comes limping, comes hobbling, without any pomp or circumstance."[386] In this very moment, I am overwhelmed by the thought that I have been able to persevere. Ah, in solitude I never wish for death. I do not understand how people can suddenly become so sluggish that they wish for death. Quite the reverse, the darker things get around me, the more I desire to live in order to persevere with myself, in order to see whether my enthusiasm was an idle word or an energizing power, whether it was a strong drink that foams by itself or a cheap beer that does indeed foam—but because of an added foreign substance. And if one can understand how terrible it can be for someone battling to become king to think of an untimely death just when he is closest to his goal, then I can understand that the person whose life is radically shaken, who has no confidant at his breast, and no *impressa vestigia* [footprints][387] for his feet, considers it important to him that death not come and make it impossible for him to find out whether this path was feasible or a mirage infatuated him, whether his resolution, which renounced all rhetorical devices, was just as full of chatter as that of the rhetoricians.

June 18. *Midnight.*
Am I guilty, then? Yes. How? By my having begun what I could not carry out. How do you understand it now? Now I

understand more clearly why it was impossible for me. What then is my guilt? That I did not understand it sooner. What is your responsibility? Every possible consequence for her life. Why every possible one, for this certainly seems to be an exaggeration? Because here it is not a matter of an event but of an act and an ethical responsibility, the consequences of which I do not dare to arm against by being courageous, for courage in this case means opening oneself to them. What can serve as your excuse? That my total individuality predisposed me to something in which I have been corroborated on all [388]sides, which, if I had sought a confidant, I would find confirmed— namely, "that a depressed person should not torment his wife with his sufferings but like a man should inclose them within himself." What is your consolation? That I, in acknowledging this guilt, also sense a Governance in it all. Precisely because I had considered this matter to the best of my ability and acted as honestly as was possible for me on the strength of what I knew, precisely for that reason I see an agency that has led me on to a point where I understood myself as I perhaps otherwise never would have, but also learned this in such a way that I shall not become haughty. What is your hope? That it can be forgiven, if not here then nevertheless in an eternity. Is there anything dubious about this forgiveness? Yes, there is—that I do not have her forgiveness; and she is and remains an intermediate court, a legitimate court, that must not be bypassed. Her forgiveness certainly cannot justify me eternally, no more than a person's implacability can harm anyone but himself, but her forgiveness is a part of a divine procedure. Why, then, do you not have it? Because I could not make myself understandable to her. It would, of course, have been much easier simply to obtain it and thus to be released from this dreadful state of suspension in which I can find a foothold only by assuming the most extreme possibility of responsibility. You were not asked about what is easiest or hardest, for one can also choose what is wrong even though one chooses the hardest. Why, then, do you not have it? Because I could not obtain it. When by letter I broke the engagement, I requested it. This she would not understand and therefore forced me to use the only means left to rescue her: to place the misunderstanding of deception between us. My pursuance of this showed me that the deception itself actually expressed the truth—that she did not understand me at all. [389]Her idea of me was that I had more worldly tastes, that I wanted my freedom because the relationship became too confining for me. Precisely because this was her idea, her pride was offended, and this was why she was reckless in using every means. [390]To her, regaining me had to depend essentially on my being led back to duty and on the arousing of my sympathy. If I had then spoken directly and said: The maintenance of the relationship is my own wish—I would not have been permitted to say more, but she would have been jubilant and said something like this: "O dear one, you do not know how happy you are making me. It is your own wish; alas, I had given up faith in that and learned to be satisfied with less until it again became your wish, but now everything is fine, in fact, more than just fine, it is splendid—you wish it and I wish it, so every hindrance is gone." What does this mean? It means that she does not understand me at all. So I chose not to make myself understood but to give her to understand that I was tired of her, that I was a deceiver, a muddlehead. Her rescue depended on my holding firmly to this. But what, then, would it mean suddenly to beg for her forgiveness? It would sound as if I were making a fool of her. The word "forgiveness" between *us* places everything on a religious basis. To inveigle forgiveness from her is not, however, what is demanded of me. If I were to speak, I would have to admit my fault; but also, if this is going to be in earnest, she must be able to understand my justification. As soon as the discussion began, she would limit herself to understanding the first half and thereupon understand none of the rest, which then means that she would misunderstand the first part. If I could have been understandable to her in my entire makeup and consequently her forgiveness could have become something other than a comedy situation, then her behavior to me would have been so shocking that she would have needed my forgiveness instead, and [391]so I would have done enough with that note. But as things stood, anything I said in the vein of truth would only contribute to making the two months even longer, for then she would be prompted to become more and more vehement in her approach—yet without gaining anything. [392]To that extent, then, the most I have to reproach myself for is the earnest words I secretly interspersed in the confusion. Thus I do not have forgiveness. An official forgiveness between two who do not understand each other is an empty gesture and just as dubious as a contract drawn up in writing between two people, one of whom can neither write nor read handwriting. The greater mutual safeguard in having a written agreement compared with a verbal agreement disappears in a double manner: the person who cannot read handwriting has only what he has heard on which to stand and has no way of knowing whether what is written there is what was read aloud to him, and his signature becomes meaningless; the other person has the burden of having to be solely responsible for both of them, although the document is really supposed to be mutual. Before I can really be forgiven, she must be able to place herself in my position; otherwise her forgiveness becomes just like a written statement from someone who cannot read handwriting—indeed, her forgiveness is even less, for the person who cannot read handwriting can very well understand what the discussion is all about, but forgiveness from the person who cannot or will not understand what the discussion is about is just as meaningless as an approval of a petition by one who does not know what is being sought in the petition. This, then, is why I have no forgiveness! I thought to honor her more by not tricking such a thing out of her; I have done what I believed to be due her or, more correctly, it happened for her sake: forgiveness has been made as difficult as possible for me. My break with actuality was of such a nature that it is a simple consequence that genuine forgiveness on her part is inconceivable, for this would indeed place me in continuity with actuality.[393]

This is the way the whole thing stands in time. As far as eternity[394] is concerned, it is my hope that there we shall understand each other and that there she will forgive me. In time it becomes a dialectical goad in my pain that wounds me in many ways because it disturbs my view of life in regard to sympathy and also in regard to the deception. It is troubling that a deception, be it ever so pious and well intentioned, should have that much power; [395]and there is always the possibility that the deception can acquire an epigrammatic power to satirize. The most poetic is also most ethical. For her it would be most poetic to remain devoted to me or to remain true to herself in her love, and this would also be the most terrible revenge on me. [396]Every prosaic revenge *eo ipso* makes my responsibility lighter because it is less ethical.

How consistent life is! There is not anything that is true in one sphere that is not true in another. What profound earnestness that the laws of life are such that everyone must serve them whether he wants to or not. The Governance that requires a conciliatory spirit of every person also knows how to affirm itself, for precisely when the individual wants to avenge himself, the affair becomes easiest for the guilty party; and on the other hand, when the one offended chooses to be conciliatory, then Governance places the emphasis of revenge in this mildness. [397]Caesar did many an illustrious deed, but even if nothing were preserved but one single statement he is supposed to have made, I would admire him. After Cato committed suicide, Caesar is supposed to have said, "There Cato wrested from me my most beautiful victory, for I would have forgiven him."[398]

My demand to life is this—that it would make it clear whether I was trapped in self-delusion or I loved faithfully, perhaps more faithfully than she. How long I must persevere is not known. Even if the age of oracles vanished long ago, there is still one thing of which the simplest and the most profound person must, if he talks about it, talk mysteriously— that is: time. Without a doubt, it is the most difficult mystery, just as it is also supposed to be the most profound wisdom, to arrange one's life as if today were the last day one lives and also the first in a sequence of years.[399]

June 19. *Morning.*
A year ago today. Yet these tears that force their way out of her eyes force out of my brain the possibility of impossibili-

ties. Even though it is a superfluous gesture, I nevertheless cannot stop doing it. Hence I shout to the world, just in case someone might hear me: I bid, I bid half my life for a half year of happiness with her: I bid it for fourteen days: I bid it for the wedding day—is there no stroke of the hammer?

No! —But I must go to work. The person who is sentenced for life is used for hazardous work; so also is it with me and with my work.

Today she said the most extraordinary thing I have ever heard from her. In a certain sense it hit right in the heart. When a shot suddenly hits dead center in target shooting, the scorekeeper takes the precaution first of ascertaining whether it was an accidental shot, a shot in the air, a shot without aim, a weapon that perhaps went off by itself. She told me that she really believed that I was mad. But upon being scrutinized it proved to be a wild shot, and perhaps nothing she has said has more clearly shown me the difference between us. To be sure, in a certain sense a depressed person is mad, but to comprehend this madness takes considerable dialectic and considerable pathos. Anyone who says this in somewhat the same way one would say of a man dressed rather ludicrously, "Oh! He is mad," shows *eo ipso* that there is not a trace of an intimation of what madness really is. The whole thing was a false alarm. It was an impetuous outburst that in its hurry did not know what else to say. And now and then she is a bit impetuous. She says that I am malevolent, not good. She said this again yesterday. Such a statement is a coveted stimulus to my nonsensical chatter, which immediately seized upon it. Well, I see it now; we do understand each other. The matter is quite simple. You merely give a statement something like this: In case something happens to me, I the undersigned declare that I do indeed feel respect. Say and write "respect" . . . . . or what was it I wanted to say? It was indeed respect that you do not feel. Everything is becoming all mixed up for me. It is in novels that one certainly has respect—so, I do not feel respect, and since true love, real love, is unimaginable without respect, then etc. As you see, it can be done in two ways. In other

VI
359

words, when respect and love join together against a person, then good night, Ole.[400] One can, however, come out of it just as well with the help of respect alone as with the help of love. In other words, if one considers what respect really is . . . . . Here I was interrupted. She cannot keep from laughing when I am really laying on the nonsense. [401]This consoles me. Basically she is suffering less from this than I, who in such a preposterous way have to work her loose.

VI
360

June 24. Midnight.

Not even what I am writing here is my innermost meaning. I cannot entrust myself to paper in that way, even though I see it in what is written. Think of what could happen! The paper could disappear; there could be a fire where I live and I could live in uncertainty about whether it was burned or still existed; I could die and thus leave it behind me; I could lose my mind and my innermost being could be in alien hands; I could go blind and not be able to find it myself, not know whether I stood with it in my hands without asking someone else, not know whether he lied, whether he was reading what was written there or something else in order to sound me out.

Recollect it I can, and more swiftly than the briefest fraction of a moment. Lessing was indeed wrong in saying that the swiftest thing of all, swifter than sound and light, is the transition from good to evil,[402] for even swifter is *das Zugleich*, the all-at-once. Indeed, transition itself is a time, but that which is all-at-once is swifter than any transition. Transition is still a qualification of time, but the speed with which that which once was and never is forgotten is present, although it was indeed present: that speed is the swiftest of all, for it is so swift that its being absent is, of course, but an illusion.

June 26. Morning.

A year ago today.

I bid my whole life for the wedding day; and we are, after all, two. No! That we are not, for she is not bidding in the same way; she wants to struggle but also to have a future. Of course, she must not leave her honor and her pride in the lurch. No stroke of the hammer.

Yesterday the nonsensical talk went on undauntedly as always. We discussed my dismissal and that this would be the most sagacious thing she could do, if I might make a recommendation. The result would be that I would soon regret it and return like a whipped cur. She took this advice with the laconic answer "Yes!" and added, "No, I don't trust you an inch." I saw from that what a poor opinion she really has of me, and what a mistaken exaggerated trust she has in the significance of her personal presence. That is a bit of luck. But then, just as the nonsensical talk was going best, she bursts into tears. A person who is in desperate need always has supranatural powers, and therefore my countenance stayed completely unaltered. Thereupon she said: Let me cry; it is a relief. By law all torture is forbidden; truly this is a dreadful torture. But I must respect the argument, but not in such a way that it disturbs me. And there is also a consolation in my not having avoided the sight from which a person in my position, when he is about to take his dismissal in a contemptible role, usually excuses himself. Then the nonsensical talk began again, and it does not seem to signify as much to her as to me.

Not to dare to say an earnest word, for it would, of course, be madness if I, the guilty one, were to admonish or comfort, but is it not also insane to sit here and look on! But the good thing about it is that it is my presence that goads her, even if against her will, to express herself this way. When I am absent, she hardly does it and perhaps does not feel the urge to do it.

Just suppose a third person had witnessed this situation! Just suppose someone who did nothing but write riddles and someone who grew old by guessing riddles were to join forces and guess [403]which of the two is suffering more, on whom the impression is deeper! Tell us then, you man of experience, of a vortex that confused existence—but I have seen a confusion in which it seemed as if the commotion would not obey the rudder of an honest will! Tell about a dead calm that was the despair of all effort—but I saw a dead calm in which a lover worked and worked and almost became the beloved's murderer—not out of malice, not by accident, but in accord with his most honest conviction.

                                        June 30. *Midnight*.
What a toil and trouble is my life! My existence is nothing but *molimina* [vain efforts]; I cannot come back to myself. Whether that will ever happen in the world of time, I do not know. And if I become free so that I can integrate myself again, I may have trouble separating the alien parts that I nevertheless do not really want to separate. If I become free, there will still be an anxiety in my inclosed reserve that she has been changed.

So it is with a mussel that lies on the seashore; it opens its shell searching for food; a child sticks a twig in between so that it cannot close up. Finally the child gets tired of it and wants to pull out the twig, but a sliver remains. And the mussel closes up, but deep inside it suffers again and cannot get the sliver out. No one can see that there is a sliver, for of course the mussel has closed up, but that it is there the mussel knows.

But away with despondency; it is a deceit against her and essentially alien to my soul. If the Jewish high priest was forbidden to tear his clothes in grief because it was too passionate and too strong an expression,[404] then [405]I, too, am forbidden to become despondent because it is too apathetic and too weak. But my having become momentarily despondent shows me that for the first time in my life I have trusted my understanding in opposition to her. I have always known what it could say to me, but I have not wanted it. The impression of that meeting has given my understanding the advantage.

My sympathy, however, finally reduces me to a beggar's staff. I am like the Englishman who was in financial difficulty even though he had a five-hundred-pound banknote in his hands—but no one in the little village where he was could change it.[406] But is an expression of sympathy supposed to be like changing large currency? I thought that sympathy was like that shilling in Fortunat's purse[407]—one continually pays it all out and continually keeps it all; if one wants to change it, the magic vanishes. See, this gives me comfort.

July 2. Morning.   VI
363

A year ago today. An eyewitness to my situation would probably say to me: You do not know what love is since you are acting this way. Possibly so, but this much I do know—I know its pain. Its pleasure I perhaps know also, although at a distance, at a very great distance. If it were possible, if it were possible—in the very same moment I breathe every tear away from her eyes, alas, as schoolchildren do lest anyone see that they have cried, then the pain is forgotten, more than forgotten. Swiftly, through the omnipotence of being in love, swiftly like the growth of plants when they are cultivated by fairies, she unfurls, lovelier than ever—through herself, through the germinating power of being in love, and through my breath and the words that are whispered into her ear. Then I take her on my arm and dash through the world with her—this much, at least, I understand about love. But this very understanding of love could easily drive me out of my mind. Never in my life until now have I felt the temptations of suicide. But the torment of sympathy and then to be the guilty one—this contradiction affects my soul the way the wrenching of one's joints out of their natural position affects one physically. But what good would suicide do? Well, it could prevent her from being offended, for then she could go on living as mine if she so wished. But suppose she some day finds out—that would indeed be terrible. If she had sense, she would of course perceive that she should never have brought me to this extremity, and thus I would have made her guilty. And by such a step I perhaps would have determined her whole life so that she would not seek her healing in finitude, where she really must seek it nevertheless.

Spiritually, she is not suffering so very much. She is not even exhausted as much as she is beginning to become a little weary, with a little admixture of being bored. Humanly speaking, this does not surprise me at all, for she has no confidant, and I am unwearied in nonsense.

The days are numbered. [408]Suppose that she became ill before the final day arrived; suppose that in a fever delirium she betrayed what is taking place between us. Her closest kin, who would believe it was all fantasy, and I, who knew it was actuality! And then when she had recovered, we would begin all over again.

July 3. Midnight.[409]

Where shall we see each other again? In eternity. So there is certainly time enough for an understanding. Where is eternity? When does eternity begin? What language is spoken there? Or is there perhaps no speaking at all? Could there not be a little intervening time? Is it always high noon in eternity? Could there not be a dawn in which one found understanding in intimacy? What is eternity's judgment? Is the judgment ready before eternity begins and eternity only its execution? How is eternity depicted? As the wide horizon where one sees nothing. This is the way it is depicted in the tombstone picture: the mourner sits in the foreground and says, "He has gone away, into the hereafter." But on the wide horizon I see nothing at all, and the passerby only sees the bereaved one in the foreground, but beyond that he sees nothing. So I do not see her, either. It is impossible. I must see her. Is this no argument, or is it a better argument that whether I will or not I must see her? Suppose she had forgotten me. Can we see each other then? Suppose she had not forgiven me. Then, of course, she would not have forgotten me. But can we see each other then? Suppose she stood beside someone else. When she stands that way within time, I am standing in her path and therefore shall go away. [410]But if I stood in her path in eternity, where should I go? Compared with eternity, is time the stronger? Has time the power to separate us eternally? I thought it had only the power to make me unhappy within time but would have to release me the instant I exchange time for eternity and am where she is, for eternally she is continually with me. If so, what then was time? It was that we two did not see each other last evening, and if she found another, it was that we two did not see each other last evening because she was out somewhere else. And whose fault was that? Yes, the fault was mine. But would I or could I nevertheless act in any other way than I have acted if the first is assumed to have happened? No! I regret the first. From that moment on, I have acted according to the most honest deliberation and to the best of my ability, [411]as I also had done the first, until I perceived my error.

But does eternity speak so frivolously about guilt? At least time does not; it will no doubt still teach what it has taught me, that a life is something more than last evening. But eternity will, of course, also heal all sickness, give hearing to the deaf, give sight to the blind and physical beauty to the deformed; hence it will also heal me. What is my sickness? Depression. Where does this sickness have its seat? In the power of the imagination, and possibility is its nourishment. But eternity takes away possibility. And was not this sickness oppressive enough in time—that I not only suffered but also became guilty because of it? After all, the deformed person only has to bear the pain of being deformed, but how terrible if being deformed made him guilty!

VI
365

So, when time is over for me, let my last sigh be to you, O God, for my soul's salvation; let the next to the last be for her, or let me for the first time be united with her again in the same last sigh!

July 6. *Midnight.*

[412]Today I saw her. How strange! A thundershower forced me to go into my old café, where I have not been since those days of expectation: *erat in eo vicinio tonstrina quaedam* [in that vicinity was a barber's shop].[413] A barber's shop such as that, said the teacher, is closest to what a café is with us. *Eo sedebamus plerumque, dum illa rediret* [Frequently we sat there until she returned]. The rain was quickly over, the air mild and inviting, everything refreshed and rejuvenated. If I had not been

absorbed in recollections, I would hardly have stayed so long. The old café owner came over and greeted me, talked with me—everything acted like a drug on me. I sat in my old place, looking out the window now and then—then she came walking by. She was walking with another young girl, both in a lively conversation; she was cheerful and healthy and happy. Was she perhaps coming from her singing lessons, my beloved songstress—is she going to her singing lessons again? Has perhaps only the song changed?

Would that for half a year I could be changed into a woman in order to understand her nature—my standard is perhaps still too high!

It seems as if everything is as it was. She goes to singing lessons, she comes from singing lessons, happy as before. But there is no one waiting for her. Here in the café there is in one sense no one, but perhaps elsewhere. After all, one often hears that a girl conquers pain and falls in love again. And here, of course, the relationship was particularly conducive to something like that, for I was certainly not her beloved but a deceiver. One also often hears that a girl could not live without a man, and it was true, but it was not that man but another man.

So we are indeed in the old situation, have come to it through change, but I have remained unchanged in it. I can truthfully say, "I continue to be" etc., but what I continue to be is not clear. I am assuming that she becomes another's—what do I continue to be, then? [414]And yet not this way, I cannot relinquish her this way. That almost insane wish to see it reestablished is now superseded by another similar one—that if she becomes another's, this other might be her first love. Then she would not have broken with the idea, would not have lost in my eyes. To be sure, what does she care about losing in my eyes. But she should not think this way, for my view is more careful of her than anyone else's. Hence I am not going to see my life-view disturbed by her; alas, how it would pain me and cripple me. If the rest of the whole world has another view, it is merely a signal for battle. The trouble is that I know nothing at all about any such earlier love. However, it must be remembered that I have been far too absorbed in myself and far too ethically engrossed to come to know something like that. To that extent it certainly would be possible. If something like that is the case, it is a little satire on me that I have been ignorant of it. She has not felt encouraged to say anything; perhaps my inclosing reserve has affected her in that way. To that extent it certainly would be possible. Would that it were also actually so. And if it is actually so and remains actual, how fortunate that I did not know it! Perhaps I would have come to take the matter too lightly, and the event would not have gained the significance for me that it has.

What do I continue to be? Well, it is hard to say. But if I myself had not experienced this story and someone else were telling it, I would think that he was talking about me, [415]so completely does it apply to me.[416]

If she becomes another's, I will be less than ever able to talk with her. [417]Should I seek a real understanding just the way she did when she played the hypocrite in bargaining about the price of the ideal? Should I speak out of the passion of truth and satirize against my will? She herself is partly to blame for the confusion, for she has disturbed the erotic by playing false in the religious. She refused to be satisfied with the erotic, with being loved or not loved and the consequences of that for her; she seized upon the religious and in responsibility became a gigantic figure for me. To be sure, war between two great powers has come about because a prince sent back a king's daughter; for me, who refused her, my conflict became just as terrible, for it was God who was her sponsor. This is how I have viewed the matter. But this terrible earnestness changes the erotic into something almost comic, because, thinking with pathos, I would have to say that if she had been as ugly as hereditary sin, as shrewish as the day is long, she would have had the same meaning for me, but this is speaking altogether unerotically. So who is to blame that I must talk in this manner? It is she, who changed an erotic relationship into a religious one.

[418]Only when I am silent can I keep my soul full of pathos

behind the deception of the comic, or behind the cover that I
have long since forgotten the whole thing.

July 7. *Morning.*

A year ago today. Let me see! My life-view was that I would
hide my depression in my inclosing reserve. My pride was
that I could do it, and my resolution was to proceed further
with it to the best of my ability. I am stranded. On what? On
the misrelation of individuality and on the wedding ceremony
as a protestation in virtue thereof. What is my life's confusion?
That the statement *ultra posse nemo obligatur* [nothing can be
obligated beyond one's capacity][419] has become meaningless
to me. What is my guilt? To have ventured into something I
could not carry out. What is my offense? To have made a person unhappy. Unhappy in what way? In possibility in such a
way that according to what she said and by virtue of possibility I have a murder on my conscience. What is my punishment? To endure this consciousness. What is my hope? That
a compassionate Governance will in actuality reduce the sentence by helping her. What does my understanding say about
her? That there is no real probability of the worst. What consequence does this have for me? None at all. An ethical commitment cannot be discharged by any calculation of probability but only by assuming the ultimate possibility of
responsibility.

VI
368   I went to see her. I approached her with unusual cheerfulness and told her that it was possible to do what she wished.
As long as one is struggling, and if one is able to understand
what sympathy commands, it is easy to explain that one can
forget this consideration precisely because one is struggling.
Sympathy usually awakens most powerfully when one has
conquered. I thought I should make this extreme attempt to
see if she, prompted by having been victorious, would not
decide to give me my freedom. No! She accepted it, but without a word reflecting sympathy; she even accepted it somewhat coldly—which pleases me, for it proves that she is
weary.

I went away. At noon I came back. An absolute resolve makes one calm; a resolution that has gone through the dialectic of the terrible makes one unterrified. Coldly and definitely I announced that it was over. She was about to abandon herself to the most violent expressions of passion, but for the first time in my life I spoke imperatively. It is terrible to have to hazard this, and yet it was the only thing to do. If she had come close to death before my eyes, I would not have been able to change my resolve. My inflexibility helped her, and what was the most rash undertaking went off in an orderly way. One more attempt to arouse my sympathy had no effect. Finally she begged me to think of her sometimes, and this was promised in a casual tone—perhaps she did not mean much by it, but on the other hand I meant it in all earnestness.

So it is all over. If she chooses the scream, then I choose the pain;[420] one becomes tired of screaming—perhaps she is already; the cycle of pain will come to me again and again.

What does my understanding teach me about the employment of the two months with regard to her? She will not grieve to the point of endangering her life. For one thing, her passion is not very dialectical in inwardness; for another, no one will be able to provide her with a more favorable situation than the one she has had: to terrify me, the guilty one, to move me by her suffering. The solicitude of a sympathizer cannot give emphasis to the outburst of pain the way my presence can. Reflection will not readily take hold of her, for by now she has gone through a considerable curriculum. What she herself can think up will not be much compared with what I have already done adequately—that is, have perfected her in to the point of nausea. She will be unable to feel any sympathy for me; if there is a little remnant, it will soon be stifled. Whether she did not have a little to reproach herself with, that she still could have acted differently toward me, will never occur to her. She will perhaps become ill, just as someone who has studied too hard for an examination becomes ill when the examination is over. One could also die from such an illness, but this does not result in an infallible conclusion to a *propter hoc* [because of this].[421] [422]—As for myself, by driving me to extremes, she has helped me extricate my personality from her as far as possible. If she, tired of the whole affair, should find herself a new love, then I shall not only be left out of it, but so will every image of me, for she has none—at least none in which there is any truth.

July 7. Midnight.

See, now I am stopping for the time being. My season of hibernation with regard to her is beginning; I am withdrawing. The third of January the unrest begins again. When one is discharged, the order is: Right face, about left, march. It is rather satirical, for my trouble is that I cannot make either a right face or an about left or march.

The time of unrest is the half year, the half year of that actuality that comes back again and again until I become free. Good that it was not a full year, for then I would have had a year of mourning in the same sense as one has a church year— the moment I was through with the old one, I had to begin the new one.

When the night watchman began to shout, an old woman used to say: Now I suppose he has lost his way. And the one who is lost does indeed shout. Thus in the period of unrest I am a shouter, a lost person.

In faithfulness to her, my resolution is with all my power[423] to remain faithful to the ideas and to my spiritual existence so that I may be convinced by experience that it is spirit that gives life,[424] that the external man can languish and the spirit conquer, creation can groan and the spirit rejoice,[425] so that I might be comforted and become happy through the spirit, renouncing all of finitude's grounds of comfort, so that I might persevere and not terminate the glory of the word in the pettiness of deeds and not witness in lofty phrases and contradict myself with deeds of finitude. It would have been better if I could have remained faithful to her; it would have been greater if my spiritual existence had countenanced everyday use in a marriage, and I would have understood life more surely and easily. This is the order of rank. Next comes what I do. If she would bleed to death in a futile passion, if she would not be saved by a help that is perhaps closer than I think or at least comes close enough when it is needed, then I must work in such a way that my existence can count for two. If she helps herself in some other way, that is superfluous.

Suppose there was a book that was printed once and could not be reprinted and in it there was no place to make corrections, but in the list of printing errors there was a reading that was much more expressive than what stood in the same place in the text—then it would have to be satisfied to remain standing among the printing errors but nevertheless with its fullness of meaning. Suppose there was a weed that grew apart from the useful grain—then it would indeed stand on the side, would indeed be a weed, and would indeed be disgraced, but suppose that nevertheless it was called Proud Henry.[426]

Here the diary ends for the time being. It deals with nothing, yet not in the sense of Louis XVI's diary, the alternating contents of which are supposed to have been: on one day, went hunting; the second day, *rien* [nothing]; the third day, went hunting.[427] It contains nothing, but if, as Cicero says, the easiest letters deal with nothing, then sometimes it is the hardest life that deals with nothing.

LETTER TO THE READER[428]

from

Frater Taciturnus

My dear reader, if you in any way are of my profession, you will immediately perceive that the character conjured up here is a demoniac character in the direction of the religious—that is, tending toward it. [429]How honestly, how amply he does his part by talking so that you can see him *(loquere ut videam)* [speak so that I may see],[430] no one knows better than I, who, often exhausted, often wearied, have been tempted to abandon him and to give up patience, which amount to the same thing, which is also why, by heeding the stars and by reading coffee grounds by virtue of my scaldic vision and eagle eye,[431] I pronounce the matchless prophecy that two-thirds of the book's few readers will quit before they are halfway through, which can also be expressed in this way—out of boredom they will stop reading and throw the book away. Since he is standing on a dialectical pinnacle, one must be able to calculate with infinitely small numbers if one wants to observe him. For a round sum, be it ever so large if it nevertheless is round, one does not buy admission to his dialectical performances, and thus one would be better off not finding it worth the trouble to observe such a puppet. [432]Yet it may well have its importance to pay attention to him, because one is able to study the normal in the aberration and, if nothing else, always learn this much, that the religious is not something to make light of as something one can easily do, or something for stupid people and unshaven striplings, since it is the most difficult of all, even though absolutely accessible and absolutely enough for everyone, which is already difficult to understand, just like the contradiction that the same water in the same place is so shallow that a sheep can wade and so deep that an elephant can swim.

The girl I have kept altogether ordinary (in particular have only had her lack religious presuppositions) and deliberately so, in order that she can better illuminate him and teach him to exert himself. It would take frightful effort, perhaps even be impossible, to raise a very small object with a hydraulic jack, or to weigh half a pound with a quarter-ton steelyard: and likewise I have also thought that if there has to be a misunderstanding, it had better be of some use.

[433]The erotic and the erotic relationship, however, are of minor concern to me. I use it mainly for orientation in the religious, so one does not become all confused and think that the religious is the first spontaneity,[434] the first immediacy, or a little bit of this and that: drives and natural impulses and youthfulness, in which with an admixture of a little spirit there is a bit of fermentation. —The girl is what one properly calls a nice girl.* In novels and plays, and actually not until the

---

* The female character, of course, is only suggested in general outlines: a very young, lovable girl within the esthetic scope of naïveté. I shall sketch her here, since otherwise she is not discussed in her totality. I continually have him *in mente*, respecting, of course, the psychological probability that she does not emerge from her esthetic naïveté. [435]*In the period of the engagement* she is reserved at first. His singularity and unerotic behavior were certainly bound to make a girl feel strange. She cannot bear it, becomes bored with it, wrinkles her nose, and puts her foot down. Then comes a little incident, and she relents; she places the chair beside her and bids him sit down while she charmingly in the most endearingly roguish manner does a little fall on her knees. But he, a miserable hero as a lover, he cannot understand this, and in no situation does he more resemble *qua* lover the immortal knight of the rueful countenance than when he is seated this way. Now he wants to leave her. In her agony, she beseeches him by God and everything holy that she can think of. She herself brings the note to him; she does not suspect that there could be anything wrong in that. Now the final struggle of separating begins. She manifests all her lovable sympathy, which is ready to be satisfied with any condition, and this is the endearing sympathetic resignation naïveté. She cannot express herself in any other way, and even if one were inconsistently to demand an indication of reflection's resignation, his deception and his desperate conduct in the deception completely prevent any genesis or expression of a reflective sympathy. Thus she is altogether charming, but nevertheless with only enough resilience, if it could be measured, so that there is the psycholog-

fifth act, "a girl like that" makes a man happy; in actuality's five acts she does the best she can; in the imaginary psychological construction [*Experiment*],[437] she cannot make him happy—not because she cannot (for she can), but because she never has a chance—that is why they make each other unhappy. By endowing her differently, I would merely have prevented my main character from being adequately illuminated. With her charm, she does him a significant service, more than any general maid who does everything, and that is already a great deal for an ordinary girl in an imaginary psychological construction, for she does not belong there.

As a lover, the male character would hardly succeed in the world. His conduct and his fidelity are so grandiose, impractical, and awkward that one could be tempted to ask along with, I think, a French author[438]—whether he became mad because he was faithful to the girl, or he remained faithful to her because he was mad, for as a lover he is mad. If he actually existed, if I were able to give flesh and blood to a character in an imaginary construction, if he lived in our day and in his interiority so that his exterior appearance would not be a deception, it would be an out-and-out comedy. How funny it would be to see such a spook, troglodyte, or cave dweller come sneaking out after listening secretly to people's romantic talk and claim to be an unhappy lover of the first rank! He

---

ical possibility of a new love affair, even if psychologically the pattern may be varied.

After the engagement she does nothing at all. Even there where the psychological possibility points most dangerously at him, in the meeting at church, it is not assumed that it is an actuality (but it is also a long way from being a psychological impossibility), for his passion sees everything there is, as in this case, despite the distance. But even if he has seen accurately, the whole thing would be a little fancy on her part, perhaps a little favor, perhaps because it now occurred to her that she had been too severe with him—a little fancy *ad modum* [like] that little fall on her knees. But he, who with respect to her has undertaken "to try to abolish fate and chance," he has naturally qualified himself to be continually led by the nose, just as he is by various remarks about her future that he, unfortunately for him, has elicited from her, remarks that did not mean much to her when she said them, whereas he feels eternally obliged repeatedly to make everything of them.[436]

would have the street urchins on his tail, that is certain. An anachronism like that in the nineteenth century!—when everyone knows that unhappy lovers are like those snakes with seven heads, whom Linné proved did not exist, were a figment of the imagination.[439] To take seriously that summary that everyone knows so well: to love once, to make each other happy, etc.—to act in virtue of that with the utmost effort in a way that is condoned only in the action of a very young person once in his life and at most for half a day, to work oneself to death in an empty ceremonial service that aims to introduce utterly obsolete customs and manners—that would really be rich material for comedy. It goes without saying that just as one learns language in one's childhood, so also in youth one provides for one's whole life and stores up among other things a little supply of beautiful idioms and enthusiastic turns of phrase that serve oneself and others for a lifetime and are sociable in friendship and friendly in society and unceasingly friendly. That idioms last for a lifetime is, of course, quite as it should be, so much the more so because they provide a somewhat varied service and are a little fanciful adornment for youth on its happiest day, a pleasantry when mamma says it, and a witticism in a very old man's mouth. But that love is supposed to have the same indestructible quality, to say nothing of unhappy love, betrays a slovenly upbringing; I at least say with Pernille: I thank my parents in my grave that I was brought up differently.[440] Indeed, who these days buys an umbrella for a whole lifetime as they did in olden days, or a silk dress, a really good one that will be useful for a lifetime, or a fur coat for eternity? One readily admits that the quality is perhaps not like that of Chinese satin; one readily admits that the owner does not treat his clothes as carefully as that Chinese satin was handled, but the advantage of being able to procure them brand-new three or four times and the advantage of being able to be careless with one's clothes are nevertheless obvious. This wisdom must not be regarded as being for the select few—luckily it is public knowledge (praised be our century!). Thus one sees an unhappy lover as rarely as one sees a cape of Chinese satin. And then to want to be an unhappy lover, although he may not even be one, yes, to make it a point of honor, that is trying in utter madness to pick a quarrel with the world; the only worse madness would be for him to assume that he was not the only one but that there was a whole tribe of the same kind. It is well known that Don Quixote believed that he himself was a knight-errant. His madness by no means reaches its climax in this idea—Cervantes is much more profound than that. When Don Quixote had been healed of his sickness and the licentiate is already beginning to hope he has recovered his mind, he wants to test him a little. He speaks to him about different things and then suddenly intersperses the news that the Moors have invaded Spain. Then there is only one way to save Spain, answers Don Quixote. "What is that?" asks the licentiate. Don Quixote refuses to tell; only to His Faithful Majesty, the King of Spain, will he disclose his secret. Finally he yields to the licentiate's pleas and, sworn to secrecy and with the solemnity of a father confessor, he receives that famous knight's confession: "The only way is for His Faithful Majesty to send out a call to arms to all the knights-errant."[441] To be a knight-errant oneself is, if you please, the work of a half-mad man, but to populate all Spain with knights-errant is truly a *delirium furibundum* [raging madness]. In this respect, my hero has more sense, for he has understood the age in such a way that he himself becomes the only knight of unhappy love [*Kjærlighed*].

Yet, to repeat, the erotic is of minor concern to me. I have utilized it as Constantin Constantius ventured to use it in a book entitled *Repetition* (Copenhagen: 1844),[442] a venture that did not, however, succeed, for he remained within the esthetic. The collision consisting of a man's becoming a poet because of a girl and therefore being unable to become her husband lies within the sphere of the esthetic. The collision itself can, of course, only awaken a young person's concern, and I do not understand why Constantin has concealed from the young man what any practical fellow easily perceives— that the collision is resolved without any difficulty. He marries her and thus does not become a poet. That is indeed what he fears; he does just the opposite and perhaps thereby becomes a poet. If not every girl can make a man into a poet, then every woman can hinder a man in becoming a poet if he marries her, that I can guarantee him, and especially and best of all the girl who was on the way to making him a poet, for the poet's association with the muse is very different from a marriage relationship; and muses, along with whatever fabulous beings belong to them, do best by keeping their distance. And since there is nothing so embarrassing for a being that has flesh and blood as to have to be a muse, the adored one will naturally do everything to frustrate him in becoming a poet and encourage his every attempt to become a real husband. This whole collision is something my hero could have invented, something he could have thought up in order to pay the girl a compliment. In saying this, I do not mean to offend that young man, for in his youthfulness he can mean it in a good way. However, such a fancy could not occur to my hero; he is much too advanced for that. All the better—that is, all the more strongly does the misunderstanding show up.

Fortunately my hero does not exist outside my imaginary construction in thought. In actuality he cannot be the butt of laughter. This is fortunate enough, but it is even more fortunate for me that my task cannot be that of having to argue with him or dialecticize him out of his dialectical difficulty. Such a person, as an actually existing individual, would be able to provide enough to do for a *Doctor Seraphicus* [Angelic Doctor]⁴⁴³ combined with a *Magister Contradictionum* [Master of Dialectic],⁴⁴⁴ and when all is said and done, they perhaps would not be able to do a thing. To whatever they would come up with, he would presumably answer: I thought of that myself; now, you just listen. And thereupon he would interpret the dialectical objection until he had gradually changed it in his favor. Nor would it help to terrify him with pathos, for he is also man enough to express the most opposite point of view with pathos.

Therefore it is by no means my intention to convince him with what I write here, but rather to become aware of something true in him and in much of what he says. I let him pass for what he is, an enthusiast [*Svœrmer*], and an enthusiast of a particular kind, not simply because he has arrived a few centuries too late. Börne has said it felicitously: "The same thing happens to individual enthusiasts in relation to one another as happens to shareholders in a tontine—gradually, as they die off, the share increases for the survivors."[445] No wonder, then, that he as an enthusiast is extraordinarily enthusiastic, since the whole capital, plus interest and interest on the interest, falls to him. Yet he is not merely an enthusiast to such a degree by being of a unique kind but also by not being an immediate enthusiast; he is an enthusiast in the form of deception under which he lives free in his enthusiasm. This is a new expression for the degree of his enthusiasm and shows that this is the highest. A spontaneous, immediate enthusiast, and to this class essentially belong all who have become well known, will either press on jubilantly through all the world's opposition and plant the banner of victory, or he will weigh heavily upon existence with his suffering—that is, despite all his enthusiasm, the enthusiast still cannot do without the world. My hero does not wish to do this at all; on the contrary, he wants to hide his enthusiasm by an exterior that expresses the opposite; so secure is he in his cause that he does not care or, as he also thinks, does not dare to express it.

I let him pass for what he is and go to the issue. This I shall discuss [446]by suggesting specific points, and in working them out I shall always have him *in mente.*

1.[447]

What Is Unhappy Love, and What Is the Variant in the Imaginary Construction?

[448]From time immemorial, poetry has had in unhappy love [*Kjærlighed*] an object for its happy love. If, as has been said, it was a mother at her child's sickbed who invented prayer, prayer that is specifically designed for such a sufferer, one could almost believe that unhappy love has invented poetry. But in that case it is no more than reasonable for poetry to reciprocate and come to the assistance of unhappy love, and it is not too much to ask that it do this willingly.

Unhappy love implies that love is assumed and that there is a power that prevents it from expressing itself happily in the lovers' union. Nothing is easier to say than this, but to be a poet, who with his divine pathos fills this void and creates with his breath, is to be removed from this trivial remark by a distance equal to the diameter of the earth. Without pathos, no poet. Pathos ranks first, but the next, which stands in an essential and absolute relation to that, is to comprehend penetratingly a profound contrast. If one were to count all the obstacles to the happiness of erotic love [*Elskov*], there would be on this scale, just as on a thermometer's, a plus and a minus range. Beginning with the insignificant obstacles, one would reach a point where the change took place and everything became different. It is possible to think of obstacles of such a nature that one would have to say: The task for erotic love is to overcome them. If a poet selects such an obstacle as constituting an unhappy love, then he is not a poet but a satirist against his will. Consequently, it must not be in love's power to remove the obstacle.

This is how the matter stands or, more accurately, it was standing at this point many years ago. The later period has the common flaw of limping on both sides, neither believing in love as the absolute passion nor choosing obstacles of *prima* quality; people negotiate with the creditors and they listen to reason—and the item "unhappy love" is dropped and instead there is just one item, "more or less happy love"; there is equality and "one kind of beer" for everyone.

Poetry is connected with immediacy and thus cannot think a duplexity. If there is any doubt for a single moment that the lovers are not absolutely reliable *qua* lovers, not absolutely prepared within themselves for love's union, if there is a single doubt, then poetry turns away from the guilty party and declares: "This is a sign to me that you do not love, and therefore I cannot become involved with you." And in this, poetry also does well, so that it does not itself become a ludicrous power, as it has frequently become in later times through a misunderstood choice of tasks.

Without passion, no poet, and without passion, no poetry.

Consequently, if one is to break out of poetry and the rounded-off sphere in which duplexity cannot be accommodated, if this exodus is not to mean losing oneself in common-sensicality and finitude, then it must take place by virtue of a higher passion. To take passion away from poetry and to compensate for what is lost with embellishments, lovely rural scenery, popular woodland scenes, enchanting theatrical moonshine, is a loss akin to wanting to make up for the badness of a book with the elegance of the binding, something that certainly cannot interest the reader but at most the book-binder. To take passion out of the lines of a play and in compensation have the orchestra fiddle a little is to prostitute poetry and is comic, just as it would be in actual life if the lover, instead of pathos in his breast, had a music box in his pocket for the crucial moment.

Not until a higher passion enters into the passion of poetry, not until then does the duplexity under discussion here commence. Now the task becomes dialectical in itself, and this the poet's task cannot and must never be. Admittedly, unhappy love, for example, has its dialectic, but it has it outside itself, not in itself. That which is intrinsically dialectical in itself contains the contradiction in itself. The poet's task, however, is single, because the contradiction comes from outside. By itself, unhappy love is bound to become happy—this is the poet's certainty, but the trouble is that there is a power outside that wants to prevent it. In poetry, therefore, love does not relate to itself but it relates to the world, and this relationship determines whether it becomes unhappy. Therefore, as soon as passion's sonority ceases to sound from the one, as soon as there is conflict in passion itself—indeed, even if a higher passion announces itself in a new sonority—as soon as the concurrent sound of doubleness is detected in it, the poet cannot become involved with it. If the passion is love, then it must be undialectical in itself so that poetry can see in him an unhappy lover. If the passion is love of the fatherland, then this must be undialectical in itself, and if the hero sacrifices an erotic relationship because of his passion, he is not called an unhappy lover but is named after the passion that is undialect-

VI
379

ical in him. In his enthusiasm for his native land, the patriotic hero does not relate himself to himself, or the enthusiasm does not relate itself to itself, but it relates itself to a surrounding world and therein also to a relationship of erotic love, to a relationship of veneration. This is how poetry must understand it. The esthetic hero must have his opposition outside himself, not in himself. That this is not the case in Hamlet is perhaps precisely the anomaly—more on that later.

Back to unhappy love. If we consider the distinctive characters among those unhappy lovers whom "song and saga" rewarded with renown, we shall promptly see that the passion is immediate and that the contradiction is from outside, somewhat as the pastor on behalf of the engaged couple publicly invites objections, for he, too, cannot imagine that in the lover's own passion there would be a contradiction, because in that case he might feel constrained like the poet, thus by a poetic call, to say of the guilty party: He does not love. Petrarch sees Laura joined to another.[449] Abelard does not feel separated from Héloise by his holy orders (for love is the absolute passion)—he is separated by Fulbert's wrath and, alas, by his cruelty.[450] Romeo does not feel the family hatred as that which separates, because it also moves in him through filial piety toward his father; it is the family feud that actually separates him from Juliet; Axel has no conscientious scruples about the close relationship, and Valborg understands only that they love each other; it is the Church with its external power that separates them.[451] Take the obstacles away, and those unhappy people are the happiest of lovers.

In our day, unhappy love does not make a good show. We go to see *Romeo and Juliet* but really do not know what to make of it; at most it is the gallery that actually weeps. Besides, it is to Shakespeare rather than to Juliet that a tear is offered, and in the theater we feel ourselves in an almost embarrassing situation. Quite simply, this is because to love, like all passion, has become dialectical to the present generation. An immediate love such as that is incomprehensible, and in our day even a grocer's boy would be able to tell Romeo and Juliet some astounding truths. It might seem that this anomaly could be overcome by being drawn into the play and brought to consciousness there so that the public would not feel completely alien in the theater but at least recognize itself in the grocer's boy. The trouble is that it does not help, for then the grocer's boy, a matter-of-fact philosopher, a pawnbroker, or whatever other representative of common sense one would use might walk off with the victory, because the threadbare side of the matter is precisely the truth. If this did not happen, then Romeo and Juliet not only would be alien to the spectators but in their eyes would lose as obstinate characters whose death was not tragic but well deserved *ob contumaciam* [because of contempt] toward all reason. Shakespeare does, of course, also have opposite viewpoints represented in his drama, but his fully definitive pathos makes him himself just as certain as Romeo and Juliet are undialectical in their passion.

VI
381
What, then, can be the consequence when people reject poetry and yet have no higher passion? This, of course—that people go astray in half-baked ideas and are made happy in fancies and self-delusions, and this generation becomes the most expeditious [*skyndsomste*] but not the most judicious [*skjønsomste*], the promising [*lovende*] and prevaricating [*lyvende*] generation without parallel, which can easily be demonstrated a priori. So, while one almost never hears mention of an unhappy lover, there is all the more competition about having been one, even more than once having suffered what those unhappy ones suffer, but also having overcome these sufferings etc. etc. etc. Poetry cannot use such people. It requires an essential expression for what one has essentially suffered and is not satisfied with the assurances of a few girlfriends who have seen her sufferings, or with a spiritual adviser's trustworthiness, not even if he had a speculative eye and discerned the necessary development. Oh, what tempting fruits for a comic poet, and if he ever shows up, my only worry is that he himself, carried away by the vision of the inexhaustibility of the subject, will die of laughter and thus be prevented from accomplishing anything.

A poet would be an especially useful figure as the main character in such a comedy; for example, Scribe, in particular, is comic despite his matchless talent, and comic because he has not understood himself, because he wants to be a *poet* and yet has forgotten that poetry and passion are inseparable, and comic because he has satisfied the age as *poet*—this whole thing is comic in the Aristophanic sense. Scribe's whole existence is a contradiction just like that which is so often found in his plays. Take *La Cameraderie*,[452] for example, his reception piece, with its masterly effect that one cannot admire enough. It describes the contemptible solidarity of some mediocre, seedy characters who in all sorts of contemptible ways know how to push their way ahead by their obtrusiveness; but a young lawyer scorns these methods and therefore becomes the object of persecution by carping criticism and lies. What happens? A young woman is so good as to take an interest in him. She is not inexperienced in intrigues, she carries all before her, and the lawyer rises to honor and status. As a result, one *cameraderie* wins over the other, one intrigue takes the power away from the other. Just as when the rubric "unhappy love" was dropped, one kind, more or less happy love, replaced the contrasts, so here the contrasts honesty/dishonesty and virtue/contemptibleness drop out and there is one kind, approximate honesty, or there ought to be a little more than honesty.

VI
382

Now when love itself has become dialectical, poetry must relinquish it, because its having become dialectical means in the first place that the poet cannot take on his task, cannot begin, inasmuch as there has been added an introduction of which the outcome is critical, and in the second place that there is no assurance that the outcome will be happy if only all the external obstacles are cleared away, and finally that in case of death there is no assurance that it will be a heroic death from love or from passion, since it might be a feverish cold of which one dies.

Now if there comes to be a consciousness that love has been given up as an absolute passion, then poetry must forsake it; and where the carcass is, there the predatory birds[453] gather, here in the shape of novelists, serial-story writers, hermaphrodites of tragicomic writers who are not sure whether they want to be writers of tragedy or of comedy and therefore are neither, for without passion there is no poet, not a comic poet, either. If poetry is to continue to exist, it must discover another passion, one just as legitimate as love was for poetry. It would not be hard to show that there is nothing like that precisely because of the distinctive synthesis of the erotic. I shall not, however, do it here, but neither shall I demand of anyone that he believe I can do it, since I do not do it. Yet there are also other passions that in the eyes of poetry are legitimate. The same thing that weakened faith in love—the lack of a sense of the infinite—will also weaken faith in the other passions. Thus, forsaken by poetry, people will work their way down into finitude until they finally reach politics in the bad sense. If politics is viewed with the passion of the infinite, it will naturally be able to yield heroes such as there were in antiquity, when people also believed in love. In the world of the infinite, it holds that whoever offends in one thing offends in all,[454] for the person who has a sense of the infinite has a sense of every infinity.

The same reflection that corroded love will also corrode the infinite passion of politics. In an age such as that, a hero is a man who will work for a finite goal, will, as he says, sacrifice his life for it, perhaps through an error does that, and through a new error is canonized as a hero. Such a character, however, is completely unusable for poetry (possibly he could be used as the sausage peddler in Aristophanes[455]): he is unpoetic and contradicts himself. To that extent it is quite consistent that modern politics does not inspire its devotees to sacrifices, for it does not inspire at all: otherwise sacrifices come naturally. It is a contradiction to be willing to sacrifice one's life for a finite goal, and in the eyes of poetry such behavior is comic, akin to dancing oneself to death or wanting to walk with spurs when one is bowlegged and falls down on them and is killed— rather than quit wearing spurs. Oh, what an enticing task for a comic poet, but without passion no poet, no comic poet, either. Subject matter he will not lack, for politics does not lack servants. A suitable main character could be a politician who, despite all his sagacity, wants to be inspired, wants to be a sacrifice but does not want to sacrifice himself, wants to fall but wants to be a witness to the acclamation himself and therefore does not manage to fall, and when, perhaps, all is said and done, has in himself the one and only person who stands in his way—an inspired person who has no intimation of what inspiration is. His pathos would culminate in this, inconceivably enough, not long since worn-out platitude: "I want to give my life as a sacrifice; no one shall say that I do not have heroic courage, but this blind courage is not the highest, and therefore I restrain myself—and go on living; therefore I restrain myself—and let someone else, someone less important, fall in my place. *Plaudite* [Applaud]."[456] It is, of course, quite in order for a sagacious politician to be also sagacious enough to perceive—something that is hidden from the more simple—how important his life is for the state, that if he lives a long time no one is going to be in want, but inspiration this is not. All inspiration has its source in the passion of infinity, where every Tom, Dick, and Harry, together with all their sagacity, vanish as nonentities. God help poetry; with the help of politics it has been put on bread and water!

Aristotle has already divided human beings into: θεολόγοι, φιλόσοφοι, πολιτικοί [theologians, philosophers, politicians].[457] The politicians come last, to say nothing of the politicians of finitude who renounce the passion of infinity—they come at the very end, or rather, come tagging along behind, which always makes for thin beer. There is no inspiration in faith in oneself, even less in faith in one's bit of shopkeeper shrewdness. All inspiration has its source either in faith in one's passion or, deeper, in faith in a providence, which teaches a person that even the death of the greatest man is a jest for a providence that has legions of angels in reserve,[458] and that he therefore should go resolutely to his death and leave his good cause to providence and his posthumous reputation to the poet. Just as one seldom sees an unhappy lover these days, likewise does one seldom see a martyr in the political world, but on the other hand there is overall competition in saying "The devil take me if I have not been willing, indeed, willing to be a martyr, if it were not obvious that it would be greater etc." And politics has a countless host of titular heroes and volunteer martyrs, not armed but *inter pocula* [between goblets]. They all have that high-mindedness of the hero death, but they also with equally heroic wisdom have perceived that "it would be better for all, for society, to go on living, that they owed it to humankind to live—and clink the glasses." There is one step left, and it is a true *non plus ultra* [no more beyond]; this is when such a generation of armchair life-insurance salesmen consider it an injustice on the part of poetry that it does not select its heroes among the worthy contemporaries. [459]But one does poetry an injustice, or rather one does not goad it so much that it ends with poetry's taking, Aristophanically, the first sausage peddler that comes along and making him a hero. In no other way can poetry be inspired when people are swearing and thumping on the table.

So poetry's day seems to be over, tragedy in particular. A comic poet will lack an audience, since not even the audience can be two places at once, on the stage and in the auditorium. Moreover, a comic poet has his own resource in a pathos that lies outside the play and shows by its existence that the day of poetry is over. Someone who pins his hope on speculative drama serves poetry only insofar as he serves the comic. If a witch or a wizard succeeds in bringing about such a thing, if by means of a speculative thaumaturgist[460] (for a dramaturgist would not suffice) it would satisfy the requirement of the age as a *poetic* work, this event would certainly be a good motif for a comedy, even though it would achieve the comic effect through so many presuppositions that it could not become popular.[461]

That the time of poetry is over really means that immediacy is at an end. Immediacy is not entirely without reflection; as poetry sees it, it has relative reflection by having its opposition outside itself. But immediacy is not actually over until the immediate infinity is grasped by an equally infinite reflection. At the same moment, all tasks are transformed and made dialectical in themselves; no immediacy is allowed to stand by itself or to be exposed to struggle only with something else, since it must struggle with itself.

Back to love. When love does not stand on its own, this means that, self-given, it does not, as in poetry, have its obstacle outside but has its obstacle within itself. Thus a task emerges that every poet must reject but that still has its significance, a task that can be varied in many ways, and one of these variations I have chosen in my imaginary psychological construction. Love is given; no obstacle is seen. On the contrary, love is favored by peace and security, an absolute calm. But when it is to be ushered into infinite reflection, it runs into difficulties. Consequently, the difficulties do not arise because love collides with the world but because love must reflect itself in the individuality. The problem is so dialectical that the fact that love provokes resentment in this way can also invite the opposite question: Is love given, then? Now, if it is not a religious collision, then the issue does not exist at all except as silly talk; for the poetic is glorious, the religious still more glorious, but what lies between is silly talk, no matter how much talent is wasted on it.

Now, love provokes resentment, or so it seems to the individual, and he states of himself that he has an unhappy love. I express myself very dubitatively and do not have the passion of my knight, but I am trying to understand him. The poet would now ask him, "What is the obstacle? Is it cruel parents who have to be pacified? Is it a family feud that has to be conciliated? Is it a papal dispensation that has to be procured? Another person who has to be eliminated? Or—alas, I must indeed grieve over myself and my situation—if it is a mite that I am to throw to you, if you need money to be happy, well, then, unless you prefer the first four situations, then I make you unhappy, but a hero." The person involved says no. Then the poet turns away and says, "Well, my good friend, then you do not love." Poetry is willing to do everything for love, is willing to embellish happy love, is willing to celebrate unhappy love in song, but in its charming naïveté it must be sure of one thing—erotic love, lest after having done everything it suddenly discovers that it was in vain because there were other obstacles.

In order to stick to the task, one must constantly make dou-

VI
386

ble-movements.[462] Anyone who cannot do that and cannot do it with ease does not see the task at all, and then he is lucky if he has not lost his delight in poetry. But if he can do it, then he also knows that infinite reflection is not something alien but is immediacy's transparency to itself.

If love is assumed to have happily undergone infinite reflection, then it is something different, then it is religious; if it runs aground along the way, then it runs aground on the religious. This may not be immediately perceptible, because very frequently even under the name "infinite reflection" one is thinking of finite reflection. In relation to any finite reflection, immediacy is essentially higher, and it is an insult for it to have to be involved with something like this. Poets understand this very well, and that is why the obstacles come from the outside, and the tragic lies precisely in this, that these obstacles have the power to triumph in a certain sense over the infinity of immediacy; only bourgeois-philistines and hermaphroditic poets understand it otherwise. But an infinite reflection is infinitely higher than immediacy, and in it immediacy relates itself to itself in the idea.[463] But this "in the idea" signifies a God-relationship of the widest scope, and within this scope there is a multiplicity of more specific determinants.

The idea is also in immediacy; the poet does indeed see it, but for his hero it does not exist, or in his relation to it he is not in relation to himself. For this very reason he is not free in his passion. That is, freedom does not at all mean that he is to give it up, but freedom means that in order to hold on to it firmly he uses the passion of infinity by which he could give it up. Such a thought the poetic hero cannot think at all, and the poet does not dare to have him think it, for then he immediately ceases to be a poetic character.

Thus in the infinite reflection freedom is gained, whether it is affirmative or negative. In my imaginary construction, I have chosen protestation; in this way the double-movements show up most clearly. Simultaneously he holds on firmly to his love, and he has no obstacles from the outside; on the contrary, everything smiles favorably and threatens to be changed to terror if he does not follow his wish, threatens him

with the certain loss of his honor, with the death of his beloved—thus he simultaneously holds on firmly to his love and
maintains that despite everything he will not, cannot make it
concrete.

The situation is so dialectical that one must not be in a
hurry, for that would result only in confusion. But if it is true
that the time of immediacy is over, then it is a matter of attaining the religious—everything temporary serves no purpose. And for the person for whom it is true that the time of
immediacy is over, for that person, too, the most difficult dialectical movement will become popular; otherwise I am very
willing to admit that my imaginary construction is far from
being popular. What makes an exposition unpopular is generally believed to be the many technical terms in the scholarly
terminology. But that is a totally incidental kind of unpopu-
larity, which scholarly windbags have in common with skip-
pers, for example, who also are unpopular because they speak
a jargon and not at all because they speak profoundly. Indeed,
time and again the terminology of a philosophy can also make
its way even to the common man, [464]and consequently its un-
popularity was, after all, incidental. It is the thought, not the
incidentals of expression, that essentially makes an exposition
unpopular. A systematic ribbon and button maker can become unpopular but essentially is not at all, inasmuch as he
does not mean much by the very odd things he says (alas, and
this is a popular art!). Socrates, on the other hand, was the
most unpopular man in Greece because he said the same thing
as the simplest person but meant infinitely much by it. To be
able to stick to one thought, to stick to it with ethical passion
and undauntedness of spirit, to see the intrinsic duplexity of
this one thought with the same impartiality, and at one and
the same time to see the most profound earnestness and the
greatest jest, the deepest tragedy and highest comedy—this is
unpopular in any age for anyone who has not realized that
immediacy is over. But neither can what is essentially unpopular be learned by rote. More on that later.

This, then, is the task I have assigned myself: an unhappy
love affair in which love is dialectical in itself and in the crisis

of infinite reflection acquires a religious aspect. It is easy to see how different this task is from any other unhappy love affair; it is easy to see if one looks at both parts at the same time— otherwise one will perhaps not see either of them.

2.

Misunderstanding as the Tragic and Comic-Tragic Principle Utilized in the Imaginary Construction

When Claudius declares that misunderstanding is really due to the fact that people do not understand one another,[465] in his naive humor [*Lune*] as spontaneous immediacy there are concealed differences that when brought out display the comic and the tragic; this is also why that naive remark varies in relation to the opposite passion with which it can be accentuated. The tautological aspect of this remark is equally capable of arousing the comic and the tragic passion; the remark itself is one of humor. Socrates, for example, could very well say ironically in the collapsed situation of the dialogue: By the gods, Polus,[466] it is surely strange that we do not understand each other. It must be due to a misunderstanding. An enthusiast would say tragically: Ah, misunderstanding—not to be able to understand each other. From the point of unity of the comic and the tragic, this remark would not be humorous but profound. In other words, as soon as misunderstanding between two people is posited, then as long as they misunderstand each other no other reason can be given for it than misunderstanding. If the reason for the misunderstanding can be given, then the *discrimen* [distinguishing element] of the misunderstanding is removed. Thus the two could go on misunderstanding each other but nevertheless also basically understand each other.

There is misunderstanding wherever the heterogeneous are brought together, a heterogeneity, please note, of such a kind that there is a possibility of a relation, for otherwise the misunderstanding *is* not—therefore it can be said that as the basis of the misunderstanding there lies an understanding, that is, the possibility of an understanding. If the impossibility is

present, then misunderstanding is not present. With the possibility, however, there is misunderstanding, and looked at dialectically it is both tragic and comic.

Poetry cannot become involved with this duplexity of misunderstanding; it must use misunderstanding either comically
or tragically. To an extent it is correct in placing the basis of
misunderstanding in some third factor outside, by the removal of which the misunderstanders understand each other.
In other words, if the misunderstanding lies in the relation to
each other of the heterogeneous ones themselves, then the relation is dialectical and the misunderstanding is just as comic
as it is tragic. But if there is a third factor outside that separates
the two in misunderstanding, then the two, viewed essentially, are not misunderstanding but understanding, as one
sees when that third factor outside is removed.

Without going too far with examples and comparisons,
[one may say that] when poetry uses misunderstanding in
connection with an unhappy love affair it locates the misunderstanding in an unfortunate event, in a mysterious occur-
rence, in an evil or foolish individual who by his interference
occasions the misunderstanding between the two. Poetry
must be sure of the real possibility of understanding—otherwise it cannot begin at all. Take away that event, that occur-
rence, that individual, and then they understand each other,
for the obstacle merely makes them unable to arrive at that. A
misunderstanding of that sort is not simultaneously comic and
tragic. The circumstance of the misunderstanding is simple,
and what makes it tragic in unhappy love is that the substance
of erotic love is posited in the lovers' passion. Take away the
substance from the misunderstanders, and the misunderstanding is comic, for by their very misunderstanding the misunderstanders are disclosed in their emptiness, and the laughter
over them is the judgment by which life is reconciled and receives satisfaction.

[467]That the contrast is simultaneous is a consideration that
is too dialectical for poetry. Even if romantic poetry places the
comic and the tragic together, it is in the form of contrast and
at most in a negative unity of a life-view not given in poetry

but rising out of it, so to speak, as a presentiment. But it is not the same as that which is simultaneously comic and tragic; the contrast is rather the separating factor, which, with the same thrust by which it pushes down low-comedy, elevates the lyrical. —In immediacy there is continually the one, and the highest form of connection is this: when the one has been, the other follows.

[468]In the *Phaedo*, Socrates develops this succession with regard to a sense impression—the pleasant and the unpleasant—so beautifully and in an illustrative situation (for one sees him sitting and rubbing with pleasure the leg from which the chain has been removed, by the removal of which he now senses pleasure, whereas it pained him when it was there), and thinks it would have been a task for Aesop to write a fable about it, how the gods, when they could not unite these opposing powers in any other way, joined them at their extremities.[469] Presumably Socrates is in this way acknowledging that the pleasant and the unpleasant are not simultaneous, but in his ironic consciousness there is a negative unity of them.

Similarly, the contrasts of poetry merely supersede each other. Therefore, poetry would never be able to comprehend the death of Socrates. Here everything is finished, and yet poetry would be able to choose only the one side—here probably the tragic. At most it would produce a comic contrast, although perhaps this is not easy. It cannot be denied that Xanthippe makes a comic figure with her screaming and noise, that her conduct is reminiscent of many a shrewish widow's grief-stricken newspaper announcement about the deceased, nor can one deny that Socrates quite ironically lets a comic light fall on the scene of Xanthippe, with her sensitivity and her hidden screaming emotion saved up all these years for a solemn moment such as this, being transported out through the door,[470] but this contrast would be a bit unfair and inadequate. Perhaps it would be better to create in fantastic style a chorus of a certain class of philologists whose "tear-jerking" comments on this paragon of a man and his martyr's death form a good contrast to Socrates' whole view. But then in turn the historical would vanish. Even Socrates' friends are

further advanced than poetry can go, for Phaedo himself says
that as a witness to that event he found himself in a curious
state, a rare combination of joy and sorrow—indeed, that
those present, especially Apollodorus, were laughing one moment and crying the next. Not to mention Socrates himself,
for the fact that those present laugh at one moment and cry
the next only shows that they have not completely understood
him. Socrates specifically posits a duplexity that poetry cannot express. If poetry wants to use the pathos of tragedy to
depict Socrates' suffering as a martyr, it had better look where
it is going, for he does not suffer at all, he has already considered how droll it is that such a ἄτοπός τις [queer one][471] comes
to his end by way of being executed. Poetry cannot comprehend him as comic, because his having by himself considered
all the comic aspects proves specifically that he is not comic;
and if there ever was anyone who was not comic it was Socrates. The tragic death of a hero is something simple, and poetry loves that, but if it simultaneously gets a hint that the man
himself assumes that the situation could also be comic, then
poetry must declare bankruptcy.

[472]Before taking leave of poetry, however, I must make one
more comment on misunderstanding when it is used esthetically. Poetry can also use misunderstanding in such a way that
this exists for the single individual precisely because there is
no point of contact for him with the person or persons who
misunderstand him. This can become either comic or tragic,
depending on the quality and the passion, but it cannot simultaneously be comic and tragic, because the point of contact is
lacking that places the misunderstanders together in a unity or
by which they situate themselves together in such a way that
they simultaneously are kept together and yet apart in misunderstanding, and yet cannot be separated because the point
of contact is there, and its existence is a relationship that is
simultaneously comic and tragic. —It is tragic when an enthusiast speaks to a generation of dunderpates and is not understood, but it is tragic only because there is no point of contact
between them because the dunderpates do not care at all for
the enthusiast. *Gulliver's Travels*[473] is comic because of fantasy

verging on madness, but the effect is only comic, and comic because the substance of qualitative passion is not present in the misunderstanding, although passion is present in the poet, for without passion there is no poet, not a comic poet, either. If the misunderstanding is entirely about unimportant matters, it becomes a careless jest. Life has plenty of examples of this. [474]A deaf man is entering a meeting hall when the meeting is in progress; he does not want to disturb and therefore opens the big double door very gently. Unfortunately, a feature of the door is that it creaks. This he cannot hear; he believes he is doing it very well, and a long sustained creaking is produced by this slow opening of the door. People become impatient; someone turns around and shushes him; he thinks he may have been opening the door too fast, and the creaking continues. This situation is a jest, and therefore neither the tragic nor the comic can properly take hold of it. [475]Yet there is a point of unity intimated here: he does not want to disturb, the assembly does not want to be disturbed, and he disturbs it. Add a dash of feeling and something else, and the result is the many situations over which one does not know whether to laugh or to cry. This is the tragic–comic, since no essential passion is posited; neither the comic nor the tragic is essentially present. In the comic-tragic both are posited and the dialectically infinitized spirit simultaneously sees both elements in the same situation.

Now to my imaginary construction. I have placed together two heterogeneous individualities, one male and one female. Him I have kept in the power of spirit in the direction of the religious; her I have kept in esthetic categories. As soon as I posit a point of unity there can be plenty of misunderstanding. This point of unity is that they are united in loving each other. The misunderstanding, then, is not due to some third factor, as if they understood each other and were separated by some alien power—no, ironically enough, everything favors their misunderstanding. There is nothing to keep them from having each other and talking together, but right there the misunderstanding begins. Now if I take away the passion, then the whole thing is an ironic situation with Greek *Heiterkeit* [serenity]; if I posit passion, then the situation is essentially tragic; if I consider it, then I say that it is simultaneously comic and tragic. The heroine, of course, cannot see it as such—she is too immediate for that. If she sees it as comic, it must, according to the law of succession, come at a later moment, when the laughter would in turn make her comic herself, for to laugh at an essential error demonstrates that one is involved in a new one, and the person who laughs this way is as little healed as "he is free who mocks his chains."[476] The hero certainly is promptly aware of the presence of the comic, which saves him from becoming comic, but yet he cannot see the relationship as I see it, I who have laid it all out in the imaginary construction. This is due to his being in a state of passion, and the level of his passion is best shown by the fact that he fortifies himself in pathos by seeing the comic. He is in a state of passion. If I were to say to him, "Try to get over it," he would promptly replace it with another one and say that it is an ignoble treatment of the girl. Thus he can certainly see the comic in the misrelation and the misunderstanding, but he perceives this interpretation as a subordinate authority, and out of it his passion evolves with ever greater pathos. The conjunction in this misunderstanding is that they love each other, but in their heterogeneity this passion must express itself in essentially different ways, and thus the misunderstanding must not come between them from outside but develops in the relationship itself that exists between them. The tragic is that two lovers do not understand each other; the comic is that two who do not understand each other love each other. That such a thing can happen is not inconceivable, for erotic love itself has its dialectic, and even if it were unprecedented, the construction, of course, has the absolute power to construct imaginatively. When the heterogeneous is sustained the way I have sustained it, then both parties are right in saying that they love. Love [*Kjærlighed*] itself has an ethical and an esthetic element. She declares that she loves and has the esthetic element and understands it esthetically; he says that he loves and understands it ethically. Hence they both love and love each other, but nevertheless it is a misunderstanding. The heterogeneous are kept separate by category, and in this way the misunderstanding is different from novelistic bartering and hindsight-opinions within purely esthetic categories.

The male character in the imaginary construction, then, sees the comic, but not as a seasoned observer sees it. He sees the comic and with this fortifies himself for the tragic. It is this in particular that engages me, for this serves to illuminate the religious. Paganism culminates in the mental fortitude to see the comic and the tragic simultaneously in the same thing. In the higher passion, which chooses the tragic part of this unity, religiousness begins—that is, the religiousness for which immediacy is over—and in our day, so they say, it is supposed to be over for everybody. As animal creation, the human being has two legs (extremities); similarly, the comic and the tragic are necessary extremities of movement for the person who wishes to exist by virtue of spirit and after having abandoned immediacy. Anyone who has only one leg and yet wants to be spirit by virtue of spirit is ludicrous, be he ever so great a genius. In the balance between the comic and the tragic lies the condition for proper walking. Hence, the misrelation may also be described as limping, being bowlegged, club-footed, etc. —The trouble with my knight is that, when he is on the point of becoming integrated in religiousness, he becomes extremely dialectical—more of this in another paragraph. Here I shall only say that he does not become dialectical in choosing the tragic higher passion out of the comic and the tragic, because then I could not make use of him at all, but he becomes dialectical in the final expression of this very passion. Without this, I could not use him, either, for therein lies precisely a demonic qualification of approximation to the religious.

In order to throw light on the imaginary construction, I shall go over the structure.

The form of the design exhibits the duplexity. In the morning he recollects actuality; at night he deals with the same story but is permeated with his own ideality. This ideality, therefore, is not an illusory anticipation that still has not seen the actuality but is an act of freedom after the actuality. This

VI
394

is the difference between esthetic and religious ideality. The esthetic is higher than the actuality prior to the actuality, that is, in illusion; the religious is higher than the actuality after the actuality, that is, by virtue of a relationship with God. The duplexity is expressed. A poet or a lover can certainly have an ideal conception of the beloved but cannot simultaneously have an actual consciousness of the extent to which it is true or an actual consciousness of the extent to which it is not true. Only the new ideality that comes after the actuality can endure this contradiction.

[477]So the story begins twice. I have allowed a half year to intervene and assume that during this time he has lived in a kind of stupor, until suddenly passion awakens on the third of January. Other conceptions could also be introduced here— my choice is made in connection with the design.

The two individualities relate inversely to each other. For her the critical point occurs in actuality, but he, who is virtually inexperienced with regard to the opposite sex, does not see it clearly and has only some intimations of it in his theoretical efforts. [478]Shakespeare has declared somewhere—I do not remember where and cannot quote, but the sense of it is: at the moment before the cure of a violent illness occurs, at the moment of the change for the better, the assault is most violent; and every evil is worst when it is taking leave.[479] The critical point for her, when the healing essentially begins, is the moment when she has staked everything in order to hold him fast, and he, then, completely consistent with his point of view, goes to the extreme to battle his way free from her. Psychologically her change for the better began the moment she felt the pain most acutely. His image, therefore, is already vanishing while he is present and when the separation is final vanishes more and more as a recollection; actuality must assist her. [480]With him it is the reverse. In the period of actuality he is stronger because he has her only as an actuality. But the moment he is to see her again, not in actuality but in the light of his own ideality, she is transformed into a gigantic figure. What he has done in actuality, the deception, by which he has actually benefited her (for the relationship is so dialectical that the deception is basically truth to her—that is, she understands it best), he cannot maintain in relation to her as soon as he himself produces her [in ideality]. In order to believe in the significance of the deception, he must have his relationship to her in actuality and actually see her. His critical moment therefore comes on the third of January the next year, for he must be religiously healed, and in this respect her actuality disturbs him; he needs to have her ideal. Just as they have misunderstood each other from the beginning, so the misunderstanding continues after the separation and precisely now manifests itself most clearly. Just when she is on the point of having forgotten him because she does not see him and is already well on the road to recovery and he has become insignificant to her, at that very moment she has become supremely significant to him precisely because he does not see her. As soon as he sees her, is with her, speaks with her, he is clearheaded and strong; as soon as he himself creates her, he loses his understanding, does not dare believe it, and the religious must work itself ahead more definitely. A ghost is always terrifying, and she becomes that for him. But what a difference between a young girl, for whom his understanding is a match, and an ideal shape that comes terrifyingly toward him, against which his understanding is capable of nothing at all! His individuality was structured ethically-religiously. This is what he is to become. She also helps him, but not by her actuality. Here, then, lies the significance of his depression. It is the concentration of possibility. But when something like that is what it means, then all talk about a young girl's cheerfulness and a marriage's ability to dissipate it is foolish talk, for it should not be dissipated. On the contrary, the deep dark night of his soul should become still darker, for then he will recover. This she cannot discern and she acts altogether consistently. Neither can he see it, for then he would not receive the finishing blow of terror in the way it falls most tellingly when it strikes with his own guilt and her distress.

[481]The idea requires that he see her again, but please note that he does not see an actuality, for then he is helped. Therefore I have had him see her again several times. But these

meetings have a distinctive correlation. From his standpoint, he quite consistently believes that he owes it to the infinity within her not to disturb with intermixed half measures. It is immediately apparent that he has only himself to deal with— and not with her as an actuality outside himself, for then the deception would emerge again. Consequently, in order not to disturb the infinity within her, he bewitches himself into a dreadful state of moribundity or demise. From his point of view, this is just as energetic an expression of his love as her violent outburst was of hers. This, of course, was mutually the worst thing they could do to each other.

So he does see her again. But precisely because in order to help her he conducts himself as if dead, he has prevented himself from receiving a single direct impression. Here he is on the point of becoming normal; his aberration consists in his still being concerned about it with all his passion. He never witnesses any event related to her or has a direct connection with any such event, never anything certain, but keeps on concerning himself about it with all his passion, appropriates everything, even the most insignificant details, and does not acquire much more by his dialectical efforts.* In other words, he becomes more and more absorbed in himself.

As for the meetings, they in fact prove nothing to him. The conclusions he draws, no one but him will draw; I put no faith in all the paleness he sees and have many other explanations. That it was the third time he saw her in Hauser Square on a Wednesday, no one else would have discovered, even less drawn the conclusion he drew from one incident. [483]Even the meeting in the church is nothing to cling to, and he actually

VI
397

---

[482]* How exhausting such an existence must be, I see from the fact that it is already exhausting to construe it in thought so that not in a single point, in a single comma, does one forget his dialectical difficulty. In the entry made at midnight, February 13, instead of the dialectical prolixity there could just as well have been this statement, "The medical estimate is that she is feeling fine." Of the book's few readers, the expeditious ones would have noticed nothing here; of the few judicious readers, perhaps only a single one asked: How does he obtain such direct information? He must have asked someone, and his strained passion still did not prevent him from doing what he must indeed regard as the most terrible in the form of possibility.

VI
396

VI
397

knows nothing at all. No doubt he realizes this himself, but from his standpoint it is consistent to let his understanding roam. He does it to honor her, out of pride on her behalf. But at the same time something else is happening to him; he is becoming more and more religiously absorbed in himself. If he became involved with her, then he would have had his understanding again and the religious progress would have been hindered. This he does not perceive himself; he does it in order to enhance her.

[484]Therefore these meetings correspond to his psychic condition; and the contact with actuality, in which he merely touches it in the direction away from it, holds him in the state of suspension in which the religious has to consolidate itself. He poetizes her now, but by virtue of a religious ideality that comes after actuality. Just as a lover by virtue of an ideality that comes prior to actuality sees beauties in the beloved that are not there, so he with the purposeful passion of repentance sees terrors that do not exist. —Here, at one and the same time, are the good and the exceptional in him, but also the demonic—that he cannot find rest and come to rest in the ultimate religious resolution but is constantly kept in a state of suspension. She determines his fate, he says, and it is true; but the untruth is that she determines it, for it is determined. That he continues to be *in suspenso* is simultaneously a passionate expression of his sympathy for her, but also of the demonic.*

He certainly ought to remain *in suspenso* or at the pinnacle of the wish, as he says, but at the same time, by virtue of the fact that for him the decision is over, he ought to have his religious resolution at rest and not let the decision become dialectical because of her. But precisely because he is not like this, in his state of suspension and in his aberration he illuminates many a religious issue, although one must remember that what he says is a reply made in individual passion. —He had sufficient

---

* Every step he takes in order to help her must be regarded in this way. But in the last, which he himself regards as a weakness, he is exalted in his suffering when he, at the moment when understanding must declare that now everything seems to be turning out all right, collapses under the thought that she is being healed only in the finite sense.

energy to endure his deception, energy enough to choose the religious, and in the very last moment or at the outer edge of the religious passion, he becomes dialectical. There seems to be a possibility that he would arrange his life differently if she came out of all this all right. Precisely in this lies the demonic—that with a presentiment of a possibility he is unwilling to relate himself to himself in his religious idea but understands her in esthetic categories and cheats the ethical a little, as if he were—if he is guilty—less guilty because she came out of it all right, less guilty even if she had dealt wrongly with him. But more on that elsewhere.

The decisive points in the heterogeneity between the two individualities will now be pointed out. The heterogeneity will have the result that the dialectic continually rearranges the relationship, which the reader himself will be aware of in the book.

(1) *He is inclosingly reserved* [indesluttet]

—she cannot even be that.[485]

Why can she not be that? All inclosing reserve is due to a dialectical reduplication that for immediacy is altogether impossible. The language of immediacy, like languages with vowels, is easily pronounced; the language of inclosing reserve is a language only in silence, or at most like the languages that place four or six consonants before a vowel. Because she is immediate in this way, her devotedness is quite properly the medium in which she, after having been overwhelmed by him for a time and having suffered wrong, thereupon prompted by a little event, expresses her passion. His reserve is shipwrecked on this devotedness—that is, he is so much more dialectical that he perceives the misrelation.

[486]Inclosing reserve can, however, signify various things. His inclosing reserve is essentially a form of depression, and his depression in turn is the condensed possibility that must be experienced through a crisis in order that he can become clear to himself in the religious. With regard to his reserve, nowhere does he explain what it implies. I have deliberately

kept him so, partly because I needed the inclosing reserve only as the frontier, the frontier of understanding that posits the misunderstanding, partly because he himself cannot even say what it contains. In other words, his reserve is neither more nor less than the condensed anticipation of the religious subjectivity. The religious subjectivity has one more dialectical element than all actuality has, one that is not prior to actuality but after actuality. Thus he can exist exceptionally well in actuality and is considered to have done so, but inclosing reserve is and remains the intimation of a higher life. It goes without saying that when it comes to the religious, such categories of actuality as the one that the outer is the inner and the inner the outer are in relation to the religious the inventions of Münchhausens who have no understanding whatever of the religious (something an enthusiast of the understanding like me can have very well without being religious). In these spheres they do just about as much good, to quote an old saying, as sticking one's tongue out the window and getting a slap for it.

Thus far, then, his inclosing reserve contains nothing at all but is there as the frontier, and it holds him, and at present he is depressed in his reserve. The most abstract form for reserve is that it closes itself in. The psychologist is well aware that while the reserved person can say a lot, and with a lightness, about what *has* made him reserved, he does not and cannot say what *is making* him reserved. Therefore, inclosing reserve can scarcely be taken from the reserved person and there is no real healing for him except religiously within himself. This is the most abstract form of the state of reserve—when it is the anticipation of a higher life in the condensation of possibility. This is why he never says what his reserve contains, but only that it is there. From the standpoint of this possibility, one can struggle ahead to religious transparency; this is what he has to do. But this he does not know, and least of all does he suspect that the road passes through the terrors of giving up his relationship with her because it is a misrelationship. If he had not found within himself the power to make the resolution of despair, if, without understanding its meaning for him or, rather, without understanding anything except that it would destroy him, he had not found the strength for it in his sympathetic enthusiasm for her, whether or not she understood it, if she had won—then he would have been lost. The progress of the development of his reserve would have been halted; he would have become active with regard to his reserve, would have closed it off, hidden it inside himself as a fixed idea, perhaps in the quiet form of mental derangement, perhaps even in the form of guilt, for both these forms are the essential forms of consolidated inclosing reserve. —He had her life on his conscience; that helped and will help him. She had his whole spiritual life upon her conscience; she has never dreamed of that.

In order to throw light upon his inclosing reserve, I have inserted into the diary a few entries in which he seems to be searching for an expression for his own reserve. He never expresses himself directly—that he cannot do—but indirectly. Therefore they must also be understood indirectly. One of them is titled "A Possibility," for him the crucial category, which therefore must be pursued to an extreme. It ends with his saying that it was an imagined guilt, a feverish dream. Here he is groping for the sin. If he had a sin on his conscience, if I had imagined him this way, then it would have been far easier to pull him out of this, but then the whole structure would not have manifested what I wanted it to.

(2) *He is depressed—she is full of the joy of life.*

But if his depression is of such a nature that it ought to be arrested, then leave it up to her; for then she will help him, as he himself so movingly speaks of it. But this is not the case. He is unaware that this depression signifies something else; he himself is crushed, and yet the pain of sympathy for her wins out and he decides to leave her without suspecting that precisely this is bound to help him. [487]On the whole, his concern for the girl is sheer enthusiasm, in itself ludicrous, tragic because of his suffering, comic because he does the most foolish things.

There is a difference between depression and depression. There is a depression that for poets, artists, and thinkers is the crisis and with women can be an erotic crisis. Thus the depression of my character is the crisis prior to the religious. If I take an artist, this crucial depression does not express itself straightway in his lamenting over his not being qualified to be an artist. Far from it; at times it is open to suspicion that the sufferer knows what it is, that his suffering is perhaps merely a rehash. No, this depression can hurl itself at everything, at the most trifling thing, and not until his essential qualification is established is it evident that this was the secret of his depression. But with the religious the crisis must come later, that is, with the kind of religiousness in which it holds true that immediacy has succumbed. The reason is the many presuppositions that are required: he must be esthetically developed in his imagination, must be able to grasp the ethical with primitive passion in order to take offense properly [488]so that the original possibility of the religious can break through at this turning point. Hence his depression must have accompanied him through the earlier stages.

VI
401

This, then, is the situation of my imaginatively constructed personage. It is precisely the terror that will help him. This he does not dream of; he thinks only about her and about his suffering in guilt. His sympathy for her inspires him to be scrupulous in hazarding the extreme. He leaves her, but not in order to give her up, but in order to persevere, just in case it might help. This he does not tell her, for since it is uncertain and unsure it is insulting to her to put her off with such a hope. It is altogether consistent, it is this that is to help, but how he does not know. One word between them and his development would surely have been disturbed.

The result, of course, will be that in the meantime she changes her mind; she cannot carry on by herself. This is as it should be; that should not be his direction, and everything is set in order for him so that he can become a proper individuality. —This is how I have designed the imaginary construction—simultaneously comic and tragic.[489]

If she had won out, he would have been lost. Even if her lightheartedness, which, after all, is a declining fund, had been capable of making him a happy married man, this was not what he was supposed to be. But of this he does not dream and merely feels his misery so deeply that he is incapable of being what everyone is capable of—being a married man.

He takes her life on his conscience, she has had his whole personality on hers and naturally has not dreamed of it.

(3) *He is essentially a thinker—she anything but that.*

[490]With the word "thinker," a certain comic light is cast upon him, for only his being exclusively occupied with thoughts accounts for what the imaginary construction assumes—that he has been able to go on living without the least acquaintance with the world and especially with the opposite sex. If he had had that, especially the latter, well, then the construction could not have been made at all, for one does not need to look around very long to see what he had to do and especially what one must do with a young girl's consternation, which is best honored by making an old verse a rule of conduct: *cantantur haec, laudantur haec, dicuntur, audiuntur; scribuntur haec, leguntur haec—et lecta negliguntur* [this is sung, is praised, is told, is heard; this is written, is read—and what is read is neglected].[491] Hence in the construction a certain ludicrous light must fall upon him as a reflex of his lack of knowledge of the world; but on the other hand his unsophisticated veneration for the opposite sex has something touching about it, plus a certain epigrammatic force superior to knowledge of the world.

That he is a thinker does not mean that he reads many books and aims to mount the lectern as an assistant professor. Thinkers such as that are well able to join things that are different, and then they have mediation also. He, however, is essentially an independent thinker, and in the sense that he must always have the idea along with him in order to exist. This engrosses him with the passion of an independent thinker, not with an assistant professor's affected trustworthiness based on assurances.

As becomes her in her immediacy, the girl has life and days before her, which is most endearing. She has nothing against his wanting to study, even if it were to study the Syro-Chal-

VI
402

daic language; she pooh-poohs learned and curious subjects, which is a lovable trait and not devoid of charm. But what preoccupies him is not the Syro-Chaldaic or the Elamitic languages, it is the life itself in which he exists.

As a result of this, they are totally unable to understand each other. She does not even know the existence of what preoccupies him, and if he were to tell her about it, it would interest her no more than if he talked about Sennacherib and Shalmaneser.[492] Nor does she ask for it, and this is very endearing of her, especially if the task had been the opposite—that to be of service to him she should not give it a thought. She of course does not grasp that her request and her dispensation do not counterbalance the ideas, and that not to express the idea not only disturbs him but that he regards it as an insult to her.

So, then, he thinks. And this he is able to think—that he can have a murder on his conscience—but not to express the idea to him is unthinkable. For a thinker, a girl's honor is the idea and consistency; for a self-thinker it is to cling firmly to it in life. If he has her honor on his conscience, then she has had his thought-existence on hers. She, of course, has had no intimation of this.

VI
403

(4) *He is ethical-dialectical—she, esthetically immediate.*

From each of these standpoints, the concept of suffering is altogether different. He cannot understand what her suffering is essentially (if there is any), namely, to lose possession of another person; she does not understand at all what his suffering is essentially—responsibility and guilt.

So they both become unhappy, and each has done the best for the other with regard to becoming unhappy: he by breaking the engagement, she by laying a murder on his conscience. To be sure, he would have had it anyway, but nevertheless she does it.

(5) *He is sympathetic—she in the sense of immediacy*
is innocently self-loving.

Unbeautiful self-love is always distinguished by reflection. There is none of this in her; however, there certainly is the

instinct for self-preservation, which by some Greek philosophers was laid down as a moral principle.[493] Their mistake was
that this cannot be done without reflection; she, however, is
without reflection, and therefore this self-love is not unbeautiful and is a sign of a natural health.

[494]Despite the partiality with which he generally views her,
he nevertheless in a way does her an injustice by saying that
there is not a trace of resignation in her. Not that he was
wrong in saying it, for it is entirely true, but the reason is that
she has no understanding at all of what it means, which at the
same time can indicate her healthiness but perhaps also an
erotic modesty. Moreover, he keeps her from understanding
it. He uses the deception to conceal his own sufferings so that
she will not be moved sympathetically. But then he forgets to
take the deception into account, that it really is keeping her
from becoming aware of the promptings of sympathy. But
just as there is a contradiction here, so also is his dialectical
position so difficult, so ambiguous, that one might think that
he would simultaneously be just as reluctant to have her sympathetically moved for her own sake as for his own sake to
have a vigorous expression of her magnanimity. But this he
has realized, for he says that he has offered her the opportunity
to give him his freedom, which he did in fact do, but this still
does not mean that he is purely sympathetic at this point but
rather bowing to what he regards as his duty. Inasmuch as he
has made this offer, he is saved from becoming demonic in the
direction of evil, which he could have become at this point;
but neither is he purely religious, that is, it is possible. The
trouble is that she does not want to understand him but only
uses every new discovery of his feeling for her to fling herself
at him with her devotedness.

It is sympathy for her, consistent, please note, as it can be
in his individuality (for his sympathy, of course, cannot speak
in her tongue), that inspires him to the steps he otherwise
would scarcely have ventured. I could have left it at that, but
in order to throw light on him I had the thought enter his
mind, and actuality seemed to encourage it, that it would
nevertheless all end in a completely natural way with her

VI
404

being quite free and unrestrained again through a *restitutio in integrum* [restitution to the original state]. Here it will come to light whether he is sympathetic, or rather, since he is disposed to be sympathetic, it will come to light that he is suffering almost more now because he thinks she loses in idea-existence. Here his sympathy is manifested most powerfully, as it must be in a thinking person to whom idea-existence is the one and only—if he had been acquainted with the world and with the opposite sex, he would have come out better, that is, if he would have cared about this knowledge.

So, then, he breaks the engagement, and the wedding ceremony performs the strange service of becoming the separating factor. The misunderstanding once again manifests itself in the latter. As said previously, she is already recuperating when he leaves her and is recuperating little by little; he suffers most afterwards. He is the one who acts, she the one who suffers, so it seems. Yet it is the reverse; he is the one who suffers, who did not venture what she ventured—to lay a responsibility such as that upon another human being. [495]She believes that he has insulted and offended her by breaking the relationship, and yet he has offended her only by beginning it. He broke it out of sympathetic enthusiasm for her. His guilt, apart from beginning it, is that he applies too high a standard to her, and this is precisely to his honor. He is guilty, and she, so he thinks, is completely innocent. Yet this is not so: if he is guilty in having begun, then she is guilty of making use of the ethical side of the relationship to bind him to herself and of risking the steps the results of which she neither dreams nor is able to estimate. He sees the comic, but with passion, so that out of that he chooses the tragic (this is the religious and something that I, who see there both elements in equilibrium, cannot understand); she sees the tragic, and so clearly that she makes it the comic. He produces no effect whatsoever externally, except what any male could do just as well, that a girl wants to die etc.; he cannot even make a girl unhappy. She produces an enormous effect. She does not think of this at all, for she thinks that if she had been permitted to make him happy, then it would have been something. He does not think of the former, for he is obliged to think that he has crushed her. He is sure of one thing—that it will be the ruination of the girl to be united with him; perhaps the girl is more sagacious in thinking that she could very well make use of him. She is sure of easily being able to make him happy, and yet, as has been pointed out, that would unconditionally have been his downfall. He makes a fool of himself by his humble deference; she makes a fool of herself with her big words.

But how, then, did he come to begin? This I believe I have clearly established. He begins with a complete life-view that he has formed for himself. I must make of him an approximation of a religious individuality, and therefore the view must be esthetic-ethical under illusion. So, in fact, it is, and it is quite in order that it must have satisfied his individuality. He sees the girl, has an erotic impression of her, but nothing more. She is taken up into his existence, and he does not want, as he says, to insult her by learning to know her more fully. One immediately sees the enthusiast, and an enthusiast he must be, but he will enter into another sphere. Time passes, he is resolute, but the erotic has not received its due at all. Now he is in it and views the matter ethically, while the religious possibility is continually deepest in his soul, as it already was in his first life-view except that he did not know of it. Now the ethical becomes clear to him in actuality, and he is shipwrecked. His affront was not breaking the engagement but, with such a life-view, to want to fall in love. The stages are structured as follows: an esthetic-ethical life-view under illusion, with the dawning possibility of the religious; an ethical life-view that judges him; he relapses into himself, and he is just where I want him to be.

I have now very briefly made the rounds of my imaginary construction. I am continually circling it, for I certainly do grasp the unity of the comic and the tragic, but I do not understand from where he has the higher passion, which is the religious. Might it be ethics, which by its negative thrust helps him past the metaphysical (for that is where I am) into the religious? I do not know.

[496]The upshot of the whole process of misunderstanding is

really that they nevertheless do not really love. But that cannot by any means be said in the beginning, and this still continually remains, that each of them has a share of the elements of erotic love. He does not love, for he lacks the immediacy, in which there is the first basis of the erotic. If he could have become hers, he still would have become a spirit who wants to do everything to indulge her wishes—but not a lover. But if he does not have immediacy, he does have the ethical element, which she does not understand at all or care about. She does not love, that is, she has the impulses and persistence of immediacy; [497]but in order to love, she must also have resignation so that it can become clear that she does not love herself.

With that the imaginary construction is completed, but in another sense in its more detailed fulfillment it is not completed or brought to an end. (On the reason for that, more later.) If I were to assume as fact and event what he suspects and is quite probable—that she would fall in love again—what then? Then he might recover from his aberration. I continually put myself in his place and certainly do see that he is not to be helped as I, if I were in his place, would long ago have helped myself. I do not want to dispute about that; I want to construct imaginatively. [498]His aberration is due to his letting her actuality disturb his integrating of himself in repentance, with the result that he cannot find peace in his repentance because she makes it dialectical for him. (More on that later.) Therefore, as soon as she is gone, he will simply have only himself to deal with; repentance unhindered will gain the ideality he needs, without being disturbed by pathos-filled passion into wanting to act or by comic sights that he himself does not bring about. To complete an individuality and put down a summary answer, that is for the great systematic thinkers, who have so much to traverse; to allow it to come into being in all its possibility is what interests one who composes imaginary constructions. Thus I could well imagine that, although I set myself this task, he would once more become dialectical. If that happens, he remains demonic. It is not the dialectical that makes a person demonic—far from it, but it is remaining in the dialectical.

The reader who has read Constantin Constantius's little book[499] will see that I have a certain resemblance to that author but nevertheless am very different, and the person who composes imaginary constructions always does well to conform to the construction.

3.

The Tragic Needs History More than the Comic Does; the Disappearance of this Difference in the "Imaginary Construction"

[500]I have often been engrossed by the circumstance that the tragic poet, in order to make sure of the proper impression on the spectators, in order to win for the play their belief and confidence and for the performance their tears, draws support from the historical, from the fact that his hero actually has performed something great, even though the poet does not simply render the historical. That this is the case no one, I am sure, will deny, and will not quote Lessing against me, since *Emilia Galotti*[501] [502]as the exception bears out the rule, and many comments by its author indicate that he himself has had the same view on the subject.[503] It is by far the common practice to utilize the historical and with considerable reservation to understand the Aristotelian dictum that the poet is a greater philosopher than the historian because he shows how it ought to be, not how it is.[504] The comic poet, however, does not need a historical foothold such as this. He may give his characters whatever names he pleases, he may have the episode take place wherever he wants it, if only the comic ideality is there so there is sure to be laughter; and, conversely, he does not gain by using Harlequin and Pierrot when he does not know how to use them except as names.

Now, is it because people are more inclined to discover the weak points of others than to see what is great, is it because it is more acceptable to laugh at something with no guarantee of quality than to cry over it, as if it did not have its validity, that a fool laughs at nothing? [505]Or may this be the reason, that the comic, lightly armed, searches its way past the ethical toward metaphysic's freedom from care and merely wants to provoke laughter by making the contradiction become obvious, whereas the tragic, on the other hand, heavily armed as it is, remains stuck in an ethical difficulty, so that the idea certainly does win the victory but the hero succumbs, which is rather bleak for the spectator, insofar as he also wants to be a hero, and rather sarcastic if he considers that he has nothing to fear for his life since it is only the heroes who die?

But whatever the reason is, what engrosses me is not the reason but the fact that the tragic seeks a foothold in the historical. This means, then, that poetry does not believe itself capable of awakening ideality in the spectator by itself, does not believe that the spectator has it, but that the historical, that is, the fact that it is historical, will probably help him to gain it. With regard to the comic, however, it never occurs to the poet to want to appeal to history or to undergird the comic figure with the help of history, for the spectator quite properly says: Make him appear to us as comic; then you may keep the historical.

But, now, does it help one to believe in what is great by knowing it is historical? No, not at all. This knowledge merely assists one into an illusion that is infatuated with the palpably material. What is that which I know historically? It is the palpably material. Ideality I know by myself, and if I do not know it by myself, then I do not know it at all, and all the historical knowledge does not help. Ideality is not a chattel that can be transferred from one person to another, or something thrown in to boot when the purchase is a large one. If I know that Caesar was great, then I know what the great is, and this is what I see—otherwise I do not know that Caesar was great. History's account—that reliable men assure us of it, that there is no risk involved in accepting this opinion since it must be obvious that he was a great man, that the outcome demonstrates it—does not help at all. To believe the ideality on the word of another is like laughing at a joke not because one has understood it but because someone else said that it was funny. In that case, the joke can really be omitted for the person who laughs on the basis of belief and respect; he is able to laugh with equal *Emphasis* [significance].

From the heading of this section, the reader will easily perceive that it is not my intention to remain in the esthetic but that I want to go on to the religious. What the tragic hero is in the esthetic, the religious prototype (of course, I am here thinking only of devout individuals etc.) is for the religious consciousness. The poet here is speaker. Here one turns again to the historical. The prototype is presented, and then the speaker declares that it is positively certain, for it is historical, and the believing congregation believes everything, even that the speaker knows what he himself is saying.

In order to grasp the ideality, I must be able to dissolve the historical in the ideality or do (to use a pious expression) what God is said to do for one who is dying: shine upon it. Conversely, I do not enter into the ideality by repeating the historical jingle. Therefore, anyone who, with regard to the same thing, does not reach the conclusion just as well *ab posse ad esse* [from possibility to actuality] as *ab esse ad posse* [from actuality to possibility] does not grasp the ideality in this same thing. He is nurtured only on fancies. Ideality as the animating principle does not automatically become historical. That which can be transmitted to me is a multiplicity of data, which is not ideality, and thus the historical is always raw material, which the person who appropriates it knows how to resolve in a *posse* [possibility] and assimilate as an *esse* [actuality]. There is nothing, therefore, more foolish in the religious sphere than to hear the commonsensical question that asks when something is being taught: Now, did it actually happen this way, for if it did one would believe it. Whether it actually happened this way, whether it is as ideal as it is represented, can be tested only by ideality, but one cannot have it historically bottled.

[506]I have been made aware of this by producing the story of suffering I have carried out as an imaginary construction. Alas, if I were a famous author, then a reading public that is energetic about believing, indefatigably energetic, would be distressed, for it would worry about the book and ask: But

did it actually happen—for if so we will surely believe it. What is it the reading public wants to believe? That it actually happened. Well, one does not get anywhere along that road. If a speaker disregards this, he may well be able to make a deep impression on his audience, but he also makes it into a satirical truth about himself, into what Socrates said about eloquence—that it is a fraudulent art.[507] The more it is emphasized that it is historical and therefore etc., the more he deceives; and if he is paid so little that it is not worth talking about the money he receives, then it is just as certain that he is putting out chitchat, perhaps a good deal of chitchat—alas, for poor pay. A historicizing speaker such as that merely contributes his share to making the learners devoid of spirit. It is spirit to ask about two things: (1) Is what is being said possible? (2) Am I able to do it? But it is lack of spirit to ask about two things: (1) Did it actually happen? (2) Has my neighbor Christophersen done it; has he actually done it? And faith is the ideality that resolves an *esse* in its *posse* and then conversely draws the conclusion in passion. If the object of faith is the absurd, then it still is not the historical that is believed, but faith is the ideality that resolves an *esse* in a *non posse* and now *wills* to believe it.

In order further to secure the religious paradigm, the religious is kept exclusively in pathos-filled categories of immediacy. The same thing happens with the speaker here as happens with the poet in regard to his tragic hero. One simply may not allow the comic to emerge. Thus the listener knows for sure that it is in earnest, and if it is in earnest then he surely can believe it. But just suppose this earnestness is a jest. Religious earnestness, like the religious, is the higher passion proceeding from the unity of the comic and the tragic. This I know precisely because I myself am not religious and have reached this standpoint (of unity) without skipping anything in advance and without finding the religious within myself. —If this is the way it is, then the historical need not trouble itself, for just as it can never help one to an ideality, it can least of all help one to a dialectical ideality. If I were a trustworthy man, it would look bad for the reading public who cannot find out in advance whether it is a jest or is in earnest. I would be forced into an explanation—there is always something good, after all, in not being trustworthy.

[508]One safeguards the religious, as well as the esthetic, by a result—but my imaginary construction is not completed. Consequently there is no result. —"I ask my esteemed thinking public to consider what it means to publish a book without a result. Fortunately no one reads it, since it is by an obscure author"—this is what a reviewer will say, even though I have implored him to refrain, not to refrain from saying this, for if he ultimately has to say something, it can surely make no difference what he says. Consequently, the result, which any busybody reader in all fairness could demand in advance, does not come at all. Would, however, that these comments might make some amends for that.

VI
411

Poetry consists in the commensuration of the outer and the inner, and it therefore shows a visible result. The result is plain and easy to grasp. However, a little circumspection does no harm, for the result has the same dialectic as the ideality. The religious lies in the internal. Here the result cannot be shown in the external. But what does the speaker do? He guarantees the result. Such a security must in every way be regarded as reassuring—for the serious and positive.

The esthetic result is in the external and can be shown. With the aid of opera glasses, it can be shown and seen even by the myopic that the hero conquers, that the magnanimous man falls in the battle and is carried in dead (of course not simultaneously) etc. This is precisely the imperfection of the esthetic. [509]—The ethical result is less capable of being shown, or, more correctly, it is actually demanded with such speed that one does not have time to look around before it is there. For example, if I exclude every other thought and think only of the ethical, I demand ethical sanction to see the good triumph with a boundless speed, to see the evil punished with boundless speed. Now, this cannot be depicted, least of all in five acts, and therefore the esthetic and the ethical have been combined. The total thought of the ethical has been retained and the boundless speed has been slowed down by esthetic categories (fate, chance), and now at the end one sees in the total thought of the ethical a world order, a Governance, providence. This result is esthetic–ethical and therefore can be shown in the external to a certain degree. But there is a dubiousness about this result, for the ethical cannot regard the esthetic in any other way than to regard a direct union with it as a misalliance. (No doubt this is why Boethius is so indignant about poet productions, I, p. 9;[510] no doubt this is why Solon forbade plays as deception;[511] no doubt this is why Plato wanted to ban poets from his state.[512]) The ethical asks only about guilty or not guilty, is itself man enough to be a match for men, has no need for anything external and visible, to say nothing of something as ambiguously dialectical as fate and chance or the tangibility of some verdict document. The ethical is proud and declares: When I have judged, then nothing more is needed. This means that the ethical wants to be separated from the esthetic and the externality that is the latter's imperfection; it desires to enter into a more glorious alliance, and this is with the religious.

The religious then plays the same role as the esthetic, but as the superior; it spaces out the limitless speed of the ethical, and development takes place. But the scene is in the internal, in thoughts and dispositions that cannot be seen, not even with a night telescope. The principle of the spirit is that the external and the visible (the world's gloriousness or its miserableness for the existing person, a result in the external or the lack of it for the one acting) exist to try faith, consequently not to deceive but in order that the spirit can be tested by placing it in the realm of the indifferent and taking itself back again. The external makes no difference—and, first of all, the result lies in the internal and, second, is continually postponed.

The esthetic outcome is in the external, and the external is the guarantee that the outcome is there; we see that the hero has triumphed, has conquered that country, and now we are finished. The religious outcome, indifferent toward the external, is assured only in the internal, that is, in faith. Indifferent toward the externality, which the esthetic needs (there must be great men, great subject matter, great events; so it becomes comic if there are small folk or petty cash), the religious is commensurate with the greatest man who has ever lived and with the most wretched, and equally commensurate, commensurate with the prosperity of nations and with a farthing, and equally commensurate. The religious is simply and solely qualitatively dialectic and disdains quantity, in which esthetics has its task. Indifferent toward the externals, which the esthetic needs in the result, the religious disdains anything like that and proclaims, jointly and individually, that the person who believes he has finished (that is, fancies that he has, for such things cannot be believed because faith is expressly the infinite)—has lost.

VI
413

And now for the speaker who handles results—what does he do? He does precisely what is possible for him to do in order to deceive his listeners. But the speaker is positive. Entirely correct, he also accepts money for what he says, and this already inspires listeners to have a certain confidence in him, for if a person lost his money or lost his reputation in order to speak truthfully, what confidence could people have in him; after all, he refutes himself, for would anything that did not bring a person money, esteem, and anything such as that be the truth!

If someone were to declare that swimming is lying on dry land and threshing around, everyone presumably would consider him mad. But believing is just like swimming, and instead of helping one ashore the speaker should help one out into the deep. Consequently, if someone were to say that believing is lying on dry land and threshing around certain of result, he is saying the same thing, but perhaps people are not aware of it.

What is expressed here about the lack of a result in the religious, I can also say in this way: the negative is higher than the positive. How lucky to be an obscure author when one imaginatively constructs with such thoughts. An esteemed author would be in an awkward situation, for by reason of his esteem the positive people probably would quickly perceive that he had arrived at a positive result, and his positive esteem would become even greater. Positives or, to use the definite article even more definitely in order to show what I mean, the positives have a positive infinity. Quite correct, a positive is finished, and once one has heard it, one is also quickly finished. Here is result in overabundance. If one seeks enlightenment from the master, Hegel, about what a positive infinity means,[513] one learns a great deal; one takes the trouble, and one does understand him. The only thing a latecomer perhaps does not understand is how a living human being or a human being during his lifetime becomes such a being that he can be calmed and reassured in this positive infinity, which usually is reserved for the deity and eternity and the deceased. As far as that goes, I cannot understand anything else than that a result is missing here, which the negatives, who are not finished, might *en passant* very eagerly look forward to see whether or not, long after the system is finished, astrology might succeed in finding on those distant planets higher beings who would be able to use it. The rest must be left up to the higher beings, but it is up to us human beings to be careful not to become all too positive, for this would really mean being fooled by life. Life is perfidious and has many charms and spells with which it tries to capture the adventurer, and the person who is captured, yes, the person who is captured—well, what is made out of him is not exactly some higher being.[514]

For a finite being, and that, after all, is what human beings are as long as they live in temporality (see Balle's *Lærebog*[515]), the negative infinity is the higher, and the positive is a dubious reassurance. Spiritual existence, especially the religious, is not easy; the believer continually lies out on the deep, has 70,000 fathoms[516] of water beneath him. However long he lies out there, this still does not mean that he will gradually end up lying and relaxing onshore. He can become more calm, more experienced, find a confidence that loves jest and a cheerful temperament—but until the very last he lies out on 70,000 fathoms of water. If immediacy is supposed to go, which indeed everyone calls for, then this enters in. There will be difficulties enough in life for all. Let the poor feel the hard stress of poverty and the cares of making a living. The person who chooses spiritual existence by virtue of the religious will have the consolation, which I can understand he needs, that he, too, suffers in life and that before God there is no respect of persons.[517] For to become positive does not procure for one personal esteem in God's eyes, even though this has become wisdom ever since the time when speculation took religion under its wing by taking away its life.

This I have understood very well, although I myself am not religious, but neither do I arrogate to myself the desire to take it by force,[518] but with the pleasure of observation I only want to understand it by imaginatively constructing. The religious seeks no foothold in the historical, does not seek it, even less and for a higher reason than the comic does. It presupposes the unity of the tragic and the comic in passion, and with a new passion or with the same one it chooses the tragic, and this relation in turn makes every historical foothold meaningless. It is never finished, at least not in time, and therefore can be represented as such only by a deception. If, then, a man who had been regularly listening to a speaker discoursing on religious matters were to go to him and say, "Now that I have listened to you so regularly, do you not think that I now have faith?" the speaker, in a fit of what one calls good nature, concerned sympathy (for which one inserts a card of thanks in the newspapers), answers, "Why, of course, that is my opinion, set your mind at ease; just don't miss my discourses, and feel free to come to me if you ever have any doubts again etc." My constructing scrutiny, devoid of all good nature and concerned sympathy, is of the opinion that he would have done better to answer, "My dear fellow, are you making fun of me? I do not even dare vouch for my wife—indeed, not even for myself, for I am lying out on 70,000 fathoms of water."

VI
415

Now, if only no one tempts me, perhaps promises me the moon and the stars, the favor of young maidens and the applause of the reviewers, but then demands an answer to the question whether my imaginary construction is a real-life story, whether it is based on something actual. Yes, certainly it is based on something actual, namely, on the categories. But for an unknown author the temptation is presumably minor. Everyone will readily see that the whole thing is a child's

prank, which, however, it is not, for it is an imaginary construction. The tragic has the interest of actuality, the comic
metaphysical disinterestedness, but the construction lies in the
invisible unity of jest and earnestness. The dialectical tension
between form and content and content and form prevents
every immediate relation to it, and in this tension the construction evades the formidable handshake of earnestness and
jest's fellowship with jolly companions. The construction always addresses the reader with the formal *De* [instead of the
familiar *du*]. The poetic hero wants to inspire by his victory,
wants to depress by his suffering (have the interest of actuality); the comic hero wants to provoke laughter, but
Quidam[519] [Someone] of the "imaginary construction" wants
nothing at all, without any claim whatsoever is at your service
in every way; he cannot inconvenience anyone, for in this respect, too, he is at your service, so that you can ignore him
without any risk at all, so much the more since it is absolutely
indeterminable whether anyone who paid attention to him
gained something thereby or was harmed by it.

4.

Repentance Dialectically Prevented
from Constituting Itself;
the Last Frontier between the Esthetic and
the Religious Lies in the Psychological

Poetry cannot use repentance; as soon as it is assumed, the
scene is internal. Naturally the system cannot use it either; for
the system, after all, has to be finished, the sooner the better,
and not until it is finished has it nothing to repent, and in order
to become finished it sees to it that it is free of repentance. The
systematic abbreviation of the pathological elements of life is
sheer ludicrousness the moment it wants to have anything but
a metaphysical significance. Thus the system is exclusively
metaphysics, and as such that is quite in order, but it is not a
system that embraces existence, for then the ethical must be
included, and to abbreviate the ethical is to make a fool of it.

On the systematic "roller coaster," as Quidam of the imaginary construction says, it goes as follows: ¶ 17, Repentance;

¶ 18, Atonement; ¶ , the system finished, with some concluding suggestions to the bookbinder with regard to the
binding. That is, bound in half-leather it is metaphysics;
bound in full calf it is the system.[520] Consequently one does
not stop with repentance. One cannot say that, since a paragraph is no eternity, not even for the person who has extremely urgent business. I, however, aim to pause for a little
moment at repentance—a composer of imaginary constructions can afford the time.

The demonic in Quidam of the construction is actually this,
that he is unable to take himself back in repentance, that at the
extreme point he becomes suspended in a dialectical relation
to actuality (see above). [521]Juno, as is known, sent a gadfly to
torment Latona so that she could not give birth;[522] similarly a
girl's actuality is a gadfly, a "perhaps" that teases him, a nemesis of actuality, an envy of life that will not let him slip out
and thereby absolutely into the religious.

When repentance is less systematically, that is, more thoroughly, developed, one ordinarily has one's eyes opened particularly in order to emphasize the Atonement. This can be
very fine, but there are also existence-difficulties elsewhere.
When repentance is posited, guilt must be assumed as clearly
and certainly substantiated. But the difficulty arises precisely
when this becomes dialectical. That is why I said previously
that if Quidam of the construction had had an actual sin, it
would have been far easier to clear him of it, for then the dialectical would have been avoided.

Whether such things are found only rarely in actual life or
not found at all makes no difference to the imaginary construction. Yet presumably it is possible that the dialectical is
found most frequently but amounts to nothing at all; for the
perfectly normal perhaps is found simply and solely in hand-
books and in lectures by men who do not exist in themselves
at all or know how to spy on life and on others.

The imaginary construction has made the situation for the
existing person as dialectical as possible. He can have a murder
on his conscience; the whole thing can be a gust of wind. He
has it because the girl lays it upon him, and if it was just a bit

of nonsense, then he has no murder. What will decide this? Actuality will. But actuality takes a little time, and when I am composing an imaginary construction I do not care for paragraph-haste. Consequently, how does he exist during that time? For repentance it is something to despair over. For me it is another matter, for I sit elated with my reckonings and look simultaneously at the comic and the tragic. The tragic girl who dies and the comic sinner who becomes a murderer, the tragic sinner who suffers and the comic girl who goes on living. A word is a word, and a man is a man—this applies only to men, who therefore ought to be cautious about talk of death. What a now dead and departed person said about death is certainly true: It recognizes no rank and no age, but nothing follows from that in advance.

A dialectical reader will promptly become aware of a difficulty here, to which Quidam of the construction pays no attention or not enough. By a deception he wants to trick out of the girl every impression she may have of him. He carries out the deception, but then he forgets to reckon it. He has strength to defy the terrors of actuality, but in relation to himself he does not have the strength to stick to it. He is higher than actuality; this he shows in the deception when he shuns no argument but sees it through. However, because of the deception the argument becomes something different from what it otherwise would be. The moment the deception is carried VI 418 out with certainty, he is indeed misleading the girl and goading her to express herself unsympathetically. She has no inkling that he himself is suffering; she must assume that he is merely determined to see an end to the relationship and then exult. Thus there is nothing that can curb her expressions. To this extent he himself is to blame that the consternation is as it is. But it must be remembered that he tried a more lenient way before resorting to the deception. But for me it is very important in the imaginary construction that he himself through the deception contributes to making everything more terrible for himself; that consequently he does not *through the deception* create an advantage for himself but a defeat. In an external sense he has conquered, the force with which actuality stands up to him is capable of nothing against him—but then a half year later he begins again within himself, wounded by that event, and now he has to give up. This throws light precisely on the religious. The religiousness that derives directly from actuality is a dubious religiousness; it can very well be esthetic categories that are used and worldly wisdom that is gained; but when actuality has not been capable of shattering and the individual succumbs by his own hand, then the religious is more distinct.

Again I see the unity of the comic and the tragic in something to which he himself does not pay sufficient attention; that is, the comic is not that he is a swaggering braggart, for then it would have to be actuality that inevitably made short work of him, but that he survives the crisis of actuality and then succumbs by his own hand. It is a task for the esthetic to have someone who fancies that he is something be shown up in actuality in his nothingness, but if the esthetic has first acknowledged that in actuality he is great, then the esthetic has no superior power over him and must acknowledge him as a hero, but then the religious says: Wait a minute, let us look at this a bit closer and see how he is in himself. This engrosses me in a purely Greek way. I imagine the blissful gods creating such a human being in order to have the enjoyment of the dialectical delight in it. They give him powers in the realm of actuality so that he is victor there, but then they give him an inwardness in which he himself goes astray. He is really capable of something great, but as soon as he has done it the event duplicates itself within him and he topples. And I imagine the gods saying to each other, "We really ought to have something for ourselves, and this is not even for the goddesses, who do not understand it, and if they did understand it would not be without compassion. This is not a laughing matter like the fabrications of poets, which we honor with the reward of our laughter; and it is not a crying matter, which we also are willing to reward with tears if it deserves it, but this is festive dialectical enjoyment of equilibrium. He cannot complain about us, for we have, after all, made him great, and

actually it is only we gods who simultaneously see his nothingness."

Quidam of the imaginary construction does not see it this
way, for in his passion he clings to the god [*Guden*] in faith
and in his own destruction does not see, as I do, the negative
unity of the comic and the tragic and nothing more but sees
his own rehabilitation; he sees himself as falling not by the
hand of actuality but by the hand of God, and therefore he is
rehabilitated. Religiously speaking, I must express myself differently, even though I here speak in a strange tongue: providence, which is infinitely concerned about each and every person, equips an individuality, to whom it gives unusual powers
in relation to actuality. "But," says providence, "lest he do
himself too much harm, I tie this power up in depression and
thereby hide it from him. What he is capable of doing, he will
never find out, but I will use him; he is not going to be humiliated by any actuality—to that extent he is more pampered
than other men, but within himself he is going to feel destroyed as no other person feels it. [523]Then and there and only
there is he going to understand me, but there he will also be
certain that it is I whom he understands." As a composer of
imaginary constructions, I can well understand this, but
otherwise not, for my mind is not at rest in passion but in
impassivity.

Consequently, repentance has become dialectical for him
and remains so for him because he must wait for information
from actuality about what he has really perpetrated. The dialectical reader will naturally be able to fashion many examples
of this kind of dialectical repentance. I will merely suggest
one. David has decided that Uriah must be put away in a subtle fashion so that Bathsheba can become his. [524] I am assuming
that he has sent a messenger with secret orders to the commander; I am assuming that it takes the messenger three days'
journey to reach the camp. The historic actuality makes no
difference here. What happens? The very same night the messenger departed, David, trying to find the rest of sleep, does
not find it but finds terror wide awake; it grips him, and he
collapses in repentance—in the next paragraph, to be sure,

comes the atonement. No, wait a minute. That same moment David realizes that it might still be possible to prevent the murder. An express messenger is sent, and David stays behind. I am assuming that this takes five days more. Five days—how much is that? After all, it is not a phrase in a paragraph; at most it is a particle, a "meanwhile" that merely begins a sentence, but five days could very well make a man gray-haired. Indeed, there is a great difference between having wanted to be a murderer and being one. Now David is in a dialectical suspension, and the composer of an imaginary construction who wants to describe his condition psychologically can employ many, many paragraphs. —Everyone easily perceives, however, that all this is a far easier case than the one in my imaginary construction. David has nevertheless wanted to make himself guilty of a murder, but Quidam of the construction wants simply to rescue. Inspired solely by sympathy, he takes an extreme risk, and just look, he has a murder on his conscience or, rather, he enters into dialectical agony. This agony is also more dialectical than it is in David's situation because in David's case the comic cannot emerge at all. For David, it could have been a relief if he could have succeeded in preventing Uriah's actual death, but a jest it would never become. Quidam of the construction, on the other hand, can become almost ludicrous if he does not parry with the help of the idea.

VI
420

The dialectical form of the repentance here is as follows: he cannot begin to repent, because what it is he ought to repent of seems to be undecided as yet; and he cannot find rest in repentance, because it seems as if he were continually about to act, to undo everything, if that were possible. —That he gives way to this is the demonic; he should only pay attention to the possibility and entirely remove repentance from this. To the extent that he is kept *in suspenso* by the first reason (that what he is supposed to repent of is still undecided), he is ironic; to the extent that it is the second reason (that he continually has to act), he is altogether sympathetic. —There is still a third factor in his repentant situation. In the system, a person repents once and for all in ¶ 17 and then goes on to ¶ 18. But if healing is to begin for the existing person, the moment must come when one lets the act of repentance go. For one single moment this has a deceptive similarity to forgetfulness. But to forget guilt is a new sin. This is the difficulty. To hold firmly to guilt is the passion of repentance, and it proudly and enthusiastically scorns the prating of forgetfulness about relief and, troubled, is itself suspicious of it. And Quidam of the construction even believes he is thereby honoring the girl—a seductive thought, especially because it is beautiful; to let go of it, to remove it so it is not just as present at every moment, is necessary for healing. When everything goes so smoothly that ¶ 18 follows upon or after ¶ 17, an internal and really dialectical treading water such as this goes unnoticed.

Appendix

A Side-glance at Shakespeare's Hamlet

Börne has written a little review of *Hamlet*. It is only a final comment[525] of his that engrosses me, and I do not even know if he himself attaches much worth to it—it is just a comment. On the whole, Börne, Heine, Feuerbach, and such authors are the individualities who have great interest for someone who is composing an imaginary construction. They frequently are well informed about the religious—that is, they know definitely that they do not want to have anything to do with it. This is a great advantage over the systematicians, who without knowing where the religious really is located take it upon themselves to explain it—sometimes obsequiously, sometimes superciliously, but always unsuccessfully. An unhappy, a jealous lover can know just as much about the erotic as the happy lover, and, similarly, someone offended by the religious can in his way be just as well informed about it as the believer. At present, when our age seldom has a great believer to show, we must always be pleased to have a few really clever ones who are offended. If someone really wanting to have something clearly explained is so fortunate that a rigorous believer in the seventeenth-century sense of the word and an offended nonbeliever in the nineteenth-century sense of the word both say the same thing—namely, that the one says, "It is thus and so, I know it for sure; therefore I do not accept it," and the other says, "Thus and so it is; therefore I believe it," and this thus and so agrees perfectly, then one can trustfully conclude his observation. Two compatible witnesses such as these provide a reliability lawyers do not know.

[526]Börne says of *Hamlet*, "It is a Christian drama." To my mind this is a most excellent comment. I substitute only the word a "religious" drama, and then declare its fault to be not that it is that but that it did not become that or, rather, that it ought not to be drama at all. If Shakespeare does not give Hamlet religious presuppositions that conspire against him in religious doubt (whereby the drama ceases), then Hamlet is essentially a vacillator, and the esthetic demands a comic interpretation. Hamlet says he has conceived his grandiose plan of being the avenger to whom vengeance belongs.[527] If one does not simultaneously see him sink religiously under this plan (whereby the scene becomes introspective and his unpoetic doubts and misgivings in the psychological sense become a remarkable form of dialectical repentance, because the repentance seems to come too early), then one demands quick action, for then he is dealing simply and solely with the external, where the poet places no obstacles in his way. If the plan remains fixed, then Hamlet is a kind of loiterer who does not know how to act; if the plan does not remain fixed, he is a kind of self-torturer who torments himself for and with wanting to be something great. Neither of these involves the tragic. [528]Rötscher quite correctly made him morbidly reflective.[529] Rötscher's explanation is excellent and also has an interest of another kind for someone who wants to see how systematicians are forced to use existence-categories.

If Hamlet is kept in purely esthetic categories, then what one wants to see is that he has the demonic power to carry out such a resolution. His misgivings have no interest whatsoever; his procrastination and temporizing, his postponing and his self-deluding enjoyment in the renewed intention at the same time as there is no outside hindrance merely diminish him, so that he does not become an esthetic hero, and then he becomes a nonentity. If he is religiously oriented, his misgiv-

VI
422

ings are extremely interesting, because they give assurance that he is a religious hero. At times people have a totally external concept of a religious hero. In Catholicism, for example, especially in the Middle Ages, there perhaps was many a one who was zealous for the Church the same way a Roman was zealous for his native land, and became a tragic hero for the sake of the Church just as the Roman did for his country, and then was regarded as a religious hero—that is, on the basis of purely esthetic categories passed through to the private oral religious examination. No, the religious is in the interior being and therefore misgivings have their essential significance.

If Hamlet is to be interpreted religiously, one must either allow him to have conceived the plan, and then the religious doubts divest him of it, or do what to my mind better illuminates the religious (for in the first case there could possibly be some doubt as to whether he actually was capable of carrying out his plan)—give him the demonic power resolutely and masterfully to carry out his plan and then let him collapse into himself and into the religious until he finds peace there. A drama, of course, can never come from this; a poet cannot use this subject, which should begin with the last and let the first shine out through it.

On a specific point, one may have a doubt, another opinion, and yet agree on the one opinion that has been the opinion of one and two and three centuries—that Shakespeare stands unrivaled, despite the progress the world will make, that one can always learn from him, and the more one reads him, the more one learns.

VI
423

5.[530]

[531]The Hero—Suffering—Tragedy Aims to Purify the Passions through Fear and Compassion—The Spectator's Sympathy Varies within the Different World Views

The esthetic hero is great by *conquering*, the religious hero by *suffering*. To be sure, the tragic hero also suffers, but in such a way that he simultaneously conquers in the external. This is what uplifts the spectator while he weeps for the dying one.

If Quidam of the imaginary construction was supposed to have been a kind of esthetic hero, he would have had to become that in the demonic (in the direction of evil) and could indeed have become one in that way, for the esthetic is not so physical that it pays attention mainly to the bloodshed or the number of the murdered in order to determine whether someone is a hero. It looks mainly at passion, except that, not emancipated from externals, it is not capable of penetrating to that solely qualitative qualification that is reserved for the religious, where a farthing is worth just as much as kingdoms and countries. So if he were to be a hero he would have to act by virtue of this consideration: I see my idea of existence being stranded on this girl, *ergo*, she must go; my road to a great goal runs over her downfall. Nor is it difficult to construct for him some brilliant idea or other he wants to fulfill. We would then see him reach his goal and the world order again bring a nemesis upon him. He would above all have to be egotistically sure of himself, and what one would see would be his undauntedness, and how he became supranatural—not as the religious individual becomes that by making sacrifices, but as the demonic oriented to evil becomes that by demanding sacrifices. But above all he must not be what he is in the construction, of a sympathetic nature, for then esthetics cannot understand his collision, and above all he must not, as in the construction, do just the opposite and regard it as the most important thing of all that he eventually suffers more than she, and be sure, as he wishes, that the step itself will become not the girl's downfall but his own.

VI
424

Quaedam of the imaginary construction lies essentially within the esthetic. The unusual trait that constitutes an esthetic heroine would here be to possess within herself sufficient ideality to cling firmly to her love and in this strength, which preserved the love, to be heightened to something extraordinary and thus herself form a nemesis upon him. A girl of that quality could not be used in the construction if the special concern is to throw light on him and to have the unity of

the comic and the tragic as the structuring principle. Therefore, I chose a girl of a rather ordinary kind. His sympathetic
nature must be illuminated from all sides, and therefore I had
to have a female character who can make the whole thing as
dialectical as possible for him and among other things can
bring him into the anguish of seeing her break with the idea,
as he calls it, even if she does nothing else (if she does that)
than that she, *sine ira et studio* [without wrath and partiality],[532]
without losing her feminine lovableness, acquires for herself a
new partner in the dance of life—in other words, if a person
cannot have the one, then take the other, unembarrassed by
prolixity of ideas, and precisely for that reason lovable. Anyone could have told him this in advance, but that does him no
good. Of course she, like any other girl, had a possibility of
becoming great, and there are moments in their relationship
when I had hoped that I could bow before her, for I, who am
an observer and thus *poetice et eleganter* [in a poetic and refined
way] a street inspector, I find great joy in bowing. I have
never envied Napoleon his greatness, but I have indeed envied
the two chamberlains who opened the door for him, the good
fortune to be the one who opened the door, bowed deeply,
and said: The Emperor! Because of the relationship this could
not be done, and it is the relationship that gives me my dialectical satisfaction. I am not interested in how they happened to
begin, in their individual fates. If I were, I would instantly be
influenced essentially by his passion, and that would be the
end of my equilibrium. As soon as I add passion and consider
each one individually and his fate, then I must say of *him* that
he is the one who eventually suffers more. He began, and by
doing so he insulted her since he did not understand the distinctive characteristic of a female existence; he began, and
therefore he deserved his suffering. Of *her*, I must say that she
is the one to whom life does the greater wrong in the imaginary construction, that by having become involved with him
she always appears in a wrong light from the moment he by
his deception prevents her from expressing the sympathy she
certainly could have felt. Because he exists in the deception, a
comic light falls upon her whatever she may do, even if she

chose to remain faithful to him. He is very sensible of this wrong against her, and yet from his viewpoint he is acting in sympathetic passion, and this is one of the coiled springs in his suffering—that from his viewpoint he is doing the utmost and yet the most lunatic thing he can do; because they do not have a common viewpoint, he does not form a contiguous angle with her. Neither from his viewpoint nor from hers is it like for like: feminine attractiveness, loveliness—and a spiritual existence by virtue of the dialectical. His most desperate efforts are of no help, do not make up for the disparity, for feminine attractiveness has a claim that demands precisely what he lacks. Here is the source of his suffering. On the other hand, the opposite holds, that a spiritual existence by virtue of the dialectical must ask with regard to feminine attractiveness as the mathematician asks: What does that demonstrate? This he does not do, for he is not in spiritual equilibrium but in passion and therefore is concerned about the former and here chooses his suffering.

[533]Suffering he has in abundance, but because of the externality that is its element the esthetic has its own thoughts about suffering. Esthetics quite properly says that suffering itself has no significance and no interest; only when it relates to the idea is it a matter of concern. This is an indisputable truth, and thus it is entirely proper for esthetics to reject sufferings such as toothache and gout. But when esthetics has to explain in more detail what it means to relate to the idea, it once again must become obvious, as touched on in section 1, that it is only an immediate relationship that concerns esthetics—in other words, that the suffering must come from without, be visible, not within the individual himself. It is for this reason that a view, superbly developed by expert estheticians, has gradually become common property even for the poorest newspaper scribblers: Not every suffering concerns esthetics—for example, sickness.

VI
426

This is entirely correct, and the result of such deliberations is: the esthetic hero, excelling by his quantitative difference, must possess within himself the conditions for being victorious, must be healthy, strong, etc.; then the difficulties come from the outside. I remember a little controversy carried on in Germany on this subject, in which one party cited the Greeks and Greek esthetics against a play in which blindness had been used as a tragic motif.[534] The other party responded by citing *Oedipus* by Sophocles. Perhaps he could better have cited *Philoctetes*, which in a way is an exception to the universal esthetic concept but yet such that the exception by no means can invalidate it but rather itself lapses.

Consequently, this is an established point in esthetics. Now, when I leave the esthetic, I remove the externality and repeat the correct principle: only the suffering that is related to the idea is of interest. This remains forever true. When a relationship to the idea does not become visible in suffering, it is to be rejected in the esthetic sphere, condemned in the religious sphere. But since the religious is only qualitatively dialectical and commensurable for everything and equally commensurable, then any suffering can *eo ipso* acquire interest, precisely because everyone can have a relationship to the idea.

There has been much talk about poetry reconciling one with life; it might rather be said that it leads one to revolt against life, for poetry does people an injustice by its quantifying; it can use only the chosen ones, but this is a mediocre reconciliation. I take, for example, illness. Esthetics responds proudly and consistently: It cannot be used. Poetry is not supposed to be a hospital. That is right, so must it be, and it is bungling to want to deal with such things esthetically. Now, if one does not have the religious, one is in an awkward position. Esthetics finally culminates in the principle concerning illness that Fr. Schlegel has stated: *Nur die Gesundheit ist liebenswürdig* [Only health is lovable].[535] Lest it degenerate into blubbering and *weinerliche* [weepy] drama, poetry is obliged to declare against poverty (when it is constrained to answer people, in which constraint the fault lies with the people, something that will be touched upon later): Only wealth is lovable or *conditio sine qua non* [the indispensable condition] if I am going to be able to use the characters. Of course, I might be able to write an idyllic piece, but that is not poverty, either.

It is certainly true that poetry, hospitable and affectionate as it is, invites everyone to lose himself in it and thus be reconciled, but it still assumes the distinction because it concerns itself only with the preferred sufferings and consequently demands more from the person who is experienced in life's unpreferred sufferings, demands more power for him to lose himself in poetry. And here poetry has already undermined itself, for indeed it cannot be denied that someone who can lose himself in poetry despite life's unpreferred pressures is greater than someone who does the same but does not suffer in this way, and yet poetry must say that it cannot find in such a person, even though he is greater, a subject for its interpretation.

As soon as one leaves poetry, which, as a friendly power of divine origin far from wanting to offend anyone, does its best to reconcile, as soon as I transfer the esthetic principle from the fenced-in precincts of poetry into actuality, then such a principle, as, for example, that health alone is lovable, is that of an altogether contemptible person. Such a person is contemptible because he is without sympathy and because in his egotism he is cowardly.

In this exigency, when that which one has learned from poetry does not reconcile one with actuality, the religious appears and says: Every suffering is commensurate with the idea, and as soon as the relation to the idea is there, it has interest—otherwise it is culpable and it is the sufferer's own fault. It makes no difference in the matter whether the suffering is not to be able to carry out his big plans or to be hunchbacked; it makes no difference at all in the matter whether it is to be deceived by a faithless lover or to be so unfortunately misshapen that even a kindly person cannot help laughing when he sees such a one, with whom it would never enter anyone's head to fall in love.

This is how I have understood the religious in composing the imaginary construction. But what is the idea-relationship that could be to the point here? It is, of course, a relationship with God. The suffering is within the individual himself; he is no esthetic hero, and the relationship is with God. But once

again restraint must be exercised, for otherwise the religious
becomes so high-spirited that it goes to the very opposite extreme and says, "The lame, the crippled, the poor are my heroes—not the privileged"[536]—which would be unmerciful of
the religious, which is indeed mercifulness itself.

I know that this is the nature of suffering as seen from the
standpoint of the religious, because I can place two men together who say the same thing. Feuerbach, who swears alle-
giance to the principle of health, says that the religious existence (more particularly the Christian) is a continual story of
suffering; he asks one just to consider Pascal's life,[537] and he
certainly has enough. Pascal says exactly the same: Suffering
is a Christian's natural condition[538] (just as health is the sensate
person's), and he became a Christian and spoke out of his
Christian experience.

"A Story of Suffering" is also related to a reader just as the
esthetic work is (except that one must note the dialectical difficulties underscored in section 3 and brought to consciousness in the form of the "imaginary construction"). On the relation of tragedy to the spectator, these are the words of the
founder Aristotle: δι' ἐλεόυ καὶ φόβου περαίνουσα τὴν τῶν
τοιούτων παθημάτων κάθαρσιν [by pity and fear accomplishing
its catharsis of such emotions].[539] Just as in the foregoing I
kept the principle in the religious by removing the externality
from the esthetic, so these words could also be maintained but
must be understood more precisely. Aristotle's meaning is
clear enough. The ability to be affected on the part of the spectator is presupposed, and tragedy assists here by awakening
φόβος [fear] and ἔλεος [pity, compassion], but it then takes
away the egotism in the affected spectator in such a way that
he loses himself in the hero's suffering, forgetting himself in
him. Without fear and compassion [*Medlidenhed*], he will sit in
the theater like a clod, but if all he gathers within himself is
selfish fear, then he sits there as an unworthy spectator.

This is not difficult to understand, but this already does
suggest that fear and compassion must have a specific nature
and that not everyone who fears and is compassionate is therefore able to see a tragedy. The purely sensuous person has no

fear whatsoever of that which preoccupies the poet—hence he feels neither fear nor sympathy. Suppose he sees a man walk a tightrope to Rosenborg Castle;[540] then he fears, and for someone who is going to be executed he has compassion. Thus someone watching a tragedy must have an eye for the idea; then he sees the poetic and in his fear and compassion is purified of all low egotistical elements.

But in turn the religious person has another conception of what awakens fear, and his compassion is therefore in another quarter. Illness and poverty do not concern the estheticist; he has no sympathy with this suffering; he has no fellow feeling for it. As Börne says somewhere, "He feels healthy and has no desire to hear anything about suffering."[541] But all healing power, that of poetry as well as of religion, is only for the sick,[542] because the healing is through fear and compassion. Börne should not have made that last statement, for here the esthetic is already defined in relation to actuality, and thus it is narrow-mindedness or callousness not to want to know anything about it. If the esthetic is maintained in its pure ideality, one does not deal with such things; that is correct, and the poet offends no one. Therefore, it is a mistake for the religious to be angry at poetry, because poetry is and remains lovable. For the spectator it is another matter if he is aware that such things exist. It is, of course, stupidity or cowardly callousness to want to be ignorant of the existence of poverty and sickness because a person is himself healthy; for even if the poet does not make it manifest, nevertheless anyone who has thought two healthy thoughts about life knows that in the next moment he can be in the same situation. It is not wrong of the spectator to want to lose himself in poetry; this is a joy that has its reward, but the spectator must not confuse theater and actuality, or himself with a spectator who is nothing more than a spectator at a comedy.

In the religious, again by means of fear and compassion, these passions are to be purified. But fear has become something different, and consequently compassion also. The poet does not want the spectator to fear what the crude person fears, and he teaches him to fear fate and to have compassion for the person who suffers under it—the subject, however, must be great and quantitatively conspicuous.

The religious man begins in another quarter; he wants to teach the listener not to fear fate, not to lose time in pity for the person who falls before fate. All this has become less important to him, which is why he, unlike the estheticist, sees all people, great and small, as equally exposed to the blows of fate. But then he says, "What you must fear is guilt, and your compassion must be for the person who falls in this way, for the danger is first here. Yet your compassion must not go astray so that you forget yourself over some other person." He will teach the hearer to sorrow, as the parish clerk, that lowly servant, by virtue of his office, a humble-proud high priest of inner emotion, tells us "that we should sorrow over our sins," something, of course, that the parish clerk does not dare say to the reverend superiors, the assistant professors in the pulpit. Fear and compassion are to be aroused by the presentation; these passions are also to be purified of egotism, but not by becoming lost in contemplation but by finding within oneself a relationship with God. "It is indeed egotism," declares the poet, "if you cannot forget the blow of fate that has struck you when you see the tragic hero; it is egotism when, by seeing the hero become a tailor, you go home anxious"— "but to dwell on one's own personal guilt," says the religious person, "to be apprehensive about one's own guilt is not egotism, for precisely thereby one is in a relationship with God!" For the religious person, fear and compassion are something different and are purified not by turning outward but by turning inward. The esthetic healing consists in this, that the individual, by staring himself into the esthetic dizziness, disappears from himself, like an atom, like a speck of dust, something thrown into the bargain along with what is the common lot of all human beings, of all humanity, disappears like an infinitely brief fractional consonance in the harmony of the spheres of life. The religious healing, conversely, consists in transforming the world and centuries and generations and millions of contemporaries to something vanishing, transforming jubilation and acclamation and esthetic hero worship into a disturbing diversion, the idea of being finished into a phantasmagoric hallucination—so that all that remains is only the individual himself—this particular individual placed in his relationship with God under the qualification: guilty/not guilty.

This is the religious according to what I have ascertained in the composing of the imaginary construction. I do not see it this way, for in the relation between the esthetic and the religious I see again the unity of the comic and tragic that they form when they are placed together. Thus also in poverty I see the tragedy in the fact that an immortal spirit is suffering and the comedy in the fact that all revolves around two shillings. I do not go beyond the unity of the comic and the tragic in the balance of spirit. I have a notion that I, if I did go further and made a beginning in the religious, might not get into the predicament where it would be doubtful whether I was guilty, and therefore I remain outside. I am not an offended person, far from it, but neither am I religious. The religious interests me as a phenomenon and as the phenomenon that interests me most. Therefore, it is not for the sake of humanity but for my own sake that it distresses me to see religiousness vanish, because I wish to have material for observation. I say this without hesitation, and I also have sufficient time for it, for an observer has time in abundance. Not so with a religious person. When he speaks it is only a monologue; occupied only with himself, he speaks aloud, and this is called preaching; if there is anyone listening, he knows nothing about his relation to them except that they owe him nothing, for what he must accomplish is to save himself. Such a right reverend monologue that witnesses Christianly, when in its animation it moves the speaker, the witnessing, because he is speaking about himself, is called a sermon. World-historical surveys, systematic conclusions, gesticulations, wiping sweat from the brow, a stentorian voice, and pulpit pounding, along with the premeditated use of all this in order to accomplish something are esthetic reminiscences that do not even know how to accentuate fear and pity properly in the Aristotelian sense. For world-historical surveys do not awaken fear any more than systematic conclusions, and a stentorian voice does not shake the soul but at most the eardrums, and wiping sweat from the brow at most arouses only sensate sympathy for the sweater. A religious speaker who, inwardly moved, does not speak about himself but about everything else should remember Gert Westphaler.[543] Gert could talk about anything, knew a great deal, and was so very perfectible that he perhaps could have managed to know everything; one thing he did not manage to know, that he himself was a *Schwatzer* [babbler]. Yet Gert is blameless, for he did not pretend to be a religious speaker.

VI
432

[544]The religious speaker who purifies these passions through fear and compassion does not in the course of his address do the astounding thing of ripping the clouds asunder to show heaven open, the judgment day at hand, hell in the background, himself and the elect triumphantly celebrating; he does the simpler and less pretentious thing, the humble feat that is supposed to be so very easy: he lets heaven remain closed, in fear and trembling does not feel that he himself is finished, bows his head while the judgment of the discourse falls upon thought and mind. He does not do the astounding thing that could make his next appearance lay claim to being greeted with applause; he does not thunder so that the congregation might be kept awake and be saved by his discourse. He does the simpler and less pretentious thing, the humble feat that is supposed to be so very easy: he lets God keep the thunder and the power and the honor and speaks in such a way that even if everything miscarried he nevertheless is certain that there was one listener who was moved in earnest, the speaker himself, that even if everything miscarried there was one listener who went home strengthened, the speaker himself, that even if everything miscarried and everyone stayed away there was still one person who in life's difficult complications longed for the upbuilding moment of the discourse, the speaker himself. He is not lavish in the dispensing of an overabundance of words and information but is attentive to the yield of the upbuilding; he scrupulously sees to it that the exhortation binds himself before it goes to anyone else, that

the comfort and truth do not leave him—in order to be communicated all the more prodigally. Therefore, says the religious person, if you were to see him in some lonely, out-of-the-way place, deserted by everyone and positive that he accomplished nothing by his speaking, if you saw him there you would see him just as inwardly moved as ever; if you heard his discourse, you would find it as powerful as always, guileless, uncalculating, unenterprising, you would comprehend that there was one person it was bound to upbuild—the speaker himself. He will not become weary of speaking, for attorneys and speakers who have secular aims or worldly importance with regard to eternal aims become weary when what they accomplish cannot be counted on their fingers, when crafty life does not delude them with the illusion of having accomplished something, but the religious speaker always has his primary aim: the speaker himself.

This is the way, according to what I have ascertained in the composing of the imaginary construction, that the religious will effect the ennobling of these passions through fear and compassion. Any other method produces confusion by introducing semiesthetic categories: by making the speaker esthetically important and by assisting the listener to swoon away into an esthetic absorption in something universal.

VI
433

Appendix

[545]*Self-inflicted Sufferings—Self-Torment*

From the point of view of the esthetic, every *heautontimorumenos* [self-tormentor][546] is comic. In that respect, different ages produce different types. Our age is not the worst, for it seems as if the whole generation were tormenting itself with the fixed idea that it was called to the extraordinary, that any moment a message for it was bound to come by way of a deputation from the council of the gods, so that it could take its place in the council meeting, for this much is certain—familiar with its task, the future of the whole human race, it seems as if at any moment it would, like Hermann von Bremenfeldt, take off to whisper in God's ear what was the right thing to do. And how lamentable that Hermann von Bremenfeldt did not manage to speak with the Elector of Saxony![547] Moreover, as do all who suffer from fixed ideas, it has a strong tendency to see espionage and persecution everywhere, and just as rheumatic people feel drafts everywhere, so does it sense pressure everywhere, the misuse of power, and knows how to explain in a satisfying way the feeble signs of life in the public spirit not on the basis that its strength is merely symptomatic and imaginary but on the basis that it is cowed by governments, somewhat as the Busybody explains that he accomplishes nothing during the day, not on the basis that he is fussy and fidgety but on the basis of the many affairs that burst in on him.[548] Enough of that.

Precisely because it is esthetically correct that all self-torment is comic, one is psychologically wise in an actual situation to use the comic explorer before dealing with self-torment another way. One of course does not bring the patient to laugh immediately at his own fixed idea but by means of analogies comes closer and closer to him. If he laughs excitedly at the analogies, then it is possible that one can take him by surprise by means of a *coup de main* [surprise stroke]. However, this can be developed specifically only in practice, but in practice there is nothing more ridiculous than to see religious categories used in deep and dumb seriousness where one should use esthetic categories with humor and jest.

Without being aware of it, Quidam of the imaginary construction acted quite correctly. With enormous passion he conceives the plan of making his whole love relationship into tomfoolery in the girl's eyes. What I find laughable, from my point of view, is his prodigious passion—otherwise he is right. There is not always peril to life just because a person screams for help. If Quaedam of the construction had been suffering tragically, she would have kept him from having a chance to use the deception. She would have collected herself inwardly and restrained herself. These are always the dangerous phenomena. Instead of that, she went to the very opposite extreme: exaggerated as much as possible and tormented herself with wanting to be an unhappy lover on the largest possible scale. But precisely this suggests that a comic treatment is correct, for a woman who is unhappy in love on the largest possible scale is silent. If she had been kept in religious categories, she would not have acted that way, either; she would have feared for herself and therefore would have feared most the responsibility she could incur by making the matter as difficult as possible for him, not so much by her personality but by an erotic counterfeit that trespasses upon the ethical and the relationship of duty.

If Quidam of the construction had had the spiritual balance to understand what he was doing, he would have been an entirely different person. But his troubled passion makes him tragic in his use of the deception, and I see the unity of the comic and the tragic precisely because he does the right thing but not for the reason he thinks—that in his sympathetic zeal he would have the power to wrest her loose from a real love affair. No, the comic is precisely this: the reason for the victory of his tragic foolhardiness is that her love does not go very deep.

The reason that the esthetic quite consistently treats all self-torment comically is easy to see, simply because it is consistent. Esthetics maintains the hero in a sound condition on the basis of the immediate relation between strength and suffering (within/from without). Therefore it considers any inward direction a desertion, and since it cannot have the deserter shot it makes him ludicrous.

I now leave the esthetic and go on to the religious. In composing my imaginary construction, I merely set the categories in motion in order to observe completely undisturbed what these require without caring to what extent someone has done it or can do it, whether Per left it alone because he was too weak, Poul because he was too smart, Mads because he saw the others leave it alone and thus he could leave it alone without any risk and be loved and esteemed, since he did not want to be better than others: in short, regardless of life-insurance wisdom, the outcome of which is, when one sheep goes to drink the other does also, what one fool does another fool does also.

The religious does not consist in an immediate relation between strength and suffering, but in the internal, when this relates itself to itself. That the "self" is accentuated here is always sufficient to show that self-torment is to be regarded differently but is not sufficient, declares the religious person, to justify the jumbling of something together by individuals who have their whole existence in the esthetic and the failure of religious speakers, despite all their platitudes and sanctimonious words, to have pure categories.

Insofar as self-torment, viewed esthetically, is comic, it is, viewed religiously, reprehensible. A religious healing is accomplished not by laughter but by repentance; self-torment is a sin like other sins.

But while the esthetic, precisely because it is not involved with the internal, quite generally dismisses self-torment as comic, the religious cannot do so. The religious individual's fear is precisely fear for himself; the religious healing consists first and foremost in arousing this fear, and from this it is easy to see that here the matter becomes more difficult. But how does the individual begin to fear himself without discovering *by himself* the danger he is in. A sly religiousness, to be sure, acts in another way. It says, "One must not evoke the dangers oneself; our Lord will surely send them if necessary." One may well say that, but it will never do to say "Amen" and end with that, for that kind of talk is dubious. Despite the religious phrase "Our Lord," instead of which someone, in order to talk even more religiously, might say "Our Savior" (as if the religious consisted of certain words and phrases), the categories are nevertheless half-esthetic. Although the talk is religious, the individual is seen only in an external relationship to God, not in an interior relationship to himself. The talk amounts to this: Our Lord can certainly bring danger and misery to your house; indeed, he can take your property, your beloved, your children, and he will surely do it if it is beneficial for you—*ergo*, since he has not done it, then there is no danger. This is esthetics with imitation religious gilding. From the religious point of view, the greatest danger is that one does not discover, that one is not always discovering, that one is in danger, even if one otherwise had money and the most lovable girl and adorable children and was king of the country or one of the quiet ones in the land, free from all cares.

As stated, one may well say that, but one must not say "Amen" and end with that, for then one deceives. On closer inspection of the talk, this is again apparent. So, then, there is a man, a real favorite [*Pamphilius*] of fortune (this phrase is very appropriate to such religious talk), who is coddled and cared for and, unacquainted with danger, is edified by the thought that Our Lord will surely . . . . . if . . . . . . What a lucky esthete, who in addition to all the *Heiterkeit* [serenity] of the esthetic has a religious safe-conduct document! But to begin with, everyone has something called imagination. So our lucky fellow hears rumors of sufferings and misery in the world! Well, he is ready and willing to give and is praised for it. But imagination is not satisfied with that. It paints for him a horrible picture of suffering, and when it is most shocking, the thought strikes him and a voice says: It could indeed happen to you also. If there is any knightly blood in him, he says: Why should I be exempt in preference to others. (Tieck has treated this somewhere in a short story in which a rich young man despairs over his wealth, not because of spleen but because of his sympathy for mankind.[549]) Of this the talk says nothing at all, and yet here is the dividing line between the esthetic callousness that does not want to know that it exists and the religious elevation through suffering. That there is a crossroad such that one cannot buy exemption by paying the welfare tax and giving a bit more—about this nothing at all is said; our Pamphilius would be happy until Our Lord, when it was found necessary, sent danger. What is the speaker doing here? He is deceiving. Instead of taking him out into danger, he is helping him by way of religious fancy to play hooky from life. Any attempt to clog up receptivity to the fact that one is in danger is esthetic deviation—callousness—not toward poetry, but toward the esthetic, as it manifests itself in relation to actuality.

If the one talking is a more religious speaker, he moves with ease in this difficulty and assists his listener in it. He speaks with the jesting of religiousness about fate and vicissitudes—our lucky Pamphilius becomes a little frightened, and the speaker has not deceived him. Now he is built up by the confidence of faith, and the religiously inspired speaker calls out to himself and to him: A religious person is always joyful.[550] This is the most glorious statement made in the world—that is, if it is true that no one, no one on earth or in heaven knows what danger is and what it is to be in danger as does the religious person, who knows that he is always in danger.[551] Thus he who truthfully and simultaneously can say that he is always in danger and always joyful is saying simultaneously the most disheartening and the most high-minded words spoken. And I, who am only an observer, *poetice et eleganter* [in a poetic and refined way] a street inspector, will already count myself lucky in daring to bow before such a person, but to speak about myself in my own categories: even though the gods have denied me greatness, that which is infinitely beyond my capacity, they have given me an uncommon ingenuity in paying attention to people, so that I neither take off my hat before I see the man nor take it off to the wrong one.

There is many a man who has been *immer lustig* [always merry] and yet stands so low that even esthetics regards him as comic. The question is whether one has not become joyful in the wrong place; and where is the right place? It is—in danger. To be joyful out on 70,000 fathoms of water, many, many miles from all human help—yes, that is something great! To swim in the shallows in the company of waders is not the religious.

It is now obvious what must be understood religiously by self-torment. It is a matter of discovering *by oneself* the full possibility of danger, and *by oneself* at every moment discovering its actuality (this the esthete would call self-torment, and the esthetic lecture would prevent one from it by imitation religious gilding), but it is simultaneously a matter of being joyous. Where, then, is the self-torment? It is at the halfway point. It is not at the beginning, for then I am speaking esthetically, but it is due to one's being unable to work one's way through to joy. And this, declares the religious person, is not comic; neither does it lend itself to evoking esthetic tears, for that is reprehensible and one *shall* work one's way through. Anyone who does not make his way through has only himself to blame, for here there are not hard-hearted fathers as with the unhappy lovers in the tragedy; here there is not the superiority of the enemy, before which the hero in the tragic drama falls; here there is not the betrayal by the person one trusted most so that the outstanding person is caught in the trap—here there is only one who can be the betrayer, oneself, and next to him, but infinitely far removed, the speaker who would advise one to leave it alone instead of doing the only thing he can do—helping one out into the depths where there are 70,000 fathoms. And when this has happened and he now perceives that he can do no more, cannot do more to help the person he loved more than his own life (as is possible in the story of the play) but only in this anxiety discovers that he has 140,000 fathoms beneath him, there is still one thing left to do; he can shout to the beloved, "If you do not become happy now, then know this, know that it is your own fault."

VI
438

And even if it is the opinion of many people, if they were to become aware of what is stated here, that such a speaker must be regarded as a national scourge and that it would be the most foolish thing of all to pay him because he made one unhappy, that is not my opinion. I would gladly pay him, and if I could become a speaker such as that I would imperturbably receive money for it, but I would not think I was rewarding him or was being rewarded, for money is incommensurable with that kind of instruction and is not even of such worth that one polemically accentuates it by refusing to accept it, as Socrates did.[552]

So much with regard to self-torment. It is extremely simple; everyone knows it, and precisely in that I again see the unity of the comic and the tragic when I consider that *everyone* knows what a human being *is*, and the observer knows what everyone is.* It is not esthetic-comic because there is more

* Although I ordinarily do not desire any comment from the critics, I almost desire it in this case if, far from flattering me, it consisted of the blunt

than an immediate relation (for the comic lies in the misrelation between an imagined possibility and actuality). Diedrik Menschenschrek[553] is comic because his courage is an imagined possibility and thus his actuality is dissolved into nothingness. But that possibility for everyone is no imagined possibility but a real possibility; he can become the highest, declares the religious person, because he is intended [*anlagt*] for the highest. It is tragic that he is not, but comic that he nevertheless is, for he cannot wipe out that possibility intended by God himself.[554] Thus, everyone knows that a human being is immortal. The observer knows what everyone *is*, and yet everyone indeed is and remains immortal. Consequently his immortality was no imagined possibility, as was D. Menschenschrek's courage, and, on the other hand, the person who, despite all the terrors of life and despite the cunning of the age and of habit, keeps faith in immortality present with him, does not become more immortal than anyone else.

Quidam of the imaginary construction is something of a self-tormenter. His first move is good and correct, but he remains in the sortie; he does not retrieve himself in joy quickly enough to repeat the movement again. Yet the point at which I have conceived him is indeed also his crisis. It is possible that things will go better for him if he is sufficiently sensible to regard a whole life as compatible with such a course of instruction and to reconcile himself to remaining a dawdler among those who are quickly finished, a retarded pupil among those who go infinitely further.

---

truth "that what I say everyone knows, every child, and the educated infinitely so much more." That is, if it only remains fixed that everyone knows it, then my position is in order and I shall surely come to terms with the unity of the comic and the tragic. If there were anyone who did not know it, I would be thrown off balance by the thought that I could possibly teach him the requisite preparatory knowledge. What occupies me so much is precisely what the educated and cultured say in our time—that everyone knows what the highest is. This was not the case in paganism, not in Judaism, and not during seventeen centuries of Christianity. Fortunate nineteenth century! Everyone knows it. What a progress since those ages when only a few knew it. Would a balance possibly require that in return we assume that there is no one at all who would do it?

That the girl is helpful in getting him out upon the deep, of that there is no doubt, and from my point of view I must say that his whole relationship with her is a happy one, for the man is always happy in love who finds a girl who is specifically designed to develop him. Thus Socrates was fortunate in being married to Xanthippe;[555] he would not have found her match in all Greece, for that old grandmaster of irony needed such a person in order to develop himself. Therefore, if Xanthippe frequently had to hear herself maligned in the world, I, on the contrary, believe that she has the gratification that the commander in chief of irony, who towers a head over the human throng, owed no person as much as he owed Xanthippe's housekeeping, where Socrates ironically debated *pro summis in ironia honoribus* [for the highest honors in irony][556] and in that connection debated himself into the ironic proficiency and equanimity with which he conquered the world.

Thus the girl is entirely suitable to him, as is meet and proper for the imaginary construction. She is lovely enough to stir him, but also weak enough to misuse her power over him. It is the former that binds him, the latter that helps him out upon the deep but also saves him. If the girl had been more spiritually qualified and less femininely lovable, if she had been very magnanimous, she would have said to him in the middle of the deception: My dear, you distress me with your deceit. I do not understand you, and I do not know whether you are irresponsible enough to want to leave me because you want to be out in the world or whether you are hiding something from me and are perhaps better than you seem. But whichever it is, I do realize that you must have your freedom; I fear for myself if I were not to give it to you, and I love you too much to deny you it. So take it, without any recriminations, without any anger between us, without any thanks on your part but with the awareness on my part that I have done the best I could. If this had happened, he would have been crushed; he would have sunk into the ground for shame, for with his passion he can superbly bear all evil when he knows himself to be better, but he would not be able to forget that he became debtor to a magnanimity such as that, the greatness of which he would discover with demonic discernment. This would have done him an injustice, because from his viewpoint he also meant well. In the construction he is humbled not by a human being but before God.

Anyone who otherwise has the desire and the aptitude to construct imaginatively with categories, without needing pageantry, settings, many characters, "and then the cows," will see how many new constructions could be made from this point by changing him or her a little and seeing what would result for him and for her, how he might have been in order to crush her (if, for example, he had cruelly made her responsible for his life and perhaps terrified her so that she never recovered from it), which he simply cannot do, or how both must have been constituted for both of them to be crushed (if, for example, he had not had religious presuppositions and perhaps in desperate pride ended by celebrating their union with suicide) instead of both being helped as they are now.

Readers of novels, of course, make other and greater demands and feel that when everything revolves around only two characters it must be boring, which it is indeed if it does not also revolve around the categories. If it does, even one character can be entertaining, and 6 billion 477,378,785 people cannot revolve around more. A reader of novels, of course, is excited only when something exciting is going on, as one says upon seeing a crowd. But if the crowd revolves around nothing, then there is still not anything going on.

6.

[557]To Repent of Nothing Is the Highest Wisdom— the Forgiveness of Sin

Hand in hand with such negative principles as: Admire nothing,[558] expect nothing, etc. is the negative principle: Repent of nothing or, to use other words that perhaps are not as ethically disturbing: Regret nothing. The real secret of this wisdom is that an esthetic principle has been embellished and given the appearance of an ethical principle. Understood esthetically from an ethical position this is entirely true, for the free spirit essentially ought not to esteem the whole range of the esthetic so highly that he regrets something. For example, if someone has become poor, then it is correct to say: To regret nothing is the highest wisdom—that is, act by virtue of the ethical. Then the principle means: continually to cut down the bridge of the past behind one in order continually to be able to act at the moment. If you have devised a plan after thorough deliberation and the outcome seems to show that your plan was mistaken, then the point is to regret nothing but to act by virtue of the ethical. Beyond a doubt, much time is wasted in the world on this kind of looking backward, and to this extent the principle can be commendable.

But if the plan was not made after due deliberation, if there was deceit in it—what then? Does it still apply: Repent of nothing in order not to be delayed? It depends upon the nature of the delay one could fear. If one fears delay and hindrance in sinking ever deeper, then it would certainly be best to shout: Repent of nothing, and to understand the poet's words *nulla pallescere culpa* [no wrongdoing to turn us pale][559] to refer to the brazenness that does not turn pale at guilt, but in that case the principle is extremely unethical. However, there are many people who rush through life with the haste of anxiety. There is nothing they fear more than the dialectical, and when they say "Repent of nothing" with regard to the past, they could with the same right say "Deliberate about nothing" with regard to the future. Thus it is rather witty of a jolly fellow in one of Scribe's plays to say that since he never made any plan, neither did he ever have the trouble of seeing it fail;[560] women often act without deliberation in this way and come out very well. In another way a very sagacious person sometimes acts without deliberation or in desperation in order to obtain a criterion. When someone is stuck in something and does not know which end is up, when everything has become so devastatingly relative that it seems as if one is being suffocated, then it may be expedient to act suddenly at one point just to get something moving and some life in all that dead flesh. An interrogator, for example, when he is in a complete quandary and everything is equally probable, suddenly directs the inquiry at one individual, not because suspicion falls most upon him, for a definite suspicion is precisely what he lacks; he passionately pursues this arbitrary clue—at times the light dawns, but in another place. If one does not know whether one is sick or well, if this condition tends to make no sense, it is good to risk doing something desperate suddenly. But even if one acts without deliberation, there is still a kind of deliberation.

Otherwise it is a matter of persevering in the dialectical with deliberation as the antecedent and with repentance as the consequent. Only the person who in deliberation has exhausted the dialectical, only he acts, and only the person who in repentance exhausts the dialectical, only he repents. Thus it seems inexplicable how that powerful thinker Fichte could assume that there was no time for the man of action to repent,[561] and all the more so because this energetic and, in the noble Greek sense, honest philosopher had a great conception of a person's actions taking place only in the internal. Yet this may be explained by the fact that with his energy he did not particularly realize (at least not in his earlier period) that this internal action is essentially a suffering, and that therefore a person's highest inward action is to repent. But to repent is not a positive movement outwards or off to, but a negative movement inwards, not a doing but by oneself letting something happen to oneself.

There are three existence-spheres: the esthetic, the ethical, the religious. The metaphysical is abstraction, and there is no human being who exists metaphysically. The metaphysical, the ontological, is [*er*], but it does not exist [*er ikke til*], for when it exists it does so in the esthetic, in the ethical, in the religious, and when it is, it is the abstraction from or a *prius* [something prior] to the esthetic, the ethical, the religious. The ethical sphere is only a transition sphere, and therefore its highest expression is repentance as a negative action. The esthetic sphere is the sphere of immediacy, the ethical the sphere of requirement (and this requirement is so infinite that the individual always goes bankrupt), the religious the sphere of fulfillment, but, please note, not a fulfillment such as when one fills an alms box or a sack with gold, for repentance has specifically created a boundless space, and as a consequence the religious contradiction: simultaneously to be out on 70,000 fathoms of water and yet be joyful.

Just as the ethical sphere is a passageway—which one nevertheless does not pass through once and for all—just as repentance is its expression, so repentance is the most dialectical. No wonder, then, that one fears it, for if one gives it a finger it takes the whole hand. Just as Jehovah in the Old Testament visits the iniquities of the fathers upon the children unto the latest generations,[562] so repentance goes backward, continually presupposing the object of its investigation. In repentance there is the impulse of the motion, and therefore everything is reversed. This impulse signifies precisely the difference between the esthetic and the religious as the difference between the external and the internal.

The infinite annihilating power of this repentance is best seen in the sympathetically dialectical character that it also has. Attention is rarely paid to this. I shall not discuss here such shabbiness as wanting to repent of a specific act and then being a jolly fellow again or wanting to have repented and to be believed, although every such expression is adequate demonstration that the one who resolves, the one who gives assurances, the one who believes it has no concept of meaning, but even the more competent expositions of repentance fail to see the dialectical side with regard to the sympathetic. An example to throw some light on this. A gambler comes to a standstill, repentance seizes him, he renounces all gambling. Although he has been standing on the brink of the abyss, repentance nevertheless hangs on to him, and it seems to be successful. Living withdrawn as he does now, possibly saved, he one day sees the body of a man drawn out of the Seine: a suicide, and this was a gambler just as he himself had been, and he knew that this gambler had struggled, had fought a desperate battle to resist his craving. My gambler had loved this man, not because he was a gambler, but because he was better than he was. What then? It is unnecessary to consult romances and novels, but even a religious speaker would very

VI
444

likely break off my story a little earlier and have it end with my gambler, shocked by the sight, going home and thanking God for his rescue. Stop. First of all we should have a little explanation, a judgment pronounced on the other gambler; every life that is not thoughtless *eo ipso* indirectly passes judgment. If the other gambler had been callous, then he could certainly conclude: He did not want to be saved. But this was not the case. Now, my gambler is a man who has understood the old saying *de te narratur fabula* [the tale is told of you];[563] he is no modern fool who believes that everyone should court the colossal objective task of being able to rattle off something that applies to the whole human race but not to himself. So what judgment shall he pass, and he cannot keep from doing it, for this *de te* is for him the most sacred law of life, because it is the covenant of humanity. If a religious speaker, who in his lack of being able to think is still able to prate, was deeply moved and benevolently wanted to help him with half categories, then my gambler is sufficiently mature to see the mirage—consequently he must press through. At the moment when he is to judge, he holds to the humble expression of a doctrine of predestination (the proud expression lies in the esthetic with artificial religious gilding) if he hopes for his own salvation. The person who does not have sympathy but has a fear of water naturally finds it unreasonable to take another person's fate so hard, but not to do so is unsympathetic and excusable only insofar as the reason is stupidity. Life certainly must still have laws; the ethical order of things is no hullabaloo in which one person escapes unscathed from the worst and another scathed from the best. But now the judgment. The idea, of course, is not that it is a proclivity to condemn that makes him so keen. But he himself cannot be saved by chance; that is thoughtlessness. And if he says that the other gambler went down despite his good intentions, then he himself goes down; and if he says that consequently the other was unwilling, then he shudders, because he still saw the good in him and because it seems as if he is making himself better.

I have deliberately sharpened the issue. Aided by the dialectical in repentance in the direction of sympathy, anyone who is not stupid is immediately shipwrecked. Although I am not a gambler, that phenomenon is sufficient, unless, of course, I am an angel. Though I have ever so little guilt on my conscience, if I have only a smidgen of thought in my brain, all human cobwebs, all of Tom, Dick, and Harry's small talk about rescue, break like sewing thread until I find the law of life. A man who goes undauntedly through life on the category that he is not a criminal but not faultless, either, is of course comic, and one must help the esthetic in having him extradited if he sneaks into the religious in order to be there also, extradited for comic treatment.

It is queer enough to see an author who certainly is unaware of the dialectic of repentance in the direction of sympathy but yet is aware of something resembling it, an expression of sympathy—to see such an author cure this suffering by making the sickness even worse. Börne, in all seriousness and not without some emotion at the thought of how easy it is for people in small towns to become misanthropes or even blasphemers and mutineers against the wise governance of providence, explains that in Paris the statistics on miseries and crimes contribute to curing [564]the impression to which they probably have contributed—and contribute to Börne's becoming a philanthropist. Well, well, what a priceless invention statistics are, what a glorious fruit of culture, what a characteristic counterpart to the *de te narratur fabula* of antiquity. Schleiermacher so enthusiastically declares that knowledge does not perturb religiousness, and that the religious person does not sit safeguarded by a lightning rod and scoff at God;[565] yet with the help of statistical tables one laughs at all of life. And just as Archimedes was absorbed in his calculations and did not notice that he was being put to death,[566] so, in my opinion, Börne is absorbed in collecting statistics and does not notice—but what am I saying! Oh, a person who is far from being as sensitive as B. will surely discover when life becomes too difficult for him, but as long as a person is himself saved from misfortune (for B. surely can easily save himself from sin by means of a non–Socratic ignorance) he certainly owes it to his good living to have means with which to keep horror away. After all, a person can shut his door on the poor, and if someone should starve to death, then he can just look at a collection of statistical tables, see how many die every year of hunger—and he is comforted.*

---

* As an example of a not imperceptible kind of mystification in which sympathy is confused with egotism, I shall quote the passage (*Sämtl. W.*, VIII, p. 96). He speaks of the danger of living in small towns and goes on to say: *Grosze Verbrechen geschehen so selten, dasz wir sie für freie Handlungen erklären, und die Wenigen, die sich ihrer schuldig machen, schonungslos verdammen* [Major crimes occur so rarely that we regard them as free acts, and the few who are guilty of them we condemn mercilessly]. (This, however, is unnecessary unless one is egotistically cowardly or very stupid. And divine justice does not let itself be intimidated as does a military tribunal by a mutiny that gets everybody pardoned because, after all, not everyone can be executed.) . . . . . *Aber ganz anders ist es in Paris* [But it is entirely different in Paris]. (In other words, there one believes in the saving power of mutiny.) *Die Schwächen der Menschen erscheinen dort als Schwächen der Menschheit* [The weaknesses of human beings appear there as the weaknesses of humanity] (well, let it have it; it is, especially when B. is talking, an imaginary quantity that can be treated cavalierly *en carnaille* [in a vulgar way], for B., I daresay, is not embarrassed by the difficult question of how the human race results from individuals and from reciprocation); *Verbrechen und Miszgeschicke* (the one as good as the other) *als heilsame Krankheiten, welche die Uebel des ganzen Körpers, diesen zu erhalten, auf einzelne Glieder werfen* [crimes and misfortune (appear) as salutary ailments that urge the maladies of the whole body upon individual members in order to preserve the whole body]. (And B. imagined himself persecuted as a demagogue! He is so aristocratic that here he is obviously ridiculing the tribune's speech about the whole body's suffering when one member suffers.[567]) *Wir erkennen dort* (in Paris) *die Naturnothwendigkeit des Bösen* [There (. . .) we recognize the necessity of evil] ("Heaven help us, how grand everything is in Paris; there nothing at all is ordinary, but everything is exactly as in summer amusement park time"[568]); *und die Nothwendigkeit ist eine beszre Trösterin als die Freiheit* [and necessity is a better comforter than freedom] (especially for those who have stopped grieving and thus need no consolation). *Wenn in kleinen Städten ein Selbstmord vorfällt, wie lange wird nicht darüber gesprochen, wie viel wird nicht darüber vernünftelt* [When a suicide occurs in small towns, how long one talks on and on about it, how much one reasons and palavers]! (However, I believe that one is through with it more quickly than if one were to introduce reason into this wisdom. Poor Paris! I wonder if it is not also true that when a coward, hiding in the crowd like an urchin under his mother's skirts, writes something in which he is not, as he usually is, wittily entertaining but

Statistical summaries are of no use to an imaginatively constructing psychologist, but then he does not need such an im-
mense conflux of people, either.

[569]Once again, imaginatively constructing, I have laid out
an issue for the religious: the forgiveness of sin. To place immediacy and the forgiveness of sins together in an immediate
relationship can certainly occur to many people; probably
they are also able to talk about it—why not? Indeed, probably
they are also able to induce others to believe that they themselves have experienced something similar and existed in this
way; probably they are even able to induce many to want to
do the same and to want to think they have done the same—
why not! The only difficulty here is that it is an impossibility.
But when it is a matter of the physiology of walking, one does
not have so much free play, and if someone were to claim that
he walked on one arm or even that everyone walked in this
manner, he would soon be discovered to be a tattle carrier
[*Rygter*], but a cattle driver [*Røgter*] in the world of spirit is
more free and easy.

An immediate relationship between immediacy and the forgiveness of sin means that sin is something particular, and this
particular the forgiveness of sin then takes away. But this is
not forgiveness of sin. Thus a child does not know what forgiveness of sin is, for the child, after all, considers himself to

---

instructive, the same thing happens to him as to the one who committed suicide—no one pays any attention to him.) . . . . . *Liest man aber in Paris die am-
tlichen Berichte über die geschehenen Selbstmorde* . . . . . *wie so viele aus Liebesnoth
sich tödten, so viele aus Armuth, so viele wegen unglücklichen Spiels, so viele aus
Ehrgeiz,—so lernt man Selbstmorde als Krankheiten ansehen* [If one reads the official announcements about suicides occurring in Paris . . . . . how so many
kill themselves because of the torments of love, so many because of poverty,
so many because of unlucky gambling, so many because of ambition]—then
one learns to regard suicide as ailments (indeed, according to the above *als
heilsamen Krankheiten* [as healing ailments]), *die wie Sterbfälle durch Schlagflusz
oder Schwindsucht in einem gleichbleibenden Verhältnisse jährlich wiederkehren* [that
as an invariable condition return annually like deadly diseases through strokes
or consumption]! And having learned this, one has become a philanthropist,
a pious person who does not mock God or presumably even rebel against his
wise order. For piety dwells in Paris and Börne is a spiritual counselor!

be basically a fine child. If only that thing had not happened
yesterday, and forgiveness removes it and the child is a fine
child. But if sin is supposed to be radical (a discovery owed to
repentance, which always precedes the forgiveness), this
means precisely that immediacy is regarded as something that
is not valid, but if it is to be considered thus, then it must be
presumed to have been canceled.

But how does one manage to exist by virtue of such an idea,
somewhat more concretely understood, for to rattle something off is not difficult? —I am well aware that speculators
and prophetic seers who scan the future of all humankind will
regard me at best as a normal-school graduate perhaps capable
of writing a catechetical commentary on a textbook for the
public schools. Be that as it may—after all, that is always
something. If only the normal-school graduates will not in
turn exclude me from their society because they know ever so
much more, and finally, if I were satisfied with being a pupil,
just so the enlightened normal-school graduate, the world-
historically concerned parish clerk, would not say: That is
really a stupid boy—he asks such foolish questions. That is of
little concern to me; my sole thought is some day to dare in
conversation to come closer to that Greek wise man whom I
admire, that Greek wise man who laid down his life for what
he had understood and once again would joyfully have risked
his life in order to understand more, since he considered being
in error the most terrible thing of all. And I am sure that Socrates would say: Surely, what you are asking about is a difficult matter, and it has always amazed me that so many could
believe that they understood a teaching such as that; but it has
amazed me even more that some people have even understood
much more. The latter I would certainly like to engage in conversation, and although as a rule I have not made a practice of
personally paying for banquets and musicians, I still would
have clubbed together with such people in order to be initiated
into their exalted, not merely suprahuman but also supradi-
vine wisdom. For Gorgias and Polos and Thrasybolus[570] and
others, who in my day had booths in the marketplace in Athens, were still only suprahuman wise men, like the gods, but

these men, who speed past the gods and for this reason certainly accept not only money but also adoration, from these
men one must be able to learn a great deal.

The difficulty with the forgiveness of sins, if it is not to be
decided on paper or be decided by declarations of a living
word, moved now in joy, now in tears, is to become so transparent to oneself that one knows that one does not exist at any
point by virtue of immediacy, yes, so that one has become
another person, for otherwise forgiveness of sin is my point
of view: the unity of the comic and the tragic.

But since immediacy is indeed something simple but also
something highly compounded, with this one difficulty (of
being annulled), together with the other, which is just like it
(that immediacy is even canceled as sin), the signal is given for
the *difficileste* [most difficult] questions, all of which are included in the one: how an immediacy comes again (or
whether the cancellation of immediacy for the existing person
means that he does not exist [*er til*] at all*), how such an im-

* Although one reads hundreds of times: Immediacy is annulled—one
never sees a single statement about how a person manages to exist in this
manner. One might conclude from this that the writers are poking fun at one
and themselves privately exist by virtue of immediacy[571] and in addition make
their living by writing books about its being annulled. Perhaps the system is
not even very difficult to understand, but what makes the appropriation very
difficult is that all the middle terms have been skipped over—about how the
individual suddenly becomes a metaphysical *I-I*, to what extent it is feasible,
to what extent permissible, to what extent all the ethical has not been set
aside, to what extent the system's eternal truth, as presupposition (with respect to the existential, psychological, ethical, and religious) does not have a
necessary little lie, for want of another introduction, and to what extent the
system's heavenly text in explanation does not offer rather shabby notes as
well as an ambiguous tradition that exempts the initiates from thinking anything decisive even about what is most decisive. An immediate genius can become a poet, artist, mathematician, etc., but a thinking person must, after all,
know his relationship to the human existence lest he, despite all the German
[*tydske*] books, become a monstrosity [*Utydske*] (with the help of the pure
being, which is an unthing). He must indeed know how far it is ethically and
religiously defensible to close himself up metaphysically, to be unwilling to
respect the claim life has—not upon his many blissfully transporting
thoughts, not upon his fancied I-I, but upon his human *you*, whether life calls
him to pleasure and happiness and enjoyment or to terror and trembling, be-

mediacy is different from an earlier one, what is lost and what is gained, what the first immediacy can do that the second one does not dare, what the first immediacy loves that the second does not dare, what certainty the first immediacy has that the second does not have, what is its joy that the second does not have, etc., for it is a very prolix matter. In another sense it is easily exhausted if one does not have the Socratic horror of being in error but has the modern foolhardiness to think that if one merely says it then one is that—just as in the fairy tale one becomes a bird by saying certain words.[573]

Although ordinarily I am not inclined to wish and am far from wanting to believe that I would be aided by the fulfilled wish, I nevertheless wish that a Socratically scrupulous man would have such an existing character come into existence before our eyes so that by hearing him we could see him. By no means do I think that if I read such a narrative one hundred times I would advance one single step if I, suffering, did not personally arrive at the same position. Praised be the righteous rule that in the world of spirit gives everyone his due and does not let someone in mortal danger and with utmost effort acquire in misery what someone else thoughtlessly and stupidly dozes into.

But the issue itself, the idea of forgiveness of sins, is extraneous to the task the imaginary construction has assigned itself, for Quidam is only a demonic figure oriented to the religious, and the issue is beyond both my understanding and my capacities. I shall not shirk it by saying that this is not the place, as if it were the place and perhaps the time and the space on paper that I lacked, since on the contrary I rather much

cause thoughtlessly to remain unaware of that is just as dubious. And if he is able thoughtlessly to disregard this, [572]then try something with that kind of a thinker: place him in Greece—and he will be laughed to scorn in that chosen land, so fortunate in its beautiful location, so fortunate in its rich language, so fortunate in its unparalleled art, so fortunate in the happy temperament of its people, so fortunate in its beautiful girls, but first and last so fortunate in its thinkers, who sought and struggled to understand themselves and themselves in existence before they tried to explain all existence.

believe that once I had understood it myself I would surely find the place and time and the space for exposition.

A Concluding Word

My dear reader—but to whom am I speaking? Perhaps no one at all is left. Probably the same thing has happened to me in reverse as happened to that noble king whom a sorrowful message taught to hurry, whose precipitous ride to his dying beloved has been made unforgettable by the unforgettable ballad[574] in its celebration of the hundred young men who accompanied him from Skanderborg, the fifteen who rode with him over Randbøl Heath, but when he crossed the bridge at Ribe the noble lord was alone. The same, in reverse, to be sure, and for opposite reasons, happened to me, who, captivated by one idea, did not move from the spot—all have ridden away from me. In the beginning, no doubt, the favorably disposed reader reined in his swift steed and thought I was riding a pacer, but when I did not move from the spot, the horse (that is, the reader) or, if you please, the rider, became impatient, and I was left behind alone: a nonequestrian or a Sunday rider whom everybody outrides.

Inasmuch as there is nothing at all to hasten after, I have forever and a day for myself and can talk with myself about myself undisturbed and without inconveniencing anyone. In my view, the religious person is the wise. But the person who fancies himself to be that without being that is a fool, but the person who sees one side of the religious is a sophist. Of these sophists I am one, and even if I were capable of devouring the others I would still not become fatter—which is not inexplicable as in the case of the lean cows in Egypt,[575] for with respect to the religious the sophists are not fat cows but skinny herring. I look at the religious position from all sides, and to that extent I continually have one more side than the sophist, who sees only one side, but what makes me a sophist is that I do not become a religious person. The very least one in the sphere of religiousness is infinitely greater than the greatest sophist.[576] The gods have alleviated my pain over this by granting me many a beautiful observation and by equipping me with a certain amount of wittiness, which will be taken away from me if I use it against the religious.

Sophists can be grouped in three classes. (1) Those who from the esthetic reach an immediate relation to the religious. Here religion becomes poetry, history; the sophist himself is enthusiastic about the religious, but poetically enthusiastic; in his enthusiasm he is willing to make any sacrifice, even lose his life for it, but does not for that reason become a religious person. At the peak of his prestige, he becomes confused and lets himself be confused with a prophet and an apostle. (2) Those who from the immediate ethical enter into an immediate relation to the religious. For them religion becomes a positive doctrine of obligation, instead of repentance being the supreme task of the ethical and expressly negative. The sophist remains untested in infinite reflection, a paragon of positive epitomization. Here is the sphere of his enthusiasm, and without guile he has joy in inspiring others to the same. (3) Those who place the metaphysical in an immediate relation to the religious. Here religion becomes history, which is finished; the sophist is finished with religion and at most becomes an inventor of the system. —The masses admire the sophists because—in comparison with the poetic intuition in which the first category loses itself, in comparison with the positive striving toward a goal outside oneself that beckons the second category, in comparison with the enormous result that the third category acquires by putting together what is finished— they are magnanimously unconcerned about themselves. But the religious consists precisely in being religiously, infinitely concerned about oneself and not about visions, in being infinitely concerned about oneself and not about a positive goal, which is negative and finite because the infinitely negative is the only adequate form for the infinite, in being infinitely concerned about oneself and consequently not deeming oneself finished, which is negative and perdition. —This I do know, but I know it with a balance of spirit and therefore am a sophist like the others, for this balance is an offense against the holy passion of the religious. [577]But this balance in the unity of the comic and the tragic, which is the infinite concern about one-self in the Greek sense (not the infinite religious concern about oneself), is not devoid of significance in illuminating the religious. Thus in a certain sense I am further from the religious than the three classes of sophists, all of whom have made a beginning in it, but in another sense I am closer, because I see more clearly where the religious is and consequently do not make the mistake by grasping something particular but make the mistake of not grasping it.

This is how I understand myself. Satisfied with the lesser—hoping that the greater may some day be granted me, engaged in the pursuits of the spirit in which it seems to me every human being is bound to have abundance enough for the longest life, even if this were composed of nothing but the longest days—I am happy in life, happy in the little world that is my environment. Some of my countrymen no doubt think that Copenhagen is a boring town and small.[578] To me, on the contrary, Copenhagen, refreshed by the sea on which it lies and without being able even in winter to surrender the recollection of beech forests, seems to be the most fortunate place of resi-dence I could wish. It is large enough to be a fair-sized city, small enough so that there is no market price on people. The statistical consolation they have in Paris over so and so many suicides,[579] the statistical joy they have in Paris over so and so many superlative people, cannot intrude disturbingly and churn the individual into a froth so that life has no meaning, his Sabbath no comfort, his festival day no joy, because every-thing slips away into emptiness or surfeit.

VI
453

Some of my countrymen find people who live in this city not lively enough, not moved quickly enough. I do not think so. The speed with which thousands in Paris form a crowd around someone may well flatter the one around whom they gather, but I wonder if it pays for the loss of the more tranquil temperament that lets the single individual feel that he, too, still has some significance? Precisely because individuals have not entirely fallen in price, as if it took so and so many dozens to make one human being, precisely because the people for-tunately are too slow to comprehend this half-hour erudition that only flatters the desperate and the hoodwinked, precisely for these reasons life in this metropolis is so entertaining for the person who knows how to delight in people, which is more entertaining and yields richer dividends than getting a thousand people to shout one's acclaim for half an hour. The error here may rather be that one individual dreams about foreign places, a second individual is absorbed in himself, a third individual is prejudiced and separatistic, etc.—consequently that all these individuals prevent themselves from taking what is offered richly, from finding what is there in overabundance when it is sought. Someone who wants to do nothing at all could still, if he had his eyes open, lead a very enjoyable life merely by paying attention to others; and the person who also has his work does well to see to it that he does not become too trapped in it. But what a pity if there were many who missed out on what costs nothing, no entrance fee, no banquet expenses, no society dues, no trouble and worry, what costs the richest and poorest just as little and yet is the richest enjoyment, who missed out on an education that is not acquired from a particular teacher but from any passerby whatsoever, from a stranger in conversation, from any chance contact. Something on which one has in vain sought enlightenment in books suddenly dawns on one upon hearing a servant girl talking with another servant girl; a phrase that one has tried in vain to torture out of one's own brain, sought in vain in dictionaries, even in the dictionary of the Academy of Sciences and Letters,[580] is heard in passing—a soldier says it and does not dream what a rich man he is. And just as someone walking in the great forest, amazed at everything, sometimes breaks off a branch, sometimes a leaf, then bends down to a flower, now listens to the screeching of birds—so does one walk around among the populace, amazed at the wondrous gift of language, plucking this expression and that in passing, delighting in it and not being so ungrateful as to forget to whom he is indebted—so does one walk among the multitude of people, sees now a manifestation of a psychological state, then another, learns and learns and only becomes more eager to learn. One does not let oneself be deceived by books, as if human nature is so rarely found; one does not read about it in newspapers; the best part of the expression, the most endearing, the little psychological trait, is not often preserved.[581]

Some of my countrymen think that the mother tongue is not adequate to express difficult thoughts. To me this seems a strange and ungrateful opinion, just as it also seems strange and inordinate to champion it so ardently that one almost forgets to rejoice in it, to defend an independence so zealously that one's zeal almost seems to suggest that one already feels dependent, and finally the polemical words become the excitement, not the delight of language the refreshment. I feel fortunate to be bound to my mother tongue, bound as perhaps only few are, bound as Adam was to Eve because there was no other woman, bound because it has been impossible for me to learn another language and thus impossible for me to be tempted to be supercilious and snobbish about my native language. But I am also happy to be bound to a mother tongue that is rich in intrinsic originality when it stretches the soul and with its sweet tones sounds voluptuously in the ear; a mother tongue that does not groan, obstructed by difficult thought, and perhaps the reason some believe it cannot express it is that it makes the difficulty easy by articulating it; a mother tongue that does not puff and sound strained when it stands before the unutterable but works at it in jest and in earnest until it is enunciated; a language that does not find far off what is close at hand or seek deep down what is readily available, because in its happy relation to the object it goes in and out like an elf, and like a child comes out with the felicitous comment without really knowing it; a language that is intense and emotional every time the right lover knows how to incite masculinely the language's feminine passion, is self-assertive and triumphant in argument every time the right master knows how to guide it, adroit as a wrestler every time the right thinker does not let it go and does not let go of the thought; a language that even though it seems impoverished at a particular point really is not but is disdained like a humble, modest sweetheart who indeed has the highest worth and above all is not shabby; a language that is not without expressions for the great, the crucial, the eminent, yet has a lovely, a winsome, a genial partiality for intermediate thoughts and subordinate ideas and adjectives, and the small talk of moods and the humming of transitions and the cordiality of inflections and the secret exuberance of concealed well-being; a language that understands jest perhaps even better than earnestness—a mother tongue that captivates its children with a chain that "is easy to carry—yes, but hard to break."[582]

Some of my countrymen think that Denmark is living on [*tære paa*] old memories. To me this seems to be a strange and ungrateful opinion that no one can approve who would rather be friendly and happy than sullen and grudging, for this only consumes [*tære*]. Others are of the opinion that Denmark faces a matchless future; some who feel misjudged and unappreciated also console themselves with the thought of a better posterity. But the person who is happy with the present and is adept at inventiveness when it comes to being satisfied with it does not really have much time for matchless expectations, and he does not let himself be disturbed by them any more than he reaches out for them. And the person who feels unappreciated by his contemporaries does indeed speak strangely in promising a better posterity. For even if it were so that he was not appreciated, and even if it were so that he would become well known in a posterity that esteemed him, it nevertheless is an injustice and a prejudice to say of this future generation that it is therefore better than the present one, that is, better because it thinks better of him. There is not that great a difference between one generation and the next; the very generation he is criticizing is in the situation of extolling what a former generation of contemporaries misjudged.

Some of my countrymen think that to be an author in Denmark is a poor way to make a living and wretched employment. They not only think that this is the case with such a dubious author as I am, one who does not have a single reader and only a few up to the middle of the book—whom they therefore do not even have in mind in their judgment—but they think this is also the case with distinguished authors. Well, after all, it is only a small country. But was it such a bad job to be a magistrate in Greece, even though it cost money to be one! Just suppose it were the case, suppose it came to be the case, that in Denmark it finally became an author's lot that he had to pay a fixed sum every year for the work involved in being an author—well, what if it were then also the case that foreigners had to say, "In Denmark it is a costly matter to be an author; therefore there are not authors by the dozens, but then in turn they do not have what we foreigners call *Stüber-fängere* [catchpennies],[583] something so unknown in Danish literature that the language does not even have a word for it."

If it were conceivable (something I have not assumed) that there is a reader who has persevered and consequently has come to read this (something I have not imagined, for then I would not have written it), if he talked with others about what he read, some of my countrymen would perhaps say, "Pay no attention to such an author, do not listen to him—he is a seducer."

And one of these "some" would perhaps go on to say, "Ordinarily one thinks of a seducer in connection with women, and even in this connection he is most often depicted in wild demonic passion, secretive and cunning. But this is not the dangerous kind of seducer even in connection with women. No, if I am to imagine such a person, then I shall imagine a young man rich in imagination and intellectually endowed. He does not crave the favor of any woman, and this indifference is not a cover for a secret passion, far from it; he is pursuing no girl, but he is an enthusiast. He does not go to dances with girls (in this respect he is far behind), but he seeks a place in a small sideroom off the ballroom and in a corner of the parlor. Then when the girls are somewhat tired from dancing, or when twilight falls and work stops and thoughts want to flap their wings, then he sits down; now it is his time. Then they listen to his talk, and with his imagination he lures them on into seductive ideals, and as he talks he stretches the expectancy of the aspiring soul and the claim of presentiment. He craves nothing for himself. And once again they seek the pleasure of the dance and the daily pursuits begin again, but secretly they ponder the lofty things he had talked about and

VI
457

they long to imbibe once again the spellbinding illusion. He himself remains unchanged, for his delight is only in the longing for the ideal in his words and thoughts. And when he is silent, it seems to him as if there were a deep sorrow in his soul; in his depression he feels like a blind old man whom talking, like a child, leads through life. So the little misses listen to him, and little by little they are seduced; they seek in vain for what he described, seek it in vain in him, seek it in vain in themselves, and yet they long for his conversation and grow old by hearing it. And when a little earlier the old aunt said to the girls, 'Be careful, girls. Don't listen to him! He is a seducer,' they smiled and said, 'He! He is the nicest man, and in his association with us is so careful, so reserved, as if he did not see us or as if he were afraid of us, and what he says is beautiful, oh, so beautiful!' A poet can be a seducer of that sort. Well, this author surely does not have such powers, nor does he chase after women, but nevertheless in a different sphere he is a seducer. Essentially he has nothing to say, is far from being dangerous—it is not for this reason I warn against him, for as a deeply philosophical friend has said to me: Anyone who looks at him with a genuinely speculative eye sees with half a glance that he, himself defrauded by life by being merely an observer, has become not the deceiver but the deception, the objective deception, the pure negation. Only in an age when temperaments are so intensely agitated that the rule 'He who is not with us is against us'[584] is doubly in force, only in an age when individuals, raised to a higher power by the great crises and the great decisions confronting them, can easily be damaged even by the least little thing, only in such an age could one be tempted to waste a word on warning against him, if it is at all necessary. He is a seducer in a different sphere. Arrayed in mockery and thereby deceptive, at heart he is an enthusiast. He also continually sits close by where people are gathered, he also loves the quieter moment when the ears of the immature young eagerly drink his false teaching. Himself intoxicated in dreams and fortified in illusions, extinct as an observer, he wants to induce everyone to believe that the single individual has infinite significance and that this is the validity of life. Therefore do not listen to him, for what he wants, yet without having any evil intention that would make him dangerous, is to seduce you in a period of ferment to sit still in the undivided estate of quietism in the futile thought that everyone is supposed to attend to himself; he wants to persuade you to betray the great tasks that need united effort but also give rich reward to all. See, because he has not understood this, because he lacks earnestness and positivity, his existence is only an optical illusion, his words are indeed as weak and impotent as a ghost's, and all his statements are only, as the poet says, like the pearl-gray color of an old gate, like snow in a summer rill.[585] But you who are alive and children of the age, are you not aware that life is quaking? Do you not hear the martial music that is signaling, do you not sense the urgency of the moment, so that not even the hour hand can keep up! From whence this frothing unless it is boiling in the depths; from whence these terrible labor pains if the age is not pregnant! Therefore, do not believe him, do not listen to him, for in his mocking and drawn-out way, which is supposed to be Socratic, he probably would say that from the labor pains one cannot directly deduce the outcome of birth since labor pains are like nausea, which is worst when one has an empty stomach. Nor does it follow that everyone who has a distended belly is about to give birth—it could also be flatulence. Likewise, neither does it follow that everyone who has an obstructed abdomen is about to give birth, since it could be something completely different, as Suetonius reminds us when he says of one of the Roman emperors: *vultus erat nitentis* [the face was that of one who is straining].[586] So do not be concerned about him at all, do not let yourselves be disturbed by him. He has not been able to legitimize himself as authorized in the age, he is not the man to come up with the least little thing the age could demand. He is unable to make a single proposal or to advance with positive earnestness in a posture of concern at the thought of the great task of the moment. But do not incite him, for then he could possibly become dangerous; let him go for what he is, a mocker and an enthusiast *in uno* [in one], a bourgeois-philistine *in toto* [throughout], a deceiver, pure negation.[587] If you do that, then he is no seducer."

VI
459

Alas, alas, alas! How fortunate that there is no reader who reads all the way through, and if there were any, the harm from being allowed to shift for oneself when it is the only thing he wishes, is, after all, like the punishment at the hand of the men of Molbo who threw the eel into the water. *Dixi* [I have spoken].[588]

SUPPLEMENT

Key To References
496

Original Title Page of
Stages on Life's Way
498

Selected Entries from Kierkegaard's
Journals and Papers Pertaining to
Stages on Life's Way
501

KEY TO REFERENCES

Marginal references alongside the text are to volume and page [VI 100] in *Søren Kierkegaards samlede Værker*, I–XIV, edited by A. B. Drachmann, J. L. Heiberg, and H. O. Lange (1 ed., Copenhagen: Gyldendal, 1901-06). The same marginal references are used in Sören Kierkegaard, *Gesammelte Werke*, Abt. 1-36 (Düsseldorf, Cologne: Diederich, 1952-69).

References to Kierkegaard's works in English are to this edition, *Kierkegaard's Writings* [*KW*], I–XXVI (Princeton: Princeton University Press, 1978–). Specific references to the *Writings* are given by English title and the standard Danish pagination referred to above [*Either/Or*, I, *KW* III (*SV* I 100)].

References to the *Papirer* [*Pap.* I A 100; note the differentiating letter A, B, or C, used only in references to the *Papirer*] are to *Søren Kierkegaards Papirer*, I–XI³, edited by P. A. Heiberg, V. Kuhr, and E. Torsting (1 ed., Copenhagen: Gyldendal, 1909-48), and 2 ed., photo-offset with two supplemental volumes, XII–XIII, edited by Niels Thulstrup (Copenhagen: Gyldendal, 1968-70), and with index, XIV–XVI (1975-78), edited by N. J. Cappelørn. References to the *Papirer* in English [*JP* II 1500] are to the volume and serial entry number in *Søren Kierkegaard's Journals and Papers*, I–VI, edited and translated by Howard V. Hong and Edna H. Hong, assisted by Gregor Malantschuk, and with index, VII, by Nathaniel Hong and Charles Barker (Bloomington: Indiana University Press, 1967-78).

References to correspondence are to the serial numbers in *Breve og Aktstykker vedrørende Søren Kierkegaard*, I–II, edited by Niels Thulstrup (Copenhagen: Munksgaard, 1953-54), and to the corresponding serial numbers in *Kierkegaard: Letters and Documents*, translated by Henrik Rosenmeier, *Kierkegaard's Writings*, XXV [*Letters*, Letter 100, *KW* XXV].

References to books in Kierkegaard's own library [*ASKB* 100] are based on the serial numbering system of *Auktionspro-*

tokol over Søren Kierkegaards Bogsamling [Auction-catalog of Søren Kierkegaard's Book-collection], edited by H. P. Rohde (Copenhagen: Royal Library, 1967).

In the Supplement, references to page and lines in the text are given as: 100:1-10.

In the notes, internal references to the present volume are given as: p. 100.

Three spaced periods indicate an omission by the editors; five spaced periods indicate a hiatus or fragmentariness in the text.

Stadier paa Livets Vei.

Studier af Forskjellige.

Sammenbragte, befordrede til Trykken og udgivne

af

Hilarius Bogbinder.

Kjøbenhavn.

Hos Universitetsboghandler C. A. Reitzel.

Trykt i Bianco Lunos Bogtrykkeri.

1845.

STAGES ON LIFE'S WAY.

Studies by Various Persons.

――――――――

Compiled, forwarded to the press and published

by

Hilarius Bookbinder.

――――――――

Copenhagen.

Available at University Bookseller C. A. Reitzel's.

Printed by Bianco Luno Press.

1845.

SELECTED ENTRIES FROM
KIERKEGAARD'S JOURNALS AND PAPERS
PERTAINING TO
STAGES ON LIFE'S WAY

See 199:25

What in a certain sense is called "spleen" and what the mystics knew by the designation "the arid moments," the Middle Ages knew as *acedia* (ἀϰήδια, aridity). Gregory, *Moralia in Job*, XIII, p. 435:[1] *Virum solitarium ubique comitatur acedia . . . . . est animi remissio, mentis enervatio, neglectus religiosae exercitationis, odium professionis, laudatrix rerum secularium* [Wherever aridity encompasses a solitary man . . . . . there is a lowering of spirit, a weakening of the mind, a neglect of religious practice, a hatred of professing, a praise of secular things].* That Gregory should emphasize *virum s o l i t a r i u m* points to experience, since it is a sickness to which the isolated person [is exposed] at his highest pinnacle (the humorous), and the sickness is most accurately described and rightly emphasized as *odium professionis*, and if we consider this symptom in a somewhat ordinary sense (not in the sense of churchly confession of sins, by which we would have to include the indifferent church member as *solitarius*) of a self-expression, experience will not leave us in the lurch if examples are required.

July 20, 1839

The ancient moralists show a deep insight into human nature in regarding *tristitia* [sloth, dejection] among the *septem vitia principalia* [seven deadly sins]. Thus Isidorus Hisp. See de Wette, translated by Scharling, p. 139, note q, top; see Gregor and Maximus Confessor in the same note—*JP* I 739 (*Pap.* II A 484) *n.d.*, 1839

In margin of Pap. II A 484:

* This is what my father called: *A quiet despair*.[2]—*JP* I 740 (*Pap.* II A 485) *n.d.*, 1839

See 325:27-28:

Leibniz tells about a Baron Andrè Taifel who had a satyr and the following Spanish inscription on his coat of arms: *mas perdido y menos arrepentido, plus perdu et moins repentant* [the more lost, the less repentant],[3] and that later a Count Villamedina, who was in love with the queen, used the same motto to indicate a hopeless passion that one nevertheless will not give up.

See Erdmann's edition of Leibniz,[4] p. 652, col. 2.—*JP* III 2362 (*Pap.* IV A 26) *n.d.*, 1842-43

See 219:35-220:18:

If I should ever be accused of something, I would immediately petition His Majesty the favor of promptly receiving the most extreme (relative to the incident) sentence, even if it were execution, and that it be carried out immediately. I would make the petition for the following reasons: (1) because the trial costs money, (2) it costs time, and I have no time to wait for men to decide what is just, which is a matter of indifference to me, anyway, if I can just get it over with, (3) because all the talk about justice is drivel, and one may just as well have oneself executed outside the law and without being sentenced as by the verdict of three courts.[5]—*JP* V 5610 (*Pap.* IV A 34) *n.d.* 1843

See 283:1-25:

Outline

Once in his early youth a man allowed himself to be so far carried away in an overwrought irresponsible state as to visit a prostitute.[6] It is all forgotten. Now he wants to get married. Then anxiety stirs. He is tortured day and night with the thought that he might possibly be a father, that somewhere in the world there could be a created being who owed his life to him. He cannot share his secret with anyone; he does not even have any reliable knowledge of the fact. —For this reason the incident must have involved a prostitute and taken place in the wantonness of youth; had it been a little infatuation or an actual seduction, it would be hard to imagine that he could know nothing about it, but now this very ignorance is the basis of his agitated torment. On the other hand, precisely because of the rashness of the whole affair, his misgivings do not really start until he actually falls in love.—*JP* V 5622 (*Pap.* IV A 65) *n.d.*, 1843

See 283:34-284:25:

Outline

IV
A 68
25

A man who for a long time has gone around hiding a secret becomes mentally deranged. At this point one would imagine that his secret would have to come out, but despite his derangement his soul still sticks to its hideout, and those around him become even more convinced that the false story he told to deceive them is the truth. He is healed of his insanity, knows everything that has gone on, and thereby perceives that nothing has been betrayed. Was this gratifying to him or not; he might wish to have disposed of his secret in his madness; it seems as if there were a fate which forced him to remain in his secret and would not let him get away from it. Or was it for the best, was there a guardian spirit who helped him keep his secret.[7]—*JP* V 5624 (*Pap.* IV A 68) *n.d.*, 1843

IV
A 68
26

See 16:18-19:

There is a place out in Gribs-Skov which is called the Nook of Eight Paths.[8] The name is very appealing to me.—*JP* V 5643 (*Pap.* IV A 81) *n.d.*, 1843

Deleted from journal; see 300:33-301:2:

At vespers on Easter Sunday in Frue Kirke (during Mynster's sermon), she nodded to me. I do not know if it was pleadingly or forgivingly, but in any case very affectionately. I had sat down in a place apart, but she discovered it. Would

IV
A 97
37

to God she had not done so. Now a year and a half of suffering and all the enormous pains I took are wasted; she does not believe that I was a deceiver, she has faith in me. What ordeals now lie ahead of her. The next will be that I am a hypocrite. The higher we go, the more dreadful it is. That a man of my inwardness, of my religiousness, could act in such a way. And yet I can no longer live solely for her, cannot expose myself to the contempt of men in order to lose my honor—that I have done already. Shall I in sheer madness go ahead and become a villain just to get her to believe it—ah, what help is that? She will still believe that I was not that before.

Every Monday morning between nine and ten she met me. I made no effort to have it happen. She knew the street I usually walk; I knew the way she

[*A page removed from the journal*]

IV
A 97
38
I have done everything in order that she may not suspect that she perhaps bears a little bit of the guilt herself. A young girl should, after all, have calmness and humility. Instead, it was she who was proud; it was I who had to teach her humility by humbling myself. Then she took my depression wrong; she believed that I was so meek and humble because she was such a matchless girl. Then she took a stand against me. God forgive it—she awakened my pride. That is my sin. I ran her aground—she deserved it, that is my honest opinion—but not what happened later. Then it was that I became depressed; the more passionately she clung to me, the more responsible I felt. It would never have been so difficult if that conflict had not taken place. Then the bond broke.—*JP* V 5653 (*Pap.* IV A 97) *n.d.*, 1843

See 287:6-35:

IV
A 105
40

IV
A 105
41
The only person with whom I have ever had obscene talk is the old China-captain I converse with in Mini's Café[9] and who thinks I am forty years old. But our conversation is rather more humorous. When he begins to tell me how in Manila everyone has a tart or about the fun he has had in his youth with tarts (it is his pet expression) in London, whom one

treats with a glass of grog, "for they are so fond of it"—the situation is humorous enough, an old China-captain (seventy-four years old) talking with me in that way about such things. But he certainly was not particularly involved himself, for there is still a purity in him that testifies for him; as a consequence what he says is more humorous than obscene.[10]—*JP* V 5656 (*Pap.* IV A 105) *n.d.*, 1843

See 262:38-263:21

What is the happiest life? It is [that of] a young girl sixteen years old, pure and innocent, who possesses nothing, neither a dresser nor a tall cupboard, but who makes use of the lowest drawer of her mother's bureau to hide her treasures—a confirmation dress and a hymnbook. . . . . . Fortunate is he who owns no more than that he can live drawer to drawer with her.

What is the happiest life? It is [that of] a young girl sixteen years old, pure and innocent, who indeed can dance but who goes to a party only twice a year.

What is the happiest life? It is [that of] a young girl sixteen years old, pure and innocent, who sits by the window busily sewing, and all the while she sews she steals glances toward the window of the ground floor apartment opposite, where the young painter lives.

What is the unhappiest life? It is [that of] that rich man of twenty-five years who lives opposite on the first floor.

Is one equally old if one is thirty summers old or thirty winters.—*JP* V 5661 (*Pap.* IV B 140) *n.d.*, 1843

Deleted from journal:

May 17

If I had had faith, I would have stayed with Regine.[11] Thanks to God, I now see that. I have been on the point of losing my mind these days. Humanly speaking, I was fair to her; perhaps I should never have become engaged, but from that moment I treated her honestly. In an esthetic and chival-

IV
A 107
41

IV
A 107
42

rous sense, I have loved her far more than she has loved me, for otherwise she would neither have treated me proudly nor unnerved me later with her pleas. I have just begun a story titled "'Guilty?'/'Not Guilty?'";[12] of course it would come to contain things that could amaze the world, for I have personally experienced more poetry in the last year and a half than [is contained in] all novels put together, but I cannot and will not do it, for my relationship to her must not become poetically diffused; it has a completely different reality [*Realitet*]. She has not become a kind of theatrical princess;* so, if possible, she will become my wife. Lord God, that was my only wish, and yet I had to deny myself that. Humanly speaking, in doing that I was perfectly right and acted most nobly toward her by not letting her suspect my agony. In a purely esthetic sense I was generous. I dare congratulate myself for doing what few in my place would do, for if I had not thought so much of her welfare, I could have taken her, since she herself pleaded that I do it (which she surely should never have done; it was a false weapon), since her father asked me to do it; I could have done a kindness to her and fulfilled my own wish, and then if in time she had become weary, I could have castigated her by showing that she herself had insisted on it. That I did not do. God is my witness that it was my only wish; God is my witness how I have kept watch over myself lest any memory of her be effaced. I do not believe that I have spoken to any young girl since that time. I thought that every rascal who happened to be engaged regarded me as a second-rate person, a villain. I have done my age a service, for in truth it was certainly [here some illegible words].

[*A page removed from the journal*]

it would surely have happened. But with respect to marriage it is not true here that everything is sold in the condition "as

In margin: *How would anyone have suspected that such a young girl could go about nursing such ideas. Then, too, it was a very immature and merely vain idea, as the future showed; for if the constituents had actually been present, then the manner in which I broke the engagement would have been absolutely decisive. Precisely such things must give a kind of elasticity. But so my girl was—first coy and beside herself with pride and arrogance, then cowardly.

IV
A 107
43

is" when the hammer falls; here it is a matter of a little honesty about the past. Here again my chivalry is obvious. If I had not honored her higher than myself as my future wife, if I had not been prouder of her honor than of my own, then I would have remained silent and fulfilled her wish and mine—I would have married her—there are so many marriages which conceal little stories. That I did not want, then she would have become my concubine; I would rather have murdered her. —But if I were to have explained myself, I would have had to initiate her into terrible things, my relationship to my father, his depression, the eternal night brooding within me, my going astray, my lusts and debauchery, which, however, in the eyes of God are perhaps not so glaring; for it was, after all, anxiety which brought me to go astray, and where was I to seek a safe stronghold when I knew or suspected that the only man I had admired[13] for his strength and power was tottering.—*JP* V 5664 (*Pap.* IV A 107) May 17, 1843

See 232:24:

I am going to try to get rid of the gloomy thoughts and black moods that still live in me by writing something which will be called:

A Leper's Self-Contemplation.[14]
—*JP* V 5666 (*Pap.* IV A 110) *n.d.*, 1843

In margin of Pap. IV A 110:

It will be a scene between two lepers—the one is compassionate and does not wish to be seen lest he disquiet people; the other wants to revenge himself by horrifying people. The one has brothers and has discovered only recently that they are in the same situation, that the whole family had incurred leprosy.[15]—*JP* V 5667 (*Pap.* IV A 111) *n.d.*

See 250:30-252:22:

I must get at my Antigone again. The task will be a psychological development and motivation of the presentiment of guilt. With that in mind I have been thinking of Solomon and David, of the relation of Solomon's youth to David, for no doubt both Solomon's intellect (dominant in the relationship) and his sensuousness are the results of David's greatness. He had had earlier intimations of David's deep agitation without realizing what guilt might rest upon him, and yet he had seen this profoundly God-fearing man give such an ethical expression to his repentance, for it would have been a quite different matter if David had been a mystic. These ideas, these presentiments, smother energies (except in the form of imagination), arouse the intellect, and this combination of imagination and intellect, where the factor of the will is lacking, is sensuousness proper.—*JP* V 5669 (*Pap.* IV A 114) *n.d.*, 1843

See 360:9:

Idea:

Recollections of My Life
by
Nebuchadnezzar
Formerly Emperor, Recently an Ox
Published
by
Nicolaus Notabene[16]

—*JP* V 5671 (*Pap.* IV A 119) *n.d.*, 1843

See 280:24-32:

Pages From the Notebook of a Street Commissioner[17]

Under this title I would like to describe particular districts of the city that have a certain poetic atmosphere about them, such as Kultorvet (this is the marketplace with the most atmosphere), street scenes, a gutter plank, etc., fishing boats. What splendid contrasts—at one moment have his thoughts sweep that boundless view over the water at Knippelsbro, the next become immersed in contemplation of cod and flounder in a tank. Characters would constantly be thrown in—love stories, maidservants, etc. On the whole, it is remarkable what a healthy sense of humor is often to be found in maidservants, especially when they are criticizing the frippery of elegant ladies.

—At present I am making an effort to get every child I meet to smile.[18]—*JP* V 5678 (*Pap.* IV A 132) *n.d.*, 1843

See 354:23-356:2:

[19]. . . . . her. If she but knew all my sufferings during the past year. She should never have discovered anything. But then my whole outlook is immediately changed. In the marriage ceremony I must take an oath—therefore I do not dare conceal anything. On the other hand there are things I cannot tell her. The fact that the divine enters into marriage is my ruin. If I do not let myself marry her, I offend her. If an unethical relationship can be justifiable—then I begin tomorrow. She has asked me, and for me that is enough. She can depend on me absolutely, but it is an unhappy existence. I am dancing upon a volcano and must let her dance along with me as long as it can last. This is why it is more humble of me to remain silent. That it humbles me I know all too well.—*JP* V 5680 (*Pap.* IV A 133) *n.d.*, 1843

See 65:25-71:12:

He could turn out to be a fine dramatic character: a man with a profound sense of humor who has established himself as a fashion designer and exerted all his influence and financial resources in making women ridiculous, meanwhile being as insinuating as possible in relation to them, charming them with his flattery and conversation, not because he wanted any favors (he was much too intellectual for that) but in order to get them to dress as ridiculously as possible and thus satisfy his contempt for women, and especially when a fine lady like that found a man who was just as much a fool. —In order to chastise him it could be dramatically planned so that everybody actually considered his malevolently introduced styles to be in excellent taste so that he was the only one who laughed, and yet with perfect right. —Then he fell in love with a girl. He wants to make an exception of her, cannot bear to see her wear the ridiculous clothes he himself has made fashionable in order to prostitute the sex. But he cannot convince her and has to bear the sight of his beloved dressed just like the others.[20]—*JP* V 5681 (*Pap.* IV A 135) *n.d.*, 1843

Addition to Pap. IV A 135:

He gets the women to want to indicate in their dress the group differences that distinguish their husbands; this wins their husbands' approval and thus everything is prostituted.— *JP* V 5682 (*Pap.* IV A 136) *n.d.*, 1843

In margin of Pap. IV A 135:

For example, he designs a new costume for women to wear to church in order to prostitute them there also.[21]—*JP* V 5683 (*Pap.* IV A 137) *n.d.*, 1843

In margin of Pap. IV A 135:

Lines: what is everything in life but fashion—piety is a fashion as well as love and hoopskirts and rings in the noses of savages—I am different from the others only in that I have realized it and come to the aid of that sublime genius in every way until I roar with laughter at the most ridiculous of all animals—man. But there comes the Baroness von der Vüe; she probably will buy herself a new fool's costume.[22]—*JP* V 5684 (*Pap.* IV A 138) *n.d.*

In margin of Pap. IV A 135:

I do not cheat my customers. I always use the best fabrics, pure gold, genuine Brussels lace. My only joy is to spoil everything in the cutting and to make something tasteless out of it, for I scorn gold and silver and genuine shawls as profoundly as I scorn the women who swaddle themselves therein.[23]—*JP* V 5685 (*Pap.* IV A 139) *n.d.*

See 279:28-280:14:

A mentally deranged person who went around scanning all children, for he believed that he had once made a girl pregnant but did not know what had become of her and now had but one concern—to find the child. No one could understand the indescribable concern with which he would look at a child.[24]—*JP* V 5691 (*Pap.* IV A 147) *n.d.*, 1843

See 7, 15:20-31:15:

The Banquet,
instead perhaps: *In vino veritas*[25]
or: Evening
(The basic mood will be different according to the title.)
The narrator goes wandering at the Nook of Eight Paths[26] seeking solitude. There he meets a friend, "although he had rather expected to find a frightened bird." He tells him all about the banquet. The contrast of the deep silence of the forest[27] makes the story about the night of pandemonium better, more fantastic.
The talk on Eros.[28]
The characters:[29] Johannes with the nickname The Seducer, Victor Eremita, Recollection's Unhappy Lover, Constantin Constantius, and "a Young Man." The last, a very young man, gives a talk in which he proves that erotic love and physical desire are the most ludicrous of all (their frightful consequences[30]—getting children, plus the fact that a person deceives himself in this lust and merely serves existence). He uses an essay by Henr. Cornel. Agrippa, *De nobilitate et praecelientia Foeminei sexus*[31] (which I have). By using its naïveté a comic and humorous effect is assured.
The condition is that each one is to base his talk on a definite and personal experience of love.[32] —The young man, however, declares that he cannot provide anything like that since

IV
A 170
63

IV
A 170
64

he has always been smart enough to stay clear of it. "One can make a fool of oneself by joining up with a girl who by nature is always a silly flirt." If one is to have anything to do with them, one must only seduce!

The banquet begins with a situation.[33] They are assembled in a festively illuminated hall where dinner music (from *Don Juan*) is being played; they themselves are dressed to the hilt and each one has a personal waiter. While the dinner music is being played, Victor Eremita rises and proposes that they first sing the ditty:

My Brimming Glass and the Lusty Sound of Song.[34]

This has an immediate effect upon the gentlemen present, who readily perceive the humor in the singing of a drinking song by such a company of dinner guests, so thoroughly out of keeping with the drinking song period.—*JP* V 5699 (*Pap.* IV A 170) *n.d.*, 1843

V
A 33
15

See 199:25-200:25:

Quiet Despair[35]
A Narrative

In his early years the Englishman Swift established an insane asylum, which he himself entered in his old age.[36] Here he is said to have observed himself frequently in a mirror and to have exclaimed: Poor old man![37]

V
A 33
16

There were a father and a son. Both were highly endowed intellectually and both were witty, especially the father. Everyone who knew their home was certain to find a visit very entertaining. Usually they discussed only between themselves and entertained each other as two good minds without the distinction between father and son. On one rare occasion when the father looked at the son and saw that he was very troubled, he stood quietly before him and said: Poor child, you live in quiet despair. But he never questioned him more closely—alas, he could not, for he, too, lived in quiet despair. Beyond this not a word was exchanged on the subject. But the father and the son were perhaps two of the most melancholy human beings who ever lived in the memory of man.

From this originates the phrase: quiet despair. It is never used otherwise, for generally people have a different conception of despair. Whenever the son merely said these words to himself, quiet despair, he always broke into tears, partly because it was so inexplicably moving, and partly because he was reminded of his father's agitated voice, since like all melancholics he was laconic but also had the pithiness of the melancholic.

And the father believed that he was responsible for his son's melancholy, and the son believed that he was responsible for his father's melancholy; therefore they never raised the subject. That outburst by the father was an outburst of his own melancholy; therefore when he said this, he spoke more to himself than to the son.—*JP* I 745 (*Pap.* V A 33) *n.d.*, 1844

See 360:22:

These days I suffer very much from a mute disquietude of thought. I am enveloped in an anxiety; I cannot even say what it is that I cannot understand. Like Nebuchadnezzar, I must ask not only for an explanation of the dream but that someone tell me what it was I dreamed.[38]—*JP* V 5743 (*Pap.* V A 71) *n.d.*, 1843

See 7-86:

Much of the content of " '*In vino veritas*' "[39] will no doubt seem to be terribly sensuous; already I hear an outcry and yet what is this compared with Goethe, for example, Philine in *Wilhelm Meister*.—*JP* V 5745 (*Pap.* V A 82) *n.d.*, 1844

See 71:26:

The Seducer's talk[40] is like what is called shower clouds.
—*JP* V 5747 (*Pap.* V A 87) *n.d.*, 1844

See 395:16:

In connection with what I read in Rötscher about the accent on the ethical,[41] it occurs to me that in my personal life I, too, used it properly, as both a poet and a speaker, inasmuch as I said with reference to my relation to Regine and breaking the engagement and her certain death: She chooses the scream, I the pain.[42] Now I can say that she did choose the scream and I did choose the pain.—*JP* V 5748 (*Pap.* V A 88) *n.d.*, 1844

See 183:38:

Lines by an Individual

"As a girl my wife taught me to write short sentences, for at times she sat with me and promised me a kiss at the end of each sentence. Then when I had learned to write short sentences, for which my critic commended me, I was married, and then my wife taught me that writing books was not worth the trouble."

In margin: Originally intended for the Judge in "The Wrong and the Right."[43]—*JP* V 5750 (*Pap.* V A 92) *n.d.*, 1844

See 24:19-21:

The stupidity of Grundtvig (who has now gone completely into vaudeville, toward which he has always had a leaning, for example, his featherbrained desire to be a prophet and seer without any intuition of how such a figure must be tempered in accordance with all the crises of Christianity) is that he always wants to have spiritual security. This accounts for his insipid outspokenness and wittiness *à la* Lars Mathiesen.[44] Luckily he selected the words: "Ladies and Gentlemen,"[45] strongly reminiscent of Dyrehavsbakken.[46] Just like his wittiness are the Ohs! and Ahs! and Eees! of the barenecks, a bodyguard of interjections, the only class of people Grundtvig has won for himself. —He hopes to produce a great effect by talking, yes, particularly in the vein of the vague. But he perhaps could also produce an effect by standing on his head. Eventually the proof of a doctrine's truth will be to sweat, knit one's brow, thump one's head, smile confidently, visibly swoon under the power of the spirit, etc. It is something like Helveg's[47] springing into the pulpit to the honor of Christianity, probably wanting to prove its truth by the fact that he could leap a foot in the air.—*JP* V 5752 (*Pap.* V A 94) *n.d.*, 1844

Report

" 'In vino veritas' "[48] is not going well. I am constantly rewriting parts of it, but it does not satisfy me. On the whole I feel that I have given far too much thought to the matter and thereby have gotten into an unproductive mood. I cannot write it here in the city; so I must take a journey.[49] But perhaps it is hardly worth finishing. The idea of the comic as the erotic is hinted at in *The Concept of Anxiety.*[50] The Fashion Designer is a very good figure, but the problem is whether by writing such things I am not deferring more important writing. In any case it must be written in a hurry. If such a moment does not come, I will not do it. At present the productivity has miscarried and makes me constantly write more than I want to write.—*JP* V 5744 (*Pap.* V A 109) August 27, 1844

The purpose of the five speakers in " '*In vino veritas*',"[51] all of whom are *Karikaturen des Heiligsten* [Caricatures of the Most Holy],[52] is to illuminate women essentially but nevertheless falsely. The Young Man understands women solely from the point of view of the sex; Constantin Constantius considers the psychic aspect: faithlessness—that is, of frivolousness; Victor Eremita conceives of the female sex psychically as sex, its significance for the male, i.e., that there is none; the Fashion Designer considers the sensuous aspect, outside the essentially erotic, of the vanity that is more pronounced in a woman's relationship to women, for as an author has said, women do not adorn themselves for men but for each other;[53] Johannes the Seducer considers the purely sensuous factor with respect to the er[otic].—*JP* V 5755 (*Pap.* V A 110) *n.d.*, 1844

Stages On Life's Way.
Studies by Various Persons.

[*deleted:* stitched together] compiled, forwarded to the press
and published

by
Hilarius Bookbinder.

(1) *in vino veritas* (2) about marriage in answer to
objections, by a married man
(3) Guilty?/Not Guilty?
—*Pap.* VI B 5 *n.d.*, 1844

To the Typesetter:

The entire work is to be printed in large format, like that of
Erslew's *Lexicon*.[54] Medium-sized type the size of that in the
lexicon is to be used. The other prefaces found in the work are
to be set in brevier. The preface to the entire book [is to be set
in type] larger than that of the text.—*JP* V 5773 (*Pap.* VI B
8:1-2) January 1845

From draft; see 3:1-6:25:

Aide-mémoire (in old style).

He had obtained it in this way. An old literatus had sent several books to him to be bound, among them these also—forgot them—he died.

He himself had often read them for diversion, yet without
understanding them, but because of the beautiful lettering and
flourishes let his children practice their penmanship*—until a
teachers-college graduate and university student, who was
supposed to instruct the children in return for his dinner (and
often preached—voice—well educated), made him aware how
lucky he was**: that by the printing of such books one could
not only contribute to the advancement of good and beneficial
learning among the children of men in these days, when faith
and money are becoming a rarity among people, but himself
earn something and large profits, for which he promptly stipulated ten rix-dollars and a pint of wine on Sunday. He was

of the opinion (my learned friend) that the books could not be by one author, but that that literatus had been the head of a fraternity or a society and therefore had preserved the files.

That this story is trustworthy, one would certainly be willing to believe in other times, but in these unbelieving times, but in these times one has—what I have indeed learned and preserved in my recollection—mistaken Magnus Eriksen[55] for a pseudonymous name.

That a bookbinder takes the trouble to publish books—but I have not done anything more than a bookbinder ordinarily does in making one book by stitching together several parts.

* and the reading of handwriting (I. Levin).

** What a glorious gift and donation God had allotted to his house.—*Pap.* VI B 6 *n.d.*, 1844

From draft; see 3:23:

. . . . . that even the best and palest people, for the literatus was not ruddy of complexion, ...

—*Pap.* VI B 7:1 *n.d.*, 1844;

From draft; see 6:23:

Christianshavn in March 1845.

—*Pap.* VI B 7:4 *n.d.*, 1844

From draft; see 6:14-20:

Should Prof. Heiberg[56] make a fuss on account of N. Notabene,[57] a sentence could be inserted about one's being deterred from writing a preface by his example, and then a little malice. This provides the added advantage of H.'s acquiring a name for himself.—*Pap.* V B 192 *n.d.*, 1844

From draft; see 7:2-19:28:

Rapport ad se ipsum
[Report to himself]

Preface [*Forord*]   Preface [*Forerindring*]⁵⁸

What is as seductively enjoyable as a secret, how greedy one can be for it, and yet how dubious it can be to have enjoyed it, how rarely does it agree with one very well! In other words, if someone believes that his only difficulty in enjoying it is seeing to it that he does not betray it, he is not very competent, for he also assumes the responsibility of not forgetting it—which is indefensible with respect to those concerned and dubious for oneself. This is how oblivion and recollection [*Erindring*] fight about the secret; for every person it must be forgotten as if it had never existed, and for oneself it must be recollected. Oblivion is the silken curtain one draws before it; recollection is the vestal virgin who never sleeps.[*] But recollection itself must be not only accurate; it must also be happy; in bottling the recollection, the fragrance of the experience must be sealed within when it is corked. In this respect recollection requires a far more careful study than one usually thinks when one confuses recollection and memory. Just as grapes cannot be pressed at any time, just as the weather at the time of pressing has great influence on the wine, so also what is experienced cannot be recollected at any time, nor are any time and any place propitious for undertaking the transformation by which what is experienced becomes recollection. For example, one can remember very well every detail of an event without being able to say that one recollects it, for memory is the antecedent condition; by means of memory the experience presents itself for the consecration of recollection.

Everyone who can remember is not therefore a poet, but everyone who can recollect has something of a poetic soul in him. This is discernible in a consideration of the difference between the generations. The old person cannot remember, loses memory, and yet the old person is regarded as prophetic and the dying as inspired, and the old person can indeed recollect.[**] The old person cannot remember, but he can recollect, has poetic farsightedness. His gaze is formed like the

[*] goes behind the curtain
[**] *In margin:* and recollection is precisely the old person's consolation

glasses with which one cannot see close at hand but only at a distance. It is the reverse in childhood, which has memory and quickness of apprehension to a high degree but really no recollection. There is an old saying that what one apprehends [*nemme*] in childhood one does not forget [*glemme*] in old age; relative to the subject at hand one could say: What the child remembers the old person recollects. At the same time old age's recollection, like childhood's happiness, is nature's gracious gift that with special solicitude embraces the two helpless[*] periods of life, and the art, on the other hand, requires coming to the assistance of nature or assisting oneself in the other period of life. The old person's weakness is that he cannot remember, that his soul becomes like his eyes, for ordinarily old people cannot see close at hand and use glasses for that; if they must see at a distance, they take off their glasses. The child's imperfection is that it cannot recollect at all; like its eyes, its soul is very nearsighted, very much in the moment, fixed in the moment, but is unable to place anything at a distance.

The art of recollection first of all requires a unity of these two contraries: to be able to remember like a child and to recollect like an old person, to be able to see the finest detail close at hand and immediately be able to place it at a distance. To be able to do this is also a gracious gift, but a gift of the spirit, and is also an act of freedom. But next it calls for a close acquaintance with and a study of contrasting moods. To be able to make this change of scene quickly and accurately and happily, which is more difficult than to be able to live both on land and in the water, to be this amphibian that is both child and old person, is achieved only through much practice. To go on living in an illusion [**] is easy enough, and in this respect the imperfect person has the advantage, but to be able to conjure oneself into an illusion, to allow it to work fully upon one, and yet continually to realize that one is in an illusion— that is a free art that unfortunately people neglect far too

[*] *In margin:* and yet in a certain sense happy
[**] *In margin:* where it is continually dawning and is never day.

much. Memory can be assisted immediately, recollection only reflectively, and therein lies the difference, a difference that manifests itself in all sorts of misunderstandings in life. For example, homesickness is not something remembered but something recollected. If a person wishes merely to remember his birthplace, he can go there and look at it; if he wishes to feel homesickness, he must be absent. But the art is to be able to feel homesickness even though one is at home; this takes proficiency in illusion. Here again memory and recollection are ordinarily confused—indeed, by means of this confusion one can properly study the depth of a person. A man has lived on a farm, his wife may have died there, and he has deeply felt this loss—then he never wants to see that place again. Obviously he fears memory and is not at all afraid of recollection. Such a person is always a prosaist, for otherwise he would especially fear recollection and soon experience that there is nothing that kills recollection better than the very sharpening of memory at the same point. Now, since that man may have lacked the inwardness of soul required in order to recollect, he behaved very properly, for he only cut off memory. If he had had sufficient depth to recollect, he probably would have learned—if to him the pain was bitter, which became gigantic precisely by recollection—to use memory against it. He would then have come to the aid of memory by visiting the same place every day; it would soon have enriched him with a mass of details that would have smothered recollection. Thus one can immediately perceive the ideality in the lovers by paying attention to whether they resort to memory or to recollection in the moment of separation. So it is with the immortality of the soul*, for one is tempted to doubt whether many a person who departs this life can be immortal since he does not take with him a single recollection but leaves behind him only a well-nourished memory.[**]

V
B 155
268

In margin: * And I pledge myself to clip thoughtlessness very lightly in such a way that if I merely fail to mention the phrase a whole congregation Sunday after Sunday will believe that I am speaking edifyingly.

[**] *In margin:* So also with respect to repentance or the actual recollection

If this is how it is, then it is easy to perceive how much practice it takes to have such self-control that with regard to illusion, which is the condition for recollection, one can help oneself in the same way as the pelican.[*] To reflect oneself out of all illusion is not so difficult, but to reflect oneself into an illusion and yet to be aware of it is a great art. It is a matter of understanding counterpoint, of knowing contrasting moods and situations and surroundings, and the happy contrast is not always the direct contrast. It is a matter—if one wishes to dig the treasure of recollection—of having, like that treasure hunter, all the magic formulas at hand, and also, as Lichtenberg says: the treasure[59]—that is, here the power to use it. An erotic situation in which the specific salient feature was forest solitude can at times be best recollected, or embalmed for recollection, in a theater, where the noise and all the surroundings force the soul to recollect; but it is not always thus.[**] It would be a mistake, however, to go out to that lonely place to recollect, for then one nourishes memory. Thus for two opposite reasons two people may wish not to see the same place again: the one fears nourishing memory lest he get something to remember; the other fears that by nourishing memory he will lose recollection.

V
B 155
269

[*] *Penciled in margin:* Themistocles wanted to forget.

[**] *In margin:* If it is defensible to use people as means, it can at times be right to use a new love precisely in order to gain the opportunity to recollect the old.—*Pap.* V B 155 *n.d.*, 1844

From draft; see 9:10:

(which is indefensible with regard to the persons concerned and precarious for oneself.*)

* since it demonstrates that it is not a *true* recollection.—*Pap.* V B 186:1 *n.d.*, 1844

---

of guilt, which is very different from remembering it. The moment a sin is committed, a person remembers every detail, and yet it has a totally different meaning when many years later he recollects it and does not remember it nearly as well.

From draft; see 10:20-27:

To recollect is not identical with to remember.

To recollect is the appropriation of ideality. This is why ordinarily very few want to recollect. One God, one faith, etc. understood in this way: out of one piece, *uno tenore* [uninterrupted].

In order to recollect, the unity of remembering and recollecting is required.

Next something beneficial. Memory can be assisted immediately, recollection not.

In margin: one can recollect only the essential—but neither can one forget what is recollected (Thor's hammer—the battle-seasoned dove).—*Pap.* V B 159 *n.d.*, 1844

From draft; see 10:22-11:12:

V
B 157
272
. . . It is the same with immortality of the soul, for many a person departs this life whose immortality one is tempted to doubt[*] since he does not take with him a single recollection but leaves behind a well-nourished and glutted memory. That is, recollection, like all ideality, makes life strenuous. There is something terrifying in an eternal recollecting; and yet recollection is the true upbuilding and the eternal protest against all Sunday prattle about how every other hour one becomes a new person, who is rejuvenated and falls in love again and becomes a veterinarian after having been a philosopher. This, of course, is the sensual person's craven wish** and is thoughtlessness[†] but nevertheless I am convinced that merely by clipping thoughtlessness and decorating it a little one would Sunday after Sunday be able to preach a whole congregation consolation and solace unto true upbuilding, whereas the person who actually would speak in an upbuilding way would inevitably be regarded as a fanatic and a hothead. It is a dubious matter that Jacobi is the only person in whom I at least have ever read the comment that it is terrible to think that one is immortal—indeed, so terrible that it sometimes seemed as

V
B 157
273

if the thought would drive him out of his mind. Poor Jacobi.[‡]
Sunday guests and those toughened pulpit orators who have
become toughened merely by pounding the pulpit no doubt
find it *gelaüfig* [easy] enough.

[*]*In margin:* Thus one at times finds people who relate recollections of their life in which there is not a trace of recollection.

In margin: **not to become something for oneself and by
oneself, but to become by accident something great in the
world and for the world.

In margin: [†]not to want to be renewed by the spirit but by
life's masquerade costumes that change people.

[‡]he certainly must have had bad nerves!

—*Pap.* V B 157 *n.d.*, 1844

From draft; see 11:8-12:

In recollection a person draws on the eternal, and everyone
is indeed allowed to do this; in this respect everyone is solvent—alas and yet how many are solvent. There are perhaps
few occasions in which fools are made of people or rather they
make fools of themselves as they do when they talk in lofty
tones about never wanting to forget (be it out of love or out
of hate). Anyone who knows anything about human beings
knows very well what this means: one or two weeks, or a
year, or once in a while if the occasion comes from without.—
Pap. V B 158 *n.d.*, 1844

From draft; see 11:8-12:5:

Posito, I assume, that one person[*] had loved only once, a
second had been married seven times—who then had more to
recollect? Or one person had pursued only a single thought,
had always been occupied with the same eternal thought; another had been an author in seven branches of science, even in
astronomy[**]—who then had more to recollect? Or one person had found rest in the one thing needful; another had

countless necessities, all of which had been satisfied—who then had more to recollect?

[*]*In margin:* had spoken day in and day out in general assemblies, had measured his fund of eloquence with even full measures and also with heaped measures, had made his wife happy even by talking at night as if he were in the general assembly—the other was silent

[**]*In margin:* and was interrupted by death just as he was about to begin veterinary science.

—*Pap.* V B 160:8 *n.d.*, 1844

From final draft; see 11:23-24:

Here a few mathematical problems that do not belong under profit sharing according to contribution. (A man loves but once, perhaps even unhappily; another marries seven times, without, however, having time to fall in love; they live the same length of time; here the question of the result is raised or who has more to recollect?)

In margin: One could make such problems an assignment.

—*Pap.* V B 186:4 *n.d.*, 1844

From draft; see 13:2:

. . . . . for remembering is an art and a collector's storeroom, not that kiss of the eternal.

—*Pap.* V B 160:11 *n.d.*, 1844

In margin of draft; see 14:6:

. . . . . or a third person, who certainly understands recollection, but does not want to hear wisdom's counsel, the dejected timorous one who fears the first pain.—*Pap.* V B 160:13 *n.d.*, 1844

From draft; see 14:36-15:3:

Only there is the difference that, insofar as what one recollects (with which by recollecting it one always becomes alone)

is something in which several are interested, one does not have the necessary caution as when it is a secret.—*Pap.* V B 156:2 *n.d.*, 1844

In margin of draft; see 15:10-19:

In other words, the scope of what I have to remember is very little (some speeches and a few minor remarks), but it has been difficult for me to grasp it with recollection.—*Pap.* V B 169:1 *n.d.*, 1844

In margin of draft; see 15:25:

If there perhaps is a difficulty with the correctness of the name the participants had given it—*in vino veritas*—insofar as the truth proclaimed by the speakers certainly was *in vino* but as *veritas* was dubious, my telling of it is at least *veritas*.—*Pap.* V B 169:2 *n.d.*, 1844

From draft; see 15:25-27:

I have not supported memory by once again visiting the places but, on the contrary, with some written notes that have the value of reliability.—*Pap.* V B 169:3 *n.d.*, 1844

From draft; see 16:16-17:

. . . . . so here I have sought to recollect the exuberance of spirit in nature's vegetative lushness.—*Pap.* V B 169:4 *n.d.*, 1844

From draft; see 16:18-19:15:

Preliminary

Albertus and his friend chance to run into each other at the Nook of Eight Paths. The friend has lost his way; Alb. is there "to put an experienced event into the framework of contrast." At first he is irritated by the encounter, but after having more or less spent his rage he is quite happy that the other person has come since now he could wish to have someone to whom he could communicate.

A. When I am alone, all this enthusiasm is meaningful to me, but not as soon as someone is present.—*Pap.* V B 161 *n.d*, 1844

From draft; see 16:18-19:15:

V
B 162
276

Fantastic. sentimental–ironic.

A. Ye gods! I could sooner have expected to see (to be developed at length) a deer or a robber

a pursued innocent or a hermit.

B. Be quiet, by the devil's skin and bones!

A. or to see a black horse (a monster, a dragon) (to be developed).

B. Be quiet—what is this harangue supposed to mean.

A. It is supposed to mean that I will retaliate when someone comes inopportunely to disturb my solitude.

B. Well, that is another matter, this is not the case with me, because you come most opportunely* for me so that I can ask you what this means more precisely out here—in other words, where am I, what is the name of this place, what people live here, how do they make a living, do they raise potatoes, are they pagans, perhaps cannibals.

V
B 162
277

A. Be quiet, by the devil's skin and bones.

B. But if I am disturbing you, I will leave immediately.

A. It's too late; you should have thought of that before.

B. And you should have said it before.

A. This is nonsense.

B. It was indeed nonsense.

A. Let's call it quits.

B. Quits.

A. Yet now it doesn't matter, for after all, you are really opportune for me—the gods have protected my solitude, and now I am qualified to communicate. The only gain that now is already detectable is that I am a bit more talkative than conversational. So be it.

*A. *ille nefasto te posuit die* [he did it on an evil day who planted you][60]—what are you here for

B. in the first place, to use the fortunate circumstance of meeting you here, to ask you: Where am I?—*Pap.* V B 162 *n.d.*, 1844

From draft; see 16:18-19:15:

Albertus—His Friend

V
B 163
277

A. Ye gods! You here! I would sooner have expected to see the snorting steed and the pursued deer, and the noble maiden's waving veil, or to see the robber rushing out of his dark hiding place, or a girl who had escaped from a robber den, or a hermit who had made this place his home for a generation, or Robinson [Crusoe], or Friday, or

FRIEND. Be quiet, by the devil's skin and bones.

A. Or the black horse grazing here, the horse on which Valdemar[61] rides by night at Lake Gurre,[62] or a monster [*Uhyre*] that lives in the forests of the Middle Ages, or Diderich from Berne arriving here when he rode away on a black horse or

FRIEND. Or someone who, although totally mad, is still not half as crazy as you; what is this harangue supposed to mean. Just yesterday I saw you in the city and you were completely sane. Has solitude had such a powerful effect on you?[*]

A. What is it supposed to mean? It is supposed to mean that I want to retaliate against anyone who comes to me inopportunely, for you must have been born on an unlucky day and left the city at an unlucky hour and come here at an unlucky moment—what do you want out here?

V
B 163
278

FRIEND. First and foremost, I want to use the lucky circumstance of meeting you to ask you what this out here means more precisely; in plain Danish, where am I, what is the name of this place, what people live here, whether they are cannibals or are they refined, what do the people live on here, whether

A. Be quiet, by the devil's skin and bones.

FRIEND. whether they raise potatoes or kohlrabi.

[*]*In margin:* just yesterday you were a rational being in the city; have you become stark raving mad in solitude?
—*Pap.* V B 163 *n.d.*, 1844

Addition to Pap. V B 163:

Tone: fantastic sentimental-ironic, to be held at a peak so that Albertus, although still in solitude, is discerned to believe what he almost derisively tosses out in his friend's presence.—*Pap.* V B 164 *n.d.*, 1844

Addition to Pap. V B 163:

N.B. The dialogue form that I at first wanted to give the Preliminary to the story cannot be used; it hinders the development, and finally that friend becomes a superfluous character.—*Pap.* V B 165 *n.d.*, 1844

From draft; see 17:15-20:

V
B 166
278

V
B 166
279

. . . . . then I dare extol my life, for in my nook I am well hidden and superbly concealed. If I do not dare interpret the poet thus and extol my life, I will still extol the nook and extol life as it appears when I regard it from that nook. And seen from a nook, everything is indeed most beautiful, the music to which one listens—ah, when later one is seated in style, one may perhaps sit more comfortably—the beloved at whom one steals a glance—ah, as soon as one is in lawful possession, then, one detects no heartbeat.—*Pap.* V B 166:1 *n.d.*, 1844

From draft; see 17:20:

. . . . . (true it is that when a person is hidden in his sequestered nook he is a totally different person than when there is a single person present).—*Pap.* V B 186:7 *n.d.*, 1844

From draft; see 17:32-33:

. . . . . in that friendly melting together before the king of heaven yet curves its way behind the mountains and arouses the admiration of everything when with its last rays it does not burn but is great as a recollection. Friendly meadow, forest so fair, grass-cool fields![63]—*Pap.* V B 166:2 *n.d.*, 1844

Continuation of Pap. V B 166:2; *see 17:34-19:15:*

Thus I had in all likelihood already been sitting in my nook a long time, for that little insect had already traversed most of the way, and the deer was standing still and looking around, and consequently I had not even moved. The stillness grew, like the shadows; the silence increased every minute and more and more became a magic incantation. I scarcely had the heart to talk with myself softly; the only thing would have been to shout so that echo would have answered. What, indeed, is as intoxicating as stillness; just as someone drinking becomes more intoxicated with every glass he drinks, so the intoxication mounts with every moment the stillness reigns, and what is the richest profusion of the foaming goblet compared with the sea of stillness and infinity! Everything so peaceful, only the quiet meadow, the silent forest, the gentle breeze, and yet I was prepared to see the most fantastic things. Yes, I expected at any moment to see that black steed from Gurre, on whom the king rides at night, grazing here in the soft whispering of evening[*]—then suddenly a noise startles me, and a human form appears nearby; a glance is exchanged, and the battle was decided! It is perhaps a robber, since I was gripped by anxiety; alas, no! It was my best friend, my one and only—who came inopportunely. If a person has been alone for just a few hours and has been secure in his solitude, has reveled in feeling sentient and has forgotten that he belongs to the vocal animals, he easily becomes shy, does not know immediately how to begin worldly chatter where he left off, he is somewhat weakened and is not immediately able to hold his own with co-

V
B 167
279

V
B 167
280

partners in language—that is, human beings from life. Only the person who has to be a co-partner in language and in turn is not a co-partner, only he understands what divine eloquence silence indeed is. My friend Theobald apologized, because very likely recollections charmed me to this place or expectancy bound me to it, and in any case he felt that he had come most inopportunely. I gladly forgave** him, and immediately tried to divert his attention by posing a problem for discussion: that sometimes one could altogether innocently come into a situation where one almost felt guilty because one had disturbed others.

[*]*Penciled in margin:* I thank the gods that no one has surprised me, for then it would have been wasted and his repentance would not help.—*Pap.* V B 167 *n.d.*, 1844

Addition to Pap. V B 167:

V
B 168
280 **and genuinely forgave him, for his offer to go his way again in order to leave me alone betrayed only little knowledge of the chaste association required by silence, which does not tolerate the slightest thing and makes everyone guilty, be he ever so innocent, yes, even the one who through ignorance and inexperience almost makes the situation ridiculous because he cannot comprehend that something is lost or something has happened. It is the same as with the silence of innocence and bashfulness; if it is violated it can become almost insanely comic to imagine a sober-minded yet deferential commonsensicality that wants to explain what bashfulness actually is. But *verloren ist verloren* [lost is lost], and what comforted me was that my friend explained how he actually had arrived on these paths (had lost his way etc.). It was great comfort to me, for it would indeed have been most disastrous[†] if I had encountered a solitary person who was seeking the very same solitary places—an associate in solitude. When I heard his story, I allowed myself a little lie about the reason for my being there and, aided by my knowledge of the locality, led him somewhat afield and thereby to the right road so that he would not very easily find my nook again. My for-

V
B 168
281

giveness was well-intentioned, and I have every reason to forgive, since I myself at times have been just as innocently guilty
of something similar. But here are tasks that are altogether
incommensurable for repentance, even if one may very deeply
feel painfully moved as the guilty one and would want very
much to apologize and beg for forgiveness. And in this purely
esthetic guilt there is something depressing as in the Greek
tragedy. At times I have surprised a pair of lovers this way in
the hiddenness of the forest. Who would be so envious of
others that he did not wish to be a guardian angel on such an
occasion, for only rarely is it the case that a little surprise is of
benefit to the lovers by creating a little situation for them and
tightening the erotic relation. Then I give myself the pleasure
of appearing in the background if I suspect any such thing, for
then I do indeed serve Eros, and the lovers really ought to
thank me, even if it is impossible for them to dispel the illusion that I am a chicaner. It is conceivable that in precisely this
manner a pair of lovers could owe someone a great deal, although they would naturally hate and loathe that person, and
this is precisely the secret that would make them snuggle their
heads closer together more erotically—but this secret naturally could never become apparent to them. —But if this is
not the case with the lovers, how unhappy I feel when by taking them by surprise I do a disfavor I can never rectify. Then
I could wish that I were like a bird that hovers voluptuously
above the heads of the lovers, to be the bird whose cry is fate-
ful for the lovers, the lark that soars jubilantly, the wren, seductive for the lovers to watch, that darts among the bushes;
[I could wish] that I were the blending that makes everything
languorous, the distant clattering of a carriage suggesting that
the others are now going away and leaving the lovers alone
(as in *D. G.* the most solitary scene is not that way because
Zerlina *is* alone but because she *becomes* alone on the stage; we
hear the disappearing of the chorus, and its distant fading
away begins Zerlina's little part[64]—this is a purely musical situation that no other power can portray). [I could wish] to be
like the disappearing of the mother, the last to bid the bride
farewell, like the nature-solitude that tempts erotic love, like

V
B 168
282

the murmuring that tightens the cord of erotic love; like the echo that shows that one is in a remote place, like the coolness of the evening that fans the lovers' intimacy.—

I was out here in order to place something experienced in the frame of the contrast (the noisy evening party—and nature's soft, quiet peace—not even night would have been such a sharp contrast, because this is already fantastic, and consequently of the same potency, while the fantastic here results from the clash).

In margin: † second to that is to become the object of an insane man's fixed idea*

—*Pap.* V B 168 *n.d.*, 1844

* or of a hysterical female's

From draft; see 17:34-19:15:

V
B 171:1
284

An apology from the one who disturbs and causes surprise and interruption is of little benefit.* One is willing enough to forgive him; he is innocent and yet he becomes guilty. How jealous solitude is of itself, how strange human life, that one in this way can become guilty purely esthetically, feel all the pain of guilt and yet be unable to repent, and yet be innocent. I have often thought about this, that I myself should never be guilty of this toward others, and yet one can never be secure or know that one is secure. How ashamed one can be there with a gnawing bitterness in one's soul when one happens to disturb others in this way. The task is altogether incommensurable for repentance; one would most willingly beg for forgiveness. The person from whom one begs it is willing, and yet he cannot actually stop being angry at one! Only rarely can surprise be of benefit, as if a pair of lovers who have sought the hiddenness of the forest do not have sufficient

In margin: *as little as his proposal to leave the solitary one to himself again betrays familiarity with the chaste association that silence requires, since his commonsensicality (which is ignorance of the danger) only makes the situation ludicrous, just as when the silence of innocence and modesty are violated, commonsensicality (which is ignorance of the danger and has not understood the difficulty before it wants to replace it) in its sober-minded knowledge quite estimably explains what modesty actually is. No! *Hin ist hin, verloren ist verloren* [What is gone is gone, what is lost is lost].

power to create a situation but need to have the erotic relation
tightened a little. If I knew this in advance, then I would give
myself the pleasure of appearing in the background, for then
if I suspect any such thing I do indeed serve Eros and the lovers really ought to thank me, even if it is impossible for them
to dispel the illusion that I am an intriguer. It is conceivable
that in precisely this manner a pair of lovers could owe someone a great deal, although they would naturally hate and
loathe that person, and this is precisely the secret that would
make them snuggle their heads closer together and more erotically. —Yet this is seldom the case, and if it is not, how unhappy I can feel by surprising them in this way; for who
would not prefer to be erotic love's guardian angel? Then I
could wish that I were like a bird that hovers voluptuously
above the heads of the lovers, to be the bird whose cry is fate-
ful for the lovers, the lark that soars jubilantly, the wren, seductive for the lovers to watch, that darts among the
bushes;[*] [I could wish] to be like the disappearing of the
mother when she is the last one in the bridal house, like the
nature solitude that tempts erotic love, like the murmuring
that tightens the cord of erotic love, like the echo that shows
that one is in a remote place, like the coolness of the evening
that fans the lovers' intimacy, like the distant clattering of a
carriage suggesting that the others are now going away and
leaving the lovers alone. Never is one so solitary as when one
hears the others going away. The most solitary of situations
is Zerlina's in *Don Giovanni*; she *is* not alone—no, she *becomes*
alone; we hear the disappearing of the chorus, and the solitude
becomes audible in the distant fading away of this sound and
solitude comes into existence as a musical situation, something only music and no other power is capable of expressing
in this way.

[*]*In margin:* to be like the summer humming that assures
one that all existence is only rapture and festivity *without work*
and like God without toil.

and in relation to solitude the point is for every third person
(for he is also a third person to the one who is alone) to understand the art of removing himself.—*Pap.* V B 171:1 *n.d.*,
1844

V
B 171:1
285

From sketch; see 20:1-33, 26:9-14:

V
B 172:1
285

It was in the month of August about nine o'clock in the evening that the participants gathered for that banquet. The date I have forgotten, just as I generally never think of noting the date or am never able to retain it when an impression over-whelms me. But the mood I can recollect, and insofar as the weather and other such things influence mood, I recollect it so

V
B 172:1
286

clearly that I inhale the same fragrance (for nothing is recollected as well as "the scent of flowers and old melodies"[65]) and become wholly contemporary with my self. The participants were seven in number: Johannes, nicknamed the Seducer; Victor Eremita; Constantin Constantius, and in addition three others, whose names I did not learn since I did not hear them called by name at all but only by an epithet: Recollection's Unhappy Lover, the Fashion Designer, the Young Man.[66] As far as I know, it was Constantin who was at the head of it and prepared the invitations to this banquet, the motto of which was: *in vino veritas* [in wine truth], because not one word was to be spoken except *in vino*, and not one truth except as it is *in vino*, so that wine would be a defense for truth and truth would be a defense for wine.—*Pap.* V B 172:1 *n.d.*, 1844

From draft; see 20:24-25:

He looked like a Ganymede,[67] but one forgot it again.— *Pap.* V B 187:1 *n.d.*, 1844

From draft; see 22:14-18:

. . . . . at him, for I believed that he actually was mad. Yet it is impossible to get a total impression of him, for he has bewitched himself, by his own will has conjured himself into a form out of which there still breaks forth a reflection. He has wanted to express a contrast but has selected it too close at hand; it would have been easier to effect a Pierrot, for example.

In margin: charmed himself
                                    —*Pap.* V B 187:4 *n.d.*, 1844

From draft; see 23:2-6:

Everything must be new, and the moment they rose from the table the proper number of workmen would have been summoned, a demolition crew, in order not to leave a splinter behind—yes, even while they drank the last glass it would be all right to hear the workmen in the next room taking out their tools and making a noise and knocking about like the Commendatore.[68]— *Pap.* V B 187:5 *n.d.*, 1844

From draft; see 23:12:

. . . . . for someone, as if there were any actuality and as if everything were not a product of the imagination, as if there were any enthusiasm to compare with the enthusiasm of demolition.—*Pap.* V B 187:6 *n.d.*, 1844

From draft; see 24:19-22:

. . . . . and because I thank Grundtvig for prostituting ladies for all eternity by his folk-high-school jargon [*Brage-Snak*] and his Ale-Nordic[69] impropriety.—*Pap.* V B 187:8 *n.d.*, 1844

From draft; see 24:26-37:

This is why those light ethereal lunches or afternoon repasts out in the country are so charming and women absolutely belong there. The Englishman is no doubt right in having the women go away when they have eaten but not right in beginning with them. There ought to be a completeness to it that promptly manifests itself in the beginning. Banquets such as are given now with men and women are just as far from poetry and idea as a four-seater wagonette is from the ideal.— *Pap.* V B 187:9 *n.d.*, 1844

From draft; see 25:31-38:

Here we encounter a difficulty, for I certainly can be prevailed upon to eat together with one single woman and have a variety of dishes but then eat only a little, and this impression I want to have from the beginning. At a banquet the impression I want to have is that hearty eating is the thing to do. Indeed, on the basis of all these reasons, which I admittedly have not set forth as reasons but which one can shape into reasons just as logic can shape all our talking into judgments and conclusions, on the basis of all these reasons, which the man of experience can easily shape into reasons against the matter, I believe that a banquet is a *pium desiderium* [pious wish], and in this respect I am so far from speaking with my friend Constantin about repetition that I believe it cannot be done the first time.

In margin: I insist upon table music
—*Pap.* V B 187:11 *n.d.*, 1844

From draft; see 26:15-16:

The place where they assembled was in Ordrup,[70] where Constantin in advance had arranged for some changes to be made in the great salon and had had a small adjoining room prepared for an orchestra.—*Pap.* V B 172:3 *n.d.*, 1844

From draft; see 27:21-28:28:

At precisely eleven o'clock the doors of a private room were opened and they entered the dining room. Never have I seen a hall more splendidly lighted—behind each table setting stood a waiter—as they entered, the table music from *D. G.*[71] began. There was no one who was not impressed. Johannes the Seducer became inflamed as by a challenge. —But a shudder went visibly through V. Eremita's soul; his body almost trembled and, beside himself, while the infirmity of his body or its languorous weakness seemed to struggle with the power of his voice, he cried out: You festive tones, you to whom my soul belongs, even more than Elvira to Don Giovanni! You seductive voice of delight and enjoyment and pleasure and the moment, which tore me like an Elvira[72] out of the solitude of a quiet monastic life to make me eternally unhappy, eternally running after you, without being able to move you, even if I sacrificed honor and family and friends: "Everything is a gift of love."[73] Here Constantin interrupted him and reminded him that it was against the rules, and now everyone took his place.—*Pap.* V B 172:7 *n.d.*, 1844

From draft; see 28:36-31:15:

. . . One rarely hears about this these days when people of course understand the matter better, for they are festive when the host wants them to be and solemn when the pastor tells them to be.

V B 187:13 326

They took their places at the table, and when V. E. noticed a centerpiece to which there was attached a piece of paper on which was written: This is a fountain, he nodded to Constantin and declared that now he was perfectly able to eat a hundred courses and drink cape wine, moreover, that the only way this could be done was beside a fountain.

The orchestra paused a moment, then Constantin proposed that they recall that jolly time with which they certainly had not been quite contemporary but which nevertheless had the charm of a fancied recollection for them: the period of the drinking song. Thereupon they sang: My brimming glass and the lusty sound of song. Nor did this proposal fail in its effect, for the contradiction that such a company sang that drinking song, in which men and women sat together, produced an altogether fantastic effect, which put an end to whatever remained of that almost solemn festivity. The Fashion Designer became so excited that he rose from the table, glass in hand, and began a speech thus: When one day I climb into the bridal bed. He was interrupted, for Constantin declared that in order to prevent the speeches from fluttering vaguely about no one

V B 187:13 372

was to speak before they had agreed to a limitation. In his opinion, they should eat and drink first and then give speeches. His first condition was that no one was to speak before he had drunk so much that he could detect in himself that he was in the power of wine.[*] Therefore before speaking each one was to declare solemnly on his honor that he was in this condition. A quantity could not be prescribed since the saturation capacity could vary, no one was to be intoxicated but was to be in that state of conflict. As for the content of the speech, he proposed to carry out what they had quite often talked about, that each one give a speech on Eros. Yet no one was to tell a love story but presumably in his view of the erotic suggest it. . . .

V
B 187:13
328

. . . These speeches I have now recorded, and I do not conceal that they were not delivered thus. If they had been delivered as drawn up, they certainly would have failed in their effect, but this is their content.

. . . He [the Young Man] was not as beautiful as before the meal, not as noble, but when he began to speak his words were more impetuous and precipitous than usual.

[*]*In margin:* not to be intoxicated but only be in the condition in which one says what one otherwise is not inclined to say, except that the coherence of thought needs to be interrupted continually by the hiccup of whimsical impulse.—*Pap.* V B 187:13 *n.d.*, 1844

From sketch; see 30:4-11:

Before they began to eat, Constantin proposed that they should sing a drinking song.

Constantin knew very well what he was doing, for this idea brought a wildness into the company, as if they were already intoxicated. With tremendous passion they sang: My brimming glass and the lusty sound of song. Nor is it easy to imagine a crazier idea on the part of such a company than to want to revive the memory of the period of the drinking song; its conviviality and sober-mindedness created an utterly fantastic background—especially when the Young Man proposed to sing: When one day I climb into the bridal bed, falderi, faldera.—*Pap.* V B 172:12 *n.d.*, 1844

From draft; see 30:16-24:

The second condition was that no one would be allowed to speak before he had drunk so much that he could detect in himself that he was intoxicated, and before he had permission to speak he must declare it on his honor. The conditions could not be made more detailed, for the necessary quantum could of course vary, and everyone could choose the wine he wanted. For that purpose, a list of wines lay at every place setting—*Pap.* V B 172:11 *n.d.*, 1844

From sketch; see 30:36-31:3:

Thereupon Constantin announced that they were to speak for or against Eros and in such a way that each one had a love story in mind, yet did not tell it, but in his view of woman intimated it—*Pap.* V B 172:10 *n.d.*, 1844

From draft; see 33:16-19:

. . . . . they do not go back to the first question. They assume that to fall in love belongs to being human as bleating belongs to being a sheep, and they are now thinking about finding someone with whom to bleat; but this, of course, is not thinking about erotic love but is assuming it, and at most is being intent on acquiring a beloved for oneself.—*Pap.* V B 175:2 *n.d.*, 1844

From draft; see 33:29:

That means, more I do not say, erotic love always becomes ludicrous to a third party.—*Pap.* V B 175:3 *n.d.*, 1844

From draft; see 34:2-13:

This perhaps seems strange to many, but it is not, not for the person who actually has understood what it is to doubt, not to speak of the person who has doubted everything. If reflection is to make something out of it, nothing immediate must be left standing anywhere.—*Pap.* V B 175:4 *n.d.*, 1844

From draft; see 35:21-36:37:

V
B 175:6
298

And the person who listens to the lovers' talk in order to hear what it is they are actually talking about is bound to lose his mind, for finally, after they have said something he is fairly able to understand, all their talk ends up with their saying that they nevertheless do not actually love for this reason, but that there is something inexplicable, something they cannot say. Yet this is not so strange, for when one observes people, there is something very strange. There would be something alarming about it if time and again people dropped dead all around and no one knew from what. But this is exactly what happens with erotic love. Today one talks with a person and can understand him fairly well, tomorrow he begins to look strange—he has fallen in love. But in a large city there is, of course, an overabundance of women; consequently the erotic cannot ordinarily be explained by the relationship between the masculine and the feminine. Sometimes a man can go on for many years before he finally one day begins to display all the symptoms of having fallen in love. Is it not comic that what is supposed to enhance and explain everything ends up in perfect confusion.

V
B 175:6
299

In margin: The one believes that it is the beloved's *teretes sures* [shapely legs],[74] the other that it is her husband's handlebar mustache, and a third speaks grandiloquently about her whole lovable nature, and then when he has brought his discourse to the highest peak he suddenly slips in the word "inexplicable," and this is supposed to please the beloved more than everything else. Me it does not please, for I do not understand one word, and understand only that the person who is supposed to explain something does not explain it and makes the whole thing dubious by not saying straightway that it is the inexplicable, for what, indeed, was everything else he said if it was not an explanation.—*Pap.* V B 175:6 *n.d.*, 1844

From draft; see 40:18-22:

It lacked only that there be a complete carrying through of what in part can be carried through, that the one lover continually finds the other ludicrous. But that the one laughs at the other when they both are in love is to me disgusting and is a pride I cannot endure, for why should the one person by virtue of his difference qua human being delude himself in this way into thinking himself to be more than human. I do not approve of this.—*Pap.* V B 175:9 *n.d.*, 1844

From draft; see 42:3-10:

. . . . . fencing positions and those strange modes of expression. I assume that I can understand that two souls want to belong to each other for all eternity; I can comprehend that when it is brought to the point of certainty he vents his feelings in words or that in his joy he goes and hangs himself because he is certain that they belong to each other for all eternity, but I do not comprehend why it occurs to them to express it in a kiss or occurs to them that a kiss is supposed to prove something. It is comic that erotic love in its highest flight ends, just like Saft, in the pantry, or in an even more dubious place—*Pap.* V B 175:11 *n.d.*, 1844

From sketch; see 42:11-43:5:

[*Penciled:* 1]
(c) the comic in the lovers' enjoying themselves in love's desire, since they are merely serving life and the race by propagation, for propagation, after all, is precisely the triumph of species over the individuals that annihilates the individuals,

and yet the news travels around the country that our mother has had a child.—*Pap.* V B 174:13 *n.d.*, 1844

From sketch; see 43:30-44:4:

[*Penciled:* 2]
(b) the comic in the enormous consequence erotic love engenders: to have children, which has no analogies whatsoever in the consequences of other pleasures (drinking oneself to intoxication one evening or eating too much). But such an enormous consequence—one does not know where it comes from or even know with certainty whether it does come—is, after all, neither one thing nor another.—*Pap.* V B 174:12 *n.d.*, 1844

From sketch; see 44:4-13:

(f) *omne animal post coitum triste* [every animal is sad after coitus], but that implies that there must have been something comic in the movement beforehand, for they always succeed each other this way.
In margin: that *tristitia* [sloth, dejection] which the initiates place next when the lovers *diversi abeunt* [depart their separate ways], *coeuntes* [coming together] no more.
—*Pap.* V B 174:18 *n.d.*, 1844

From draft; see 44:5:

that a stagnant state sets in.*
In margin: *or that a *tristitia* sets in, which suggests that desire is comic, even if for a reason other than erotic love, because that *tristitia* which sets in also in relation to erotic love is most compounded, for the initiates say this: *neque diversi abeunt amantes vero* [nor do they depart their separate ways, loving truly].—*Pap.* V B 175:12 *n.d.*, 1844

From sketch; see 44:14-22:

(d) The comic in the fact that erotic love's desire is an exertion, consequently what follows presumably must be the essential desire, that is, to have children (the highest desire of that love is so significant to the lovers that accordingly they assume new names, and the man is called father and the woman mother).—*Pap.* V B 174:14 *n.d.*, 1844

From sketch; see 44:26-45:33, 45:30:

(e) To be a father is the strangest thing of all, and if a man does not according to custom want to be a father and a noble father,* he would then see the ridiculousness in his position; either it has eternal significance** that he is the child's father, which is nonsense, or it has only an animal significance. Therefore, one can in truth say what Magdelone somewhere in Holberg says in a somewhat different sense to Jeronymus when he refers to being the child's father: It is delusion.[75]— *Pap.* V B 174:15 *n.d.*, 1844

Addition to Pap. V B 174:15:

. . . . . *it is said that the greatest benefaction a man can do for another is to be his father—and yet the father gratified his own desire.

I do not wish to abolish piety, far from it. I can understand it, it contains no contradiction, but I want to think myself into this instance and have clarity.—*Pap.* V B 174:16 *n.d.*, 1844

V
B 174:16
296

V
B 174:16
297

In margin of Pap. V B 174:15:

. . . . . **but if it has this, then placing a child into the world and giving him life is the most terrible thing, far more terrible than killing a person.—*Pap.* V B 174:17 *n.d.*, 1844

From sketch; see 45:34-47:2:

For these reasons I have kept myself out of erotic love. Suppose that in the decisive moment the erotic appeared to me as the comic and I started to laugh; then I would certainly have offended the girl, which I do not wish to do at all if she did not understand that the erotic is the comic. If she understood this, the erotic understanding would be rendered impossible, and moreover it would displease me that the beloved had acquired foreknowledge to this degree. With regard to the erotic, it is preferable to take them without foreknowledge.—*Pap.* V B 174:19 *n.d.*, 1844

From sketch; see 47:26:

No. 2

Constantin Constantius's [*changed from:* Victor Eremita's] speech.

—*Pap.* V B 176:1 *n.d.*, 1844

From sketch; see 49:1-21:

A girl's being can be disintegrated in silly chatter within a half hour; therefore a person must never become entirely involved with her, lest he become disgusting to himself by seeing his own being, which one has of course surrendered in love when it is total, go the same way. To catch oneself in silliness, that the substance of one's whole life was silliness, must be the most disgusting of all, enough to lose one's mind over, much more than to be a robber and murderer (of which one can repent).—*Pap.* V B 176:5 *n.d.*, 1844

From sketch; see 49:31-51:14:

V
B 176:6
301

Nor can one fight with a girl. One does not have the heart to use all one's strength (compassion), and what triumph [is there] in being victorious over a woman. On the other side, if she sees her opportunity, she runs off with the victory—always compassion, one cannot hate, cannot rage, cannot set passions in motion—and yet one is made much more of a fool by talking with her.—*Pap.* V B 176:6 *n.d.*, 1844

V
B 176:6
302

Deleted from sketch; see 51:15-53:10:

V
B 178:6
306

What follows now from this, that man is indebted not to woman for anything but only to his own ideality. Therefore marry, but in a particular way. Every woman by nature has a born genius for all nonsense; one develops this to the point of virtuosity, and then the joke is priceless. Just as others practice balancing a cane on the nose or handling a glass or dancing among eggs, so one has one's amusement from being married. One continually believes one's wife, does what she wants, but since a woman is never transparent to herself, sheer confusion results, which is not attained by saying anything contrary to her, for that helps her. This marriage, that is, this amusement, this game, produces conversations no other game produces.—*Pap.* V B 178:6 *n.d.*, 1844

V
B 178:6
307

From draft; see 52:28-53:28:

In the erotic sense, one believes her absolutely; in the intellectual sense, one credits her with everything. Socrates should have done that with Xanthippe instead of squabbling with her, for what benefit did he have from, as he himself says, practicing on her like a riding master, in comparison with this *himmelhoch jauchende* [shouting-to-the-skies-with-delight] amusement.

So much is being said and written about feminine faithfulness, and about her unfaithfulness. Yet why has there never been willingness to see it in the right light? What new and daring discoveries are not owed to a woman in this respect. Only one must not regard her [*deleted:* ethically].[*] That is incorrect and thus the amusement is left out. No, just make token gestures continually in this direction, and then see what comes of it. Great and incomprehensible is feminine faithfulness, but especially when it is declined. This I have expressed and it is the law.

[*]*Penciled in margin:* esthetically.

—*Pap.* V B 177:3 *n.d.*, 1844

From sketch; see 53:23-26:

"Great is feminine faithfulness, especially when it is declined."—*Pap.* V B 176:4 *n.d.*, 1844

From sketch; see 53:30-55:27:

Response to the Young Man. One sees that it is a young man who has spoken; inexperienced, he mentions such an unfaithfulness, that a girl who had pledged her troth to a man deceived him. Alas, I know something much stranger, a girl who had begged a man to remain faithful to her. He did so, although with much sacrifice on his part, and when he came home after being abroad for a year, she was already far gone, if not *by* another then with another. On this occasion, he resolved to celebrate a festival day in her honor every month, on which day he sang this verse:

> Cheers for me and you, I say
> The day will never be forgotten
> No, cheers for me and you, I say
> The day will never be forgotten.

—*Pap.* V B 176:3 *n.d.*, 1844

In margin of sketch; see 53:32-55:27:

see the Young Man's speech as it is in the sketch; some of this on the first page [*Pap.* V B 174:4] is suitable* for him.—*Pap.* V B 176:2 *n.d.*, 1844

Addition to Pap. V B 176:2:

*my explanation of the contradiction in life that our Young Man has discovered is that to place [*essentially the same as Pap.* V B 174:4]. . . .

It is good for the girls that they are not to be buried every time they die; it would be very expensive.—*Pap.* V B 176:7 *n.d.*, 1844

From sketch; see 53:32-55:9:

[*]My only explanation is this, to place the first love in connection with that idea that unhappy love is certain death—and

then it is all right. As soon as the erotic relation ceases, one dies of unhappy love; fourteen days later one falls in love again, and the second love is not some defective reprint but is the first, as is natural, since by having died one awakens to a new life. Therefore, if the lovers expressed themselves correctly, with their help everything would be confused. For example, I knew a man who once made a casual remark about his departed first love. I was moved by the idea, but see, the man was speaking correctly. Some time later, in his company, I meet on the street a gentleman and a lady with whom I had become acquainted just the day before. I greet them, and since I seem to detect on his face that he also knew them, I ask him about it, and he answers: Oh, yes, very well, indeed, intimately, for it was my late departed. What late departed one, I ask. My late departed first love. Alas, it was indeed a sad story; she took her death of grief and unhappy love, and thereupon she took a husband and now compels me to speak like Bollingbrocke: When my wife was living, it was then that I lived with my wife.[76]

V
B 174:4
294

[*]*Penciled in margin:* Constantin Const.

—*Pap.* V B 174:4 *n.d.,* 1844

From draft; see 56:10:

. . . . . from which one in fairness dares to conclude that they are worth thanking God for. Yet other times, other customs—gratitude to the gods does not seem to be in fashion.— *Pap.* V B 179:1 *n.d.,* 1844

From sketch; see 56:6-60:3:

Plato, as we know, thanks the gods for four things—an older philosopher had already thanked them for three; it increases. I go back further and thank them for one, but all the more fervently, that I became man and not woman. Woman is basically made a fool of in life; she is never allowed to mean anything on her own but only through her relationship. As a

V
B 178:8
307

V
B 178:8
308

child the girl is esteemed less than the boy; future care of the girl occupies the parents very early and worries them. She grows up, and, see, now a rich suitor casts his eyes on her. Presto—the sweet Camilla becomes in the parents' eyes a most precious child (a blatant lie; it is a matter of the son-in-law and his money). He wooes her and for fourteen days of billing and cooing he buys a lifetime of slavery. This whole wooing business in particular is an unparalleled joke on her. Even the crudest male, even the public executioner, when he lays down his *fasces* in order to go a-wooing, even he makes his approach with a certain ingratiation and obsequiousness— and even the most cultured man is absolutely changed as soon as he becomes a married man.[77] If I were a woman I would first and foremost petition that all wooing be abolished. I would say to the man: If you want me, then take me. I will bear your children. I will manage your house. I know that I am the weaker sex, but you have not made me that; I take that humbly from God's hand. But all wooing disgusts me; it is a lie—you may rather hit me. —Eventually she dies and now the husband becomes sentimental and consoles himself with the reunion. But I hope that by that time she will have perceived herself differently and will receive him most kindly in a better world. For this blessed reunion the man prepares himself by taking a new wife, even if he still believes that a second marriage cannot be as beautiful as the first, but only a reprint. In olden days, one believed that immortality was proved by erotic love, somewhat like this: these two love each other for all eternity, ergo, there ought to be an eternity; nowadays one proves it by having loved very frequently, for is not a perfectibility such as this proof of an immortal spirit!

If we leave this bourgeois world in order to enter the world of poetry and fiction, then a fool is once again made of woman. She is supposed to be, so it is claimed, the one who inspires. How many amorous flutists have played this theme, and how many shepherdesses have listened to it. She inspires the warrior; she rewards him with her love. But if one thinks about that more carefully, one perceives that unhappy love in particular makes the bravest warrior, and if she does it once,

then possession is the knight's very downfall, for now he acquires something else entirely to think about—ergo, it is in a
very figurative sense that she does it. —She inspires the poet.
She? Which she? The beloved, quite right, but not the beloved
he won as his wife, by no means. Is there one single example
of a happy love that has made a man a poet? So it is a lie and
falsehood, and it is only the man's ideality that is aroused by
the lies. If he had won the beloved, then good night, good
peaceful night, Mr. Married Peter.[78] Thus everywhere she is
the object of ridicule. No man has ever become a poet because
of a woman. It happens in two ways, either by loving only
one, whom he does not win, or by loving many, but *summa
summarum* [sum of sums, in the long run] loving many is indeed also an unhappy love, for the point in all happy love is
that there is only one.—*Pap* V B 178:8 *n.d.*, 1844

V
B 178:8
309

From sketch; see 56:26-30:

Women and slaves were always placed in [the same] category by the Greeks.—*Pap.* V B 178:4 *n.d.*, 1844

Deleted from final copy; see 57:18:

Richard III was, as he himself says, *en[t]stellt, verwahrlost
von der tückischen Natur* [deformed, unfinished by dissembling
nature].[79]—*Pap.* VI B 8:5 *n.d.*, 1844

Deleted from final copy; see 57:26:

Richard's fury over being a love-smitten specimen of a human being would probably have been even more terrible if it
were conceivable that with a higher reflection he could catch
himself having to be helped from the frying pan into the fire.
—*In the sense of Richard III

In margin: *In the sense of a deformed person

—*Pap.* VI B 8:6 *n.d.*, 1844

From sketch; see 59:6-7:

V
B 179:3
309

It is also my opinion that ideality enters into life by way of women, and to that extent I am far from agreeing with Con-

V
B 179:3
310

stantin that she is a joke. What is man without woman? It is altogether correct; but as soon as this high-sounding talk is understood more closely, then it goes just like the transition from Juliane to Mrs. Petersen.—*Pap.* V B 179:3 *n.d.*, 1844

From sketch; see 59:19-22:

. . . It is very wisely arranged by life that a man shall not owe one person everything.—*Pap.* V B 178:7 *n.d.*, 1844

From sketch; see 60:34-61:21:

The true ideality and true verification in the proof again rest first in unhappy love.—*Pap.* V B 179:4 *n.d.*, 1844

From draft; see 61:32-62:2:

The view once again begins to be so grandiloquent, as if she were even capable of becoming more guilty than the man, and in the next moment ends with one's saying to her or to oneself about her: Don't trouble yourself about it, dear child; you certainly have been forgiven for it long ago.—*Pap.* V B 179:5 *n.d.*, 1844

From draft; see 62:15-64:26:

V
B 179:6
310

Now if this is the way it is with woman, what position to her is the man to take? In my opinion, he is to stay on the outside completely and attend to saving his soul from such meaninglessness, which ultimately enervates his strength. A man who has much to do with women eventually, just like her, in an imaginary moment becomes something extraordinary and in actuality nothing. Wherever woman is involved, there is this unavoidable hiatus, a hiatus that begins with

opening the mouth so wide that it is impossible to speak because of sheer overexcitement and when one finally shuts
one's mouth ends in finding that basically it is not worth talking about. So it is with marriage—which especially in our day
begins with a hodgepodge[*] of sacred and secular, of pagan
and Christian, bourgeois grandiloquence, so one can make
neither head nor tail of whether it is that inexplicable eroticism, that *Wahlverwandtschaft* [elective affinity] between like-
minded souls, or it is duty or it is a partnership or an expediency in life or the custom in certain countries, whether one
is to listen to the tunes of the cither in the evening or to organ
music or to the admonishing words, the edifying discourse,
of the clergyman or of the police inspector.

[*]*In margin*: just as the turtle has a taste of everything possible

V
B 179:6
311

—*Pap.* V B 179:6 *n.d.*, 1844

From draft; see 63:10-14:

If, however, she remains faithful, then good night, Ole and
Ideality.—*Pap.* V B 180:1 *n.d.*, 1844

From draft; see 63:18:

. . . . . only death is more decisive.—*Pap.* V B 181:2 *n.d.*,
1844

From draft; see 64:1-3:

. . . . . passage that is unlike anything else, for not even
death can be compared, since as simple it no doubt is terrible
but is not complex. Consequently such a composite passage—
Pap. V B 181:3 *n.d.*, 1844

From draft; see 64:21-26:

As he sees it afterwards, he gradually sees exactly the opposite, and in the course of two weeks one can, by observing

him and his speech, receive the opposite explanations, for his life lacks unity.

Just as I have thanked the gods that I became man and not woman, so let us also thank the gods that none of us has been so infatuated with any woman that he has received employment for life, a lifetime employment of continually having to think afterwards.—*Pap.* V B 181:4 *n.d.*, 1844

From sketch; see 64:27-65:14:

Victor Eremita's Speech

Lines. After all, a seducer has always been a difficult subject for me. Certainly no one has ever begun with wanting to be a seducer,* but it is a man who has been unable to decide to belong to one girl for his whole life. He has had sufficient ideality to grasp this thought but not to go through with it. Thus a seducer is also an unhappy lover, and the first love's yield is what he plows under, and this plowing under nourishes his autumn affair. But in this way a seducer is the most dependent.—*Pap.* V B 178:1 *n.d.*, 1844

In margin of Pap. V B 178:1:

. . . . . *no more than a girl at first wants to let herself be seduced. Yet we have an example (police inspector Götsche,[80] a "freeborn," who as a maiden became a public prostitute, robbed the man, and he reported the theft but also believed that she could not be a public prostitute since she was a maiden).—*Pap.* V B 178:3 *n.d*, 1844

From sketch; see 64:27-65:14:

To be a benedict—is rubbish; to be a seducer is also rubbish; but to be an exceptional husband and on the quiet seduce every girl—seemingly to be a seducer and yet hide all the ardor of romance in his soul—this is the task. To me this reduplication is necessary. I have difficulty articulating myself. This reduplication is like the embellishment in the Slavic languages. For this reason no immediate subjectivity can understand me or articulate me. For this reason I cannot marry, for my wife cannot articulate me. (After all, every man in his youth has felt this urge for reduplication, but then they become cowardly.)—*Pap.*   V   B   178:5   *n.d.*, 1844

From sketch; see 65:5-27:

But this reduplication shows that his relationship to woman is not something essential but that through her he merely relates to himself. A reduplication such as that is like the embellishment in the words of several languages, it makes it impossible for woman to articulate him. An immediate subjectivity cannot understand or articulate this reflectiveness in which man's ideality is actually first posited.

But even conceived in this way, the relationship to woman in one way or another still remains a concession, for even if a concession is revoked by being drawn up into a second power it is nevertheless a concession in the first power. Therefore, what was my first word is my final word, that I thank the gods I became a man and not a woman.

If a woman can do the same as the man, then there can still be no relationship between them, no more than an erotic relationship between man and man, and for her to be regarded as man would of course be unbeautiful.

—*Pap.* V B 179:7 *n.d.*, 1844

From sketch; see 65:25-67:9:

The Fashion Designer

If anyone knows woman, then it is I; I know her from her advantageous side: adornment, and what else is she able to do or for what else does she have any sense than for adorning herself. see journal, p. 71 [*Pap.* IV A 135-139].[81]

—*Pap.* V B 182:1 *n.d.*, 1844

From sketch; see 66:10-15:

Indeed, if fashion meant nothing more than that a woman in the concupiscence of lust throws off everything, that would still be something. But that is not the way it is. Fashion is not open sensuality; it is not tolerated dissipation; it is authorized propriety. This, its pettiness, is what is really so loathsome about it. In a country where Jews are not tolerated, one at times sees a Jew roaming around and hawking; in the same way fashion's sneaking sensuality fears morality's commandment and therefore makes no big business deals, nothing that could intimidate, but in very small, almost microscopic parts (for the feminine reflection is infinite) one hawks the forbidden but in such a retail way that no devil can check on it. . . . —*Pap.* V B 182:5 *n.d.*, 1844

From sketch; see 68:13-70:12:

V
B 182:7
314

. . . See, there she stands; now she pushes her lips aprior- ally, then gesticulates aposteriorally; now she wriggles her hips, then she lisps with her tongue and then with her feet; now she sinks casually into an upholstered armchair while I obsequiously hand her a flacon, recommend a new kind of perfume to her, and say to her that she is in fashion. In every- thing, everything, every minute she wants to be in fashion. Fashion, *pro dii immortales* [ye immortal gods], what is woman when she is not in fashion, and what is woman when she is in fashion! Say to her when she blissfully sinks to your breast and lisps incomprehensibly, "Yours forever," and hides her face in your bosom, say, "Sweet Katy, your hairdo is in style"— and everything is forgotten.[*] From my boutique the glad gospel [*essentially the same as 69:26-35*] I put everything in or- der,** and when she looks crazier than someone who has es- caped from the loony bin, indeed, as crazy as someone who could not even be admitted there, then I escort her out, hurry past her, open the door of my boutique, bow adoringly before her, cross my arms, allow myself to throw her an admiring kiss.

V
B 182:7
315

[*]I am the most dangerous man in the kingdom.
**[*See last line of Pap.* V B 182:8]
                                        —*Pap.* V B 182:7 *n.d.*, 1844

From sketch; see 68:24-37:

Say to her as she adoringly falls on your breast, "Dear Catherine, one of your curls is falling down"—and then she has forgotten everything over that. Say to her when she kneels before God that her shawl has fallen down too far (the woman Diogenes saw, who lay worshiping in a somewhat immodest position and he asked her whether she did not believe that the gods could see her from behind).—*Pap.* V B 182:3 *n.d.*, 1844

From sketch; see 70:8-71:12:

All girls, not merely the exclusive ones, pay homage to fashion. This I can see in my young girls who sew for me and on whom I lavish a little. They look half lunatic, and I the high priest look utterly disconsolate. Whether I am serving the devil or the god I do not know, but I am right. And I press my right. I see a little bourgeois girl who, ordinary and nice, pays no attention to fashion and corsets. Soon she is mine. I measure her first with a contemptuous look; she perishes from fright, alas, for I am the Fashion Designer κατ᾽ ἐξοχήν [par excellence]. Thereupon I deck her out, and blissful she leaves me.—*Pap.* V B 182:8 *n.d.*, 1844

From sketch; see 70:15-20:

When a seducer says that every woman's virtue is for sale, I do not believe him. But she lets herself be brought into the realm of fashion; she cannot resist the temptation. And yet she is more incurably corrupted by this than by being seduced, for this self-reflection lets her perish as one σκωληκόβρωτος [eaten by worms],[82] and it can be stopped at a hundred places, but it breaks out once again.—*Pap.* V B 182:4 *n.d.*, 1844

From final copy; see 70:20:

. . . . . for this sickness cannot be stopped, and fashion's prey always ends up as one σκωληκο´βρωτος [eaten by worms].[83]—*Pap.* VI B 8:7 *n.d.*, 1844

From sketch; see 70:20:

The most wretched of all must still be to have been a woman who went about with padded hips in order to please men and to have fuller hips than her friends.
—*Pap.* V B 182:2 *n.d.*, 1844

From sketch; see 70:21-24:

I always use women as spies and to incite.—*Pap.* V B 182:9 *n.d.*, 1844

From sketch; see 71:27-72:2:

V
B 183:1
315

Johannes the Seducer's Speech

When Johannes was about to speak and consequently first declare that he was intoxicated or in the condition in which the power of the wine and the power of consciousness are wrestling, objections were raised. Constantin insisted that he was not in the condition.* During the meal it had struck me that although Johannes drank much more than all the others he was so far removed from becoming drunk that he became more and more sober-minded; just a certain coolness spread over his whole being, and he spoke more slowly and in very short sentences. It seemed as if his reflection made it impossible for him to become drunk. He retained all his dignity, and when it appeared to him that a waiter did not understand how to serve champagne, he took the bottle from him and did it himself, but with a marvelous graciousness. Now he stood up, his napkin in hand, and declared that if he was not intox-

V
B 183:1
316

icated now he never would be.** So he received permission to speak.

In margin: *At this point the uniform succession of the speeches was interrupted by a deliberation over whether or to what extent experimenting reflection—to drink in order to see if one can become drunk—does not make it impossible to become so.

In margin: **but if it could set their minds at rest, he would have a huge bottle of champagne brought;[†] he drank it.

[†]so that my eyes may be red with tears, as Falstaff says.[84]

—*Pap.* V B 183:1 *n.d.*, 1844

From sketch; see 72:21-26:

One should not demand of woman an ideality she does not have, that she be faithful or make something of the man, but one should take her as she is and have one's joy of her.—*Pap.* V B 183:3 *n.d.*, 1844

From sketch; see 72:21-26:

I am not surprised that in this company such strange conclusions are arrived at with respect to woman, for all the other speakers seem to me to be unhappy lovers, since he, too, is an unhappy lover who has conjured up a notion of womanly ideality that cannot be found. Such a thing has never occurred to me.—*Pap.* V B 183:4 *n.d.*, 1844

From sketch; see 73:24-28:

It seems almost like a conspiracy against the opposite sex; if no one will speak to its honor, then I surely will.

Eulogy on Woman

For this he uses an essay by Hen. Corn. Agrippa,[85] which I own. Because of its naïveté the comic and humorous effect is assured.—*Pap.* V B 183:2 *n.d.*, 1844

From sketch; see 76:14-21:

The god [*Guden*] formed her out of man; as this derivative she promptly manifests herself as being collective.—*Pap.* V B 183:15 *n.d.*, 1844

From sketch; see 77:3-26:

V
B 183:12
318

. . . . . light as the bird, although she bears a world of bliss within her

elegant of gait

V
B 183:12
319

light and ethereal as if formed of the mists of the summer night, swift, vanishing like a wren until once again she betrays her hiding place, mischievous as a child at play who peeks out of his hiding place, and in the same way she peeks out of her hiding place. Calm as the stillness of evening when not a leaf stirs, calm as the thought that has nothing to think about, calm as the consciousness that is aware of nothing, for she knows nothing, and yet the devotee of erotic love who listens with stethoscopic probity discovers all the craving of desire therein. Silent as the solitude of the forest, talkative as twittering birds.

carefree

—*Pap.* V B 183:12 *n.d.*, 1844

From sketch; see 77:16-21:

confidential as if it were oneself; surprising as the sight of a revelation, necessary in life, and yet like the riddle of life—strange, as if one were looking at oneself outside oneself, inexplicable as that which did not arise in one's heart.—*Pap.* V B 183:13 *n.d.*, 1844

From sketch; see 77:21-26:

The Young Man is perfectly right in saying that love is a contradiction, and if one wants to reflect oneself into it one will never attain it. Begin in another way; understand that it

is recklessness and the greatest genius of all recklessness.—
Pap. V B 183:5 *n.d.*, 1844

From sketch; see 77:27-78:9:

. . . . . when the gods had finished her in this way, they hid
all this from her in the modesty* that nevertheless is a form of
sensuality.**

  *for the gods did not dare tell her how beautiful she was
  for fear of acquiring someone who shared the secret and
  could betray it and hinder the deception.

  **and the devotee of erotic love who like Pyramis places
  his ear against the partition of modesty has intimations
  of all that is behind it.

   inviting by her shrinking from notice, constraining
   by her fleeing, irresistible by her continual resisting.
       —*Pap.* V B 183:20 *n.d.*, 1844

V
B 183:20
320

V
B 183:20
321

From draft; see 80:17:

You do woman a great injustice. I also am certainly aware
of the unloveliness, but it is not her fault—and in that case she
is not with her seducer.—*Pap.* V B 185 *n.d.*, 1844

Penciled in sketch; see 71:26:

. . . . . his speech consists of nothing but shower clouds
       —*Pap.* V B 183:8 *n.d.*, 1844

From draft; see 81:1-4:

To break off requires strength. To break off is an art, precisely because the strength expresses itself only negatively,
and therefore is not seen, indeed, in a way lets itself be
feigned, insofar as what should indeed be an act of freedom
happens to one, for that something stops and that it is broken
off are by no means identical, and yet in a certain sense the
result is the same. This is why to most people the pleasure of
breaking off is and remains a secret, something cryptic that

nevertheless in their minds is not confused with strength *ad modum* [in the manner of] *Kryptkirke* and *Kraftkirke*,[86] for they have no knowledge at all that it exists.—*Pap.* VI B 1:1 *n.d.*, 1844

From draft; see 82:18-23:

As police agents, it is true, and yet the night had made it possible to assume that they themselves were rowdies. Not a word was said, but each, as wary and concealed as possible, took his place; then Victor burst out: Oh, my God, it's Judge William and his wife.

In margin: was about to take his place

in order to surround the terrain

—*Pap.* VI B 1:3 *n.d.*, 1844

From sketch; see 83:4-8:

It is not so with married people, but of course they have a trustworthiness to cling to that the lovers do not have; they have the confirmation of the Church and of the state. Certainly this is not very difficult to obtain, but they have made for themselves a chain of testimony. [*Deleted:* The tea stood on the table.] Married folk they were, but how long—*Pap.* VI B 1:4 *n.d.*, 1844

From draft; see 85:18-29:

. . . He pressed a kiss upon her lips and with a passion with which married people are seldom credited, and, taking her by the arm as if to lean on her for support, he went out of the arbor, and the last words he said were these: You see, I cannot consider the matter seriously; I have too many "ors" for that.

The participants in the banquet, hidden in the foliage, had listened and looked, and it had made a singular impression upon them. Constantin had made a few parodying witty asides, and Johannes said to the Young Man: What do you say now that you have seen this, and he answered: I see nothing, my eyes are shut to anything I call spiritual trial.[*] The five still stood there while the Judge, accompanied by his lovely spouse, went into a bypath, and they looked just like rowdies. And if anyone up to now had had the right to call them that only in a figurative sense, V. E. suddenly qualified himself further. For what happens—without saying a word he runs to a room opening onto the garden. . . .

[*]*In margin:* and around this paradise those enemies had pitched their camp.—*Pap.* V B 189 *n.d.*, 1844

From draft; see 85:22-28:

. . . . . the plunder [*Bytte*] they had taken was a peculiar kind of outcome [*Udbytte*]. Only V. E. would not go home empty-handed. Without saying a word he turns to a garden room with a door standing open . . . . .

Presumably, V. E. was not satisfied with this outcome,

In margin: None of them was satisfied with this outcome; the others were satisfied with making a malicious remark.— *Pap.* VI B 1:7 *n.d.*, 1844

From draft; see 87:1-4:

Some Reflections on Marriage
in Answer to Objections
by
a Married Man.

(On Marriage, Married Happiness,
Married Love, etc.)
by
A Married Man.
—*Pap.* V B 190:1 *n.d.*, 1844

In margin of draft; see 92:28:

Let them heap together all the arguments to marriage; I will certainly be ready, if I just have time and opportunity. I promptly classify them in two sections: the objections which one best answers, as Hamann so splendidly says of particular individuals, by saying "Bah." With them I am quickly finished, and I will also be finished with those worth answering.—*Pap*. V B 190:2 *n.d.*, 1844

From draft; see 112:25-27:

He is a poor wretch or he is a brazen mutineer, and I could easily be tempted to say of him what stands in an old book
[*two blank lines*]
In margin: somewhere in Agrippa, *De matrimonio*[87]
                                —*Pap*. V B 190:5 *n.d.*, 1844

From draft; see 131:11-16 fn.:

                    p. CLXXVII. line 1 from top.
Note
Precisely because I do not want to appeal to the theater arts, which also could seem precarious since here everything concentrates on the demand of the moment, it is all the more joy for me to see . . . . . —*Pap*. VI B 4:1 *n.d.*, 1844

See 131:11-132:43:

On an attached sheet.
                                —*Pap*. VI B 8:8 *n.d.*, 1844

From draft; see 131:11-132:10-34 fn.:

VI
B 2
74

            To Be Added Somewhere in the Judge's Papers.

Without wanting to appeal to the theater arts, it is nevertheless always a joy to find the true and to find the truth therein. The actress who really portrays the feminine is Mme. Nielsen.

VI
B 2
75

The character she portrays and the voice with which she moves us is precisely what must be called: the essentially feminine. Many an actress has become great and admired because of virtuosity in an accidental aspect of the feminine, but from the beginning this admiration is time's booty when the accessories have vanished on which the triumphal performance rested. This is not the case with Mme. N. [*deleted:* since she was young] and therefore time has no power over her. In every period of her life [*deleted:* since she was young] she will express the essential just as she began her beautiful career with it, and if she becomes one hundred years old she will continue to be perfect. I know of no more noble triumph for an actress than this, that the person who in the whole kingdom is most afraid of offending such an actress, that he, as I do, with confidence dares to mention the one hundred years, which ordinarily is the last thing one mentions about an actress. She will in turn portray a great-grandmother by means of the essential, just as the young girl did not produce an effect by some extraordinary beauty or by being able to dance but by the dedication that is the pact of pure femininity with the imperishable. Ordinarily I detest the pandering in calling artists priests, but Mme. N. could justifiably be called a priestess. And although it is easy at the theater to think about the vanity of life and youth and beauty and charm, one is safe in admiring her because one knows that it does not pass away.—*Pap.* VI B 2 *n.d.*, 1844

Addition to Pap. VI B 2:

The essential in the exalted and the essential in the corrupted, whereas a chance portrayal along the latter line produces, despite all virtuosity, either the one or the other deviation: that one forgets that the corrupted one is a woman or that one thinks her to be better than she appears because one does not see the corruption lying in the essentially feminine and consequently does not see that she is and remains a woman but has suffered damage to her soul in demonic passion, in a hardening of mind, in worldly, vain, soft, voluptuous, aristocratic license. An actress who does not have the exalted in her power will portray the corrupted in such a way that one involuntarily comes either to believe that it is an exaggeration or has excuses readily at hand, that her surroundings, her upbringing, have corrupted her. But Mme. Nielsen's performance is always within the boundaries of femininity, and yet in such a way that one comprehends, yes, almost in a tangible way, that such a woman is herself the

VI
B 3
75

VI
B 3
76

original inventor of the corruption, that she has the corrupted at first hand as a *primus motor* [first mover] that could corrupt the entire sex precisely because she still belongs essentially to the sex.—*Pap.* VI B 3 *n.d.*, 1844–45

From draft; see 136:4-7:

. . . . . and just as cream rises from milk in the pantry from morning until evening, just so ever new deliciousness continually rises from this happy domestic life.—*Pap.* V B 190:11 *n.d.*, 1844

From draft; see 141:2:

. . . . . (who in this respect make just as disgusting an impression upon me as when a crowd of louts rushes at the poor peasant's* nice assortment of foodstuffs, not in order to buy, but in order to carry them away)
*The story is told about the 3 per cent bonds.[88]
—*Pap.* V B 190:12 *n.d.*, 1844

In margin of final copy; see 146:15-20:

A place in *Serapionsbrüder*. Must be looked into.—*Pap.* VI B 8:9 *n.d.*, 1844

In margin of final copy; see 152:18:

N.B.

See *Aus meinem Leben, Sämtlich. W.*, the small edition,[89] XXV, p. 292, or Book 10 at the very beginning.—*Pap.* VI B 8:10 *n.d.*, 1844

From draft; see 176:38-177:1:

. . . . . *an arrow in Epaminondas's*[90] *heart*, enough for one life [*penciled in margin:* N.B.]
— *Pap.* V B 190:20 *n.d.*, 1844

In margin of draft; see 182:7-14:

The god [*Guden*] continually avenges himself, as on Prometheus,[91] on the person who wants to trick him out of something or wants to trick him out of spirit and does not want to receive it as it has pleased the god to apportion it. But in these spheres, even if there is a justification, there is this cunning, that the god strikes with his revenge.—*Pap.* V B 190:24 *n.d.*, 1844

From draft; see 183:36-184:8:

And yet I shall throw you away, you wretched pen—my choice is made; I follow the beckoning and the invitation. Let a wretched author sit trembling when thoughts present themselves in a lucky moment, trembling lest someone disturb him—I am not afraid of it. Tomorrow, if I have the time, the day after tomorrow, in a week, I shall write further, more about marriage, but not now, even if I could convince the whole world; I am breaking off; even if it means that I never write again. As a girl she taught me to write short sentences, for at times she sat beside me, and at the end of each sentence I would talk with her, and she rewarded me with a kiss for each sentence; if as wife she prevents me from becoming an author, I am in turn satisfied with a kiss. . . . —*Pap.* V B 190:26 *n.d.*, 1844

From draft; see 185:

Guilty?/Not-Guilty?
A Story of Suffering
An Imaginary Psychological Construction
[*deleted:* edited]
by
Frater Taciturnus
—*Pap.* V B 142 *n.d.*, 1844

From draft; see 185:

Guilty?/Not-Guilty?

My life's question
My need   *portio mea et poculum* [my portion and cup][92]
My pain
My stopping
My annihilation

—*Pap.* V B 144 *n.d.*, 1844

From draft; see 185, 199-200, 232-34, 250-52, 276-88, 360-63:

The short articles to be inserted into " 'Guilty?'/'Not-Guilty?' "

1. Father-concern. See journal, pp. 25 and 26 top. See p. 77 top [*Pap.* IV A 65, 147].[93]

2. A Leper's Self-Contemplation. See journal, p. 55 [*Pap.* IV A 110, 111].

3. See journal, p. 57; cf. p. 75 bot. and p. 76 top [*Pap.* IV A 114, 144].[94]

4. Recollections of My Life by Nebuchadnezzar. See journal, p. 59 [*Pap.* IV A 119].

5. Abelard. See journal, p. 96 bot. and p. 13 top [*Pap.* IV A 177, 31].

6. Quiet despair. See journal, p. 121 [*Pap.* V A 33].

7. See Fenelon's *Lebensbeschreibungen und Lehrsätze der alten Weltweisen.* Periander's life noted in my copy on pp. 79 ff.[95]

—*Pap.* V B 124 *n.d.*, 1844

From final draft; see 190:4-8:

. . . . . torn from the New Testament containing four verses from John's Epistle, and other similar articles that only to the owner can have a value equal to the very valuable jewelry. The manuscript is entirely unchanged as I found it.—*Pap.* V B 143:3 *n.d.*, 1844

From final draft; see 190:32:

As for the date, by my own calculation and Mr. Bonfil's published table I have found that the whole thing fits the year 1750 or the year the Seven Years' War began. One is compelled to go somewhat back in time or to assume that an error crept into the information, or that the whole thing is a poetic venture, and that he threw it into the water because he was tired of it.

As for reviewers—unless there suddenly emerged a new and authorized reviewer—I shall speak quite honestly: it is my wish that they keep perfectly quiet. If one is able to acquire a claim to a person's gratitude in such an easy manner, lucky fellow: unless the reviewers could not possibly keep silent. *N.B.* see p. 7

—*Pap.* V B 143:6 *n.d.* 1844

Addition to Pap. V B 143:6; *see 191:7-13:*

Continuation of the Preface.

All of us will accept a little psychological insight, some powers of observation, but when this science or art manifests itself in its interminable amplitude, when it abandons minor transactions on the streets and in the dwellings in order to scurry after its favorite: the person inclosingly reserved—then men grow weary.—*JP* V 5721 (*Pap.* V B 147) *n.d.*, 1844

Deleted from margin of draft; see 193:6:

"Guilty?"/"Not-Guilty?"

My life question.
Portio mea et poculum
[My portion and cup].[96]
My daily consuming.

—*Pap.* VI B 8:11 *n.d.*, 1844

From draft; see 195:1:

V
B 191
334

The Wrong and the Right.
Preface.

Perhaps it is my fault, perhaps it is just as much the fault of several others, perhaps it is not the fault of any of us. To me it seems that the empty courtesy with which one enters into a social group, the empty courtesy with which one leaves it is the weak side of social life, a Chinese seasoning that clashes with and works against the animating principle: the meaninglessness that is the key to and the screen around the light game of conversation and the droll intermingling of incidentals and the cheerful carefreeness of sociality, lest something meaningful and serious enter in disturbingly.[*] Even if there is the prospect of meeting pleasant company, the foolish importance of an introduction can easily appear to someone as too high an entrance fee, and what is worse, it can easily waste a half hour before one arrives at the happy interplay—indeed, what is worse, can transform the whole evening into a boring children's game. Even if one has passed a pleasant hour, perhaps even two, and wishes to preserve the mood, the leave-taking's return to stiff, unnatural importance can easily seem to one to be too high a tax, indeed, what is worse, can easily spoil the enjoyment.

V
B 191
335

In the same way it seems to me that upon the publication of a book a preface is the weak side, is a dubiousness one must try to slip past as quietly as possible. This, you see, is why I say nothing at all, my dear reader, but carry you *in medias res non secus ac notas* [into the middle of things as if already known], as the poet says, and furthermore do what the poet bids the poet: *quae desperat tracata nitescere posse relinquit* [what he fears he cannot make attractive with his touch he abandons].[97] The elegant bow of the preface I believe myself unable to perform with elegance, because I continually bear in mind what the busybody says: To the point, please, to the point.[98]

deadly
[*]*In margin:* with its insipid and haughty hollowness.

Therefore, if you like, I blurt out what I have to say without a single word about how I as editor am connected with this little book. Anyone who wishes introductory compliments, the painful silence of the beginning, the monotonous sound of what is usually said on this occasion, can be justifiably angry at me for breaking with ceremony. Anyone who instead of wanting to read a book would rather read what can activate his conjectural criticism, the untruths, theories, and fables as one finds them in a preface, let him shrug his shoulders at me for not being man enough to think up a single lie, but let him also bear in mind that by not saying a single word I open up the widest territory to his research. The reader who desires to read a book, my reader who desires to read this book, no doubt says with the busybody: To the point, please, to the point.

V
B 191
336

That is what I say, to repeat, and only add: Where there is a wrong, there is also a right; thus on the one side the wrong, on the other the right, or on the one side the right and on the other side the wrong, without its thereby having been decided on which side is the right or who has the right on his side.

—*Pap.* V B 191 *n.d.*, 1844

In top margin of draft; see 187:1, 195:1:

[*Heading, crossed out with pencil:* Notice: Owner Sought]
Above the beginning of text:

N.B. What is written in the morning is the reproduction of the love affair, consequently what happened the year before. What is written at midnight is something later, what happens in the current year.—*Pap.* V B 99:1-2 *n.d.*, 1844

From draft; see 195:1:

The insertions in " 'Guilty?'/'Not–Guilty?' " should all be dated the fifth [*changed in pencil from:* the third) of each month. It begins the third of January.—*Pap.* V B 134 *n.d.*, 1844

In margin of draft; see 197:12-16:

I also desired a little joy in life, a little joy in existence; I will stake everything on her. When I experience happy times, how blessed to share, indeed, to keep less for myself. And I will surely constrain the darkness within me; at least she must not come to suffer under it.—*Pap.* V B 99:7 *n.d.*, 1844

From draft; see 198:17:

. . . . . it should be a third person who will tell me about a girl, and I should know what I know about her staying power, I think that conversation should not be like a lonely one with myself in tears but in laughter. The demon of wittiness . . . . .
—*Pap.* V B 99:8 *n.d.*, 1844

From draft; see 198:19:

. . . . . a little Emeline, who will die of love.[99]
—*Pap.* V B 99:9 *n.d.*, 1844

In margin of draft; see 198:37-199:3:

My God, do the summoners of eternity look like this; when I see this paleness, this almost glazed look, death walks over my grave.—*Pap.* V B 99:10 *n.d.*, 1844

From draft; see 198:38-199:22:

. . . . . who can calculate this impression. If she dies, merciful God, I will shoot a bullet through my head. But not before, alas I have surely been tempted, but if I do it before, I will provide her with an explanation, and to keep that away from her I would sacrifice my life. —Therefore be cold, calm, levelheaded, almost childishly open, moreover attentive to everything, aware of everything, weighing what my eyes, when the occasion is there, teach me and what the reports contain. To be truthful, when I became engaged to her I was not an intriguer; now I have become one.—*Pap*. V B 99:11 *n.d.*, 1844

From final draft; see 199:25:

No. 1

Quiet Despair

—*Pap*. V B 128 *n.d.*, 1844

From draft; see 201:20:

. . . . . and vanish without a trace. I can almost feel it as a pain because the nature of life is such that a young girl's life is to be thrown to the wolves in such a way that I, if I were a brute, could allow myself to make love to her. It is certainly true that society does punish philanderers, that we laugh at them, condemn them, but what is that compared with the harm that they do?—*Pap*. V B 100:1 *n.d.*, 1844

From draft; see 201:31-35:

. . . . . then I would no doubt become so terrified that nothing more would comfort me, because I would not believe her even if she maintained the opposite, since I would believe that she did it in order to spare me.—*Pap*. V B 100:2 *n.d.*, 1844

From draft; see 202:7-8:

. . . . . but also the nagging pain that I have interfered with the religious, and then where would I find recourse.—*Pap*. V B 100:3 *n.d.*, 1844

From draft; see 205:35-38:

. . . . . for, good Lord, it is not an illusion I foster, is it? I who am so reflective as if I were sheer reflection, and would it be the reason that I feel happier in the distance of possibility? Terrible! But it is not so.—*Pap*. V B 100:8 *n.d.*, 1844

From draft; see 207:19:

. . . . . this is a risk I dare not take. In that case, I would rather choose an unhappy love, which still makes only one person unhappy.—*Pap.* V B 100:12 *n.d.*, 1844

From draft; see 214:17:

—It is clear, however, that the only thing I know for sure about the girl is that I am in love with her.—*Pap.* V B 100:18 *n.d.*, 1844

From draft; see 215:1-4:

. . . . . have damaged her soul by becoming shrewd—and it is supposed to be my fault, my silence is supposed to have corrupted her, corrupted her even more than if I had seduced her.—*Pap.* V B 100:19 *n.d.*, 1844

From draft; see 216:26-28:

. . . . . but with God; it is a religious battle that gathers over me; it is my view of life that demands a rebirth. What sorrow. There I sit with the suffering in my soul, and with me sits the young girl; she does not suspect how this pertains to her. Only I see the sword over our head, and I grow old, and she—she is my beloved.—*Pap.* V B 100:20 *n.d.*, 1844

From draft; see 218:6-10:

It is difficult at times, but I have learned especially to be attentive to being able to break off in an entirely casual but, please note, dispassionate, merely conversational manner. I myself have used the opposite tactic with an inclosingly reserved person; therefore I know the difficulties.—*Pap.* V B 100:23 *n.d.*, 1844

From draft; see 218:12:

The point is to be able to look at him in the same second, for if one speaks longer with him, then he dispels the impression by means of discourse.—*Pap.* V B 100:24 *n.d.*, 1844

From draft; see 219:5-6:

. . . . . to have him in such a way that he is bound as the police desire it, because I could divulge his life and thereby can coerce him . . . . . —*Pap.* V B 100:25 *n.d.*, 1844

From draft; see 220:28-30:

Then it must be because a girl according to her nature is babble, that she babbles away and in the mental sense as well has a monthly emptying so that she forgets everything and begins from the beginning.—*Pap.* V B 100:27 *n.d.*, 1844

Deleted from sketch; see 222:21-26:

Morning

She is silent
I have read a sermon to her.
I wonder what she is thinking of my emotion? That it is the rapture of love, that it should be she who moved me thus.

—*Pap.* V B 97:1 *n.d.*, 1844

From draft; see 223:3:

. . . . . I who knew that I surpassed even my father in this virtuosity . . . . . —*Pap.* V B 100:29 *n.d.*, 1844

From draft; see 224:18:

Truly she will be busy with recollection; she has enough, for to have been involved with a person who is the epitome of all reflection gives work in abundance.—*Pap.* V B 100:30 *n.d.*, 1844

From sketch; see 224:28-31:

If my honor were not at stake, if my pride were not violated—I wanted it but was incapable of it. If she had abandoned me—what then—then it all would have amounted to nothing.— —*JP* V 5663 (*Pap.* IV B 142) *n.d.*, 1843

From draft; see 225:30-31:

But from my earliest years I have lived almost only intellectually. Thought, ideas, dialectics, that is my life, my highest.—*Pap.* V B 100:31 *n.d.*, 1844

From draft; see 228:19:

. . . . . highest, that I could really make her proud as she once was.—*Pap.* V B 100:34 *n.d.*, 1844

From draft; see 229:18-26:

Faithless reflection, the person who treads on you, let him be on the alert. Then this thought surely must be taken on also. One might think that the person embraced by a reflection of that sort would be suffocated, and yet I know that this reflection is so elastic that she does not notice it at all.

I read aloud to her, I speak with her, she seems to find a certain pleasure in it. Yet she is quiet, silent, reticent.—*Pap.* V B 100:35 *n.d.*, 1844

Deleted from sketch; see 229:8-11, 33-34:

Midnight

Everyone creates God in his image; as an intriguer, I believe that God is that also.

Penciled in margin:
    Wer keinen hat muss auch zu Bett
    [Who has none must also to bed].[100]

                    —*Pap.* V B 97:6 *n.d.*, 1844

From draft; see 230:11-231:25:

And thus I use other hours of the day for recollecting that relationship, and the night hours for devising schemes and for keeping myself up to scratch.—*Pap.* V B 100:36 *n.d.*, 1844

From draft; see 232:16-18:

. . . . . a matter of a life's substance, of what makes a young person's age that of an oldster.—*Pap.* V B 100:37 *n.d.*, 1844

From sketch; see 235:16-234:32:

    The leper has concocted a salve that can conceal his leprosy from others, but it is still contagious—the one now wants to take revenge upon the people; the other wishes to remain out there among the gravestones.

V
B 126
220

    Ah, stupid human language, who is entitled to compassion if not someone who is unfortunate, and yet it is the reverse, it is the unfortunate one who has compassion on the fortunate one.

V
B 126
221

        the pauper who has fallen into the hands of the
        Jewish peddler, with what does it end, it ends in
        the debtors' prison, and so it is with human
        compassion, when at no risk to themselves people
        can practice usury with their charity and obtain a
        hundredfold return in the next life—but
        ordinarily it ends with their sending the one
        person out here.
        the other one is called Manasse.

                  —*Pap.* V B 126 *n.d.*, 1844

From final draft; see 234:32:

But then silence, so that no one ever comes to know anything, for of what use is it otherwise.—*Pap.* V B 129:1 *n.d.*, 1844

From draft; see 235:27-29:

. . . . . religiously I am equal to everyone, and religiously I have humbled myself under this relationship. If a young girl were to get such a confounded idea, that an old man should become an idolater through her.—*Pap.* V B 101:2 *n.d.*, 1844

Deleted from sketch; see 235:6-7, 236:37:

Morning

She no doubt thinks I am making a fool of everyone but her.

> *In margin:* see, do you dare to say
> by God.
> —*Pap.* V B 97:4 *n.d.*, 1844

From draft; see 237:2:

. . . . . where religiousness consists of summarily expecting to obtain what one desires.—*Pap.* V B 101:4 *n.d.*, 1844

Deleted from sketch; 241:8-33:

Morning

I speak with her as with a child. She does not reflect at all; I cannot say a word without its being reflective.

Small talk—yet in many ways I am qualified to be a husband.

> *In margin:* She is silent.
> —*Pap.* V B 97:2 *n.d.*, 1844

In margin of draft; see 241:36:

. . . . . should be a Wednesday.

—*Pap.* V B 101:10 *n.d.*, 1844

Deleted from sketch; see 242:4-6, 244:35-245:5:

Midnight.

Meeting on the street.
If I were not so scrupulous, I would have
moved into her neighborhood in order to train
her in seeing me. It is desirable that she
not become dull.

—*Pap.* V B 97:9 *n.d.*, 1844

From draft; see 243:17-19:

. . . . . feeling talented in comparison with the particular
individual with whom I spoke and secretly expecting that
nothing would ever come of me other than a queer fellow
who walked up and down the floor and smoked tobacco.—
Pap. V B 101:12 *n.d.*, 1844

Deleted from sketch; see 243:3-38:

Midnight.

She wanted to be something extraordinary. I am lying and
waiting in the pilot boat in order to help her secretly—*Pap.* V
B 97:17 *n.d.*, 1844

From draft; see 244:1-10:

. . . . . then I shall rejoice in her and in my heart know that
I have secretly worked for her to the utmost of my capacity.
In margin: the anonymous novella[101] about which I was mis-
taken.

—*Pap.* V B 101:13 *n.d.*, 1844

From sketch; 244:12-19:

Morning

I confess to her that she is sacrificing herself for me; I have asked her forgiveness for pulling her along in this way.—*Pap.* V B 97:5 *n.d.*, 1844

In margin of draft; see 244:12:

. . . . . should be a Wednesday.

—*Pap.* V B 101:15 *n.d.*, 1844

Deleted from sketch; 244:12:

Midnight

Meeting on the street.

—*Pap.* V B 97:10 *n.d.*, 1844

Deleted from sketch; 244:12:

Midnight.

She is looking for me. Hauser Square.

—*Pap.* V B 97:11 *n.d.*, 1844

Deleted from sketch; 245:6-246:6:

Midnight.

The letter to her at second hand.

—*Pap.* V B 97:8 *n.d.*, 1844

From draft; see 245:28-29:

I do not understand how the whole affair about the letters of the schoolteacher Bæren[102] can arouse such a great sensation; my correspondence is always transmitted by way of friendship.—*Pap.* V B 101:16 *n.d.*, 1844

Deleted from sketch; 248:18-38:

Morning

She is silent.

I can do everything with my artificial leg. We are merry and a pair of young lovers, she by virtue of her seventeen years—and I—on my artificial leg. I am learning the comic from the ground up, and yet it is enough to make one lose one's mind.

In margin: Captain Gribskopf
I shall reach the religious; it is a
precaution, like contributing to a widow's
fund.

—*Pap.* V B 97:3 *n.d.*, 1844

In margin of draft; see 249:1:

. . . . . should be a Wednesday
—*Pap.* V B 101:17 *n.d.*, 1844

Deleted from sketch; see 250:12-28:

In Part 1
Morning

Throughout almost the whole month of March it merely says very briefly: no new symptom. Somewhat indifferently narrated and embellished.—*Pap.* V B 97:19 *n.d.*, 1844

Deleted from sketch; see 250:12-28:

[*In margin:* In Part 2]

March. Morning.
And when a happy prospect for our future has appeared, then I rush to her; when I have joy to bring, I never seek a long way around—*Pap.* V B 97:22 *n.d.*, 1844

From draft; see 250:13:

. . . . . symptom. Through the religious I am attaining more and more actuality. When . . . . . —*Pap.* V B 101:18 *n.d.*, 1844

See 250:30:

This piece[103] could be called "Solomon's Dream," in which a melancholy youth has the impression of David that he was not God's chosen one but only pretending to be so while inwardly his bad conscience preyed on him.—*Pap.* V B 125 *n.d.*, 1844

From final draft; see 251:11-12:

. . . . . the son of the chosen one, and the royal purple that already blinds a mortal eye blinded double when David stepped forth in full array, because he was a king of the spirit.—*Pap.* V B 130:2 *n.d.*, 1844

From final draft; see 252:4:

. . . . . everything, and he was offended at God.
                              —*Pap.* V B 130:4 *n.d.*, 1844

From final draft; see 252:12:

. . . . . strength, and the budding shoot of action was snapped off by one winter frost, and he never attained his strength—*Pap.* V B 130:5 *n.d.*, 1844

Deleted from sketch; see 252:24-254:2:

Midnight.

My head is tired; oh, if only I dared to be a little sad, to recollect—but then I am deceiving her. Why am I doing all this? For the sake of the idea, because it is freedom's highest passion, and my nature's deepest necessity—Simon Stylites's mistake was not that he did it but that he invited others to watch him.—*Pap.* V B 97:15 *n.d.*, 1844

Deleted from sketch; see 254:29-255:37:

In Part 2
Midnight.

Suppose she were to become a governess—I am like a child writing a drill-exercise on specified words.
a word about her father's driving out to a country manor.

Midnight.
Drives out there. Eighty miles. Postilion.
                    —*Pap.* V B 97:29 *n.d.*, 1844

Deleted from sketch; see 257:28-261:4:

Midnight.
An actual religious individuality I am not. I am a superbly constituted possibility for it, discover the whole religious turning point primitively, but while I am grasping for the religious patterns my prodigious philosophical doubt enters in. It is dreadful to be able to understand the need for the religious so deeply and yet have a doubt such as that. Yet I will stick it out;* I will not turn away; I will not seek the company of a yodeling saint who when contemplating world history and existence yodels in half Norwegian: It is so wonderful.

The Comic

*as soon as I am through with my relationship to her, that is the moment to plunge myself absolutely down into this.— *Pap.* V B 97:16 *n.d.*, 1844

From draft; see 258:7:

If one has a little talent, it is not difficult to preach in any style whatsoever and continually satisfy some people with each style, but it is difficult to become intelligible to oneself. Fine.—*Pap.* V B 102:2 *n.d.*, 1844

From draft; see 258:14-15:

. . . . . that I never dare confide to any person. In the midst of all my need and misery, I constantly have an ear with which I listen to what is being achieved in our day. Yes, that's a fine help.—*Pap.* V B 102:3 *n.d.*, 1844

From draft; see 258:35-259:10:

I will not be satisfied with talking about it because others are satisfied with it; I will not be clever with phrases by which one says here is not the place, this is not the time for us to talk about it. Neither will I seek association with a sect with a yodeling saint, who when he contemplates life and existence and the course of world history yodels in Norwegian: It is so wonderful.—*Pap.* V B 102:4 *n.d.*, 1844

From draft; see 259:22-27:

If only this were done, if instead of wasting time on criticism and preliminaries and systems, or wasting words on judging and denouncing the hypocrisy of the enthusiasts [*Opvakte*] one had a good comic drawing of such a figure.— *Pap.* V B 102:5 *n.d.*, 1844

From draft; see 260:11-38:

V
B 102:6
194
. . . . . on the contrary, it was my one and only wish to do it, and even if I had not wished it I still would have married. I always believe that obedience is more pleasing to God than the fat of rams,[104] and God does not stand in need of any human being. Such rashness was truly far from my soul. I often think of how deeply offended I would be if a high-ranking man ever arrayed himself in his superiority and rightfully— please note, rightfully—said to me, who had wanted to elbow

my way to the front: Stay where you are, just as I myself at times also say of a fool: Shoemaker, stick to your last. And if anyone can be superior, God in heaven can. How dreadful if I were to vanish into a nothing before his majesty, and this is called: Stay where you are. Perhaps I would never recover. Yet I think a pietist [*Hellig*] would find this talk facetious; he would no doubt want me to curse piously just as one otherwise curses impiously. But if I sensed this terror in this way, would it not be earnestness? Why do people know so well how to talk about a high-ranking man's superiority, why do they understand so well how humbling it must be to vanish in this way like a lie before his superiority, and why should one not understand the same about God?—*Pap.* V B 102:6 *n.d.*, 1844

V
B 102:6
195

From draft; see 261:7-8:

Perhaps, despite all my efforts, I have become somewhat changed, but good Lord, nine months in such sufferings and such tensions—one cannot keep oneself totally unchanged— yet I am ready at once, but as yet the counterorder is in force.—*Pap.* V B 102:7 *n.d.*, 1844

From draft; see 261:27-28:

in short, suppose that we in truth were separated, suppose that she, according to her own statement as reported to me today, had never cared for me at all.—*Pap.* V B 102:8 *n.d.*, 1844

Deleted from sketch; see 262:38-263:21:

In Part 2
Morning

What is the happiest life? It is [that of] a young girl sixteen years old. (to be found in the black Berlin portfolio that lies in the mahogany box in which everything pertaining to this affair is to be found).—*Pap.* V B 97:30 *n.d.*, 1844

From draft; see 262:38-263:21:

What is the happiest life? It is [that of] a young girl eighteen years old.

> (This little piece is in my Berlin portfolio, which is in the mahogany box, where all these papers pertaining to Guilty/and Not–Guilty? are kept.)

—*Pap*. V 102:9 *n.d.*, 1844

From draft; see 263:38-264:16:

Is this not like the time when the rescue equipment was in the house close to the beach where the dying person lay, but the keys to the building were with the Commander, who* was not at home. Indeed, if only I were afloat myself, I would promptly be there in my boat. How just one word can awaken much in a person and have an infinite power over the soul.

In margin: *lived far away from there and

—*Pap*. V B 102:10 *n.d.*, 1844

From draft; see 264:23:

. . . . . in the wind, like a mermaid's streaming hair.

—*Pap*. V B 102:11 *n.d.*, 1844

Deleted from sketch; see 265:10:

> disabled.
> The Clothes of Gladness

—*Pap*. V B 97:31 *n.d*, 1844

Deleted from sketch; see 265:25:

> *Midnight.*

I actually suffer sympathetically; the formative for me in this.—*Pap*. V B 97:32 *n.d.*, 1844

From draft; see 266:27-267:8:

. . . . . but I can despair over an eternal responsibility.
—*Pap*. V B 102:12 *n.d.*, 1844

Deleted from sketch; see 267:10-30:

At the beginning of April, conditions are such that he has to check on the effect this has had upon her, how the whole situation stands, and look, she says that she does not care for him at all. She does not want to answer, is simply devil-may-care peevish: O depression, how you do make a fool of a person; here I have worked to the best of my ability, continually worried about making her unhappy, and the whole thing is a false alarm. —All my depression is gone, and I can treat her just the way I have treated everyone else.—*Pap*. V B 97:20 *n.d.*, 1844

From draft; see 267:17-19:

The whole thing *ad modum* [in the manner of] (Benedick's*) and Beatrice's declaration of love in *Viel Lärmen um Nichts* [*Much Ado about Nothing*], act V, sc. 4, p. 196 bot., in vol. VII of Tieck and Schlegel.
*for I did not play Benedick
—*Pap*. V B 102:13 *n.d.*, 1844

From draft; see 267:33-35:

If only I were absolutely confident, so that I would dare to use force against her because I would be certain of making her happy—*Pap*. V B 102:14 *n.d.*, 1844

Deleted from sketch; see 268:21-274:12:

Midnight

What if she now became insane
Nina[105]

a psychological construction of feminine insanity
In margin: to have to experience insanity sympathetically
—*Pap.* V B 97:33 *n.d.*, 1844

From draft; see 268:27-269:12:

I could consult a poet. Nina became insane from love, it says in the play, and the poster says the same. She saw the beloved, whom she could not have, leap into the sea; she saw a bloody head bob up—and the daylight of consciousness was changed into the fog of insanity. This is inappropriate. She has not seen me jump into the water, nor has she seen a bloody head bob up, ergo—. What a consolation to have a poet who has the psychological genius to pose the problem. For Nina became insane from love; and it was not from fear or horror over the bloody head, it was not even a consequence of the dreadful irony by which the father had changed their relationship into a jest and in jest had given his consent. One would think that sufficient to make a girl insane, more than sufficient, but the poet makes use of the bloody head.—*Pap.* V B 102:15 *n.d.*, 1844

From draft; see 275:9:

I dispute *colloquio privatissimo* [in a private colloquium] with God in heaven.—*Pap.* V B 102:17 *n.d.*, 1844

From draft; see 275:12-20:

she has said, and which forms depression's dark dream.* In that sense I need no relief; it does not help me. It cannot be done, the case has gone to the highest court. I do not care about any degree or about *gradus ad Parnassum* [a step toward Parnassus]; I care only about my responsibility.
Penciled in margin: *I could not wish that, for then she would come to be totally insignificant.—*Pap.* V B 102:18 *n.d.*, 1844

From draft; see 276:17-21:

Even in her refractoriness there is an acknowledgment of my power for she is like a little girl who is mocking her father. If she felt herself to be my betrothed she would of course know that she has just as much power as I, and the person who has the power never behaves that way.—*Pap.* V B 102:19 *n.d.*, 1844

From sketch; see 276:23-288:38:

No. 4

Father-concern[*]

V
B 131
222

In a little country village there lived a very tall and slender man; every day he walked a set course outside his house; all the children knew him.[**]

Some claimed that in his youth he had been in love with a queen of Russia—

V
B 131
223

But at certain times of the year he went on a journey, going away notably at the time the stork came. Thus he traveled widely, and when he was at home there was only one thing that engrossed him. He looked at them so closely that it was terrible, went home and looked into big books, checking and checking. For he had a very large library, but only of physiological works.[†]

Hameln.[106]

He believed he was a father—a lapse in his youth—did not know what had become of the girl or who she was or whether there was a child. Now he was studying the physiological laws, family resemblance, etc.

This happened very early in his youth. Several years had passed without his really thinking about it; then it suddenly

[*]*In margin:* A possibility
The Prodigal Son
[**]*In margin:* in Christianshavn
(the idyllic to be developed)
[†]*In margin:* He could also be called The Ratcatcher from—what was the name of the city—the one who led all the children away with his playing.

became very vivid to him. Now he withdrew from the world and sank into brooding thoughts. The only relative he had was an old uncle, who was a man rather experienced in life, now old, and not exactly venerable, but with the kind of old man's witticism so unbecoming to gray hair. He often talked about such things and always used to say that no one could know how many children he had.[*]

So he became insane and lived on in this way.

Every two weeks he went [*deleted:* to the club][**] and spoke with an old ship captain, who thought that he was sixty years old although he was only thirty-nine.

V
B 131
224

[*Deleted:* journal, p. 49 (*Pap.* IV A 105), can be used.]

[*] *In margin:* And this silence and this witticism worked upon him so long that his understanding finally decided to move away [*skifte*] because it could not bear serving in a household such as that, and he exchanged [*omskifte*] understanding for insanity.

[**] *In margin:* At a café in Christianshavn. There I have seen him laugh.

—*Pap.* V B 131 *n.d.*, 1844

From draft; see 276:34:

In this respect, life on the streets and alleys of a metropolis at times has something very humbling for the elite and at times something charming for the simpler class, for His Lordship must jump off the sidewalk and yield to the maidservant with her market basket, and the omnibus driver blows his horn at the gentlemen's carriages, for if he cannot drive out of the way for them, they have to drive out of the way for him.—*Pap.* V B 135:2 *n.d.*, 1844

From draft; see 277:8-14:

Magnificence is not to be found out there, and misery is so at home that it does not even occur to the miserable to want to escape from it across the ocean *per mare pauperiem fugiens* [fleeing poverty through sea].[107]—*Pap.* V B 135:4 *n.d.*, 1844

From draft; see 277:28-278:2:

Christianshavn is like a market town. Christianshavn has a great deal of atmosphere.[*] —When one stands on Snurre Bridge. The orphanage. A couple of doomed individuals who have a conversation near Frelsers Church.

Christianshavn, like market towns, has several characters whom everyone knows. Just as almost every market town has a mentally deranged person.

[*]*In margin:* sadness.

—*Pap.* V B 135:6 *n.d.*, 1844

From draft; see 280:10-23:

The situation often stirred me deeply, for here the charitableness had acquired a strange equality. The poor woman needed money, she received it, but on the other hand the poor woman would not easily be tempted to be envious of the fortunate, for she no doubt felt that this man, her noble benefactor (this, of course, is the poor people's expression) was more unfortunate than she. Therefore she had a double joy in being grateful to him. If he had been a happy individual, she perhaps would have been hurt by the thought that he did not care much for her gratitude. If he who was her benefactor had been a fortunate individual who passed her by without once touching his hat or looking at her, she would have been hurt; now, however, she was placated by the thought of his suffering.— *Pap.* V B 135:12 *n.d.*, 1844

From draft; see 288:6-10:

. . . Eventually the bookkeeper died[*]. . . .

[*]*In margin:* —he was ill several days, and his delusion faded away; death remedied it; he had had nothing to worry about as far as that possibility was concerned.—*Pap.* V B 135:22 *n.d.*, 1844

From sketch; see 285:18-20:

For no. 1. The man who in jest repeated a stock joke that no one could know how many children he had. —This contributed to his becoming insane. His pathos-filled despair and the flippancy of the other man.—*Pap.* V B 127 *n.d.*, 1844

Penciled in margin of draft; see 276:23, 288:38, 289:1:

April 5 *Midnight*
A Possibility.
—*Pap.* V B 103:1 *n.d.*, 1844;

Deleted from sketch; see 290:3-27:

Midnight.

I was at a party; some brilliant women who hinted that if the girl is not intelligent enough, then it is all right to break the engagement.

Ah, to have to be silent lest she find out something. — Otherwise I should have crushed them.

In margin: summa summarum [sum of sums] of her hidden and manifest charms.

love—[*deleted:* whore]
play—drink—love N.B.

—*Pap.* V B 97:36 *n.d.*, 1844

From draft; see 293:12:

Recensenten og Dyret[108]
—*Pap.* V B 103:2 *n.d.*, 1844

From draft; see 293:23-294:18:

[*Deleted:* One should not change the language. I am thinking of a line by the servant in *Kong Salomon og Jørgen Hatte-mager:* Play as much as you want to, drink as much as you want to, love as much as you want to.[109] Father Holberg would not have been timorous; he would have said: Whore as much as you wish.]

But falling in love gives absolute meaning, and faithfulness in one's love is the ideality. Although ordinarily I do not attend funerals, I would gladly attend the funeral of the lowliest servant girl who was faithful in her love.—*Pap.* V B 103:5 *n.d.*, 1844

Deleted from final copy; see 293:24:

Therefore one should not, as an author has done whose linguistic merit is otherwise worthy of respect, one should not have the servant in *Kong Salomon og Jørgen Hattemager* say: . . . . . —*Pap.* VI B 8:12 *n.d.*, 1844

Deleted from sketch; see 295:12-21:

Midnight.

I have everything ready, just for the sake of possibility. At the second-hand furniture store a complete set of furniture is ready at my expense. My apartment is large enough. If only the moment arrives, that very second I will make up for everything, will apply all my ingenuity to enchant her.—*Pap.* V B 97:37 *n.d.*, 1844

From draft; see 295:35-38:

. . . . . it not at all. In a little Swedish ballad it says, "In a pinch, one must oneself be the godparent," that is, when one cannot find any godparents, and likewise when one cannot find a wife.—*Pap.* V B 103:7 *n.d.*, 1844

From draft; see 295:35-38:

. . . . . is an extremely serious matter, and just as two pennies are important to the conscientious accountant lest the account be confused, so here every insignificant thing is important to me, and just as an accountant can be happy when the account balances down to two pennies, so I shall be happy or, more correctly, infinitely more happy, if I obtain permission to draw up my account.—*Pap.* V B 103:8 *n.d.*, 1844

From draft; see 297:16-28:

If she wants to begin and presumably in order to say something entirely different, I interrupt again and say: But good Lord, my dear girl, can't you remember it*—partly because she fears that I, like Gert Westphaler,[110] will attack her, like Jørgen Handskemager, in the flank, if she wants to carry on any political and curious discourse whatsoever. If I exchange a word with her alone, it is always about unimportant things, only when I converse in company do I slip in hints, but always with inverse passion, for I do not wish other parties to it.

In margin: *indeed, it was yesterday evening, or was it (and at the same moment my face is changed for a second and is understandable only to her) three nights ago. (Three nights ago we were not enemies.)—*Pap.* V B 103:9 *n.d.*, 1844

From draft; see 298:13-14:

And yet if this prompted a defiance in her soul, if she became for me what I once was for the person who loved me more than anyone has, an object of grave concern! But this is why I do not remove the religious—under this we are both still equal—and this is why I do not withdraw my attention from her, for I am more watchful now than ever.—*Pap.* V B 103:10 *n.d.*, 1844

From draft; see 298:18-21:

Most people perhaps would be inclined to take something like that as an exaggeration, as was indeed the case with that man. And yet in a curious way he was both right and wrong. Which is why he has always interested me as a psychological phenomenon.—*Pap.* V B 103:11 *n.d.*, 1844

From draft; see 298:29-30:

When there is a high mortality among women in confine-
ment, one sometimes takes the precaution of suppressing information about it to the living, but why should anyone think
of taking precaution with regard to me.—*Pap.* V B 103:12
n.d., 1844

From draft; see 298:33-38:

How much I have suffered in this way. If my path is otherwise strewn with thorns, these random contacts are a unique
kind that pain bitterly. In poetry, in random comments, in
mystifications in newspapers, I am continually seeing clues,
ghosts, and I do not ever dare to let it be noticed that I am
terrified. Since I myself am initiated into and am practiced in
countless mystifications, I cannot refrain from crediting her
with similar proficiency. I actually believe a policeman could
learn something from me. He should see me when I come to
some place or other where I know that she also comes; he
should see me make a search if I believe that she has been
there. Indeed, if one is entitled to order all the hiding places to
be opened, this is not so difficult, but if one must come up
with an idea in order to have permission to look into a table
drawer, if one must admire a vase of artificial flowers in order
to see if there might be a slip of paper in the big flower, if one
must stumble because only in that position can one look under
a work table etc.—that is something else.—*Pap.* V B 103:13
n.d., 1844

V
B 103:13
199

V
B 103:13
200

Deleted from sketch; see 298:26-37:

Midnight.

Yesterday I read in the newspaper about a young girl who
had taken her own life. I understand all sorts of lines personally.
Penciled: tradesmen's wives—death in the newspaper
— *Pap.* V B 97:40 *n.d.*, 1844

From draft; see 299:36:

Underscored with pencil and with N.B. *penciled in margin:* her mother

—*Pap.* V B 103:14 *n.d.*, 1844

Deleted from sketch; see 300:25-301:18:

Midnight.

In the church
—*Pap.* V B 97:12 *n.d.*, 1844

Deleted from sketch; see 300:25-301:18:

Midnight

The second time in the church
see journal [*Pap.* IV A 97]
The method is changed.
—*Pap.* V B 97:13 *n.d.*, 1844

From draft; see 300:31:

Whether she knows it, I do not know, but I go to the churches I customarily attend and almost always sit in my usual place.—*Pap.* V B 103:16 *n.d.*, 1844

From draft; see 301:4-302:16:

Whether it was the tension she was in or whatever it was, she looked very troubled. Nevertheless, I understood this greeting in my own way. I lifted my head and let it fall down on my chest, somewhat like one who is bidding at an auction and says Yes, but did it also like one who is singing a hymn very loudly;* at least I have noticed Hiorthøy[111] doing it. Then she disappeared; I saw her no more.

In margin: *Which I also did, so that the people standing nearby looked at me; she also could do it all the more safely.—*Pap.* V B 103:17 *n.d.*, 1844

From draft; see 302:21:

Suppose I myself were the one who had to give her this message—what a situation: I with my wish, and a wish for both of us, and she has lost the sense for this language.—*Pap.* V B 103:18 *n.d.*, 1844

From draft; see 305:4-5:

And I do not deny that I have signed—certainly not indifferently but yet calmly—more than one death sentence—that is, from my standpoint I have had to judge that this kind of life was slovenly.—*Pap.* V B 103:19 *n.d.*, 1844

From draft; see 306:10:

In this respect I have in the past probed her under the guise of laughter and flippancy. This was not exactly out of character for me, but truly not one serious word was exchanged between us about what she should do.—*Pap.* V B 103:20 *n.d.*, 1844

From draft; see 307:19-21:

And yet I have perhaps made too strong an impression. It is so seldom that I want anything in the world of finitude; therefore it is certainly possible that I, if I do want something with decided passion, as was the case here, have made the strongest impression precisely by the short, simple statement. It is certainly possible that when a girl is altogether ignorant of a person's passion, and the time comes when not only with all his passion but also with its opposite, with calm self-possession, he says these words, "It is you I have sought; it is you I am seeking—I love you"—that this can make too powerful an impression, and far more powerful than all erotic gestures. Suppose it were so, that she was indeed taken by surprise! Well, so it goes.—*Pap.* V B 103:22 *n.d.*, 1844

From draft; see 308:1-3:

This, then, was an event. It is good that it happened. And yet it actually was not entirely right for her to want to communicate with me in this manner. She has no idea at all of the impression she can make on me; but presumably she relies on my ability to endure everything.—*Pap.* V B 103:23 *n.d.*, 1844

From draft; see 308:23-25:

. . . . . and so it is settled with her, my proud sun or, rather, with her, my bright moon—"as warm as the sun, as amorous as the moon."[112] Yes, she enchants me. That so much can happen in so short a time!—*Pap.* V B 103:25 *n.d.*, 1844

From draft; see 309:33-310:23:

. . . . . part of the fear. I am not expecting death, or insanity, or an intensification of her temporal existence, or an energetic expression indicating that she is destroyed, or a grand religious movement.

Thus I could have spared all my effort. Yet I do not regret it, and I am ever ready at all times once again to spend a whole day on the most trivial thing that could pertain to her. And yet I achieve nothing. In a certain sense I am the most sagacious person around, and in another sense I am the most stupid. Within my presupposition, I am the most intelligent, but this presupposition, which is always ideal, makes me with all my sagacity the most stupid of persons; thus someone who is half as sagacious as I am but who does not become involved with such presuppositions is actually far more sagacious than I am.

But I do not repent my ideal presupposition; in it I hold her and myself in honor.—*Pap.* V B 103:26 *n.d.*, 1844

See 310:3-323:23:

In a section about Periander in Fénelon's *Lebensbeschreibungen und Lehr-Satze*, Frankfurt and Leipzig, 1748, I read something which I had never read before and which is extremely interesting and poetic.

The passage is from pp. 80 bottom-87 bottom.—*JP* V 5736 (*Pap*. V A 45) *n.d.*, 1844

Deleted from sketch; see 310:35-38:

Midnight.

Sadness is actually sorrow's grace; but one must creep before one learns to walk and shriek before one learns to be sad.—*Pap*. V B 97:14 *n.d.*, 1844

From draft; see 312:4-15:

I now have my being entirely in my power. In this respect that misunderstanding has harmed me. She certainly notices that I look serious. She probably thinks that it is because of that quarrel. How maddening it is.—*Pap*. V B 103:27 *n.d.*, 1844

From draft; see 315:20:

—This is my pellet.

— *Pap*. V B 103:28 *n.d.*, 1844

Deleted from margin of sketch; see 316:30:

Midnight.

Whether I could not provide her with a more lenient impression of me—although I dislike these half explanations—to a certain degree—*Pap*. V B 97:44 *n.d.*, 1844

Deleted from margin of sketch; see 316:32-317:29:

Midnight.

The more lenient interpretation she must be provided with—now the imaginary construction is being developed.— *Pap*. V B 98:3 *n.d.*, 1844

From draft; see 317:36-37:

And yet this criterion is the current one—Yes, what is more, it is what poets* use when they portray heroes; Goethe does not have as much as one proper villain or one serious character in his repertoire—they are all fabricated people. Scribe is the cleverest of them all.

In margin: *Goethe

—*Pap.* V B 103:29 *n.d.*, 1844

Deleted from margin of sketch; see 318:35-319:10:

Midnight.

The story about Pericles in the second part of Plutarch, pp. 239 and 238. He weeps for his son, repeals the law about legitimate children; the Athenians believe that he is being punished by the gods.—*Pap.* V B 97:45 *n.d.*, 1844

From sketch; see 323:22-328:4:

My Reading Lesson.*
My Lesson
Periander.

*It is prepared for use in schools and therefore it is not considered necessary to become involved in the difficulties with respect to the two Perianders and the distinction in Herodotus etc.

In margin: Bookmark.
Reading for Diversion
—*Pap.* V B 133 *n.d.*, 1844

From draft; see 323:22-328:4:

My Reading Lesson.[*]
Periander.

Whether the tyrant P. is also the wise P., whether some statements by him ought to be attributed to another person with the same name, P. of Ambracea, whether the distinction in antiquity's perceptions determine an essential distinction: all this cannot occupy us or justifiably attract the attention of someone who is only preparing a reading book for beginners, and so regards the tale with which he is passing the time.

[*]*In margin:* "more crushed than repentant"
—*Pap.* V B 136:1 *n.d.*, 1844

From draft; see 330:13-17:

. . . . . She begs me for God's sake, she begs me in memory of my mother not to leave her.—*Pap.* V B 104:3 *n.d.*, 1844

From draft; see 330:20-25:

It is God's name and my late mother's name. Indeed, the person who dares to and is justified to use these weapons against me has power over me.—*Pap.* V B 104:4 *n.d.*, 1844

Deleted from sketch; see 331:20-332:8:

Morning

So come, then, for the last time, you mighty one, irony— help me.

> "Moon, lend me your ease in changing."
> Lauge Urne in
> *Eric and Abel.*[113]

a religiously unifying point we cannot have under such conditions.

In margin:
Thus I am as if married to her.
God—and my dead mother.
it is an unerotic action.
frivolously to risk her honor
—*Pap.* V B 97:24 *n.d.*, 1844

From sketch; see 331:18-332:4; 373:19-21:

In Part 3 (the two months)
Morning

. . . . . to have so much at stake on one play; her father is just as dear to me as she is, the whole family . . . . . —*Pap.* V B 97:18 *n.d.*, 1844

From sketch; see 332:34:

Midnight reports that correspond approximately to Part 3 in the story.—*Pap.* V B 98:1 *n.d.*, 1844

Deleted from sketch; see 335:4-31:

Midnight.

I have seen her. There is a movement in her face; whether it is weeping or laughter I do not know; I could write a whole book about it.—*Pap.* V B 97:42 *n.d.*, 1844

Deleted from sketch; see 335:4-31:

Midnight.

I have seen her. There is a movement in her face. Is it weeping or laughter? Bosom—throat muscles.—*Pap.* V B 98:10 *n.d.*, 1844

From draft; see 335:34-36:

V
B 114
207

I can remember once hurrying down one of the streets in the vicinity of Nicolai Tower.[114] I was supposed to be somewhere at precisely three o'clock, and I thought it was past three. Then I heard one stroke from the tower. I realized that I had arrived too late, that the time was a quarter past three. And yet it was wrong. The transmission of sound has a limit one does not consider when the line of demarcation is so close. The bell actually struck three; it was the last stroke. But when the hour was struck on the second stroke I still was not close

V
B 144
208

enough to hear the church bell. That is why I thought it was a quarter past three.—*Pap.* V B 114 *n.d.*, 1844

From draft; see 338:16-19:

As for the planned jealousy, I actually do not fear it; it is hardly my concern. After all, it would be most ridiculous for me to become jealous because another person obtained what I did not want. Jealousy demands that I myself want to have it and then another person obtains it.

In margin: for Augustine (in *De doctrina christiana*) declares very correctly: *non enim in carendo difficultas, nisi quum est in habendo cupiditas* [for there is no difficulty in abstaining, unless there is lust in enjoying].[115] —*Pap.* V B 115:1 *n.d.*, 1844

From draft; see 339:10-12:

I do believe that Young is wrong, and later Talleyrand, when they say that language is for the purpose of concealing thoughts; I believe also that a more recent author is wrong when he says that the purpose of language is not for concealing thoughts but for concealing the fact that one has no thoughts . . . . .[116] —*JP* III 2322 (*Pap.* V B 115:2) *n.d.*, 1844

From draft; see 340:27-32:

. . . . . because to be a model of virtue or a saint is for one thing a very embarrassing position in life; for another—and this is the most dangerous—precarious for virtue and sanctity. It is so satisfying, it is inspiring, to know that one is serving *pro virili* [according to one's capacity] what one considers to be the good and does it gratis. The person who really loves some study or other with enthusiasm will reluctantly make this study his job, even if he is awake early and late for it. Similarly the person who really loves the good does not want this enthusiasm of his to become a job enthusiasm, nor does he want to be persecuted by the world as if this were a proof of one's being so virtuous; above all, neither does he wish to

V
B 115:3
208

V
B 115:3
209

have a dozen applauding friends. If one really wishes to have
security about oneself, it is always best to exist under a form
of deception. The deception can be twofold: one can deceive
by being a villain at heart and yet so decent externally; one can
also deceive in the opposite way.—*Pap.* V B 115:3 *n.d.*, 1844

From draft; see 342:32:

Of course, that requires a kind of self-denial, which in my
view is not great, namely, to be nothing and have meaning in
one's life instead of seeming to be something in which there is
no meaning, and unctuously demand the same of others. But
. . . . . —*Pap.* V B 115:5 *n.d.*, 1844

From draft; see 342:37-343:34:

I am well aware that everyone would smile at me if I initiated him into my doubt, for what the pastor says everyone
can indeed understand, and what I say is confused. Yet I was
willing to give my life for the truth of my objection, but it
would be inconsistent of me to initiate anyone into it, for
there I would have to fancy that I was supposed to prepare the
Lord's way for others by proclaiming doubt. But I do not delude myself; I have only with myself to do.
    With regard to her, it is another matter . . . . . —*Pap.* V B
115:6 *n.d.*, 1844

From draft; see 346:22-33:

I certainly do not blame her for it; I have never searched for
my guilt in any other person. Even if my adolescent years
were disturbed by impressions which the child should be
spared, I never seek guilt in any other person but in myself, in
the fact that the disturbing factor had a disturbing effect on
me. Of what use is it to blame another person—and to live
without meaning, for there is no meaning in the fact that
someone else is able to damage me. Every such observation is

only a secular diversion that does not want to understand ethically something that demands a religious reassurance.—*Pap.* V B 115:7 *n.d.*, 1844

Deleted from sketch; see 347:6-9:

> ## Midnight.

To go away on a journey will never do; she could enter into an illusion.—no, the thing to do is to remain absolutely the same, to do nothing at all.—*Pap.* V B 98:2 *n.d.*, 1844

From draft; see 348:22-24:

It is a beautiful falling in love when one looks to see if it pays; it is even more beautiful than if a pastor, during the enthusiasm of his discourse, could see how much each one was putting in the collection box! If only I can keep the inwardness of prayer to my last breath, I ask nothing more. In its enthusiasm I am strong enough to forsake everything, and without it I am more wretched than a sucking calf—of what use to me then is the world's glory!—*Pap.* V B 115:8 *n.d.*, 1844

From draft; see 348:38-349:2:

This is just as ludicrous as when a man is unable to speak except to a general assembly—indeed, infinitely more ludicrous. But, of course, since one indeed knows that one can talk to God gratis, one must see to having a little benefit from it in another way. So it is with people. Let a man work to the utmost of his capacity in order to find the truth, but let him in addition have sufficient enthusiasm (bearing in mind that a dancer ought never be seen to be panting) to say: It costs nothing—then the world says: He is a selfish man. Let a man work half as much, but say: It costs so and so much—then the world says: That is a really clever man, a useful member of society. And why is he clever and useful? Because he lets himself be paid.

Yet I would rather not argue about this with anyone, much less have an esteemed public or a crowded congregation to feel that they are called to decide who is right. It is my final, my deepest conviction that every human being is equally near to God if he or she wants it. If anyone is unwilling to understand this, if anyone would rather waste his and my time in friendly squabbling, he will not fool me, for my exterior is especially designed to be free of all partnership.—*Pap.* V B 115:9 *n.d.*, 1844

From sketch; see 349:12-28:

Morning

During these two months I am doing everything to confuse her; only one thing do I insist on, and I say it to her earnestly, that she always was good enough for me, it is the last thing I said to her and as earnestly as possible. I do not have the heart to hurt her.

Every week I ask her whether we should part or keep on quarreling.

She joins in the laughter up to a certain point; then she stops laughing and the tears come; consequently she does not have any infinitude.

No trace of resignation on her part. And all this is taking place between us. No one suspects anything.

—*Pap.* V B 97:28 *n.d.*, 1844

From sketch; see 349:25-29:

Midnight.

A very inflamed response prompted by rage over lost honor and shattering of pride. —Can honor put on a leg, says Falstaff; no, but lost honor can trip one up.

—*Pap.* V B 98:15 *n.d.*, 1844

From draft; see 350:3-7:

. . . . . My soul would be rocked in the recollection of her by the monotonous waves of the sea, in winter I would deceive myself as I hurried to her.

In margin: Then I would walk out to the customshouse and fancy that she was arriving by steamship; then I would sit in my old café and watch her walk by.—*Pap.* V B 116:1 *n.d.*, 1844

From draft; see 350:9-11:

I have only the responsibility of eternity, and for me the branch of recollection is no almond staff[117] but a sword of judgment over my head.—*Pap.* V B 116:2 *n.d.*, 1844

Deleted from margin of sketch; see 350:11-15:

Midnight.

Nor do I dare recollect her. Adam could not and dared not recollect Eden—the angel with the sword.[118] —*Pap.* V B 98:5 *n.d.*, 1844

From draft; see 350:11-15:

Do you recollect . . . . . If he himself wanted to return to Eden, the angel with the flaming sword would indeed be standing there; would not the same angel be standing before the recollection.

It was sad for Petrarch that Laura belonged to another, but he nevertheless dared to think of her.[119] He had no other reproach than the fact that the pain became more bitter the more he dreamed, but no higher power forbade him that.—*JP* III 3240 (*Pap.* V B 116:3) *n.d.*, 1844

Deleted from sketch; see 350:17-37:

Midnight.

In all my depression I was an enthusiast; my depression is actually a form of my enthusiastic nature. At an early age I saw through people; then I would collect all the romantic fire in my soul, while outwardly I would be cold common sense. It was judging the world indirectly. Yet my shield must be clean. Now everything is confused; I have gotten a stain on my shield;[120] I was, after all, cold, commonsensical, shabby. See! It is my ruin, worse even than hers.—*Pap.* V B 98:6 *n.d.*, 1844

From draft; see 352:4-8:

If I will not resign myself to bear the cross of necessity, if I will not resign myself to suffer the pain of necessity, then I am annihilated and am nothing at all and have nowhere to be but among men in misunderstanding. Only when I bear this cross and feel this pain, only then will the cross be changed into a star and the pain into rejoicing.—*Pap.* V B 116:6 *n.d.*, 1844

From draft; see 352:17-353:11:

I know you, you horrifying thoughts, which still are alien to my being, I know that one can infatuate her with words, I understand how Richard III could overpower a woman who was his sworn enemy and change her into his mistress, I know that there is nothing that works so effectively on her as untruth, a lie, when it is rendered with the flaming of wild enthusiasm, with the noxious excitement of lust, I know it; she actually does not love such a person, she almost loathes him, but she becomes dizzy, drugged, she surrenders. It was as if an evil spirit wanted to bring me into his power (for these spiritual trials run down and one becomes weary of shrieking, weary of crying, weary of raging, if nothing comes of it). It already offered me as deposit a presentiment of superhuman powers by which I would accomplish great things—in that way rescue my pride and save my honor. Oh, it is a hard road, the transition from being larger than life in the power of evil to being nothing, nothing whatsoever, less than nothing, and even less than nothing through the antecedent aberrations of thought.—*Pap.* V B 116:7 *n.d.*, 1844

From draft; see 356:15-21:

. . . . . for my sake. I occupy myself essentially only with her, she occupies herself essentially only with herself, and yet I cannot stop loving her.—*Pap.* V B 107:3 *n.d.*, 1844

From draft; see 358:28-29:

. . . . . that the idea of a seduction almost comes from her. Thus the whole relationship is jolted as in an earthquake—that ultimately a casual offhand expression for our understanding should be chosen because my faithfulness was too high-strung to be satisfied with the most faithful expression.—*Pap.* V B 108:1 *n.d.*, 1844

From draft; see 359:15:

. . . . . into the discussion (her falling in love, our separation, whether she has respect for me and in such a way that she certainly does have respect but does not feel love, her future) . . . . . —*Pap.* V B 108:2 *n.d.*, 1844

From draft; see 359:36-360:7:

. . . . . then she would be far better off by having an unhappy love affair in which she has no guilt, holds it firmly, and makes a religious transfer. But she is unable to do that; to start it is of no use at all, and if she had been such a person she would not have behaved as she is behaving.—*Pap.* V B 108:3 *n.d.*, 1844

From sketch; see 360:9-363:15:

Nebuchadnezzar.

Sits on his throne. The wise men are summoned to explain how it happened that he became an ox; they could not.

Thereupon he has an accurate story drawn up depicting himself, and a slave has to be present at all times to represent him as he looked when he was an ox.

He orders a great festival to be held every year in remembrance of his having been an ox.

In margin: Was ich erlebte [What I experienced][121] when I was an ox.—*Pap.* V B 132 *n.d.*, 1844

Penciled in draft; see 360:10-363:15:

Eusebius *praeparatio evangelica*, 9, 41.[122]

—*Pap.* V B 139 *n.d.*, 1844

From draft; see 360:9-363:15:

V
B 137
231
Nebuchadnezzar's Last Will and Testament and His End

[*First three verses almost identical with first three in text*]

V
B 137
232
4. And great was my wisdom and like a dark saying that none of the wisest could explain.

5. That they could not tell me what I had dreamed, and I had them executed.

6. But the Mighty One, the Lord, is more powerful, and his wisdom is like a dark saying in action—indeed, like the deepest darkness in its inexplicableness. . . .

V
B 137
233
16. And my nails grew long like claws, and no one knew what I knew, that I was Nebuchadnezzar.

17. And the Mighty One, the Lord, has no treasurers and bailiffs, and no slingers and watchmen, and yet he has done it alone. . . .

20. Behold, this is why I will praise him as the One who is mightier than N. and seek his friendship so that I could learn to do the same.

22. And I summoned all the wise men so that they could

explain to me on pain of loss of my favor how it happened to me.

23. But they threw themselves on their faces and said: Great Nebuchadnezzar, it is a hallucination, who is capable of doing this.

24. But now Babel is not the powerful Babel, and my armies do not protect my throne, and it does not help that the night watchmen sit watching when the enemy come.

In margin: 24. [*changed in pencil to:* verse 17 add.] And I pondered long in my own thoughts and kept my thoughts to myself, for no one could perceive anything but a voice resembling an animal's. . . .

V
B 137
234

27. But I, I Nebuchadnezzar, will not be envious of him, even if I do not believe in him, nor will I give back his silver and gold vessels, but I want this to be preserved. . . .

29. And the wisest among the people will be led through the streets and be dressed as an animal, and all the people shall shout: The Lord, the Lord, the Lord is the Mighty One. . . .
—*Pap.* V B 137 *n.d.*, 1844

Addition to Pap. V B 137:

[6] The Mighty One the Lord

[8] for this king is not like a border neighbor, a nation with whom one can fight. he has no boundaries.

It is true that I do not believe in him, but I owe it to him to confess that he is the Mighty One, I Neb.—

[18] In his hands, a king's brain is like wax in the melting furnace, and kings' thoughts like a sewing thread in a child's hands.

[10] And although it was prophesied I nevertheless did not believe it. I still do not believe it.

[27] But I owe it to him to let his power be justly honored.

[28] Therefore every seventh year a festival shall be held in recollection of and in honor of him who was greater than Nebuchadnezzar.

[22-23] And I summoned the wise men to see if they could explain to me how this happened. But they answered and said: Great N., it is a hallucination, and I had them executed.

[20] If I could learn how he conducted himself, I would be just as powerful.

[25] But I have no joy from my might, of what use are all my spearmen, since I do not know whether I may become a bird that they mistake and shoot, or a tree from whose branches they make arrows.—*Pap.* V B 140 *n.d.*, 1844

In margin of draft; see 363:15:

NB
June 5
Midnight
Nebuchadnezzar

—*Pap.* V B 118:1

In margin of sketch; see 363:17-365:12:

Midnight

As a child I believed that the little fishing pond was the great ocean—to be developed—now it is just the same, this little girl is the whole world for me.—*Pap.* V B 98:13 *n.d.*, 1844

From draft; see 364:29-365:12:

In this respect, all my suffering is altogether a favor, for even the most gifted mind does not begin to understand himself unless a situation helps him in this way.

In margin: Even if I never finish there where she is finished. For suppose she became another's; then I would always still have the possibility of spiritual struggle, the possibility that it would suddenly strike me (through reading a book—through a casual word, which sometimes has the most powerful effect) or by myself I would discover that my depression was not chronic or that a marriage could be built in spite of it—suppose this happened; then I would have the opportunity to perceive the pain purely esthetically.—*Pap.* V B 118:2 *n.d.*, 1844

From draft; see 365:20-21:

I am like a human being that could be used in world-histor-ical crises; I am like a guinea pig that life uses in order to see on me how it looks. Similarly, an artist has a sketch to which he now adds a little and from which he now removes a little before and while he works on his work of art; similarly, the chemist drafts a calculation and makes a new calculation be-fore he proceeds to carry it out. And similarly, I am a sketch, a calculation.—*Pap.* V B 118:3 *n.d.*, 1844

V
B 118:3
213
V
B 118:3
214

From draft; see 365:36:

Relative earnestness is really narrow-mindedness.—*Pap.* V B 118:5 *n.d.*, 1844

Deleted from sketch; see 368:8-17:

Midnight.

I was walking with another person, we met her, I knew he was not acquainted with her, I said: How miserable the girl looks, he answered: No. It made me indescribably happy. By chance, she happened to return the very same way, we met her again, and I said: You are right, she does not look miser-able, and he said: That's just what I said. What luck. This way I obtained an expert appraisal.—*Pap.* V B 97:43 *n.d.*, 1844

From sketch; see 369:27-370:38:

Morning

During this whole operation of irony, he secretly ponders whether it could not be done. Then she throws herself away at so low a price, and his misgivings nevertheless were indeed essentially sympathetic. He is thinking this over for his own sake also, how much easier it will make his life.* Then he runs up against the wedding and thereby his own inclosing reserve; even if he would do everything and she permitted it, he must

V
B 97:51
180
V
B 97:51
181

take an oath. By an oath he binds himself and has only himself to deal with; he could eschew a wedding; a purely romantic connection is an insult. The idea absolutely dishonored.

In margin: *Also with respect to all those around her, who are entirely to his liking. To have so much at stake on one play.

A benefaction to her, and I am her benefactor—God spare me that—if she is suffering from stifled sighs, then I am suffering from stifled thoughts—one sobs—the fish gasps.—*Pap.* V B 97:51 *n.d.*, 1844

From draft; see 369:27-370:4:

But could I not yield to her for my own sake? If I am allowed to remain the person I am, and she will put up with everything, then I do indeed see what joy it could be for me that there was a person who would care about me fervently as a woman can. And if she now not only puts up with everything but begs me, begs me for it as for a benefaction for which she will thank me all her life, a benefaction for which almost all those (whom, as I expected, I have found to be lovable) around her will come to thank me.

In margin: when I made myself believe that my break with the idea was commendable, since it was for her sake, and so took her at her word, her impassioned words—*Pap.* V B 109:1 *n.d.*, 1844

From draft; see 370:20-26:

When someone who has been changed by evil spirits to the likeness of an animal sees himself, he despairs, and if I were to come to see myself and saw that I had been changed: that I had become a benefactor, her benefactor!—*Pap.* V B 109:2 *n.d.*, 1844

Deleted from sketch; see 371:10-28:

Morning.

A casual remark at a dinner party that becoming engaged makes one thin, but getting married makes one fat. He cites his father, who has been married two times and yet became thin.—*Pap.* V B 97:49 *n.d.*, 1844

Deleted from sketch; see 372:28-380:2:

Midnight.

In the Middle Ages a person saved his soul by saying his beads a certain number of times. If I could save my soul that way by repeating the story of my sufferings, I would be saved. —Is it perhaps because my repetition is not praying? But of course one does also have to work.

In margin: but nevertheless it was also curious. Everything was superbly arranged, the family as I wished it, she also, it progressed—and then suddenly came my depression—yet now I understand that my depression makes all confidentiality impossible for me.

A thank-you to God.

learn to know medical officer D, and the sympathizing families instead of God.

Penciled in margin: My excuse

—*Pap.* V B 98:8 *n.d.*, 1844

From draft; see 373:31-32:

. . . . . would from her side become a misalliance since I would acquire all the power, she none whatsoever, I would become the depository of the content of her whole soul, she only insofar as it pleases myself.—*Pap.* V B 119:1 *n.d.*, 1844

From draft; see 374:8-10:

I can concern myself about a person as perhaps not many are able to do, but I cannot accept the concern of another person who is supposed to be my confidant, for he nevertheless will not become that.—*Pap.* V B 119:2 *n.d.*, 1844

From draft; see 374:21-375:12:

Flee from it I cannot; I must bear the thought until I find a religious reassurance, and only then am I free until something

V
B 98:8
182

V
B 98:8
183

V
B 119:3
214

new comes along. For example, once I was seized by the thought that it must be horrifying to be buried alive. Instantly it became clear to me that this might happen to me, for although I have the most inspired conception that God is love, I also have the conception that in time and temporality one must be prepared to suffer everything and that it is only sensate and physical conceptions of God that believe one is exempted from this.[*] At first I tried to find some means or other of protecting myself. I once jotted them all down, and someone who is not very scheming would surely be astonished at the cunningness of my calculations. But then my depression impounded my cleverness and now I had to think up just as ingenious objections, until it was clear that there was no certainty at all in the whole wide world; even if I had all the cleverness of the world, even if all mankind were to do everything for me, there was no protection against it possibly happening to me. What then? Then I had to see about finding a religious reassurance. So I practice thinking the thought and include my conception of God's love. Gradually I become intimate with it, intimate with the thought that it might happen to me, but also with the thought that God is still love and that everything will turn out for the good and that one dies only once, even if one is buried alive. Now and then I am visited by the thought. It lasts but a minute, the very same minute I am reoriented in my religious view, and the whole thing does not disturb me at all; but I do nevertheless have the thought.

With respect to the person who wants something finite, the point is to keep the terrors away; with respect to the religious, the point is to be receptive to the terrors, to open oneself to them—but also to be led to victory through this process of annihilation.

[*]*In margin:* A blending of Judaism and Christianity

—*Pap.* V B 119:3 *n.d.*, 1844

From draft; see 375:27-30:

If the task were to conceal one's depression, then I would be *omnibus numeris absolutus et perfectus* [absolute and perfect in

V
B 119:3
215

all details],[123] and all, of course, declare the task to be that, and I believed it myself until I realized that the wedding is a divine protest against it.—*Pap.* V B 119:4 *n.d.*, 1844

From draft; see 381:10-383:34:

. . . . . sides; even in this moment I am certain that almost anyone I would consult about what a depressed man should do in order not to torture a wife would answer: He should inclose it within himself like a man. To that I would answer: I am just the man for that, and then he would smile suspiciously at me, as if I were a braggart, but he would not understand my doubt, that to be inclosingly reserved is in conflict with the ethical commitment in marriage. This does not mean that a married man is supposed to blab out everything, but it does mean that he must not hide something about which he can say, "I cannot disclose that to her."—*Pap.* V B 119:11 *n.d.*, 1844

Deleted from margin of sketch; see 381:10-383:34:

Midnight.

That I have not received her forgiveness—light to be thrown on the impossibility of this.—*Pap.* V B 98:17 *n.d.*, 1844

From sketch; see 382:4-6:

Morning

She has said that she did perceive that I would be better off being free, but I would never be happy in any case, so I could just as well take her along.—*Pap.* V B 97:27 *n.d.*, 1844

From draft; see 382:4-6:

She herself said that I would be much happier without her.—*Pap.* V B 119:12 *n.d.*, 1844

From draft; see 382:8-15:

In her opinion, it was a matter of moving me religiously by the authority of duty and of the sacred, to move me sympathetically by her misery. If I had spoken at this point, I would have had to say, "It is my highest wish to remain with you, and I am not exactly tempted to leave you and my pride in the lurch." She very likely would not have taken time to hear the latter, she would have been jubilant, she would have said . . . —*Pap.* V B 119:13 *n.d.*, 1844

From draft; see 382:37-38:

Then she could also have become mine.—*Pap.* V B 119:14 *n.d.*, 1844

From draft; see 383:3-6:

This, you see, is why I do not have it. She cannot complain about it, for her demand to me has become infinitely much more than she could make it by herself. An official . . . . . — *Pap.* V B 119:15 *n.d.*, 1844

From draft; see 383:34:

I also found a religious point of departure for the whole thing only by virtue of a break by which I became guilty because I saw a divine protest against the whole affair. This is my last resort. On an intermediate level I have to the utmost of my capacities done everything my understanding could teach me to be of service to her. I have made it possible for her to assume that I was a deceiver, a twaddler, an irresponsible person, and all such categories come naturally to her; this is something she can understand.—*Pap.* V B 119:16 *n.d*, 1844

From draft; see 384:3-5:

I shudder when I think about her suddenly beginning to understand *cum emphasi* [with emphasis] how I am still clinging

to her. What confusion, and what a satire on various ones.—
Pap. V B 119:17 *n.d.*, 1844

From draft; see 384:8-9:

Compared with this, every prosaic dabbling at wanting to
revenge oneself, for example by taking another, is only a
jest.—*Pap.* V B 119:18 *n.d.*, 1844

From draft; see 384:19-25:

This is and continues to be for me my rich consolation, my
original faith in the consistency of existence: that it must become clear . . . —*Pap.* V B 119:19 *n.d.*, 1844

From draft; see 386:6-8:

What consoles me is that his view is found in her soul, once
she is worked upon by other interpreters, whom I shall incite
against me in such a way that they help her.—*Pap.* V B 110:1
n.d., 1844

From draft; see 387:33-388:4:

. . . . . what this situation means.*
In margin: *And guess, then, what does it mean? Why is the
girl crying? And he who is with her, who is he? And which of
them is suffering more? What if he who is with her had no
religious premises and after having seen this agony could only
find rest in the wildest diversions, even if he became a seducer,
he would still only see in the seduced girl the resemblance to
her because he loved only her. But since he is not at all the
kind of a person to cause such fears, he will surely cling to her
memory, alas, till his last breath. Come then and tell him
something, you who have seen the dreadful in life, you who
have traveled widely, tell him, you tried and tested sea-hero,
that you have lain at sea where the ship would not obey the
rudder, where the anchor could not hold it, Good God, he has
even seen or thought he saw a confusion in the laws of exist-

ence where the state of upheaval would not obey the rudder of an honest will. Tell about a dead calm—he was a poor wretched lover who desperately had every sail out to catch the wind, but there was none—tell about upheavals—he was a poor wretched lover who murdered the one he loved not by accident but in accord with his most honest conviction.—*Pap.* V B 111 *n.d.,* 1844

From draft; see 388:25-27:

. . . . . be it forbidden me to become despondent. Moreover, I have no reason yet, and as soon as I have the reason, I know very well that I shall not become despondent. This despondency is a fruit of possibility.—*Pap.* V B 121 *n.d.,* 1844

From sketch; see 390:4-9:

Morning.

Suppose she suddenly became ill through all this—and I who carry the heavy burden of my dissimulation.—*Pap.* V B 97:26 *n.d.,* 1844

Deleted from sketch; see 152:7-9, 383:36, 390:10-391:11:

Midnight.

Almost all the reports in the last part will deal on occasion with a reunion in eternity.

Klopstock[124]—Meta—must try to find.

In margin: Recollections of her come on occasion, of her life with him, precisely because he now believes he has to give her up in the infinite sense.—*Pap.* V B 98:7 *n.d.,* 1844

From draft; see 390:32-33:

In time I shall be an unhappy lover; more I do not ask. I have never understood that time was any good for anything else but making a person unhappy—and thus happy in a consciousness of eternity.—*Pap.* V B 122:1 *n.d.,* 1844

From draft; see 391:10-11:

. . . . . and basically have always loved her more than my-self, in so doing unhappy, so unhappy that everyone would say it was untruth.—*Pap.* V B 122:2 *n.d.*, 1844

Deleted from sketch; see 391:30-392:22:

Midnight.

I saw her today. She did not see me. She was walking with another girl, cheerful and happy. So perhaps she becomes pale only when she sees me. I am as if sentenced at the king's pleasure.[125] As soon as I see her happy and healthy, my fate is mitigated. If she were to marry, I would be released.

In margin: By chance I went into my old café. Thus everything was like the old days.—*Pap.* V B 98:18 *n.d.*, 1844

From draft; see 392:27-393:11:

Indeed, if in the beginning I had suspected someone else, I believe it would have been almost impossible for my depression to take hold of me, but I would have known better how to evaluate her passion and her facial expressions.

In margin: And it is her first love to which she returns—thus she has lost nothing in my eyes. Absorbed in myself, I have not noticed that anything like that was in her; she has not had occasion to say anything, and thus it nevertheless is possible. That such a thing could have happened to me is, after all, a little joke on me, but it makes no difference if only she is held in the idea; then I ask no more. She possibly would have disturbed my life-view; now she does not. It is good that I never knew of any such person; it would have disturbed me in my grieving.—*Pap.* V B 122:3 *n.d.*, 1844

V
B 122:3
218

V
B 122:3
219

From draft; see 393:14-15:

. . . . . for it fits my nature so completely that I can say: Thus and only thus could I feel my way in the erotic. As soon as I dare to call it an incident, the incident is precisely just as

comic as it is tragic. The comic consists in our having exchanged roles. She screams, I suffer, she dies, I live, she loves
again, I remain the same, she becomes happy a second time, I
continue to be the unhappy one. And what is even more
comic, only in this way can my story become intelligible to
others. I would hardly dare to confess the truth of the matter
on my deathbed lest the esteemed funeral procession burst
into unseemly laughter at burying such an unhappy lover.—
Pap. V B 122:4 *n.d.*, 1844

From final copy; see 393:15:

As soon as I have peace and she is free and consequently I
dare to call the whole thing an incident, then I may say: It is
precisely just as comic as tragic. The comic consists in our
having exchanged roles. She laments, I suffer, she dies, I live,
she loves again, I remain the same, she becomes happy a second time, I am and remain the unhappy one and there the matter rests. And what is even more comic is that as soon as I shall
talk about it with someone I must talk in such a way that she
is the suffering one, I the one who walks jauntily, for otherwise he believes that I am poking fun at him, and I must go
on this way lest the esteemed funeral procession that some day
will follow me to the grave burst into unseemly laughter at
burying such an unhappy lover.—*Pap.* VI B 8:14 *n.d.*, 1844

From sketch; see 393:17-19:

What should I say? Should I change the deception a bit and
seek an understanding in: Jack does it, you do it, everyone
does it[126]—that, after all, would be a new untruth, for I am
absolutely unchanged, and it never occurred to me to think of
any other girl.—*Pap.* V B 122:5 *n.d.*, 1844

From draft; see 393:38-394:2:

No, only when I am silent can I keep my soul full of pathos
so that she and life's whirlpool do not hurl me into the ludicrous. I am as prepared as possible for what will happen; it is

my consolation that I believe myself able to hold back.—*Pap.*
V B 122:6 *n.d.*, 1844

From draft; see 395:38-396:5:

   As for myself, my understanding teaches me that I have
benefited from these two months, that she has even less of an
idea of me and my personality. To me it would be a terrible
thought to be separated from a person to whom I had entrusted some of the innermost content of my life, especially
from a young girl who perhaps would speedily enough fall in
love again and then have the content of my life to dabble in
during the love embrace. Let them hug and kiss; it is of no
concern to me, but my personality was and is a closed book
for her. If my inclosing reserve has crushed me, it has also
benefited me in that it has made me suspicious even of the
person I called my beloved.—*Pap.* V B 113 *n.d.*, 1844

*From final copy, with penciled parentheses and underlining; see
396:23:*

   . . . . . *(and with the utmost labor yet continually hidden in the
chaste modesty of the deception),* . . . . . —*Pap.* VI B 8:15 *n.d.*,
1844

From sketch; see 398:1:

                Postscript by Frater Taciturnus
                          —*Pap.* V B 148:1 *n.d.*, 1844

Deleted from sketch; see 371:3-372:18:

   My dear reader, if you are in any way a professional, you
will readily see that the character I have constructed is a demonic individuality tending toward and approximating the
religious. That kind of thing is always of interest especially to
the religious—and to *Liebhabere* [amateurs]. As for the female
individuality with whom he, to use a ballet term, performs
the routine figures, she is altogether ordinary. She is a charm-

ing girl etc. I have clung firmly to only one thing in the construction for the specific purpose of illuminating him, and that
is that she lacks religious presuppositions.

The girl is kept altogether ordinary;[*] precisely such a person illuminates him best; because of that he has the added suffering of wanting with the strain of despair to have her be
something great.

[*]*In margin:* she is what is called a nice girl.

— *Pap.* V B 148:4 *n.d.*, 1844

In margin of sketch; see 398:24-399:2:

My interest is not to be a poet but to make out the meaning
of the religious. *That it will not be thought that the religious is for
striplings* and stupid people—that is my aim in this story.

In margin: *and the unshaven

—*JP* V 5722 (*Pap.* V B 148:5) *n.d.*, 1844

Deleted from draft; see 399:23-400:27:

[*Penciled in margin: N.B.*]

V
B 154
260*In the period of engagement*, she does everything that a lovable
girl would do. She is reserved, no wonder, since all his singularity is not exactly cheering to a young girl. Then erotic
love emerges; then she gives him a most charming little curtsey, and he understands it in his categories. Then she be-
V
B 154
261seeches him* to remain with her. She shows him every possible sympathy by wanting to put up with everything in him; it
is and remains sympathy, even if he has another concept of it.
After that time, she does nothing at all, but his passion sees
everything. Even if she is assumed to have nodded to him in
church, the distance is such that it was difficult to observe, and
even if it is so, for we have no factual certainty, then it would
be just like that curtsey, and only for his eyes does this have
enormous meaning.

In margin: *in a little note she herself brings

— *Pap.* V B 154 *n.d.*, 1844

Deleted from sketch; see 399:11-402:25:

I shall now tease him a little. For example, by reminding him of a remark by another author, by asking him whether he became mad by being faithful to her, or did he remain faithful to her because he was mad. Indeed, in a certain sense it is funny to see a horror like that, a troglodyte or cave dweller, come sneaking out after secretly having listened to human talk and now wanting to imitate them. In the nineteenth century. It is good he does not appear in the external actuality, for then he would have the boys chasing him. To take seriously the whole rigmarole that everyone knows so well about loving only once etc., something one condones only in a young person, and that only once in his life, and in someone drunk. The time of youth is indeed the time of preparation, and therefore in it we lay up supplies for life; thus everyone takes along a little mouthful of romantic sayings to help himself through life according to the specification: he is sociable in friendship, is friendly in society, and on the whole pleasant and continually friendly. But it is only something one says; it is a kind of putty or paste with which one glues social life together.

Yet the erotic interests me less. The religious is the main consideration, and he has in fact established an ethical point of view before he becomes engaged. He is unable to love; for the girl he can become a powerful ministering spirit who, like the jinni of the lamp, indulges her in everything, or he can become what he became, but a lover he is not.

Otherwise, the remarkable thing about this horror is that he is not at all visible in the external and to that extent he cannot have the boys chasing him. Unlike other enthusiasts, he does not wish to transform the world and express his enthusiasm; he is free in his enthusiasm, not bound, for precisely the form of opposition makes him free.—*Pap.* V B 148:34 *n.d.,* 1844

Deleted from draft; see 404:24-25:

. . . . . in two sections: (1) about the erotic relation, (2) about the religious, and under each of these I shall bring the thought back again to specific points, in the working out of which I always have him *in mente* [in mind].

What is unhappy

A

The erotic relation.

—*Pap.* V B 150:2 *n.d.*, 1844

From sketch; see 405:26-452:13:

V
B 149:2
252

[*Deleted:* A

The erotic relation]

[*Penciled*: para. 1]

   (1) unhappy love

       [*Penciled*: para. 2]

   (2) misunderstanding as the principle for the tragic

       his misunderstanding in relation to her

comparison with Hamlet

       he has not offended her by

       what happened later but by

       beginning see p. 11 bottom [*Pap.* V B 148:34]

       [*Penciled*: para. 3]

   (3) the need for the historical in the tragic, greater than in the comic, and the disappearance of this difference in the form of the imaginary construction.

       [*Penciled*: para. 4]

   (4) dialectical repentance as transition to ethical repentance*

       the boundary between the

       esthetic and the ethical

see the black book, p. 3 top [*Pap.* V B 148:9]

       [*Penciled:* p. 6 (*Pap.* V B 148:27-28)]

[*Penciled:* David (Uriah)]

       He himself has some guilt because of

       the deception, that he had such an awful time.

V
B 149:2
253

*one cannot come to repent, because it is as if one should act—or the reverse, to stop thinking about one's guilt is it not to cease to repent, and yet it can be necessary.

> This state of suspension is
> like treading water.
> —*Pap*. V B 149:2 *n.d.*, 1844

Deleted from sketch; see 404:29-416:4:

The book will end with a few added remarks explaining that this construction is specifically different from the famous unhappy love stories of the past.

> Petrarch.
> Abelard.
> Romeo.
> Axel.

and showing what meaning this could have for esthetics. —A little reference to Heiberg's stupid remarks about the drama that the times now demand—that is, what Martensen and other cavaliers are applauding.—*Pap*. V B 148:2 *n.d.*, 1844

From draft; see 412:11-15:

But poetry cannot have anything to do with self-contradiction, and it is not inspired by assurances from the man himself or from his friend, who swears that one evening when they were out walking he heard him say: I will sacrifice my life for the good cause; or from a visitor, who in his own living room heard him say: I will present myself to the king and speak in this manner etc.—*Pap*. V B 150:4 *n.d.*, 1844

V
B 150:4
254

V
B 150:4
255

From draft; see 412:29:

Certainly speculative drama must be what the times demand, and the times indeed are advancing. When this drama comes, we shall then see what an enormous advance has been made since Shakespeare.—*Pap*. V B 150:5 *n.d.*, 1844

From draft; see 415:20-36:

Thus I have heard women hawkers using Kantian phrases. No, that which is unpopular, that which people who could rattle off terminologies could not do, is to stick to one thought, and that which always is and remains unpopular is to think with ethical passion.—*Pap.* V 150:7 *n.d.*, 1844

From sketch; see 417:35-418:5:

The comic and the tragic in pairing unlikes together in erotic love, like her and him here.

> (What Socrates says in *Phaedo* about the chain that is taken off and has caused pain but now causes a sense of well-being, and the comic and the tragic in this, which Aesop is supposed to have composed.)

Penciled in margin: see p. 2 [*Pap.* V B 148:4-8]
see p. 6 [*Pap.* V B 147:27-28]
see p. 7 [*Pap.* V B 148:29]
see p. 11 bot. [*Pap.* V B 148:34]—
Pap. V B 148:21 *n.d*, 1844

From draft; see 418:8-19:

That the opposite is simultaneous, poetry cannot accept, for in the very same moment it itself ceases.—*Pap.* V B 150:8 *n.d.*, 1844

Deleted from sketch; see 419:21-420:25:

Misunderstanding has its comic side. I had a maid who wanted to do everything to please me and to care for me, but she could not understand anything but that it was lovely in winter to have enough firewood and to make a fire, and I could not bear warm temperatures—and she stoked the fire and yet was indescribably fond of me.

In margin: Gulliver's Travels

—*Pap.* V B 148:22 *n.d.*, 1844

Deleted from sketch; see 420:7-15:

A deaf man who slowly opens a door that squeaks—he believes that he is doing it so well, instead of doing it quickly so that it would be over.—*Pap.* V B 148:23 *n.d.*, 1844

From draft; see 420:16-25:

In other respects, one will see that there is a kind of weak point of unity here, for he indeed does not want to disturb; therefore the comic and the tragic are also present in a dim twilight, but not essentially, for the substance of passion is not posited. Another example, about which one must say that one does not know whether to laugh or to cry, because there is a little more emotion but still no pathos. A man takes a poor old man into his house as his servant. He is very kind to him, and the faithful servant is utterly devoted to him. The man is prosperous, and the servant comes from straitened circumstances. Someone who has lived as that poor man had knows that poor people are accustomed to saying and thinking that it must be wonderful in winter to have enough firewood for the stove. The rich man has enough firewood, but, indulged to the nth degree, he can tolerate only a certain temperature. The faithful servant stokes and stokes the fire and cannot understand anything else than that he is doing the best thing. But here, too, no essential passion is posited.—*Pap.* V B 150:9 *n.d.*, 1844

Deleted from sketch; see 423:11-15:

Therefore the story begins twice. The night reports are interpretations of possibility and of his own ideality. It is a good contrast to those who blaze most intensely in the first moment. In the morning reports he has already perceived (i.e. consequently in actuality) that it is not so bad; he has imagined her bound to another, and in the night reports it takes a long time before he achieves that. —So it is with depression.—*Pap.* V B 148:7 *n.d.*, 1844

V
B 150:9
255

V
B 150:9
256

Deleted from sketch; see 423:20-424:35:

. . . . . the verse from Shakespeare in Börne, vol. VII, p.
245.[127] Her most dangerous and most critical moment is when
she has staked everything and in the two months when she
sees him, his image vanishes, and even more so when he has
left her. With him it is the reverse; she becomes greater and
greater, until his sympathy becomes despondent; it is the crisis
of strength and health.—*Pap.* V B 148:8 *n.d.*, 1844

Deleted from sketch; see 423:33-36:

(1) The girl became far greater to him after he left her.
     The difference between the morning and midnight re-
     ports.
(2) What his inclosing reserve means, he never says.
        He does say what once bound him in depression,
        but not what binds him.

                              —*Pap.* V B 148:6 *n.d.*, 1844

Deleted from sketch; see 424:36-427:11:

V
B 148:30
246
I have deliberately shaped his entire situation in life so that
he never has an event, a certainty, but everything becomes
dialectical for him.

V
B 148:30
247
        He sees her, she is pale, this actually proves nothing
        whatsoever, can have many reasons.
        He sees her three times on Hauser Square. Can be
        purely accidental
        He sees her in church—proves nothing whatsoever,
        perhaps it is not even as he thinks.
I could not make him otherwise; unlike novelists I have no
actuality to hold on to. The idea requires that he get to see
her again, but the idea requires that he get to see her in such
a way that he has no certainty, no fact.—*Pap.* V B 148:30
n.d., 1844

Deleted from sketch; see 425:30-39 fn.:

How fatiguing it must be to be inclosingly reserved, I can best see in the fact that it is fatiguing to think it, indeed, exhausting and wearisome to take care of small details.

For example, the piece dated midnight, February 13. It could simply have said, "According to the medical report, she feels well." Most readers would very likely have found that enough, and yet the whole design would have been spoiled, for then there would have been one single little point at which he would have received a direct piece of information instead of his needing to have everything dialectical so that he never acquires factual certainty. The good reader would also have immediately asked: How did he obtain this medical report.— *Pap*. V B 148:31 *n.d.*, 1844

From sketch; see 425:28-426:1:

Addenda to Guilty?/Not-Guilty?

[*Deleted:*
(1) the whole situation in the church amounts to nothing; at that distance she may have been nodding to someone else, perhaps did not nod at all.

(1) such a right reverend monologue etc., addendum that witnesses about the Christian faith.

(2) "a possibility" the significance of this story is that Quidam of the imaginary construction thinks through the category* that is the form of the depression. see end of journal.
    *and has it lead to insanity.]

(3) himself deceived by life etc., addendum by wanting to be an observer.

[*Deleted:*
(4) I do not see it this way; I see only the unity of the comic and the tragic—*is it perhaps because I am not the person* involved. these words are to be deleted.]
             —*Pap*. V B 153 *n.d.*, 1844

Deleted from sketch; see 426:9-38:

One can almost always grant that there is much good in an inclosingly reserved person, but he is also a fine confectioner and one must also turn out his threadbare side. —I shall certainly manage him; I myself have conjured him up, although I cannot argue with him, for the devil himself cannot do that.—*Pap.* V B 148:32 *n.d.*, 1844

Deleted from sketch; see 427:17-36:

He [is] essentially* inclosingly reserved—she could not be that even if she wanted to (why not? A woman cannot express dialectical reduplication, just as she cannot express many consonants preceding one vowel but only the vowels).

*The significance of the portions entered the fifth of each month.—*JP* V 5723 (*Pap.* V B 148:25) *n.d.*, 1844

Deleted from sketch; see 427:39-429:12:

What his inclosing reserve contains, he never says.

Let us simply assume that his depression has no content at all. He who is depressed can name many cares that hold him in bondage, but the one that binds him he is unable to name. Or let it be guilt. Or mental derangement.

—*JP* V 5724 (*Pap.* V B 148:29) *n.d.*, 1844

Deleted from draft; see 429:32-35:

On the whole, the reader will perhaps pay heed to the respect with which he treats the girl, to whom he is greatly superior, but he does not know it and does not want to know it. —*Pap.* V B 150:12 *n.d.*, 1844

From draft; see 430:15-18:

. . . . . not until then can the original possibility of the religious that must be given in childhood's impression break through.—*Pap.* V B 150:13 *n.d.*, 1844

From draft; see 430:35:

. . . . . and whereas one only rarely sees in actuality the deep respect for a girl that he has, one sees often enough that a girl does not understand herself.—*Pap.* V B 150:14 *n.d.*, 1844

Deleted from draft; see 431:7-435:8:

He cannot at all understand that which essentially becomes her suffering, and she cannot at all understand that which essentially becomes his suffering (the responsibility).

> [*Penciled:* p. 11 bot. (*Pap.* V B 148:34)]
> He is essentially a thinker, she anything but.—
> He is religious—she is of the world (in the good sense)
> he is sympathetic (since he suffers sympathetically a second time)—she egoistic (but see p. 10 [*Pap.* V B 148:33])
> he suffers afterward—she at once.
> he remains the same—she despairs and then is comforted
> Impression for eternity
> He acting—she passive, and yet it is reversed.
> he guilty—she innocent, and yet they both are guilty.
> > see p. 6 bot. [*Pap.* V B 148:28].
> > —*Pap.* V B 148:24 *n.d.*, 1844

Deleted from sketch; see 433:6-21:

When he says of her that she lacks feminine resignation, it is true, but not that she has no sympathy whatsoever for his sufferings, for at this point he forgets to bear in mind that by his deception he himself does indeed prevent her from seeing that he is suffering. Thus, the better his deception is, the less she discovers anything.

> Here I have him in a predicament.
> —*Pap.* V B 148:33 *n.d.*, 1844

Deleted from sketch; see 434:19-435:30:

She believes that he has insulted her by breaking up, and yet he actually insulted her only by beginning, which she does not believe at all*
*how did he come to begin?—*Pap.* V B 148:26 *n.d.*, 1844

Deleted from sketch; see 435:38-436:13:

The expression for the misunderstandings pointed out is really that he cannot love, nor can she (see p. 11 bot. [*Pap.* V B 148:34]). He has chosen the ethical expression of love; she has chosen the self-loving expression.

> he lacks the immediacy, has the power of will; she
> has the immediate perseverance, cannot live
> without him, but this is not loving, for she lacks
> the resignation so that it can truly be said that
> she loves him.
>
> See p. 11 bot. [*Pap.* V B 148:34]
> —*Pap.* V B 148:28 *n.d.*, 1844

In margin of draft; see 436:11-13:

If it had not come to a turning point, they could have become extremely happy in a certain sense, but unfortunately it cannot be thought away—*Pap.* V B 150:16 *n.d.*, 1844

Deleted from sketch; see 436:23-437:2:

If he now becomes free and she becomes another's, what then? —Will he then have a fling? No, it is a psychological impossibility; only then will he really begin to repent, not, however, that he gave her up (that is an esthetic observation he has already long ago put behind him) but that he began it and became a murderer. This thought he will now be able to hold fast in the ideality of his conception, undisturbed by actuality, which he was not when he had to worry about whether she actually would die etc. —He is once again inclosed within himself and has all his ideality.—*Pap*. V B 148:27 *n.d.*, 1844

Deleted from sketch; see 437:12-439:33:

Hitherto, the defect in the tragic is that it had to be about great men and great events historically certain. —Disbelief in the idea—therefore hitherto the comic has had a higher ideality; we are more inclined to believe that a person is ridiculous than that he is great (see notes on esthetics [*Pap*. IV C 102-27, especially 121] in the tall cupboard next to the door).

Likewise with the religious prototypes. The person who in this connection does not understand *ab posse ad esse valet consequentia* [a conclusion of actuality from possibility] does not understand *ab esse ad posse valet consequentia* [a conclusion of possibility from actuality] either but imagines that he does. Only ideality is the true norm; actuality and historical accuracy are nonsense as a norm.—*JP* I 150 (*Pap*. V B 148:17) *n.d.*, 1844

Deleted from margin in final copy; see 437:20-32:

. . . . . since the exception only proves the rule, and an exception like Lessing expressly demonstrates that his discovering eyes, his sharp understanding of what went before, were necessary in order that *Emilia Galotti* could see the light of day, and Lessing's mastery in constructing a plot and writing dialogue [were necessary] in order to provide entrance for the piece.—*Pap*. VI B 8:18 *n.d.*, 1844

From draft; see 437:37-438:9:

I shall not decide this matter but rather give the explanation that the comic lies in metaphysical categories, the tragic in esthetic categories. The comic therefore leaves a total impression, for, since it points out the contradiction to the idea, existence is reconciled, inasmuch as the spectator laughs at it. The tragic does not reconcile with existence. I see the hero fall and the idea conquer, but the hero's fall does indeed contain a sorrowful consideration for the spectator, who is not even a hero.—*Pap.* V B 150:17 *n.d.*, 1844

Deleted from sketch; see 439:34-440:22:

The person who would ask me if my imaginary construction was a true story has not understood it at all, for the understanding lies precisely in its being infinitely unimportant; it is the spirit's intrepid assurance that is needed. It is spirit to ask about two things: (1) Is it possible? (2) Am I able to do it? It is lack of spirit to ask about two things: (1) Is it true? (2) Has my neighbor Christophersen actually done it?—*Pap.* V B 148:20 *n.d.*, 1844

Deleted from sketch; see 441:4-444:23:

If it had been an esthetic story, the result ought to have been given, but a religious exposition has no result, for it has its surest result safeguarded only in faith. (The negative higher than the positive praised by stupid people, including several geniuses.) To believe that one is finished is precisely perdition. The stupid pastors who have results and believe that to have faith is to roll around on dry land, when it is to swim, and consequently believe that to swim is to roll around on dry land. All tasks lie in the invisible (whether one actually has done it) and are indifferent to quantitative differences (the esthetic hero is supposed to be famous, esteemed, etc.—it revolves just as well around a dog as around kingdoms and lords).—*Pap.* V B 148:19 *n.d.*, 1844

Deleted from sketch; see 441:29-442:19:

The ethical result see *Æsthetica* in tall cupboard p. 1, column 2 mid. [*Pap.* IV C 115].

—*Pap.* V B 148:18 *n.d.*, 1844

From draft; see 444:23:

For example, if we take the two characters in the imaginary construction, it is clear that the heroine is a totally different positive character than the hero. She does not venture into the uncertain; she sticks to the positive.—*Pap.* V B 150:19 *n.d.*, 1844

Deleted from sketch; see 447:13-17:

Latone could not give birth because a gadfly was tormenting her—similarly this girl is a gadfly for him, and I have deliberately kept the contrast as strong as possible.—*Pap.* V B 148:9 *n.d.*, 1844

Deleted from draft; see 450:19-24:

Precisely for that reason he will want to endure actuality and yet continually be in my service.—*Pap.* V B 150:20 *n.d.*, 1844

Deleted from sketch; see 453:6-30:

Rötscher

Börne who *en passant* [casually] calls *Hamlet* a "Christian tragedy." The mistake in Shakespeare is precisely that Hamlet does not have religious doubts. If he does not have them, then it is sheer nonsense and indecision if he does not settle the matter straight away.—*JP* II 1561 (*Pap.* V B 148:16) *n.d.*, 1844

From draft; see 453:27-30:

Rötscher has quite rightly interpreted him as being morbidly reflective [*deleted:* and it is incredible that Goethe has taken such great pains to uphold Hamlet]. Rötscher's development is excellent, and it also has something else of interest for one who wants[*] to check the systematicians a bit more closely; for R. is, as is known, a Hegelian, but in the psychical development of esthetic characters he is different and is constrained to use and does continually use existential categories such as the leap, for example, although he does not emphasize it as much as Vigilius Haufniensis does, and to me it is inconceivable that one can use them without noting the consequences for the system.

[*]*In margin:* to see how the systematicians are constrained to use existential categories such as the leap, for example.—*JP* III 2344 (*Pap.* V B 150:21) *n.d.*, 1844

Deleted from final copy; see 454:30:

> The religious relation
> para. 1.
> —*Pap.* VI B 8:19 *n.d.*, 1844

From sketch; see 454:31-460:15:

> [*Deleted: The religious*]
> Para. 1 [*changed to:* 5]

The concept of hero—suffering—"tragedy must arouse fear and cleanse the passions"—the spectator's sympathy (different within the various views of the world)

> Para. 2 [*changed to:* 6]

The principle: not to repent is the highest wisdom

> Para. 3 [*changed to:* 7]

The forgiveness of sin

> —*Pap.* V B 149:3 *n.d.*, 1844

From sketch; see 454:31-460:15:

V
B 148:37
250

What is it to be a hero?

If he, my character, had been a hero in the ordinary sense, he would have had to become that demonically by saying: I see that my idea of existence requires that she must go, ergo, and this road over her leads me to my great goal. On the other hand, he must not say conversely that for him the main point was that he should suffer more than she. That is a religious hero. He is the greatest hero who wins the most. —He is the greatest hero who suffers the most.

> Feuerbach in *Wesen des Christenthum* is scandalized at Pascal's life, that it is a story of suffering.
> Fr. Schlegel in *Lucinde*: that only health is lovable.[*]

She also could have become a heroine, but only esthetically. I have not wished to keep her that way, for a new light should fall upon his sympathy; how it pains him that she breaks with the idea.

If she had become a heroine, I would have bowed before her (although the esthetic interests me less) for there is nothing I would rather do than bow; would to God that there were someone to bow before; most people, however, believe that there is a great deal to stoop for in the world.

I am *poetice et eleganter* [in a poetic and refined way] a street inspector; I think of the two chamberlains who opened the door for Napoleon and said: The Emperor.

Anyone could be made a hero if he will confide in me. I shall bring him into mortal danger; then it will turn out all right.

Baggesen's lines fit most people (the majority):

> Our Lord took a bit of sausage meat
> And said: Become a man
> Become sausage-witted and sausage-happy.[128]

—Pap. V B 148:37 n.d., 1844

V
B 148:37
251

Addition to Pap. V B 148:37:

[*]To make health the highest good is an animalistic principle; this is the way an animal is regarded—if it is not in good health, it is not worth anything. But man is spirit. To assert this principle is sin against the Holy Spirit, the most dreadful revolt against fellow-feeling.—*JP* I 913 (*Pap*. V B 148:38) *n.d.*, 1844

From sketch; see 457:19-465:23:

There is a lot of prating about the impossibility of using certain sufferings (illness etc.—*Philoctetes*) as the subject of poetic interpretation and poetic interest. My story of suffering is not poetry, either. But that statement is comparable to saying to a child asking a question: It is a stupid child, instead of saying that one is oneself unable to answer.

Every suffering in which the suffering also becomes an occasion for something higher, a battle in which the nobler is developed, is *eo ipso* poetic. In the same way, poverty could become that.

Moreover, genuine spectator compassion is not an unshaven immediacy but must be formed in dialectic.

Aristotle: must *arouse fear compassion and purify*

In margin: see Börne, *S. S.* II, p. 165 etc.

—*Pap.* V B 148:35 *n.d.*, 1844

From draft; see 464:12-465:16:

VI
B 10
83

Note.[*] What is said in the text is not my own but the religious person's position; here, however, I want to do what the religious person probably would not do—in order to illuminate a bit more the illusory positivity with regard to the religious,** to sketch a speculative and historicizing sermon in order to see what the positive is.

(A) *The Speculative Sermon*

Let the theme be: Christian joy. The text is read, the theme is off to a proper start by means of, for example, a contrasting movement, but this is unimportant—now the discourse begins. In the first place, Christian joy is not (1) the world's joy. This is developed rhetorically in proportion to the speaker's talents, yet not very rigorously, for he is not talking to criminals and adulterers but to cultured people. And the distinguished sins, the demonic passions—one does not dare to touch on these. At the conclusion of this point one is in a

[*]*In margin:* to p. 406 [*SV* VI 432].
In margin: **and pertaining to the qualifications: fear and compassion.

pleasant, almost complacent, mood. (2) Christian joy is not the satisfaction that poetry and art confer. Here is something for the cultured; they do not have time themselves to read the system, so they get it in church, and it is always something in return for the preacher's annual gratuity. But the clergyman does not have a splendid leisure either, and what he knows here is soon used up. That he does not have leisure is nothing to sneer at, is even praiseworthy, but the one who knows what scholarship is never dabbles in the subject in the pulpit. The satisfaction of poetry and art is *appearance*. The point here is to get this word introduced—it is so speculative. If one wishes to talk still more speculatively, one says: the external appearance. This is found even in children's reading books. In a long series of such books there has been a story called: *Appearances are Deceiving*[129]—an English crime story. In a more recent speculative reading book, probably published under the direction of such a clergyman, the title is *External Appearances are Deceiving*. (3) Christian joy is not the spirit's repose in itself that scholarship bestows upon its cultivators. One has a little stock of sayings and one could, if the clergyman had time, point out to him especially many passages in Aristotle where there is discussion of the blessedness of the gods—these lend themselves excellently for use in a pagan address, and in our time also in a sermon. —But let us see what time it is. Good gracious, it is eleven o'clock! So there are only a few moments left. *Gebet Acht* [Attention, please], ladies and gentlemen—now comes the positive: the Christian joy is higher than all this. Amen. This is positive speculation in the pulpit. The theme has not even been talked about.* If anyone

In margin: *In order quite perfectly and genuinely speculatively to conceal this irregularity, the speaker would need only to say: Yet this is not the place to talk about it (but, to be sure, about art, poetry, and scholarship). This category, this is not the place, must be regarded as the system's main cornerstone, which holds up the enormous construction, which one can never storm—because this is not the place—just as the man who obtained the royal dispensation to choose the manner of his death was never executed because he very kindly explained regarding each particular manner of death that this was not the place or this was not the way he would choose.

VI
B 10
84

VI
B 10
85

says that the Christian joy is unutterable—well, then this is what is to be discussed, and the theme becomes *the unutterable joy*. It is even a beautiful theme, but then there must be discussion of the unutterable, why it is unutterable, etc. On the other hand, one does not discuss the unutterable by talking about something else which is so easy to utter that one can even say it by rote. To talk about the unutterable in this manner is similar to the language in Behrend's advertisement: when he had lost a silk umbrella and out of fear that someone would keep it if he came to know that it was made of silk, he advertised that a linen umbrella had been lost.[130] This kind of positive talk is an outright waste of the listener's time. He who has anything to do with scholarship does not wish to hear such a one-shilling course, and he who does not have anything to do with scholarship does not understand it anyway, and a good listener wishes first and last for the simple biblical teaching. If the clergyman still ventures the incredible, he says the following in the pulpit: the innermost center—but this is not particularly gripping for the person who is accustomed to move about in such scholarly phrases, and a respectable citizen who sits in a church is disturbed because he only knows these words from target-practice in the national guard.

That which really should be accentuated in religious joy is suffering and the idea that is the hinge of the category, namely, that the joy of poetry, art, and scholarship stands in an accidental relationship to suffering, because one person becomes a poet without suffering, another by suffering, a thinker without suffering (as a genius), another by suffering, but religious joy is in the danger. From here on it is easy to show why it is unutterable.—*JP* I 625 (*Pap.* VI B 10) *n.d.*, 1844

Continuation of Pap. VI B 10:

B. *A Historicizing Sermon*

In this sphere, grammar, dialectic, plan, design, consistency, train of thought, and everything that constrains are cast off together with the Roman yoke. The free spirit naturally

has free speech, and free speech is thereby different from ordinary speech in that whereas one usually has a beginning, an
intention for the thought that is clear in the beginning and
achieved in the conclusion (the speculative address perhaps
has the defect of merely beginning), free speech is remarkable
in the fact that it begins by virtue of an event so that the beginning comes upon the speaker just like Christmas Eve. But
once begun, free speech is again remarkable in that there is no
compelling reason for it to stop. Just as that worthy performer
in the Dyrehave summer amusement park draws the rope out
of himself, just so free speech rushes on, and to such an extent
that two performers could be necessary: the speaker who produces the continuous web of free speech and the clerk who
measures with an authorized yardstick and clips it off when
the piece has come to be so long that it is a sermon. Remember
what Pastor Grundtvig so rightly said in the preface to his
sermons: "to preach is not to write with pen and ink,"[131] from
which it would also follow that every child who no longer
writes on a slate but in a copy book (consequently with pen
and ink) had been preaching. But even if this is so, even if—
because of this* matchless discovery[132]—the staff is broken on
all who write and everything written, it still does not follow
that every ever so noisy sound issued by a Peder Ruus[133] is
therefore a sermon.

Therefore, even though it is with pen and ink, let us make
an attempt. Let the theme be: The Word of the Church. One
goes back quite a few centuries, one gropes about in the darkness of the Middle Ages, the intolerable Roman yoke, the papal power with its nightmare pressed upon consciences until
Martin Luther, the man of the word, made a visual demonstration of the thick darkness in which the papists groped and
won the decisive battle on the church door in Wittenberg,
where he shut the mouth of the excessively erudite tongue-
thrashers and word-distorters. But then the darkness fell again
for three centuries, until the matchless discovery [was made]
here in the North, when the Living Word was set free and

In margin: *marvelous, well-nigh

installed in its rightful place as the most beautiful field and meadow of Denmark's mother tongue, in spite of German schoolmasters. And the folk-mouth and the folk-tongue shall not be bound, but all shall talk in the spirit when the golden age arrives, the matchless future of which the seer catches a glimpse with a hawk's eye and proclaims on a mouth harp when the Living Word, the Church's Word, God's Word, which was from the beginning, sounds in Denmark. May this come to pass! Amen, yes, amen, in all eternity, amen.

Such an address is no sermon, even in its best form, yes, even if a genius opened his purse-strings and scooped information out of the horn of plenty. Clarified by occasional glints of thought, at times stirred in mood, this is a historical lecture. In relation to the religious, it holds true that all historical knowledge is negative. In relation to the religious, all historical presentation is a diversion. The listener forgets himself over the papists and the twilight, over Luther and the sunrise, over the matchless discovery that was made in Copenhagen. But in relation to the religious it is precisely negative to forget oneself.* A religious speaker must not be different from his listeners as the teachers *ex cathedra* [from the chair] are different. The richer in spirit and the more knowledgeable the religious speaker is, the greater is the self-possession required in order to achieve unity with the listener. The religious speaker should be distinguished by his having existentially made sure of what the simplest of men also know. A hawk's-eye view of world history does not replace a sober insight into oneself: the most matchless discoveries, even the discovery of gunpowder, do not compensate as a substitute for a lack of self-knowledge and of maieutic skill in relation to others.

In margin: *and the positive is to be made self-active.

—*JP* I 626 (*Pap.* VI B 11) *n.d.*, 1844–45

From sketch; see 465:25-471:19:

Para. 5.
Appendix.

about self-inflicted sufferings.

esthetically they are to be treated comically.
A sly religiousness that says that
God can certainly bring them upon one;
therefore we are not to promote them ourselves.[*]
This, however, is the principle of callousness,
for if I block out receptivity, then let us see what
God is able to do.
The principle is to discover the terror, but
to force one's way through, if I do
not force my way through, then the
suffering is self-inflicted.
[*]*In margin*: always being happy.

—*Pap.* V B 149:4 *n.d.*, 1844

Deleted from draft; see 472:10:

If a king, in order to disguise himself, walked around dressed as a butcher and resembled a certain butcher I knew and resembled him so that they could not be distinguished from each other, there would be a unity of the comic and the tragic in the relationship of the two. One would laugh at the butcher because he was not the king, and one would laugh at the other butcher because he was the king.—*Pap.* V B 150:23 *n.d.*, 1844

From sketch; see 474:30-481:19:

About the principle:
To repent of nothing is the highest wisdom an esthetic principle (dialectical in the direction of fate and decrees of providence) that has used an ethical expression.
one sees that another person succumbs, how this sympathetically affects one, and how one is to judge him, or whether one should leave it alone and keep to oneself.
the dreadfulness of such views as in Börne, VIII, pp. 96 and 97,[134] which he himself nevertheless believes to be wisdom. it is designed to blunt sympathy.
[*Penciled:* the elder Fichte.]

Imaginatively constructing, I have once again laid out everything here for the religious: the forgiveness of sins.

In margin: I have taken my gambler to the extreme; it is necessary when one pays attention to the dialectical in the direction of sympathy.—*Pap.* V B 148:39 *n.d.*, 1844

From draft; see 479:22-24:

. . . . . the impression.* He cites an example from his own practice. A fine lady in Paris had a maid who died in a pitiable way. The lady takes it hard, but what does B. do—with the aid of statistical surveys he convinces her that such things have occurred before, and she is consoled. Yet one can do that only in Paris, as B. correctly observes, where there is such a confluence of people.

In margin: *and presumably contribute to—Börne's having become a philanthropist.—*Pap.* V B 150:24 *n.d.*, 1844

From sketch; see 481:3-485:2:

The Principal Result

What he actually runs aground on is the issue of [*deleted:* the forgiveness of sins* and] the wedding. Between these fixed points, his reflection is continually at work to find a way to rescue her.

Penciled above: N.B.

—*Pap.* V B 97:23 *n.d.*, 1844

From sketch; see 481:3-485:2:

V
B 148:36
249

Actually the whole exposition tends toward *the forgiveness of sin.*

But here the point is that repentance is dialectical, whether or not there ought to be action, whether there is not something to do, whether it is not to be done over again.

It is easy enough when one assumes the guilt to be finished and fixed, and now repentance has only to consume it, but here the difficulty is whether repentance could not rather intervene in time and prevent the guilt from becoming established.

Take David, for example (Uriah and Bathsheba), imagine it has happened (Uriah has fallen—Bathsheba his wife), now he repents; but suppose he has issued the order to place Uriah in a difficult spot and now begins to repent and now cannot find out whether it has happened, this situation *in suspenso*.

The forgiveness of sin is a difficult issue in other respects. Earnest people have spoken well and competently to demonstrate that it exists, but how it now expresses itself, how human existence, not the whole world and humanity, which are so superior, but how one single individual exists by virtue of it, what influence it has upon him, what it takes away and what it allows him to keep, whether the whole esthetic side of life returns again. —Here much existence-information is needed.—*Pap.* V B 148:36 *n.d.*, 1844

V
B 148:36
250

Deleted from draft; see 483:22:

. . . . . (just as Hegel's whole life is a rather miserable immediacy, in which the most extreme crisis is: which university is more suitable to him as assistant professor*)

*something even his most zealous admirers have admitted, but without irony and humor, not even in company, much less in existing.—*Pap.* V B 150:25 *n.d.*, 1844

Deleted from draft; see 484:32-38 fn.:

. . . . . to saunter from student to professor, then let such a thinker* go hang, and if this was his conviction, if he did this, if he manfully defied every temptation in this direction because it would not be respected, then truly his style would swell with pathos because it would have become a life issue for him.

*who would be laughed to scorn in Greece.
—*Pap.* V B 150:26 *n.d.*, 1844

Deleted from final copy; see 486:38-487:9:

Sophist no. 3 is finished once and for all; I remain at every moment finished in the balance of the contradictions; but the religious person is continually striving because he is continually in passion.—*Pap.* VI B 8:20 *n.d.*, 1844

From draft; see 489:3:

For example, how much has been written about compassion for the needy, how many examples of it, how often the newspapers mention such examples, and yet the best part of it, the most endearing, the little psychological trait that gives the gift infinite worth and the lack of which changes the sum of money into jingling coins is not described. I knew a man who himself lived in poor circumstances and did not have much to give away and was never mentioned, indeed, was not even able to send his contribution pseudonymously, and yet I have learned more from him than from all publicity. He sometimes gave money to a poor person on the street, but when he gave, as secretly as possible, he always took off his hat to the poor person as respectfully as if he were a superior, and in as friendly a manner as if he were an equal. Four shillings or one mark is too little to be mentioned in the newspaper, but neither does the inwardness, the humanity get into the newspaper either.—*Pap.* V B 150:27 *n.d.*, 1844

Deleted from final copy; see 494:1:

. . . . . who goes to church on Sunday, to Fredriksberg in the afternoon, and when there has been a fire at night outside the gate goes out the next afternoon to look at the site of the fire.—*Pap.* VI B 8:21 *n.d.*, 1844

VI
B 184
254

A Wish Occasioned by a Literary Blunder
in *Berlingske Tidende*, no.   [135]

In *Berlingske T.*, no.   , under the rubric "Literature," I find my name brought in such close association with various pseudonymous works that even the heading of the article has my name. The reviewer* of those books and the exhibitor of my person, after being introduced or pushed into literature this way, is ingenious enough to assume and to put this same assumption before a highly esteemed public that I have a divining rod [*Ønskeqvist*, wishing twig]—if I have indeed, as rumor says, written a good many books. Yes—if!

The world being as it is now, when a pseudonymous book comes out, as a matter of course someone or other also asks who the author presumably is. As a matter of course, for two weeks the guilty or innocent suspect is persecuted by many an ingenious question, many a little quip—and then, fortunately again as a matter of course, the matter is forgotten. If the matter is forgotten, then it would be inept to rake it up again, for if it might be momentarily interesting to learn to know it, since one was a little curious, it is boring to get to know something that one does not care about now. It is boring even if one did get to know the truth, for when the heat of curiosity has subsided, one perceives oneself that its object was a trifle.

As it is related here, so it has also happened to me that now and then I have been tested in this distress, which, short and brief, is to have been regarded as an author. But I nevertheless ought to confess that even in private association people have shown much tact and I appreciate that no one has sought in print to draw me into an authorship into which I do not wish to be drawn.

Now once again a pseudonymous book has come out, and since everyone long ago has become indifferent to the question of who the author is, suddenly a reviewer is so good as to want to insinuate in the *Berlingske Tidende* that it is I. I think most people feel as I do the tactlessness of this. For if an author does not want to be named, let him be pseudonymous, unless a higher earnest consideration caused an authorized individuality to demand the name. But a little curiosity is no legitimate

---

* Note. What speedily found name is there for a person who writes something in a newspaper about a book.

power in relation to pseudonymity, and to do it at a time when no one is interested in it anymore is inept.

Consequently, if I, as rumor has it, am author of several pseudonymous books (a charge that is impossible to disclaim since not even all of them are named)—then I do have a divining rod or then one would almost have to believe that I have a divining rod.

Alas! I am willingly satisfied with less, willingly satisfied to be regarded as the author of a smaller number of books, and of course it would indeed always be disagreeable if it went so far that I was not even regarded as the actual author of the books that bear my name. But it is I; I do assert it. These books I have actually written; I do wish to have them linked to my name. However, I have always regarded pseudonymity as a bill of divorcement between an author and his work and in any case curiosity, when it is disagreeable to an author and annoying to a reading public by chattering afterwards, is not justified in joining what wants to be separated.

Upbuilding discourses I have written, it is true, and now I have written three discourses on imagined occasions. This authorship I cannot deny, even if I have not been much inclined to do something about acknowledging it or proving its authenticity, mainly because I do not have a particularly great notion of the solemn act and declaration of being reviewed in a newspaper. Therefore, until now I have successfully avoided having them reviewed, as it is called,* or described by a literary endorser. This was achieved in a simple way, by not sending newspapers any free copies. It is always good that people understand one another in this way.

Meanwhile the inept anonymous author in *B. T.* has interjected the discourses in order to have an opportunity to mention my name in connection with the anonymous books. It is precisely this blunder that is unpleasant for me. Without exactly daring to flatter myself with many readers, perhaps not wishing it either, I found something satisfying, something charming, something inspiring in daring to believe that he did

VI
B 184
256

In margin: * Note. This little innocent hint in *Portefeuille*[136]

exist, "that single individual whom I with joy and gratitude call my reader," that in his concealment he had enough sympathy for the modest undertaking to be just as unobtrusive on his part as I sought to be. Therefore, I am really pleased that fate so ordained it that when an installment of my discourses was published, there was also published some flashier pseudonymous book, and that many of the curious promptly hurried to it, while my reader secretly took the little book and let the others concern themselves about the bigger one. It was rather nice to think of being assured that that single individual grasped how one reads an upbuilding discourse, and above all, as remote from criticism as possible. Obeying the prompting in my inner being, I feel no need for prompting from without; inspired by the thought of "my reader," I take pride in my requirement of him. I want to be, not the master, the teacher, the guide, but the servant, not to be loved by him but to love him, not that he will be proud of me but that I shall be proud of him. This, you see, is why I wished no review. What I did wish to know, whether my reader felt himself built up by the reading, I could never find out in the newspaper, for such things are not written about in the newspaper, and if they are written about there, it would not be by my reader. Of the other things one can come to know in the newspaper, of all the other things, I prefer to be ignorant, also out of sympathy for my reader, lest they disturb him. Criticism is always disturbing; the most flattering recognition is also disturbing.

That the rather experienced but still beginning author perhaps could very well wish a word from an authority is true. I was all the more cheered that that commanding firm Kts,[137] who, when in his incognito he appears in literature, is recognized like Harun Al-Rashid[138] by every functionary, that firm, which, when he appears, arouses the wonder of the less knowledgeable, just as when the crowd sees the ordinarily dressed person suddenly approached deferentially by the police because he is the chief, that firm to whom the young have learned from their fathers to show respect, and to whom I, who find it hard to comprehend how I would become any person's teacher, have easily understood my relation as a

VI
B 184
257

learner and fear only that it might seem immoderate if in strong expressions I [*han*] were to say how much I think I have learned from him—that that firm in passing dropped a kind word, a little command for him who is all too pleased to obey. Just as that word cheered me, so "my reader" cannot have had anything but gain from it when he read it. For (yes, again I acknowledge what I owe to just that little article) it is no criticism (probably because the authority knows how dubious it is to place criticism in relation to the upbuilding), but the few words were also an upbuilding discourse, that is, it was more upbuilding than one whole discourse of mine.

And now the wish (which perhaps is not needed, although it still could not very well fail to appear, since the inept reviewer in *B. T.*, has made the attack), the wish that with the same tactfulness as before the journalists* will perceive the mistake of wanting in any way to reveal the identity of an author or to identify someone as author, i.e., to bore the readers and to annoy the innocent or guilty suspect, also that my upbuilding discourses will be left, as heretofore, unmentioned, and finally that a good beginning will be made by not discussing this article.

I have nothing further to add. The article in *B. T.* concerns only me insofar as I have been mentioned as the author and as the author of the upbuilding discourses. Whatever else can be said must, of course, be left to the pseudonymous authors to share.[**] To be summoned before the reading public in order to be praised by a sutler, to be shown a place in literature (in one respect even the most prominent place) by a voting member, to be ordered to proceed by one versed in merchandise— alas, I do not envy them! That is, since the reviewer (in fact, what speedily found name is there for a person who writes something in a newspaper about a book) is anonymous and thus deprived of reliability, and since his style and interpretation *höchstens* [at best] betray a bookseller's apprentice, it is

VI
B 184
258

In margin: * Note. Of course, I count wholesaler Nathanson[139] among them, for the article, after all, is not by him but by an anonymous writer.

[**] *In margin:* They certainly will not disagree about sharing the flattering recognition but will rather agree about . . . . .

indeed rather droll to read him when he speaks in a manner that undeniably would have great significance if it were, for example, the legitimate ruler in Danish literature, Professor Heiberg, or a European ranking scholar, Professor Madvig,[140] or that authoritative firm Kts—speaks in a manner that would have great significance if in the piece itself the writer demonstrated the authority to speak. It is rather curious—one does not, after all, assume that every student, every bookseller, every bookseller's apprentice, is qualified to be an author; on the other hand, one assumes that every appreciative or demolishing bookseller's apprentice is capable of assigning an author a place in literature and capable of encouraging him by his approbation. It is rather curious. An unauthorized censure at times is brushed aside, but an unauthorized recognition is allowed to pass.—*Pap.* VI B 184 *n.d.*, 1845

The Relation between *Either/Or* and the *Stages*

VI
A 41
16

In *Either/Or* the esthetic component was something present battling with the ethical, and the ethical was the choice by which one emerged from it. For this reason there were only two components, and the Judge was unconditionally the winner, even though the book ended with a sermon and with the observation that only the truth that builds up is the truth for me (inwardness—the point of departure for my upbuilding discourses).

In the *Stages* there are three components and the situation is different.

1. The esthetic-sensuous is thrust into the background as something past (therefore "a recollection"), for after all it cannot become utterly nothing.

The Young Man (thought-depression); Constantin Constantius (hardening through the understanding). Victor Eremita, who can no longer be the editor (sympathetic irony); the Fashion Designer (demonic despair); Johannes the Seducer (perdition, a "marked" individual). He concludes by saying that woman is merely a moment. At that very point the Judge

VI
A 41
17

begins: Woman's beauty increases with the years; her reality [*Realitet*] is precisely in time.

2. The ethical component is polemical: the Judge is not giving a friendly lecture but is grappling in existence, because he cannot end here, even though with pathos he can triumph again over every esthetic stage but not measure up to the esthetes in wittiness.

3. The religious comes into existence in a demonic approximation (Quidam of the imaginary construction) with humor as its presupposition and its incognito (Frater Taciturnus).—*JP* V 5804 (*Pap.* VI A 41) *n.d.*, 1845

From sketch of Postscript:

A story of *suffering*; suffering is precisely the religious category.

In the *Stages* the esthete is no longer a clever fellow frequenting B's living room—a hopeful man etc., because he still is only a possibility; no, he is existing [*existere*].

"It is exactly the same as *Either/Or*."

Constantin Constantius and the Young Man united in Quidam of the imaginary construction. (advanced humor.)

    as a point of departure for the beginning

      of the religious.—

    just as the tragic hero was used to bring out faith.

Three Stages and yet an Either/Or.

        —*JP* V 5805 (*Pap.* VI B 41:10) *n.d.*, 1845

William Afham's part (in *Stages*) is so deceptively contrived that it is praise and high distinction to have stupid fussbudgets pass trivial judgment on it and say that it is the same old thing. Yes, that is just the trick. I never forget the anxiety I myself felt about not being able to achieve what I had once accomplished, and yet it would have been so very easy to choose other names. This is also the reason Afham states that Constantius said that never again would he arrange a banquet, and Victor Eremita, that he would never again speak admiringly of *Don Giovanni*.[141] But the Judge declares that he can keep on repeating.* As the author himself suggested, wherever it is possible and wherever it is not possible.

*"that only thieves and gypsies say that one must never return where one has once been."[142]

—*JP* V 5823 (*Pap.* VI A 78) *n.d.*, 1845

The *Stages* will not have as many readers as *Either/Or*, will barely make a ripple. That is fine; in a way it rids me of the gawking public who want to be wherever they think there is a disturbance. I prophesied this myself in the epilogue to " 'Guilty?'/'Not Guilty?' "[143]—*JP* V 5824 (*Pap.* VI A 79) *n.d.*, 1845

Situation

With modification it could have been used in the imaginary psychological construction (" 'Guilty?'/'Not Guilty?' "): Quidam of the construction, for example, was a theological candidate who became a pastor, lived in the country, came to the capital, at the request of one of his friends preaches at the morning service, delivers the good sermon, everything fine, takes out a piece of paper that is a list of those for whom wedding banns are to be read from the pulpit—and reads: For the third time—here followed the name of the girl to whom he had been engaged and now another name.—*JP* V 5834 (*Pap.* VI A 94) *n.d.*, 1845

For a man engaged in saving himself there is something dreadful about seeing another person go down because of the very same error (this is touched upon in " 'Guilty?'/'Not Guilty?' " in Frater Taciturnus's discussion of sympathetic repentance).[144] But if it is true that I do not have the right to compare myself with others in order to praise and exalt myself but need only to relate myself to the ideal, then it is also true that I do not have the right to compare myself with others in order to despair over myself, but here again I must keep to myself and to the truth and never permit myself either

proudly or sympathetically to want to understand the truth
through the fate of a third person whom I can never know;
instead I must grasp the eternal truth.—*JP* I 924 (*Pap*. VI A
137) *n.d.*, 1845

Hilarius Bookbinder, my chief, has been flattered in *The
Corsair*.

> Frater Taciturnus
> In charge of part 3 of
> *Stages on Life's Way*.[145]
> —*JP* V 5862 (*Pap*. VII[1] B 6) *n.d.*, 1845

Note for Postscript:

VII[1]
B 83
276

For p. 217 [*SV* VII 246]

> A note that was not printed because it was
> prepared later, although it was rough-drafted,
> and for certain reasons I did not want to change
> or add the least thing in the manuscript as it
> was delivered lock, stock, and barrel to Luno the
> last days of December, 1845.

Note. This imaginary construction [*Experiment*]
(" 'Guilty?'/'Not Guilty?' ") is the first attempt in all the
pseudonymous writings at an existential dialectic in double-
reflection. It is not the communication that is in the form of
double-reflection (for all the pseudonymous works are that),
but the existing person himself exists in this. Thus he does not
give up immediacy, but he keeps it and yet gives it up, keeps
erotic love's desire and yet gives it up. Viewed categorically,
the construction relates to "The Seducer's Diary" in such a

VII[1]
B 83
277

way that it begins right there where the Seducer ends, with
the task he himself suggests: "to poetize himself out of a girl."
(See *Either/Or*, I, p. 445, *KW* III [*SV* I 412].) The Seducer is
egotism; in *Repetition* feeling and irony are kept separate, each
in its representative: the Young Man and Constantin. These
two elements are put together in the one person, Quidam of
the construction, and he is sympathy. To seduce a girl expresses masculine superiority; to poetize oneself out of a girl

is also a superiority but must become a *suffering* superiority when one considers the relationship between masculinity and femininity and not a particular silly girl. Masculinity's victory is supposed to reside in succeeding; but the reality [*Realitet*] of femininity is supposed to reside in its becoming a story of suffering for the man. Just as it is morally impossible for Quidam of the construction to seduce a girl, so it is metaphysically-esthetically impossible for a seducer to poetize himself out of a girl when it is a matter of the relationship between masculinity and femininity, each in its strength, and not of a particular girl. The Seducer's egotism culminates in the lines to himself: "She is mine; I do not confide this to the stars . . . . . not even to Cordelia, but say it very softly to myself." (See *Either/Or*, I, p. 424, *KW* III [*SV* I 392].) Quidam culminates passionately in the outburst: "The whole thing looks like a tale of seduction."[146] What is a triumph to the first one is an ethical horror to the other.—*JP* V 5865 (*Pap.* VII[1] B 83) *n.d.*, 1846

From The Book on Adler[147]

VII[1]
A 150
97

. . . . . There are examples in Adler of a style in an uncontrolled form no doubt familiar (esthetically and artistically) to Frater Taciturnus, since he, himself using a completely different style, has Quidam of the imaginary construction express himself in this stylistic form. To construct rhetorically upon a conditional clause and then have the main clause amount to nothing, an abyss from which the reader once again shrinks back, as it were, to the antecedents; to plunge into a tentative effort as if this wealth were inexhaustible and then the very same second discontinue it, which is like the trick of pulling up short at full gallop (most riders fall off—usually one first breaks into a gallop and then into a trot); to be at the head of a cavalry of predicates, the one more gallant and dashing than the other, to charge in, and then swerve; the leap in modulation; the turning to the concept in one single word; the unexpected stop etc. Just as the voice of all passionate peoples, all southern peoples (the Jews, for example) continually breaks, just as every passionate person talks in this manner, so is it also possible to produce this effect stylistically.

But this would take me much too far afield, and how many are there, after all, who have any intimation of how prose can be used lyrically—and of the task I am committed to, to pro-

VII¹
A 150
98

duce in prose a stronger lyrical effect than in verse—if people would only learn how to read and to insist on thought in every word, whereas verse always has a little padding. So I cut this short; it would concern only authors anyway. In this respect, all of the pseudonyms have an unqualified linguistic value in having cultivated prose lyrically. It is clear that Adler, too, has learned something from them, but what his flattering reviewer says in the *Kirketidende*,[148] that he began just about the same time as the pseudonyms, is not true, for he began after them, and the style of his four latest works is markedly different from that of his sermons,[149] where he had not as yet been so strongly influenced. On the other hand, what his reviewer says about the presence of passages in Adler (four latest books)[150] thoroughly reminiscent of the pseudonyms is true, but I see nothing meritorious in that, neither in copying another nor in forgetting that by having had a revelation of one's own one has entirely different things to think about than language exercises.—*JP* V 5939 (*Pap*. VII¹ A 150) *n.d.*, 1846

From The Book on Adler:

VII²
B 235
14

. . . The art in all communication is to come as close as possible to actuality, to contemporaries in the role of readers, and yet at the same time to have the distance of a point of view, the reassuring, infinite distance of ideality from them. Permit me to illustrate this by an example from a later work. In the imaginary psychological construction [*psychologiske Experiment*] " 'Guilty?'/'Not Guilty?' " (in *Stages on Life's Way*), there is depicted a character in tension in the most extreme mortal danger of the spirit to the point of despair, and the whole thing is done as though it could have occurred yesterday. In this respect the production is placed as close as possible to actuality: the person struggling religiously in despair hovers, so to speak, right over the head of the contemporaries. If the imaginary construction has made any impression, it might be like that which happens when wing strokes of the wild bird, in being heard overhead by the tame birds of the same kind who live securely in the certainty of actuality, prompt these to beat their wings, because those wing strokes simultaneously are unsettling and yet have something that fascinates. But now comes what is reassuring, that the whole thing is an imaginary construction, and that an imaginary constructor stands by. Spiritually understood, the imaginatively constructed character is in a civic sense a highly dangerous character, and such people are usually not allowed to walk alone without being accompanied by a pair of policemen—for the sake of public security. Thus, for the reassurance of public security, in that work an imaginary constructor is along also (he calls himself a street inspector)[151] who very quietly shows how the whole thing hangs together, theoretically educes a life-view that he completes and rounds out, while he points interpretively to the imaginatively constructed character in order to indicate how he makes the movements according to the drawing of the strings. If this were not an imaginary construction, if no imaginary constructor were along, if no life-view were represented—then such a work, regardless of the talent it could display, would merely be debilitating. It would be alarming to come in contact with it, because it simply conveyed the impression of an actual person who probably in the next moment would become mad. It is one thing to portray a passionate person when there is the accompaniment of someone more powerful and a view of life that can control him (and I would still like to see how many contemporary critics would be capable of handling the imaginatively constructed character so powerfully, to toss him about as the imaginary constructor does); it is something else that a passionate person, in his own personal actuality with the help of a book, by becoming an author, breaks forth and, as it were, assaults the rest of us with his unexplained doubt and his torments.—*Pap.* VII[2] B 235 *n.d.*, 1846-47

VII[2]
B 235
15

Strangely enough, the Chinese have the same custom as the Jews. Confucius's name is *Khu* or *Ju*, but when the name appears in the sacred books, the people are forbidden to utter it—it is prescribed instead that they read it as *Mou*. It is exactly the same as with *Jehovah*. The loose way in which the name of Christ is used in Christendom is really all wrong. Curiously, I have personally experienced long periods in which I have been unable to mention Christ's name to anyone because I regard it as too solemn. I have expressed this, also, in the "imaginary psychological construction," where Quidam says (p. 254 bottom [*SV* VI 309]) that the girl has pledged herself to him with the name which he does not dare utter, that is, the name of Christ.

See *China, historisch-malerisch*,[152] Karlsruhe, p. 223.—*JP* VI 6324 (*Pap.* X[1] A 73) *n.d.*, 1849

"The Seducer's Diary" had to come first in order to shed light on the "Imaginary Psychological Construction." The latter lies in the *confinium* [border territory] between the interesting and the religious. If "The Seducer's Diary" had not come out first, the result would have been that the reading world would have found it interesting. "The Seducer's Diary" was a help, and now it was found to be boring—quite rightly so, for it is the religious. Frater Taciturnus himself also explains this.[153]—*JP* VI 6330 (*Pap.* X[1] A 88) *n.d.*, 1849

X[1]
A 377
242

Something about the drama *Søstrene paa Kinnekullen*[154]

In the preface the author says that the idea was not borrowed from a fairy tale, but neither is it his own. This is a curious kind of honesty and perhaps, after all, dishonesty. It is honest to say that it is not his own; it is dishonest not to say more. For if he gave his source and the more pertinent particulars—perhaps, who knows, perhaps he both owed another more than one thinks, and perhaps he used badly that which he borrowed.

Instead of getting married, a girl becomes avaricious—sits upon the mountain and spins gold—this is detected twenty-

five years later at the other sister's silver wedding (incidentally, it could have been quaint to make it fifty years because
of the golden wedding). The mountain creature explains that
it is true not only of this girl but of so many that, lost in something abstract (or the like), they actually do not live but
merely waste their lives. The idea is that there is an abstract
life that means simply to lose life.

Fine. That may very well be what was borrowed, the part
about the abstract life. What has the poet done with it? He has
taken a particular example, and what? Avarice—how
thoughtless. If one wishes to pinpoint discerningly the falsity
in abstract life, then one must select something essentially innocent. The avaricious maiden's defect is not abstract life—
but avarice.

Thus the author has picked a wrong example. Thereupon
he makes, as they say, a universal of the particular and puts it
in the mouth of the mountain creature. But it is precisely that
which is not illuminated by the example, for the example was
erroneously selected.

On the other hand, if one wishes to validate the concrete
life in contrast to the abstract, then one must see to it that one
does not go too far afield. For the authentic religious life, in
contrast to what people generally understand by concretion
and what this poet no doubt understands by it—is an abstract
life: to suffer, to "be sacrificed."

X¹
A 377
243

The poet has had no inkling of this at all. For example, he
has not grasped how the problem should be placed in proper
relation to the ethical, which will forbid not only the sin but
also an abstract life, or in contrast to the religious, which in a
completely different sense affirms the abstract life. From a categorical point of view, the author has bungled in every respect; his categories are confused.

Now take a look at the pseudonyms. In the conviction that
life, such as most men "live" and live concretely, is wasted,
wasted also in this sense of concretion, the attempt here is to
achieve the legitimate abstract life. For this purpose there is
used: (a) an esthetic eccentric whose very defect is an erro-

neous abstract life, without being patently sinful—and (b) the ethicist, but in such a way that he points to the religious.

This is the process in all the pseudonyms' endeavors.

But, of course, such a grand endeavor is probably also an abstract life—then it is more concrete to seize with muddled categories a particular idea, to turn the whole thing wrong, to confuse all the spheres—and then "momentarily" make a big hit as a profound thinker.

If I were to take a particular example for the pseudonyms, I could use the passage in *Either/Or*[155] where the esthete divides men into two classes, those who work in order to live and those who do not need to, and then shows that it would be a self-contradiction if the purpose of life is supposed to be to work in order to live, since the purpose of living, after all, cannot be to produce the prerequisites for living.

On this basis the piece could be constructed. But then the piece would also have to point out the religious. In *Either/Or* the ethicist rounds off life with marriage, but the whole work is also only an element in the endeavor.

X[1]
A 377
244

Obviously there should have been three sisters, a third, a Christian "Mary"; then perhaps the play would have had value. [*In margin:* or an "Anna" (patience in expectancy)[156] in order to show the abstraction of the religious life to be true abstraction.]

Here Quidam of the imaginary psychological construction has the great merit of making clear that "the wish" must be preserved in suffering. The ethicist rightfully condemns waiting for fantasies and wasting life as being esthetically eccentric, but from behind the ethical emerges the religious again: that to live abstractly (ideally) is to live. Only one man has lived absolutely ideally abstractly in this way: the God-Man.

Oh, but what do they know, these poets who assume the pose of being so profound!—*JP* VI 6410 (*Pap.* X[1] A 377) *n.d.,* 1849

. . . Phase IV

I see that there must be a separation.

Here—honest with her and traitorous to myself—I advised

her not to attempt to fight with the weapon of pride, for that would make it much easier for me, but with submission.

But there had to be a break—I send her back her ring in a letter, which word for word is printed in the imaginary psychological construction.[157] . . . —*JP* VI 6482 (*Pap.* X[1] A 667) *n.d.*, 1849

. . . 8. But there was a divine protest, so it seemed to me. Marriage. I would have to keep too much from her, base the whole marriage on an untruth.

I wrote to her and sent back her ring. The note is found verbatim in the imaginary psychological construction.[158] I deliberately made it purely historical, for I have spoken to no one about it, not one single person, I who am more silent than the grave. If she should happen to see the book, I simply wanted her to be reminded of it.

9. *In margin:* Some of the lines are also factual. For example, the one about its not being quite as stated, that one gets fat when one marries,[159] that I knew a person (here I mentioned my father to alter the story) who was married twice and did not get fat. The lines: that one can break an engagement in two ways, with the help of love as well as the help of respect. Her remark: I really believe that you are mad.[160] . . . —*JP* VI 6472 (*Pap.* X[5] A 149) *n.d.*, 1849

The Fashion Designer (in *Stages*)[161] gets the idea of starting a fashionable boutique, one section devoted entirely to dressing corpses; thus for the corpse to be dressed in vogue is equivalent to being buried in Christian ground, that is, the latest interpretation.—*JP* VI 6331 (*Pap.* X[5] A 152) *n.d.*, 1849

[*In margin: Stages on Life's Way*]

They are indeed remarkable words with which the book ends, the last in Frater Taciturnus's closing words about himself: Do not incite him, for then he could become dangerous.[162]

—*Pap.* X[2] A 405 *n.d.*, 1850

The Turn the World is Taking

As I demonstrated in the last section of the review of *Two Ages*,[163] the punishment will conform to the guilt, and for this very reason [the punishment will be] to have no government, so that the tension but also the forward step will necessarily be that everyone must himself learn in earnest to be master, to guide himself without the supportive indulgence of having leaders and rulers (which was an amelioration, but rejected by the generation). Thus religiously the step forward[164] and the tension will be that everyone must carry within himself the ambivalence of realizing that Christianity conflicts with the understanding and then still believe it. This is the signal that the age of immediacy is over. Just as in the imaginary psychological construction Quidam is no spontaneously unhappy lover (he himself perceives that the matter is comic and yet tragically clings to it by virtue of something else, but therefore with a constant split, which is the sign that immediacy is over), so also with the religious.—*JP* VI 6604 (*Pap* X² A 622) *n.d.*, 1850

See 68:31-33:

A Misprint in *Stages on Life's Way*

No doubt there are many and various misprints in my books, and I actually have never been very concerned about them. But curiously enough, there is one in *Stages on Life's Way*[165] that I have not forgotten over the years and that I would like to eradicate.

It is in "The Banquet," in one of the lines spoken by the Fashion Designer. There it reads: *Pro dii immortales* [By the immortal gods], what, then, is a woman when she is not in fashion; *per deos obsecro* [I swear by the gods], what is she when she is not in fashion! Obviously there should be no "not" in the second clause; it should read: what is she when she is in fashion.

Oddly enough, indifferent as I am about such things, this misprint has plagued me year after year, and it has always bothered me not to have it corrected. The lines become so very trivial when the "not" is used twice, which certainly was not the case in the manuscript, and on the other hand it is so characteristic if the latter "not" is not there.

In that very phrase is implied the demonic sarcasm as well as the proof that the Fashion Designer is not a fool who too solemnly believed in the reality of his craft, as if he solemnly believed that woman amounted to something when she is in fashion. No, "what is she when she is not in fashion" is ironic sarcasm; now comes the far more profound "*per deos obsecro*, what is she when she is in fashion."—*JP* VI 6858 (*Pap.* XI¹ A 49) *n.d.*, 1854

Woman

What the Judge in the second part of *Either/Or*[166] says in his way about women is to be expected from a married man who, ethically inspired, champions marriage.

Woman could be called "the lust for life." There is undoubtedly lust for life in man, but essentially he is structured [*lagt an paa*] to be spirit, and if he were alone, left all alone to himself, he would not know (here the Judge is right) how to begin, and he would never really get around to beginning.

But then "the lust for life," which is within him indefinitely, becomes manifest to him externally in another form, in the form of woman, who is the lust for life: and now the lust for life awakens.

Likewise, much is true in what the Seducer (in *Stages*)[167] says about woman being bait. And strange as it may seem, it is nevertheless a fact that the very thing that makes the seducer so demonic and makes it hard for any poet to contrive such a character is that in the form of knowledge he has at his disposal the whole Christian ascetic view of woman—except that he employs it in his own way. He has knowledge in common with the ascetic, the hermit, but they take off from this knowledge in completely different directions.—*JP* IV 4999 (*Pap.* XI¹ A 164) *n.d.*, 1854

A Breach [et Brud]—*A Bride* [en Brud]

With his demonic wisdom, the Seducer says: A bride and a breach correspond to one another as male and female.[168]

With a quite different meaning, Christianity says (when one reflects on its calling the believer a bride and Christ the bridegroom): A breach and a bride—that is, in order to become a bride you must make a breach between the world and everything and yourself. Consequently, not a [en] bride and a [et] breach but a [et] breach and a [en] bride.—*JP* III 3778 (*Pap.* XI¹ A 283) *n.d.*, 1854

EDITORIAL APPENDIX

ACKNOWLEDGMENTS

Preparation of manuscripts for *Kierkegaard's Writings* is supported by a genuinely enabling grant from the National Endowment for the Humanities. The grant includes gifts from the Dronning Margrethes og Prins Henriks Fond, the Danish Ministry of Cultural Affairs, the Augustinus Fond, the Carlsberg Fond, the Konsul George Jorck og Hustru Emma Jorcks Fond, Lutheran Brotherhood Foundation, and the A. P. Møller og Hustru Chastine Mc-Kinney Møllers Fond.

The translators–editors are indebted to Grethe Kjær and Julia Watkin for their knowledgeable observations on crucial concepts and terminology.

John Elrod, Per Lønning, and Sophia Scopetéa, members of the International Advisory Board for *Kierkegaard's Writings*, have given valuable criticism of the manuscript on the whole and in detail. Rune Engebretsen, Catherine Gjerdingen, Craig Mason, Jack Schwandt, and Julia Watkin have helpfully read the manuscript. Kathryn Hong, copy editor for *KW*, Kierkegaard Library, scrutinized the manuscript and prepared the index. The Greek has been checked by James May. Translations of German quotations are by Rune Engebretsen. The entire work has been facilitated by George Coulter and Lavier Murray.

Acknowledgment is made to Gyldendals Forlag for permission to absorb notes to *Søren Kierkegaards samlede Værker*.

Inclusion in the Supplement of entries from *Søren Kierkegaard's Journals and Papers* is by arrangement with Indiana University Press.

The book collection and the microfilm collection of the Kierkegaard Library, St. Olaf College, have been used in preparation of the text, Supplement, and Editorial Appendix.

The original manuscript was typed by Dorothy Bolton. Word processing of the final manuscript was done by Kennedy Lemke and Francesca Lane Rasmus. The volume has been guided through the press by Cathie Brettschneider.

COLLATION OF *STAGES ON LIFE'S WAY*
IN THE DANISH EDITIONS OF KIERKEGAARD'S
COLLECTED WORKS

Vol. VI Ed. 1 Pg.	Vol. VI Ed. 2 Pg.	Vol. 7 Ed. 3 Pg.	Vol. VI Ed. 1 Pg.	Vol. VI Ed. 2 Pg.	Vol. 7 Ed. 3 Pg.
7	13	9	43	51	41
8	13	9	44	52	41
9	14	10	45	54	42
10	16	11	46	55	43
11	17	11	47	56	44
14	20	14	48	57	45
15	21	15	49	58	46
16	21	15	50	59	47
17	23	16	51	60	48
18	24	17	52	61	49
19	25	18	53	62	50
20	26	19	54	64	51
21	27	20	55	65	52
22	28	21	56	66	53
23	29	22	57	67	54
24	30	23	58	68	55
25	32	24	59	69	56
26	32	24	60	70	56
27	34	25	61	71	57
28	35	26	62	72	58
29	36	27	63	74	60
30	37	28	64	75	61
31	38	29	65	76	61
32	39	30	66	77	62
33	40	31	67	78	63
34	41	32	68	80	65
35	42	33	69	81	65
36	44	34	70	82	67
37	45	35	71	83	67
38	46	36	72	84	68
39	47	37	73	85	69
40	48	38	74	86	70
41	49	39	75	87	71
42	50	40	76	89	72

Vol. VI Ed. 1 Pg.	Vol. VI Ed. 2. Pg.	Vol. 7 Ed. 3 Pg.	Vol. VI Ed. 1 Pg.	Vol. VI Ed. 2 Pg.	Vol. 7 Ed. 3 Pg.
77	90	73	121	137	114
78	91	74	122	138	114
79	92	75	123	139	115
80	93	76	124	140	116
81	94	77	125	142	117
82	96	78	126	143	118
83	97	79	127	144	120
86	100	82	128	144	120
87	101	83	129	146	121
88	101	83	130	147	122
89	103	84	131	148	123
90	104	85	132	149	124
91	105	86	133	150	125
92	106	87	134	151	125
93	107	88	135	152	126
94	108	89	136	153	127
95	109	90	137	154	128
96	110	90	138	156	129
97	110	91	139	157	130
98	112	92	140	158	131
99	113	93	141	159	132
100	114	94	142	160	133
101	115	95	143	161	134
102	116	96	144	162	135
103	117	97	145	164	136
104	118	97	146	165	137
105	119	98	147	166	138
106	121	99	148	167	139
107	122	100	149	168	140
108	123	101	150	169	141
109	124	102	151	170	142
110	125	103	152	171	143
111	126	104	153	173	144
112	127	105	154	174	145
113	128	106	155	175	146
114	129	107	156	176	147
115	131	108	157	177	148
116	132	109	158	178	148
117	133	110	159	179	149
118	134	111	160	180	150
119	135	112	161	182	151
120	136	113	162	183	152

Vol. VI Ed. 1 Pg.	Vol. VI Ed. 2 Pg.	Vol. 8 Ed. 3 Pg.	Vol. VI Ed. 1 Pg.	Vol. VI Ed. 2 Pg.	Vol. 8 Ed. 3 Pg.
163	184	153	208	233	41
164	185	154	209	234	42
165	186	155	210	235	42
166	187	156	211	236	43
167	188	157	212	237	44
168	189	158	213	238	45
169	190	159	214	239	46
170	191	160	215	240	47
171	193	161	216	241	48
172	194	162	217	242	49
173	195	163	218	243	50
174	196	164	219	245	51
177	199	11	220	246	52
178	200	11	221	247	53
179	201	12	222	248	54
180	202	13	223	249	55
181	203	14	224	250	56
183	205	17	225	251	57
184	206	18	226	252	58
185	207	19	227	254	59
186	208	19	228	255	60
187	209	20	229	256	61
188	210	21	230	257	62
189	211	22	231	258	63
190	212	23	232	260	64
191	214	24	233	261	65
192	215	25	234	262	66
193	216	26	235	263	67
194	217	27	236	264	68
195	218	28	237	265	69
196	219	29	238	266	70
197	220	30	239	267	71
198	221	31	240	269	72
199	223	32	241	270	73
200	224	33	242	271	73
201	225	34	243	272	74
202	226	35	244	273	75
203	227	36	245	274	76
204	228	37	246	275	77
205	229	38	247	276	78
206	230	39	248	278	79
207	231	40	249	279	80

Vol. VI Ed. 1 Pg.	Vol. VI Ed. 2 Pg.	Vol. 8 Ed. 3 Pg.	Vol. VI Ed. 1 Pg.	Vol. VI Ed. 2 Pg.	Vol. 8 Ed. 3 Pg.
250	280	81	293	330	124
251	281	82	294	331	125
252	282	83	295	332	126
253	283	84	296	333	126
254	284	85	297	334	127
255	285	86	298	335	128
256	287	87	299	336	129
257	288	88	300	338	130
258	289	89	301	339	131
259	290	90	302	340	132
260	291	91	303	341	133
261	293	92	304	342	134
262	294	93	305	343	135
263	295	94	306	344	136
264	296	95	307	345	137
265	297	96	308	346	138
266	299	97	309	347	139
267	300	98	310	348	139
268	301	99	311	350	140
269	302	100	312	351	141
270	303	101	313	352	142
271	305	102	314	353	143
272	306	103	315	354	144
273	307	104	316	356	145
274	308	105	317	357	146
275	309	106	318	358	147
276	310	107	319	359	148
277	311	108	320	360	149
278	312	109	321	361	150
279	313	110	322	363	151
280	314	111	323	364	152
281	316	112	324	365	153
282	317	113	325	366	154
283	318	114	326	367	155
284	319	115	327	368	156
285	320	116	328	369	157
286	322	117	329	370	158
287	323	118	330	372	159
288	324	119	331	373	160
289	325	120	332	374	161
290	326	121	333	375	162
291	327	121	334	376	163
292	329	122	335	377	164

Vol. VI Ed. 1 Pg.	Vol. VI Ed. 2 Pg.	Vol. 8 Ed. 3 Pg.	Vol. VI Ed. 1 Pg.	Vol. VI Ed. 2 Pg.	Vol. 8 Ed. 3 Pg.
336	378	165	379	427	206
337	380	165	380	428	208
338	381	166	381	429	207
339	382	167	382	430	209
340	383	168	383	432	210
341	384	169	384	433	210
342	385	170	385	434	211
343	386	171	386	435	212
344	388	172	387	436	213
345	389	173	388	437	214
346	390	174	389	438	215
347	391	175	390	439	216
348	392	176	391	440	217
349	394	177	392	441	218
350	395	178	393	443	219
351	396	179	394	444	220
352	397	180	395	445	221
353	398	181	396	446	222
354	400	182	397	447	223
355	401	183	398	448	224
356	402	184	399	449	225
357	403	185	400	451	226
358	404	186	401	452	227
359	405	187	402	453	228
360	306	188	403	454	229
361	307	189	404	455	230
362	409	190	405	457	230
363	410	191	406	458	231
364	411	192	407	459	232
365	412	193	408	460	233
366	413	194	409	461	234
367	414	195	410	462	235
368	415	196	411	463	236
369	417	197	412	465	237
370	418	197	413	466	238
371	419	199	414	467	239
372	420	199	415	468	240
373	421	200	416	469	241
374	422	201	417	470	242
375	423	202	418	471	243
376	424	203	419	472	244
377	425	204	420	474	245
278	426	205	421	475	246

Vol. VI Ed. 1 Pg.	Vol. VI Ed. 2 Pg.	Vol. 8 Ed. 3 Pg.	Vol. VI Ed. 1 Pg.	Vol. VI Ed. 2 Pg.	Vol. 8 Ed. 3 Pg.
422	476	246	441	497	264
423	477	247	442	498	265
424	478	248	443	499	266
425	479	249	444	500	267
426	480	250	445	501	268
427	481	251	446	502	269
428	483	252	447	504	269
429	483	253	448	504	271
430	484	254	449	505	272
431	486	255	450	506	272
432	487	256	451	508	273
433	488	257	452	509	274
434	489	258	453	510	275
435	490	259	454	511	276
436	491	260	455	512	277
437	492	261	456	513	278
438	494	262	457	514	279
439	495	262	458	515	283
440	496	263	459	516	281

NOTES

TITLE. See Supplement, p. 516 (*Pap.* VI B 5).

Hilarius Bookbinder. For a special reference to the author's name, see Corsair *Affair*, p. 111 and note 94, *KW* XIII.

LECTORI BENEVOLO! and "IN VINO VERITAS"

1. "To the kindly disposed reader," a common Latin heading in learned works. See Supplement, pp. 516-17 (*Pap.* VI B 6).

2. Cf. Sirach 10:10.

3. See *Pap.* III A 201.

4. See Supplement, p. 517 (*Pap.* VI B 7:1).

5. In February 1845, Israel Salomon Levin solicited contributions from about 130 persons for *Album af nulevende danske Mænds og Qvinders Haandskrifter* (Copenhagen: 1846; *ASKB* 1955) designed especially to give school pupils practice in reading handwriting. See Historical Introduction, p. ix and note 8; Supplement, p. 516 (*Pap.* VI B 6); *Letters,* Letters 122-23, *KW* XXV.

6. A line by Per, not Henrich, in Ludvig Holberg, *Jacob von Tyboe Eller Den stortalende Soldat,* I, 4; *Den Danske Skue-Plads,* I-VII (Copenhagen: 1788; *ASKB* 1566-67), III, no pagination.

7. A church in the old shipping town of Christianshavn on Amager, an island linked to Sjælland by the bridge Langebro and the drawbridge Knippelsbro.

8. See Supplement, p. 517 (*Pap.* V B 192).

9. See Supplement, pp. 516-17 (*Pap.* VI B 7:4, 8:2).

10. Literally, "in wine truth." The piece is patterned on Plato's *Symposium* (sometimes translated as *The Banquet*; Latin: *Convivium*). See *Platonis quae exstant opera,* I-XI, ed. Friedrich Ast (Leipzig: 1819-32; *ASKB* 1144-54), III, pp. 429-548, esp. pp. 440-41; *Udvalgte Dialoger af Platon,* I-VIII, tr. Carl Johan Heise (Copenhagen: 1830-59; *ASKB* 1164-67, 1169 [I-VII]), II, pp. 1-104, esp. pp. 12-13; *The Collected Dialogues of Plato,* ed. Edith Hamilton and Huntington Cairns (Princeton: Princeton University Press, 1963), pp. 527-74, esp. p. 531 (176 e-177 a): "Very well, then, said Eryximachus, since it is agreed that we need none of us drink more than we think is good for us, I also propose that . . . we spend our evening in discussion of a subject which, if you think fit, I am prepared to name [love]." See Supplement, pp. 511-13 (*Pap.* IV A 170; V A 82).

11. Literally, "by himself." See Supplement, p. 517 (*Pap.* V B 155, p. 265): "Report *ad se ipsum* [to himself]."

12. G. C. Lichtenberg, "*Ueber Physiognomie wider die Physiognomen*," *Georg Christoph Lichtenberg's vermischte Schriften*, I-IX (Göttingen: 1800-06; *ASKB* 1764-72), III, p. 479. See "The Activity of a Traveling Esthetician," *Corsair Affair*, p. 40, *KW* XIII (*SV* XIII 424); *Postscript*, *KW* XII (*SV* VII 244).

13. Two Danish words, *Forord* and *Forerindring*, which is used here, are usually translated as "preface." *Forerindring*, a word very rarely used now in Danish (therefore marked with a comet sign in the large Danish dictionary, *Ordbog over det danske Sprog*), literally means "prerecollection." Not only is the Preface here a discussion of recollection and a preface to a recollection, but the Nook of Eight Paths portion is also itself a recollection. See Supplement, p. 518 (*Pap.* V B 155).

14. See Judges 14:14; *JP* I 875 (*Pap.* II A 513). Kierkegaard's Danish is a direct translation of the Hebrew and retains the play on "eat" and "eating," which is lost in the Danish translation of his time.

15. For continuation of the sentence, see Supplement, p. 521 (*Pap.* V B 186:1).

16. On the distinction between memory and recollection, see, for example, Plato, *Philebus*, 34 a-c; *Opera*, VIII, pp. 56-57; *Dialogues*, p. 1112:

> SOCRATES: Memory it would, in my opinion, be right to call the preservation of sensation.
>
> PROTARCHUS: Quite so.
>
> SOCRATES: Then by 'recollection' we mean, do we not, something different from memory?
>
> PROTARCHUS: I suppose so.
>
> SOCRATES: I will suggest the point of difference.
>
> PROTARCHUS: What is it?
>
> SOCRATES: When that which has been experienced by the soul in common with the body is recaptured, so far as may be, by and in the soul itself apart from the body, then we speak of 'recollecting' something. Is that not so?
>
> PROTARCHUS: Undoubtedly.
>
> SOCRATES: And further, when the soul that has lost the memory of a sensation or what it has learned resumes that memory within itself and goes over the old ground, we regularly speak of these processes as 'recollections.'

17. With reference to the following three sentences, see Supplement, p. 522 (*Pap.* V B 159). With reference to the following eleven sentences, see Supplement, pp. 518-20 (*Pap.* V B 155).

18. See F. H. Jacobi, *Beylagen zu den Briefen über die Lehre des Spinoza*, *Friedrich Heinrich Jacobi's Werke*, I-VI (Leipzig: 1812-25; *ASKB* 1722-28), IV², p. 68.

19. The Latin *callere* as an intransitive verb means "to have thick skin" and as a transitive verb, "to understand completely."

20. With reference to the following two sentences, see Supplement, p. 523 (*Pap.* V B 158).

21. With reference to the following sentence, see Supplement, p. 524 (*Pap.* V B 186:4). With reference to the remainder of the paragraph, see Supplement, pp. 523-24 (*Pap.* V B 160:8).

22. See Plutarch, "Marcus Cato," 27, 1, *Lives*; *Plutark's Levnetsbeskrivelser*, I-IV, tr. Stephan Tetens (Copenhagen: 1800-11; *ASKB* 1197-1200), III, p. 458; *Plutarch's Lives*, I-XI, tr. Bernadotte Perrin (Loeb, Cambridge: Harvard University Press, 1968-84), II, p. 383: "And in one thing he was even more savage, namely, in adding to his vote on any question whatsoever these words: 'In my opinion, Carthage must be destroyed.' "

23. According to a royal decree of June 29, 1753, the newly established royal orphanage was given a lottery monopoly; the drawing of numbers was done by some of the orphans.

24. Thor, the thunder god in Norse mythology, had a hammer (*Miølner*) with the remarkable feature of returning to him when it was thrown.

25. See Cicero, *De oratore*, II, lxxxvi, 350-51; *M. Tullii Ciceronis opera omnia*, I-IV and index, ed. Johann August Ernesti (Halle: 1756-57; *ASKB* 1224-29), I, pp. 501-02; *Cicero De Oratore*, I-II, tr. E. W. Sutton (Loeb, Cambridge: Harvard University Press, 1942), I, pp. 463-65 (Antony speaking): "'I have given you my view in regard to the discovery and the arrangement of topics; I will also add something on the subject of memory, in order to lighten the task of Crassus and to leave him nothing else to discuss except the method of elaborating these subjects.' . . . 'But to return to the subject,' he continued, 'I am not myself as clever as Themistocles was, so as to prefer the science of forgetting to that of remembering; and I am grateful to the famous Simonides of Ceos, who is said to have first invented the science of mnemonics.'" For a continuation of the sentence, see Supplement, p. 524 (*Pap.* V B 160:11).

26. The Christian evangelical counsels or counsels of perfection are traditionally chastity, obedience, and renunciation of personal property.

27. See Supplement, p. 524 (*Pap.* V B 160:13).

28. This is the case of the young man in *Repetition* (*KW* VI; *SV* III 173-264) in relation to Constantin Constantius.

29. With reference to the remainder of the paragraph, see Supplement, pp. 524-25 (*Pap.* V B 156:2).

30. With reference to the remainder of the paragraph, see Supplement, p. 525 (*Pap.* V B 169:1).

31. See Supplement, p. 525 (*Pap.* V B 169:2).

32. With reference to the following sentence, see Supplement, p. 525 (*Pap.* V B 169:3).

33. See Supplement, pp. 511-12 (*Pap.* IV A 170).

34. With reference to the remainder of the sentence, see Supplement, p. 525 (*Pap.* V B 169:4).

35. With reference to the following three paragraphs, see Supplement, pp. 525-28 (*Pap.* V B 161-65).

36. Gribs-Skov, about twenty miles northwest of Copenhagen, is the largest and most beautiful forest in north Sjælland.

37. See Supplement, pp. 503, 511 (*Pap.* IV A 81, 170).

38. The Latin root of "triviality" means "three paths" or "three roads."

39. A version of an expression attributed to Caesar Augustus. See Suetonius, "The Deified Augustus," 25, *The Lives of the Caesars; Caji Suetonii Tranquilli Tolv første Romerske Keiseres Levnetsbeskrivelse*, I-II, tr. Jacob Baden (Copenhagen: 1802-03; *ASKB* 1281), I, p. 109; *Suetonius*, I-II, tr. J. C. Rolfe (Loeb, New York: Macmillan, 1914), I, p. 159: "He thought nothing less becoming in a well-trained leader than haste and rashness, and, accordingly, favourite sayings of his were: 'More haste, less speed'; 'Better a safe commander than a bold'; and 'That is done quickly enough which is done well enough.' "

40. See John 3:8.

41. See *Either/Or*, I, p. 29, *KW* III (*SV* I 13-14).

42. Ovid, *Tristia*, III, iv, 25-26; *P. Ovidii Nasonis quae supersunt*, I-III, ed. Antonius Richter (Leipzig: 1828; *ASKB* 1265), III, p. 207; *Ovid Tristia Ex Ponto*, tr. Arthur Leslie Wheeler (Loeb, New York: Putnam, 1924), p. 117: "Let me tell thee, he who hides well his life, lives well; each man ought to remain within his proper position."

43. With reference to the remainder of the sentence and the following sentence, see Supplement, p. 528 (*Pap.* V B 166:1).

44. For continuation of the sentence, see Supplement, p. 528 (*Pap.* V B 186:7).

45. With reference to the remainder of the sentence, see Supplement, p. 528 (*Pap.* V B 166:2).

46. With reference to the following paragraph, see Supplement, pp. 529-33 (*Pap.* V B 167-68, 171:1).

47. Challenged to drain a drinking horn, Thor did not realize, until he was told later, that the end of it was in the sea. See Adam Gottlob Oehlenschläger, "*Thors Reise til Jothunheim*," IV, 34-40, V, 24-29, *Nordiske Digte* (Copenhagen: 1807; *ASKB* 1599), pp. 86-88, 111-12; Snorri Sturluson, *The Prose Edda*, tr. Arthur Gilchrist Brodeur (New York: American-Scandinavian Foundation, 1916), pp. 63-64, 67.

48. See Exodus 19:12-13.

49. Wolfgang Amadeus Mozart, *Don Juan*, tr. Laurids Kruse (Copenhagen: 1807), I, 18, p. 57; *Don Giovanni*, tr. Ellen H. Bleiler (New York: Dover, 1964), p. 129.

50. With reference to the following seven paragraphs, see Supplement, p. 534 (*Pap.* V B 172:1).

51. The equator. See *Letters*, Letter 218, *KW* XXV.

52. With reference to the following two paragraphs, see Supplement, pp. 511-12 (*Pap.* IV A 170).

53. Originally there were seven: Johannes, Victor Eremita, Constantin Constantius, and three with the designations of Recollection's Unhappy Lover, Fashion Designer, and Young Man. The seventh is the narrator. See Supplement, p. 534 (*Pap.* V B 172:1). Johannes the Seducer is from *Either/Or*,

I, of which Victor Eremita is the editor. Constantin Constantius and the Young Man are from *Repetition*. The Fashion Designer is a new character. Judge William, whom they visit after the banquet, is from *Either/Or*, II.

54. With reference to the following clause, see Supplement, p. 534 (*Pap.* V B 187:1).

55. For continuation of the sentence and with reference to the remainder of the paragraph, see Supplement, pp. 534-55 (*Pap.* V B 187:4).

56. Presumably the café of Madame Fousanée, Østergade 70.

57. See Luke 14:19-20.

58. An allusion to the line "Speak now or forever hold your peace" in the marriage banns or the wedding service.

59. See Proverbs 15:23.

60. Cf. "*Tischchen deck dich, Goldesel, und Knüppel aus dem Sack,*" *Kinder- und Haus-Märchen. Gesammelt durch die Brüder Grimm*, I-III (Berlin: 1819-22; *ASKB* 1425-27), no. 36, I, pp. 182-84; "The Wishing-Table, the Gold-Ass, and the Cudgel in the Sack," *The Complete Grimm's Fairy Tales*, tr. Margaret Hunt, rev., cor. and compl. James Stern (New York: Pantheon, 1944), pp. 180-86.

61. With reference to the following sentence, see Supplement, p. 535 (*Pap.* V B 187:5).

62. For continuation of the sentence, see Supplement, p. 535 (*Pap.* V B 187:6).

63. A Danish expression used by the host or hostess after a guest has expressed thanks for a meal. Literally, "May it be of good to you."

64. Cf. Ecclesiastes 1:8.

65. Literally, "from the temple" or "on the spot," "immediately." In the Danish Bible of the time (18 pr., 1830; *ASKB* 7), the Greek εὐθύς is translated as *strax* (immediately).

66. With reference to the remainder of the sentence, see Supplement, p. 535 (*Pap.* V B 187:8).

67. See Supplement, p. 514 (*Pap.* V A 94). Nicolai Frederik Severin Grundtvig (1783-1872), Danish poet, mythologist, historian, politician, and preacher, was also the inspiration for the Danish Folk High-school movement. His *Brage-Snak* (Copenhagen: 1844; *ASKB* 1548), a volume of Greek and Scandinavian myths, has "for Ladies and Gentlemen" in the title. The title itself literally means "Skaldic Talk," narratives about the Norse and Greek gods. Brage in Norse mythology is the son of Odin and is a god of words rather than of deeds. *Brag* means "poem," and Brage is the deification of Odin's gift of poetry to the skalds. *Brage-Snak* has come to mean "obscure outpourings," "elaborate outpourings."

68. With reference to the following four sentences, see Supplement, pp. 535-36 (*Pap.* V B 187:9).

69. In Greek mythology there were nine Muses and three Graces.

70. See Johann Wolfgang v. Goethe, *Faust*, I, Auerbach's cellar sc., *Goethe's Werke. Vollständige Ausgabe letzter Hand*, I-LX (Stuttgart, Tübingen: 1828-42;

ASKB 1641-68 [I-LV]), XII, pp. 114-15; *Faust*, tr. Bayard Taylor (New York: Random House, 1950), pp. 80-81.

71. See Seneca, "On Providence," III, 10; *L. Annaeus Seneca's Werke*, I-IV, tr. J. Moser (Stuttgart: 1828-35; *ASKB* 1280-80c), III, p. 351; *Seneca Moral Essays*, I-III, tr. John W. Basore (Loeb, Cambridge: Harvard University Press, 1958-70), I, p. 21.

72. With reference to the remainder of the paragraph, see Supplement, p. 536 (*Pap.* V B 187:11).

73. With reference to the following sentence, see Supplement, p. 536 (*Pap.* V B 172:3).

74. A draft names Ordrup, about five miles north of Copenhagen. See Supplement, p. 536 (*Pap.* V B 172:3).

75. With reference to the following three paragraphs, see Supplement, pp. 536-37 (*Pap.* V B 172:7), and to the following eight paragraphs, see Supplement, pp. 511-12 (*Pap.* IV A 170).

76. See Kruse, I, 20, p. 61; Bleiler, p. 133.

77. See Supplement, pp. 536-37 (*Pap.* V B 172:7).

78. See *Either/Or*, I, pp. 49, 73, *KW* III (*SV* I 33, 55).

79. See, for example, *Philosophical Fragments, or A Fragment of Philosophy*, p. 8, *KW* VII (*SV* IV 178); *Three Discourses on Imagined Occasions*, *KW* X (*SV* V 228).

80. See Kruse, I, 21, p. 63, where the Italian text is rendered as "Every one of us is free."

81. For continuation of the paragraph and with reference to the following nine paragraphs, see Supplement, pp. 537-38 (*Pap.* V B 187:13).

82. With reference to the following sentence, see Supplement, pp. 538-39 (*Pap.* V B 172:12).

83. See *Visebog indeholdende udvalgte danske Selskabssange*, ed. Andreas Seidelin (Copenhagen: 1814; *ASKB* 1483), p. 307.

84. With reference to the remainder of the paragraph, see Supplement, p. 539 (*Pap.* V B 172:11).

85. With reference to the following paragraph, see Supplement, p. 539 (*Pap.* V B 172:10), and to the following two paragraphs, see Supplement, p. 511 (*Pap.* IV A 170).

86. See Supplement, p. 514 (*Pap.* V A 110).

87. See Genesis 43:34, where the Danish Bible (18 pr. 1830; *ASKB* 7) has *drukne* (drunk), as in the text of *Stages*, and RSV has "merry."

88. A salutation used by Roman senators.

89. See Supplement, pp. 511-12 (*Pap.* IV A 170).

90. See *Either/Or*, I, pp. 75-78, *KW* III (*SV* I 57-60).

91. With reference to the remainder of the paragraph, see Supplement, p. 539 (*Pap.* V B 175:2).

92. For continuation of the sentence, see Supplement, p. 539 (*Pap.* V B 175:2).

93. See G.W.F. Hegel, *Vorlesungen über die Aesthetik*, III, *Georg Wilhelm*

Friedrich Hegel's Werke. Vollständige Ausgabe, I–XVIII, ed. Philipp Marheineke et al. (Berlin: 1832-45; *ASKB* 549-65), X³, pp. 533-34; *Sämtliche Werke. Jubiläumsausgabe [J.A.]*, I–XXVI, ed. Hermann Glockner (Stuttgart: Frommann, 1927-40), XIV, pp. 533-34; *The Philosophy of Fine Art*, I–IV (tr. of *V.A.*, 1 ed., 1835-38; Kierkegaard had this ed.), tr. F.P.B. Osmaston (London: Bell, 1920), IV, pp. 301-02.

94. For continuation of the sentence, see Supplement, p. 539 (*Pap.* V B 175:3).

95. See *Symposium*, 208 e–209 a; *Opera*, III, pp. 512-15; Heise, II, p. 75; *Dialogues*, p. 560 (Socrates relating Diotima's speech):

> Well then, she went on, those whose procreancy is of the body turn to woman as the object of their love, and raise a family, in the blessed hope that by doing so they will keep their memory green, 'through time and through eternity.' But those whose procreancy is of the spirit rather than of the flesh—and they are not unknown, Socrates—conceive and bear the things of the spirit. And what are they? you ask. Wisdom and all her sister virtues; it is the office of every poet to beget them, and of every artist whom we may call creative.

96. With reference to the following sentence, see Supplement, p. 540 (*Pap.* V B 175:4).

97. An allusion to Descartes and Hegel and their influence. See *Johannes Climacus, or De omnibus dubitandum est*, pp. 113-72, *KW* VII (*Pap.* IV B 1).

98. There is no subsequent "in the second place." Various contradictions that make love comic are included in a draft. See Supplement, pp. 540-44 (*Pap.* V B 174:12-19). Pp. 42-44 constitute "in the second place," although the designation is not given.

99. See *Symposium*, 204 e–205 a; *Opera*, III, pp. 504-05; Heise, II, pp. 67-68; *Dialogues*, p. 557 (Socrates conversing with Diotima):

> Well then, she went on, suppose that, instead of the beautiful, you were being asked about the good. I put it to you, Socrates. What is it that the lover of the good is longing for?
>
> To make the good his own.
>
> Then what will he gain by making it his own?
>
> I can make a better shot at answering that, I said. He'll gain happiness.
>
> Right, said she, for the happy are happy inasmuch as they possess the good, and since there's no need for us to ask why men should want to be happy, I think your answer is conclusive.
>
> Absolutely, I agreed.

100. See Horace, *Odes*, I, 22; *Q. Horatii Flacci opera* (Leipzig: 1828; *ASKB* 1248), pp. 55-57; *Horace The Odes and Epodes*, tr. C. E. Bennett (Loeb, Cambridge: Harvard University Press, 1978), p. 65.

101. See *Symposium*, 189 d–193 b; *Opera*, III, pp. 468-77; Heise, II, pp. 37-44; *Dialogues*, pp. 542-45:

First of all I must explain the real nature of man, and the change which it has undergone—for in the beginning we were nothing like we are now. For one thing, the race was divided into three; that is to say, besides the two sexes, male and female, which we have at present, there was a third which partook of the nature of both, and for which we still have a name, though the creature itself is forgotten. For though 'hermaphrodite' is only used nowadays as a term of contempt, there really was a man-woman in those days, a being which was half male and half female.

And secondly, gentlemen, each of these beings was globular in shape, with rounded back and sides, four arms and four legs, and two faces, both the same, on a cylindrical neck, and one head, with one face one side and one the other, and four ears, and two lots of privates, and all the other parts to match. They walked erect, as we do ourselves, backward or forward, whichever they pleased, but when they broke into a run they simply stuck their legs straight out and went whirling round and round like a clown turning cartwheels. And since they had eight legs, if you count their arms as well, you can imagine that they went bowling along at a pretty good speed.

. . . And such, gentlemen, were their strength and energy, and such their arrogance, that they actually tried—like Ephialtes and Otus in Homer—to scale the heights of heaven and set upon the gods.

At this Zeus took counsel with the other gods as to what was to be done. They found themselves in rather an awkward position; they didn't want to blast them out of existence with thunderbolts as they did the giants, because that would be saying good-by to all their offerings and devotions, but at the same time they couldn't let them get altogether out of hand. At last, however, after racking his brains, Zeus offered a solution.

I think I can see my way, he said, to put an end to this disturbance by weakening these people without destroying them. What I propose to do is to cut them all in half, thus killing two birds with one stone, for each one will be only half as strong, and there'll be twice as many of them, which will suit us very nicely. They can walk about, upright, on their two legs, and if, said Zeus, I have any more trouble with them, I shall split them up again, and they'll have to hop about on one.

So saying, he cut them all in half just as you or I might chop up sorb apples for pickling, or slice an egg with a hair. And as each half was ready he told Apollo to turn its face, with the half-neck that was left, toward the side that was cut away—thinking that the sight of such a gash might frighten it into keeping quiet—and then to heal the whole thing up. So Apollo turned their faces back to front, and, pulling in the skin all the way round, he stretched it over what we now call the belly—like those bags you pull together with a string—and tied up the one remaining opening so as to form what we call the navel. As for the creases that were left, he smoothed most of them away, finishing off the chest with the sort of tool a cobbler uses to smooth down the leather on the last, but he left a few puckers round about the belly and the navel, to remind us of what we suffered long ago.

Now, when the work of bisection was complete it left each half with a desperate yearning for the other, and they ran together and flung their arms around each other's necks, and asked for nothing better than to be rolled into one. So much so, that they began to die of hunger and general inertia, for neither would do anything without the other. And whenever one half was left alone by the death of its mate, it wandered about questing and clasping in the hope of finding a spare half-woman—or a whole woman, as we should call her nowadays—or half a man. . . .

. . . So you see, gentlemen, how far back we can trace our innate love for one another, and how this love is always trying to redintegrate our former nature, to make two into one, and to bridge the gulf between one human being and another. . . .

And so all this to-do is a relic of that original state of ours, when we were whole, and now, when we are longing for and following after that primeval wholeness, we say we are in love. For there was a time, I repeat, when we were one, but now, for our sins, God has scattered us abroad, as the Spartans scattered the Arcadians. Moreover, gentlemen, there is every reason to fear that, if we neglect the worship of the gods, they will split us up again, and then we shall have to go about with our noses sawed asunder, part and counterpart, like the basso-relievos on the tombstones. And therefore it is our duty one and all to inspire our friends with reverence and piety, for so we may ensure our safety and attain that blessed union by enlisting in the army of Love and marching beneath his banners.

102. With reference to the remainder of the paragraph and the following paragraph, see Supplement, pp. 540-41 (*Pap.* V B 175:6).

103. See Acts 2:4.

104. See Matthew 13:31-32; Mark 4:30-32.

105. See Johann Karl August Musäus, "*Liebestreue,*" *Volksmärchen der Deutschen,* I-V (Vienna: 1815; *ASKB* 1434-38), III, p. 133. See also *Either/Or,* II, p. 29, *KW* IV (*SV* II 28).

106. The source has not been located.

107. See Thomas Overskou and Anton Ludvig Arnesen, *Capriciosa, eller Familien i Nyboder,* II; *Det Kongelige Theaters Repertoire,* 139 (1842), no pagination. The play was first presented at the Royal Theater June 11, 1836.

108. With reference to the remainder of the paragraph, see Supplement, p. 541 (*Pap.* V B 175:9).

109. An allusion to paragraph 26 of the Danish constitution, 1665, which established an absolute monarchy.

110. With reference to the remainder of the paragraph, see Supplement, p. 541 (*Pap* V B 175:11).

111. The reference is to Lycaenium in Longus, *Daphnis and Chloe; Longi Pastorale,* ed. E. E. Seiler (Leipzig: 1843; *ASKB* 1128); *Longus Hirtengeschi-*

chten, tr. Friedrich Jacobs (Stuttgart: 1832; *ASKB* 1130); *Daphnis & Chloe*, tr. George Thornley, rev. J. M. Edmonds (Loeb, New York: Putnam, 1916).

112. Surgeon Brause says of his assistant, Saft: "How like the devil he twists and turns so that he ends up either in the pantry or in the wine cellar." A. G. Oehlenschläger, *Sovedrikken*, I (Copenhagen: 1808), p. 27 (ed. tr.). See also *Fragments*, p. 105, *KW* VII (*SV* IV 267); Supplement, p. 541 (*Pap.* V B 175:11).

113. With reference to the following thirteen sentences, see Supplement, pp. 541-42 (*Pap.* V B 174:13).

114. With reference to the following three paragraphs, see Supplement, pp. 511-12 (*Pap.* IV A 170).

115. See note 101 above.

116. With reference to the following six sentences, see Supplement, p. 542 (*Pap.* V B 174:12).

117. With reference to the remainder of the paragraph, see Supplement, p. 542 (*Pap.* V B 174:18).

118. For continuation of the sentence, see Supplement, p. 542 (*Pap.* V B 175:12).

119. With reference to the following four sentences, see Supplement, pp. 542-43 (*Pap.* V B 174:14).

120. With reference to the remainder of the paragraph, see Supplement, p. 543 (*Pap.* V B 174:15).

121. The source has not been located. Cf. *Either/Or*, II, pp. 340-54, *KW* IV (*SV* II 306-18).

122. An allusion to the Christology in the Nicene and Athanasian creeds.

123. See Aristotle, *Eudemian Ethics*, II, 6, 1222 b; *Aristoteles graece*, I-II, ed. Immanuel Bekker (Berlin: 1831; *ASKB* 1074-75), II, p. 1222; *The Complete Works of Aristotle*, I-II, ed. Jonathan Barnes (rev. Oxford tr., Princeton: Princeton University Press, 1984), II, p. 1936: "Every substance is by nature a sort of principle; therefore each can produce many similar to itself, as man man, animals in general animals, and plants plants."

124. See Ludvig Holberg, *Erasmus Montanus eller Rasmus Berg*, III, 6; *Danske Skue-Plads*, V, no pagination; *Comedies by Holberg*, tr. Oscar James Campbell, Jr., and Frederic Schenck (New York: American-Scandinavian Foundation, 1935), p. 157 (III, 7):

> *Jeronimus*. Listen, wife: you must know that I am the head of the house, and that I am her father.
>
> *Magdelone*. You must also know that I am the mistress of the house, and that I am her mother.
>
> *Jeronimus*. I say that a father is always more than a mother.
>
> *Magdelone*. And I say not, for there can be no doubt that I am her mother, but whether you—I had better not say any more, for I am getting excited.

See also Supplement, p. 543 (*Pap.* V B 174:15).

125. With reference to the following paragraph, see Supplement, pp. 543-44 (*Pap.* V B 174:19).

126. Cf. Genesis 2:24; Mark 10:29.

127. See Matthew 5:28.

128. See Supplement, p. 544 (*Pap.* V B 176:1).

129. See Ecclesiastes 3:7.

130. See Augustin-Eugène Scribe, *Brahma og Bayaderen*, I, 1; *Repertoire*, 93 (1841), no pagination. The play was first presented at the Royal Theater May 15, 1841.

131. Presumably an allusion to Nicolai Frederik Severin Grundtvig's emphasis on "the living word" (in the Apostles' Creed and words of institution in the Sacraments), which his adherents called a "matchless discovery." See, for example, Grundtvig's review of Jakob Peter Mynster, *Om Begrebet af den Christelige Dogmatik*, in *Maanedsskrift for Christendom og Historie*, ed. Jacob Christian Lindberg, I, 1831, p. 609 (ed. tr.):

What I nevertheless in the most urgent way must and will request of him, as well as of all *Christian* pastors and theologians in Denmark and Norway, is only that they will give my explication of the independent universal validity of the confession of faith the keen kindly disposed attention undeniably deserved by a discovery that promises Christ's Kingdom on earth amendment of its bonds and opens the brightest prospects, not only of victory over all enemies, but of an increasing enlightenment and free development of power the world will be compelled to call matchless.

For another use of "matchless," see Grundtvig, *"Blik paa Kirken i det første Aarhundrede," Theologisk Maanedsskrift*, ed. N.F.S. Grundtvig and Andreas Gottlob Rudelbach, X, 1827, pp. 3-4.

See also, for example, *Postscript, KW* XII (*SV* VII 23-33); *JP* V 5089-91, 5356 (*Pap.* I A 60-62; II A 300); *Letters*, Letter 120a, *KW* XXV.

132. See I Timothy 2:14.

133. With reference to the following ten sentences, see Supplement, p. 544 (*Pap.* V B 176:5).

134. With reference to the remainder of the paragraph, see Supplement, p. 544 (*Pap.* V B 176:6).

135. See Herodotus, *History*, VII, 34-35; *Die Geschichten des Herodotos*, I-II, tr. Friedrich Lange (Berlin: 1811; *ASKB* 1117), II, pp. 157-58; *Herodotus*, I-IV, tr. A. D. Godley (Loeb, Cambridge: Harvard University Press, 1981-82), III, pp. 347-49:

Beginning then from Abydos they whose business it was made bridges across to that headland, the Phoenicians one of flaxen cables, and the Egyptians the second, which was of papyrus. From Abydos to the opposite shore it is a distance of seven furlongs. But no sooner had the strait been bridged than a great storm swept down and brake and scattered all that work.

When Xerxes heard of that, he was very angry, and gave command that the Hellespont be scourged with three hundred lashes, and a pair of fetters be thrown into the sea; nay, I have heard ere now that he sent branders with the rest to brand the Hellespont. This is certain, that he charged them while they scourged to utter words outlandish and presumptuous: "Thou bitter water," they should say, "our master thus punishes thee, because thou didst him wrong albeit he had done thee none. Yea, Xerxes the king will pass over thee, whether thou wilt or no; it is but just that no man offers thee sacrifice, for thou art a turbid and a briny river." Thus he commanded that the sea should be punished, and that they who had been overseers of the bridging of the Hellespont should be beheaded.

136. See Shakespeare, *Othello*, V, 2; *William Shakspeare's Tragiske Værker*, I-IX, tr. Peter Foersom and Peter Frederik Wulff (Copenhagen: 1807-25; *ASKB* 1889-96), VII, pp. 180-204; *W. Shakspeare's dramatische Werke*, I-VIII, tr. Ernst Ortlepp (Stuttgart: 1838-40; *ASKB* 1874-81), V, pp. 141-60; *Shakspeare's dramatische Werke*, I-XII, tr. August Wilhelm v. Schlegel and Ludwig Tieck (Berlin: 1839-41; *ASKB* 1883-88), XII, pp. 117-34; *The Complete Works of Shakespeare*, ed. George Lyman Kittredge (Boston: Ginn, 1936), pp. 1280-84.

137. See Kruse, I, 6, pp. 16-25; Bleiler, pp. 96-102.

138. See Aristophanes, *The Clouds*; *Des Aristophanes Werke*, I-III, ed. Johann Gustav Droysen (Berlin: 1835-38; *ASKB* 1052-54), III, pp. 23-124; *Aristophanes*, I-III, tr. Benjamin Bickley Rogers (Loeb, Cambridge: Harvard University Press, 1979-82), I, pp. 266-401. See also *The Concept of Irony, with Continual Reference to Socrates, KW* II (*SV* XIII 214-41).

139. With reference to the following three paragraphs, see Supplement, pp. 544-45 (*Pap.* V B 178:6).

140. A loan word from German with a Danish ending and modified spelling, *gevaldig* in modern Danish.

141. With reference to the remainder of the paragraph and the following paragraph, see Supplement, p. 545 (*Pap.* V B 177:3).

142. A play on a line from J. H. Wessel, *Kierlighed uden Strømper*, III, 3, *Johan Herman Wessels samtlige Skrivter*, I-II (Copenhagen: 1787), I, p. 42 (ed. tr.):

> Everyone who sees the smoke ascend
> (Smoke is my aria)
> Must think, if not say,
> There is fire where it comes from.

143. See Holberg, *Den Stundesløse*, II, 1; *Danske Skue-Plads*, V, no pagination; *The Fussy Man, Four Plays by Holberg*, tr. Henry Alexander (Princeton: Princeton University Press, for the American-Scandinavian Foundation, 1946), p. 26. In response to Vielgeschrey's boast about his little black hen, Christoffer, reading the record book, says: "It's just as you say, sir, forty eggs. What else she has given is not put down."

144. See Diogenes Laertius, *Lives of Eminent Philosophers*, II, 36-37; *Diogenis*

Laertii de vitis philosophorum, I-II (Leipzig: 1833; *ASKB* 1109), I, pp. 77-78; *Diogen Laërtses filosofiske Historie,* I-II, tr. Børge Riisbrigh (Copenhagen: 1812; *ASKB* 1110-11), I, pp. 72-73; *Diogenes Laertius,* I-II, tr. R. D. Hicks (Loeb, Cambridge: Harvard University Press, 1979-80), I, p. 167:

> When Xanthippe first scolded him and then drenched him with water, his rejoinder was, "Did I not say that Xanthippe's thunder would end in rain?" When Alcibiades declared that the scolding of Xanthippe was intolerable, "Nay, I have got used to it," said he, "as to the continued rattle of a windlass. And you do not mind the cackle of geese." "No," replied Alcibiades, "but they furnish me with eggs and goslings." "And Xanthippe," said Socrates, "is the mother of my children." When she tore his coat off his back in the market-place and his acquaintances advised him to hit back, "Yes, by Zeus," said he, "in order that while we are sparring each of you may join in with 'Go it, Socrates!' 'Well done, Xanthippe!' " He said he lived with a shrew, as horsemen are fond of spirited horses, "but just as, when they have mastered these, they can easily cope with the rest, so I in the society of Xanthippe shall learn to adapt myself to the rest of the world."

145. With reference to the following sentence, see Supplement, p. 545 (*Pap.* V B 176:4).

146. With reference to the following three paragraphs, see Supplement, p. 546 (*Pap.* V B 176:3).

147. With reference to the remainder of the paragraph and the following two paragraphs, see Supplement, pp. 546-47 (*Pap.* V B 176:2,7, 174:4).

148. See *Poetics,* 1454 a; Bekker, II, p. 1454; *Works,* II, p. 2327: "In the characters there are four points to aim at. First and foremost, that they shall be good. There will be an element of character in the play, if (as has been observed) what a personage says or does reveals a certain choice; and a good element of character, if the purpose so revealed is good. Such goodness is possible in every type of personage, even in a woman or a slave, though the one is perhaps an inferior, and the other a wholly worthless being."

149. Kierkegaard may have had in mind Henrik Hertz's *Svend Dyrings Hus,* first presented March 15, 1837, and published the same year. In I, 2, the ghost of Fru Helvig makes an appearance and delivers a monologue.

150. The source has not been located.

151. A version of the refrain in the ballad "*Manden og Konen satte dem ned, Talte i Fryd og Gammen.*" See Anton Caén, *Folkevisebog,* I-II (Copenhagen: 1849), II, p. 18. See also *Letters,* Letters 49, 69, pp. 91, 140, *KW* XXV.

152. An application of the ironical phrase usually used by Kierkegaard in reference to those who think they have gone beyond Socrates, Hegel, and faith. See, for example, *Fear and Trembling,* pp. 5, 69, *KW* VI (*SV* III 57, 118); *Fragments,* p. 24, *KW* VII (*SV* IV 193).

153. See, for example, Plato, *Timaeus,* 42 a-b, 90 e; *Opera,* V, pp. 164-65, 274-75; *Dialogues,* pp. 1170-71, 1210; Aristotle, *Politics,* 1259 a-1260 b; Bekker, II, pp. 1259-60; *Works,* II, pp. 1999-2000.

154. With reference to the following six paragraphs, see Supplement, pp. 547-48 (*Pap.* V B 178:8).

155. See Lucius Firmianus Lactantius, *Institutiones divinae*, III, 19; *Firmiani Lactantii opera*, I-II, ed. Otto Fridolin Fritzsche (Leipzig: 1842-44; *ASKB* 142-43), I, p. 152; *The Divine Institutes*, tr. Mary Francis McDonald, *The Fathers of the Church*, I-LXIX, ed. Roy J. Deferrari (Washington, D.C.: Catholic University of America Press, 1943-78), XLIX, pp. 218-19:

> Cicero in his *Consolation* [fragment 11] says it is "best by far not to be born, and not to come up against these rocks of life, but, if you are born, it is next best to escape as it were from the fire of fortune as quickly as possible." It is clear that he believed that very foolish saying, because he added something of his own that he might adorn it. I wonder, therefore, for whom he thinks it is best not to be born, since there is no one at all who may be sensible of it, for the senses effect that something be good or bad. Then, why did he think that all life was nothing else than rocks and burning? As if it were in our power either not to be born, or that chance bestowed life on us, not God, or that the plan of living might seem to have some similarity to a burning.
>
> That theory of Plato's is not dissimilar, because he said that he was thankful to nature, first, because he was born a man rather than a dumb beast; then, because he was a man rather than a woman, a Greek rather than a foreigner; and, finally, because he was an Athenian and of the time of Socrates.

See also Plutarch, "Caius Marius," 46, *Lives*; Tetens, IV, pp. 338-39; Loeb, IX, p. 595; Supplement, pp. 547-49 (*Pap.* V B 178:8).

156. Thales (640-546 B.C.). See Diogenes Laertius, I, 33; *Vitis*, I, p. 15; Riisbrigh, I, p. 14; Loeb, I, p. 35: "Hermippus in his *Lives* refers to Thales the story which is told by some of Socrates, namely, that he used to say there were three blessings for which he was grateful to Fortune: 'first, that I was born a human being and not one of the brutes; next, that I was born a man and not a woman; thirdly, a Greek and not a barbarian.' "

157. For continuation of the sentence, see Supplement, p. 547 (*Pap.* V B 179:1).

158. With reference to the remainder of the paragraph, see Supplement, p. 549 (*Pap.* V B 178:4).

159. See Supplement, p. 549 (*Pap.* VI B 8:5).

160. See Supplement, p. 549 (*Pap.* VI B 8:6).

161. The character as described is not found in Tieck's writings, but there are comparable characters in reverse: the farmhand Gottlieb who appears as king and later is knighted and the tailor's apprentice who becomes emperor. See *Der gestiefelte Kater*, III, 6-7, and *Leben des berühmten Kaisers Abraham Tonelli*, *Ludwig Tieck's sämmtliche Werke*, I-II (Paris: 1837; *ASKB* 1848-49), I, pp. 486-88; II, pp. 133-57.

162. A bundle of sticks tied together with an ax in the middle and carried by the halberdiers of high Roman officials as a symbol of their authority.

163. With reference to the following sentence, see Supplement, p. 550 (*Pap.* V B 179:3).

164. With reference to the following two sentences, see Supplement, p. 550 (*Pap.* V B 178:7).

165. A daily Copenhagen paper founded in 1768 and specializing in obituaries, commercial news, a lost-and-found column, and announcements of ship movements, auctions, real estate and products for sale, help wanted, and jobs wanted.

166. See Holberg, *Barselstuen*, II, 2, *Danske Skue-Plads*, II, no pagination.

167. With reference to the following paragraph, see Supplement, p. 550 (*Pap.* V B 179:4).

168. See I Corinthians 2:9.

169. With reference to the following four sentences, see Supplement, p. 550 (*Pap.* V B 179:5).

170. See Genesis 39:7-20.

171. With reference to the following six paragraphs, see Supplement, pp. 550-51 (*Pap.* V B 179:6).

172. With reference to the following two sentences, see Supplement, p. 551 (*Pap.* V B 180:1).

173. For continuation of the sentence, see Supplement, p. 551 (*Pap.* V B 181:2).

174. An allusion to a novel by Goethe, *Wahlverwandtschaften*, *Werke*, XVII, esp. pp. 52-57; *Elective Affinities*, tr. Elizabeth Mayer and Louise Bogan (Chicago: Regnery, 1963), esp. pp. 36-44.

175. Oehlenschläger, *Aladdin*, III, *Adam Oehlenschlägers Poetiske Skrifter*, I-II (Copenhagen: 1805; *ASKB* 1597-98), II, p. 241; *Aladdin or the Wonderful Lamp*, tr. Henry Meyer (Copenhagen: Gyldendal, 1968), p. 143.

176. With reference to the remainder of the sentence, see Supplement, p. 551 (*Pap.* V B 181:3).

177. With reference to the following sentence, see Supplement, pp. 551-52 (*Pap.* V B 181:4).

178. See Horace, *Satires*, I, 4, 62; *Opera*, p. 401 ("*disjecti membra poetae*"); *Horace Satires, Epistles and Ars Poetica*, tr. H. Rushton Fairclough (Loeb, Cambridge: Harvard University Press, 1978), p. 53: ". . . even when he is dismembered, you would find the limbs of a poet."

179. With reference to the following two paragraphs, see Supplement, pp. 552-53 (*Pap.* V B 178:1,5).

180. An allusion to the esthetic and the ethical qualitative stages. See Historical Introduction, pp. viii-ix. See also, for example, *Postscript*, *KW* XII (*SV* VII 159-60, 203-04, 287); *JP* III 3665-96 and pp. 910-11.

181. With reference to the remainder of the paragraph and the following paragraph, see Supplement, p. 553 (*Pap.* V B 179:7).

182. Victor Eremita means "Victorious Hermit."

183. With reference to the following two paragraphs, see Supplement, p. 553 (*Pap*. V B 182:1).

184. With reference to the Fashion Designer's speech, see Supplement, pp. 509-11 (*Pap*. IV A 135-39).

185. See *Either/Or*, I, p. 90, *KW* III (*SV* I 71).

186. With reference to the following two sentences, see Supplement, pp. 510, 554 (*Pap*. IV A 138; V B 182:5).

187. With reference to the following sentence, see Supplement, p. 510 (*Pap*. IV A 139).

188. See Luke 15:13.

189. See Supplement, p. 514 (*Pap*. V A 110).

190. With reference to the remainder of the paragraph and the following two paragraphs, see Supplement, pp. 554-55 (*Pap*. V B 182:7).

191. With reference to the following five sentences, see Supplement, pp. 554-55, 662-63 (*Pap*. V B 182:3; XI¹ A 49).

192. See Diogenes Laertius, VI, 37; *Vitis*, I, p. 265; Riisbrigh, I, p. 245; Loeb, II, p. 39: "One day he [Diogenes of Sinope] saw a woman kneeling before the gods in an ungraceful attitude, and wishing to free her of superstition, according to Zoïlus of Perga, he came forward and said, 'Are you not afraid, my good woman, that a god may be standing behind you?—for all things are full of his presence—and you may be put to shame?' "

193. With reference to the remainder of the paragraph, see Supplement, p. 510 (*Pap*. IV A 137).

194. With reference to the following paragraph, see Supplement, p. 555 (*Pap*. V B 182:8).

195. With reference to the following sentence, see Supplement, p. 555 (*Pap*. V B 182:4).

196. See Supplement, p. 556 (*Pap*. V B 182:2; VI B 8:7).

197. With reference to the following sentence, see Supplement, p. 556 (*Pap*. V B 182:9).

198. Presumably an allusion to Socrates.

199. See Supplement, p. 513 (*Pap*. IV A 138).

200. With reference to the following paragraph, see Supplement, pp. 556-57 (*Pap*. V B 183:1).

201. With reference to the speech by Johannes the Seducer, see Supplement, pp. 513, 559 (*Pap*. V A 87, B 183:8).

202. See Terence, *Andria*, I, 126; *P. Terentii Afri comodeiae sex*, ed. M. Benedict Friedrich Schmieder and Friedrich Schmieder (Halle: 1819; *ASKB* 1291), p. 16; *Terentses Skuespil*, I-II, tr. Frederik Høegh Guldberg (Copenhagen: 1805; *ASKB* 1293-94), I, p. 25; *The Lady of Andros*, *Terence*, I-II, tr. John Sargeaunt (Loeb, Cambridge: Harvard University Press, 1983-86), I, pp. 14-15; Horace, *Epistles*, I, 19, 41; *Opera*, p. 252; Loeb, p. 265.

203. The source has not been located.

204. Christiansfeld is a small Danish town in southern Jylland, founded by a colony of Moravian Brethren (*Herrnhuter Brüdergemeinde*) who had here es-

tablished schools to which members sent their children. Kierkegaard's father and the family of Emil Boesen, Kierkegaard's closest friend, were associated with the group in Copenhagen during Kierkegaard's early years.

205. With reference to the following seven sentences, see Supplement, p. 557 (*Pap.* V B 183:3-4).

206. A decorated birch branch with which Danish children, in accordance with old custom, awaken their parents on Shrove Monday.

207. The primary female character in "The Seducer's Diary," *Either/Or*, I, pp. 301-445, *KW* III (*SV* I 273-412).

208. A reference to Friedrich Ludwig Schröder, *Ringen, No. 1* and *No. 2* (Hamburg: 1789, 1792). *Ringen No. 2* in Danish, *Ringen eller Det af Delicatesse ulykkelige Ægteskab*, tr. Friderich Schwartz (Copenhagen: 1792), was presented at the Royal Theater five times from 1830 to 1833.

209. With reference to the following two sentences, see Supplement, p. 557 (*Pap.* V B 183:2).

210. See Homer, *Odyssey*, XI, 582-92; *Homers Odyssee*, I-II, tr. Christian Wilster (Copenhagen: 1837), I, pp. 162-63; *Homer The Odyssey*, I-II, tr. A. T. Murray (Loeb, Cambridge: Harvard University Press, 1976-80), I, pp. 427-29:

> "Aye, and I saw Tantalus in violent torment, standing in a pool, and the water came nigh unto his chin. He seemed as one athirst, but could not take and drink; for as often as that old man stooped down, eager to drink, so often would the water be swallowed up and vanish away, and at his feet the black earth would appear, for some god made all dry. And trees, high and leafy, let stream their fruits above his head, pears, and pomegranates, and apple trees with their bright fruit, and sweet figs, and luxuriant olives. But as often as that old man would reach out toward these, to clutch them with his hands, the wind would toss them to the shadowy clouds."

211. See, for example, "Pandora" (the first woman), Paul Friedrich A. Nitsch, *neues mythologisches Wörterbuch*, I-II, rev. Friedrich Gotthilf Klopfer (Leipzig, Sorau: 1821; *ASKB* 1944-45), II, pp. 410-11; Hesiod, *Theogony*, 570-93; *Hesiod The Homeric Hymns and Homerica*, tr. Hugh G. Evelyn-White (Loeb, Cambridge: Harvard University Press, 1982), pp. 121-23:

> But the noble son of Iapetus [Prometheus] outwitted him and stole the far-seen gleam of unwearying fire in a hollow fennel stalk. And Zeus who thunders on high was stung in spirit, and his dear heart was angered when he saw amongst men the far-seen ray of fire. Forthwith he made an evil thing for men as the price of fire; for the very famous Limping God formed of earth the likeness of a shy maiden [Pandora] as the son of Cronos willed. . . .
>
> But when he had made the beautiful evil to be the price for the blessing, he brought her out, delighting in the finery which the bright-eyed daughter of a mighty father had given her, to the place where the other gods and

men were. And wonder took hold of the deathless gods and mortal men when they saw that which was sheer guile, not to be withstood by men.

For from her is the race of women and female kind: of her is the deadly race and tribe of women who live amongst mortal men to their great trouble, no helpmeets in hateful poverty, but only in wealth.

212. With reference to the following three sentences, see Supplement, p. 558 (*Pap.* V B 183:15).

213. See Genesis 2:21-24.

214. See note 101 above.

215. With reference to the following paragraph, see Supplement, p. 558 (*Pap.* V B 183:12,13).

216. With reference to the following sentence, see Supplement, pp. 558-59 (*Pap.* V B 183:5).

217. With reference to the following paragraph, see Supplement, p. 559 (*Pap.* V B 183:20).

218. See Oehlenschläger, *Aladdin*, II; *Poetiske Skrifter*, II, p. 192; Meyer, p. 105.

219. See Ovid, *Metamorphoses*, IV, 54-70; Richter, II, pp. 76-77; *Ovid Metamorphoses*, I-II, tr. Frank Justus Miller, rev. G. P. Goold (Loeb, Cambridge: Harvard University Press, 1984), I, p. 183:

"Pyramus and Thisbe—he, the most beautiful youth, and she, loveliest maid of all the East—dwelt in houses side by side, in the city which Semiramis is said to have surrounded with walls of brick. Their nearness made the first steps of their acquaintance. In time love grew, and they would have been joined in marriage, too, but their parents forbade. Still, what no parents could forbid, sore smitten in heart they burned with mutual love. They had no go-between, but communicated by nods and signs; and the more they covered up the fire, the more it burned. There was a slender chink in the party-wall of the two houses, which it had at some former time received when it was building. This chink, which no one had ever discovered through all these years—but what does love not see?—you lovers first discovered and made it the channel of speech. Safe through this your loving words used to pass in tiny whispers."

220. An allusion to Socrates. See, for example, Plato, *Apology*, 23 b-c; *Opera*, VIII, pp. 112-13; *Dialogues*, p. 9 (Socrates speaking in the court): "That is why I still go about seeking and searching in obedience to the divine command, if I think that anyone is wise, whether citizen or stranger, and when I think that any person is not wise, I try to help the cause of God by proving that he is not. This occupation has kept me too busy to do much either in politics or in my own affairs. In fact, my service to God has reduced me to extreme poverty."

221. See Supplement, p. 664 (*Pap.* XI¹ A 283).

222. See *Either/Or*, I, p. 391, *KW* III (*SV* I 358). In Roman Catholicism the expression refers to the Eucharist.

223. See Supplement, p. 559 (*Pap.* V B 185).

224. With reference to the remainder of the paragraph, see Supplement, pp. 559-60 (*Pap.* VI B 1:1).

225. With reference to the remainder of the paragraph, see Supplement, p. 560 (*Pap.* VI B 1:3).

226. The pseudonymous author of *Either/Or*, II, *KW* IV (*SV* II).

227. With reference to the following two sentences, see Supplement, p. 560 (*Pap.* VI B 1:4).

228. From the ballad "*Manden og Konen sætte dem ned*"; Caén, p. 18.

229. With reference to the following six sentences, see Supplement, pp. 560-61 (*Pap.* V B 189).

230. With reference to the following five sentences, see Supplement, p. 561 (*Pap.* VI B 1:7).

231. *Either/Or*, II, *KW* IV (*SV* II).

232. See Hegel, *Encyclopädie, Die Logik*, para. 87, *Werke*, VI, p. 168; *J.A.* (*System der Philosophie*), XIX, p. 207; *Hegel's Logic* (tr. of *L.*, 3 ed., 1830; Kierkegaard's ed., 1840, had the same text plus *Zusätze*), tr. William Wallace (Oxford: Oxford University Press, 1975), p. 127: "But this mere Being, as it is mere abstraction, is therefore the absolutely negative: which, in a similarly immediate aspect, is just **Nothing**."

233. The singular of "manuscript" is a token of Kierkegaard's early intention to publish the first half of *Stages* as a separate work under the title *"Vrangen og Retten"* ["The Wrong and the Right"]. See Historical Introduction, pp. viii-ix, and Supplement, pp. 568-69 (*Pap.* V B 191). " 'Guilty?'/'Not Guilty?' " was to follow as a separate volume.

SOME REFLECTIONS ON MARRIAGE

1. See Supplement, p. 561 (*Pap.* V B 190:1).

2. Plutarch, *On the Fame of the Athenians*, 5; *Plutarchs moralische Abhandlungen*, I-V, tr. Johann Friedrich S. Kaltwasser (Frankfurt am Main: 1873; *ASKB* 1192-96), III, p. 365; *Plutarch's Moralia*, I-XV, tr. Frank Cole Babbitt et al. (Loeb, Cambridge: Harvard University Press, 1967-84), IV, p. 509:

And for the dramatic poets, the Athenians considered the writing of comedy so undignified and vulgar a business that there was a law forbidding any member of the Areopagus to write comedies. But tragedy blossomed forth and won great acclaim, becoming a wondrous entertainment for the ears and eyes of the men of that age, and, by the mythological character of its plots, and the vicissitudes which its characters undergo, it effected a deception wherein, as Gorgias remarks, "he who deceives is more honest than he who does not deceive, and he who is deceived is wiser than he who is not deceived." For he who deceives is more honest, because he has done what he promised to do; and he who is deceived is wiser, because the mind which is not insensible to fine perceptions is easily enthralled by the delights of language.

See also *JP* IV 4840 (*Pap.* V A 80).

3. See Homer, *Odyssey*, II, 1-4; *Homers Odyssee*, I-II, tr. Christian Wilster (Copenhagen: 1837), I, p. 3; *Homer The Odyssey*, I-II, tr. A. T. Murray (Loeb, Cambridge: Harvard University Press, 1976-80), I, p. 3.

4. Cf. II Corinthians 3:18.

5. A character in *Jean de France*, *Mascarade*, and other comedies by Ludvig Holberg.

6. In Rome the punishment for patricide. See Cicero, "*Pro Sex. Roscio Amerino*," 10-11, 30, *Oratio*; *M. Tullii Ciceronis opera omnia*, I-IV and index, ed. Johann August Ernesti (Halle: 1756-57; *ASKB* 1224-29), II[1], pp. 42-43; *The Orations of Marcus Tullius Cicero*, I-II, tr. C. D. Yonge (London: Bell, 1903), I, pp. 45-46:

> For after they perceived that the life of Sextus Roscius was protected with the greatest care, and that there was no possibility of their murdering him, they adopted a counsel full of wickedness and audacity, namely, that of accusing him of parricide; of procuring some veteran accuser to support the charge, who could say something even in a case in which there was no suspicion whatever; and lastly, as they could not have any chance against him by the accusation, to prevail against him on account of the time; for men began to say, that no trial had taken place for such a length of time, that the first man who was brought to trial ought to be condemned; and they thought that he would have no advocates because of the influence of Chrysogonus; that no one would say a word about the sale of the property and about that conspiracy; that because of the mere name of parricide and the atrocity of the crime he would be put out of the way, without any trouble, as he was defended by no one. . . . And yet they crown and add to them by other nefarious deeds,—they invent an incredible accusation; they procure witnesses against him and accusers of him by bribery; they offer the wretched man this alternative,—whether he would prefer to expose his neck to Roscius to be assassinated by him, or, being sewn in a sack, to lose his life with the greatest infamy.

7. See I Corinthians 14:32-35.

8. Laocoön had hurled his spear at the Greek wooden horse in the city of Troy, and his fate was interpreted by the Trojans as a penalty for a crime. See Virgil, *Aeneid*, II, 199-227; *Virgils Aeneide*, tr. Johan Henrik Schønheyder (Copenhagen: 1812), pp. 63-65; *Virgil*, I-II, tr. H. Rushton Fairclough (Loeb, Cambridge: Harvard University Press, 1978), I, p. 309 (Aeneas speaking):

> "Hereupon another portent, more fell and more frightful by far, is thrust upon us, unhappy ones, and confounds our unforeseeing souls. Laocoön, priest of Neptune, as drawn by lot, was slaying a great bull at the wonted altars; and lo! from Tenedos, over the peaceful depths—I shudder as I tell the tale—a pair of serpents with endless coils are breasting the sea and side by side making for the shore. Their bosoms rise amid the surge, and their crests, blood-red, overtop the waves; the rest of them skims the main behind and their huge backs curve in many a fold; we hear the sound sent from foaming seas. And now they were gaining the fields and, with blazing

eyes suffused with blood and fire, were licking with quivering tongues their hissing mouths. Pale at the sight, we scatter. They in unswerving course fare towards Laocoön; and first each serpent enfolds in its embrace the youthful bodies of his two sons and with its fangs feeds upon the hapless limbs. Then himself too, as he comes to their aid, weapons in hand, they seize and bind in mighty folds; and now, twice encircling his waist, twice winding their scaly backs around his throat, they tower above with head and lofty necks. He the while strains his hands to burst the knots, his fillets steeped in gore and black venom; the while he lifts to heaven hideous cries, like the bellowings of a wounded bull that has fled from the altar and shaken from its neck the ill-aimed axe. But, gliding away, the dragon pair escape to the lofty shrines, and seek fierce Tritonia's citadel, there to nestle under the goddess' feet and the circle of her shield."

9. In a letter from Johann Georg Hamann to Jacobi, January 22, 1785, *Friedrich Heinrich Jacobi's Werke*, I–VI (Leipzig: 1812-25; *ASKB* 1722-28), IV³, p. 34 (ed. tr.): "There is doubt that must be dismissed with no reasons or replies but simply with a Bah!" See also Supplement, pp. 561-62 (*Pap.* V B 190:2); *JP* I 624; III 2489 (*Pap.* V A 47; X¹ A 324).

10. See Daniel 3:15.

11. See Daniel 3:28.

12. After victory over the pagan Wends on the island of Rügen in 1169, "King of the Wends" became part of the title, symbolized by a wivern, of Valdemar (the Great) I (1131-1182). After the conquest of Gotland in 1361, "King of the Goths" became part of the title, symbolized by a lion surmounting nine hearts, of Valdemar (Atterdag) IV (c. 1320-1375). In 1460, when Christian I was elected Duke of Slesvig and Holsten, that title, symbolized by a pair of lions and the nettle leaf of Holsten, was incorporated in the royal title.

13. Cf. Supplement, p. 548 (*Pap.* V B 178:8) and note 77; *Either/Or*, II, p. 125, *KW* IV (*SV* II 114).

14. See Aesop, "The Boasting Traveller," *The Fables of Aesop*, ed. Thomas Bewick (New York: Paddington, 1975), p. 59. See also, for example, G.W.F. Hegel, *Grundlinien der Philosophie des Rechts*, *Georg Wilhelm Friedrich Hegel's Werke. Vollständige Ausgabe*, I–XVIII, ed. Philipp Marheineke et al. (Berlin: 1832-45; *ASKB* 549-65), VIII, pp. 18-19; *Sämtliche Werke. Jubiläumsausgabe* [*J.A.*], I–XXVI, ed. Hermann Glockner (Stuttgart: 1927-40), VII, pp. 34-35; *Hegel's Philosophy of Right* (tr. of *P.R.*, 1 ed., 1821; Kierkegaard had 2 ed., 1833), tr. T. M. Knox (Oxford: Oxford University Press, 1978), p. 11:

The instruction which it may contain cannot consist in teaching the state what it ought to be; it can only show how the state, the ethical universe, is to be understood.

Ἰδοὺ Ῥόδος ἰδοὺ καὶ τὸ πήδημα
Hic Rhodus, *hic* saltus
[*Here* is Rhodes, jump *here*].

To comprehend what is, this is the task of philosophy, because what is, is reason. Whatever happens, every individual is a child of his time; so philosophy too is its own time apprehended in thoughts. It is just as absurd to fancy that a philosophy can transcend its contemporary world as it is to fancy that an individual can overleap his own age, jump over Rhodes. If his theory really goes beyond the world as it is and builds an ideal one as it ought to be, that world exists indeed, but only in his opinions, an unsubstantial element where anything you please may, in fancy, be built.

With hardly an alteration, the proverb just quoted would run:

Here is the rose, dance thou here.

15. After Aeneas and his people had been shipwrecked and beached, he tried to console them by casting present distress into future recollection and pointing hopefully toward their goals. See Virgil, *Aeneid*, I, 198-207; Schønheyder, p. 15; Loeb, I, p. 255 (Aeneas speaking):

"O comrades—for ere this we have not been ignorant of evils—O ye who have borne a heavier lot, to this, too, God will grant an end! Ye drew near to Scylla's fury and her deep-echoing crags; ye have known, too, the rocks of the Cyclopes; recall your courage and put away sad fear. Perchance even this distress it will some day be a joy to recall. Through divers mishaps, through so many perilous chances, we fare towards Latium, where the fates point out a home of rest. There 'tis granted to Troy's realm to rise again; endure, and keep yourselves for days of happiness."

16. An allusion to the placing of the vowel symbols below consonants in Hebrew.

17. See Genesis 33:4.

18. See John 4:24.

19. See *Either/Or*, II, Supplement, p. 384, *KW* IV (*Pap.* IV A 234).

20. Presumably an allusion to Nicolai Frederik Severin Grundtvig (1783-1872), Danish historian, mythologist, poet, politician, and preacher.

21. See *Either/Or*, II, pp. 62-88 *KW* IV (*SV* II 57-80).

22. Oehlenschläger, *Aladdin*, III, *Adam Oehlenschlägers Poetiske Skrifter*, I-II (Copenhagen: 1805; *ASKB* 1597-98), II, pp. 216-21; *Aladdin or the Wonderful Lamp*, tr. Henry Meyer (Copenhagen: Gyldendal, 1968), pp. 124-27.

23. See Johannes Climacus's observations on Judge William's expression, *Postscript*, *KW* XII (*SV* VII 150, 463).

24. A free version of a comment in Hamann's letter to Johann G. Lindner, July 3, 1759, regarding objections by David Hume to Christianity. See *Hamann's Schriften*, I-VIII, ed. Friedrich Roth and G. A. Wiener (Berlin, Leipzig: 1821-43; *ASKB* 536-44), I, p. 406. See also *JP* II 1539 (*Pap.* I A 100).

25. See *Either/Or*, II, p. 68, *KW* IV (*SV* II 63).

26. See Herodotus, *History*, I, 32; *Die Geschichten des Herodotos*, I-II, tr. Friedrich Lange (Berlin: 1811; *ASKB* 1117), I, p. 19; *Herodotus*, I-IV, tr.

A. D. Godley (Loeb, Cambridge: Harvard University Press, 1981-82), I, pp. 39-41 (Solon speaking to Croesus):

> "Many men of great wealth are unblest, and many that have no great substance are fortunate. Now the very rich man who is yet unblest has but two advantages over the fortunate man, but the fortunate man has many advantages over the rich but unblest: for this latter is the stronger to accomplish his desire and to bear the stroke of great calamity; but these are the advantages of the fortunate man, that though he be not so strong as the other to deal with calamity and desire, yet these are kept far from him by his good fortune, and he is free from deformity, sickness, and all evil, and happy in his children and his comeliness. If then such a man besides all this shall also end his life well, then he is the man whom you seek, and is worthy to be called blest; but we must wait till he be dead, and call him not yet blest, but fortunate. Now no one (who is but man) can have all these good things together, just as no land is altogether self-sufficing in what it produces: one thing it has, another it lacks, and the best land is that which has most; so too no single person is sufficient for himself: one thing he has, another he lacks; but whoever continues in the possession of most things, and at last makes a gracious end of his life, such a man, O King, I deem worthy of this title. We must look to the conclusion of every matter, and see how it shall end, for there are many to whom heaven has given a vision of blessedness, and yet afterwards brought them to utter ruin."

27. Cf. John 5:24.

28. See "The Dog and the Shadow," *Aesop*, p. 117.

29. Cf. Numbers 21:8.

30. With reference to the following two clauses, see Supplement, p. 562 (*Pap.* V B 190:5).

31. See Matthew 22:11-13.

32. In Greek mythology, the Milky Way was attributed to Hera (Roman Juno), wife of Zeus, in connection with her nursing the infant Hercules. See "Hera," Paul Friedrich A. Nitsch, *neues mythologisches Wörterbuch*, I-II, rev. Friedrich Gotthilf Klopfer (Leipzig, Sorau: 1821; *ASKB* 1944-45), I, p. 814.

33. See Psalms 1:3, 128:3.

34. See Matthew 25:35-46; James 2:15-16; Luke 17:10.

35. Cf. Matthew 6:2,5.

36. See Horace, *Odes*, I, 32, 1; *Q. Horatii Flacci opera* (Leipzig: 1828; *ASKB* 1248), p. 77 ("*Poscimur*"); *Horace The Odes and Epodes*, tr. C. E. Bennett (Loeb, Cambridge: Harvard University Press, 1978), p. 87: "I am asked for a song."

37. The Phoenicians bargained with the Libyans for as much land as could be encompassed by a bull's hide, which they then cut into very fine strips that enclosed a large tract. See Virgil, *Aeneid*, I, 365-68; Schønheyder, p. 25; Loeb, I, p. 267 (Venus speaking to Aeneas): "'They came to the place where now thou seest the huge walls and rising citadel of new Carthage, and bought

ground—Byrsa they called it therefrom—as much as they could encompass with a bull's hide.'"

38. See Exodus 20:5.

39. On "reality" and "actuality," see *JP* III 3651-55 and pp. 900-03.

40. See, for example, *"Legenden von Rübezahl,"* Johann Karl August Musäus, *Volksmärchen der Deutschen,* I-V (Vienna: 1815; *ASKB* 1434-38), II, p. 70.

41. Wolfgang Amadeus Mozart, *Figaros Givtermaal,* tr. Niels Thoroup Bruun (Copenhagen: 1817), II, 2, p. 40; *The Marriage of Figaro,* ed. Nicholas John (New York: Riverrun Press, 1983), p. 68.

42. See Galatians 4:4.

43. In Greek mythology, Orpheus, after the death of his wife, Eurydice, went to Hades to secure her release. The gods, charmed by his music, agreed, but he disobeyed their injunction not to look at her before they reached the earth, and she vanished. See Nitsch, II, p. 368.

44. Danish: *Forklaring,* which means both "explanation" and "transfiguration."

45. See p. 63.

46. An allusion to Socrates. See, for example, Plato, *Gorgias,* 490 e-491 a; *Platonis quae exstant opera,* I-XI, ed. Friedrich Ast (Leipzig: 1819-32; *ASKB* 1144-54), I, pp. 572-73; *Udvalgte Dialoger af Platon,* I-VIII, tr. Carl Johan Heise (Copenhagen: 1830-59; *ASKB* 1164-67, 1169 [I-VII]), III, p. 111; *The Collected Dialogues of Plato,* ed. Edith Hamilton and Huntington Cairns (Princeton: Princeton University Press, 1963), p. 273:

> CALLICLES: Shoes! You keep talking nonsense.
>
> SOCRATES: Well, if that is not what you mean, here it is perhaps. A farmer for instance who is an expert with good sound knowledge about the soil should have a larger share of seed and use the most seed possible on his own land.
>
> CALLICLES: How you keep saying the same things, Socrates!
>
> SOCRATES: Not only that, Callicles, but about the same matters.
>
> CALLICLES: By heaven, you literally never stop talking about cobblers and fullers and cooks and doctors, as if we were discussing them.

See also *Fragments,* p. 72, *KW* VII (*SV* IV 236).

47. See Pius Alexander Wolff, *Preciosa,* tr. Caspar Johannes Boye (Copenhagen: 1822), p. 25. The piece (with music by Carl Maria von Weber) was first performed at the Royal Theater October 29, 1822, and in 1843 on January 5. See also Supplement, pp. 652-53 (*Pap.* VI A 78).

48. See *Fear and Trembling,* p. 121, *KW* VI (*SV* III 166).

49. See p. 84 and note 2.

50. See Matthew 26:49; Mark 14:45; Luke 22:47.

51. An allusion to Helene, a Greek princess, in Henrik Hertz's drama *Svanehammen* (Copenhagen: 1841), I, 4, pp. 24-27.

52. See *Either/Or,* II, Supplement, p. 380, *KW* IV (*Pap.* IV A 246).

53. Cf. Mark 12:17.

54. See Judges 13:22; cf. Isaiah 6:5.

55. See Diogenes Laertius, *Lives of Eminent Philosophers*, I, 26; *Diogenis Laertii de vitis philosophorum*, I-II (Leipzig: 1833; *ASKB* 1109), I, p. 12; *Diogen Laërtses filosofiske Historie*, I-II, tr. Børge Riisbrigh (Copenhagen: 1812; *ASKB* 1110-11), I, p. 10; *Diogenes Laertius*, I-II, tr. R. D. Hicks (Loeb, Cambridge: Harvard University Press, 1979-80), I, pp. 26-27.

56. See pp. 71-80.

57. See John 2:14.

58. In Kierkegaard's published works and in his journals and papers, "primitive" in its various forms denotes an individual's original capacity to receive an impression without being influenced by "the others" or by current views. See *JP* III 3558-61 and pp. 887-88; VII, p. 76.

59. Together with *De incertitudine et vanitate omnium scientiarum & artium liber* etc. (Frankfurt, Leipzig: 1622 [first published in Cologne, 1527]; *ASKB* 113). See Supplement, p. 511 (*Pap.* IV A 170).

60. On May 28, 1831, the Provincial Consultative Assemblies were announced and subsequently were established on May 15, 1834. The Twenty-eighth of May Society was formed in 1832 and was promptly banned. The day was celebrated annually, however, during the following decade. The speech is presumably Kierkegaard's invention.

61. Agrippa, no pagination.

62. See Ecclesiastes 1:18.

63. With reference to the following sentence, see Supplement, p. 562 (*Pap.* VI B 4:1). With reference to the following footnote, see Supplement, pp. 562-64 (*Pap.* VI B 2-3, 8:8).

64. Anna Helene Dorothea Nielsen (1807-1850) was a member of the Royal Theater company from 1821 until her death. One of the great favorites of the critics, she portrayed especially the Danish woman of all ages from a young girl to a grandmother. See *Letters*, Letter 170, Dedication 15(b), *KW* XXV; Supplement, pp. 562-64 (*Pap.* VI B 2-3).

65. See Horace, *Epistles*, II, 1, 199-207; *Opera*, p. 636; *Horace Satires, Epistles and Ars Poetica*, tr. H. Rushton Fairclough (Loeb, Cambridge: Harvard University Press, 1978), pp. 413-15:

> But for the authors—he would suppose that they were telling their tale to a deaf ass. For what voices have ever prevailed to drown the din with which our theatres resound? One might think it was the roaring of the Garganian forest or of the Tuscan Sea: amid such clamour is the entertainment viewed, the works of art, and the foreign finery, and when, overlaid with this, the actor steps upon the stage, the right hand clashes with the left. "Has he yet said anything?" Not a word. "Then what takes them so?" 'Tis the woollen robe that vies with the violet in its Tarentine dye.

66. See Poul Martin Møller, *En Danske Students Eventyr, Efterladte Skrifter*, I-III (Copenhagen: 1839-43; *ASKB* 1574-76), III, p. 42.

67. See Exodus 25:20-21.

68. See Isaiah 22:13; I Corinthians 15:32.

69. See Horace, "The Poet's Prayer," 17-20, *Odes*, I, 31; *Opera*, p. 76; Loeb, p. 85: "Grant me, O Latona's son, to be content with what I have, and, sound of body and of mind, to pass an old age lacking neither honour nor the lyre!"

70. See Job 29:18. The reference is probably also to King Frederik III, who, when advised to flee when Copenhagen was about to be besieged by the Swedes on August 8, 1658, replied, "I shall die in my nest."

71. *Othello*, III, 3, 166-67, Kierkegaard's Danish version of the Schlegel-Tieck German translation. *Shakspeare's dramatische Werke*, I-XII, tr. August Wilhelm v. Schlegel and Ludwig Tieck (Berlin: 1839-40; *ASKB* 1883-88), XII, p. 63; cf. *William Shakspeare's Tragiske Værker*, I-IX, tr. Peter Foersom and Peter Frederik Wulff (Copenhagen: 1807-25; *ASKB* 1889-96), VII, p. 97; *W. Shakspeare's dramatische Werke*, I-VIII, tr. Ernst Ortlepp (Stuttgart: 1838-40; *ASKB* 1874-81), V, p. 76; *The Complete Works of Shakespeare*, ed. George Lyman Kittredge (Boston: Ginn, 1936), p. 1263 (Iago speaking): "the green-ey'd monster, which doth mock / The meat it feeds on."

72. In Norse mythology, Valhalla was the abode of slain heroes, who were carried into immortality by the Valkyries.

73. With reference to the remainder of the sentence, see Supplement, p. 564 (*Pap.* VI B 190:11).

74. See Luke 4:4.

75. The only desire of the Roman people, according to Juvenal, *Satires*, X, 80-81; *D. Junii Juvenalis Satirae*, tr. F. G. Findeisen (Berlin, Leipzig: 1777; *ASKB* 1249), p. 374; *Juvenal and Persius*, tr. G. G. Ramsay (Loeb, Cambridge: Harvard University Press, 1979), p. 199: "Bread and Games!" See *Either/Or*, I, p. 286, *KW* III (*SV* I 258).

76. See Hamann, "*Hirtenbriefe*," 5, *Schriften*, II, pp. 424-25. See also *JP* I 265 (*Pap.* II A 12).

77. Part of Strøget, now the main pedestrian street in Copenhagen.

78. Literally, the flower of a "thousandfold joy."

79. See Matthew 25:1-13.

80. *Othello*, II, 1, 244-47; Foersom and Wulff, VII, p. 56; Ortlepp, V, p. 44; Schlegel and Tieck, XII, pp. 37-38 (ed. tr.); Kittredge, p. 1254.

81. See Proverbs 15:23; 25:11.

82. With reference to the remainder of the sentence, see Supplement, p. 564 (*Pap.* V B 190:12).

83. See *Othello*, V, 2, 40; Foersom and Wulff, VII, p. 182; Ortlepp, V, p. 143; Schlegel and Tieck, XII, p. 119; Kittredge, p. 1280 (Desdemona, in reply to Othello's saying "Think on thy sins"): "They are loves I bear to you." See also Jacobi, *Werke*, III, p. 37 (ed. tr.): "Yes, I . . . will lie just as Desdemona, dying, lied."

84. See *Either/Or*, I, p. 34, *KW* III (*SV* I 18).

85. See Wolfgang Amadeus Mozart, *Don Juan*, tr. Laurids Kruse (Copen-

hagen: 1807), II, 20, p. 125; *Don Giovanni*, tr. Ellen H. Bleiler (New York: Dover, 1964), p. 198.

86. On Holger Danske, see Just Matthias Thiele, *Danske Folkesagn*, I-II (Copenhagen: 1819-23; *ASKB* 1591-92), I, pp. 24-25.

87. Jean Paul (Johann Paul Friedrich Richter), *Flegeljahre*, I, 14, *Jean Paul's sämmtliche Werke*, I-LX (Berlin: 1826-28; *ASKB* 1777-99), XXVI, p. 113.

88. See Mark 10:9.

89. See p. 56.

90. With reference to the remainder of the sentence, see Supplement, p. 564 (*Pap.* VI B 8:9).

91. See Ernst Theodor Amadeus Hoffmann, *"Ein Fragment aus dem Leben dreier Freunde,"* *Die Serapions-Brüder*, E.T.A. *Hoffmann's ausgewählte Schriften*, I-X (Berlin: 1827-28; *ASKB* 1712-16), I, p. 175. The scene centers on the secretary, Nettelmann, who wears a paper crown and states that his general has vanquished the Bulgarians. On a ruler he has an apple that he presents. Essentially and in other details the scene is correctly represented.

92. G. C. Lichtenberg, *"Litterarische Bemerkungen,"* *Georg Christoph Lichtenberg's vermischte Schriften*, I-IX (Göttingen: 1800-06; *ASKB* 1764-72), II, p. 278.

93. A free version of Augustine, *De bono viduitatis*, 28; *Sancti Aurelii Augustini . . . opera et studio monachorum*, I-XVIII (Bassani: 1797-1807; *ASKB* 117-34), XI, col. 820.

94. The source has not been located.

95. See Matthew 13:25.

96. Karl Friedrich Hieronymus v. Münchhausen (1720-1797) was a legendary German teller of tall tales. See *Baron von Münchhausens vidunderlige Reiser, Feldtog og Hændelser, fortalte af ham selv* (Roeskilde: 1834); Rudolph Erich Raspe, *The Surprising Adventures of Baron Munchausen* (New York: Crowell, 1902).

97. Johann Wolfgang v. Goethe, *Aus meinem Leben. Dichtung und Wahrheit, Goethe's Werke. Vollständige Ausgabe letzter Hand*, I-LX (Stuttgart, Tübingen: 1828-42; *ASKB* 1641-68 [I-LV]), XXVI, pp. 5-39; *The Autobiography of Goethe*, I-II, tr. John Oxenford (London: Bell, 1881), I, pp. 389-407. See also *JP* II 1458 (*Pap.* V A 57).

98. Christian Winther, *"Hjertesorg,"* *Haandtegninger* (Copenhagen: January 23, 1840; *ASKB* 1593; one of only five books known to bear Kierkegaard's signature), p. 28 (ed. tr.):

> He went away calm and quiet
> In a courteous manner;
> Finally in my mother's house
> We saw him no more.

99. A Danish civil-law commission established July 10, 1795.

100. The motto of the notorious Caesar Borgia (1478-1507), soldier and politician, son of Pope Alexander VI.

101. See Goethe, *Aus meinem Leben*, *Werke*, XXVI, pp. 214–23; *Autobiography*, I, pp. 504–09. Edward Young (1683-1765), English poet, was best known throughout Europe for his *Night Thoughts* (1742-46). See, for example, *Either/Or*, I, p. 2, *KW* III (*SV* I title page).

102. See *Aus meinem Leben*, *Werke*, XXV, pp. 290–93; *Autobiography*, I, pp. 342-44.

103. See p. 160.

104. See Supplement, p. 564 (*Pap.* VI B 8:10).

105. See *Aus meinem Leben*, *Werke*, XXIV, pp. 61–65; *Autobiography*, I, pp. 29–31.

106. See *Aus meinem Leben*, *Werke*, XXV, pp. 251-54; *Autobiography*, I, pp. 320–22.

107. See *Aus meinem Leben*, *Werke*, XXVI, pp. 305–09; *Autobiography*, II, pp. 33-35.

108. See J. L. Heiberg, "*Det astronomiske Aar*," *Urania. Aarbog for 1844*, ed. Johan Ludvig Heiberg (Copenhagen: 1843; *ASKB U* 57), pp. 102-07.

109. See *Aus meinem Leben*, *Werke*, XXVI, pp. 120–23; *Autobiography*, I, pp. 453–55.

110. Cf. Matthew 6:24; Luke 16:13.

111. See Proverbs 18:22.

112. See Philippians 1:6.

113. See Diogenes Laertius, II, 33; *Vitis*, I, p. 76; Riisbrigh, I, p. 71; Loeb, I, p. 163. See also *Either/Or*, I, pp. 38–40, *KW* III (*SV* I 22-24).

114. See Diogenes Laertius, I, 26; *Vitis*, I, p. 12; Riisbrigh, I, p. 11; Loeb, I, p. 27.

115. See Exodus 12:12.

116. See Song of Solomon 1:8, 5:9.

117. See Homer, *Iliad*, III, 146-60; *Homers Iliade*, I-II, tr. Christian Wilster (Copenhagen: 1836), I, p. 46; *Homer The Iliad*, I-II, tr. A. T. Murray (Loeb, Cambridge: Harvard University Press, 1976-78), I, pp. 127-29:

> And they that were about Priam and Panthous and Thymoetes and Lampus and Clytius and Hicetaon, scion of Ares, and Ucalegon and Antenor, men of prudence both, sat as elders of the people at the Scaean gates. Because of old age had they now ceased from battle, but speakers they were full good, like unto cicalas that in a forest sit upon a tree and pour forth their lily-like voice; even in such wise sat the leaders of the Trojans upon the wall. Now when they saw Helen coming upon the wall, softly they spake winged words one to another: "Small blame that Trojans and well-greaved Achaeans should for such a woman long time suffer woes; wondrously like is she to the immortal goddesses to look upon."

118. Oehlenschläger, *Aladdin*, II, *Poetiske Skrifter*, II, p. 151 (ed. tr.); Meyer, p. 151.

119. Cf. *Either/Or*, II, pp. 212-17, *KW* IV (*SV* II 191-94).

120. See *JP* II 1941-43 and pp. 594-95; VII, p. 48.

121. See Ludvig Holberg, *Nicolai Klimii inter Subterraneum* (Leipzig, Copenhagen: 1741); *Niels Klims Reise under Jorden* (Copenhagen: 1742; 2 ed., 1745); *Journey of Niels Klim to the World Underground* (London: 1745; Lincoln: University of Nebraska Press, 1960).

122. A version of an expression ("*sande Skin*," true appearance) used by Hans Lassen Martensen in "*Betragtningen over Ideen af Faust*," *Perseus*, I-II, ed. Johan Ludvig Heiberg (Copenhagen: 1837-38; *ASKB* 569), I, p. 120. See Hegel, *Vorlesungen über die Aesthetik, Werke*, X¹, p. 13; *J.A.*, XII, p. 29; *Philosophy of Fine Art*, I-IV (tr. of *V.A.*, 1 ed., 1835-38; Kierkegaard had this ed.), tr. F.P.B. Osmaston (London: Bell, 1920), I, pp. 9-10.

123. See, for example, Plato, *Symposium*, 174 a; *Opera*, III, pp. 434-35; Heise, II, pp. 6-7; *Dialogues*, p. 528.

124. See Oehlenschläger, *Aladdin*, III, *Poetiske Skrifter*, II, pp. 224-30; Meyer, pp. 129-34.

125. Oehlenschläger, *Hugo von Rheinberg* (Copenhagen: 1813), p. 101 (ed. tr.). The lines were omitted in later editions.

126. See Matthew 13:44-46.

127. Cf. I Corinthians 13:12.

128. A saying attributed to Cleobulus, one of the Seven Wise Men of Greece. See Diogenes Laertius, I, 91; *Vitis*, I, p. 43; Riisbrigh, I, p. 41; Loeb, I, p. 95.

129. A picture by the German artist Ferdinand Piloty (1786-1844) representing the moment before the farewell kiss in III, 5.

130. Cf. Suetonius, "The Deified Julius," 1, *The Lives of the Caesars; Caji Suetonii Tranquilli Tolv første Romerske Keiseres Levnetsbeskrivelse*, I-II, tr. Jacob Baden (Copenhagen: 1802-03; *ASKB* 1281), I, p. 2; *Suetonius*, I-II, tr. J. C. Rolfe (Loeb, New York: Macmillan, 1914), I, pp. 3-5:

> Everyone knows that when Sulla had long held out against the most devoted and eminent men of his party who interceded for Caesar, and they obstinately persisted, he at last gave way and cried, either by divine inspiration or a shrewd forecast: "Have your way and take him; only bear in mind that the man you are so eager to save will one day deal the death blow to the cause of the aristocracy, which you have joined with me in upholding; for in this Caesar there is more than one Marius."

Cf. also Genesis 38:23.

131. See Genesis 2:24. Cf. Mark 10:28-29; Luke 18:28-29.

132. See p. 22 and note 58.

133. Cf. Hebrews 13:14.

134. Cf. I Corinthians 13:9.

135. See I Samuel 15:22.

136. An allusion to Johan Ludvig Heiberg (1791-1860), who, in addition to being the leading Danish literary critic, Danish Hegelian, and a prominent dramatist, editor, and poet, was a devoted amateur astronomer. See, for ex-

ample, *"Det astronomiske Aar,"* *Urania* . . . *1844*, pp. 77-160; *Prefaces*, *KW* IX (*SV* V 17, 23-30, 51-54, 61-64, 69).

137. See Psalm 90:10; Ecclesiastes 4:6-8.

138. See Ecclesiastes 1:7.

139. See Virgil, *Aeneid*, VI, 424-29; Schønheyder, p. 274; Loeb, I, pp. 535-37: "The warder buried in sleep, Aeneas wins the entrance, and swiftly leaves the bank of that stream whence none return. At once are heard voices and wailing sore—the souls of infants weeping, whom, on the very threshold of the sweet life they shared not, torn from the breast, the black day swept off and plunged in bitter death."

140. Cf. *Fragments*, p. 72, *KW* VII (*SV* IV 236).

141. In Athens, voting on ostracism was done by marking fragments of earthenware.

142. See Revelation 3:15.

143. See Horace, *Epistles*, I, 2, 23-31 and 19, 17-20; *Opera*, pp. 549, 612; Loeb, pp. 265, 383:

> You know the Sirens' songs and Circe's cups; if, along with his comrades, he had drunk of these in folly and greed, he would have become the shapeless and witless vassal of a harlot mistress—would have lived as an unclean dog or a sow that loves the mire. We are but ciphers [*numerus*], born to consume earth's fruits, Penelope's good-for-naught suitors, young courtiers of Alcinous, unduly busy in keeping their skins sleek, whose pride it was to sleep till midday and to lull care to rest to the sound of the cithern.

> So if by chance I lost my colour, these poets would drink the bloodless cummin. O you mimics, you slavish herd [*pecus*]! How often your pother has stirred my spleen, how often my mirth!

144. See Ephesians 4:30.

145. Johann Peter Hebel (1760-1826), German dialect poet and popular writer. See *J. P. Hebels Sämmtliche Werke*, I-III (Karlsruhe: 1832), III, p. 405.

146. See Longus, *Daphnis and Chloe*, Proem, 2; *Longi pastoralia graece & latine*, ed. Ernst Edward Seiler (Leipzig: 1843; *ASKB* 1128), p. 4; *Daphnis & Chloe*, tr. George Thornley, rev. J. M. Edmonds (Loeb, New York: Putnam, 1916), p. 9: "For there was never any yet that wholly could escape love, and never shall there be any, never so long as beauty shall be, never so long as eyes can see. But help me that God to write the passions of others; and while I write, keep me in my own right wits." See also Virgil, *Eclogues*, X, 69; Loeb, I, p. 75: "'Love conquers all; let us, too, yield to Love!'" See also *JP* V 5587 (*Pap.* IV A 30).

147. With reference to the following clause, see Supplement, p. 564 (*Pap.* V B 190:20).

148. See Matthew 5:26.

149. See, for example, Cicero, *Tuscalanarum disputationum*, V, 62; *Opera*, IV, p. 444; *Cicero Tusculan Disputations*, tr. J. E. King (Loeb, Cambridge: Harvard University Press, 1971), pp. 487-89:

There were perfumes, garlands; incense was burnt; the tables were loaded with the choicest banquet: Damocles thought himself a lucky man. In the midst of all this display Dionysius had a gleaming sword, attached to a horse-hair, let down from the ceiling in such a way that it hung over the neck of this happy man. And so he had no eye either for those beautiful attendants, or the richly-wrought plate, nor did he reach out his hand to the table; presently the garlands slipped from their place of their own accord; at length he besought the tyrant to let him go, as by now he was sure he had no wish to be happy. Dionysius seems (does he not?) to have avowed plainly that there was no happiness for the man who was perpetually menaced by some alarm.

150. The source has not been located.

151. See, for example, *Anxiety*, pp. 129-32, *KW* VIII (*SV* IV 396-99).

152. In Greek mythology, Deianeira, the wife of Hercules, gave him a poisoned shirt that drove him to mount a funeral pyre. The Lydian queen Omphale, who owned Hercules as a slave for a period, had him work in women's clothes.

153. See I Corinthians 4:13, 15:19.

154. With reference to the following sentence, see Supplement, p. 565 (*Pap.* V B 190:24).

155. See Genesis 2:24.

156. With reference to the remainder of the paragraph, see Supplement, p. 565 (*Pap.* V B 190:26).

157. See Supplement, p. 514 (*Pap.* V A 92).

158. See *Letters*, Letter 148, pp. 209-10, *KW* XXV.

"GUILTY?"/"NOT GUILTY?"

1. With reference to the title page, see Supplement, p. 565 (*Pap.* V B 142, 144, 124). See also Historical Introduction, pp. viii-ix, xi.

2. See Supplement, p. 569 (*Pap.* V B 99:1-2); Historical Introduction, pp. viii-ix and note 9.

3. See *JP* V 5106 (*Pap.* I A 69).

4. See Psalm 130:1.

5. See, for example, *Anxiety*, pp. 123-29, *KW* VIII (*SV* 391-96).

6. With reference to the remainder of the sentence, see Supplement, p. 566 (*Pap.* V B 143:3).

7. See *Letters*, Letter 40, p. 85, *KW* XXV.

8. Carl Andreas Reitzel (1789-1853) operated a bookstore and as a publisher printed many of Kierkegaard's books.

9. Carl Joseph Julius Bonfils (1814-?). See Holger Lund, *Borgerdydsskolen: Kjøbenhavn 1787-1887* (Copenhagen: 1887), p. 290.

10. The Seven Years' War, 1756-1763, was fought by France and Austria against England and Prussia and ended with the Peace of Paris (1763), which

gave England decisive advantage over France in North America and in India. See also Supplement, p. 567 (*Pap.* V B 143:6).

11. Literally, "nothing to me," "nothing to you."

12. See *Repetition*, Subtitle note, pp. 357-62, *KW* VI.

13. With reference to the following sentence, see Supplement, p. 567 (*Pap.* V B 147).

14. See Supplement, p. 567 (*Pap.* VI B 8:11).

15. From Johann Georg Hamann's letter to Johann Gotthelf Lindner, May 2, 1764, *Hamann's Schriften*, I-VIII, ed. Friedrich Roth and G. A Wiener (Berlin, Leipzig: 1821-43; *ASKB* 536-44), III, p. 224. See *Postscript*, *KW* XII (*SV* VII 248); *JP* V 5673; VI 6154 (*Pap.* IV A 123; IX A 48).

16. For the draft of an unused preface, see Supplement, pp. 568-69 (*Pap.* V B 191). See also Supplement, p. 569 (*Pap.* V B 99:1-2, 134).

17. An avenue near Kastellet and the harbor customs house in Copenhagen.

18. In Norse mythology, Loki's wife held a bowl under the snake that was dripping poison on him.

19. With reference to the remainder of the paragraph, see Supplement, p. 570 (*Pap.* V B 99:7).

20. For continuation of the sentence, see Supplement, p. 570 (*Pap.* V B 99:8).

21. For continuation of the sentence, see Supplement, p. 570 (*Pap.* V B 99:9).

22. With reference to the following two sentences, see Supplement, p. 570 (*Pap.* V B 99:10).

23. With reference to the remainder of the paragraph and the following three paragraphs, see Supplement, pp. 570-71 (*Pap.* V B 99:11).

24. See Supplement, pp. 501, 512-13, 571 (*Pap.* II A 484-85; V A 33, B 128).

25. See *Either/Or*, I, p. 21, *KW* III (*SV* I 5) and note.

26. For continuation of the paragraph, see Supplement, p. 571 (*Pap.* V B 100:1).

27. With reference to the remainder of the sentence, see Supplement, p. 571 (*Pap.* V B 100:2).

28. With reference to the remainder of the sentence, see Supplement, p. 571 (*Pap.* V B 100:3).

29. See Johann Wolfgang v. Goethe, *Wahlverwandtschaften, Goethe's Werke. Vollständige Ausgabe letzter Hand*, I-LX (Stuttgart, Tübingen: 1828-42; *ASKB* 1641-68 [I-LV]), XVII, p. 212; *Elective Affinities*, tr. Elizabeth Mayer and Louise Bogan (Chicago: Regnery, 1963), p. 157 (British navy ropes with an identifying red strand).

30. See Diogenes Laertius, *Lives of Eminent Philosophers*, VI, 41; *Diogenis Laertii de vitis philosophorum*, I-II (Leipzig: 1833; *ASKB* 1109), I, p. 267; *Diogenes Laërtses filosofiske Historie*, I-II, tr. Børge Riisbrigh (Copenhagen: 1812; *ASKB* 1110-11), I, p. 247; *Diogenes Laertius*, I-II, tr. R. D. Hicks (Loeb, Cambridge: Harvard University Press, 1979-80), II, p. 43: "One day he got a thor-

ough drenching where he stood, and, when the bystanders pitied him, Plato said, if they really pitied him, they should move away, alluding to his vanity."

31. Terence, *Phormio*, I, 88-90; *P. Terentii Afri comoediae sex*, ed. M. Benedict Friedrich Schmieder and Friedrich Schmieder (Halle: 1819; *ASKB* 1291), I, 2, 38-40, p. 415 ("*inde iret*"); *Terentses Skuespil*, I-II, tr. Frederik Høegh Guldberg (Copenhagen: 1805; *ASKB* 1293-94), II, p. 242; *Terence*, I-II, tr. John Sargeaunt (Loeb, Cambridge: Harvard University Press, 1983-86), II, p. 15.

32. With reference to the following four sentences, see Supplement, p. 571 (*Pap.* V B 100:8).

33. See Luke 10:41-42.

34. For continuation of the paragraph, see Supplement, p. 572 (*Pap.* V B 100:12).

35. A street running alongside Rosenborg Castle.

36. An allusion to Antaeus, son of Poseidon, sea god, and Gaea, earth goddess. When Hercules lifted him off the earth, he lost his strength and lost the match.

37. See Johann Karl August Musäus, "*Rolands Knappen*," *Volksmärchen der Deutschen*, I-V (Vienna: 1815; *ASKB* 1434-38), I, pp. 105-06.

38. See Acts 3:6.

39. Horace, *Ars poetica*, 78; *Q. Horatii Flacci opera* (Leipzig: 1828; *ASKB* 1248), p. 669; *Horace Satires, Epistles and Ars Poetica*, tr. H. Rushton Fairclough (Loeb, Cambridge: Harvard University Press, 1978), p. 457.

40. See Anselm Ritter v. Feuerbach, *Kaspar Hauser* (Ansbach: 1832), pp. 109-13; *Either/Or*, II, p. 303, *KW* IV (*SV* II 271).

41. For continuation of the paragraph, see Supplement, p. 572 (*Pap.* V B 100:18).

42. See Psalm 6:5.

43. With reference to the remainder of the paragraph, see Supplement, p. 572 (*Pap.* V B 100:19).

44. See Genesis 25:22 (Rebekah).

45. For continuation of the sentence and with reference to the remainder of the paragraph, see Supplement, p. 572 (*Pap.* V B 100:20).

46. See p. 151 and note 101.

47. The new calendar inaugurated by Pope Gregory in 1582.

48. With reference to the following two sentences, see Supplement, p. 572 (*Pap.* V B 100:23).

49. For continuation of the text, see Supplement, p. 573 (*Pap.* V B 100:24).

50. See Isaiah 26:18.

51. With reference to the following phrase and clause, see Supplement, p. 573 (*Pap.* V B 100:25).

52. A popular Danish expression for imaginatively making much out of little or nothing. See, for example, Hans Christian Andersen, "*Suppe paa en Pølsepind*," *Nye Eventyr og Historier. Første Række. Første Samling* (Copen-

hagen: 1858), pp. 1-20; "How to Cook Soup upon a Sausage Pin," *Hans Christian Andersen The Complete Fairy Tales and Stories*, tr. Erik Christian Haugaard (Garden City, N.Y.: Doubleday, 1974), no. 81, pp. 516-27.

53. With reference to the following paragraph, see Supplement, p. 502 (*Pap.* IV A 34).

54. Stock characters in European pantomime, also in the pantomime theater in Copenhagen's Tivoli.

55. Jeroni(y)mus is a stock elderly character in Ludvig Holberg's *Abracadabra*, *Erasmus Montanus*, and other comedies. Cassandra is a similar character in Italian comedies.

56. The logical (not theological) principle of the excluded middle. See Aristotle, *Metaphysics*, 1011 b-1012 a; *Aristoteles graece*, I-II, ed. Immanuel Bekker (Berlin: 1831; *ASKB* 1074-75), II, pp. 1011-12; *Aristoteles Metaphysik*, I-II, tr. Ernst Wilhelm Hengstenberg (Bonn: 1824; *ASKB* 1084), I, p. 76; *The Complete Works of Aristotle*, I-II, ed. Jonathan Barnes (rev. Oxford tr., Princeton: Princeton University Press, 1984), II, p. 1597:

> Let this, then, suffice to show that the most indisputable of all beliefs is that contradictory statements are not at the same time true, and what consequences follow from the denial of this belief, and why people do deny it. Now since it is impossible that contradictories should be at the same time true of the same thing, obviously contraries also cannot belong at the same time to the same thing. For of the contraries, no less than of the contradictories, one is a privation—and a privation of substance; and privation is the denial of a predicate to a determinate genus. If, then, it is impossible to affirm and deny truly at the same time, it is also impossible that contraries should belong to a subject at the same time, unless both belong to it in particular relations, or one in a particular relation and one without qualification.

> But on the other hand there cannot be an intermediate between contradictories, but of one subject we must either affirm or deny any one predicate. This is clear, in the first place, if we define what the true and the false are. To say of what is that it is not, or of what is not that it is, is false, while to say of what is that it is, and of what is not that it is not, is true; so that he who says of anything that it is, or that it is not, will say either what is true or what is false; but neither what is nor what is not is said to be or not to be.—Again, either the intermediate between the contradictories will be so in the way in which grey is between black and white, or as that which is neither man nor horse is between man and horse. If it were of the latter kind, it could not change, for change is from not-good to good, or from good to not-good; but as a matter of fact it evidently always does, for there is no change except to opposites and to their intermediate. But if it is really intermediate, in this way too there is a difficulty—there would have to be a change to white, which was not from not-white; but as it is, this is never seen.

57. With reference to the following sentence, see Supplement, p. 573 (*Pap.* V B 100:27).

58. Shakespeare, *Cymbeline*, III, 4, 42-46; *Shakspeare's dramatische Werke*, I-XII, tr. August Wilhelm v. Schlegel and Ludwig Tieck (Berlin: 1839-41; *ASKB* 1883-88), XII, p. 196; *The Complete Works of Shakespeare*, ed. George Lyman Kittredge (Boston: Ginn, 1936), p. 1352.

59. *Cymbeline*, III, 4, 56; Schlegel and Tieck, XII, p. 196; Kittredge, p. 1352.

60. See, for example, Xenophon, *Memorabilia*, II, 6, 32-33; *Xenophontis opera graece et latine*, I-IV, ed. Karl August Thieme (Leipzig: 1801-04; *ASKB* 1207-10), IV, pp. 111-12; *Xenophons Sokratiske Merkværdigheder*, tr. Jens Bloch (Copenhagen: 1802), pp. 185-86; *Xenophontis memorabilia*, ed. F. A. Bornemann (Leipzig: 1829; *ASKB* 1211), pp. 137-38; *Xenophon Memorabilia and Oeconomicus*, tr. E. C. Marchant (Loeb, New York: Putnam, 1923), pp. 142-43. See also *Anxiety*, p. 70 fn., *KW* VIII (*SV* IV 339 fn.).

61. With reference to the following six sentences, see Supplement, p. 573 (*Pap.* V B 97:1).

62. For continuation of the sentence, see Supplement, p. 573 (*Pap.* V B 100:29).

63. See Matthew 6:2,5,16.

64. For continuation of the paragraph, see Supplement, pp. 573-74 (*Pap.* V B 100:30).

65. See, for example, Aristotle, *Prior Analytics*, 57 a-b; Bekker, I, p. 57; *Works*, I, pp. 91-92:

> It is clear then that if the conclusion is false, the premisses of the argument must be false, either all or some of them; but when the conclusion is true, it is not necessary that the premisses should be true, either one or all, yet it is possible, though no part of the deduction is true, that the conclusion may none the less be true; but not necessarily. The reason is that when two things are so related to one another, that if the one is, the other necessarily is, then if the latter is not, the former will not be either, but if the latter is, it is not necessary that the former should be. But it is impossible that the same thing should be necessitated by the being and by the not-being of the same thing. I mean, for example, that it is impossible that B should necessarily be great if A is white and that B should necessarily be great if A is not white. For whenever if this, A, is white it is necessary that that, B, should be great, and if B is great that C should not be white, then it is necessary if A is white that C should not be white. And whenever it is necessary, if one of two things is, that the other should be, it is necessary, if the latter is not, that the former should not be. If then B is not great A cannot be white. But if, if A is not white, it is necessary that B should be great, it necessarily results that if B is not great, B itself is great. But this is impossible. For if B is not great, A will necessarily not be white. If then if this is not white B must be great, it results that if B is not great, it is great, just as if it were proved through three terms.

66. The view of the pre-Socratic philosophers Democritus and Leukippus. See, for example, Aristophanes (who attributes the view to Socrates), *The Clouds*, I, 6, 380, V, 1, 1471; *Des Aristophanes Werke*, I-III, tr. Johann Gustav Droysen (Berlin: 1835-38; *ASKB* 1052-54), III, pp. 49, 122; *Aristophanes*, I-III, tr. Benjamin Bickley Rogers (Loeb, Cambridge: Harvard University Press, 1979-82), I, pp. 300-01, 398-99.

67. With reference to the following sentence, see Supplement, p. 574 (*Pap*. IV B 142).

68. See Galatians 1:16.

69. With reference to the following sentence, see Supplement, p. 574 (*Pap*. V B 100:31).

70. See pp. 94-95 and note 15.

71. See Exodus 16:3.

72. For continuation of the sentence, see Supplement, p. 574 (*Pap*. V B 100:34).

73. See Isaiah 40:6-8; Psalm 90:5-6.

74. See Philippians 4:7.

75. Text added to the evening signal (taps) sounded in German military camps. See Supplement, p. 575 (*Pap*. V B 97:6).

76. With reference to the remainder of the paragraph and the following paragraph, see Supplement, p. 574 (*Pap*. V B 100:35).

77. With reference to the following sentence, see Supplement, pp. 574-75 (*Pap*. V B 97:6).

78. See Genesis 1:26.

79. See G. C. Lichtenberg, "*Fragmente*," *Georg Christoph Lichtenberg's vermischte Schriften*, I-IX (Göttingen: 1800-06; *ASKB* 1764-72), I, p. 162.

80. Most likely Johan Arndt, *Sämtliche geistreiche Bücher vom wahren Christenthum* (Tübingen: n.d.; *ASKB* 276); *Fire Bøger om den sande Christendom* (Christiania: 1829; *ASKB* 277); *True Christianity*, rev. and ed. Charles F. Schaeffer (Philadelphia: General Council Publication House, 1917).

81. With reference to the remainder of the paragraph and the following paragraph, see Supplement, p. 575 (*Pap*. V B 100:36).

82. See John 16:4,12.

83. See *Fear and Trembling*, pp. 54-67, *KW* VI (*SV* III 104-16).

84. Hamlet, for example.

85. With reference to the remainder of the sentence, see Supplement, p. 575 (*Pap*. V B 100:37).

86. See Supplement, p. 507 (*Pap*. IV A 110).

87. See Matthew 26:6; Mark 14:3; Luke 17:12; Supplement, p. 507 (*Pap*. IV A 110-11).

88. See Genesis 2:18.

89. With reference to the following six paragraphs, see Supplement, p. 507 (*Pap*. IV A 111).

90. With reference to the remainder of the paragraph and the following three paragraphs, see Supplement, p. 575 (*Pap*. V B 126).

91. See Luke 16:22.

92. See Matthew 8:11.

93. See Titus 2:14.

94. For continuation of the paragraph, see Supplement, p. 576 (*Pap.* V B 129:1).

95. See Luke 17:12.

96. With reference to the remainder of the sentence, see Supplement, p. 576 (*Pap.* V B 97:4).

97. With reference to the remainder of the sentence, see Supplement, p. 576 (*Pap.* V B 101:2).

98. With reference to the remainder of the sentence, see Supplement, p. 576 (*Pap.* V B 97:4).

99. The multiplication table from 2 to 10.

100. Danish: *Sletdaler*, an old coin worth four marks; the *Rigsdaler* was worth six marks. See Ludvig Holberg, *Den Stundesløse*, I, 9; *Den Danske Skue-Plads*, I-VII (Copenhagen: 1788; *ASKB* 1566-67), V, no pagination; *The Fussy Man, Four Plays by Holberg*, tr. Henry Alexander (Princeton: Princeton University Press, for the American-Scandinavian Foundation, New York, 1946), p. 21. For continuation of the sentence, see Supplement, p. 576 (*Pap.* V B 101:4).

101. See Matthew 10:29.

102. See Psalm 90:4,10; II Peter 3:8.

103. See *Point of View*, *KW* XXII (*SV* XIII 556).

104. See Luke 18:10.

105. See Matthew 23:23.

106. Cf. *Anxiety*, pp. 102, 107-10, *KW* VIII (*SV* IV 371-72, 376-78).

107. Peter Wessel (1690-1720), called Tordenskjold (Thunder Shield), celebrated Norwegian-Danish naval hero. See *JP* IV 4106 (*Pap.* V A 77). His soldiers have become proverbial; see, for example, *Fragments*, p. 7, *KW* VII (*SV* IV 177).

108. With reference to the following paragraph, see Supplement, p. 576 (*Pap.* V B 97:2).

109. See Supplement, p. 577 (*Pap.* V B 101:10).

110. With reference to the following three sentences, see Supplement, p. 577 (*Pap.* V B 97:9).

111. See Shakespeare, *Macbeth*, V, 3, 11-17; *W. Shakspeare's dramatische Werke*, I-VIII, tr. Ernst Ortlepp (Stuttgart: 1838-40; *ASKB* 1874-81), I, p. 100; Schlegel and Tieck, XII, p. 350; Kittredge, p. 1141:

> The devil damn thee black, thou cream-fac'd loon!
> Where got'st thou that goose look?
> . . . What soldiers, whey-face?

112. With reference to the following two paragraphs, see Supplement, p. 577 (*Pap.* V B 97:17).

113. With reference to the remainder of the sentence, see Supplement, p. 577 (*Pap*. V B 101:12).

114. With reference to the following paragraph, see Supplement, p. 577 (*Pap*. V B 101:13).

115. With reference to the following six sentences, see Supplement, p. 578 (*Pap*. V B 97:5).

116. With reference to the following sentence, see Supplement, p. 578 (*Pap*. V B 101:15, 97:10-11).

117. A square opposite Kultorvet near the end of Købmagergade in the center of Copenhagen.

118. With reference to the following two sentences, see Supplement, p. 577 (*Pap*. V B 97:9).

119. With reference to the following two paragraphs, see Supplement, p. 578 (*Pap*. V B 97:8).

120. A coastal city about forty miles west of Copenhagen.

121. With reference to the following sentence, see Supplement, p. 578 (*Pap*. V B 101:16).

122. Danish: *Hexebrev*, literally "witch's letter," a magiclike set of picture segments of people and animals that recombine when unfolded and turned. See *Anxiety*, p. 159, *KW* VIII (*SV* IV 425); *Either/Or*, II, p. 258, *KW* IV (*SV* II 232).

123. See I Corinthians 4:10.

124. Cf. Matthew 6:24.

125. See II Corinthians 3:6.

126. With reference to the following entry, see Supplement, p. 579 (*Pap*. V B 97:3).

127. A character in Gottlieb Stephanie, *Apothekeren og Doktoren*, tr. Lars Knudsen (Copenhagen: 1789), p. 1 (ed. tr.): "Gribskov, a disabled captain, with a wooden leg and a patch on one eye."

128. See Supplement, p. 579 (*Pap*. V B 101:17).

129. With reference to the following entry, see Supplement, p. 579 (*Pap*. V B 97:19,22).

130. See Supplement, p. 580 (*Pap*. V B 101:18).

131. Cf. I Kings 3:15. See Supplement, pp. 507, 566, 580 (*Pap*. IV A 114; V B 124, 125).

132. See I Kings 3:16-28.

133. See Genesis 9:20-23.

134. With reference to the remainder of the sentence, see Supplement, p. 580 (*Pap*. V B 130:2).

135. See I Kings 1:8-46.

136. For continuation of the sentence, see Supplement, p. 580 (*Pap*. V B 130:4).

137. For continuation of the sentence, see Supplement, p. 580 (*Pap*. V B 130:5).

138. Cf. II Chronicles 9:1-11.

139. With reference to the following three paragraphs, see Supplement, pp. 580-81 (*Pap.* V B 97:15).

140. The Danish *du*, the familiar second-person singular pronoun, until recently was used only in addressing family members and close friends. To drink *dus* was the formal ceremony betokening a close relationship that allowed the address of *du*.

141. See Hebrews 4:12.

142. Simon Stylites (d. 459?), Syrian hermit who lived thirty-five years on a small platform on the top of a high pillar—hence, Stylites. His feast day is January 5. See *From the Papers of One Still Living, Early Polemical Writings, KW* I (*SV* XIII 54); *JP* V 5659 (*Pap.* IV B 78).

143. See Matthew 25:1.

144. With reference to the following three paragraphs, see Supplement, p. 581 (*Pap.* V B 97:29).

145. Regine Olsen (1822-1904), Kierkegaard's fiancée at one time, became a governess in another sense when her husband, Johan Frederik Schlegel (1817-1896), became governor of the Virgin Islands in 1854. See Kierkegaard's conversation with Emil Boesen as told by Boesen and reported in *Af Søren Kierkegaards Efterladte Papirer*, I-IX, ed. Hans Peter Barfod and Hermann Gottsched (Copenhagen: 1869-81), VIII (1854-55), Appendix, p. 593 (ed. tr.): " 'I was afraid she would become a governess; that she did not become, and yet she is now in the West Indies.' "

146. See Shakespeare, *Richard III*, V, 4, 13; *William Shakspeare's Tragiske Værker*, I-IX, tr. Peter Foersom and Peter Frederik Wulff (Copenhagen: 1807-25; *ASKB* 1889-96), VI, p. 378; Ortlepp, VII, p. 428; Schlegel and Tieck, III, p. 372; Kittredge, p. 835: "A horse! a horse! my kingdom for a horse!"

147. With reference to the following five paragraphs, see Supplement, p. 581 (*Pap.* V B 97:16).

148. See p. 125 and note 58.

149. For continuation of the text, see Supplement, pp. 581-82 (*Pap.* V B 102:2).

150. With reference to the remainder of the sentence, see Supplement, p. 582 (*Pap.* V B 102:3).

151. With reference to the following three sentences, see Supplement, p. 582 (*Pap.* V B 102:4).

152. An allusion to Nicolai Frederik Severin Grundtvig. See *Kort Begreb af Verdens Krønike* (Copenhagen: 1814), pp. xxiv, xxx-xxxi, 3-5; *Udsigt over Verdens-Krøniken* (Copenhagen: 1817; *ASKB* 1970), pp. 116, 601, 662-65. See Supplement, pp. 581, 582 (*Pap.* V B 97:16, 102:4).

153. See Supplement, pp. 514-15 (*Pap.* V A 94).

154. A trick snuffbox from which a clerical figure pops when the sides are pressed.

155. With reference to the following two sentences, see Supplement, p. 582 (*Pap.* V B 102:5).

156. Radbodus (d. 719), king of the Frisians. See Ludvig Holberg, *Almindelig Kirke-Historie*, I-II (Copenhagen: 1740), I, pp. 295-96.

157. See Hebrews 3:7,13,15, 4:7.

158. Prison labor in Denmark included the rasp-filing of dyewood, work that was arduous and dangerous to health.

159. With reference to the following nine sentences, see Supplement, pp. 582-83 (*Pap.* V B 102:6).

160. See I Samuel 15:22.

161. See Hebrews 12:29.

162. Attributed to Archimedes: Give me a place to stand and I will move the world. See Plutarch, "Marcellus," 14, *Lives; Plutark's Levnetsbeskrivelser,* I-IV, tr. Stephan Tetens (Copenhagen: 1800-11; *ASKB* 1197-1200), III, p. 272; *Plutarch's Lives,* I-XI, tr. Bernadotte Perrin (Loeb, Cambridge: Harvard University Press, 1968-84), V, p. 473: ". . . Archimedes, who was a kinsman and friend of King Hiero, wrote to him that with any given force it was possible to move any given weight; and emboldened, as we are told, by the strength of his demonstration, he declared that, if there were another world, and he could go to it, he could move this." See also *Either/Or,* I, p. 295, *KW* III (*SV* I 266); *Repetition,* p. 186, *KW* VI (*SV* III 221); *JP* V 5099 (*Pap.* I A 68).

163. With reference to the following sentence, see Supplement, p. 583 (*Pap.* V B 102:7).

164. With reference to the remainder of the sentence, see Supplement, p. 583 (*Pap.* V B 102:8).

165. A Copenhagen social club organized in 1783, active in sponsoring balls, performances, and the like.

166. With reference to the following five paragraphs, see Supplement, pp. 505, 583-84 (*Pap.* IV B 140; V B 97:30, 102:9).

167. See Genesis 3:16.

168. When Ixion, king of Thessaly, who had been given refuge on Olympus by Zeus (Roman Jupiter), sought to embrace Hera (Roman Juno), Zeus substituted a cloud in her shape. A monster, Centaur, was born from this union. Ixion was chained to a fiery wheel in Hades as punishment for his act. See Paul Friedrich A. Nitsch, "Ixion," *neues mythologisches Wörterbuch,* I-II, rev. Friedrich Gotthilf Klopfer (Leipzig, Sorau: 1821; *ASKB* 1944-45), II, pp. 122-23; *JP* V 5100 (*Pap.* I A 75).

169. With reference to the remainder of the paragraph and the following sentence, see Supplement, p. 584 (*Pap.* V B 102:10).

170. For continuation of the sentence, see Supplement, p. 584 (*Pap.* V B 102:11).

171. See Shakespeare, *King Lear,* V, 3, 11-18; Foersom and Wulff, II, p. 195; Ortlepp, III, p. 145; Schlegel and Tieck, XI, p. 117; Kittredge, p. 1235 (Lear speaking to Cordelia):

> So we'll live,
> And pray, and sing, and tell old tales, and laugh
> At gilded butterflies, and hear poor rogues
> Talk of court news; and we'll talk with them
> too—

> Who loses and who wins; who's in, who's out—
> And take upon 's the mystery of things,
> As if we were God's spies; and we'll wear out,
> In a wall'd prison, packs and sects of great ones
> That ebb and flow by th' moon.

172. See Supplement, p. 584 (*Pap*. V B 97:31).

173. With reference to the remainder of the sentence, see Supplement, p. 584 (*Pap*. V B 97:32).

174. See Ossian, "*Carric-thura*," *Ossians Digte*, I-II, tr. Steen Steensen Blicher (Copenhagen: 1807-09; *ASKB* 1873), I, p. 38 (ed. tr.): "Sweet is the joy of melancholy"; "*Crothar*," ibid., II, p. 219: "There is joy in melancholy when peace dwells in the sorrower's breast." "Caric-thura," *The Poems of Ossian*, tr. James Macpherson, I-II (New York: Dixon and Sickels, 1827), I, p. 40: "Pleasant is the joy of grief"; "Croma," ibid., p. 86: "There is joy in grief, when peace dwells in the breast of the sad."

175. With reference to the remainder of the paragraph, see Supplement, p. 585 (*Pap*. V B 102:12).

176. With reference to the following two paragraphs, see Supplement, p. 585 (*Pap*. V B 97:20).

177. With reference to the following sentence, see Supplement, p. 585 (*Pap*. V B 102:13).

178. See, for example, Shakespeare, *Much Ado about Nothing*, V, 4, 72-83; Ortlepp, III, pp. 285-86; Schlegel and Tieck, VII, pp. 195-96; Kittredge, pp. 190-91 (Benedick and Beatrice speaking):

> *Bene*. Soft and fair, friar. Which is Beatrice?
> *Beat*. [*unmasks*] I answer to that name. What is your will?
> *Bene*. Do not you love me?
> *Beat*. Why, no; no more than reason.
> *Bene*. Why, then your uncle, and the Prince, and Claudio
>   Have been deceived, for they swore you did.
> *Beat*. Do not you love me?
> *Bene*. Troth no; no more than reason.
> *Beat*. Why, then my cousin, Margaret, and Ursula
>   Are much deceiv'd; for they did swear you did.
> *Bene*. They swore that you were almost sick for me.
> *Beat*. They swore that you were well-nigh dead for me.
> *Bene*. 'Tis no such matter. Then you do not love me?
> *Beat*. No, truly, but in friendly recompense.

179. A Latin gloss on Sophocles, *Antigone*, 620-23; *The Complete Greek Tragedies*, I-IV, ed. David Grene and Richmond Lattimore (Chicago: University of Chicago Press, 1960), II, p. 180 (Chorus speaking):

> Word of wisdom it was when someone said,
> "The bad becomes the good
> to him a god would doom."

180. With reference to the following sentence, see Supplement, p. 585 (*Pap.* V B 102:14).

181. With reference to the following nine paragraphs, see Supplement, pp. 585-86 (*Pap.* V B 97:33).

182. With reference to the following paragraph, see Supplement, p. 586 (*Pap.* V B 102:15).

183. The Danish rix-dollar [*Rigsdaler*] was divided into six marks of sixteen shillings each. With the rix-dollar worth about $5.00 (1973 money), four shillings would be about four nickels. See *Letters*, pp. 450, 454, *KW* XXV.

184. See "*Ridder Stig og Findal eller Runernes Magt*," V, 62, *Udvalgte danske Viser fra Middelalderen*, I-V, ed. Werner Hans Abrahamson, Rasmus Nyerup, and Knud Lyne Rahbek (Copenhagen: 1812-14; *ASKB* 1477-81), I, p. 301 (ed. tr.): "She sleeps every night by the side of Knight Stig Hvide." See also *Fear and Trembling*, p. 45, *KW* VI (*SV* III 95).

185. The Latin is a revision of a line used on the title page of a published Latin dissertation. With reference to the following sentence, see Supplement, p. 586 (*Pap.* V B 102:17).

186. With reference to the remainder of the paragraph, see Supplement, p. 586 (*Pap.* V B 102:18).

187. Possibly Michael Nielsen (1776-1846), principal of Borgerdyds School, which Kierkegaard attended.

188. With reference to the following two sentences, see Supplement, p. 587 (*Pap.* V B 102:19).

189. With reference to the following section, see Supplement, pp. 502-05, 511, 590, 586-87 (*Pap.* IV A 65, 68, 105, 147; V B 103:1, 131). See also *Anxiety*, pp. 155-62, *KW* VIII (*SV* IV 421-28).

190. A bridge connecting the island of Sjælland (Copenhagen) with the island of Amager (Christianshavn).

191. For continuation of the paragraph, see Supplement, p. 588 (*Pap.* V B 135:2).

192. Cf. Horace, *Odes*, I, 32, 1; *Opera*, p. 77; *Horace The Odes and Epodes*, tr. C. E. Bennett (Loeb, Cambridge: Harvard University Press, 1978), p. 87: "I am asked for a song" ("*Poscimur*"). With reference to the sentence, see Supplement, p. 588 (*Pap.* V B 135:4).

193. With reference to the remainder of the paragraph, see Supplement, p. 589 (*Pap.* V B 135:6).

194. June 25, 1817.

195. A street running alongside the canal in Christianshavn.

196. With reference to the remainder of the paragraph, see Supplement, p. 589 (*Pap.* V A 135:12).

197. With reference to the following paragraph, see Supplement, p. 509 (*Pap.* IV A 132), and to the following five paragraphs, see Supplement, p. 511 (*Pap.* IV A 147).

198. A character in "*Die Königsbraut*." See Ernst Theodor Amadeus Hoff-

mann, *Die Serapions-Brüder*, *E.T.A. Hoffmann's ausgewählte Schriften*, I-X (Berlin: 1827-28; *ASKB* 1712-16), IV, p. 267.

199. According to an old custom, someone dressed as a goat who jested and made sport with children at Christmas parties.

200. See Ecclesiastes 11:9.

201. With reference to the following two paragraphs, see Supplement, p. 502 (*Pap.* IV A 65).

202. With reference to the following paragraph, see Supplement, p. 503 (*Pap.* IV A 68).

203. According to an old definition of adulthood as beginning at the age of forty. See Supplement, p. 588 (*Pap.* V B 131).

204. See Ecclesiastes 1:14, 4:16.

205. With reference to the following sentence, see Supplement, p. 590, (*Pap.* V B 124).

206. See Supplement, p. 504 (*Pap.* IV A 105).

207. With reference to the following two sentences, see Supplement, p. 589 (*Pap.* V B 135:22).

208. See Revelation 14:13.

209. See Supplement, p. 590 (*Pap.* V B 103:1).

210. The strait separating Sjælland from southern Sweden.

211. Queen Scheherazade, narrator of the stories in *The Arabian Nights' Entertainments* (*Thousand and One Nights*).

212. With reference to the following paragraph, see Supplement, p. 590 (*Pap.* V B 97:36).

213. See Luke 3:16; John 1:27.

214. See Shakespeare, *Henry IV*, *I*, V, 4, 75-77; Foersom and Wulff, III, p. 171; Ortlepp, VI, p. 241; Schlegel and Tieck, I, p. 310; Kittredge, p. 578:

> Enter *Falstaff*.
> *Fal*. Well said, Hal! to it, Hal! Nay, you
> shall find no boy's play here, I can tell you.
> Enter *Douglas*. He fighteth with *Falstaff*, who
> falls down as if he were dead. [*Exit Douglas*.]

215. A version of the refrain in a drinking song in Holberg, *Jeppe paa Bjerget*, I, 6, *Danske Skue-Plads*, I, no pagination; *Jeppe of the Hill, Comedies by Holberg*, tr. Oscar James Campbell, Jr., and Frederic Schenck (New York: American-Scandinavian Foundation, 1914), p. 10.

216. See *Two Ages*, *KW* XIV (*SV* VIII 3-105).

217. The author of *First Love* and other dramas. See *Either/Or*, I, pp. 231-79, *KW* III (*SV* I 205-51).

218. See, for example, Hegel, *Encyclopädie der philosophischen Wissenschaften, Erster Theil. Die Logik*, para. 63, *Georg Wilhelm Friedrich Hegel's Werke. Vollständige Ausgabe*, I-XVIII, ed. Philipp Marheineke et al. (Berlin: 1832-45; *ASKB* 549-65), VI, pp. 128-31; *Jubiläumsausgabe* [*J.A.*], I-XXVI, ed. Hermann Glockner (Stuttgart: Frommann, 1927-40) (*System der Philosophie*),

VIII, pp. 166-69; *Hegel's Logic* (tr. of *L.*, 3 ed., 1830; Kierkegaard's ed., 1840, had the same text, plus *Zusätze*), tr. William Wallace (Oxford: Oxford University Press, 1975), pp. 97-99: "But, seeing that derivative knowledge is restricted to the compass of finite facts, Reason is knowledge underivative, or Faith. . . . With what is here called faith or immediate knowledge must also be identified inspiration, the heart's revelations, the truths implanted in man by nature, and also in particular, healthy reason or Common Sense, as it is called. All these forms agree in adopting as their leading principle the immediacy, or self-evident way, in which a fact or body of truths is presented in consciousness." See also Hegel, *Philosophische Propädeutik*, para. 72, *Werke*, XVIII, p. 75; *J.A.*, III, p. 97. See *Fear and Trembling*, pp. 55, 69, 82, *KW* VI (*SV* III 105, 118, 130); *JP* I 49; II 1096 (*Pap.* V A 28; I A 273, which includes a reference to Hegel).

219. See p. 55 and note 152.

220. See James 2:10.

221. Characters, a bookbinder and a printer, in J. L. Heiberg, *Recensenten og Dyret*, *Skuespil*, I-VII (Copenhagen: 1833-41; *ASKB* 1553-59), III, pp. 185-288.

222. See Holberg, *Erasmus Montanus*, II, 1, *Danske Skue-Plads*, V, no pagination; Campbell and Schenck, p. 131.

223. See Jens Baggesen, *"Min Gienganger-Spøg, eller den søde Kniv," Jens Baggesens danske Værker*, I-XII (Copenhagen: 1827-32; *ASKB* 1509-20), VI, p. 144.

224. See Supplement, p. 590 (*Pap.* V B 103:2).

225. With reference to the remainder of the paragraph and the following paragraph, see Supplement, pp. 590-91 (*Pap.* V B 103:5).

226. See Supplement, p. 591 (*Pap.* VI B 8:12).

227. Presumably a reference to the Order of the Iron Cross, created in Prussia by Friedrich III, March 10, 1813, during the War of Liberation against France, as a token of courage and determination in the field as well as at home. See Johann Kasper Friedrich Manso, *Geschichte des Preussischen Staates vom Frieden zu Hubertusburg bis zum zweyten Pariser Frieden zu Hubertusburg bis zu der Zweyten Pariser Abkunft*, I-III (Frankfurt am Main: 1819-20), III, p. 129.

228. See Matthew 8:22.

229. See Terence, *Phormio*, I, 82; Schmieder (I, 2, 32), p. 414; Guldberg, II, p. 242; Loeb, II, p. 15.

230. With reference to the following paragraph, see Supplement, p. 591 (*Pap.* V B 97:37).

231. See Herodotus, "Darius," *History*, V, 105; *Die Geschichten des Herodotos*, I-II, tr. Friedrich Lange (Berlin: 1811; *ASKB* 1117), II, p. 59; *Herodotus*, I-IV, tr. A. D. Godley (Loeb, Cambridge: Harvard University Press, 1981-82), III, p. 127:

> Onesilus, then, besieged Amathus. But when it was told to Darius that Sardis had been taken and burnt by the Athenians and Ionians, and that Aristagoras the Milesian had been leader of the conspiracy for the weaving

of this plan, at his first hearing of it (it is said) he took no account of the Ionians,—being well assured that they of all men would not go scatheless for their rebellion,—but asked who were the Athenians; and being told, he called for his bow, which he took, and laid an arrow on it and shot it into the sky, praying as he sent it aloft, "O Zeus, grant me vengeance on the Athenians," and therewithal he charged one of his servants to say to him thrice whenever dinner was set before him, "Master, remember the Athenians."

232. For continuation of the sentence, see Supplement, p. 591 (*Pap*. V B 103:7).

233. With reference to the remainder of the sentence, see Supplement, pp. 591-92 (*Pap*. V B 103:8).

234. See note 183 above.

235. With reference to the remainder of the paragraph, see Supplement, p. 592 (*Pap*. V B 103:9).

236. With reference to the following two sentences, see Supplement, p. 592 (*Pap*. V B 103:10).

237. With reference to the following two sentences, see Supplement, p. 592 (*Pap*. V B 103:11).

238. With reference to the following paragraph, see Supplement, p. 593 (*Pap*. V B 97:40).

239. With reference to the following sentence, see Supplement, p. 593 (*Pap*. V B 103:12).

240. With reference to the remainder of the paragraph, see Supplement, p. 593 (*Pap*. V B 103:13).

241. With reference to the following phrase, see Supplement, p. 594 (*Pap*. V B 103:14).

242. With reference to the following paragraph, see Supplement, p. 594 (*Pap*. V B 97:12,13).

243. For continuation of the paragraph, see Supplement, p. 594 (*Pap*. V B 103:16).

244. See Supplement, pp. 503-04 (*Pap*. IV A 97).

245. With reference to the following five sentences, see Supplement, p. 594 (*Pap*. V B 103:17).

246. See Diogenes Laertius, VIII, 17; *Vitis*, II, pp. 97-98; Riisbrigh, I, pp. 371-72; Loeb, II, pp. 335-37:

The following were his watchwords or precepts: don't stir the fire with a knife, don't step over the beam of a balance, don't sit down on your bushel, don't eat your heart, don't help a man off with a load but help him on, always roll your bed-clothes up, don't put God's image on the circle of a ring, don't leave the pan's imprint on the ashes, don't wipe up a mess with a torch, don't commit a nuisance towards the sun, don't walk the highway, don't shake hands so eagerly, don't have swallows under your own roof, don't keep birds with hooked claws, don't make water on nor stand upon your nail- and hair-trimmings, turn the sharp blade away, when you go abroad don't turn round at the frontier.

This is what they meant. Don't stir the fire with a knife: don't stir the passions or the swelling pride of the great. Don't step over the beam of a balance: don't overstep the bounds of equity and justice. Don't sit down on your bushel: have the same care of to-day and the future, a bushel being the day's ration. By not eating your heart he meant not wasting your life in troubles and pains. By saying do not turn round when you go abroad, he meant to advise those who are departing this life not to set their hearts' desire on living nor to be too much attracted by the pleasures of this life. The explanations of the rest are similar, and would take too long to set out.

247. For continuation of the paragraph, see Supplement, p. 595 (*Pap.* V B 103:18).

248. Cf., for example, *Fear and Trembling*, p. 36, *KW* VI (*SV* III 87).

249. See Supplement, pp. 654-55 (*Pap.* VII¹ B 83). See also, for example, *Postscript, KW* XII (*SV* VII 53, 56-61, 68, 210, 233, 548); *JP* I 632, 649, 653 (*Pap.* VI B 38; VIII² B 81, 85).

250. The strait separating Sjælland and southern Sweden.

251. See Genesis 45:4-5, 50:20.

252. With reference to the remainder of the sentence, see Supplement, p. 595 (*Pap.* V B 103:19).

253. See, for example, *JP* III 2679 (*Pap.* XI² A 91).

254. For continuation of the paragraph, see Supplement, p. 595 (*Pap.* V B 103:20).

255. See Mark 12:42; Luke 21:1-4.

256. See Genesis 8:8-12.

257. With reference to the following sentence, see Supplement, p. 595 (*Pap.* V B 103:22).

258. With reference to the following sentence, see Supplement, p. 596 (*Pap.* V B 103:23).

259. With reference to the remainder of the sentence, see Supplement, p. 596 (*Pap.* V B 103:25).

260. With reference to the remainder of the sentence and the following paragraph, see Supplement, p. 596 (*Pap.* V B 103:26).

261. See François de Salignac de la Mothe-Fénelon, *Herrn von Fenelons kurze Lebens-Beschreibungen und Lehr-Sätze der alten Welt-Weisen* (Frankfurt am Main, Leipzig: 1748; *ASKB* 486 [Leipzig: 1741]), pp. 80-87; Supplement, pp. 596-97, 566 (*Pap.* V A 45, B 124).

262. With reference to the following paragraph, see Supplement, p. 597 (*Pap.* V B 97:14).

263. With reference to the following paragraph, see Supplement, p. 597 (*Pap.* V B 103:27).

264. For continuation of the paragraph, see Supplement, p. 597 (*Pap.* V B 103:28).

265. See Job 38:1-2.

266. See, for example, Plato, *Phaedo*, 90 c-d; *Platonis quae exstant opera*, I-XI, ed. Friedrich Ast (Leipzig: 1819-32; *ASKB* 1144-54), I, pp. 552-55; *Udvalgte Dialoger af Platon*, I-VIII, tr. Carl Johan Heise (Copenhagen: 1830-59; *ASKB* 1164-67, 1169 [I-VII]), I, pp. 68-69; *The Collected Dialogues of Plato*, ed. Edith Hamilton and Huntington Cairns (Princeton: Princeton University Press, 1963), p. 72 (Socrates speaking):

Well, then, Phaedo, he said, supposing that there is an argument which is true and valid and capable of being discovered, if anyone nevertheless, through his experience of these arguments which seem to the same people to be sometimes true and sometimes false, attached no responsibility to himself and his lack of technical ability, but was finally content, in exasperation, to shift the blame from himself to the arguments, and spend the rest of his life loathing and decrying them, and so missed the chance of knowing the truth about reality—would it not be a deplorable thing?

267. With reference to the following two paragraphs, see Supplement, p. 597 (*Pap.* V B 97:44, 98:3).

268. See, for example, Thomasine Gyllembourg(-Ehrensvärd), *En Hverdagshistorie*, a serial in J. L. Heiberg's *Kjøbenhavns flyvende Post*, II, 69-76, August 29-September 22, 1828; *Noveller gamle og nye, af Forfatteren til "En Hverdags-Historie,"* I-III, ed. Johan Ludvig Heiberg (Copenhagen: 1833), I, pp. 1-67.

269. With reference to the following sentence, see Supplement, p. 598 (*Pap.* V B 103:29).

270. See Augustin-Eugène Scribe, *Oscar*, I, 1; *Det Kongelige Theaters Repertoire*, 153 (1844), p. 1.

271. See Galatians 1:16.

272. With reference to the following paragraph, see Supplement, p. 598 (*Pap.* V B 97:45).

273. See Plutarch, "Pericles," 36-37, *Lives*; Tetens, II, pp. 236-39; *Plutarch's Werke*, I-VI, tr. J. G. Klaiber (Stuttgart: 1827-30; *ASKB* 1190-91), pp. 470-72; Loeb, III, pp. 103-09.

274. See, for example, *Either/Or*, I, p. 22, *KW* III (*SV* I 6).

275. Charlotte Stieglitz, who committed suicide December 29, 1834, in the hope that the deep sorrow of her husband, the German poet Heinrich Stieglitz, would give impetus to his poetic endeavors. See *Charlotte Stieglitz, ein Denkmal*, ed. Theodor Mundt (Berlin: 1835).

276. See Shakespeare, *Romeo and Juliet*, IV, 3, 59; Foersom and Wulff, II, p. 377; Ortlepp, VIII, p. 509; Schlegel and Tieck, IV, p. 208; Kittredge, p. 1037.

277. See J. H. Wessel, *Kierlighed uden Strømper*, I, 2, V, 4, *Johan Herman Wessels samtlige Skrivter*, I-II (Copenhagen: 1787), I, pp. 6-7, 79.

278. Danish: *Indenads-Lectien*. Cf. *Indenadslæsning*, in the church service "the reading" of the text before the sermon. See, for example, *Works of Love*, *KW* XVI (*SV* IX 128). With reference to the following section, see Supplement, pp. 598-99 (*Pap.* V B 133, 136:1).

279. See Fénelon, pp. 80-87. See also Supplement, pp. 596-97, 598-99 *Pap.* V A 45, B 133, 136:1).

280. See Diogenes Laertius, I, 98-99; *Vitis*, I, p. 47; Riisbrigh, I, pp. 44-45; Loeb, I, p. 103: "Sotion and Heraclides and Pamphila in the fifth book of her *Commentaries* distinguish two Perianders, one a tyrant, the other a sage who was born in Ambracia. Neanthes of Cyzicus also says this, and adds that they were near relations. And Aristotle maintains that the Corinthian Periander was the sage; while Plato denies this."

281. A golden statue erected after he won the chariot race at the Olympics. See Diogenes Laertius, I, 96; *Vitis*, I, p. 46; Riisbrigh, I, p. 43; Loeb, I, p. 99.

282. See Diogenes Laertius, I, 99; *Vitis*, I, p. 47; Riisbrigh, I, p. 45; Loeb, I, p. 103: "Practice makes perfect."

283. See Diogenes Laertius, I, 94-96; *Vitis*, I, pp. 45-46; Riisbrigh, I, pp. 42-43; Loeb, I, pp. 97-99:

> By her [Lysida] he had two sons, Cypselus and Lycophron, the younger a man of intelligence, the elder weak in mind. However, after some time, in a fit of anger, he killed his wife by throwing a footstool at her, or by a kick, when she was pregnant, having been egged on by the slanderous tales of concubines, whom he afterwards burnt alive.
>
> When the son whose name was Lycophron grieved for his mother, he banished him to Corcyra. And when well advanced in years he sent for his son to be his successor in the tyranny; but the Corcyraeans put him to death before he could set sail. Enraged at this, he dispatched the sons of the Corcyraeans to Alyattes that he might make eunuchs of them; but, when the ship touched at Samos, they took sanctuary in the temple of Hera, and were saved by the Samians. . . .
>
> Aristippus in the first book of his work *On the Luxury of the Ancients* accuses him of incest with his own mother Crateia, and adds that, when the fact came to light, he vented his annoyance in indiscriminate severity.

284. Cf. Diogenes Laertius, I, 98; *Vitis*, I, p. 47; Riisbrigh, I, p. 44; Loeb, I, p. 101: "Betray no secret."

285. Cf. Johannes Stobaeus, *Florilegium*, III, 79; *Ioannis Stobaei sententiae* (Lugduni: 1555; *ASKB* 244 [Basel: 1549]), p. 117 (ed. tr.): "*Infortunium tuum celato, ne gaudio inimicos afficias* [Conceal your misfortunes, lest you please your enemies]."

286. See Diogenes Laertius, I, 98; *Vitis*, I, p. 47; Riisbrigh, I, p. 44; Loeb, I, pp. 100-01.

287. Cf. Diogenes Laertius, I, 97; *Vitis*, I, p. 47; Riisbrigh, I, p. 44; Loeb, I, p. 101: "He said that those tyrants who intend to be safe should make loyalty their bodyguard, not arms."

288. See note 287 above.

> Grieve not because thou hast not gained thine end,
> But take with gladness all the gods may send;
> Be warned by Periander's fate, who died
> Of grief that one desire should be denied.

289. See Supplement, p. 502 (*Pap.* IV A 26).

290. See Diogenes Laertius, I, 100; *Vitis*, I, p. 48; Riisbrigh, I, p. 45; Loeb, I, p. 105:

Thrasybulus to Periander

"I made no answer to your herald; but I took him into a cornfield, and with a staff smote and cut off the over-grown ears of corn, while he accompanied me. And if you ask him what he heard and what he saw, he will give his message. And this is what you must do if you want to strengthen your absolute rule: put to death those among the citizens who are pre-eminent, whether they are hostile to you or not. For to an absolute ruler even a friend is an object of suspicion."

291. See *Fear and Trembling*, p. 3, *KW* VI (*SV* III 56).

292. See Diogenes Laertius, I, 94; *Vitis*, I, p. 45; Riisbrigh, I, p. 42; Loeb, I, pp. 96-97.

293. See Herodotus, III, 50-53; Lange, I, pp. 249-52; Loeb, II, pp. 63-71.

294. See Supplement, pp. 660-61 (*Pap.* X⁵ A 149:8; X¹ A 667).

295. With reference to the remainder of the sentence, see Supplement, p. 599 (*Pap.* V B 104:3).

296. With reference to the following sentence, see Supplement, p. 599 (*Pap.* V B 104:4).

297. With reference to the remainder of the paragraph and the two following paragraphs, see Supplement, p. 599 (*Pap.* V B 97:24).

298. With reference to the following sentence, see Supplement, p. 600 (*Pap.* V B 97:18).

299. See Supplement, p. 600 (*Pap.* V B 98:1).

300. See Psalm 35:20.

301. Cf. Petrarch, *Rimes*, I, 7; *Sämmtliche italienische Gedichte*, I-VI, tr. F. W. Brückbrau (Munich: 1827; *ASKB* 1932-33), I, p. 288; *Petrarch's Lyric Poems The* Rime sparse *and Other Lyrics*, tr. and ed. Robert M. Durling (Cambridge: Harvard University Press, 1976), 237, p. 394:

> The sea has not so many creatures among its waves,
> nor up there beyond the circle of the moon
> were so many stars ever seen by any night,
> nor do so many birds dwell in the woods,
> nor did any field ever have so much grass, or any meadow,
> as I have cares in my heart every evening.

302. With reference to the following paragraph, see Supplement, p. 600 (*Pap.* V B 97:42, 98:10).

303. The royal gardens around Rosenborg Castle in the center of Copenhagen.

304. With reference to the following sentence, see Supplement, pp. 600-01 (*Pap.* V B 114).

305. In Greek mythology, the place of punishment as far below Hades as

the earth is below heaven, sometimes regarded as one of the two parts (Elysium and Tartarus) of Hades. See Nitsch, I, pp. 563-67.

306. Augustine, *De doctrina christiana*, III, 18; *Sancti Aurelii Augustini . . . opera et studio monachorum*, I-XVIII (Bassani: 1797-1807; *ASKB* 117-34), III, col. 69; *The Confessions. The City of God. On Christian Doctrine*, tr. Marcus Dods and J. F. Shaw (Chicago: Encyclopedia Britannica, 1952), p. 665.

307. Cf. Romans 12:11.

308. See Supplement, p. 601 (*Pap.* V B 115:2); *Anxiety*, p. 108, *KW* VIII (*SV* IV 376).

309. See *JP* V 5937-38; VI 6680 (*Pap.* VII^1 A 147-48; X^3 A 450). See also Scribe, [*Puf eller*] *Verden vil bedrages*; *Repertoire*, no no. (n.d.).

310. See Holberg, *Erasmus Montanus*, I, 4, *Danske Skue-Plads*, V, no pagination; Campbell and Schenck, p. 127.

311. For continuation of the sentence and with reference to the following two sentences, see Supplement, pp. 601-02 (*Pap.* V B 115:3).

312. See Mark 1:3.

313. For continuation of the paragraph, see Supplement, p. 602 (*Pap.* V B 115:5).

314. See Acts 13:2; Romans 1:1.

315. With reference to the remainder of the paragraph, the next paragraph, and the following sentence, see Supplement, p. 602 (*Pap.* V B 115:6).

316. See J. L. Heiberg, *Kong Salomon og Jørgen Hattemager*, 26, *Skuespil*, II, p. 386 (ed. tr.) (Chorus): "We depend upon his word and gown."

317. See "The Difference between a Genius and an Apostle," *Without Authority*, *KW* XVIII (*SV* XI 93-109).

318. Socrates.

319. With reference to the remainder of the paragraph, see Supplement, pp. 602-03 (*Pap.* V B 115:7).

320. See Ecclesiastes 1:9.

321. With reference to the following sentence, see Supplement, p. 603 (*Pap.* V B 98:2).

322. See Horace, *Epistles*, I, 1, 46; *Opera*, p. 541; Loeb, p. 255: "fleeing poverty through sea, through rocks, through flame." See *Either/Or*, II, p. 202, *KW* IV (*SV* II 182).

323. See, for example, *JP* I 703 (*Pap.* IV A 57).

324. See, for example, Plato, *Theaetetus*, 155 d; *Opera*, II, p. 41; *Dialogues*, p. 860: "This sense of wonder is the mark of the philosopher. Philosophy indeed has no other origin . . . ." Aristotle, *Metaphysics*, 982 b; Bekker, I, p. 982; *Works*, II, p. 1554: "For it is owing to their wonder that men both now begin and at first began to philosophize . . . ." On *Forundring* and *Beundring*, see, for example, *Fragments*, p. 310, note 35, *KW* VII.

325. With reference to the following sentence, see Supplement, p. 603 (*Pap.* V B 115:8).

326. With reference to the remainder of the sentence, see Supplement, pp. 603-04 (*Pap.* V B 115:9).

327. See J. L. Heiberg, *Recensenten og Dyret*, 16, *Skuespil*, III, p. 243 (ed. tr.) (Trop speaking): "She never sings except to a horse; she is accustomed to hearing the whip, and without it she can do nothing."

328. With reference to the following three paragraphs, see Supplement, p. 604 (*Pap*. V B 97:28).

329. With reference to the remainder of the paragraph, see Supplement, p. 604 (*Pap*. V B 98:15).

330. With reference to the remainder of the sentence, see Supplement, p. 605 (*Pap*. V B 116:1).

331. With reference to the remainder of the sentence, see Supplement, p. 605 (*Pap*. V B 116:2).

332. With reference to the remainder of the paragraph, see Supplement, p. 605 (*Pap*. V B 98:5, 116:3).

333. See Genesis 3:18.

334. With reference to the remainder of the paragraph, see Supplement, p. 606 (*Pap*. V B 98:6).

335. See John 6:68.

336. See John 15:16; Supplement, p. 606 (*Pap*. V B 116:6).

337. See Adelbert v. Chamisso, *Peter Schlemihl's wundersame Geschichte* (Nuremberg: 1835; *ASKB* 1630); *Peter Schlemihl's forunderlige Historie*, tr. Frederik Schaldemose (Copenhagen: 1841); *The Wonderful History of Peter Schlemihl*, tr. Ilsa Barea (Emmaus, Pa.: Story Classics, n.d.).

338. With reference to the remainder of the paragraph, see Supplement, pp. 606-07 (*Pap*. V B 116:7).

339. See Shakespeare, *Richard III*, I, 2, 43-223; Foersom and Wulff, VI, pp. 184-96; Ortlepp, VII, pp. 279-87; Schlegel and Tieck, III, pp. 242-49; Kittredge, pp. 792-94 (Richard and Anne in dialogue).

340. See Shakespeare, *Henry IV*, I, V, 1, 133-43; cf. Foersom and Wulff, III, p. 155; Ortlepp, VI, p. 231; Schlegel and Tieck, I, p. 300; Kittredge, p. 575:

> Can honour set to a leg? No. Or an arm? No. Or take away the grief of a
> wound? No. Honour hath no skill in surgery then? No. What is honour? A
> word. What is that word honour? Air. A trim reckoning! Who hath it? He
> that died a Wednesday. Doth he feel it? No. Doth he hear it? No. 'Tis in-
> sensible then? Yea, to the dead. But will it not live with the living? No.
> Why? Detraction will not suffer it. Therefore I'll none of it. Honour is a
> mere scutcheon—and so ends my catechism.

341. See Revelation 21:1.

342. See Luke 7:37-50.

343. With reference to the following two paragraphs, see Supplement, p. 509 (*Pap*. IV A 133).

344. With reference to the remainder of the sentence and the following two sentences, see Supplement, p. 607 (*Pap*. V B 107:3).

345. See Plutarch, "Pyrrhus," 21, *Lives*; Tetens, IV, p. 182; Loeb, IX, p. 417:

> The two armies [of Epirus and Rome] separated; and we are told that Pyrrhus said to one who was congratulating him on his victory [at Asculum], "If we are victorious in one more battle with the Romans, we shall be utterly ruined." For he had lost a great part of the forces with which he came, and all his friends and generals except a few; moreover, he had no others whom he could summon from home, and he saw that his allies in Italy were becoming indifferent, while the army of the Romans, as if from a fountain gushing forth indoors, was easily and speedily filled up again, and they did not lose courage in defeat, nay, their wrath gave them all the more vigour and determination for the war.

346. See Shakespeare, *Henry VI*, *II*, III, 2, 388-96; Schlegel and Tieck, III, p. 71; Kittredge, p. 729 (Suffolk speaking to Queen Margaret):

> If I depart from thee, I cannot live;
> And in thy sight to die, what were it else
> But like a pleasant slumber in thy lap?
> Here could I breathe my soul into the air,
> As mild and gentle as the cradle-babe
> Dying with mother's dug between its lips;
> Where, from thy sight, I should be raging mad
> And cry out for thee to close up mine eyes,
> To have thee with thy lips to stop my mouth.

347. J. L. Heiberg, *Den farlige Taushed*, *Digte og Fortællinger*, I-II (Copenhagen: 1834-35; *ASKB* 1551-52), I, p. 149.

348. Presumably an allusion to Johann Georg Hamann. See *JP* II 1556, 1558 (*Pap*. VI A 5; VIII[1] A 251).

349. With reference to the remainder of the sentence, see Supplement, p. 607 (*Pap*. V B 108:1).

350. For continuation of the phrase, see Supplement, p. 607 (*Pap*. V B 108:2).

351. See Daniel 3:4-30.

352. With reference to the remainder of the paragraph, see Supplement, p. 607 (*Pap*. V B 108:3).

353. See Supplement, pp. 508, 566, 608 (*Pap*. IV A 119; V B 124, 132).

354. See Daniel 2:4; Supplement, p. 608 (*Pap*. V B 139).

355. With reference to the following section, see Supplement, pp. 610-12 (*Pap*. V B 137, 140).

356. See Daniel 4:32-33.

357. See Supplement, p. 513 (*Pap*. V A 71); *JP* V 5325 (*Pap*. II A 757).

358. See Supplement, p. 610 (*Pap*. V B 118:1).

359. With reference to the following three paragraphs, see Supplement, p. 610 (*Pap*. V B 98:13).

360. Cf. *Johannes Climacus*, p. 121, *KW* VII (*Pap.* IV B 1, pp. 107-08); *Repetition*, p. 166, *KW* VI (*SV* III 204-05).

361. Cf. *JP* III 3065-66; V 5303; VI 6445 (*Pap.* XI¹ A 195-96; II A 210; X¹ A 546).

362. With reference to the remainder of the paragraph and the following paragraph, see Supplement, p. 610 (*Pap.* V B 118:2).

363. Terence, *The Self-Tormentor*, I, 25; Schmieder, p. 213; Guldberg, I, p. 276; Loeb, I, pp. 124-25.

364. With reference to the following sentence, see Supplement, p. 611 (*Pap.* V B 118:3).

365. For continuation of the paragraph, see Supplement, p. 611 (*Pap.* V B 118:5).

366. See, for example, Plato, *Symposium*, 223 c-d; *Opera*, III, pp. 546-48; Heise, II, pp. 103-04; *Dialogues*, p. 574: "Socrates was arguing with the others—not that Aristodemus could remember very much of what he said, for, besides having missed the beginning, he was still more than half asleep. But the gist of it was that Socrates was forcing them to admit that the same man might be capable of writing both comedy and tragedy—that the tragic poet might be a comedian as well."

367. "Mediation" is the Danish (and English) version of the German *Vermitt(e)lung*. See, for example, Hegel, *Wissenschaft der Logik*, I, *Werke*, III, pp. 100, 105, 110; IV, p. 75; *J.A.*, IV, pp. 110, 115, 120, 553; *Hegel's Science of Logic* (tr. of *W.L.*, Lasson ed., 1923; Kierkegaard had 2 ed., 1833-34), tr. A. V. Miller (New York: Humanities Press, 1969), pp. 99, 103, 107, 445; *Encyclopädie, Die Logik, Werke*, VI, pp. 133-34, 138; *J.A.*, VIII, pp. 171-72, 176; *Hegel's Logic*, pp. 101, 105. See also *Anxiety*, pp. 81-93, *KW* VIII (*SV* IV 350-63); *JP* II 1578; III 3072, 3294 (*Pap.* II A 454; III A 108; IV A 54).

368. Holberg, *Jacob von Tyboe*, III, 5, *Danske Skue-Plads*, III, no pagination; *Letters*, Letter 37, *KW* XXV.

369. See J. L. Heiberg, *Kong Salomon og Jørgen Hattemager*, 26; see note 316 above.

370. With reference to the following three paragraphs, see Supplement, pp. 611-12 (*Pap.* V B 97:51).

371. With reference to the following five sentences, see Supplement, p. 612 (*Pap.* V B 109:1).

372. With reference to the following two sentences, see Supplement, p. 612 (*Pap.* V B 109:2).

373. With reference to the following paragraph, see Supplement, pp. 612-13 (*Pap.* V B 97:49).

374. With reference to the following ten paragraphs, see Supplement, p. 613 (*Pap.* V B 98:8).

375. See I Corinthians 8:4.

376. With reference to the following clause, see Supplement, p. 600 (*Pap.* V B 97:18).

377. With reference to the remainder of the sentence, see Supplement, p. 613 (*Pap.* V B 119:1).

378. With reference to the following sentence, see Supplement, p. 613 (*Pap.* V B 119:2).

379. With reference to the remainder of the paragraph, see Supplement, pp. 613-14 (*Pap.* V B 119:3).

380. With reference to the remainder of the paragraph, see Supplement, pp. 614-15 (*Pap.* V B 119:4).

381. See Hegel, *Wissenschaft der Logik, Werke,* IV, pp. 177-83; *J.A.,* IV, pp. 655-61; *Science of Logic,* pp. 523-38; *Encyclopädie, Logik, Werke,* VI, pp. 275-81; *J.A.,* VIII, pp. 313-19; *Hegel's Logic,* pp. 197-200. See also *Either/Or,* I, pp. 3-4, *KW* III (*SV* I v-vi).

382. An allusion to N.F.S. Grundtvig's "matchless discovery." See p. 48 and note 131.

383. An allusion to Grundtvig. See Supplement, pp. 581, 582 (*Pap.* V B 97:16, 102:4); *Postscript, KW* XII (*SV* VII 33).

384. Danish: *Kjøbstad,* literally "buying place."

385. See p. 125 and note 58.

386. See Baggesen, "*Til Danfanas Døttre,*" *Værker,* III, p. 60 (ed. tr.); *Danfana* (Copenhagen: 1816-17; *ASKB* 1508), January 1816, p. 9.

387. Cf. Cicero, *Orator,* III, 12; *M. Tullii Ciceronis opera omnia,* I-IV and index, ed. Johann August Ernesti (Halle: 1756-57; *ASKB* 1224-29), I, p. 656; *Brutus Orator,* tr. H. M. Hubbell (Loeb, Cambridge: Harvard University Press, 1971), pp. 313-15: "There indeed is the field for manifold and varied debate, which was first trodden by the feet of Plato."

388. With reference to the remainder of the paragraph, see Supplement, p. 615 (*Pap.* V B 98:17, 119:11).

389. With reference to the following sentence, see Supplement, p. 615 (*Pap.* V B 97:27, 119:12).

390. With reference to the following two sentences, see Supplement, p. 616 (*Pap.* V B 119:13).

391. With reference to the remainder of the sentence, see Supplement, p. 616 (*Pap.* V B 119:14).

392. With reference to the following two sentences, see Supplement, p. 616 (*Pap.* V B 119:15).

393. For continuation of the paragraph, see Supplement, p. 616 (*Pap.* V B 119:16).

394. See Supplement, p. 618 (*Pap.* V B 98:7).

395. With reference to the remainder of the sentence, see Supplement, pp. 616-17 (*Pap.* V B 119:17).

396. With reference to the following sentence, see Supplement, p. 617 (*Pap.* V B 119:18).

397. With reference to the following two sentences and the following line, see Supplement, p. 617 (*Pap.* V B 119:19).

398. See Plutarch, "Caesar," 54, *Lives;* Loeb, VII, p. 569: "Being eager to

take Cato alive, Caesar hastened towards Utica, for Cato was guarding that city, and took no part in the battle. But he learned that Cato had made away with himself, and he was clearly annoyed, though for what reason is uncertain. At any rate, he said: 'Cato, I begrudge thee thy death; for thou didst begrudge me the preservation of thy life.' "

399. Attributed to Bias, one of the Seven Wise Men of Greece. See Diogenes Laertius, I, 87; *Vitis*, I, p. 41; Riisbrigh, I, p. 38; Loeb, I, p. 91: "He advised men to measure life as if they had both a short and a long time to live."

400. An allusion to the sandman lullaby about Ole Lukøie (Ole Shut-Eye).

401. With reference to the following two sentences, see Supplement, p. 617 (*Pap.* V B 110:1).

402. See "*Doctor Faust*," 3, *Gotthold Ephraim Lessing's sämmtliche Schriften*, I-XXXII (Berlin, Stettin: 1825-28; *ASKB* 1747-62), XXIII, p. 177 (ed. tr.): "No more and no less than the transition from good to evil."

403. With reference to the remainder of the paragraph, see Supplement, pp. 617-18 (*Pap.* V B 111).

404. See Leviticus 21:10.

405. With reference to the remainder of the sentence, see Supplement, p. 618 (*Pap.* V B 121).

406. See *JP* V 5738 (*Pap.* V A 52).

407. See L. Tieck, *Fortunat*, III, 1, *Ludwig Tieck's sämmtliche Werke*, I-II (Paris: 1837; *ASKB* 1848-49), I, p. 234.

408. With reference to the remainder of the paragraph, see Supplement, p. 618 (*Pap.* V B 97:26).

409. See Supplement, p. 618 (*Pap.* V B 98:7).

410. With reference to the following sentence, see Supplement, p. 618 (*Pap.* V B 122:1).

411. With reference to the remainder of the sentence, see Supplement, p. 619 (*Pap.* V B 122:2).

412. With reference to the following three paragraphs, see Supplement, p. 619 (*Pap.* V B 98:18).

413. A variation of the lines on p. 204.

414. With reference to the remainder of the paragraph, see Supplement, p. 619 (*Pap.* V B 122:3).

415. With reference to the remainder of the sentence, see Supplement, pp. 619-20 (*Pap.* V B 122:4).

416. For continuation of the paragraph, see Supplement, p. 620 (*Pap.* VI B 8:14).

417. With reference to the following sentence, see Supplement, p. 620 (*Pap.* V B 122:5).

418. With reference to the following paragraph, see Supplement, pp. 620-21 (*Pap.* V B 122:6).

419. A principle in Roman law.

420. See Supplement, p. 514 (*Pap.* V A 88).

421. The fallacy of *post hoc, ergo propter hoc* (after this, therefore because of this).

422. With reference to the remainder of the paragraph, see Supplement, p. 621 (*Pap.* V B 113).

423. For continuation of the sentence, see Supplement, p. 621 (*Pap.* VI B 8:15).

424. See John 6:63; II Corinthians 3:6.

425. See Romans 8:2, 22; II Corinthians 4:16.

426. Danish: *Stolten-Hendrik*, literally "Proud Henry." The English version is "Good-King-Henry," designating an herb of the goosefoot family (*Chenopodium bonus-henricus*).

427. The source has not been located. The reference is to Louis XVI (1754–1793), king of France.

428. See Supplement, p. 621 (*Pap.* V B 148:1).

429. With reference to the remainder of the paragraph, see Supplement, pp. 621-22 (*Pap.* V B 148:4).

430. According to Erasmus, Socrates was supposed to have said this to a boy. See Erasmus, *Apophthegmata*, III, 70; *Opera*, I-VIII (Basel: 1540), IV, p. 148 (ed. tr.):

> Quum diues quidam filium adolescentulum ad Socratem misisset, ut indolem illius inspiceret, ac paedagogus diceret, Pater ad te, O Socrates, misit filium, ut eum videres: tum Socrates ad puerum, Loquere igitur, inquit, adolescens, ut te videam: significans, ingenium hominis non tam in vultu relucere, quam in oratione, quod hoc sit certissimum [When a certain wealthy man had sent his very young son to Socrates to observe his genius, and his slave said, "His father sent his son to you that you might see him, Socrates": thereupon Socrates said to the boy, "Speak, lad, so that I may see you": thus signifying that the character of a man comes to light not so much in his countenance as in his manner of speaking, in which this is most certain].

See also Hamann, *Aesthetica. in. Nuce, Schriften*, II, pp. 261-62: "*Rede, dasz ich Dich sehe! . . . Reden ist ü b e r s e t z e n . . .* [Speak, so that I may see you! . . . Speaking is *translating . . .*]." See also, for example, *Irony*, *KW* II (*SV* XIII 110, 450); *Either/Or*, II, p. 275, *KW* IV (*SV* II 246); *Letters*, Letter 8, *KW* XXV; *JP* II 2115 (*Pap.* VI B 53:16).

431. An allusion to N.F.S. Grundtvig. See pp. 48, 101 and notes 131, 20.

432. With reference to the following sentence, see Supplement, p. 622 (*Pap.* V B 148:5).

433. With reference to the following two paragraphs, see Supplement, p. 623 (*Pap.* V B 148:34).

434. See, for example, *JP* II 1123; V 6135 (*Pap.* VIII[1] A 649, 650).

435. With reference to the remainder of the paragraph, see Supplement, p. 622 (*Pap.* V B 154).

436. In the final manuscript, the long footnote is on an attached sheet.

437. See *Repetition*, pp. xxi-xxvii, 357-62, *KW* VI.

438. The German writer Karl Ludwig Börne (1786-1837), who lived in Paris for many years. See *"Die Leichtthurm,"* *Gesammelte Schriften von Ludwig Börne*, I-VIII (Hamburg: 1835-40; *ASKB* 1627-29), I, p. 77 (ed. tr.): "Does one need to be a Parisian to ask: Has Herr Ulrich lost his mind because he has so faithfully loved his wife, or has he faithfully loved her *because* he has lost his mind?"

439. See Carl v. Linné, *Systema naturae*, I-XIV (Stockholm: 1766), I^1, p. 358.

440. See Holberg, *Jacob von Tyboe*, III, 2, *Danske Skue-Plads*, III, no pagination (ed. tr.): "My dear parents out in their graves."

441. See Cervantes, *Don Quixote*, V, 1; *Den sindrige Don Quixote af Mancha*, I-IV, tr. Charlotte Dorothea Biehl (Copenhagen: 1776-77; *ASKB* 1937-40), III, pp. 2-4; *The Ingenious Gentleman Don Quixote de la Mancha*, ed. Samuel Putnam (New York: Modern Library, 1949), pp. 512-14.

442. *Repetition*, pp. 125-231, *KW* VI (*SV* III 171-264).

443. The scholastic mystic Bonaventura (1221-1274).

444. The pre-Reformation reformer Johann Wessel (Gansfort) v. Groningen (c. 1420-1489), also called *Doctor controversiarum* (Doctor of Dialectic).

445. A tontine is a group-annuity arrangement of Italian origin whereby the survivors annually divide the interest and the final survivor receives the entire fund. See Börne, *"Ueber den Umgang mit Menschen,"* *Schriften*, III, pp. 241-42.

446. With reference to the remainder of the sentence, see Supplement, pp. 622-23 (*Pap.* V B 150:2).

447. With reference to the following four sections (1-4), see Supplement, pp. 624-25 (*Pap.* V B 149:2).

448. With reference to the following section, see Supplement, p. 625 (*Pap.* V B 148:2).

449. Petrarch (1304-1374), the Italian poet, first saw Laura in Avignon in 1327. Married to another, she became the inspiration for his love poems.

450. Peter Abelard (1079-1142), prominent French philosopher and teacher, was in love with Héloise, niece of Fulbert, canon of Notre Dame, who opposed the match. See Supplement, p. 566 (*Pap.* V B 124). See also *JP* V 5609, 5703 (*Pap.* IV A 31, 177).

451. Axel and Valborg, in an old Danish ballad. See Adam Gottlob Oehlenschläger, *Axel og Valborg*, *Oehlenschlägers Tragødier*, I-X (Copenhagen: 1841-49; *ASKB* 1601-05 [I-IX]), V, pp. 3-111; *Axel and Valborg*, tr. Frederik Strange Kolle (New York: Grafton, 1906).

452. Augustin-Eugène Scribe's *La Cameraderie* was published in 1836, the year in which he was elected a member of the French Academy (hence the designation "reception piece"). It was first performed in Copenhagen at the Royal Theater November 14, 1839.

453. See Luke 17:37.

454. See James 2:10.

455. A character in Aristophanes, *The Knights*. See Droysen, II, pp. 312-431; Loeb, I, pp. 123-259.

456. A conventional closing in Latin comedies.

457. The trio together has not been located in a single passage in Aristotle.

458. See Matthew 26:53.

459. With reference to the remainder of the paragraph, see Supplement, p. 625 (*Pap*. V B 150:4).

460. Presumably an allusion to Hans Lassen Martensen's review (*Fædrelandet*, 398-400, January 10-12, 1841, col. 3205-24) of J. L. Heiberg's *Nye Digte* (Copenhagen: 1841; *ASKB* 1562). Martensen stresses the importance of *Nye Digte* as an expression of "the spirit of the new age" and of the teachings of speculative philosophy. See *Irony, KW* II (*SV* XIII 393).

461. For continuation of the paragraph, see Supplement, p. 625 (*Pap*. V B 150:5).

462. See, for example, *Fear and Trembling*, pp. 36-38, 42, 119, *KW* VI (*SV* III 87-89, 93, 164-65).

463. Cf., for example, *Sickness unto Death*, pp. 13-14, *KW* XIX (*SV* XI 127-28).

464. With reference to the remainder of the paragraph, see Supplement, pp. 625-26 (*Pap*. V B 150:7).

465. In the report of a fictional conversation between the Emperor of Japan and Asmus. See Matthias Claudius, "*Die Audienz*," *ASMUS omnia sua SECUM portans oder Sämmtliche Werke des Wandsbecker Bothen, Werke*, I-IV (1-8) (Hamburg: 1838; *ASKB* 1631-32), I, 3, p. 53 (ed. tr.): "The misunderstanding in the world is usually due to the fact that the one does not understand the other."

466. A character in Plato's *Gorgias*.

467. With reference to the following three sentences, see Supplement, p. 626 (*Pap*. V B 150:8).

468. With reference to the following paragraph, see Supplement, p. 626 (*Pap*. V B 148:21).

469. See Plato, *Phaedo*, 60 a-c; *Opera*, I, pp. 478-79; Heise, I, pp. 6-7; *Dialogues*, p. 43.

470. See Plato, *Phaedo*, 116 b; *Opera*, I, pp. 614-15; Heise, I, p. 120; *Dialogues*, p. 96.

471. Cf., for example, Plato, *Symposium*, 215 a; *Opera*, III, p. 528; Heise, II, p. 87; *Dialogues*, p. 566.

472. With reference to the following paragraph, see Supplement, p. 626 (*Pap*. V B 148:22).

473. See Jonathan Swift, *Satyrische und ernsthafte Schriften von Dr. Jonathan Swift*, I-VIII (Hamburg, Leipzig, Zurich: 1756-66; *ASKB* 1899-1906), V.

474. With reference to the following four sentences, see Supplement, p. 627 (*Pap*. V B 148:23).

475. With reference to the remainder of the paragraph, see Supplement, p. 627 (*Pap*. V B 150:9).

476. Cf. Lessing, *Nathan der Weise*, IV, 4; *Schriften*, XXII, p. 181; *Nathan the Wise*, tr. Patrick Maxwell (New York: Bloch, 1939), p. 295.

477. With reference to the following paragraph, see Supplement, p. 626 (*Pap*. V B 148:7).

478. With reference to the remainder of the paragraph, see Supplement, p. 628 (*Pap*. V B 148:8).

479. See Shakespeare, *King John*, III, 4, 114-15; Foersom and Wulff, VIII, p. 75; Ortlepp, V, p. 615; Schlegel and Tieck, I, p. 53; Kittredge, p. 490 (Pandulph speaking): "Evils that take leave / On their departure most of all show evil." See also Supplement, p. 628 (*Pap*. V B 148:8).

480. With reference to the following three sentences, see Supplement, p. 628 (*Pap*. V B 148:6).

481. With reference to the following four paragraphs, see Supplement, p. 628 (*Pap*. V B 148:30).

482. With reference to the following footnote, see Supplement, p. 629 (*Pap*. V B 148:31).

483. With reference to the following sentence, see Supplement, p. 629 (*Pap*. V B 153).

484. With reference to the following paragraph and footnote, see Supplement, p. 630 (*Pap*. V B 148:32).

485. With reference to the heading and the following paragraph, see Supplement, p. 630 (*Pap*. V B 148:25).

486. With reference to the following two paragraphs, see Supplement, p. 630 (*Pap*. V B 148:29).

487. With reference to the following sentence, see Supplement, p. 630 (*Pap*. V B 150:12).

488. With reference to the remainder of the sentence, see Supplement, p. 630 (*Pap*. V B 150:13).

489. For continuation of the sentence, see Supplement, p. 631 (*Pap*. V B 150:14).

490. With reference to the following eleven paragraphs, see Supplement, p. 631 (*Pap*. V B 148:24).

491. See Gottfried Wilhelm Leibniz, *Nouveaux Essais*, I, 2, 11; *God. Guil. Leibnitii opera philosophica . . .*, I-II (with continuous pagination), ed. Johann Eduard Erdmann (Berlin: 1840; *ASKB* 620), I, p. 216; *New Essays on Human Understanding*, tr. and ed. Peter Remnant and Jonathan Bennett (Cambridge: Cambridge University Press, 1981), p. 95. See also *JP* V 5585 (*Pap*. IV A 22).

492. Sennacherib (714-696 B.C.) and Shalmaneser (d. 722 B.C.) were Assyrian kings. See, for example, II Kings 18:9,13.

493. Chrysippus and other Stoics. See Diogenes Laertius, VII, 85; *Vitis*, II, p. 38; Riisbrigh, I, pp. 312-13; Loeb, II, p. 193:

An animal's first impulse, say the Stoics, is to self-preservation, because nature from the outset endears it to itself, as Chrysippus affirms in the first book of his work *On Ends*: his words are, "The dearest thing to every animal is its own constitution and its consciousness thereof"; for it was not likely that nature should estrange the living thing from itself or that she should leave the creature she has made without either estrangement from or affection for its own constitution. We are forced then to conclude that nature in constituting the animal made it near and dear to itself; for so it comes to repel all that is injurious and give free access to all that is serviceable or akin to it.

494. With reference to the following six sentences, see Supplement, p. 631 (*Pap.* V B 148:33).

495. With reference to the remainder of the paragraph and the following paragraph, see Supplement, p. 632 (*Pap.* V B 148:26).

496. With reference to the following paragraph, see Supplement, p. 632 (*Pap.* V B 148:28).

497. With reference to the remainder of the sentence, see Supplement, p. 632 (*Pap.* V B 150:16).

498. With reference to the remainder of the paragraph, see Supplement, pp. 632-33 (*Pap.* V B 148:27).

499. *Repetition*, pp. 124-231, *KW* VI (*SV* III 172-264).

500. With reference to the following six paragraphs, see Supplement, p. 633 (*Pap.* V B 148:17).

501. Lessing, *Emilia Galotti, Schriften,* XXI, pp. 185-304; *Five German Tragedies*, ed. and tr. F. J. Lamport (Baltimore: Penguin, 1969), pp. 31-103.

502. With reference to the remainder of the sentence, see Supplement, p. 633 (*Pap.* VI B 8:18).

503. See Lessing, *Hamburgische Dramaturgie,* 14, 19, 23, 87-88, 91, *Schriften,* XXIV, pp. 103-09, 138-44, 165-71; XXV, pp. 246-59, 272-79; *Hamburg Dramaturgy,* tr. Helen Zimmern (New York: Dover, 1962), pp. 38-40, 51-53, 58-62, 221-29, 236-39.

504. See Aristotle, *Poetics*, 1451 a-b; Bekker, II, p. 1451; *Aristoteles Dichtkunst,* tr. Michael Conrad Curtius (Hanover: 1753; *ASKB* 1094), p. 19; *Works,* II, p. 2323: "The distinction between historian and poet is not in the one writing prose and the other verse—you might put the work of Herodotus into verse, and it would still be a species of history; it consists really in this, that the one describes the thing that has been, and the other a kind of thing that might be. Hence poetry is something more philosophic and of graver import than history, since its statements are of the nature rather of universals, whereas those of history are singulars."

505. With reference to the remainder of the paragraph, see Supplement, pp. 633-34 (*Pap.* V B 150:17).

506. With reference to the following paragraph, see Supplement, p. 634 (*Pap.* V B 148:20).

507. See, for example, Plato, *Gorgias,* 463 a-b, 465 b-e; *Opera,* I, pp. 298-99, 302-05; Heise, III, pp. 41-42, 46-47; *Dialogues,* pp. 245-46, 247-48:

SOCRATES: Well then, Gorgias, the activity as a whole, it seems to me, is not an art, but the occupation of a shrewd and enterprising spirit, and of one naturally skilled in its dealings with men, and in sum and substance I call it 'flattery.' Now it seems to me that there are many other parts of this activity, one of which is cookery. This is considered an art, but in my judgment is no art, only a routine and a knack. And rhetoric I call another part of this general activity, and beautification, and sophistic—four parts with four distinct objects.

To be brief, then, I will express myself in the language of geometricians—for by now perhaps you may follow me. Sophistic is to legislation what beautification is to gymnastics, and rhetoric to justice what cookery is to medicine. But, as I say, while there is this natural distinction between them, yet because they are closely related, Sophist and rhetorician, working in the same sphere and upon the same subject matter, tend to be confused with each other, and they know not what to make of each other, nor do others know what to make of them. For if the body was under the control, not of the soul, but of itself, and if cookery and medicine were not investigated and distinguished by the soul, but the body instead gave the verdict, weighing them by the bodily pleasures they offered, then the principle of Anaxagoras would everywhere hold good—that is something you know about, my dear Polus—and all things would be mingled in indiscriminate confusion, and medicine and health and cookery would be indistinguishable.

Well, now you have heard my conception of rhetoric. It is the counterpart in the soul of what cookery is to the body.

508. With reference to the following eight paragraphs, see Supplement, p. 634 (*Pap.* V B 148:19).

509. With reference to the remainder of the paragraph, see Supplement, p. 634 (*Pap.* V B 148:18).

510. See Boethius, *De consolatione philosophiae Severini Boethii libri V* (Agriae: 1758; *ASKB* 431); *The Consolation of Philosophy*, tr. W. V. Cooper (New York: Modern Library, 1943), pp. 4-5:

When she [Philosophy] saw that the Muses of poetry were present by my couch giving words to my lamenting, she was stirred a while; her eyes flashed fiercely, and said she, "Who has suffered these seducing mummers to approach this sick man? Never do they support those in sorrow by any healing remedies, but rather do ever foster the sorrow by poisonous sweets. These are they who stifle the fruit-bearing harvest of reason with the barren briars of the passions: they free not the minds of men from disease, but accustom them thereto. I would think it less grievous if your allurements drew away from me some uninitiated man, as happens in the vulgar herd. In such an one my labours would be naught harmed, but this man has been nourished in the lore of Eleatics and Academics; and to him have ye reached? Away with you, Sirens, seductive unto destruction! leave him to my Muses to be cared for and to be healed."

Their band thus rated cast a saddened glance upon the ground, confessing their shame in blushes, and passed forth dismally over the threshold.

511. See, for example, Plutarch, "Solon," 29, *Lives*; Tetens, I, pp. 360-61; Klaiber, II, pp. 268-69; Loeb, I, p. 489:

> Thespis was now beginning to develop tragedy, and the attempt attracted most people because of its novelty, although it was not yet made a matter of competitive contest. Solon, therefore, who was naturally fond of hearing and learning anything new, and who in his old age more than ever before indulged himself in leisurely amusement, yes, and in wine and song, went to see Thespis act in his own play, as the custom of the ancient poets was. After the spectacle, he accosted Thespis, and asked him if he was not ashamed to tell such lies in the presence of so many people. Thespis answered that there was no harm in talking and acting that way in play, whereupon Solon smote the ground sharply with his staff and said: "Soon, however, if we give play of this sort so much praise and honour, we shall find it in our solemn contracts."

512. See, for example, Plato, *Republic*, 605 a-c; *Opera*, V, pp. 70-73; *Dialogues*, p. 830 (Socrates speaking with Glaucon):

> This consideration, then, makes it right for us to proceed to lay hold of him and set him down as the counterpart of the painter, for he resembles him in that his creations are inferior in respect of reality, and the fact that his appeal is to the inferior part of the soul and not to the best part is another point of resemblance. And so we may at last say that we should be justified in not admitting him into a well-ordered state, because he stimulates and fosters this element in the soul, and by strengthening it tends to destroy the rational part, just as when in a state one puts bad men in power and turns the city over to them and ruins the better sort. Precisely in the same manner we shall say that the mimetic poet sets up in each individual soul a vicious constitution by fashioning phantoms far removed from reality, and by currying favor with the senseless element that cannot distinguish the greater from the less, but calls the same thing now one, now the other.
>
> By all means.
>
> But we have not yet brought our chief accusation against it. Its power to corrupt, with rare exceptions, even the better sort is surely the chief cause for alarm.

513. See, for example, Hegel, *Wissenschaft der Logik*, I, *Die objective Logik*, *Werke*, III, pp. 147-73; *J.A.*, IV, pp. 157-83; *Science of Logic*, pp. 137-56.

514. For continuation of the paragraph, see Supplement, p. 635 (*Pap.* V B 150:19).

515. Nicolai Edinger Balle, *Lærebog i den Evangelisk-christlige Religion indrettet til Brug i de danske Skoler* (Copenhagen: 1824; *ASKB* 183), VIII, 1, pp. 110-11.

516. See, for example, *Postscript*, *KW* XII (*SV* VII 114, 171, 195, 246); *JP* II

1142, 1402; IV 4937; V 5792, 5961 (*Pap.* X⁴ A 114, 494, 290; VI B 18; VII¹ A 221).

517. See Acts 10:34.

518. See Matthew 11:12.

519. Because the main characters in "'Guilty?'/'Not Guilty?'" are anonymous, Frater Taciturnus uses the Latin *quidam* and *quaedam* in referring to them. In *Postscript, KW* XIII (*SV* VII 247-49), Johannes Climacus regards Quidam as a name, and therefore the initial letter is capitalized. The same form is used in the present volume.

520. Cf. Holberg, *Erasmus Montanus*, I, 4, *Danske Skue-Plads*, V, no pagination; Campbell and Schenck, p. 126.

521. With reference to the following sentence, see Supplement, p. 635 (*Pap.* V B 148:9).

522. In Greek mythology, Io, not Leto (Roman Latona), was changed by Zeus into a heifer to protect her against the wrath of Hera, and, tormented by a gadfly sent by Hera, Io wandered over the earth. In later versions, the wanderings of Leto (in the same triangular relation to Zeus and Hera) were linked to Hera's jealousy. See Nitsch, I, pp. 34-35.

523. With reference to the following two sentences, see Supplement, p. 635 (*Pap.* V B 150:20).

524. See II Samuel 11.

525. Börne, "Hamlet, *von Shakspeare*," *Schriften*, II, p. 197 (ed. tr.): "*Hamlet* is a Christian tragedy."

526. With reference to the following paragraph, see Supplement, p. 635 (*Pap.* V B 148:16).

527. See Deuteronomy 32:35; Romans 12:19; Hebrews 10:30.

528. With reference to the following two sentences, see Supplement, pp. 635-36 (*Pap.* V B 150:21).

529. See Heinrich Theodor Rötscher, *Cyclus dramatischer Charaktere*, II of *Die Kunst der dramatischen Darstellung*, I-II (Berlin: 1841-44; *ASKB* 1391), II¹, p. 99.

530. See Supplement, p. 636 (*Pap.* VI B 8:19).

531. With reference to the section heading, see Supplement, p. 636 (*Pap.* V B 149:3). With reference to the section heading and the following eleven paragraphs, see Supplement, pp. 636-37 (*Pap.* V B 148:37,38).

532. See Tacitus, *Annals*, I, 1; *Cajus Cornelius Tacitus*, I-III, tr. Jacob Baden (Copenhagen: 1773-97; *ASKB* 1286-88), III, p. 541; *Des C. Cornelius Tacitus sämmtliche Werke*, I-III, tr. Johann Samuel Müllern (Hamburg: 1765-66; *ASKB* 1283-85), III, pp. 604-05; *Tacitus: The Historical Works, Germania and Agricola*, I-II, tr. Arthur Murphy (Everyman, New York: Dutton, 1907), II, p. 317.

533. With reference to the following fourteen paragraphs, see Supplement, p. 638 (*Pap.* V B 148:35).

534. See Börne, "*Das Bild*," *Schriften*, II, pp. 132-68, part of a controversy

between Börne and the *Tübinger Literaturblatt* over Ernst v. Houwald's tragedy *Das Bild*.

535. *Lucinde* (Stuttgart: 1835), p. 27 (*die Gesundheit allein liebenswürdig ist*); *Friedrich Schlegel's* Lucinde *and the Fragments*, tr. Peter Firchow (Minneapolis: University of Minnesota Press, 1971), p. 57. See *Irony, KW* II (*SV* XIII 357-70), a discussion of Friedrich Schlegel's *Lucinde*.

536. See Matthew 11:5.

537. See Ludwig Andreas Feuerbach, *Das Wesen des Christenthums* (Leipzig: 1843; *ASKB* 488), pp. 90-92; *The Essence of Christianity*, tr. George Eliot (New York: Harper, 1957), pp. 61-63.

538. Ibid., p. 425 fn.

539. See Aristotle, *Poetics*, 1449 b; Bekker, II, p. 1449; Curtius, p. 12; *Works*, II, p. 2320. See also 1452 b-1453 a; Bekker, II, pp. 1452-53; Curtius, pp. 25-26; *Works*, II, p. 2325:

> We assume that, for the finest form of tragedy, the plot must be not simple but complex; and further, that it must imitate actions arousing fear and pity, since that is the distinctive function of this kind of imitation. It follows, therefore, that there are three forms of plot to be avoided. A good man must not be seen passing from good fortune to bad, or a bad man from bad fortune to good. The first situation is not fear-inspiring or piteous, but simply odious to us. The second is the most untragic that can be; it has no one of the requisites of tragedy; it does not appeal either to the human feeling in us, or to our pity, or to our fears. Nor, on the other hand, should an extremely bad man be seen falling from good fortune into bad. Such a story may arouse the human feeling in us, but it will not move us to either pity or fear; pity is occasioned by undeserved misfortune, and fear by that of one like ourselves; so that there will be nothing either piteous or fear-inspiring in the situation. There remains, then, the intermediate kind of personage, a man not preeminently virtuous and just, whose misfortune, however, is brought upon him not by vice and depravity but by some fault, of the number of those in the enjoyment of great reputation and prosperity; e.g. Oedipus, Thyestes, and the men of note of similar families.

540. A reference to Christian Roat, a daring tightrope walker from Holland, who twice attempted the ascent to one of the tower windows of Copenhagen's Rosenborg Castle (June 6 and 12, 1827). Because of friction of the rope against the stonework, the rope broke the second time and Roat was fatally injured. See Eiler Nystrøm, *Offentlige Forlystelser i Frederik Den Sjettes Tid*, I-II (Copenhagen: 1910-13), II, pp. 133-36.

541. A compaction of "*Das Bild*," *Schriften*, II, pp. 143-48.

542. Cf. Mark 2:17.

543. The main character in a Holberg play of the same name. See *Danske Skue-Plads*, I, no pagination.

544. With reference to the following paragraph, see Supplement, pp. 638-42 (*Pap.* VI B 10-11).

545. With reference to the heading and the following thirteen paragraphs, see Supplement, pp. 642-43 (*Pap.* V B 149:4).

546. The title of a play by Terence. See Schmieder, pp. 212-306; Guldberg, II, pp. 269-393; Loeb, I, pp. 113-229.

547. See Holberg, *Den politiske Kandestøber*, II, 1 (Gert Bundtmager speaking), *Danske Skue-Plads*, I, no pagination; *The Political Tinker*, Campbell and Schenck, p. 63.

548. Vielgeschrey, the main character in Holberg's *Den Stundesløse*. See I, 6, *Danske Skue-Plads*, V, no pagination; *The Fussy Man*, *Four Plays*, p. 11.

549. Presumably Balthasar, although he is not a young man, in *Der Alte vom Berge* (1828). See *Ludwig Tieck's gesammelte Novellen*, I-XII (Berlin: 1852-54), VIII, pp. 208-13.

550. See I Thessalonians 5:16.

551. Presumably an allusion to Hans Adolph Brorson, "*Jeg gaaer i Fare, hvor jeg gaaer.*" See *Psalmer og aandelige Sange*, ed. Jens Albrecht Leonhard Holm (Copenhagen: 1838; *ASKB* 200), 168, pp. 513-14.

552. See, for example, Plato, *Apology*, 19 d-20 a; *Opera*, VIII, pp. 104-05; *Dialogues*, p. 6 (Socrates speaking):

> The fact is that there is nothing in any of these charges, and if you have heard anyone say that I try to educate people and charge a fee, there is no truth in that either. I wish that there were, because I think that it is a fine thing if a man is qualified to teach, as in the case of Gorgias of Leontini and Prodicus of Ceos and Hippias of Elis. Each one of these is perfectly capable of going into any city and actually persuading the young men to leave the company of their fellow citizens, with any of whom they can associate for nothing, and attach themselves to him, and pay money for the privilege, and be grateful into the bargain.

553. See Holberg, *Diderich Menschen-Skræk*, 20, *Danske Skue-Plads*, IV, no pagination; *Diderich the Terrible*, *Seven One-Act Plays*, pp. 103-32.

554. For continuation of the paragraph, see Supplement, p. 643 (*Pap.* V B 150:23).

555. See p. 53 and note 144.

556. A version of the terminology used in presenting a doctoral dissertation.

557. With reference to the heading and the following ten paragraphs, see Supplement, pp. 643-44 (*Pap.* V B 148:39).

558. See Horace, *Epistles*, I, 6, 1-11; *Opera*, p. 561; Loeb, p. 287:

> "Marvel at nothing [*Nil admirari*]"—that is perhaps the one and only thing, Numicius, that can make a man happy and keep him so. Yon sun, the stars and seasons that pass in fixed courses—some can gaze upon these with no strain of fear: what think you of the gifts of earth, or what of the sea's, which makes rich far distant Arabs and Indians—what of the shows, the plaudits and the favours of the friendly Roman—in what wise, with what feelings and eyes think you they should be viewed?

> And he who fears their opposites "marvels" in much the same way as
> the man who desires: in either case 'tis the excitement that annoys, the mo-
> ment some unexpected appearance startles either.

559. Horace, *Epistles*, I, 1, 61; *Opera*, p. 542; Loeb, pp. 254-55.

560. The source has not been located.

561. See J. G. Fichte, *Die Bestimmung des Menschen* (Berlin: 1838; *ASKB*
500), p. 202; *Johann Gottlieb Fichte's sämmtliche Werke*, I-VIII (Berlin: 1845-46;
ASKB 492-99), II, p. 311; *The Vocation of Man, The Popular Works of Johann
Gottlieb Fichte*, I-II, tr. William Smith (London: 1889), I, pp. 470-71: "My
mind is for ever closed against embarrassment and perplexity, against uncertainty, doubt, and anxiety;—my heart against grief, repentance, and desire.
There is but one thing that I may know,—namely, what I ought to do; and
this I always know infallibly."

562. See Exodus 20:5.

563. Cf. Horace, *Satires*, I, 1, 69-70; *Opera*, p. 361; Loeb, pp. 8-11. Cf. II
Samuel 12:7.

564. With reference to the remainder of the sentence, see Supplement, p.
644 (*Pap.* V B 150:24).

565. See Friedrich Daniel Ernst Schleiermacher, *Über die Religion. Reden an
die Gebildeten unter ihren Verächtern* (Berlin: 1843; *ASKB* 271), p. 77; *On Religion: Addresses in Response to Its Cultured Critics*, tr. Terrence N. Tice (Richmond, Va.: Knox, 1969), p. 112:

> Indeed, if you yourselves are still capable of being seized with reverence
> before the great powers of nature, tell me: Does this depend on your own
> security or on your lack of it? Are you prepared to mock and laugh at the
> thunder when you stand under the protection of your lightening rods? Well
> then, is what is protective and sustaining in nature any more or less an
> object of worship than this is?

566. Plutarch recounts ("Marcellus," 19, *Lives*) that when a soldier commanded Archimedes to come to Marcellus, Archimedes said he wanted to
finish working on some geometrical figures, whereupon the soldier killed
him. See Tetens, III, pp. 183-84; Loeb, V, pp. 486-87.

567. See Livy, *History*, II, 32; *T. Livii Patavini historiarum libri*, I-V, ed.
August G. Ernesti (Leipzig: 1801-04; *ASKB* 1251-55 [ed. stereo., n.d.]), I,
pp. 105-06; *Livy*, I-XIV, tr. B. O. Foster et al. (Loeb, Cambridge: Harvard
University Press, 1965-84), I, pp. 323-25:

> There was a great panic in the City [Rome], and mutual apprehension
> caused the suspension of all activities. The plebeians, having been aban-
> doned by their friends, feared violence at the hands of the senators; the
> senators feared the plebeians who were left behind in Rome, being uncer-
> tain whether they had rather they stayed or went. Besides, how long would
> the seceding multitude continue peaceable? What would happen next if
> some foreign war should break out in the interim? Assuredly no hope was

left save in harmony amongst the citizens, and this they concluded they must restore to the state by fair means or foul. They therefore decided to send as an ambassador to the commons Agrippa Menenius, an eloquent man and dear to the plebeians as being one of themselves by birth. On being admitted to the camp he is said merely to have related the following apologue, in the quaint and uncouth style of that age: In the days when man's members did not all agree amongst themselves, as is now the case, but had each its own ideas and a voice of its own, the other parts thought it unfair that they should have the worry and the trouble and the labour of providing everything for the belly, while the belly remained quietly in their midst with nothing to do but to enjoy the good things which they bestowed upon it; they therefore conspired together that the hands should carry no food to the mouth, nor the mouth accept anything that was given it, nor the teeth grind up what they received. While they sought in this angry spirit to starve the belly into submission, the members themselves and the whole body were reduced to the utmost weakness. Hence it had become clear that even the belly had no idle task to perform, and was no more nourished than it nourished the rest, by giving out to all parts of the body that by which we live and thrive, when it has been divided equally amongst the veins and is enriched with digested food—that is, the blood. Drawing a parallel from this to show how like was the internal dissension of the bodily members to the anger of the plebs against the Fathers, he prevailed upon the minds of his hearers.

568. Cf. J. L. Heiberg, *De Danske i Paris*, II, 4, *Skuespil*, V, p. 77.

569. With reference to the following seven paragraphs, see Supplement, pp. 644-45 (*Pap.* V B 97:23, 148:36).

570. Presumably Thrasymachus; see Book I of Plato's *Republic*.

571. For continuation of the sentence, see Supplement, p. 645 (*Pap.* V B 150:25).

572. With reference to the remainder of the sentence, see Supplement, p. 645 (*Pap.* V B 150:26).

573. See W. Hauff, "*Die Geschichte von Kalif Storch*," *Wilhelm Hauff's Sämmtliche Werke*, I-X (Stuttgart: 1840), V, pp. 14-28.

574. A ballad about Queen Dagmar and King Valdemar II, "*Dronning Dagmars Død*." See Abrahamson, Nyerup, and Rahbek, II, pp. 87-94.

575. See Genesis 41:1-4,17-21,26-31.

576. Cf. Matthew 11:11.

577. With reference to the remainder of the paragraph, see Supplement, p. 646 (*Pap.* VI B 8:20).

578. In 1840, greater Copenhagen had a population of about 123,000.

579. See Börne, *Aus meinem Tagebuche*, XII, *Schriften*, VIII, p. 96.

580. *Dansk Ordbog udgiven under Videnskabernes Selskabs Bestyrelse*, I-VIII (Copenhagen: 1793-1905).

581. For continuation of the paragraph, see Supplement, p. 646 (*Pap.* V B 150:27).

582. See Steen Steensen Blicher, "*Fløitetoner elskovsømme, bløde,*" *Trækfuglen* (Randers: 1838; *ASKB* 1525), 11, pp. 23-24.

583. A German word with a Danish ending.

584. See Matthew 12:30.

585. See Baggesen, "*Min Gienganger-Spøg, eller den søde Kniv,*" *Værker*, VI, p. 135.

586. See Suetonius, "Vespasian," 20; *Caji Suetonii Tranquilli Tolv første Romerske Keiseres Levnetsbeskrivelse*, I-II, tr. Jacob Baden (Copenhagen: 1802-03; *ASKB* 1281), II, p. 211; *Suetonius*, I-II, tr. J. C. Rolfe (Loeb, New York: Macmillan, 1914), II, pp. 312-13.

587. See Supplement, p. 646 (*Pap.* VI B 8:21).

588. Customary closing words in Latin orations: *Dixi et liberavi cor meum* (I have spoken and delivered my heart).

SUPPLEMENT

1. See Wilhelm Martin Leberecht de Wette, *Lærebog i den christelige Sædelære*, tr. Carl Emil Scharling (Copenhagen: 1835; *ASKB* 871), p. 139.

2. See pp. 199-200.

3. See p. 325.

4. *God. Guil. Leibnitii opera philosophica . . .*, I-II, ed. Johann Eduard Erdmann (Berlin: 1840; *ASKB* 620), with continuous pagination.

5. See p. 220.

6. See p. 283.

7. See pp. 283-84.

8. See pp. 16-19.

9. Jacob M. Mini's café on Kongens Nytorv 3.

10. See p. 287.

11. Regine Olsen (1822-1904). See Historical Introduction, pp. xiv-xv.

12. See pp. 185-397.

13. Kierkegaard's father, Michael Pedersen Kierkegaard (Dec. 12, 1756-Aug. 9, 1838).

14. Cf. p. 285.

15. See p. 233.

16. See pp. 360-63. Note the intended attribution to Nicolaus Notabene, the pseudonymous author of *Prefaces*, *KW* IX (*SV* V 1-71).

17. See Supplement, p. 509 (*Pap*. IV A 132); *JP* V 5564 (*Pap*. III A 245). This projected writing was not completed. Kierkegaard, however, without appointment as "Street Commissioner," was Copenhagen's foremost peripatetic and street observer and conversationalist. See, for example, Andrew Hamilton, *Sixteen Months in the Danish Isles*, I-II (London: 1852), II, p. 269: "The fact is *he walks about town all day*, and generally in some person's company . . . . When walking he is very communicative."

18. Cf. pp. 262-63.

19. Two pages of the journal are missing, and the remainder of the entry given here is crossed out.

20. See pp. 70-71.

21. See p. 69.

22. See p. 70.

23. See pp. 66-67.

24. See p. 280.

25. See p. 7. The title of Plato's *Symposium* in Latin is *Convivium* (Banquet).

26. See p. 16.

27. See pp. 17-18.

28. All the speeches are on love. See especially pp. 31-47, the Young Man's speech.

29. See p. 20.

30. See pp. 43-45.

31. See p. 126.

32. See pp. 31-32.

33. See pp. 27-30.

34. See *Visebog indeholdende udvalgte danske Selskabssange*, ed. Andreas Seidelin (Copenhagen: 1814; *ASKB* 1483), pp. 203-04.

35. See Supplement, p. 501 (*Pap.* II A 485).

36. See *Either/Or*, I, p. 25, *KW* III (*SV* I 5). Cf. Johann von Breitenfels, "*Vorrede*," *Satyrische und ernsthafte Schriften von Dr. Jonathan Swift*, I-VIII (Hamburg, Leipzig, Zurich: 1756-66; *ASKB* 1899-1906), I, no pagination.

37. See Johann Georg Hamann, *Hamann's Schriften*, I-VIII, ed. Friedrich Roth and G. A. Wiener (Berlin, Leipzig: 1821-43; *ASKB* 536-44), II, pp. 61-62; letters from Hamann to Jacobi, April 25, 1786, March 30, 1788, *Friedrich Heinrich Jacobi's Werke*, I-VI (Leipzig: 1812-25; *ASKB* 1722-28), IV³, pp. 211, 402.

38. Cf. *Prefaces, KW* IX (*SV* V II).

39. See p. 7 and note 10.

40. See pp. 70-80.

41. See Heinrich Theodor Rötscher, *Die Kunst der dramatischen Darstellung*, I-II (Berlin: 1841-44; *ASKB* 1391), I, pp. 394-96.

42. See *Pap.* V B 52.

43. See p. 195 and note 1.

44. Lars Mathiesen (1769-1852), the well-known convivial restaurateur in Fredriksberg Gardens, west of Copenhagen.

45. See Nicolai Frederik Severin Grundtvig, *Brage-Snak om Græske og Nordiske Myther og Oldsagn for Damer og Herrer* (Copenhagen: 1844; *ASKB* 1548).

46. A summer amusement park on the northern outskirts of Copenhagen.

47. Hans Friedrich Helveg (1816-1901), who preached occasionally in Grundtvig's church in Vartov, a philanthropic institution in central Copenhagen.

48. See pp. 7-86.

49. Kierkegaard did not take another writing sabbatical in Berlin. He did, however, make a considerable number of excursions to areas outside Copenhagen. See *JP* V, note 1127.

50. See *Anxiety*, pp. 69-70, *KW* VIII (*SV* IV 338-39).

51. See pp. 31-80; Supplement, pp. 511-12 (*Pap.* IV A 170).

52. See Henrich Steffens, *Caricaturen des Heiligsten*, I-II (Leipzig: 1819-21; *ASKB* 793-94).

53. See p. 67.

54. Thomas Hansen Erslew, *Almindeligt Forfatter-Lexicon for Kongeriget Danmark med tilhørende Bilande, fra 1814 til 1840*, I-III (Copenhagen: 1841-53), *Supplement, fra 1840 til 1853*, I-III (Copenhagen: 1858-68; *ASKB* 954-69 [I-III and two fascicles of *Supplement*, I]).

55. A reference to Magnús Eiríksson (1806-1881), who in April 1844 had published *Om Baptister og Barnedaab*.

56. Johan Ludvig Heiberg (1791-1860), the leading Danish literary critic of the time.

57. Nicolaus Notabene, the pseudonymous author of *Prefaces*, *KW* IX (*SV* V 1-71), and the intended publisher of the "Nebuchadnezzar" section.

58. See p. 9 and note 13.

59. The source has not been located.

60. See Horace, *Odes*, II, 13, 1; *Q. Horatii Flacci opera* (Leipzig: 1828; *ASKB* 1248), p. 119; *Horace The Odes and Epodes*, tr. C. E. Bennett (Loeb, Cambridge: Harvard University Press, 1978), p. 139: "The man who first planted thee did it upon an evil day and reared thee with a sacrilegious hand, O tree, for the destruction of posterity and the countryside's disgrace."

61. The Danish king Valdemar Atterdag (c. 1320-1375).

62. Valdemar Atterdag's Gurre Castle was on the shore of Lake Gurre.

63. See Oehlenschläger, *"Morgen-Vandring," Langelands-Reise*, Adam Oehlenschlägers Poetiske Skrifter, I-II (Copenhagen: 1805; *ASKB* 1597-98), I, p. 362.

64. See Wolfgang Amadeus Mozart, *Don Juan*, tr. Laurids Kruse (Copenhagen: 1807), I, 18, p. 57; *Don Giovanni*, tr. Ellen H. Bleiler (New York: Dover, 1964), p. 129.

65. Adam Gottlob Oehlenschläger, *Erik og Abel*, I, *Oehlenschlägers Tragødier*, I-X (Copenhagen: 1841-49; *ASKB* 1601-05 [I-IX]), V, p. 138 (ed. tr.).

66. The seventh, of course, was William Afham.

67. In Greek mythology, a beautiful youth, cupbearer to the gods of Olympus.

68. See Kruse, II, 20, pp. 123-26; Bleiler, pp. 196-99. The Commendatore is the avenging statue come to life at the end of the opera.

69. Danish: *Ølnordisk*, a play on *Øl* (ale) and *Oldnordisk* (Old Norse) and an allusion to Grundtvig's great interest in Norse mythology.

70. A town and woods about seven miles from Copenhagen.

71. See Kruse, II, 17, pp. 114-17; Bleiler, pp. 189-92.

72. See Kruse, I, 6, p. 18; Bleiler, pp. 98-99.

73. Kruse, I, 6, p. 18 (Elvira speaking); Bleiler, p. 98.

74. Horace, *Odes*, II, 4, 21; *Opera*, p. 45; Loeb, pp. 116-17 ("*suras*").

75. See Ludvig Holberg, *Erasmus Montanus eller Rasmus Berg*, III, 6, *Danske Skue-Plads*, I-VII (Copenhagen: 1788; *ASKB* 1566-67), V, no pagination; *Comedies by Holberg*, tr. Oscar James Campbell, Jr., and Frederic Schenck (New York: American-Scandinavian Foundation, 1914), p. 157 (III, 7).

76. Viscount Bolingbroke (Henry St. John), English politician (1678-1751), notorious for his libertinism, in Augustin-Eugène Scribe, *Et Glas Vand eller Liden Tue kan vælte stort Læs*, tr. Thomas Overskou, I, 2, *Det Kongelige Theaters Repertoire*, 134 (1841), no pagination.

77. Danish: *Ægte-Mand*, ordinarily spelled *Ægtemand*, therefore here with an emphasis on the first part, "married."

78. Danish: *Ægtepær* (*Ægte* + *Pær*, *Per* [Peter]), a play on *Ægtepar* (married couple) and meaning a somewhat cowed, boring husband.

79. Shakespeare, *Richard III*, I, 1, 19-20; *William Shakspeare's Tragiske Værker*, I-IX, tr. Peter Foersom and Peter Frederik Wulff (Copenhagen: 1807-25; *ASKB* 1889-96), VI, p. 176; *W. Shakspeare's dramatische Werke*, I-VIII, tr. Ernst Ortlepp (Stuttgart: 1838-39; *ASKB* 1874-81), VII, p. 272: "*Geschändet von der tückischen Natur, / Entstellt, verwahrlost*"; *Shakspeare's dramatische Werke*, I-XII, tr. August Wilhelm v. Schlegel and Ludwig Tieck (Berlin: 1839-41; *ASKB* 1883-88), III, p. 235; *The Complete Works of Shakespeare*, ed. George Lyman Kittredge (Boston: Ginn, 1936), p. 789: "Cheated of feature by dissembling Nature, / Deform'd, unfinish'd." See also *Fear and Trembling*, p. 105, *KW* VI (*SV* III 152).

80. Nicolai Edinger Balle Gøtzsche (1797-1866), appointed Copenhagen police inspector in 1830.

81. See Supplement, pp. 510-11.

82. See Acts 12:23.

83. Ibid.

84. See Shakespeare, *Henry IV*, *I*, II, 4, 423-24; Foersom and Wulff, III, p. 186; Ortlepp, VI, p. 81; Schlegel and Tieck, I, p. 251; Kittredge, p. 560: "to make my eyes look red, that it / may be thought I have wept . . . .."

85. See p. 126.

86. The Danish *Kraftkirke* (underground church, literally, "strength-church") is an adaptation of *Kryptkirke* (literally, "crypt-church"), hence a confusion or identification of *Kraft* and *Krypt*.

87. *Henrici Cornelii Agrippae de sacramento matrimonij libellus*, together with *De nobilitate et praecelientia foemenei sexus* etc. (Frankfurt, Leipzig: 1622; *ASKB* 113).

88. See *Postscript*, *KW* XII (*SV* VII 533).

89. Johann Wolfgang v. Goethe, *Goethe's Werke. Vollständige Ausgabe letzter Hand*, I-LX (Stuttgart, Tübingen: 1828-42; *ASKB* 1641-68 [I-LV]).

90. Epaminondas (d. 362 B.C.), Greek general of Thebes, won a complete victory at Mantinea but died of his wounds.

91. In Greek mythology, Prometheus, a Titan, was punished (for bringing

fire to the earth) by Zeus by being chained to a Caucasian mountain. A vulture ate away at his liver until he was freed by Hercules.

92. See Psalm 16:5.

93. See Supplement, p. 590 (*Pap.* V B 127).

94. See Supplement, p. 580 (*Pap.* V B 125).

95. François de Salignac de la Mothe-Fénelon, *Herrn von Fenelons kurze Lebens-Beschreibungen und Lehr-Sätze der alten Welt-Weisen* (Frankfurt am Main, Leipzig: 1748; *ASKB* 486 [Leipzig: 1741]), pp. 78-91.

96. See Psalm 16:5.

97. See Horace, *Ars poetica*, 148-50; *Opera*, p. 678; *Horace Satires, Epistles and Ars Poetica*, tr. H. Rushton Fairclough (Loeb, Cambridge: Harvard University Press, 1978), p. 463.

98. Cf. Vielgeschrey in Holberg, *Den Stundesløse*, II, 8; *Danske Skue-Plads*, V, no pagination; *Four Plays*, p. 40 (sc. 9).

99. See *Either/Or*, I, pp. 274-76, *KW* III (*SV* I 246-47); *JP* V 5913, 5999 (*Pap.* VII¹ A 126, p. 67; VIII¹ A 100).

100. Cf. p. 229.

101. Anon., *Udtog af en ung Piges Dagbog og Brevskaber. En Novelle* [Selections from a Young Girl's Diary and Letters. A Novella] (Copenhagen: 1842).

102. Cf. *Fædrelandet*, 1690, September 24, 1844, col. 13541; *Kjøbenhavnsposten*, 274, November 22, 1844, col. 1097-98.

103. See Supplement, p. 566 (*Pap.* V B 124), no. 3.

104. See I Samuel 15:22; Micah 6:7-8.

105. See J. L. Heiberg, *Nina, eller Den Vanvittige af Kjærlighed, Skuespil*, I-VII (Copenhagen: 1833-41; *ASKB* 1553-59), V, pp. 111-294.

106. See Ludwig Achim (Joachim) v. Arnim and Clemens Brentano, "*Der Rattenfänger von Hameln*," *Des Knaben Wunderhorn*, I-III (Heidelberg: 1819; *ASKB* 1494-96 [2 ed., 1834]), I, pp. 44-46.

107. Horace, *Epistles*, I, 1, 46; *Opera*, p. 541; Loeb, pp. 254-55.

108. J. L. Heiberg, *Skuespil*, III, pp. 185-288.

109. Sc. 5, ibid., II, p. 324.

110. See Holberg, *Mester Gert Westphaler eller Den meget talende Barbeer*, III, 2; cf. V, 7, *Danske Skue-Plads*, I, no pagination.

111. Presumably Christian Julius Hiorthøy (d. 1843), councilor and royal archivist.

112. Adam Gottlob Oehlenschläger, *Aladdin*, III, *Poetiske Skrifter*, II, p. 241 (ed. tr.).

113. Oehlenschläger, *Erik og Abel, Tragødier*, V, p. 134 (line by Lauge Gudmundsøn, ed. tr.).

114. The tower of Nicolaj Church near Kongens Nytorv.

115. Augustine, *De doctrina christiana*, III, 18; *Sancti Aurelii Augustini . . . opera et studio monachorum*, I-XVIII (Bassani: 1797-1807; *ASKB* 117-34), III, col. 69; *The Confessions. The City of God. On Christian Doctrine*, tr. Marcus Dods and J. F. Shaw (Chicago: Encyclopedia Britannica, 1952), p. 665.

116. See Edward Young, *Love of Fame*, II, 203-10; *Satiren auf die Ruhmbe-*

gierde, II, *Einige Werke von Dr. Eduard Young*, I-III, tr. Johann Arnold Ebert (Braunschweig, Hildesheim: 1767-72; *ASKB* 1911), III, p. 36; *Edward Young The Complete Works Poetry and Prose*, I-II, ed. James Nichols (Hildesheim: Olms, 1968), I, p. 360:

> With generous scorn how oft hast thou survey'd / Of court and town the noontide masquerade; / Where swarms of knaves the vizor quite disgrace, / And hide secure behind a naked face; / Where Nature's end of language is declined, / And men talk only to *conceal* the mind; / Where generous hearts the greatest hazard run, / And he who trusts a brother is undone!

Talleyrand is reputed to have said to the Spanish envoy Isquierdo, "*La parole a été donnée à l'homme pour désguiser sa pensées* [Speech was given to man to conceal his thoughts]." The "more recent author" is Vigilius Haufniensis, the pseudonymous writer of *Begrebet Angest* (1844). See *Anxiety*, p. 108, *KW* VIII (*SV* IV 376). See also *JP* I 623 (*Pap.* V A 19).

117. See Numbers 17:1-8.

118. See Genesis 3:24.

119. See p. 407 and note 449.

120. See Oehlenschläger, *Palnatoke*, V, 2, *Tragødier*, II, p. 298 (Palnatoke speaking).

121. An allusion to the title of Henrich Steffens's autobiography, *Was ich erlebte. Aus der Erinnerung niedergeschrieben*, I-X (Breslau: 1843; *ASKB* 1834-43).

122. Eusebius Pamphili (E. of Caesarea), *Eusebii Pamphili Caesareae Palaestinae Episcopi Praeparatio Evangelica* (Cologne: 1658), pp. 456-58; *Preparation for the Gospel*, I-II, tr. Edwin Hamilton Gifford (Grand Rapids, Mich.: Baker, 1982), I, pp. 484-86: "I found also the following statements concerning Nebuchadnezzar in the work of Abydenus *Concerning the Assyrians*: . . . ."

123. Cf., for example, Cicero, *De natura deorum*, II, 13, 37; *M. Tullii Ciceronis opera omnia*, I-IV and index, ed. Johann August Ernesti (Halle: 1756-57; *ASKB* 1224-29), IV, p. 523; *Cicero De natura deorum, Academica*, tr. H. Rackham (Loeb, Cambridge: Harvard University Press, 1979), pp. 158-59: "'Neque enim est quicquam aliud praeter mundum cui nihil absit quodque undique aptum atque perfectum expletumque sit omnibus suis numeris et partibus [In fact there is nothing else beside the world that has nothing wanting, but is fully equipped and complete and perfect in all its details and parts].'"

124. See p. 152.

125. According to old Danish law, if the death sentence was considered by royal officials or the king to be too severe, the condemned could be imprisoned for a period dependent upon conduct or other factors. See *Repetition*, p. 214, *KW* VI (*SV* III 247).

126. See Seidelin, pp. 353-55.

127. Ludwig Börne, *Gesammelte Schriften*, I-VIII (Hamburg: 1835-40; *ASKB* 1627-29).

128. Jens Baggesen, *"Over Baldrian," Jens Baggesens danske Værker*, I-XII (Copenhagen: 1827-32; *AKSB* 1509-20), I, p. 234 (ed. tr.) ("Nature took . . .").

129. See *Ny Danske Læsebog for de første Begyndere*, ed. Morten Hallager (Copenhagen: 1800, 23 pr. 1844), p. 84.

130. See *JP* I 140 (*Pap.* II A 571).

131. N.F.S. Grundtvig, *Christelige Prædikener eller Søndags-Bog*, I-III (Copenhagen: 1827-30; *ASKB* 222-24), I, p. i.

132. See p. 48 and note 131.

133. See Holberg, *Peder Paars* (Copenhagen: 1798), II, 1, pp. 129-30.

134. See note 127 above.

135. *Berlingske Tidende*, 108, May 6, 1845.

136. See *Ny Portefeuille*, pub. Georg Johan Bernhard Carstensen, ed. Jørgen Christian Schythe, II, 13, June 30, 1844, col. 309 (ed. tr.): "We have spoken with various people who immediately seemed to betray a certain acquaintance with Nicolaus Notabene's *Prefaces* as well as with Vigilius Hafniensis's book *The Concept of Anxiety* and S. Kierkegaard's *Philosophical Fragments* and his new *Upbuilding Discourses*. But, strangely enough, every time we wanted to go into one or another of these works a little, they always reverted to the comments about Prof. Heiberg in *Prefaces*."

137. Jakob Peter Mynster (1775-1854), Bishop of Sjælland, used this pseudonym formed from the initial consonant of the second syllable in each of his three names.

138. The famous Arabian caliph (764-809), about whom many tales are told in the *Arabian Nights' Entertainments* (*Thousand and One Nights*). See, for example, Nights 431, 559, 754-55, *Tausend und eine Nacht*, I-IV, tr. Gustav Weil (Stuttgart, Pforzheim: 1838-41; *ASKB* 1414-17), II, pp. 612-13; III, pp. 314-19; IV, pp. 82-87.

139. Mendel Levin Nathanson (1780-1868), merchant, author, and editor (1838-58, 1865-66) of *Berlingske Tidende*.

140. Johan Nikolai Madvig (1804-1886), philologist and politician, professor of philology, University of Copenhagen (1829), editor of acclaimed scholarly editions of Cicero and Livy, and author of numerous works on language.

141. P. 27.

142. P. 118.

143. P. 398.

144. Pp. 477-81.

145. See Corsair *Affair*, p. 96, *KW* XIII.

146. P. 311.

147. Adolph Peter Adler (1812-1869) was a pastor in Hasle and Rutsker, on the Danish island Bornholm, who in 1843 published *Nogle Prædikener* (*ASKB* u 9), in the preface of which he claimed direct divine revelation. Later in the journals, Kierkegaard refers frequently to Adler and in 1846-47 wrote *Bogen*

om Adler, which remained unpublished until it appeared posthumously in Kierkegaard's *Papirer* (VII² B 235). See *The Book on Adler, KW* XXIV.

148. See Hans Frederik Helweg, "*Mag. Adlers senere Skrifter*," *Kirketidende*, no. 45, 46, July 19, 26, 1846.

149. *Nogle Prædikener* (Copenhagen: 1843; *ASKB* 49).

150. *Nogle Digte; Studier og Exempler; Forsøg til en kort systematisk Fremstilling af Christendommen i dens Logik; Theologiske Studier* (Copenhagen: 1846; *ASKB* 1502, 411-13).

151. Pp. 456, 470.

152. Anon., *China, historisch, romantisch, malerisch* (Karlsruhe: n.d.; *ASKB* 2036).

153. Pp. 398-99.

154. Anon. [Johannes Carsten Hauch], *Søstrene paa Kinnekullen* (Copenhagen: 1849).

155. I, p. 31, *KW* III (*SV* I 15).

156. See Luke 2:37-38; Romans 8:25; "Patience in Expectancy," *Two Upbuilding Discourses, Eighteen Upbuilding Discourses, KW* V (*SV* IV 69-113).

157. Pp. 329-30.

158. Pp. 329-30.

159. P. 371.

160. P. 385.

161. Pp. 22, 65-71.

162. P. 493.

163. *Two Ages*, pp. 107-09, *KW* XIV (*SV* VIII 100-02).

164. See *JP* VI 6255 (*Pap.* IV B 63:7).

165. P. 68.

166. *Either/Or*, II, pp. 306-16, *KW* IV (*SV* II 275-83).

167. Pp. 75-76.

168. P. 79.

BIBLIOGRAPHICAL NOTE

For general bibliographies of Kierkegaard studies, see:

Jens Himmelstrup, *Søren Kierkegaard International Bibliografi.* Copenhagen: Nyt Nordisk Forlag Arnold Busck, 1962.

Aage Jørgensen, *Søren Kierkegaard-litteratur 1961-1970.* Aarhus: Akademisk Boghandel, 1971. *Søren Kierkegaard-litteratur 1971-1980.* Aarhus: privately published, 1983.

François H. Lapointe, *Sören Kierkegaard and His Critics: An International Bibliography of Criticism.* Westport, Connecticut: Greenwood Press, 1980.

Kierkegaard: A Collection of Critical Essays, ed. Josiah Thompson. New York: Doubleday (Anchor Books), 1972.

Kierkegaardiana, XII, 1982.

Søren Kierkegaard's Journals and Papers, I, ed. and tr. Howard V. Hong and Edna H. Hong, assisted by Gregor Malantschuk. Bloomington, Indiana: Indiana University Press, 1967.

For topical bibliographies of Kierkegaard studies, see *Søren Kierkegaard's Journals and Papers*, I-IV, 1967-75.

INDEX

Abelard, 407, 625

Abrahamson, Werner Hans, Rasmus Nyerup, and Knud Lyne Rahbek, *Udvalgte danske Viser fra Middelalderen*, 716, 741

absolute, the, 48-49; esthetic, 129

abstraction, the abstract: and being, 693; and concretion, 114-15, 658-59; and falling in love, 174; and ideality, 114-15; inhumanity of, 174; and intellectuality, 171; and marriage, 174-75; and the metaphysical, 476; religious, 172-73, 175-76, 659-60; and resolution, 114-15; and temporality, 175

absurdity, the absurd, 163-64

accident(s), the accidental, 10, 12, 80, 129

accounting, *see* analogy

actor/actress, 131-32

actuality, the actual, xii, 23, 26, 30, 62; break with, 177; and communication, 656; and erotic love, 32; and the esthetic, 459; and imaginary construction, 191; and love, 160; and possibility, 205, 328-29, 439, 472; and reality, 698; and reflection, 160; and the religious, 428; and the writer, xiv-xv

Adam: and Eden, 350, 605; and Eve, 36, 127, 489

Adler, Adolph Peter, 655-56; *Forsøg til en kort systematisk Fremstilling af Christendommen i dens Logik*, 749; *Nogle Digte*, 749; *Nogle Prædikener*, 748; *Studier og Exempler*, 749; *Theologiske Studier*, 749

admiration, 27, 28, 243, 251; as unfaithfulness, 158; of women, 51, 58, 159

Adresseavisen, 60

adulthood, definition of, 717

Ægtemand, 93, 745

Ægtepær, 745

Aeneas, 694, 696, 697, 704

Aesop, 418, 626; fables: "Boasting Traveller," 695; "Dog and the Shadow," 697

Afham, William, *see* KIERKEGAARD, pseudonyms

age, aging, 287; the current, 465-66, 492-93; and memory, 9, 518-21; and recollection, 10, 12, 520-21; and women, 133-34

Agrippa, Heinrich Cornelius: *De incertitudine et vanitate omnium scientiarum & artium liber . . .* , 699; *De nobilitate et praecelientia foeminei sexus, eiusdemque; supra virilem eminentia libellus*, 126, 511, 557, 745; *de sacramento matrimonio libellus*, 562, 745

Aladdin, vii, 78; and Gulnare, 103; wedding of, 103-04, 164; wish of, 103-04

Albertus, 525-28

Alcibiades, 687

Alexander, Henry, *Four Plays by Holberg*, 686

Alexander VI, 701

Al-Rashid, Harun, 649

Amager, 675, 716

analogy(ies), 466; accounting, 591-92; bargain, 176; bear and fly, 358; beer, 308, 380; books, 364; body parts, 480; Chinese satin, 401-02; christening, 99; clock, 335, 347, 600-01; compass, 299; consonants and vowels, 97; corns, 128-29; daisy, 138; deaf man, 420,

633; and women, 48–49, 59, 550, 557

illusion, 13, 48, 145–46; happiness as, 108; and reflection, 521; unhappiness of, 316. *See also* women

imaginary construction, x, xiii, 31–32, 185, 191; explained, 398–494, 654–58; love as, 32; religious in,458–60; structure of, 422–27, 467; unity of comic and tragic in, 435, 437, 455–56, 463, 467, 471–72, 643. See also *Experiment*

imaginary constructor, xii–xiii, 437, 657

imagination, 27, 52, 469; and actuality, 26; and intellect, 508; and sensuousness, 508; and will, 508

immediacy, the immediate, x, xi, 12; Aladdin as, 104; annulment of, 483; anxiety of, 103; and contradiction, 366; as divine category, 23; end of, 412; and erotic love, 100, 102, 166–68; and esthetics, 476–77; faith and, 292, 718; and falling in love, 103, 121, 156, 158–59, 162; first, 484; and the idea, 414; language of, 427; love and, 160, 407; and marriage, 64, 101–02; new, 163, 484; pathos of, 152; and poetry, 105; and reason, 718; and reflection, 123, 157, 162, 412, 414; and the religious, 162, 166–67, 169, 172, 415, 422, 440; and resolution, 102, 147, 162; and seduction, 104; and spirit, 65

immortality, 472; and birth, 45; consciousness of, 60–61; and death, 11; and erotic love, 548; and memory, 520; and recollection, 10, 520, 522; terror of, 10. *See also* eternity

Imogen, 220–21

in vino veritas, 26, 28, 525, 534

inclosing reserve, 189, 230. *See also* Quidam

Indesluttedhed, 189

Indesluttet, 187, 427

indirect method, xv

individuality(ies), 230, 261, 269, 271, 316, 430; authorized, 345, 647; esthetic, 420; ethical, 145; and imaginary construction, 191; justified, 104, 120; and love, 413; poet as, 154; religious, 153, 231, 318, 420, 435, 581; repenting, 317; and resolution, 109, 171; and τέλος, 101; and spirit, 171, 297; unhappy, 120

individual(s): and existence, 483–84, 487–88, 492–93; and recollection, 10; and the religious, 486; and self, 342–45; and species, 43, 541–42

inexplicable, the, 35–40, 63, 540–41

infinity, the infinite, 410. *See also* eternity

inner: and the outer, 375, 428, 441

insanity: bookkeeper's, 279; feminine, 270, 585–86; slow, 269; sudden, 269

inspiration, 411. *See also* women

intellect, the intellectual: and abstraction, 171; and imagination, 508; and sensuousness, 508; vs. spirituality, 170; and will, 508

internal, the, 441–42, 468, 476, 477

intoxication, 18, 30, 529, 538–39, 556–57

Io, 737

irony, 50, 57, 157; and gallantry, 146; Socrates', 156

Ixion, 714

Jacob, 97

Jacobi, Friedrich Heinrich, 10, 522–23, 695, 700, 743; *Beylagen zu den Briefen über die Lehre des Spinoza*, 676; *Werke*, 676

Jacobs, Friedrich, *Longus Hirtengeschichten*, 683–84

ADVISORY BOARD